The Creative Spirit

THIRD EDITION

The Creative Spirit

An Introduction to Theatre

Stephanie Arnold

Lewis & Clark College

Mc
Graw
Hill

Boston   Burr Ridge, IL   Dubuque, IA   Madison, WI   New York
San Francisco   St. Louis   Bangkok   Bogotá   Caracas   Kuala Lumpur
Lisbon   London   Madrid   Mexico City   Milan   Montreal   New Delhi
Santiago   Seoul   Singapore   Sydney   Taipei   Toronto

The McGraw·Hill Companies

Higher Education

THE CREATIVE SPIRIT: AN INTRODUCTION TO THEATRE, THIRD EDITION
Published by McGraw-Hill, a business unit of The McGraw-Hill Companies, Inc., 1221 Avenue of the Americas, New York, NY 10020. Copyright © 2004 by The McGraw-Hill Companies, Inc. All rights reserved. Previous editions © 2001, 1998 by Mayfield Publishing Company. No part of this publication may be reproduced or distributed in any form or by any means, or stored in a database or retrieval system, without the prior written consent of The McGraw-Hill Companies, Inc., including, but not limited to, any network or other electronic storage or transmission, or broadcast for distance learning.
Some ancillaries, including electronic and print components, may not be available to customers outside the United States.

2 3 4 5 6 7 8 9 0 DOC/DOC 0 9 8 7 6 5 4 3

Vice president and editor-in-chief: *Thalia Dorwick*
Publisher and sponsoring editor: *Christopher Freitag*
Marketing manager: *Lisa Berry*
Production editor: *Holly Paulsen*
Manuscript editor: *Kay Mikel*
Art director: *Jeanne M. Schreiber*
Design manager: *Cassandra Chu*
Cover and interior designer: *Linda Robertson*
Art manager: *Robin Mouat*
Art editor: *Emma Ghiselli*
Photo research coordinator: *Nora Agbayani*
Research assistant: *Zack Ross*
Production supervisor: *Tandra Jorgensen*

The text was set in 10/12 Janson Text by G&S Typesetters, Inc. and printed on acid-free, 45# New Era Matte, PMS 301, by R. R. Donnelley, Crawfordsville.

Cover image: METAMORPHOSES, written and directed by Mary Zimmerman, based on a translation by David Slavitt of Ovid's "Metamorphoses." Sets by Daniel Ostling; costumes by Mara Blumenfeld; lighting by T. J. Gerckens. Photo by Joan Marcus.

The credits for this book begin on page C-1, a continuation of the copyright page.

Library of Congress Cataloging-in-Publication Data
Arnold, Stephanie.
    The creative spirit : an introduction to theatre / Stephanie Arnold.—3rd ed.
      p. cm.
    Includes bibliographical references and index.
    ISBN 0-07-255831-8
    1. Theater. 2. Drama. I. Title
PN1655.A75 2003
792—dc21
                                    2003056115

www.mhhe.com

For Mark and for Daniel—
who provide the inspiration and the joy.

Preface

I wrote *The Creative Spirit* for students like mine, whose interest in live theatre is critical to its future. My goal has been to give students the information they need for an in-depth understanding of the way theatre creates meaning. Rather than using a multitude of examples from plays that students may not have seen, I have chosen to focus on fewer works in greater detail, allowing students to become immersed in the worlds of the plays, the lives of the characters, and the choices involved in bringing these texts to the stage. My teaching has convinced me that students gain the most comprehensive understanding of theatre when plays are presented both in the context of culture and history and in relation to performance.

FIVE COMPLETE PLAYSCRIPTS

At the core of the text are five complete plays: *Joe Turner's Come and Gone* by August Wilson, *And the Soul Shall Dance* by Wakako Yamauchi, *Angels in America: Millennium Approaches* by Tony Kushner, *Dog Lady* by Milcha Sanchez-Scott, and *Buried Child* by Sam Shepard. (These plays are set off from the rest of the text by a blue background.) Four of the plays are used to illustrate chapter themes: in Chapter 3 *Joe Turner's Come and Gone* illustrates the playwright's vision; Chapter 9 includes *And the Soul Shall Dance* as an example of expressing a worldview through realism; in Chapter 11 *Angels in America: Millennium Approaches* is included as an example of expressing a worldview through theatricalism; and in Chapter 14 *Dog Lady* illustrates the genre of comedy. The final play, *Buried Child*, is meant for a group project, although it may also be used as an additional or alternative example for other chapters. These five works demonstrate the power of contemporary American theatre to address the questions and concerns of our time.

EXAMPLES FROM A RANGE OF CULTURES AND PERIODS

In addition to the five complete plays, extended examples from classic and contemporary drama are included throughout. Chapter 1, for example, details ritual performance among the Hopi Indians of the Southwestern United States, and Chapter 2 includes an extended discussion and a scene from *The Oresteia* by Aeschylus. Medieval mystery cycles, Elizabethan drama, Iranian theatre, the Beijing Opera of China, seventeenth-century French comedy, European modernism, and mid-twentieth-century American musicals are among the types of drama represented. The primary focus, however, remains on the rich diversity of contemporary American theatre. And because the theatre's eloquence depends on visual imagery as well as on language, *The Creative Spirit* is supported by 200 production shots, design sketches, renderings, and drawings that highlight the exciting work of today's theatre artists.

AN INTEGRATED APPROACH: CONTEXT AND PERFORMANCE

I have tried to show students how to explore the text of a play as a theatre practitioner might, and how this exploration enriches their experiences as audience members as well. Each of the book's five complete playscripts is accompanied by a discussion of the playwright's other works, his or her sources, and the historical and cultural context that informs the play's plot, setting, and characters. In Context boxes provide timelines related to the play; for example, a list of key dates in the African American experience offers some background for *Joe Turner's Come and Gone*. Following each playscript (except the project text *Buried Child*) is a section on the performance and production of the play at one or more representative American theatres. The theatres range from small, innovative theatres, such as the Eureka Theatre and East West Players, to large regional companies, such as the Oregon Shakespeare Festival and the Mark Taper Forum, to Broadway playhouses. This integrated approach is most apparent in these "case study" chapters, but I have also discussed cultural context and performance choices in the book's ten other chapters.

VOICES OF THEATRE ARTISTS

In writing *The Creative Spirit*, I wanted to bring to the forefront the energy, passion, and commitment of artists working in the theatre today. I wanted students to hear playwrights, actors, designers, and directors explain, in their own words, the choices and methods they use in their work. To obtain this material, I interviewed more than 40 theatre artists. Playwrights Milcha Sanchez-Scott and Wakako Yamauchi; directors Libby Appel, Clinton Turner Davis, and Tony Taccone; actors LeWan Alexander and BW Gonzalez; designers Deborah Dryden, Ming Cho Lee, and R. Eric Stone; and dramaturg Oscar Eustis are among the commentators on plays and productions discussed in the text.

NEW TO THE THIRD EDITION

- A **new chapter order** presents the material on acting, directing, design, and musical theatre earlier in the book. This reordering makes for a better fit with many college syllabi. The new chapter order also spreads out the complete playscripts, alternating them with other kinds of chapters rather than grouping them together. This should make for a better pacing of course reading.

- A **new part structure** organizes the chapters into four parts instead of three. The book now addresses why we do theatre (Part One) and how we do theatre (Part Two) before continuing on to the analysis of dramatic style (Part Three) and dramatic structure and genre (Part Four).

- A **new play**, *Dog Lady* by Milcha Sanchez-Scott, strengthens the book's presentation of comedy and genre while introducing students to the one-act form. Scene designer Ming Cho Lee collaborated on this material, offering an insider's look at the design process.

- **Coverage of musical theatre is expanded**, with the addition of a section on the work of composer/lyricist Stephen Sondheim and choreographer-director Susan Stroman. The material on Sondheim fills out the historical presentation of the development of American musical theatre and further defines the role of the lyricist. The section on Stroman includes two of the most significant recent productions on the musical stage, *Contact* and *The Producers*.

- A **new photo essay** on recent productions of *The Oresteia* reinforces the significance of Greek tragedy for contemporary society. **Forty new photographs** throughout the text provide coverage of many new and important productions.

- **Discussions of plays that explore contemporary events**, such as Tony Kushner's *Homebody/Kabul* and Anne Nelson's *The Guys*, show how theatre responds to the challenges of the present time.

- **Updates for the Suggestions for Further Reading and new questions in Topics for Discussion and Writing** keep the text fresh and current.

SUPPLEMENTS

The following supplements are available through a McGraw-Hill sales representative.

- A **Theatre-Goer's Guide** helps students make the most of their theatre experiences. Suggestions for writing about a performance are also included.
- An **Online Learning Center**, located at www.mhhe.com/arnold3, offers chapter quizzes, extensive Web links, exercises, and more.
- The **Instructor's Manual and Test Bank** (ISBN 0-07-255834-2) offers a variety of resources for instructors, including assignment ideas; chapter summaries; and multiple-choice, short-answer, and essay questions.

ACKNOWLEDGMENTS

As *The Creative Spirit* enters its third edition, I am deeply appreciative of the many people who have contributed to its evolution. A large number of theatre artists have given generously of their time in helping to build the case studies of the various productions or in contributing additional interview material. The playwrights, actors, directors, and designers whose insightful commentary is found throughout the text have added immeasurably to the book's specificity and vitality. For the third edition, I thank Libby Appel, BW Gonzalez, and Joan Arhelger for their commentaries. Many theatres have provided visual material and supported my investigations of their productions. For contributions to the third edition, I extend my gratitude to the American Conservatory Theatre, Arena Stage, Berkeley Repertory Theatre, Betty Nansen Theatre, the Court Theatre, the Denver Theatre Center, the Guthrie Theatre, Imago Theatre, Ma-yi Theatre, Pan Asian Repertory Theatre, Pearl Theatre, and Seattle Repertory Theatre. I also wish to thank Roger Lee of the York Wagon Plays Board and Erik Hansen-Hansen.

A growing number of people have reviewed the manuscript at different stages of the project. I wish to thank the following reviewers for their invaluable comments and suggestions for the third edition:

Margaret Anich
University of North Carolina at Charlotte

Tony Arduini
University of Dubuque

Mark Branner
Antelope Valley College

Patricia Clark
East Carolina University

Amy Cuomo
State University of West Georgia

Thomas H. Empey
Casper College

Kathryn Ervin
California State University, San Bernardino

Judy Garey
Ventura College

Kerry Graves
Eastern Michigan University

Juliet Hampel
Westchester University

Mychelle Hopkins
Western Michigan University

Gregory Justice
Virginia Polytechnic Institute and State University

Catherine F. Norgren
State University of New York at Buffalo

George Emilio Sanchez
College of Staten Island

John C. Watson
University of Oregon

Evan Winet
University of Kansas

I also wish to express my appreciation to Lionel Okun who has provided thoughtful suggestions and guided me to valuable resources. During the work on the third edition, Zack Ross has been my research assistant, tackling the photo requests and permissions. Zack has been meticulous, patient, and imaginative in helping to prepare the manuscript, and I feel particularly fortunate to have had the pleasure of working with him.

The third edition sees the transition from Mayfield Publishing Company to McGraw-Hill. The Mayfield staff nurtured the book with great care and wisdom for which I continue to be profoundly grateful. The McGraw-Hill staff has brought new energy and new perspectives that have been particularly helpful in addressing the evolving structure of the book. I thank Allison McNamara and Chris Freitag, the book's new sponsoring editor. In bridging the staff changes, Cynthia Ward and Ashaki Charles provided excellent support and continuity. And much thanks to the production staff for bringing the project to successful conclusion: Holly Paulsen, production editor; Cassandra Chu, design manager; Emma Ghiselli, art editor; and Nora Agbayani, photo research coordinator.

Once again, I would like to include a few words about my students. I have been most fortunate in my teaching career to have worked closely with many remarkable students. As I have taught them in acting and dramatic literature classes or directed them in plays, we have had the great joy of making discoveries together, of learning from each other, and together, reaching an understanding of the value of the theatre in our lives. I salute their talent, their openness, their idealism, and their commitment. Finally, I acknowledge the loving support of my family, who have never flagged in their enthusiasm for the project or their willingness to undertake all the necessary tasks to make the book possible and to keep my sense of humor intact.

Brief Contents

Contents

Chapter **5**   **The Director**   149

Chapter 11   **Expressing a Worldview Through Theatricalism** 309

Looking at *Angels in America: Millennium Approaches* by Tony Kushner

Chapter **14**   **Choosing a Genre: Comedy**   408
Looking at *Dog Lady* by Milcha Sanchez-Scott

Chapter **15**   **The Project**   434
Looking at *Buried Child* by Sam Shepard

The Nature of Theatre

For thousands of years, in almost all cultures, the theatre has been an essential part of human expression. In his book *The Rainbow of Desire*, Brazilian theatre director Augusto Boal calls theatre the first human invention because it is through theatre that we step back from ourselves to observe and interpret our own behavior. Through the theatre, we reflect on our experiences and we imagine new possibilities. Making theatre is a way of understanding the world around us and our place in it. We also find this process of projecting ourselves into strange or familiar circumstances immensely entertaining.

In the theatre, the **playwright** and the **actor** together present stories in the form of action. The stage action invites audience members to enter a created, fictional world. The energy of the actors and the energy of the audience fuse to charge the theatre event with an

1

intensity that carries the performance beyond ordinary existence into a magical realm of the human spirit. Into theatre performances we pour our dreams, our myths and stories, our struggles and fears. The conflicts that divide us and the laughter that makes us whole take their place on the stage. We make a journey through space and time that is limited only by our imagination.

Before the electronic age, the theatre provided much or all of a community's dramatic entertainment. Today, drama takes place on small and large screens and over the airwaves as well as in the theatre. But although it has much in common with its electronic relatives, the theatre is distinguished by the very fact that it is a live event dependent on the presence of actor and audience in the same space. The live actor-audience relationship offers countless possibilities for envisioning human experience.

This book presents a study of contemporary American plays and productions as a way of understanding the theatre in our own time. To lay a foundation for this approach, we begin by examining the nature of performance and the way performance responds to deep human needs. We look at the impulse to perform that draws actors onto the stage. We then consider the power of the theatre in society. Just as performance exerts a strong pull on individuals, the theatre generates a forceful presence in the life of a community. By introducing some of the great theatre traditions worldwide, we begin a discussion of the many forms that theatre may take and the complex relationship between theatre and society.

CHAPTER 1

The Impulse to Perform

One of the strangest and most distinctive elements of human behavior is the impulse to **perform,** to create a character that is part of ourselves but somehow separate from us. When we **act** a part, when we take on a role, we seek to transform ourselves through the construction of a new identity. This process of transformation is fundamental to human nature and is at the heart of the theatre.

The idea of **performance,** or creating roles, may seem strange because as a society we place a high value on a stable, consistent sense of identity. We mistrust people whose surface appearance proves to be an illusion. Aliases are for criminals or for people in witness protection programs, people who have somehow become social outcasts. Presenting a false identity in a relationship is considered a betrayal. And displaying multiple identities is perceived to be a sign of mental illness. Yet we are fascinated by the ability of actors to re-create their self-images, and we ourselves continuously take on roles as we move through the shifting demands of our daily lives.

Performance can also seem superficial. In contemporary life we are surrounded by performers in a continuous array of filmed dramas, from movies to television shows to music videos.

Partly because so much of the performance we see involves car chases, gun battles, or soap opera seductions, it is easy to view performance as trivial, escapist entertainment rather than an activity that has primary significance for both individuals and society.

In actuality, the impulse to perform is part of the way we survive. We adapt to changes in our circumstances by making adjustments in the identity that we present to other people. The human mind is elastic and imaginative in the construction of identity. Part of growing up depends on observing successful "role" models and experimenting with identities that make us feel comfortable in the face of changing social pressures or demands. Identity is fluid rather than fixed; we may be one person with our families and quite a different person at work or in public situations.

Sometimes we feel that we cannot know certain people until we can break through the masks that they wear to protect themselves or, perhaps, to take us in. Consider on one hand the politician who puts on a different face for every new situation or constituency. We may even doubt that such a person has a core identity at all. On the other hand, we may believe that we cannot really know someone until we recognize that he or she is made up of different identities. Certainly we understand the great release in letting go of certain "expectations" of behavior and trying out a role that is "nothing like us." In the theatre, actors build on this fundamental human impulse to perform in order to describe and interpret human existence for an audience. As audience members, we take great pleasure in watching the work of actors who have made an art out of an impulse that is part of human nature.

We begin our study of the theatre by exploring the place of performance in human behavior. What human needs are met through performance? What are the psychological, social, and cultural conditions that motivate performance? For the purposes of our discussion, we separate performance into three different areas: (1) personal performance—the kind of performance or role shifting that occurs in daily life, (2) community performance—ritual dramas enacted to benefit a group of people sharing common beliefs, and (3) professional performance—the performance that we see in the theatre and in the movies. All three of these areas of performance share overlapping characteristics. Understanding the functions of personal and community performance in our lives provides a basis for approaching the professional performance of the actor, whose work is the essence of the theatre.

PERSONAL PERFORMANCE

If we observe children at play, we see that many of them pretend to be the adults who are prominent in their lives. Children often start their role-taking by "playing house" or "playing school"—pretending to be parents or teachers. Children living in war zones play out the violence that surrounds them at a very early age. Certainly children's imitation of the behavior they observe is a way of learning about or preparing themselves for roles they expect to assume. But there is more to dramatic play than social conditioning.

Imagine a four-year-old boy going shopping with his mother. Before leaving the house he insists on putting on his cape and strapping on his sword. Whether he sees himself as Superman, Batman, Spiderman, or the latest incarnation of a superhero, his impersonation is a serious business. At four, he is old enough to know that the world can be a threatening place. He is aware that he is physically small and lacks the special skills of older children, such as reading, that would give him more control in a dangerous and confusing environment. So he puts on the costume or "signs" of what he recognizes as power. And through wearing the cape and bearing the sword, he takes on a role that enables him to share in the power of his hero.

We recognize in this small boy's actions a pattern of behavior that occurs in a variety of situations and at different ages. Life is difficult

These children, living in Kosovo, use dramatic play to imitate and interpret the violence that governs their lives.

and full of obstacles. In certain situations, we enact roles; we make adjustments in the way we present ourselves, particularly in ways that make us feel more powerful. The small child is not concerned about being obvious as he carts around his sword. He wants threatening forces, whether real or imaginary, to be clear about his new identity. As adults we try to be more subtle as we put on the clothes and accessories of power, assume certain postures, and alter our language or vocal intonation. Actor Bill Irwin, whose work is discussed later in the chapter, says he approaches many of his characterizations by asking himself two questions: (1) "What am I afraid of right now?" (2) "What are all the mechanisms that I'm putting into play to show that I'm not really afraid of that?"[1]

COMMUNITY PERFORMANCE

The story of the little boy and his superhero battle gear is one of many examples of individual role playing. But humans also engage in forms

of collective dramatic expression that are fundamental to the community. Through **dramatic rituals** we reinforce community values and act out community stories that preserve a way of life. The term *ritual* refers to a ceremonial observation that is repeated in a specified way in order to confer certain benefits on the participants. Rituals are highly symbolic events with densely coded meanings. There are sacred rituals, and there are distinctly secular rituals. Indeed, some of the richest forms of ritual dramatic expression take place as part of religious observances such as the enactment of the birth of Christ at Christmas in the Christian community or the observation of the Seder meal at Passover in the Jewish community.

Weddings and graduations exemplify two types of major community rituals. In a traditional wedding, a sacred ritual, the bride, the groom, and the attendants wear elaborate and highly ceremonial clothes, and the couple enact their vows according to the custom of their religious faith. Many believe that such a ceremony strengthens the marriage and subsequently the community, whose members participate as witnesses and join in the celebration; they see the wedding ceremony as essential to the stability of the community. Although rituals tend to change slowly because their form needs to be fixed to be effective, they can also be somewhat flexible. One element of the wedding ritual currently undergoing significant change is giving away the bride. At one time this gesture symbolized shifting authority over a woman from her father to her husband. Today other family members or friends may "give the bride away," or the couple may choose to eliminate this custom altogether.

The secular ritual of the high school graduation is of great significance to towns and cities across the United States. The graduation ceremony is a formal rite of passage for the community's young people, a way for them to be accepted into adulthood. Robes and hats are worn; solemn music is played; the graduates accept their diplomas and congratulations and best wishes for the future from their community leaders. Most students play their parts with an unusual amount of dignity. To complement the formality of the actual graduation ceremony, many graduating classes develop their own more ecstatic, freer ritual festivities to mark the significance of this event.

Other secular rituals include sporting events, particularly college and professional football games. Sports fans wear costumes and makeup as part of their identification with the drama enacted on the playing field. Beauty pageants, too, are community rituals, as are parades, such as the gay-pride parades that occur in a number of communities and involve many dramatic elements of costume and impersonation.

Community rituals bind community members together by reinforcing their common history and shared goals for the future. They help shape the yearly calendar and the many rites of passage in the human life cycle. Because the United States is made up of many religious faiths and cultural groups, our national rituals tend to be secular, which may be one reason sports have become so important to us. Nonetheless, some community rituals in the United States are a form of worship that interpret religious history or values and also allow for intense identification with the most sacred beliefs of the community. For some communities, dramatic religious rituals are central to community life and govern a great deal of community activity throughout the year. It is from such entrenched dramatic ritual that many of the major dramatic traditions worldwide have evolved.

We turn to the dramatic rituals of a small Native American community, the Hopi, as a source for our further examination of the impulse to perform. This community has been chosen for two primary reasons: the richness of its ceremonial performances and the fact that this community's rituals—as well as other Native American ceremonial drama—represent one of the earliest dramatic forms indigenous to our continent.

Ritual Performance Among the Hopi

In an elaborate sequence of dramatic ceremonies, the Hopi Indians of the southwestern United States **personate** the *kachinas*, whom Barton Wright describes as "the spiritual guardians of the Hopi people and their way of life."[2] According to Dorothy K. Washburn, "Kachinas are the messengers and intermediaries between men and gods."[3] The concept of the kachina is associated with the clouds from which rain falls and with the dead, whom the Hopi believe become part of the clouds and return to earth as rain. The Hopi believe that the intervention of the kachinas will bring rain to the arid landscape of the high desert and ensure the success of their crops.

With their brilliant costumes and **masks** incorporating animal and plant images, the ceremonial dramas make the kachina spirits visible to the Hopi community. Because most elements of the costumes and masks have a symbolic meaning, the Hopi figuratively "wear their world" when they are in their ceremonial dress.[4] For example, different colors represent

The performance of the kachina cycle binds the Hopi community together through the preservation of a belief system and a way of life. Kachina dolls like the one shown here are carved by Hopi artists as a sacred representation of the kachina ritual. The preferred Hopi word for kachina is katsina *and, in the plural form,* katsinam.

the different geographic and spiritual directions and the weather and resources represented by those directions. Tortoiseshell rattles refer to the water of the ponds and springs where the tortoises live. Eagle and turkey feathers become the flight of prayers.

Kachina Performances

The kachina ceremonies are central to the Hopi worldview and may have originated as early as the twelfth or thirteenth centuries. There are more than three hundred different kachinas, and kachina rituals are spread over much of the year. From December to July a great epic cycle of kachina performances involves all members of the community in varying responsibilities for the ongoing ritual drama. In fact, the Hopi villages are built around the plazas in which the ceremonial dances take place. The kachina performances are at the center of the community physically as well as spiritually and socially.

The first observation of the **kachina cycle** occurs at the winter solstice, *Soyal,* in December, to break the darkness and prepare for the new year. *Niman,* the last ceremony, anticipating a successful harvest, occurs in July. Following this final Home Dance, the kachinas are believed to return to the San Francisco Mountains

west of the Hopi villages, where they remain until they rejoin the Hopi at the winter solstice. Between the initiation of the cycle in December and the conclusion in July, the kachinas perform a series of ceremonies in which seeds are planted, children are initiated, community members are taught discipline, and, finally, crops are harvested. Rain, fertility, and maintaining social order are the underlying goals of all kachina activity. The dramatic ritual is a highly complex way of exerting control over the environment—that is, the physical, social, and spiritual world.

The kachina ceremonies are frequently serious and sometimes even frightening. But humor is also an essential part of the ritual; laughter is understood as basic to human survival. Clowns appear among the kachinas, and they offer a critique of negative behavior through **parody** by performing outrageous acts that would be unacceptable outside of the ritual observation.

The Hopi Performer

The Hopi man who personates a kachina is transformed (women do not participate as performers). He transcends his own being and becomes the kachina spirit that he personifies.

He takes on the presence and the power of the kachina and therefore can act for the kachina in the ceremonies. Through the ritual dance, a transaction takes place between the human and the supernatural, a merging of the two levels of existence (Color Plate 1).

Like personal performance, community performance is very much tied to the quest for power. But in sacred community performance in particular, performers become separated from their status as mere mortal beings. They become elevated. By the nature of their special religious knowledge, their enactment of the ceremony, and their performance skills, they become "magicians" who act on behalf of the other members of the community.

The professional actor is also a kind of magician. Actors can do what we, the audience, cannot. Like the ceremonial performers in the kachina ritual, they act for us. Sometimes through words, sometimes through actions, sometimes with dance and song, they create the presence of characters, of human spirits. They draw us into a world apart where life is at its most intense. Their **characters** take us on journeys in the form of stories that let us see into their souls so that we may see into our own. To create such an experience, actors must possess extraordinary skills, both physical and mental. By using their bodies and voices as expressive instruments and by calling on acute powers of observation, intuition, analysis, and emotional response, actors project a vibrant sense of life onstage that lifts us out of ourselves to meet them halfway.

Performance as Community Obligation

Although the kachina rituals provide entertainment for the Hopi community, they are, first and foremost, ceremonies that will have a beneficial effect on the lives of the Hopi people. That is why we say the performances are community-centered. The men who perform are fulfilling a community obligation. Although women do not participate in the

actual impersonation, they have other ceremonial responsibilities.

The professional theatre in the United States does not have the same place in society that the kachina dramas have in Hopi community life. Plays or performances may deal with political or social problems. They may create a community of the people who come to form the audience. And there may be long-term benefits for the people who attend. Some would say a healthy society depends on having a healthy theatre. But modern professional dramas are unique expressions of the playwrights and the actors. They are not tied through ritual to the shared beliefs of the community. Each performance is made up of the ideas of the individuals involved rather than community-held beliefs that have evolved over generations.

PROFESSIONAL PERFORMANCE: FOUR STORIES

To investigate the performance impulse in the professional theatre, we consider here the work and backgrounds of four actors who have captured the imagination of U.S. audiences. Three of the following actors perform in theatre pieces that they have developed themselves as well as in works written by others. Thus we are able to examine their choices and passions under circumstances over which they have more control than many other actors do. By examining the paths these individual actors have taken, we will broaden our assessment of the impulse to perform.

Bill Irwin: Physical Humor

I feel about the theatre the way a sailor must feel about the sea. I'm drawn to it, but I'm frightened.[5]
—BILL IRWIN

Bill Irwin wanders onstage wearing a baggy suit and an odd hat. With his horn-rimmed glasses and thoughtful expression, he appears to be one

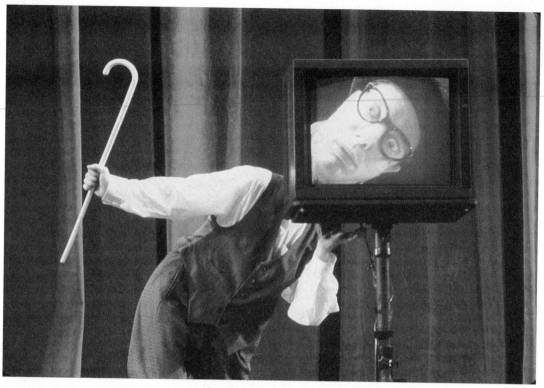

In 1989 in the play Largely New York, *Bill Irwin played a bewildered character trying to make sense of the changes in the world around him—changes that ranged from technological advances to break dancers confronting him on the street.* Largely New York, *written and directed by Irwin, was staged through mime, dance, and video. Other original Irwin vaudeville pieces for the theatre include* The Regard of Flight, *discussed here, and* Fool Moon *(Color Plate 2).*

of those people who knows what he is about. But before long, if he approaches the curtain or the wings, an invisible force, an unseen hand, begins to pull him off the stage. Of course, there is no offstage force, only the actor's ability to make us see what is not there by his heroic efforts to resist being dragged away.

Throughout his hilarious attempts to defeat the unseen demons, Bill Irwin does not speak. What he does as a performer is most closely related to the world of the circus clown or the old vaudeville and film routines of the Marx Brothers or Buster Keaton. And like the clowns who find themselves in impossible situations, jumping off burning buildings or being squashed by the dozen in a tiny car, Bill Irwin

finds himself battling the malevolent forces around him for some measure of control. He runs and trips and falls, finally leaping off the stage, frantically trying to avoid the villain who is chasing him, only to land on a trampoline hidden in the orchestra pit, which bounces him back onto the stage and into the middle of his troubles again. With the training of a gymnast, a dancer, and a mime, he executes unbelievable stunts, extreme blown-up versions of what we all go through in life. And we laugh until our sides ache, and we say, "Ah yes, life is like that."

Bill Irwin was born in California in 1950 and grew up in Tulsa, Oklahoma, where his father worked as an aeronautical engineer. The oldest of three children, he remembers an early fascination with the bizarre and the theatrical. He began clowning in part to entertain his younger siblings with such routines as "the man who couldn't get on the couch." By the time he began his freshman year at UCLA in 1968, he already knew that he wanted to study theatre.

The late 1960s was a time of intense political conflict on U.S. college campuses. Antiwar protests, sit-ins, and confrontations with police were a regular part of college life. And Irwin had spent the year before he started college as an exchange student in Belfast, Ireland, the heart of the ongoing strife between Catholics and Protestants. Irwin recognized even as a college freshman that he needed to find new theatre material and a new way of performing that would respond to the political upheaval of the times:

> The turmoil of the time, the ethical and moral questioning that was all around, led me to wonder why, with the whole country popping, I was working backstage at "Kiss Me Kate." It seemed obscene, in 1968, to do the usual spring musical.[6]

It was not theatre that Irwin doubted but theatre that asked no questions, that posed no challenge for the audience. Bill Irwin began his search for a theatre of new meanings by joining experimental theatre director Herbert Blau, first at the California Institute of the Arts and then at Oberlin College in Ohio. Blau was engaged in intense experimentation with a small company of students called Krakken. Although Irwin found Blau's work politically and aesthetically provocative, he longed for what he describes as a more "grassroots experience." He wanted theatre that would engage a large audience of different ages.

In a remarkable shift of direction, Bill Irwin left the circumscribed world of **avant-garde** college theatre for the rough-and-tumble atmosphere of the Clown College of Ringling Brothers Barnum and Bailey Circus. He knew that for him physical action was the key to establishing the relationship he wanted with his audience. What he learned at Clown College Irwin describes simply as "how to trip and fall down":

> The school is a weird and wonderful place. You're stretching on the same mats that they use for the circus and the old timers are telling you, "When you do a fall, fellas, always turn your face to the side because that thing has been soaked in tiger urine."[7]

At Clown College, Bill Irwin discovered the basics of a performance style that would become his life's work. Honed through street performances, birthday party clowning, and then the Pickle Family Circus, Irwin worked and reworked the ability to "trip and fall down." But the ability to fall also became the ability to fly and, in that flight, to carry audiences beyond the limits of earthbound reality.

Anna Deavere Smith: The Power of Words

When Anna Deavere Smith performs, she brings a whole community of people with her: people who have experienced the upheaval of the 1992 Los Angeles riots in response to police brutality or the 1990 crisis in Crown Heights, New York, in which a black child and a Jewish student were killed. Although only Smith is actually present on the stage, the people of Los Angeles or New York speak through her. Smith plays as many as thirty different characters by simply changing a costume piece and her attitude. She portrays old and young, female and male, black and white. She finds the essence of her characters in what she calls their "speech rhythms." In rehearsal, she creates her characters by memorizing words that she has previously tape-recorded in interviews. As she repeats the language of a black teenage gang member, former Los Angeles Police Chief Darryl Gates, or a Korean shop owner over and over again, their physical mannerisms, posture, and facial expressions begin to take shape. As an actor, she tries to make her own personality disappear.

Anna Deavere Smith grew up in Baltimore, the oldest of five children, in a family that

Anna Deavere Smith changes characters by changing costume pieces and props. For each character, she establishes different speech rhythms, postures, gestures, and facial expressions and handles different objects, presenting multiple points of view on the same subject.

House Arrest, staged in 2000, explores the American presidency and the limitations placed on the inhabitants of the White House since the early days of the nation. Smith again plays a variety of roles. Here she portrays a photographer who has his own way of capturing the current holder of the office.

particularly valued language and reading. Her mother taught remedial reading and insisted that everyone could learn to read. Smith's grandfather also exerted a lifelong influence on her attitude toward language when he told her that "if you say a word often enough, it becomes you."[8] Her grandfather's idea, in fact, eventually formed the basis of her approach to teaching acting and to working as an actor herself.

Smith's experience of segregation and integration also contributed to her heightened awareness of the power of speech to reveal or conceal identity. During the 1950s and 1960s, when Smith was a child, Baltimore was changing rapidly; the integration of some neighborhoods was followed by white flight. She felt that she grew up in an "experiment."[9] She began her education at an all-black elementary school and then moved to a largely white junior high school.

> I was excited by the different ways we talked and held ourselves, and I became very interested in language.[10]

As a child she was also deeply moved by the troubles of others:

> I wanted to be a psychiatrist, but my mother told me I couldn't, because I was too sensitive. A movie like *West Side Story* would make me cry for two days straight.[11]

Her empathetic nature and passion for language would lead her to acting. Her concern with building bridges between people brought

Storm Reading, performed by Access Theatre of Santa Barbara, California, under the direction of Rod Lathim, was based on the journals and writings of Neil Marcus and toured across the country. The sequence shown above was a dance done by Marcus to his own poetry: "Every dream I ever had, came true. The person that I never thought I could be, I am."

her to focus on race as one of the major subjects of her work.

Neil Marcus: Storyteller and Dancer

People are watching me. They are watching me all the time. They're watching me even when they're pretending not to watch me. They're watching me to see how well I do this thing called human.[12]

—NEIL MARCUS

Neil Marcus rolls onstage in a wheelchair. His arms and legs jerk in spasms beyond his control; and when he does speak, his words are hard to understand. He seems to be playing a character like Christy, the man portrayed by actor Daniel Day Lewis in the movie *My Left Foot*. But Marcus is not creating a disabled character. The disability is real, and what Marcus is performing is in part the story of his own life. With two other actors—Mathew Ingersoll, who speaks as the voice of Marcus's imagination, and Kathryn Voice, who interprets the whole play in American Sign Language as she also plays her roles—Marcus performs sketches about his struggles to be recognized as a complete human being with both his own special talents and his own special needs. Marcus does not create a character who is completely separate from himself. Rather, his performance is based on his own poetry and journals, which represent years of evaluating his own experiences.

Neil Marcus was born in White Plains, New York, in 1954, the youngest of five children. He was a lively, active child who loved the stories his mother wrote and the camping and hiking outings he shared with his father after they moved to Ojai, California. Nothing in those early years predicted the wrenching change that confronted him when he was eight years old. What began as tremors in one arm would eventually take over Marcus's whole body. Responding to what they thought was a psychological problem, his parents sent him to summer camp to spend time with other children when the first symptoms of his rare condition, dystonic musculorum deformans, began.

When Marcus returned from camp, he could not hold a pencil, and his hands were no longer open but had become clenched fists. He walked with a limp, and his leg began to turn inward. Speech was becoming as hard to manage as moving his arms and legs. He could no longer be understood. For four months the condition progressed, transforming his once coordinated body into twisting, jerky spasms out of his control. He had no idea what was happening to him or what the outcome would be.

Coping with the new circumstances of his life presented enormous challenges that would take years to overcome. It took fifteen years for Marcus to accept what dystonia had made of his body. He felt a constant pressure to overcome his disability but not an acceptance of his limitations. Although teachers and fellow students were helpful and supportive, the emphasis was on ignoring rather than embracing his difference. And so he grew up feeling the need to hide. He avoided eye contact with other people to persuade himself that he wasn't being seen, that his physical difference wasn't constantly apparent. His effort to disappear, not to be different, brought him a profound sense of separation and isolation.

The story of Neil Marcus's becoming an actor, then, is the story of a young man coming out of hiding. It is a story of transforming a desire to withdraw into an activism in the civil rights movement for people with disabilities. It is the story of a passion so strong to touch the lives of other people that it propelled this man to take center stage in his wheelchair and then rise up out of that chair to dance.

Frances McDormand: Creation of Character

Each time Frances McDormand appears on-stage or in a movie, she seems to be an entirely different person. As Marge Gunderson, the small-town police chief in *Fargo*—the role for which she won a 1997 Academy Award—McDormand transformed herself into a plain and very pregnant woman, waddling through the snow in a maternity snowsuit and a furry police hat with earflaps. With a heavy Minnesota accent marking her down-to-earth observations about both police work and the meaning of life, the character's intelligence and warmth sets in sharp relief the mindless violence that surrounds her.

Whether she is acting in a turn-of-the-century Russian play by Anton Chekhov or a contemporary comedy by Wendy Wasserstein, whether she is filming a psychological thriller such as *Primal Fear* or a political drama such as *Mississippi Burning*, McDormand seeks to reshape herself according to the needs of the story and the character.

For her role in the film Fargo, *Frances McDormand set out to create a character truthful to the circumstances of the situation. The small-town police chief Marge Gunderson emerged as an original character, memorable for her combination of earthiness and wisdom.*

I'm an actor. I can make you believe I am almost anything using artifice and imagination onstage or on film. I've got from the bottom of my feet to the top of my head to do it. I'm already limited enough in the film business by being a woman. I'm not going to let them limit me more than that.[13]

In her process of character creation, McDormand draws on her own emotional experiences and collaborates closely with makeup and costume designers to invent a physical reality that seems truthful for each different character. For *Fargo*, she deliberately set out to contradict traditional ideas of movie glamour.

I figured what would this woman put on herself everyday when she got up? . . . A little blue eyeliner that she'd worn every day since high school in Brainerd, Minnesota. She'd have broken blood vessels cause it's always cold. . . . We gave her very pink cheeks. The wig was an ugly hairstyle.[14]

McDormand describes herself as a working actor who uses her craft to create an imaginative stage life. She believes she is responsible to the script and that the characters she creates must fulfill the ideas of the play or film. She also has a responsibility to the other actors to listen honestly to them and base her reactions on their words and actions. She sees herself as an interpreter, not as a personality:

I have friends who are movie stars, and I think it's just as hard a job as being a working actor. But it's a different job, and it's not the one I want.[15]

Born in Illinois to Canadian parents, McDormand spent her childhood moving around the Midwest as her family accompanied her father, a traveling Disciples of Christ minister. When they finally settled in Pennsylvania and she could participate in school activities, McDormand discovered the theatre. She played Lady Macbeth in a high school production:

I did the sleepwalking scene and it was the first time I'd ever done anything that I felt was mine. I took it much more seriously than the other kids. When we were backstage, for example, I knew it was important to be quiet when other people were acting. It seemed like I knew the ethics of the theater environment intuitively. It became clearer and clearer to me that acting was the only thing I knew how to do.[16]

After completing the graduate acting program at the Yale School of Drama, McDormand started dividing her time almost immediately between the theatre and film. In 1984, in addition to making her first movie, *Blood Simple*, directed by Joel and Ethan Coen, McDormand also made her New York stage debut in *Painting Churches*, by Tina Howe. In 1988, the year that she was nominated for a Tony award for her performance as Stella in Tennessee Williams's *A Streetcar Named Desire*, at the Circle in the Square Theatre in New York, she was nominated for an Academy Award for her work in *Mississippi Burning* with Gene Hackman and Willem Dafoe. Although McDormand has received acclaim for her film work, she finds that the theatre provides her with the best opportunity to grow as an actor:

> After becoming dissatisfied with the benefits I reaped as an actor in television and film, I found a new commitment to doing theatre, at least two or three plays a year. There I found my ethical community. . . . If there's longevity involved, if you see yourself being an actor until the day you die and living a healthy life, then that is the moment when you truly take responsibility for your technique.[17]

Most recently she arranged her schedule to appear in the films *City By the Sea* and *Laurel Canyon* and still act onstage in *To You, The Birdie* with the Wooster Group and *Far Away* by Caryl Churchill at the New York Theatre Workshop.

Why They Perform

Bill Irwin, Anna Deavere Smith, Neil Marcus, and Frances McDormand are all collectors of human experience and human behavior. They are supreme observers of the large and small moments in their own lives and the lives of the people around them. They continually study the efforts made by people to overcome obstacles, to successfully live through another day. In their own unique ways they record the details of what they see and hear and feel because it is through the selection and arrangement of details that they compose the life they put on the stage.

Irwin collects moments of the ridiculous, such as a man bent over to pick up a dropped item while those around him mimic his momentary loss of dignity. Smith chooses the most revealing "language acts" of the people she interviews, which she also calls "living evidence." For Marcus the significant evidence is other people's responses to his disability: the man taking his order at Burger King who becomes almost paralyzed when he cannot understand Marcus's speech. And McDormand seeks out details of appearance that define character. She shops for costume pieces and searches for props that will enable her to create a world that the character and the audience may enter.

Irwin, Smith, Marcus, and McDormand are all actors, although they describe their own work quite differently. Bill Irwin sees laughter as a crucial connecting point between actors and the audience. Laughter is a common denominator that brings people together. For Irwin it is the physical portrait that captures the essence of the human condition, physical humor that generates the most profound laughter. And he sees that the laughter that comes from physical humor can also lead to questioning:

> When an audience laughs at physical humor, it's not like any other kind of laughter. It's deeper, weightier somehow, than laughter at something that's said. If no one laughs (when you fall), it's painful. But if people laugh, you feel nothing. The laughter cushions every thud. It's like floating down. In clowning you're always breaking through that fourth wall that separates audiences from actors in the traditional theater.[18]

Irwin brings his idea of physical comedy to plays by Samuel Beckett and Molière in which he speaks as well as to his own silent creations.

Smith sees acting as a way of learning about herself through studying the community around her. Over a period of more than ten years she has developed a series of theatre pieces entitled *On the Road: A Search for American Character*, which has culminated in *Fires in the Mirror*, about Crown Heights, and *Twilight: Los Angeles, 1992*, about the Rodney King incident. "My goal has been to find American character in the ways people speak," Smith says.[19] She seeks to discover what lies underneath the surface of a statement, what may be revealed about people in the breaks and disruptions of their sentences: "I call myself a repeater or a reiterator, rather than a mimic. The roots of what I do are in the black tradition of oral history."[20] Smith approaches speech as a process of thought that increases awareness:

> The sections of the interviews I repeat onstage, word for word, are those where people have come into a greater understanding of themselves. I'm not just repeating the words, I'm re-enacting a slight lift in consciousness. My re-enactment, slightly, ever so slightly, lifts my own consciousness. That's the only way I know how to learn.[21]

Smith sees acting as an opportunity for studying human behavior, individually and collectively. She is struggling to understand where we are as a society, particularly in matters of race. She sees herself as an observer, and she tries to give life to what she observes around her. Curiously, even though she plays all the parts herself, the intention is not to focus on her life or her own virtuosity but on the lives of people from communities caught in crisis:

> There's not a lot of flash about me . . . my job is to disappear. I'm not interested in myself at all. I'll probably be 90 before I'll do a day in the life of Anna Deavere Smith.[22]

In her job as an actor, Smith believes she should disappear as a person. Neil Marcus is an actor who cannot disappear. The continuous motion of his body makes him very visible and constantly attracts attention. Since people have always looked at him or tried not to look at him, he feels that, in some way, he has always been center stage: "The lives of people with disabilities are very dramatic."[23] He wants people to look at him, but in ways that will take them into his heart and mind. Marcus sees his own life as a vehicle, a starting point from which others can consider issues relating to disability. In the play *Storm Reading*, Marcus presents a personal commentary that begins with his own life experiences.

Unlike the other actors in this chapter, Frances McDormand performs only in the scripted works of playwrights and screenwriters. Like most actors, she does not perform in works that she creates herself. Therefore, all of her creative efforts are focused on realizing characters who have been originated by someone else. She feels a deep obligation to discover the place of her character in relationship to the script and to the other characters and to contribute to a collaborative effort of expressing an idea.

McDormand looks outside of herself for details that provide clues to a character's physical identity. But she also draws heavily on her own emotional history as a major source for the inner life of the character:

> I allow my emotional life and the pain and joy of my past to be a present fact of my life and not something I merely relive in memory. But because the scar tissue never forms entirely, the past never fully becomes memory, it remains an active part of my present. Not that I keep everything so present. Some wounds just naturally have to be submerged. But even they will rise to the surface when I both need them as an actor and am ready to handle them as a person.[24]

These actors have remarkably different points of departure for structuring their performances, yet what they share is a commitment to appearing on a stage, in front of an audience, using only their own personal resources to interpret life for an audience. Musicians have instruments between themselves and the audience; painters, a canvas. But for actors, whatever the audience sees must come through the actors' presence, their bodies and voices, their emotional and intellectual responses. In that sense the actor is the most vulnerable of artists. No other artist is subject to the same personal scrutiny. And yet there is a special kind of exhilaration in overcoming that vulnerability. The actor feels a sense of personal power, of expansiveness, of living fully.

Irwin, Smith, Marcus, and McDormand all give charismatic performances. They have a remarkable ability to move audiences in some profound way and are exemplary representatives of their profession. As we read about their work and the experiences that have influenced them, we cannot help recognizing that they are deeply affected by social and political forces. These forces influence the works they have created as well as their choices to perform the works of other playwrights and filmmakers.

But whether actors perform their own material or that of other playwrights, one cannot think of an actor as just a clean slate or a piece of clay to be molded in the shape of one role and then to be returned to an unformed state until the next role. Like all of us, actors have their insecurities; unlike most of us, they have an extraordinary ability to change and reconstruct their identities in visible ways. For many actors, the impulse to perform is connected to their passions and convictions about the human condition. Although there are surely actors who perform only out of vanity, they can show us only themselves. They cannot lead us into a process of discovery where we can say, "That is true for me as well."

SUMMARY

Performance is a vital part of human expression that may involve playing roles in daily life, participating in community rituals, or working as a professional actor. Performance is an essential human activity that relates to successful personal adaptation. Children use performance to test new roles; adults use performance to adjust to changes in their circumstances. Much of the shifting of roles in daily life relates to our attempts to become more powerful.

Through dramatic rituals, communities reach out to supernatural forces to secure control over their environment. Ceremonial performances, such as the kachina cycle of the Hopi, are central to the social and religious

organization of the community. The individual who takes on a ceremonial role goes through a process of transformation.

For professional actors, performance becomes the key to interpreting human behavior. Actors such as Bill Irwin, Anna Deavere Smith, Neil Marcus, and Frances McDormand combine remarkable expressive skills with acute powers of observation to create memorable characters. Actors use many different approaches to create a stage life that entertains as it contributes to the understanding of human nature. In the next chapter, we examine performance as part of the theatre and look at the significance of theatrical performance for society.

TOPICS FOR DISCUSSION AND WRITING

1. If you act or perform, answer the following questions in terms of yourself. If you do not do any acting, interview a student actor, a community actor, or a professional actor. The purpose of the exercise is to discover what compels people to act on the stage. Questions: Why do you perform? What are your performance impulses? What needs are satisfied by acting? What were your starting points? How have they changed?

2. The purpose of this exercise is to examine the way "personal performance" is used in everyday life. Choose "nonactors" for your observations. Where do you see people performing in daily life? That is, under what circumstances do people make some kind of switch in how they present themselves, taking on a different role, putting on a mask, or dramatically aggrandizing their behavior? What is the purpose of the "performance"? Observe people in five different situations. Write approximately one-half page for each observation.

3. Discuss the ways in which the Hopi kachina cycle benefits the Hopi community. Do you know of any dramatic ceremonial performances that are part of your community?

NOTES

1. Bill Irwin, quoted in Bruce Weber, "Just Clowning Around with Intellect," *New York Times*, 3 March 1993, C1.

2. Barton Wright, *Kachinas: A Hopi Artist's Documentary* (Phoenix: Heard Museum, 1973), 2.

3. Dorothy K. Washburn, *Hopi Kachina: Spirit of Life* (San Francisco: California Academy of Sciences, 1980), 40.

4. Washburn, 41.

5. Bill Irwin, quoted in Janice Ross, "Bill Irwin: Getting Physical with Comedy," *Dancemagazine*, June 1982, 70.

6. Bill Irwin, quoted in Sylviane Gold, "He's a Clown with a Mission," *New York Times*, 8 August 1982, 19.

7. Irwin, quoted in Weber, C8.

8. Anna Deavere Smith, introduction to *Fires in the Mirror* (New York: Doubleday, 1993), xxiv.

9. Barbara Lewis, "The Circle of Confusion: A Conversation with Anna Deavere Smith," *Kenyon Review* 15, no. 4 (1993): 62.

10. Anna Deavere Smith, quoted in Ralph Rugoff, "One Woman Chorus," *Vogue*, April 1993, 242.

11. Smith, quoted in Rugoff, 238.

12. Neil Marcus, Rod Lathim, and Roger Marcus, *Storm Reading*, unpublished manuscript.

13. Frances McDormand, quoted in Janet Sonenberg, *The Actor Speaks* (New York: Random House, 1996), 252.

14. Frances McDormand, quoted in Merle Ginsberg, "A Gosh-Darn Good Actress," *The Oregonian*, 5 April 1997.

15. Frances McDormand, quoted in Rebecca Ascher-Walsh, "Interview with Frances McDormand," *Entertainment Weekly*, 12 April 1996, 36.

16. Frances McDormand, quoted in Graham Fuller, "How Frances McDormand Got into Minnesota Nice," *New York Times*, 17 March 1996, 28.

17. McDormand, quoted in Sonenberg, 252.

18. Irwin, quoted in Gold, 19.

19. Smith, introduction to *Fires in the Mirror*, xxiii.

20. Anna Deavere Smith, quoted in Richard Stayton, "The Voices of the City," *Los Angeles Times*, 25 April 1993, 7.

21. Anna Deavere Smith, quoted in Stephen Foehr, "Creating Community," *Houston Chronicle*, 17 January 1994, 3.

22. Smith, quoted in Stayton, 7.

23. Neil Marcus, interview with author, 30 May 1994.

24. McDormand, quoted in Sonenberg, 253.

SUGGESTIONS FOR FURTHER READING

Blau, Herbert. *The Audience*. Baltimore: The Johns Hopkins University Press, 1990.

A complex discussion of the relationship between the performance and the audience.

Boal, Augusto. *The Rainbow of Desire*. Translated by Adrian Jackson. New York: Routledge, 1995.

An analysis of the nature of theatre and its importance to society from the viewpoint of a director-producer who uses theatre to empower the oppressed; an accessible presentation of theory supported by many examples of performance techniques and themes, including a discussion of improvisational, participant-centered theatre.

Deegan, Mary Jo. *The American Ritual Tapestry: Social Rules and Cultural Meanings*. Westport: Greenwood Press, 1998.

An examination of social rituals in the United States in the late twentieth century, the rapidity with which "hyper-modern" society generates change in ritual patterns, and the global impact of American social rituals.

Goffman, Erving. *The Presentation of Self in Everyday Life*. New York: Doubleday, 1959.

A detailed study of the construction of social roles using the language of the theatre as the foundation for describing human interaction.

Hawthorn, Audrey. *Kwakiutl Art*. Seattle: University of Washington Press, 1994.

A detailed description of Northwest Coast native rituals, including both the ceremonial performances and the art objects such as masks, musical instruments, and feast vessels that were essential to the rituals; over four hundred illustrations in color and black and white.

Jenkins, Ron. *Acrobats of the Soul: Comedy and Virtuosity in Contemporary American Theatre*. New York: Theatre Communication Group, 1988.

> A book on American clowning, including an excellent chapter on Bill Irwin, with a detailed description of his performance style and an excerpt from the script of *The Regard of Flight*.

Kirby, E. T. *Ur-Drama: The Origins of Theatre*. New York: New York University Press, 1975.

> An investigation of the nature of shamanistic practice (religious ritual) as the basis for the development of theatre forms in different parts of the world; includes a brief discussion of Kwakiutl rituals as well as a more extended consideration of early Greek and Chinese practices.

Sealey, Jenny, ed. *Grae*ae *Plays: New Plays Redefining Disability*. London: Aurora Metro Publications, 2002.

> An anthology of plays addressing disability written by disabled playwrights. The plays have all been developed in association with Grae*ae*, "Britain's premiere professional theatre company of disabled people."

Smith, Anna Deavere. *Fires in the Mirror*. New York: Anchor Books, 1993.

> The text of Smith's play about the conflict between black and Jewish residents of Crown Heights, New York; contains photographs of the actual community as well as pictures of Smith performing the work. This published edition of the play includes very helpful introductory material, both about Smith's approach to theatre as well as background on the subject of the play.

Smith, Anna Deavere. *Twilight: Los Angeles, 1992*. New York: Anchor Books, 1994.

> The script of Smith's play about the riots in Los Angeles in 1992. The script was based on 200 interviews with participants and observers.

CHAPTER 2

Theatre and Society

THE POWER OF THE THEATRE

On February 2, 1940, Vsevolod Emilievich Meyerhold was shot to death while he was being held by Soviet authorities in a Moscow prison. Within a few weeks, Meyerhold's wife, Zinaida Raikh, was stabbed to death by attackers who were never apprehended, and Meyerhold's personal papers were stolen. What made these two people a danger to the Soviet system? They had broken no laws, yet how had they become a threat serious enough to lead to execution without being formally charged with a crime or publicly tried?[1]

Most people believe that both killings were instigated by the Soviet regime and, more particularly, were authorized by Andrey Zhdanov, a close collaborator of Stalin's who was responsible for the Soviet cultural policy.[2] Vsevolod Meyerhold was a theatre director. Zinaida Raikh was an actor who played major roles in many of the productions staged by Meyerhold. Together they represented a style of theatre that the Soviet authorities found unacceptable. The plays that Meyerhold directed did not present the "truth" that government officials wanted to be acted out onstage, nor did Meyerhold's theatre follow the style of **socialist realism** that the

state had designated as the appropriate form of expression, a style that was suited to an idealistic presentation of life under the Soviet system.

On June 21, 1956, American playwright Arthur Miller was called before the House Un-American Activities Committee (**HUAC**) of the U.S. Congress to answer questions about his views on communism and to identify other writers who might be communists. When Miller refused to provide the committee with the names of writers who might have communist associations, Miller was cited for contempt of Congress and received a jail sentence that was eventually suspended.

Other playwrights, screenwriters, and actors did not emerge from their encounters with HUAC with suspended sentences. Those who refused to name names, to identify supposed participants in the "communist conspiracy" to overthrow the American government, went to jail, and those who were named by witnesses as communists were blacklisted. No judicial proof of any wrongdoing was required; no due process was observed. Innuendo was enough. Blacklisting ruined careers and lives, and suicide was not an infrequent outcome of this attempt to control the free expression of ideas.

Ta'ziyeh ("Mourning") is a heroic, epic drama from Iran, dating from the eighteenth century, that takes on ceremonial importance when performed in Iranian communities. It tells the story of the prophet Muhammed's grandson, Imam Hussein, through some 200 different episodes. The Battle of Karbal, fought in 680, is the center of this ritual, music drama. Three episodes of the Ta'ziyeh were performed for the first time in the United States at the 2002 Lincoln Center Festival in New York City. This photograph shows a performance in Iran.

The climate of fear and intimidation created by what would come to be called witch-hunts functioned as a potent form of censorship that spread throughout the arts in the United States, particularly in the late 1940s and 1950s. Among the many people across the spectrum of American life who were attacked during the "red scare" were labor leaders, college professors, scientists, and government employees. But it was the theatre and film communities that attracted HUAC's most concentrated attention. Just as the Soviet government demanded that artists and writers use socialist realism to celebrate the heroic nature of the workers' struggle and the benefits of the Soviet system, so the congressional committee lectured its subpoenaed witnesses on the virtues of art that expressed the triumphs of capitalism and democracy.

Both incidents, Meyerhold's death and the attempted intimidation of Arthur Miller, point to the power of the theatre as a social force. The governments of these two modern powers with opposing ideologies felt that what was at stake was worth murder in the first case and the suppression of freedom of speech in the second. These examples are far from unique. Many societies, past and present, have persecuted actors and playwrights, and many have worshiped them, sometimes simultaneously. Actors and playwrights have been slaves, and they have been military leaders. They have been social outcasts and the confidants of kings. In our own times, Ronald Reagan, an actor, served as president of the United States, and Vaclav Havel, a playwright, was elected the first president of the Czech Republic.

In this chapter we examine the relationship between theatre and society by studying examples of theatres from different nations and different historical periods; we study both the subjects and ideas of the particular theatres and the aesthetics of the different styles of performance. As we move from theatre to theatre, we explore some of the issues that have arisen from the volatile relationship between theatre and society: issues of religion and politics, race and gender, social stability and revolution.

Society and Aesthetic Expression

The impulse to perform, to interpret human existence through the presentation of characters on a stage, has evolved into an astonishing variety of theatre traditions. Just as the human capacity for speech has produced many languages, so the impulse to perform has found expression in many distinct forms. In Indonesia shadow puppets play out complicated stories of kings and battles; in China animal gods fight with demons as actors in highly stylized makeup and costumes perform a combination of sensational gymnastics and martial arts; in India barefoot women with painted faces, hands, and feet perform eloquent dances made up of densely coded, intricate gestures. Sometimes actors speak, sometimes they dance, sometimes they sing. Actors may wear masks or elaborate symbolic costumes, or they may wear the clothes of everyday life. They may inhabit mythical regions, historical locations, or realistic, contemporary environments. They may use elevated speech and gestures or language and actions that correspond with contemporary behavior.

From culture to culture and continent to continent, the theatre responds to the unique worldviews of differing human communities and develops forms of expression that reflect specific community concerns and community aesthetics. By community concerns, we mean the ideas or subjects of theatre performances. By **community aesthetics,** we mean the actual nature of the elements that construct the performance itself, elements that have precise meaning for a particular community and that contribute to the images with which the community describes itself.

For example, in Chapter 1 we discussed the Hopi kachina performances, which emphasize the importance of the harvest and the place of the entire agricultural process in maintaining social order. The relationship between agriculture, the natural environment, and the social order of the community is shaped by the proper regard for a spiritual presence. This complex interaction is the subject of the ritual;

(Left), *Shadow puppets are carved from stiff leather, sometimes with intricate use of color. Backlit from behind simple screens, the puppets are manipulated in relation to the light to create changes in the size and definition of the image. Frequently the puppet plays are part of lengthy community gatherings; music accompanies the telling of stories, which can continue for many hours.* (Right), *Sudha Rani Narasimhan, a member of the Abhinaya Dance Company of San Jose, California, is shown here in a pose depicting Lord Nataraja, the Supreme Dancer, in the Bharatanatyam style of classical dance from southern India.*

it is what the dramatic cycle is about. The performances themselves are created through certain sequences of dance steps performed by celebrated characters wearing symbolic costumes and carrying iconographic props, all of which form images that express the Hopi view of the world. These characteristics of performance are part of the aesthetic expression of this particular people. Geography, the physical environment, material culture, family structure, social organization, history, religion, and

philosophy are some of the basic forces that shape artistic expression.

The Collective and Public Nature of Theatre

Sometimes the theatre retells the sacred stories of a community. Sometimes individual playwrights forge the body of work that interprets the life of the social group. Myths, legends, history, contemporary events, and personal

The Handspring Puppet Company of South Africa produced Ubu and the Truth Commission *in response to the actual Truth and Reconciliation Commission that held hearings in South Africa on the crimes committed under apartheid. Busi Zokufa appears as Ma Ubu.*

experience filtered through the imagination of the playwright may all serve as sources for theatrical expression. Celebrated plays of individual playwrights may come to function as sacred stories, anchoring community values or providing a measure against which new experience can be tested. But whatever balance is struck between sustaining stories and the innovations of individuals, the formation and evolution of the theatre takes place in a public forum in a collective endeavor. A community of artists gathers to present a performance for a community audience.

Theatre as a Social Force

It is particularly the collective and public nature of the theatre that makes it such a potent social force. The theatre is a gathering place for the public presentation of ideas. Because ideas are expressed through characters caught in difficult or dangerous situations, the theatre creates an intensely emotional experience for the audience. And the impact of the work is then magnified by the number of people present. A collective emotional response is a force of enormous energy and can function in different ways. On one hand, theatre can evoke a collective sigh of relief, an emotional release: sometimes when a group of people have laughed very hard together or cried together, they feel that they can more easily accept the difficulties of their daily lives or the pressures that face the entire community. On the other hand, theatre can generate and focus collective anger or outrage, which can then take form as a revolutionary force.

The relationship between theatre and society is complex because the theatre has so much potential power. Theatre can be a conservative force that contributes to stability and reinforces the status quo, or it can be part of an experimental process through which a society redefines itself. Theatre can release social tensions, or it can lead to social upheaval. Theatre can be part of social debate, part of the free exchange of ideas, or it can be used for the dissemination of propaganda. Because of its unique power as a collective, public form, theatre has always been of great interest to philosophers and governments.

THEATRE AND RELIGIOUS FESTIVALS

We begin our study of selected theatre traditions by examining two very different European theatres that both developed in conjunction with religious festivals: the Greek theatre of Athens in the fifth century B.C.E. and the medieval mystery cycles, specifically those of England, which reached their high point between 1350 and 1550. Although both of these theatres were associated with community celebrations and ceremonies, the Greek theatre developed into a forum for highly sophisticated philosophical debate about the place of human beings in the universe, whereas the medieval theatre produced a pageant that functioned as a form of devotion, an affirmation of accepted religious beliefs.

THE GREEK THEATRE: ATHENS, FIFTH CENTURY B.C.E.

By the fifth century B.C.E., Athens had become the dominant force in the group of city-states politically, culturally, and geographically linked on the peninsula and islands of Greece. The century produced a dazzling record of the Athenian genius for the arts, for learning, for government, and for the building of an empire. The Athenian theatre and literature of the fifth century B.C.E. has inspired much of the theatre and literature in later eras and throughout the world. The great **tragedies** that came from this period, *Prometheus Bound*, *Oedipus Rex*, *Antigone*, and *Medea*, were intricately bound to the religious as well as the political life of the community.

The Origin of Greek Theatre in the Worship of Dionysus

Early on in the development of theatre in Greece, plays were associated with festivals to honor the god **Dionysus**. There is much debate among theatre historians and anthropologists about whether the plays actually evolved out of ritual worship of Dionysus or whether they grew out of the more secular impulses of individual playwrights. Whatever path the evolution of Greek drama followed, the worship of Dionysus was central to the place of theatre in Greek culture.

Dionysus was the Greek god of the life force; he represented new growth for vegetation, new life for herds and flocks, and fertility for human beings. A god of nature, wine, and fertility, Dionysus was honored in the spring with festivals that celebrated regeneration and renewal. These were ecstatic celebrations in which social inhibitions were supplanted by liberated, intoxicated behavior. The worship of Dionysus supposedly began with his followers' tearing apart his body and eating it in order to absorb his power into themselves. In the spring following the dismemberment of the god, Dionysus was miraculously restored to life, resurrected. In its evolution, the worship of Dionysus at first actually involved human sacrifice; later, animals were used for the communion ritual. Stories and songs celebrating the life of Dionysus were added to the ritual observations, which grew into community festivals involving civic and religious activity. Finally, in the sixth century B.C.E., dramas were added to the various activities of the festival of Dionysus, setting the stage for the brilliant Athenian **drama** that would emerge in the fifth century B.C.E.

In Context

ORIGINS OF THE THEATRE IN GREECE

Date	Event
1300–1200 B.C.E.	Worship of Dionysus introduced to Greece from the Middle East
c. 800 B.C.E.	The *Iliad* and the *Odyssey* composed by Homer
534 B.C.E.	Dramatic competition established at City Dionysia
523–456 B.C.E.	Life of Aeschylus
508 B.C.E.	Athenian democracy established
496–406 B.C.E.	Life of Sophocles
490 B.C.E.	Defeat of the Persians by the Greeks at Marathon
480–406 B.C.E.	Life of Euripides
c. 460–430 B.C.E.	Rule of Pericles
458 B.C.E.	*The Oresteia,* by Aeschylus
431 B.C.E.	*Medea,* by Euripides
430 B.C.E.	*Oedipus Rex,* by Sophocles
429–347 B.C.E.	Life of Plato
404 B.C.E.	Athens defeated in Peloponnesian War
384–322 B.C.E.	Life of Aristotle
c. 330 B.C.E.	*The Poetics,* by Aristotle

Although the Greek dramas that came to dominate the festival of Dionysus are profoundly different from the Hopi kachina cycle discussed in Chapter 1, certain remarkable similarities are apparent. For both cultures, the drama is central to community observations concerned with renewal and regeneration. The transformation of actors into characters concerned with issues of social and religious order coincides with the transformation of nature to sustain human existence once more. The suffering and rebirth of Dionysus became a model for the theatre, which explores the suffering and triumph of the human community. This transformative function for the drama would recur in the Christian drama of medieval times, when pageants celebrating the Christian history of the world were performed in conjunction with the Corpus Christi festivals held throughout Europe in the late spring to celebrate the sacraments of the church associated with the body of Christ.

Like the Hopi ritual performances, the Greek theatre was part of the soul of the community, essential to the basic fabric of the life of the city-state. Through plays, the Greeks examined the relationships necessary to sustain human existence as they understood it. Family relationships, social organization, the relationships and obligations of individuals to the larger society, and the interplay between human action and the actions of the gods dominated the dramas written by playwrights such as Aeschylus (523–456 B.C.E.), Sophocles (496–406 B.C.E.), and Euripides (480–406 B.C.E.). By raising ethical and political questions, the Greek plays helped shape the emergence of democracy in Athens.

There are, however, significant differences between the kachina cycle and the theatre of Greece. The kachina performances evolved over generations of community participation; no single playwright shaped the ideas and images. By contrast, in the Greek theatre it was the imagination of the individual playwright that was celebrated. The presentation of plays, in fact, took the form of a competition, at the festival known as the **City Dionysia,** and prizes were given each year to the outstanding playwright. Further, the kachina performances reinforce an accepted set of religious beliefs, whereas Greek theatre questioned the nature of fate and the very existence of the gods.

The Greek plays were presented each year over a period of several days. Most traditional work stopped, and 15,000 community members or more would gather on a hill outside the city where a rudimentary theatre had been constructed. From wooden benches built into the hillside, the audience would look down on an

The theatre at Epidauros dates from about 300 B.C.E., which is later than the period we have been studying. However, these well-preserved ruins give a sense of the scale and setting of the theatre of Dionysus in Athens in the fifth century B.C.E. The theatre at Epidauros seated 14,000 spectators and was known for its excellent acoustics. In spite of the vast size of the theatre, the actors could be heard by everyone present. Our knowledge of Greek theatre practice is based on fragmentary evidence and involves much speculation on the part of theatre historians. We imagine that the actors in the fifth century B.C.E. performed on a circular, unraised playing area, with a wooden building behind that served as a place to change costumes and masks and from which actors entered and exited the stage. The wooden building might have created the sense of a palace facade. The roof of the scene building also provided a raised level for the appearance of the gods.

open-air playing space. At the back of this circular playing area was a plain stone building that provided for the entrances and exits of the actors and served as a place for costume changes and storage for simple stage machinery. Beyond the theatre lay the sea. The audience and the actors gathered in the middle of the geographic features that delineated the external boundaries of the Athenian world as they witnessed or acted the plays that probed the internal nature of that world. From early morning to late afternoon, the playwrights staged dramas to entertain, to illuminate, and to reflect on the concerns of the huge audience. We now examine one of the Greek dramas, *The Oresteia*, to explore the merging of ideas and aesthetics in the Greek theatre. Accompanying our discussion of *The Oresteia* are photos drawn from a few of the many recent productions of this work, some returning to the Greek tradition of masked

actors and some exploring more contemporary approaches. *The Oresteia* continues to be compelling for modern producers and audiences because of its treatment of cyclical violence and because it laid the foundation for addressing many social conflicts still prevalent today.

The Oresteia, *by Aeschylus*

The Oresteia was written by Aeschylus in 458 B.C.E. If the dates that are commonly used for this period are accurate, Aeschylus would have been sixty-five when he wrote *The Oresteia* and at the end of his illustrious career as a highly respected civic and military leader and playwright. *The Oresteia* is actually a collection of three plays, called a **trilogy.** Together, the three plays, named for the central character, Orestes, tell a bloody story of murder and revenge as disturbing as some of today's films. Violence in the

An important character in the story of Agamemnon and his brother Menelaus is Menelaus's wife, Helen. According to The Oresteia, the Trojan War was fought by the two Greek generals to recapture Helen and punish the Trojans for having taken her. In a production at the Denver Center for the Performing Arts in 2000 entitled Tantalus, the playwright John Barton drew on the works of Aeschylus, Sophocles, and Euripides as well as earlier writings to present his own version of the upheaval in Greece caused in part by Helen, played here by Annalee Jefferies, supposedly the most beautiful of women, when she left Menelaus for Paris, the son of King Priam of Troy.

drama and in the conduct of human affairs is not a uniquely contemporary phenomenon.

Dramatic Structure   The Oresteia focuses on the conflicts in the family of Agamemnon, the legendary king of Argos (in eastern Greece). Agamemnon and his brother, Menelaus, were the leaders of the Greek navy that decimated the city-state of Troy after ten long years of vicious warfare. The play begins at the time of Agamemnon's return from the Trojan War. Aeschylus takes his departure point for *The Oresteia* from Homer, whose epic poems, the *Iliad* and the *Odyssey*, describe the Trojan War and its aftermath. Aeschylus, however, arranged the material and emphasized selected incidents and relationships in order to present his own

concerns and observations about life in Athens in the fifth century B.C.E.

Summarized very simply, the plot of *The Oresteia* follows a cycle of murder and vengeance in the family of Agamemnon; this cycle repeats itself until a system of justice can be established to stop the pattern of violence that threatens to plunge the entire society into chaos. In our own times, a similar pattern of violence answering violence, retaliation provoking retaliation, can be seen in such conflicts as the gang warfare in U.S. cities or the centuries of feuding that have produced the ethnic hatred in Kosovo between ethnic Albanians and Serbians or in the Middle East between Israelis and Palestinians.

In the first play, *Agamemnon*, the warrior Agamemnon is murdered upon his return from the Trojan War by his wife Clytaemnestra and her lover Aegisthus. The murder is ferocious. Clytaemnestra hacks Agamemnon to pieces with a sword while he is defenseless in his bath. In her own defense, we learn from Clytaemnestra that she plotted the deed throughout the ten years of Agamemnon's absence to avenge the death of her daughter, Iphigeneia. We learn that unfavorable winds kept the Greek navy from setting sail at the beginning of the Greek campaign against the Trojans and that it was Agamemnon who sacrificed his own teenage daughter, Iphigeneia, to secure the winds that would carry the Greek armada across the Aegean Sea to Troy.

Aegisthus, the lover, joins with Clytaemnestra in attacking Agamemnon as a way of revenging himself on Agamemnon's father, Atreus. Atreus was Aegisthus's uncle and the brother of Aegisthus's father, Thyestes. In a dispute over the throne a generation earlier, Atreus had murdered two of Thyestes' children, the brothers of Aegisthus, and had served them to Thyestes as part of a vile banquet of reconciliation. Thyestes had begun to eat his own children before he realized the nature of the deception. The play *Agamemnon* chronicles a family history filled with the most appalling violence of parent against child, uncle against

In Context

FAMILY TREE FOR *THE ORESTEIA*

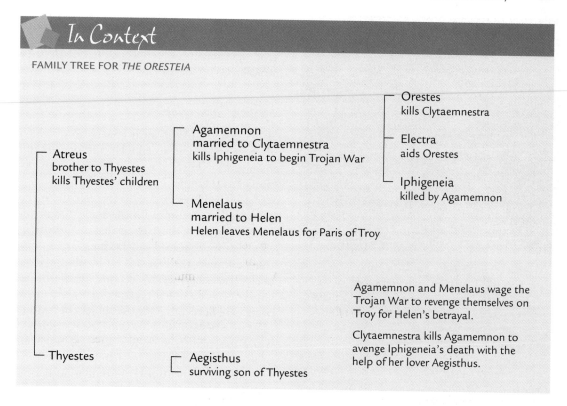

Atreus
brother to Thyestes
kills Thyestes' children

Agamemnon
married to Clytaemnestra
kills Iphigeneia to begin Trojan War

Menelaus
married to Helen
Helen leaves Menelaus for Paris of Troy

Orestes
kills Clytaemnestra

Electra
aids Orestes

Iphigeneia
killed by Agamemnon

Thyestes

Aegisthus
surviving son of Thyestes

Agamemnon and Menelaus wage the Trojan War to revenge themselves on Troy for Helen's betrayal.

Clytaemnestra kills Agamemnon to avenge Iphigeneia's death with the help of her lover Aegisthus.

nephews, brother against brother, and wife against husband.

In the second play of the trilogy, *The Libation Bearers*, Orestes and Electra, the surviving children of Clytaemnestra and Agamemnon, plan the murder of their mother to answer for the death of their father. Orestes stabs to death both Clytaemnestra and Aegisthus, carrying out what he believes to be his obligation to his father and the gods. Unlike Clytaemnestra, Orestes does not exult in the blood he has shed but instead embarks on a journey to cleanse his spirit of his gruesome deed.

Finally, in the third play, *The Eumenides*, Orestes stands trial for the murder of his mother, Clytaemnestra. The trial, held in Athens, is described as the first trial by jury, and ten citizens are selected to decide the fate of Orestes. When at the end of the trial the jury is deadlocked, the goddess Athena casts the

tie-breaking vote in favor of Orestes, setting him free.

***Interpreting* The Oresteia**   It is difficult to say with certainty what *The Oresteia* meant to audiences in its own day; the three plays may have had an entirely different impact on ancient audiences than they have on modern audiences. Certainly the plays are concerned with achieving peace and justice. The responsibility of democratic institutions, such as the court system, for maintaining stability through a considered judicial process is also a significant issue. But what are we to make of the fate of Clytaemnestra? Today we find her motives for the murder of her husband, Agamemnon, understandable if not excusable. He has sacrificed their daughter. Yet from the beginning of the trilogy she is vilified. And at the end, the play identifies Agamemnon as the victim, deserving

Several recent productions of The Oresteia *have sought ways to expand the presence of Iphigeneia, the daughter sacrificed by Agamemnon to secure favorable conditions for the Greek navy's crossing of the Aegean Sea to Troy. In the Denver production of* Tantalus *directed by Peter Hall, an entire episode focusing on the Iphigeneia/Agamemnon relationship was included in which Agamemnon, portrayed by Greg Hicks, is reluctant to kill his daughter, but Iphigeneia, played by Mia Yoo, and her mother, Clytaemnestra, insist on Iphigeneia giving her life. This interpretation adds depth to the character of Agamemnon but conflicts with the versions of the story told by Aeschylus in which Clytaemnestra, not Agamemnon, mourns the loss of Iphigeneia and by Euripides in which Agamemnon is condemned for his failure to place the life of his own child above the misdeeds of Helen, his brother's unfaithful wife.*

issues would have resonated quite differently in Greek culture, where women were restricted from participating in public life, than they would today (Color Plate 3).

Staging Conventions

Every theatre has its own conventions, which are understood and accepted by performers and audience members alike. **Theatrical conventions** are the unique devices of dramatic construction and performance that facilitate the presentation of stories on the stage. One convention in Greek theatre was that no more than three actors appeared on the stage at any one time; another was that the actors always wore masks. Although we know some of the major conventions used in Greek performance, many others are unrecorded or the subject of continuing intense debate. However, using evidence from the plays themselves as well as from other writings, artwork, and archaeological investigation, we can imagine some aspects of a performance.

Male Actors We know that women did not participate in the Greek theatre in any way, which means that all of the roles, male and female, were played by men. We also know that the Greeks used only a small number of actors, two or three, to play all of the individual speaking parts in the play. We must shift our contemporary perspective then to imagine two or three men at a time, all wearing masks and costumes to indicate the roles they are assuming. And after the actors finished one scene or section of the play, they would exit to change their costumes and masks so that they could appear as other characters. The same actor could play a man, a woman, and a god all within a few scenes.

Offstage Violence The many murders in *The Oresteia* bring us to a particularly noteworthy convention of Greek theatre. All of the violence was performed offstage. Frequently, dead bodies were wheeled onstage on a special wagon

sympathy, and Clytaemnestra as the force of passion, violence, and disruption that must be subdued. The play obviously has a great deal to say about the balance of male-female relationships in the family and in society. The gender

In a production entitled Agamemnon and His Daughters at the Arena Stage in Washington, D.C., Clytaemnestra, played by Gail Grate, holds the knife she has used to kill Agamemnon while her children Orestes and Electra look on. Together, Orestes and Electra will plot the death of their mother in revenge for the murder of their father. This production, directed by Molly Smith in 2001, used parts of other plays by Euripides such as Iphigeneia in Aulis and Iphigeneia in Tauris to augment the relationships presented by Aeschylus in The Oresteia.

called the **ekkyklema.** The audience heard in gory detail from messengers about the violent encounters that resulted in the loss of life, and they saw the reactions from the other characters. But the Greek audience did not witness the fight scenes, the murders, and the beheadings that played a prominent part in their dramas and that have essentially taken center stage in contemporary plays and films.

The Mask   Another convention of the Greek theatre that sharply contrasts with contemporary theatre practice is the use of the mask. The mask has been a vital element of theatrical expression in a variety of cultures and had a number of significant functions in the Greek theatre. For the Greeks the mask had practical implications as well as aesthetic ones. As our discussion of *The Oresteia* demonstrates, masks allowed one actor to play a number of roles. The same actor probably would have played the Watchman, Agamemnon, and then Aegisthus, Agamemnon's enemy. Masks also enabled male actors to play female roles. All the female characters—Clytaemnestra, Cassandra, and Electra, as well as the female choruses—would have been played by men. And masks allowed mortals to play the roles of the gods. Both Apollo and Athena have large roles in the third play of the trilogy and must project the power and authority of Olympian deities. Because the Greek plays took place in huge outdoor theatres, the mask also increased the visibility of the actor, who would have been at a considerable distance from many of those in the audience. And in the case of the Greeks, the mask put yet more emphasis on the importance of the voice in conveying the meaning of the text and holding the audience's attention.

The mask also significantly affected the nature of acting. Whereas contemporary performance is frequently dominated by the personality and appearance of the actor, the use of masks in the Greek theatre put the emphasis in performance on the character rather than on the actor. The mask allowed the character to emerge as an entity separate from the actor who wore it. The mask shifted the expressive emphasis to the voice and gestures, although the positioning of the head would have been very expressive in the absence of changing facial expression. In the Greek theatre, the gestures and body positions would have had to be large and striking to communicate across the vast space of the amphitheatre. The most sharply drawn contrast with performance today would be to the close-up of the

The Guthrie Theatre of Minneapolis encouraged renewed interest in The Oresteia *with a landmark production in 1967 entitled* The House of Atreus *adapted by John Lewin and directed by John Houseman. The all-male cast wore elaborate costumes and masks designed by Tania Moisevitch, giving the actors an imposing presence. The figures of the gods were created on an enormous scale to communicate their power. Here Athena sits on her throne ready to pass judgment on Orestes' guilt or innocence.*

actor in a film where the most subtle and natural expressions of the face suggest great depth of feeling. The eyes that turn inward, the mouth that trembles slightly can convey significant meaning. The Greek actor had to work with an entirely different apparatus and on a much larger scale to make his meaning clear.

Any actor who wears a mask experiences some degree of transcendence as he or she identifies with the spirit of the mask. For actors such as the Hopi engaged in a religious ceremony, the mask is an essential intermediary that transports the actor into the spirit world. In more secular performances, masks can still have the effect of lifting the actors out of themselves to identify with the essence of what the masks represent. Finally, for the audience, masks transform the stage or playing space into a magical world inhabited by larger-than-life characters who prompt a shift in the audience's consciousness. The audience members feel that they are in the presence of powerful, archetypal figures who bring onto the stage a cosmic drama.

The Chorus   The **chorus,** like the mask, was another convention of the Greek theatre. Although audiences today are familiar with singing choruses of all kinds, they might find a speaking or chanting chorus on the contemporary stage somewhat strange. A group of twelve to fifteen characters dressed alike and speaking in unison would not seem to represent the world as we see it. In his movie *Mighty Aphrodite,* Woody Allen gets hilarious mileage out of having contemporary characters confide in a Greek chorus. But for the Greek audience, the chorus was an expected part of the theatre experience. The chorus first appeared in early religious festivals, when groups of fifty would sing choral hymns in honor of Dionysus. Some theatre historians believe tragedy had its beginning when one of the chorus members initiated a dialogue between himself—as a single speaker or character—and the rest of the chorus. This legendary first speaker, Thespis, is the source of the word **thespian,** meaning actor.

Sometimes the Greek chorus spoke in **dialogue** and sometimes in longer poetic passages. In the sections of dialogue, the chorus played opposite major characters, asking questions and then listening, serving as a confidant who allowed the central characters to explain themselves. In the poetic or choral passages, the chorus gave much of the family history; in

The Berkeley Repertory Theatre's 2001 production of The Oresteia *was played with the actors unmasked, emphasizing their individual suffering. Here Cassandra, played by Francesca Faridany, cries out her warnings to the chorus of the bloodshed to come. In this production, directed by Tony Taccone and Stephen Wadsworth, the chorus was played by women rather than the chorus of old men called for in the original text.*

The Oresteia, for example, the chorus tells the story of the sacrifice of Iphigeneia to start the Trojan War and explains the references to the murder of Thyestes' children by Agamemnon's father, Atreus. The choral passages also contained many references to other mythological situations, and these allowed the playwright to expand on the significance of the immediate dramatic conflict. He built a complex background through the choral commentary.

In addition to functioning as both a character and a storyteller, the chorus had rhythmic and visual functions. The choral sections were accompanied by music and had their own meter, which contrasted with the dialogue episodes and heightened the growing tensions. The staging of the choruses involved intricate choreography and were an important part of the visual spectacle.

Visualizing a Scene from The Oresteia

With these theatrical conventions in mind, we can now visualize a **scene** from *The Oresteia*. Agamemnon has brought a captive with him from Troy—Cassandra, the youngest daughter of the defeated Trojan king. Cassandra is a prophet, and she tries to warn the chorus, the elders of Argos, that Clytaemnestra is a killer. Clytaemnestra has already persuaded Agamemnon to enter the palace, and she now presses Cassandra to go into the palace as well, where she can trap and kill Agamemnon and Cassandra together. Clytaemnestra cannot withhold her rage when she speaks to Cassandra:

CLYTAEMNESTRA: I have no leisure to stand
    outside the house and waste
  time on this woman. At the central
    altarstone
  the flocks are standing, ready for the
    sacrifice
  we make to this glad day we never hoped to
    see.
  You: if you are obeying my commands at all,
    be quick.
  But if in ignorance you fail to comprehend,
  speak not, but make with your barbarian
    hand some sign.
CHORUS: I think this stranger girl needs some
    interpreter
  who understands. She is like some captive
    animal.
CLYTAEMNESTRA: No, she is in the passion of her
    own wild thoughts.
  Leaving her captured city she has come to us

untrained to take the curb, and will not
understand
until her rage and strength have foamed
away in blood.
I shall throw down no more commands for
her contempt.

(*Clytaemnestra goes back into the house.*)

CHORUS: I, though, shall not be angry, for I pity
her.
Come down, poor creature, leave the empty
car. Give way
to compulsion and take up the yoke that
shall be yours.

(*Cassandra descends from the chariot*)³

Cassandra starts her part of the scene by
calling on the god Apollo. It is Apollo who gave
Cassandra the ability to foresee the future, but
because she had refused his sexual advances, he
cursed her by making sure that even though she
told the truth she would not be believed.

CASSANDRA: Oh shame upon the earth!
Apollo, Apollo!
CHORUS: You cry on Loxias in agony? He is not
of those immortals the unhappy supplicate.
CASSANDRA: Oh shame upon the earth!
Apollo, Apollo!
CHORUS: Now once again in bitter voice she
calls upon
this god, who has not part in any
lamentation.
CASSANDRA: Apollo, Apollo!
Lord of the ways, my ruin.
You have undone me once again, and
utterly.
CHORUS: I think she will be prophetic of her
own disaster.
Even in the slave's heart the gift divine
lives on.
CASSANDRA: Apollo, Apollo!
Lord of the ways, my ruin.
Where have you led me now at last? What
house is this?

CHORUS: The house of the Atreidae. If you
understand
not that, I can tell you; and so much at least
is true.

Cassandra begins to have a vision that reveals
the history of violence connected to the house
of Atreus, particularly the death of Thyestes'
children. She then is drawn to images of
Clytaemnestra, who will kill Agamemnon while
he is in his bath, and she speaks of Clytaemnestra's catching Agamemnon (whom she refers to
as "the bull") in a net. The chorus recognizes
the danger of Cassandra's words but cannot
make sense of her fragments and riddles.

CASSANDRA: No, but a house that God hates,
guilty within
of kindred blood shed, torture of its own,
the shambles for men's butchery, the
dripping floor.
CHORUS: The stranger is keen scented like some
hound upon
the trail of blood that leads her to
discovered death.
CASSANDRA: Behold there the witnesses to my
faith.
The small children wail for their own death
and the flesh roasted that their father fed
upon.
CHORUS: We had been told before of this
prophetic fame
of yours: we want no prophets in this place
at all.
CASSANDRA: Ah, for shame, what can she
purpose now?
What is this new and huge
stroke of atrocity she plans within the
house
to beat down the beloved beyond hope of
healing?
Rescue is far away.
CHORUS: I can make nothing of these
prophecies. The rest
I understood; the city is full of the sound of
them.

CASSANDRA: So cruel then, that you can do this
thing?
The husband of your own bed
to bathe bright with water—how shall I
speak the end?
This thing shall be done with speed. The
hand gropes now, and the other
hand follows in turn.
CHORUS: No, I am lost. After the darkness of
her speech
I go bewildered in a mist of prophecies.
CASSANDRA: No, no, see there! What is that
thing that shows? Is it some net of death?
Or is the trap the woman there, the
murderess?
Let now the slakeless fury in the race
rear up to howl aloud over this monstrous
death.
CHORUS: Upon what demon in the house do
you call, to raise
the cry of triumph? All your speech makes
dark my hope.
And to the heart below trickles the pale drop
as in the hour of death
timed to our sunset and the mortal radiance.
Ruin is near, and swift.
CASSANDRA: See there, see there! Keep from his
mate the bull.
Caught in the folded web's
entanglement she pinions him and with the
black horn
strikes. And he crumples in the watered bath.
Guile, I tell you, and death there in the
caldron wrought.
CHORUS: I am not proud in skill to guess at
prophecies,
yet even I can see the evil in this thing.
From divination what good ever has come
to men?
Art, and multiplication of words
drifting through tangled evil bring
terror to them that hear.

After Cassandra foretells the death of
Agamemnon, she acknowledges that she must
die with him.

CASSANDRA: Alas, alas for the wretchedness of
my ill-starred life.
This pain flooding the song of sorrow is
mine alone.
Why have you brought me here in all
unhappiness?
Why, why? Except to die with him? What
else could be?
CHORUS: You are possessed of God, mazed at
heart
to sing your own death
song, the wild lyric as
in clamor for Itys, Itys over and over again
her long life of tears weeping forever grieves
the brown nightingale.
CASSANDRA: Oh for the nightingale's pure song
and a fate like hers.
With fashion of beating wings the gods
clothed her about
and a sweet life gave her and without
lamentation.
But mine is the sheer edge of the tearing iron.
CHORUS:
Whence come, beat upon beat, driven of
God,
vain passions of tears?
Whence your cries, terrified, clashing in
horror,
in wrought melody and the singing speech?
Whence take you the marks to this path of
prophecy and speech of terror?

Cassandra then turns to the history of her own
city, Troy, whose downfall began when Paris,
her brother, kidnapped Helen, the wife of
Agamemnon's brother, Menelaus. The wedding
of Paris and Helen brought the Greek army to
decimate Troy. Cassandra is the last survivor.

CASSANDRA: Oh marriage of Paris, death to the
men beloved!
Alas, Scamandrus, water my fathers drank.
There was a time I too at your springs
drank and grew strong. Ah me,
for now beside the deadly rivers, Cocytus
and Acheron, I must cry out my prophecies.

CHORUS: What is this word, too clear, you have uttered now?
A child could understand.
And deep within goes the stroke of the dripping fang
as mortal pain at the trebled song of your agony shivers the heart to hear.
CASSANDRA: O sorrow, sorrow of my city dragged to uttermost death.
O sacrifices my father made at the wall.
Flocks of the pastured sheep slaughtered there.
And no use at all
to save our city from its pain inflected now,
And I too, with brain ablaze in fever, shall go down.

. . .

But this is evil, see!
Now once again the pain of grim, true prophecy
shivers my whirling brain in a storm of things foreseen.
Look there, see what is hovering above the house,
so small and young, imaged as in the shadow of dreams,
like children almost, killed by those most dear to them,
and their hands filled with their own flesh, as food to eat.
I see them holding out the inward parts, the vitals,
oh pitiful, that meat their father tasted of. . . .
I tell you: There is one that plots vengeance for this,
the strengthless lion rolling in his master's bed,
who keeps, ah me, the house against his lord's return;
my lord too, now that I wear the slave's yoke on my neck.
King of the ships, who tore up Ilium by the roots,
what does he know of this accursed bitch, who licks

his hand, who fawns on him with lifted ears, who like
a secret death shall strike the coward's stroke, nor fail?
No, this is daring when the female shall strike down
the male. What can I call her and be right? What beast
of loathing? Viper double-fanged, or Scylla witch
holed in the rocks and bane of men that range the sea;
smoldering mother of death to smoke relentless hate
on those most dear. How she stood up and howled aloud
and unashamed, as at the breaking point of battle,
in feigned gladness for his salvation from the sea!
What does it matter now if men believe or no?
CHORUS: Thyestes' feast upon the flesh of his own children
I understand in terror at the thought, and fear
is on me hearing truth and no tale fabricated.
The rest: I heard it, but wander still far from the course.
CASSANDRA: I tell you, you shall look on Agamemnon dead.
CHORUS: Peace, peace, poor woman; put those bitter lips to sleep.
CASSANDRA: Useless; there is no god of healing in this story.
CHORUS: Not if it must be; may it somehow fail to come.
CASSANDRA: Prayers, yes; they do not pray; they plan to strike, and kill.
CHORUS: What man is it who moves this beastly thing to be?
CASSANDRA: What man? You did mistake my divination then.
CHORUS: It may be; I could not follow through the schemer's plan.

CASSANDRA: Yet I know Greek; I think I know it
    far too well.
CHORUS: And Pythian oracles are Greek, yet
    hard to read.

After Cassandra calls Clytaemnestra "the woman lioness," she imagines the torture that this animal-like Clytaemnestra is planning. Cassandra also blames Apollo for her fate and rips off the items of clothing that she wears that are associated with prophecy.

CASSANDRA: Oh, flame and pain that sweeps me
    once again! My lord,
    Apollo, King of Light, the pain, aye me, the
      pain!
    This is the woman-lioness, who goes
      to bed
    with the wolf, when her proud lion rages far
      away,
    and she will cut me down; as a wife mixing
      drugs
    she wills to shred the virtue of my
      punishment
    into her bowl of wrath as she makes sharp
      the blade
    against her man, death that he brought a
      mistress home.
    Why do I wear these mockeries upon my
      body,
    this staff of prophecy, these flowers at my
      throat?
    At least I will spoil you before I die. Out,
      down,
    break damn you! This for all that you have
      done to me.
    Make someone else, not me, luxurious in
      disaster. . . .
    Lo now, this is Apollo who has stripped me
      here
    of my prophetic robes. He watched me all
      the time
    wearing this glory, mocked of all, my dearest
      ones
    who hated me with all their hearts, so vain,
      so wrong;

    called like some gypsy wandering from door
      to door
    beggar, corrupt, half-starved, and I endured
      it all.
    And now the seer has done with me, his
      prophetess,
    and led me into such a place as this, to die.
    Lost are my father's altars, but the block is
      there
    to reek with sacrificial blood, my own.

Finally, Cassandra tells of the coming of Orestes, who will avenge her death and that of Agamemnon, Orestes' father.

CASSANDRA: We two
    must die, yet die not vengeless by the gods.
      For there
    shall come one to avenge us also, born to
      slay his mother, and to wreak death for
      his father's blood.
    Outlaw and wanderer, driven far from his
      own land,
    he will come back to cope these stones of
      inward hate.
    For this is a strong oath and sworn by the
      high gods,
    that he shall cast men headlong for his
      father felled.
    Why am I then so pitiful? Why must
      I weep?
    Since once I saw the citadel of Ilium
    die as it died, and those who broke the city,
      doomed
    by the gods, fare as they have fared
      accordingly,
    I will go through with it. I too will take my
      fate.
    I call as on the gates of death upon these
      gates
    to pray only for this thing, that the stroke be
      true,
    and that with no convulsion, with a rush of
      blood
    in painless death, I may close up these eyes,
      and rest.

CHORUS: O woman much enduring and so
    greatly wise,
  you have said much. But if this thing you
    know be true,
  this death that comes upon you, how can
    you, serene,
  walk to the altar like a driven ox of God?
CASSANDRA: Friends, there is no escape for any
    longer time.
CHORUS: Yet longest left in time is to be
    honored still.
CASSANDRA: The day is here and now; I can not
    win by flight.
CHORUS: Woman, be sure your heart is brave;
    you can take much.
CASSANDRA: None but the unhappy people ever
    hear such praise.
CHORUS: Yet there is a grace on mortals who so
    nobly die.
CASSANDRA: Alas for you, father, and for your
    lordly sons.
    Ah!
CHORUS: What now? What terror whirls you
    backward from the door?
CASSANDRA: Foul, foul!
CHORUS: What foulness then, unless some
    horror in the mind?
CASSANDRA: That room within reeks with blood
    like a slaughter house.
CHORUS: What then? Only these victims
    butchered at the hearth.
CASSANDRA: There is a breath about it like an
    open grave.
CHORUS: This is no Syrian pride of frankincense
    you mean.
CASSANDRA: So. I am going in, and mourning as
    I go
  my death and Agamemnon's. Let my life be
    done.
  Ah friends,
  truly this is no wild bird fluttering at a
    bush,
  nor vain my speech. Bear witness to me
    when I die,
  when falls for me, a woman slain, another
    woman,

and when a man dies for this wickedly mated
    man.
  Here in my death I claim this stranger's grace
    of you.

An anguished young woman pours out her final grief to the sympathetic but bewildered old men of Argos. But the horror is contained by the formal presentation of the scene, the masked male actor portraying Cassandra, surrounded by the masked chorus of elders moving in choreographed rhythms around her:

CASSANDRA: Yet once more will I speak, and not
    this time my own
  death's threnody. I call upon the Sun in
    prayer
  against that ultimate shining when the
    avengers strike
  these monsters down in blood, that they
    avenge as well
  one simple slave who died, a small thing,
    lightly killed.
  Alas, poor men, their destiny. When all goes
    well
  a shadow will overthrow it. If it be unkind
  one stroke of a wet sponge wipes all the
    picture out;
  and that is far the most unhappy thing of all.

The Greek theatre of Athens in the fifth century B.C.E. reinforced the existing social structure and celebrated Athenian democracy. But it was also a theatre of questions. The playwrights recognized that life is full of contradictions and that the future can be neither predicted nor controlled. The dramas that have come down to us call the community to account for its actions and charge individuals with responsibility for their choices. Characters struggle toward self-knowledge, but their view is frequently distorted by arrogance and passion. Wisdom follows only from catastrophic suffering.

THE MEDIEVAL MYSTERY CYCLE

Medieval society was organized largely around the Catholic Church, and it was as part of religious observation that the theatre developed in medieval Europe. The great medieval **mystery cycles** that were staged across western Europe from the thirteenth to the sixteenth centuries are a fascinating example of a religious theatre tradition that depended on the same kind of broad community participation found in the Hopi kachina cycle.

Originally initiated by the Catholic Church in the tenth century to make Christian teachings more accessible to a largely illiterate population, the mystery cycles dramatizing the Christian history of the world grew into elaborate pageants associated with the late spring festivals of Corpus Christi. Towns in England, France, Germany, Italy, and Spain all staged similar variations of these performances, which focused on biblical events from the creation of the world, to the birth and crucifixion of Jesus, to the last judgment. The number of episodes presented ranged from forty to as many as one hundred. Not only did the normal work of the communities cease during the time the plays were performed—as it did during the City Dionysia in Athens and as it continues to do during the kachina cycle in Hopi communities—the entire town was responsible for the presentation of the elaborate sequence of plays.

Staging and Production: A Community Endeavor

In England, production of the plays was organized through the business community and specifically through workers' unions known as guilds. Different guilds were responsible for the production of the different plays. In fact, the work of a particular guild would sometimes

The pageant wagon was a popular style of stage for the mystery plays performed in medieval England. Mystery cycles were performed throughout Europe; and although the stages varied from country to country, all the staging relied on telling the complex Christian history through a series of episodes. The pageant wagons themselves may have had their own compartments for changing costumes, as well as machinery for special effects. The action of the play might have also spilled off the stage into the street before the wagon. Here is a re-creation of the York Cycle as it is performed regularly today outside York Cathedral.

relate to the subject of its assigned play: the boatwrights produced *Noah's Ark*, and the bakers were responsible for *The Last Supper*.

The individual playlets of the English cycles were staged on **pageant wagons,** or carts that were drawn through the town by horses, each one essentially a miniature traveling stage. In the town of York, for example, forty plays were presented beginning at the earliest morning light and continuing far into the night. Each play was performed at twelve different sites throughout the town. People would gather at the designated locations along the "parade" route, and the plays would come to them. Food and music added to the air of great festivity and celebration.

The involvement of the guilds in the production of the plays is not unlike the corporate sponsorship of contemporary entertainments, including parades. The huge nationally televised parades, such as the Tournament of Roses parade on New Year's Day in Pasadena, California, with its flower-covered floats, and the Macy's Thanksgiving Day parade in New York, with its huge balloon characters, are supported by both commercial enterprises and city and state governments.

However, perhaps closer in spirit to the community involvement in the medieval mystery cycles is the small-town parade on the Fourth of July or another day dear to the heart of a local community. The high school bands, groups of riders on horseback, veterans, civic dignitaries, Shriners, and floats sponsored by local businesses—all represent community institutions and community values. The people who line the parade route recognize their friends and neighbors in the parade, and they clearly understand the significance of the celebration.

The kind of community effort that was required to produce the medieval mystery cycles is hard for us to imagine, because most of our elaborate entertainments are put on by professionals and involve a variety of commercial considerations. Over a hundred male actors, and sometimes several hundred, were involved in the mystery plays, as were dozens of men to build scenery and arrange the stage or pageant wagons. Numerous musicians played during or between episodes. And a director and technicians in charge of special effects coordinated the many participants. The undertaking was so complex and demanding of community resources that productions took place only every few years rather than on an annual basis.

Aesthetic Expression: A Shared, Sacred Language

We have seen that the Greek theatre of the fifth century B.C.E. developed a distinct life of its own in part because of the brilliant playwrights who shaped the ideas in the plays and the conventions of performance. In fact, the Greek playwrights directed their own plays, therefore exercising virtually complete control over the material. The medieval theatre, in contrast, was guided by no such original thinking. Rather, it can be seen as one element in an overall pattern of aesthetic expression influenced by the Catholic Church. Because artwork was done for the glory of God, the artists, including visual artists, were all anonymous. We know neither the names of the playwrights nor the identity of the artisans who made the glorious stained glass windows of the great medieval cathedrals. Art was seen as a collective effort of devotion rather than as something done for personal aggrandizement. Instead of focusing on individual innovation or style, artists used the same system of signs and symbols that had evolved within the church and that functioned as a kind of sacred language or writing understood by the entire community. The theatre and the various forms of visual art all used the same subjects, the same ideas of organization, the same details of character, and the same symbols of religious significance.

Story and Symmetry   We have already observed that the mystery cycles were organized in an **episodic,** or processional, manner, constituting a number of separate incidents all related to one epic story. The visual art forms of the time, such as stained glass windows and paintings, were also structured as a group of individual panels with episodes or story incidents all related to one larger theme. Within each panel the figures were organized in a symmetrical and hierarchical manner. For example, three angels at the top of a panel might be balanced by three devils at the bottom, or a certain number of virtuous characters might be depicted to the right of Jesus, with a comparable number of sinners to the left. Functioning as a background in many of these visual images was often a small building or emblematic structure that indicated the location of the scene. The same small buildings became the scenic units placed on the pageant wagons. The arrangement and spacing of the characters probably drew on the same principles of symmetry and hierarchy.

Performance and Special Effects   The simplicity and order of the staging, however, did not restrict the exuberance of the performances, which were far from stiff religious exercises. The point of the performances was to give the audience a chance to identify with Christ's suffering, to feel the power of the miracles and the degradation of the devils and those who had sinned. The central subject of the entire pageant was salvation itself. To have a powerful and useful effect on the audience, the staging had to be clever, magical, lively, and humorous.

Much effort went into the staging of special effects, such as fire, flying angels, ascensions, flowing water, and the bouncing head of St. John the Baptist. One of the most popular parts of the spectacle was the hell mouth, a gaping, monstrous structure emitting smoke and fire and discharging devils in fantastic costumes out into the audience. And the small plays themselves all had compelling details of human interest that connected the situations of the characters to the immediate

hardships and joys experienced by those in the audience.

The Role of the Mystery Cycles in Medieval Society

There are several ways to view the relationship of the Christian mystery cycles to society. On one level they must be seen as a celebration that gave people a break from their routine tasks and a chance to work together to re-create primary community stories. Participants had the double satisfaction of contributing their own skills to the performances and enjoying the results of their neighbors' contributions. Although the mystery plays quickly grew beyond

The mystery cycles were performed in a holiday atmosphere. Music, food, large crowds, and the interruption of work contributed to the audience's anticipation of the performance. Fire, smoke, and the appearance of devils who interacted with the audience all made for very lively entertainment.

the walls of the church buildings themselves, they served to tie the church and community together. The plays reinforced people's faith by allowing community members to identify with Christ's suffering and triumph and to act on their devotion through the production of the plays.

At the same time, the plays served the interests of the ruling classes and the Catholic Church. They reinforced the social organization of the time, which held people in rigidly structured hierarchical positions with almost no possibility of upward mobility. The plays were full of lessons based on accepting one's position in society no matter what the degree of poverty or deprivation; the true rewards of human existence, the plays taught, were to be received in the hereafter.

The relationship of the mystery cycles to society can be seen clearly in the changes that occurred in England in the sixteenth century. In medieval times the mystery cycles benefited both church and state, but after the Protestant Reformation (beginning in 1511), the religious theatre became embroiled in the political upheavals of the day. In England, Henry VIII broke with the pope in 1534 over issues of autonomy in general and divorce in particular. His daughter, Elizabeth I, governed a nation with an expanding sense of national identity and power and a newly established Church of England, which allowed Christian worship without papal interference. Up to this time, the performance of the mystery cycles had reinforced a strong Catholic presence in England. Worried that continued performances would provide a rallying ground for supporters of the pope and Catholicism, the English government set about eliminating the mystery cycles. Manuscripts recording the plays were destroyed, regulations against religious performances onstage were enforced, and plays expressing Catholic views were not licensed. The mystery cycles, long considered a fundamental part of English society, were suppressed when they no longer served the interests of the state.

THE PROFESSIONAL THEATRE

The Greek theatre of the fifth century B.C.E. and the medieval mystery cycles were both associated with religious festivals and appeared only seasonally. The plays in both cases were community endeavors involving large numbers of community members and resources. The production of plays was considered a civic and religious responsibility and brought together religious leaders, civic leaders, business interests, and community members. The participants in the performances themselves consisted of a few semiprofessional theatre practitioners, but the majority were nonprofessionals.

We turn now to two professional theatres with different aesthetics and different conditions of performance: the theatre of Shakespeare and the **Beijing Opera** (also called the Chinese Opera). Unlike the Greek and medieval theatres, both of these theatres involved professional practitioners engaged full-time in the production of plays. Commercial considerations were vital to the financial well-being of each theatre. Attracting a regular and substantial paying audience and securing the patronage of the aristocracy were equally important. Although the theatres of Shakespeare and the Beijing Opera represent extremely different cultural traditions, they share staging conventions that focus on the abilities of actors working on a bare stage to engage the imagination of the audience.

THE ELIZABETHAN THEATRE

Elizabeth I, the daughter of Henry VIII by Ann Boleyn, came to the English throne in 1558. She inherited the English crown when England was entering an era of adventure and expansion, when the spirit of the Renaissance was firing the English imagination. But her reign began in the shadow of English civil wars, the Wars of the Roses, that had bled the nation during the

TUDOR AND JACOBEAN ENGLAND

Date	Event
1455–1485	Wars of the Roses
1485	Battle of Bosworth in which Richard III is defeated by the first Tudor king, Henry VII
1509–1547	Reign of Henry VIII (father of Elizabeth I)
1534	Henry VIII breaks with the pope and founds the Church of England
1547–1553	Reign of Edward VI
1553–1558	Reign of Mary I
1558–1603	Reign of Elizabeth I
1588	Defeat of the Spanish Armada by the English navy
1564–1623	Life of Shakespeare
c. 1590–1610	Shakespeare's theatre career in London
1603–1625	Reign of James I (referred to as the Jacobean period)

preceding century. And Elizabeth faced an ongoing religious struggle between Protestants and Catholics, initiated when her father, Henry VIII, broke with the pope in 1534 and established himself as head of the Church of England. Elizabeth reigned for almost fifty years, until 1603, and she did much to stabilize the nation, creating an atmosphere conducive to spectacular achievements in science, exploration, and the arts. But she held together a contentious society that would return to civil war some years following her death, and there was a price to be paid for the peace that she maintained.

The Theatre in Society

The Elizabethan theatre inherited much from both the Greek theatre and the medieval theatre that immediately preceded it, but it took quite a different place in the English society of the late sixteenth and early seventeenth centuries than did those theatres in their societies. The production of Greek and medieval plays merged religious observation with performances that entertained as they reinforced community values. Regular citizens were involved at every level of the productions, so productions were community-based and amateur in nature. In both Greece and medieval Europe, theatre festivals were held at special times of the year when the normal life of the community stopped to allow the presentation of plays.

In contrast, Elizabethan theatre was a secular theatre operated by professional actors and playwrights who supported themselves with their theatre activities on a year-round basis. This secular theatre interpreted the ambitions and the tremendous changes in worldview of the age. Elizabethan theatre was fascinated by the power struggles of kings and the inner turmoil provoked by such struggles. But in spite of seizing on the political maneuverings of the human community as one of its principal subjects, the theatre was cautious in keeping its distance from the political debates that swirled around the throne of Elizabeth I.

The unique circumstances of the late sixteenth century in England afforded the opportunity for a national theatre. The intellectual and artistic curiosity of the Renaissance prepared the way for sophisticated plays such as those of Shakespeare. The stability of the long reign of Elizabeth I allowed the economy to prosper and with it the theatre. The patronage of the nobility protected playwrights and actors and allowed them to continue to work, even when some religious and civic leaders saw the theatre as either a moral danger or an actual physical danger through the spread of the plague. The growth of London—with a population of 200,000, the largest city in Europe—provided a lively audience eager for frequent theatre performances. And the English language, already rich in expressive words and rhythmic possibilities, was open to the

The 1999 film Elizabeth, with Cate Blanchett in the title role, chronicled the evolution of Elizabeth I into a monarch with an iron will, strong enough to withstand the threats to her throne and the power struggles surrounding her. In a remarkable performance, Blanchett begins as a lively and emotional girl and gradually builds up her defenses until she withdraws behind the mask of the invulnerable Queen. Elizabeth I brought considerable stability to England, allowing the theatre, including the work of William Shakespeare, to flourish.

playwright's inventive vocabulary and phrasing, unfettered by rigid rules or academic restrictions.

The Nature of Elizabethan Drama

Elizabethan drama focused on the complexity of human motivation. The human mind and human action were placed center stage. Human action was played out against a background of religious and political concerns, but it was the internal struggles of the characters that became the major subject of the drama. The most compelling characters from Elizabethan drama were those whose vision for themselves outreached their abilities to live the lives they imagined. It was the drama of an age of human possibility, full of startling opportunities for the expansion of human understanding, underscored by the expansion of the European nations on the high seas and on vast, distant continents. The unknowns were enormous, but the possibilities were exhilarating. A new view of human existence was emerging from Renaissance philosophy and science; at the same time, however, medieval thinking still persisted.

A play that offered an illuminating prologue for the Elizabethan dramas to follow, particularly the plays of William Shakespeare, was *Doctor Faustus*, by Christopher Marlowe. *Doctor Faustus* explores the mind of a man with a consuming ambition to understand the nature of the world and the universe. But his science proves to be no more than a magician's tricks. Faustus's hope for the mind of man shatters his faith in God. He dies in despair, unable to achieve the heights of human understanding that he envisions but also unable to repent for his desire to know. In his quest for knowledge, he is damned by his own conscience as well as the prevailing morality of his society. Faustus has lost the comfort of the medieval worldview, a view that he has yet to escape.

Doubts and questions also torment Shakespearian characters whose burning ambitions lead them to ill-conceived courses of action. Macbeth pursues a course of murder to gain the crown but cannot silence his conscience. King Lear divides up his kingdom in order to receive the adulation of his daughters and is driven mad by the consequences of his actions. In his greatest play, Shakespeare creates a character, Hamlet, who is forced to deal with the murderous ambition of his uncle Claudius. The play explores the questioning mind of a character who cannot make sense of the political realities confronting him.

William Shakespeare

As we examine Elizabethan theatre, we focus on William Shakespeare, the playwright whose soaring achievements became synonymous with the age. A number of other playwrights, such as Christopher Marlowe and Ben Jonson, contributed to the vitality and brilliance of this remarkable period of theatre, but as the theatre became central to Elizabethan and Jacobean England, so Shakespeare became central to the theatre.

Shakespeare's Career   Shakespeare's career in the theatre illuminates the characteristics of the professional London stage of the late sixteenth and early seventeenth centuries. Between approximately 1590 and 1610 Shakespeare wrote thirty-seven plays that together are considered the greatest achievement of any playwright in the history of world theatre.

Shakespeare emerged from an obscure background in Stratford to become one of the important members of the Lord Chamberlain's Men, a small but prominent professional theatre company in London. As part of this company, Shakespeare was an actor, a shareholder, a part owner of the Globe Theatre, and, most significantly, a playwright. Shakespeare's membership and participation in the Lord Chamberlain's Men greatly facilitated his career as a playwright. He worked with a company that had a continuing need for new material, and he knew the strengths and weaknesses of the company, the specialized skills of individual members, and the range of the different actors. In fact, he knew who would play the roles as he wrote them—which actor excelled at comedy, which actor had a good singing voice, which boy actor was available to play a woman's role and how many lines he could be expected to handle.

Although images of Shakespeare exist, he continues to be an elusive historical figure, known through the eloquence of his plays but not through substantial biographical materials. We can only imagine the life he led in London as a member of the Lord Chamberlain's Men who sometimes wrote as many as three plays a year to keep up with the demands of his company and his audience.

There was a continuous interplay between the playwright and the company as he crafted his work to take advantage of the gifts of his fellow company members.

The Sources of Shakespeare's Plays   Shakespeare was not an original story maker. Rather, he was a genius at taking materials from other sources—historical chronicles, romances, and even other plays—and dramatizing them for his company, his theatre, and his lively audience, which consisted of royalty, aristocrats, merchants, and laborers. Written histories of the dynastic struggles that led to the triumph of the House of Tudor provided the material for his chronicling of the English kings. His comedies were modeled on the Latin comedies of Plautus and on Italian romances; his tragedies derived from violent stories and plays of revenge. But no matter how indebted he may have been to his sources, Shakespeare's particular genius—his brilliant language, his facility with plot and action, and his deep understanding of human nature expressed through his unparalleled array of characters—allowed him to bring a series of dramas to the stage that made his company the most successful in London.

Although the struggle for political power was a prominent subject of his plays, Shakespeare generally managed to focus on character rather than on political analysis, which might have been seen as commentary on the national debate over succession. One of the most striking of his history plays, *The Tragedy of Richard III*, however, reveals the manipulation of history in the drama (Color Plate 4). Drawing on the distortions in Thomas More's biography of Richard III, also repeated in the Holinshed *Chronicles* (histories of England, Scotland, and Ireland), Shakespeare created a portrait of a monstrous, misshapen villain who murders the two boys who are the true heirs to the throne and slashes his way across England to revenge himself for his bitter life. As a study of evil, *Richard III* conveniently justifies the killing of Richard by Henry VII and Henry's subsequent usurpation of the throne. Henry VII was the grandfather of Shakespeare's sovereign, Elizabeth I. The portrait of Richard III immortalized by Shakespeare obviously justifies the presence of Elizabeth on the throne. That Richard was actually far different from Shakespeare's character has generally been lost to history, so vivid was Shakespeare's rendering of his villain.

Elizabethan Staging

The Globe and Other Theatres   A cluster of professional theatres was built across the River Thames from the city of London, just beyond the jurisdictional reach of a city government that was dubious about the wisdom of a growing theatrical presence. But theatre owners saw profit to be made from theatrical entertainments that drew 3,000 spectators at a time to their large, round, wooden theatres. The most famous of these public, commercial theatres, the Globe, was the home of Shakespeare's company, the Lord Chamberlain's Men, from 1599 to 1609. The name of the Globe not only reflected the circular shape of the theatre but also described the way the physical structure of the theatre contained the universe as the Elizabethans saw it. And this point of view, encompassed by the theatre building, echoed the same combination of medieval and Renaissance thinking as did the structure of the plays.

Because the theatre was partly open to the sky, the stage was protected by a canopy that might have had stars painted on it to represent the heavens. The stage platform itself was the world, the level of human endeavor, while the area below the stage, accessible through trap doors, suggested hell, with its ghosts and spirits. This hierarchical representation was similar to the understanding of the universe expressed by the medieval stage. The difference was the expansion of the human arena, where most of the action took place.

Of the three theatres discussed so far, the medieval theatre had the most elaborate scenic effects. The Elizabethan stage—like the stage of the Beijing Opera discussed later in this chapter—was an empty space with minimal stage properties, a table, a chair, banners. As such, it was through the playwright's eloquent language that the Elizabethan actor defined the space.

Language as an Element of Staging   Like the Greek theatre, the Elizabethan stage relied on vivid, energetic, and evocative **language** to fill the stage space and shape the **action.** In scene after scene, the playwright framed the action with only a few poetic words to create setting or time of day. In *Hamlet*, the sunrise is created with the following memorable lines:

> But, look, the morn, in russet mantle clad,
> Walks o'er the dew of yon high eastern hill.[4]

The Globe Theatre was built for the Lord Chamberlain's Men and was the site of the premiere performances of some of Shakespeare's most famous plays. This photo shows a reconstruction of the Globe that is now used for theatre performances in London.

In *King Lear*, a storm is created when Lear pours out a description of the weather that also describes the breaking of his heart:

LEAR: Blow, winds, and crack your cheeks!
    Rage! Blow!
  You cataracts and hurricanoes, spout
  Till you have drench'd our steeples, drown'd
    the cocks!
  You sulph'rous and thought-executing
    fires,
  Vaunt-couriers of oak-cleaving thunderbolts,
  Singe my white head! And thou, all-shaking
    thunder,
  Strike flat the thick rotundity o' th' world!

Crack nature's moulds, all germens spill at
  once
That makes ingrateful man![5]

The entering or exiting of characters indicated a change of scene, and frequently characters referred to their next destination as they went. All the information needed by the audience to follow the action was contained in the language. The importance of the language points to an audience prepared to listen closely to the words and rapidly process verbal cues, although there were certainly visual cues as well.

The performance of Shakespeare depended on the imagination of the audience. *Henry V*

The exterior of the reconstructed Globe Theatre is seen against a view of contemporary London. In Elizabethan times the River Thames served as a boundary between the city of London and the theatres that were kept by law outside the city limits.

opens with a prologue in which a character called Chorus asks the audience to fill in the images suggested by the actors so that the stage might become a battlefield where a few actors become armies led by kings:

> Piece out our imperfections with your
>   thoughts;
> Into a thousand parts divide one man,
> And make imaginary puissance;
> Think, when we talk of horses, that you see
>   them
> Printing their proud hoofs i' th' receiving
>   earth.
> For 'tis your thoughts that now must deck
>   our kings,
> Carry them here and there, jumping o'er
>   times,
> Turning the accomplishment of many years
> Into an hour-glass.[6]

As suggested in these lines, Elizabethan plays involved numerous characters acting out complicated events in rapidly shifting locations over extended periods of time. This expansiveness of space and time was a direct inheritance from the medieval stage, which told the entire history of the Christian world in a single production. The Greek drama, in contrast, generally offered a concentrated representation of human experience, portrayed by only a few characters in one location in a very compressed passage of time: human action reduced to its essence. Shakespeare and his contemporaries looked to show the variations of human action by writing complex plays with multiple plots or subplots. To accomplish this sweeping presentation of action, the Elizabethan stage depended on the alertness of its audience and the language of the playwright.

Acting in Elizabethan Dramas

The professional English actor was a master of speech. In discussions of Elizabethan acting, the most famous acting teacher was Shakespeare himself, who through the character of Hamlet instructs a group of traveling actors on their craft:

> Speak the speech, I pray you, as I pronounced it to you, trippingly on the tongue; but if you mouth it, as many of your players do, I had as lief the town-crier had spoke my lines.[7]

Hamlet goes on to emphasize a natural acting style, performed with moderation rather than exaggeration.

> Nor do not saw the air too much with your hand, thus, but use all gently; for the very torrent, tempest, and, as I may say, the whirlwind of passion, you must acquire and beget a temperance that may give it smoothness. . . . Suit the action to the word, the word to the action; with this special observance, that you o'erstep not the modesty of nature. For anything so overdone is from the purpose of playing, whose end, both at the first and now, was and is, to hold, as 'twere, the mirror up to nature; to show virtue her own feature, scorn her own image, and the very age and body of the time his form and pressure.[8]

In fact, the actor would frequently perform very close to the audience, again more like the medieval theatre than the Greek. The platform stage extended into the audience space, and audience members would have stood on three sides of the stage pressing close against it. The actor playing at the edge of the stage would have been able to address the audience easily and intimately in his soliloquies and asides. Even the audience seated in boxes placed around the walls of the audience space would have been close enough to the stage to observe the details of character action. The proximity of the audience to the actors suggests that broad gestures and exaggerated speech were unnecessary. Furthermore, the indication is that the speech was delivered with considerably more speed than it would be today, making a broad style of delivery impossible to maintain.

THE BEIJING OPERA OF CHINA

China is a nation with ancient origins that date back to around 4000 B.C.E. The theatre has played a significant part in the rich Chinese cultural heritage for more than 3,000 years and has taken many forms over that remarkable span of time. The relatively recent form that we examine here, the Beijing Opera, draws on many earlier theatre movements or styles but is usually recognized as being established in 1790. It was at the eightieth birthday party of the reigning emperor in that year that new forms of performance were introduced to Beijing, the capital of China.

A Formal Society

The teachings of Confucius, who lived in the fifth century B.C.E., at the same time as the major Greek playwrights, provided the foundation for the organization of Chinese society. Confucian ideas of family, respect for and deference to elders, acceptance of one's place in the hierarchy, and the importance of formal codes of conduct evolved over a period of centuries into a society governed officially by a vast bureaucracy and internally by a complex and pervasive network of rules and obligations. Although Confucius adhered to ideals that included democracy, what resulted from the modifications of his principles led to a society committed to conformity as a way of maintaining social stability.

At the center of Chinese society was the extended family. The effective functioning of the family as the basic social and political unit depended on the observation of intricate rules that governed relationships and the demonstration of appropriate regard for the elders who headed the family and the ancestors who had preceded them. The dramas of the Beijing Opera took this organization of the family as one of its major subjects. The theatre developed its own precise rules of style and detailed codes for the presentation of character types in response to the formal organization of Chinese society.

Playwrights and Plays

Like the Greek dramatists and Shakespeare, the playwrights for the Beijing Opera drew on earlier sources, such as historical novels, myths, and legends. But the goal of the Chinese

In Context

THE BEIJING OPERA AND CHINESE HISTORY

Date	Event
1644	Manchus conquer China. China is ruled by Manchu dynasties until 1911.
1790	Beijing Opera introduced at the eightieth birthday celebration of Emperor Ch'ien Lung.
1911	Revolution breaks out against dynastic rule. After 1911, women slowly begin to appear on the stage in traditional plays as well as more westernized drama.
1912	China becomes a republic. A period of great instability begins, involving continuous military and political struggles over the next thirty-seven years, including feuding warlords, Japanese invasion, and civil war between Chiang Kai-shek and the communists.
1921	Creation of the Communist Party.
1930/1935	The actor Mei Lan-Fang tours Japan, the United States, and Russia, where he is seen by Bertolt Brecht.
1937	War with Japan.
1942	Talks at Yan'an Forum on Art and Literature, during which Mao Zedong presents his theories of art and theatre serving the political cause.
1949	Communist takeover of China.
1966	Cultural Revolution. Harshest period of censorship of the arts under supervision of Mao's wife, Jiang Qing. Substitution of model plays for traditional Chinese theatre.
1976	Death of Mao. Overthrow of the "gang of four." Revival of traditional theatre forms.
1989	Massacre at Tiananmen Square. Crackdown against democracy movement.

dramatist was not to create a work that would stand on its own philosophical or poetic merit but to provide a vehicle for the actor. The Chinese playwright was an anonymous arranger of a text, bringing together functional passages that would support the actor's creation. And the audience members who gathered in large restaurant-like theatres, drinking tea and eating during the performances, did not hang on every word but paused in their noisy activity to pay close attention only to the most exciting or clever parts.

The plays were loosely divided into two areas of focus: civil plays that dealt with domestic and social situations and military plays that maximized the opportunity for the action of warriors, outlaws, and demons. Plays were constructed around a set of instantly recognizable stock characters: four categories—male, female, painted-face, and comic—were divided into representative types whose characteristics were predetermined through generations of performances. A male character could be the hero, the official, the warrior, or the patriarch. A female character could be the virtuous and demure woman, the lively but untrustworthy woman, the warrior woman, or the matriarch. As in the Greek, medieval, and Elizabethan theatres, men played the women's roles, and because these were professional actors, female impersonation became a highly refined art. The gender issues related to female impersonation were complicated further by the social and sexual position of the male actors who undertook these roles in Chinese society. We return to the issue of female impersonation later in the chapter.

The painted-face characters brought the fantastic, the grotesque, and the supernatural into the world constructed by the Chinese theatre. Animal gods, outlaws, and warriors were given a larger-than-life appearance with bold and colorful makeup applied in such strong patterns that it functioned much like a mask. Finally, the comic roles included characters who contradicted expectations: the elderly soldier who was foolish rather than wise, the peasant who was cunning rather than simple.

A Language of Gesture

Although the form of the Beijing Opera is absolutely distinct from the other major forms of theatre in Asia, such as the **kabuki** theatre of Japan, the **kathakali** theatre of India, and the dance drama of Bali, certain basic principles guide all of the traditional theatres of Asia. Just as text is the dominating force in the Western theatre, so gesture is the language of the actor in the Eastern theatre. In the West, the scripts of famous playwrights have been handed down through the centuries, and theatre is largely a verbal, language-based art. In Asian theatre, the gestures, stylized and intricate, convey codes of meaning that can be "read" by an audience just as plainly as we in the West can interpret the actor's speech.

The text of the Beijing Opera may lack the power of the finest writing for the Western stage; similarly, the use of character types may have precluded the development of highly individualized, psychologically developed characters such as Oedipus and Hamlet, whose struggles have made them central to Western culture. But the Beijing Opera developed a poetry of theatrical expression that we cannot yet approximate. And the speech of Asian theatre, which is totally unlike Western conversational stage speech, is as stylized and removed from the everyday world as the actor's movement patterns.

Acting and Staging

The movement and the speech or singing of the Asian theatre demand a technical proficiency achievable only after years of the most disci-

The Beijing Opera involves a spectacular display of gymnastics, martial arts, and pantomime that demands the most rigorous training. Children begin their training at an early age, much like Olympic athletes, in order to be able to perform the intricate and explosive choreography required of the Beijing Opera form. The costumes provide the visual focus in the Beijing Opera. Layers of fabric, heavily embroidered patterns, gorgeous colors and textures, and fabulous headdresses and wigs create a sumptuous visual presentation that does not need further definition from scenery.

plined training, which begins when the actors are children. It is through such rigorous training that the physical interpretation of a role can be passed from generation to generation, even over centuries.

With the conventions of the Chinese theatre in mind, we can imagine a performance of the Beijing Opera in the mid-nineteenth century. The actor stood alone on a bare, platform stage. Although elaborate scenery was in use throughout European and American theatres at

The Peony Pavilion *represents a form of Chinese Opera called* kungku, *which is less acrobatic and more lyrical than the Beijing Opera. The* Peony Pavilion, *written in 1598, tells the story of a scholar, Liu Mengmei, who rescues his beloved, Du Liniang, from the underworld. Told in fifty-five episodes, which take nineteen hours to perform,* The Peony Pavilion *was revived in 1999 with performances at Lincoln Center in New York City and in Shanghai, China.*

this time, in the Beijing Opera there were no clever scenic elements to capture the audience's imagination, no special lighting effects to focus their attention. The actor had to use his own resources to create everything that the audience would see. And for this, the actor was singularly well-prepared. With a few steps he crossed an invisible threshold and entered a new room or building. With a flick of his whip he rode a nonexistent horse; with a swaying motion he was carried down the river in an imaginary boat. Dressed in sumptuously embroidered robes and wearing an elaborate wig and headdress, the Chinese actor created a compelling presence (Color Plate 5).

Later in the performance the subtle pantomime that created both environment and action gave way to more spectacular choreography. A battle scene took place, and the combatants seemed to come flying across the stage. With enormous swords in hand, the actors performed acrobatic feats that had the audience shouting their approval. Bodies hurtled about the stage at unbelievable speeds, performing multiple flips and somersaults in the air, akin to the flights of Olympic gymnasts. All of the action, the entrances and exits, the pantomimed sequences, and the acrobatic choreography, were accompanied by musicians seated in view of the audience playing drums, gongs, cymbals, flutes, and traditional Chinese string instruments. The actors' lines, which had their own stylistic patterns, were sung and chanted rather than spoken.

A few basic pieces of furniture were all that helped designate location. A table and two chairs in different configurations changed the scene from a palace to a law court to a bedroom or indicated a wall, a bridge, or a mountain. A stagehand whose invisibility was an accepted convention of the Chinese theatre appeared as needed to reposition the furniture or to add or remove the few additional props that gave further definition to the changing space. The flexible approach to staging meant that performances could easily accommodate multiple locations and shifting conditions, such as time of day and weather. This style of performance emphasized the bond between the actor's skill and the audience's imagination. It also depended heavily, as so many performance traditions do, on a body of theatrical conventions accepted and understood by all participants in the dramatic event.

The Beijing Opera and the Communist Revolution

The history of the Beijing Opera in the twentieth century was closely intertwined with the rise of the Communist Party to power and its subsequent cultural policies. In the first part of the twentieth century approximately 3,000 opera companies performed the traditional repertoire throughout China. A typical company was a private, commercial endeavor organized around one or more star performers that played regular engagements in a theatre and also was hired to perform for various festivals, both public and private.

The most famous company was headed by the actor Mei Lan-Fang, who was revered throughout China for his brilliant performances and for the innovations he brought to the traditional theatre form. Mei Lan-Fang also achieved an international reputation by undertaking a series of tours with his company in the 1920s and the 1930s to Japan, the United States, and Russia. He made an enormous impression on Western theatre practitioners, particularly the German director and playwright Bertolt Brecht, who would become one of the defining forces in twentieth-century theatre.

The Chinese communists saw the arts as essential to their goals for transforming Chinese society. From the early days of communist activity in China, Mao Zedong and his followers encouraged the development of a political theatre that would serve the revolutionary cause. In 1942, seven years before the communists came to power in China, Mao officially articulated his theories about the relationship between politics and art and literature at the Yan'an Forum on Art and Literature. According to his view, the only acceptable function for art was to celebrate and serve the proletariat:

> If everyone agrees on the fundamental policy of art serving the workers, peasants and soldiers and on how to serve them, such should be adhered to by all our workers, our schools, publications and organizations in the field of literature and art and in all our literary and artistic activities. It is wrong to depart from this policy. Anything at variance with it must be duly corrected.

The implications of this policy would be as wrenching for the Beijing Opera as the upheaval and strife generated by Mao and his wife, Jiang Qing, would be for the Chinese nation as they reformed what they perceived to be the corruptions of the past. Because of its enormous popularity, the Beijing Opera was targeted as a major vehicle for communist propaganda. During the **Cultural Revolution** (1966 to 1976), the traditional Beijing Opera was almost completely suppressed and replaced with eight model plays that dealt with contemporary themes and emphasized heroic, sacrificial actions on behalf of the revolution and the workers. Enormous sums of money and human resources were lavished on the development of the model productions. Productions such as *The Red Lantern* and *The White-Haired Girl* demonstrated the class struggle at the heart of the Chinese revolution and clearly identified the corrupt, capitalist enemies of the people.

Although these plays are not without strong characters and rising tension, they are extremely didactic. And although the model productions held the attention of audiences during this intense period of upheaval in China, they undermined the ability of the opera form to sustain itself when the political winds changed. The old actors and stories were gone. Audiences became wary of overtly political theatre. The model productions had laid no groundwork for the development of new material, and the companies had no other plays available with which to attract audiences.

The manipulation of the Beijing Opera to present communist propaganda had the long-term effect of practically destroying the theatre form itself; this development was not unlike the elimination of the mystery cycles in Elizabethan England as part of the government's policy to create a nation removed from the pope's influence. In China, the Beijing Opera was appropriated to promote the social change envisioned by Mao Zedong and his wife, Jiang Qing.

The Beijing Opera, like the Elizabethan theatre, the Greek theatre, and the medieval theatre, was at the center of its society. All four of these theatres functioned as the mirror that, in Hamlet's words, revealed the "form and pressure" of "the very age and body of the time." The performance traditions and the subjects of the plays reflected the concerns of the community and the way the community understood and expressed itself.

Thus far we have observed the way the theatre has reflected religious beliefs, political organization, and social relationships. As we try to understand what the theatre has to tell us about the past, we are struck particularly by one theatrical convention shared by all of these theatres from vastly different periods and with extremely different political and religious points of view: although women characters appeared on the stage, all of the female roles were written and played by men.

THEATRE AS A MIRROR OF SOCIETY

In the theatres that we have studied in this chapter, women did not participate in any way except as audience members. The exclusion of

In this production of Shakespeare's As You Like It *at Shakespeare and Company in Lenox, Massachusetts, Judith McSpadden plays Jacques, a role originally written for a male actor. Such casting challenges assumptions based on gender.*

women from participation in the theatre reflected a significant aspect of a social organization that excluded women from the public discourse. Just as women did not vote, hold office, or participate in the educational system or the government—with the exception of Elizabeth I—so they were not allowed to be part of the theatre. Women were represented, but they did not represent themselves. The female behavior constructed onstage was considered appropriate or even ideal. But men created all of the images that represented women, both physically and psychologically.

Today, some theatre historians and social critics see this representation of women by men as an absence. That is, any actual sense of women was completely missing. The female characters were part of a man's world but not part of a woman's world. The female characters may have become erotic objects for the male characters or they may have reflected male attitudes toward women, but they did not genuinely represent the actual nature and concerns of women themselves.

In the Greek theatre, masks and costumes designated the gender of the characters, and because three actors played all of the individual roles, actors moved back and forth between male and female characters. In the unmasked Elizabethan theatre, boys or young men played the female parts. In the Beijing Opera, elaborate makeup, costuming, and wigs were used to complete the illusion. In the Asian theatre, actors were designated at an early age to take female roles, and their whole training focused on techniques of impersonation. These actors, called *dan* in the Beijing Opera, then played female roles throughout their careers. In the Chinese theatre, female-character actors had to wear and master special blocked shoes that gave the impression that the character had bound feet. Later, beginning in 1911, when women began to appear onstage and bound feet had been outlawed in China, the women had to learn from the male actors how to create the accepted stage impression of a woman's bound foot.[9]

The exclusion of women from the theatre has had a number of significant consequences. The theatre has always been a central institution for the exchange of ideas and the evolution of culture. By being excluded from the early forms of theatre, women lost a valuable opportunity to participate in the life of the community. Their voices were not heard, creating a serious distortion of what both women and men in a given society saw as "believable" female behavior. Because the theatre functions as a major source of culturally accepted gender identity, ideas or models of behavior were generated that defined women's roles and their nature, even though women had no part in their creation. As a result, women may have shaped or distorted their own behavior or adopted styles of dress or attitude in response to what had been repre-sented in the theatre. This distortion resulted from both the selection of character qualities to be represented—that is, what was chosen and what was left out—and from the context in which the female characters were placed.

THEATRE AND SOCIAL CHANGE

U.S. society today is vitally concerned with issues of gender and race. These concerns are reflected in legislation, education, economic initiatives, public debate, and theatre. The theatre not only mirrors the roles human beings take in their respective societies but also plays an important part in changing the way we see ourselves. Many contemporary plays, including those represented in this book, directly address questions of race and gender and challenge us to rethink issues of equity and citizenship. In such recent plays as *Joe Turner's Come and Gone*, *And the Soul Shall Dance*, *Angels in America*, and *Dog Lady*, identity is considered in connection to the individual psychology of the characters, but it is also explored in terms of the way social expectations condition human behavior.

Plays and theatrical movements have frequently been a significant factor in challenging prevailing points of view and bringing about social change. We must always remember that although the theatre is vulnerable to government intervention, it is the power of theatre that provokes government scrutiny. For example, in the 1960s in the United States, a protest movement aimed at ending U.S. participation in the war in Vietnam eventually gathered such strength that the U.S. government ended its military involvement there. An important part of that protest movement was theatre. Theatre performances in the streets, on college campuses, and in traditional, professional, and community theatres were a powerful way of bringing people together and expressing the suffering and the futility of war. Processions created by the Bread and Puppet Theatre involved huge puppets representing Vietnamese

Since its founding in 1965, the Bread and Puppet Theatre has provided commentary on American politics, government, business, and social structure. Through startling puppets that can be grotesque or exquisitely beautiful and are frequently overwhelming in size, Peter Schumann and his company create an imaginative spectacle that simultaneously transports audiences to a different world and critiques the world we live in.

women that moved silently through the streets of New York City. Political parodies were staged in cabarets, and theatre companies performed Euripides' antiwar play *The Trojan Women,* among other Greek tragedies. The performances promoted discussion and action, adding the energy of the collective artistic experience to the political activity.

In the 1960s in the fields of California, another theatre movement sprang up that contributed to social change. César Chávez began to organize migrant farmworkers in strikes and demonstrations for better working conditions and wages. Luis Valdez brought actors into the fields on the backs of flatbed trucks to perform short plays about the lives of the farmworkers, thus bringing theatre into the farmworkers' movement. These were exuberant plays that energized audiences with their satiric treatment of worker-employer relationships. These "actos" performed in the fields became the foundation of the Teatro Campesino, one of the early Latino theatres in the United States that would subsequently make a major contribution to the Hispanic theatre movement and to the American theatre.

Most recently the theatre has become part of our collective national effort to respond effectively to the attacks on the United States of September 11, 2001. Rather than providing answers to difficult questions or formulating a call to action, the theatre presents a forum that allows for the examination of individual experience as well as social and political concerns. In the words of playwright Tony Kushner, plays can "prove generative of thought, contemplation, discussion."[10] The first play written about the collapse of the towers at the World Trade Center, *The Guys* by Anne Nelson, opened in December 2001. It serves in part as a memorial, a eulogy for firefighters whose lives were lost. A year later, in September 2002, three days of plays entitled *Brave New World* were staged, bringing together more than 130 actors, playwrights, and musicians who produced fifty plays that wrestled with various implications resulting from terrorism on U.S. soil. At a time of national soul searching, we recognize the significance of dramatic storytelling in trying to make sense of individual loss as well as changes in our national consciousness, a process with no fixed timetable or outcome.

Before the September 11 attacks, Tony Kushner had written a play about Afghanistan that was scheduled to go into rehearsal in October of 2001 at the New York Theatre Workshop. Homebody/Kabul *opened on December 19, 2001. Although the play was stunningly timely, it was not written or rewritten to respond specifically to the events of September 11 but rather to address the complex historical and political circumstances in Afghanistan. In the 2002 Berkeley Repertory Theatre production directed by Tony Taccone, Priscilla Ceiling, played by Heidi Dippold, is searching for her mother, who has disappeared in Kabul.*

THE SUSTAINING POWER OF THE THEATRE: *WAITING FOR GODOT* IN SARAJEVO

In conclusion, we turn to the story of a small theatre in a small community where the performance of a play became part of the survival effort in a war-torn nation. In 1991 Yugoslavia broke up into smaller states and entered a pe-

riod of disastrous conflict that has yet to be fully resolved. The city of Sarajevo, the capital of Bosnia and Herzegovina, only a decade earlier the site of the Olympic Games, became one of the casualties of this civil war. Its gracious buildings were turned to rubble, its economy was ruined, and its citizens were left scrounging for any kind of fuel to get them through the bitter winters.

Susan Sontag, an American writer, philosopher, and theatre director, wanted somehow to stand with the people of Sarajevo in their desperate situation. She went to Sarajevo in 1993 to put on a play. The play she chose, *Waiting for Godot*, by Samuel Beckett, is about characters who exist in a bleak and comfortless landscape, seeking somehow to pass the time while they wait for someone who never comes. Asked if *Godot* might be too pessimistic a play choice under the circumstances, Sontag wrote,

> In Sarajevo, as anywhere else, there are more than a few people who feel strengthened and consoled by having their sense of reality affirmed and transfigured by art.[11]

The example of Susan Sontag's work in Sarajevo is included in this book because she has written about her experiences and therefore provided a way for us to understand the conditions of this theatre production. The actors worked under very difficult conditions. Before rehearsals began at ten o'clock in the morning, the actors spent hours procuring water for their families and carrying heavy jugs up many flights of stairs. Most of the actors suffered from malnutrition. They had difficulty memorizing their lines because of their health and the obvious distractions of rehearsing while shells and sniper fire exploded in the city streets around them, injuring or killing their fellow Sarajevans. Fatigue was a continuous factor; the actors needed to lie down on the stage floor to rest every time there was a break in the rehearsal. The stage was lit only by a handful of candles, and reading from the poorly duplicated scripts made the rehearsals halting and slow.

Susan Sontag (top right) *joins the actors of* Waiting for Godot *on the stage in Sarajevo.*
Photo © Annie Leibovitz.

But even under such circumstances, the production of a play drew the actors to the theatre:

> Putting on a play means so much to the local theatre professionals in Sarajevo because it allows them to be normal, that is to do what they did before the war; not just haulers of water or passive recipients of "humanitarian aid."[12]

When *Waiting for Godot* was performed in Sarajevo, all the seats were taken and people had to be turned away. In this performance of a painful play under difficult circumstances, the relationship between theatre and the surrounding community, the society, became clearly defined. We recognize that the actors needed to be in each other's presence rehearsing their parts; we also recognize that the audience members needed to gather together with each other and with the actors, even in an auditorium dimly lit by candles, with sniper fire outside the theatre door. For the audience members, watching a film recorded in another place and at another time could not have equaled the experience of being with live actors, who became their companions in a performance that celebrated humanity at a time when inhumanity threatened to engulf their world. The sharing of the performance, the connection between actors and audience, became its own candle, lit to offset the despair darkening Sarajevo.

SUMMARY

The power of the theatre derives from its collective public nature, from the combined energies of the community of artists and the community audience. Theatre addresses issues of religion and politics, gender and race, social stability and revolution. It functions as a mirror to society, reflecting both the themes and subjects that concern the people and the forms of aesthetic expression deemed appropriate and acceptable in that community.

Some theatre traditions developed in association with religious festivals. The theatre of Athens in the fifth century B.C.E. arose from festivals celebrating the transformative powers of Dionysus, god of the life force. Performed outdoors in natural amphitheatres overlooking the sea, the Greek dramas provided the occasion for thousands of Athenians to gather for a few days every year to experience community myths and legends in the form of drama. Greek theatre employed certain well-understood conventions of performance, including the mask and the chorus. Through drama, the Greeks explored difficult questions about human existence. *The Oresteia*, a trilogy by Aeschylus, addresses issues of guilt, responsibility, and retribution.

Like Greek theatre, the medieval mystery cycles were religious in origin and purpose. Every few years, community members, working through their guilds, re-created the story of Christianity in a series of playlets presented during the late spring festival of Corpus Christi. Plays were staged on pageant wagons that moved from place to place in the town. The conventions of the medieval theatre were derived from the shared, sacred language of signs and symbols used to evoke and represent Christianity. Stories were simple and told in episodic fashion, both in the plays and in medieval visual art forms such as stained glass windows; the works of playwrights and artists were anonymous and emphasized order and symmetry. In the medieval cycles, religious meaning merged with the humorous and exuberant performances to create an event that was highly entertaining as well as deeply moving. The plays reinforced the hierarchical structure of medieval society with stories that encouraged obedience and humility.

Unlike the Greek and medieval theatres, which were basically religious and depended on community participation, Elizabethan theatre and the Beijing Opera were secular and professional. Elizabethan drama focused primarily on human motivation and the internal struggles of psychologically complex characters. Reflecting the curiosity and expansiveness of the Renaissance, Elizabethan drama took on the whole realm of human endeavor. The vitality of Elizabethan drama came from vivid and poetic language, most highly regarded in the works of William Shakespeare. Performing on a bare platform stage during Shakespeare's time, the actors were able to create a constantly changing panorama of events and locations through the playwright's expressive words.

Before the Cultural Revolution (from 1966 to 1976), Chinese plays focused on domestic, social, and military situations, supporting the existing values of society. The Chinese playwright's goal, however, was not to create an immortal work but to provide a vehicle for the highly trained Chinese actor. The Beijing Opera was a theatre of stylized gesture and choreographed, acrobatic movement. The conventions of this theatre included a refined movement vocabulary that conveyed meaning just as spoken scripts do in Western theatre.

Theatre has always reflected religious belief, social organization, and issues of concern to the community. In the twentieth century, the theatre began to question the construction of identity in relation to race and gender. No matter what its specific concerns, however, theatre is a community endeavor with the power to reinforce, to celebrate, to challenge, and to sustain.

TOPICS FOR DISCUSSION AND WRITING

1. Greek tragedies involved a great deal of violence. However, all of the violent incidents took place offstage and were then described in detail to the audience by messengers who had witnessed the violence. The dead bodies were also frequently brought onstage as a display of what had happened. What reasons might the Greeks have had to place the violence offstage? What do you think the effect would have been on the audience? What would happen to contemporary drama and films if the violence occurred offstage? What is the effect of onstage and onscreen violence on audiences today?

2. Based on the examples discussed in the chapter, what differences do you find between religious and secular theatre?

3. What makes theatre a useful tool for propaganda?

4. The chapter discusses the exclusion of actual women from the theatres of the past. How were women represented on the stage? What conventions were used to create female characters? Are there any such conventions used today for the representation of women or men in the theatre, film, or television?

NOTES

1. In *The Theatre of Meyerhold* (New York: Drama Book Specialists, 1979), Edward Braun notes that the killing of both Meyerhold and Raikh by Soviet authorities is the version of the events accepted by their families (p. 286). Also see Zygmunt Hubner, *Theater and Politics* (Evanston: Northwestern University Press, 1992), 194.

2. John Elsom, *Cold War Theatre* (London: Routledge, 1992), 9.

3. All passages from *The Oresteia* are from Aeschylus, *The Oresteia*, trans. David Grene and Richard Lattimore (Chicago: University of Chicago Press, 1967), 74–87.

4. Hamlet, in *The Complete Plays and Poems of William Shakespeare*, ed. William Allen Neilson and Charles Jarvis Hill (Cambridge: Riverside Press, 1942), 1049. (I, i)

5. *King Lear*, in *The Complete Plays*, ed. Neilson and Hill, 1158. (III, ii)

6. *Henry V*, in *The Complete Plays*, ed. Neilson and Hill, 711. (Prologue)

7. *Hamlet*, 1068. (III, ii)

8. *Hamlet*, 1068. (III, ii)

9. A. C. Scott, *The Theatre in Asia* (New York: Macmillan, 1972), 261.

10. Tony Kushner, "An Afterword," *Homebody/Kabul* (New York: Theatre Communications Group, 2002), 144.

11. Susan Sontag, "Godot Comes to Sarajevo," *New York Review*, 21 October 1993, 52.

12. Sontag, 54.

SUGGESTIONS FOR FURTHER READING

Aeschylus. *The Oresteia.* Translated by Robert Fagles. New York: Viking Press, 1977.

> A passionate and poetic translation of the three plays that make up the only surviving trilogy of Greek tragedy, with an exceptional introduction that clarifies the themes and structure of the work.

Arnott, Peter D. *Public and Performance in the Greek Theatre.* London: Routledge, 1991.

> A lively and accessible exploration of audience, actor, staging, and physical space in the ancient Greek theatre.

Bate, Jonathan, and Russell Jackson, eds. *Shakespeare: An Illustrated Stage History.* Oxford: Oxford University Press, 1966.

> A thoughtful chronicle of the changing styles of performing Shakespeare from Elizabethan times to the present. Models of theatre buildings and stages, set and costume designs, directorial approaches, and actor's commentary on their roles all create a vivid impression of each age. The text

highlights issues in the plays as well as the concerns and values of different time periods.

Beadle, Richard, ed. *The Cambridge Companion to Medieval English Theatre*. Cambridge: Cambridge University Press, 1994.

A contemporary overview of the development of the medieval theatre, with a particular focus on the themes and production of the mystery cycles; reviews the traditional scholarship in light of new research and offers fresh ideas in a clear and straightforward manner.

Flanagan, Hallie. *Arena*. New York: Duell, Sloan and Pearce, 1940.

A documentation of the one attempt in American history to forge a major relationship between the government and the theatre. This book outlines the history of the Federal Theatre project set up during the Depression to provide work for the unemployed and to encourage theatrical participation and expression throughout the nation. It explores the triumphs of major theatrical innovations, the brilliance of such artists as Orson Welles and John Houseman, and the relationship between the many theatre ventures and the United States government, which first mandated a national theatre and then, for political reasons, shut it down.

Macherras, Colin, ed. *Chinese Theatre: From Its Origins to the Present Day*. Honolulu: University of Hawaii Press, 1983.

A strong overview of the forms of Chinese theatre from its early origins in the thirteenth century A.D. to the present. This book is particularly useful in assessing the relationship between theatre and society in China, including the upheavals and complexities of the twentieth century.

Sorell, Walter. *The Other Face: The Mask in the Arts*. New York: Bobbs-Merrill, 1973.

An exploration of the place of masks in various communities and in various types of performance, including dance, plays, and puppetry. With 121 illustrations of historical and modern uses of masks, Sorell provides philosophical and psychological insight into artistic expression through masks.

Werthein, Albert. *The Dramatic Art of Athol Fugard: From South Africa to the World*. Bloomington: Indiana University Press, 2000.

A study of the work of South African playwright Athol Fugard, who is also a highly regarded actor and director. Plays discussed include *The Blood Knot, A Lesson from Aloes, Sizwe Bansi Is Dead*, and *Master Harold and the Boys*. These plays exemplify Fugard's concerns with relationships, race, and the significance of the theatre and art in bringing about social change.

Yan, Haiping, ed. *Theatre and Society: An Anthology of Contemporary Chinese Drama*. New York: M. E. Sharpe, 1998.

A collection of the most recent plays from China, including music drama and modern spoken drama; discusses the revival of drama in China following the damage done to the theatre during the Cultural Revolution.

The Nature of Performance

The Theatre Practitioners

In Chapter 2 we considered the centrality of theatre for societies earlier than our own, societies in which dramas could only be presented live, not through the film media prevalent today. We now shift our attention to the significance of the theatre in modern society, particularly the American theatre, and the work that must be done to realize theatre productions on the contemporary stage. As we expand our references to American playwrights and productions, we quickly see that no one playwright speaks for the nation as Shakespeare did in Elizabethan England, nor do we have a national theatre like the Greek and medieval theatres, with a set of myths and signs recognized by everyone. Furthermore, the American theatre is not dominated by a particular place or group of producers. For many decades the center of the American theatre was considered to be New York City.

The acceptance of any new play depended on a production in one of the prestigious theatres clustered on and around **Broadway.** Other parts of the nation would see what Broadway had sanctioned through touring productions or the gradual passage of successful plays to smaller theatres around the country. But the energy of the American theatre is no longer focused in one geographic area. Although New York is certainly still a leader in the development of plays and performance styles, large and small theatres play a vital part in communities throughout the country and collectively help to form an evolving idea of the American theatre.

Producing theatre depends on a collaborative process, usually begun by a playwright who is joined by actors, a director, and designers. In this section of the book, we turn our attention to the work of these theatre practitioners. First we examine the way the contributions of the different participants come together to build ideas, images, dramatic action, and character development. Through a study of the play *Joe Turner's Come and Gone* by August Wilson in a production at the Oregon Shakespeare Festival, we explore the playwright's creation and then the collective effort of producing the play for an audience. We see the play as a work of art and an exploration of historical and social issues.

Following the discussion of the play in production, we take a closer look at the unique arts of the actor, the director, and the designers. We separate and examine the special abilities and skills required of each theatre artist and the kinds of training necessary to prepare for the intense demands of theatre work. Whether a playwright, a performer, a director, or a visual artist, all theatre practitioners share the need to merge creativity and discipline, intuition and analysis, imagination and technique. Only through years of training does the skilled artist emerge. The section concludes with a history and analysis of the American musical theatre that allows us to include the composer, the lyricist, and the choreographer in our assessment of the work of theatre practitioners and to consider the way music and dance contribute to the theatrical experience.

CHAPTER 3

The Playwright's Vision

Looking at Joe Turner's Come and Gone *by* August Wilson

When August Wilson was a fifteen-year-old high school student living in Pittsburgh with his mother, he wrote a paper on Napoleon for his history class. The quality of the paper was so high that the teacher had two responses: he gave the paper an A+, and he told the young African American student that he would have to prove that the work in the paper was really his. Wilson pointed to the bibliography and footnotes but otherwise refused to plead his case. The teacher then changed the grade to an F. On that day, August Wilson quit school and never went back.

He turned instead to the public library and began to educate himself through the books he found there. And at age twenty he began his writing career, first as a poet and then as a writer of short stories. As a young man who had been rejected by the institutions of white culture, he began "remaking the world in his own image through the act of writing."[1] But while he responded to his own experiences, he also started listening to the stories and experiences of the people he met on the street, people such as the elderly black men who hung around the cigar store, "swapping tales, discussing the day's headlines, arguing and needling."[2] Their lives and memories were long, going back to

To write is to fix language, to get it down and fix it to a spot and have it have meaning and be fat with substance. It is in many ways a remaking of the self in which all of the parts have been realigned, redistributed, and reassembled into a new being of sense and harmony. You have wrought something into being, and what you have wrought is what you have learned about life, and what you have learned is always pointed toward moving the harborless parts of your being closer to home. To write is to forever circle the maps, marking it all down, the latitude and longitude of each specific bearing, giving new meaning to something very old and very sacred—life itself.[3]

—AUGUST WILSON

the postslavery days in the South and the great migration to the North.

Eventually Wilson would prove that he had a rich and unique way of presenting history: the history of African Americans, too frequently left out of American history books. Wilson ultimately turned to playwriting in order to present this history on the stage, where his characters could come to life and share their revelations with audiences across the country.

In the early 1980s Wilson began writing a cycle of plays chronicling African American life in the United States. These plays interpret periods of history through the stories of ordinary people rather than the powerful or famous individuals who are usually considered historical figures. For each decade of the twentieth century, Wilson has focused on a representative group of characters whose struggles and dreams reflect the events and attitudes of the larger society. Thus far, Wilson has completed nine plays in this ambitious cycle. In his first play, *Ma Rainey's Black Bottom*, originally produced in 1984 and set in the 1920s, Wilson explores the world of black jazz musicians who seek recognition for themselves and ownership of the music that they are making. *Fences* looks at life in the America of the 1950s. A former baseball player, forced by racial circumstances to become a garbage hauler, battles with his son to justify his own life.

In *The Piano Lesson*, representing the 1930s, a brother and sister fight over the fate of the old family piano. Carved on the piano's legs are the faces of relatives who were slaves. By selling the piano, the brother hopes to make enough money to buy land and secure a place for himself in America. For the sister, the piano symbolizes the presence of their ancestors, a presence that she cannot part with.

In *Two Trains Running*, the characters gather in Memphis Lee's diner, where they find the determination in each other's company to take their places with dignity in the hostile urban environment of Pittsburgh in 1969. *Seven Guitars*, set in 1940s Pittsburgh, returns to the struggles of a musician, this time singer and guitar player Floyd Barton, and the events that led up to his death.

Three more of Wilson's plays are set in Pittsburgh: *King Hedley II*, *Jitney*, and *Joe Turner's Come and Gone*. *King Hedley II* looks at the struggles of an ex-convict trying to make a life for himself in the 1980s. *Jitney*, written in 1979, was recently revised and given a new series of productions beginning in 1996. Set in the 1970s, *Jitney* reflects the tensions of inner-city life through the world of unlicensed cab drivers who drive their "jitneys" through the decaying streets of Pittsburgh, beyond the boundaries of the legal taxi trade. *Joe Turner's Come and Gone*, set in 1911, represents one of

In Context

AUGUST WILSON'S DRAMATIC CYCLE

Play (first production date)	Decade Represented
Gem of the Ocean (2003)	1900s
Joe Turner's Come and Gone (1986)	1910s
Ma Rainey's Black Bottom (1984)	1920s
The Piano Lesson (1987)	1930s
Seven Guitars (1995)	1940s
Fences (1985)	1950s
Two Trains Running (1990)	1960s
Jitney (1982)	1970s
King Hedley II (2001)	1980s

the earliest time periods in Wilson's cycle and brings us characters who are closest to the experience of slavery (Color Plate 6).

The focus of this chapter is the artistic vision of the playwright, a vision that emerges from the playwright's imagination and is shaped by the playwright's personal history and responses to cultural influences. By studying the text of *Joe Turner's Come and Gone* and a production of the play at the Oregon Shakespeare Festival, we explore the foundation of August Wilson's work and the way his vision is realized in performance. The entire text of the play is included in the chapter.

EXPLORING THE TEXT OF
JOE TURNER'S COME AND GONE

Joe Turner's Come and Gone is about the aftermath of slavery, about the damage done to the spirit, which must be healed before people can take their rightful place in the world. Following the end of slavery, white plantation owners resorted to new forms of forced labor. The worst of these continuing injustices was the chain gang. The play's central character, Herald Loomis, has just served seven years on Joe Turner's chain gang in Tennessee. Now he has come North to search for his wife from whom he was separated when he was kidnapped and imprisoned by Joe Turner. He joins a group of characters he meets at a boardinghouse in Pittsburgh, most of whom are part of the migration of African Americans leaving the South in search of a better life.

PLOT AND CHARACTERS:
A MEETING OF TWO WORLDS

The play begins in Seth and Bertha Holly's boardinghouse, where two dollars a week pays for a room, two meals a day, and a fried chicken dinner on Sunday. The boardinghouse is a haven for struggling, young black men and women, charged with energy and full of longing, trying to make a start in a northern city. Bertha provides the roomers with biscuits and sensible counsel. Bynum, a "rootworker," offers his own special wisdom accompanied by herbs and powders. The transient characters look to Seth and Bertha for the practical necessities of life. Bynum offers them a mystical vision to help them find themselves. Everyone at the boardinghouse has a story to tell, and the characters share their tales around the big dining table.

The contentious but cheerful atmosphere of the boardinghouse is interrupted by the arrival of a threatening stranger. He is as withdrawn and abrupt as the other characters are open and at ease. In his long dark coat and hat, the stranger, Herald Loomis, keeps himself hidden. For Herald Loomis the chain gang has been an extension of slavery, and he hides the torment and shame of that legacy. Joe Turner and the chain gang represent all three hundred years of slavery, with its endless sorrow and dislocation. The ghost of Joe Turner haunts Herald Loomis. The play's title says Joe Turner has "come and gone." But for Herald Loomis, Joe Turner is not yet gone. Loomis must rid himself of the ghost of Joe Turner before he can find himself and begin life as a free man.

HISTORICAL AND CULTURAL CONTEXTS OF THE PLAY

In creating this remarkable play, which is both a social document and the dramatization of a heroic struggle, August Wilson is responding to a unique cultural context—that is, the personal, historical, social, and artistic forces that combine to create his particular perspective. That perspective is shaped by the experiences of being a black American as well as through the inspiration of other artists. For example, Wilson came of age in the explosive 1960s, when black cultural awareness led to a major reassessment of American history and the relationship of black Americans to the society in which they lived. For Wilson, ideas of "self-determination, self-respect, and self-defense" became crucial to his outlook.[4]

During this time he also discovered **the blues,** which provided an oral and a musical rendering of the history and texture of black American life. As we will discuss shortly, Wilson's fascination with great blues artists such as Bessie Smith led him to the work of another

artist, this time a painter, Romare Bearden. Bearden had found a way to create visual narratives out of the life sung about in the blues. Wilson wanted to put the life of the blues into a dramatic verbal form just as Bearden had created visual stories through paint and collage.

We begin our study of *Joe Turner's Come and Gone* by examining in this section the historical and cultural contexts of the play; in the following section we look at some of August Wilson's sources. The historical and cultural contexts and Wilson's personal sources will help us to understand the world of this particular play and at the same time provide insight into the creative process of the playwright in making theatre.

Theatre as History

The theatre has always been a major repository of history. Some plays, such as Shakespeare's histories, interpret the lives and actions of actual historical figures—in Shakespeare's case, the kings who preceded Elizabeth I. Some plays feature legendary characters who symbolize the conflicts and concerns of their own times.

In Context

THE AFRICAN AMERICAN EXPERIENCE

Date	Event
1518	African people first brought to New World as slaves by Spaniards
1619	First African slaves in North America arrive in Virginia on a Dutch ship
1860	Slaves number 3.5 million in the United States, about one third the total population of slave-holding states
1860–1865	Civil War
1863	Lincoln's Emancipation Proclamation, freeing slaves in Confederate states
1865	13th Amendment to the Constitution, prohibiting slavery in the United States
1865–1877	Reconstruction: Federal government is involved in governing former Confederate states
1880	Beginning of Jim Crow legislation in the South, legalizing segregation and discrimination, including the loss of voting rights for black American citizens. The Jim Crow laws were part of the institutionalized oppression that shut off economic opportunity for southern African Americans.
1890–1930	Migration of African Americans from rural South to urban North

Greek tragedies are full of larger-than-life characters such as the mythological heroes who fought the Trojan War.

By using a historical frame, August Wilson gives us something of the past and something of the present. In the case of *Joe Turner's Come and Gone*, he gives us certain information about life for African Americans at the turn of the century: the harshness of labor conditions in the South, from sharecropping to the chain gang; a sense of life on the road for a migrating people searching for a more fulfilling life; and the difficulties of re-making life yet once again, this time in northern cities eager for African American labor but resistant to sharing wealth and accepting cultural difference. Wilson also shows us individuals engaged in a struggle to gain control of their own lives and to make connections with others that will sustain them. That struggle, of course, continues today and includes all of us.

The Aftermath of Slavery: Peonage and Sharecropping

Following the Civil War, African Americans experienced a period of promise. But the promise of freedom quickly turned to the reality of reenslavement. Across the South horrifying, new forced-labor practices emerged to compensate for the loss of slave labor. Particularly in the production of cotton, turpentine, and tobacco, black Americans were forced to work as part of prison gangs or under circumstances known as peonage. White employers would claim that black workers owed them money for rent or wages that had been advanced and would then insist that the workers remain in their employment until the debt was discharged. Obligations were frequently manipulated so that the worker could never be free of debt. The peonage system was dominated by violence. A worker who tried to escape would be hunted and beaten or shot. Any form of resistance could result in imprisonment or lynching.

In Wilson's play, Herald Loomis's wife tries to keep up their sharecropper's plot when he is sentenced to the chain gang. Sharecroppers farmed on land owned by someone else and paid their rent with part of their crop. Sharecropping was part of the vicious cycle that kept black Americans in debt and unable to achieve any economic security. In the play, Martha finds she cannot meet the sharecropper's obligation alone and goes to live with her mother. But "trouble" follows her, and the growing violence motivates her to take to the road. The migrating characters who gather at the Pittsburgh boardinghouse contrast sharply with Herald Loomis, a man bound by both physical and spiritual chains.

Migration to the North

Several of the plays in this book deal with the consequences of migration. Although each play examines the realities of migration for specific communities, migration is in fact one of the essential experiences that has shaped U.S history and culture. We all share in the process and consequences of migration, from the migration from south to north represented in *Joe Turner's Come and Gone* to the migration that has brought groups of immigrants to the United States from all over the world and has set off large movements across the continent from east to west.

The year 1911, the time period of *Joe Turner's Come and Gone*, represents the early stages of African American migration to the North. Beginning in 1890 hundreds of thousands of black Americans moved from the farms and plantations of the South to the cities of the North, a process accelerated by factory employment needs during World War I. By 1930, the African American populations of New York, Chicago, Detroit, and Pittsburgh had doubled and then tripled, as southern blacks fled from the poverty and violence that followed the period of Reconstruction after the end of the Civil War.

They brought the energy and strength that had made southern agriculture flourish in the eighteenth and nineteenth centuries to the growing industrial base that would shape American life in the twentieth century. Although the journey was one of hope and optimism, it was begun in fear and deprivation and was characterized by the confusion of a people uprooted first from their ancestral home, Africa, and then driven out of their second home by massive economic and social discrimination and repression.

The Metaphor of the Road

Herald Loomis has suffered more than any of the other characters in August Wilson's play. But all the characters share in this history of violence and intimidation. That is why the metaphor of the road becomes so important to the play. Freedom of movement, the chance to move on in search of opportunity, the chance to settle your own land and determine your own future—these ideas have always been synonymous with America.

The road is one of the dominant images of August Wilson's play as the characters set out on journeys of discovery. The road, of course, suggests the passage from the South to the North. And although the road connects people to new opportunities and new ways of seeing the world, for Wilson's characters the journey also serves as a process of searching to find oneself. For black Americans leaving the South, the road had another significance as well. It represented a freedom of movement that had been denied them in slavery and then by the forced labor symbolized in the Joe Turner chain gang. The road, then, symbolizes a celebration of life and possibility.

The Oral Tradition

Beginning in the southern plantation fields, enslaved Africans—who were cut off from almost all cultural expression—adapted African work songs to their brutal new environment. Forbidden the use of their eloquent drums, the displaced Africans poured all of their heartache into song. These slave songs were a collective expression of oppression and sorrow. After the Civil War, as black Americans farmed alone or took to the road in search of work, the collective songs of the fields were elaborated and reinterpreted by the individual: "Each man had his own voice, and his own way of shouting—his own life to sing about."[5]

But poverty, lack of opportunity, and violence still characterized life for black Americans. By 1890 these songs of overcoming hardship, of lost love, of loneliness, of determination not to be defeated had become the blues. Throughout the South, on the docks, on the rivers, on the railroads, on the farms, and in the woods, the blues became a crucial form of communication, a way of rebuilding a collective sense of the black American experience. The blues were concerned with social issues and personal problems; they offered a social critique and a form of rebellion or resistance. They were also the basis for social gatherings that brought the community together to dance and sing and shout. These social gatherings were an opportunity for communal emotional expression, for letting go of feelings, just as the lyrics of the blues provided a communal text, an oral, rather than a written, history that described the lives of people who had the doors of literacy closed in their faces.

In his book *Looking Up at Down*, William Barlow explains the importance of the oral tradition to the development of culture:

> The legions of folk musicians and songsters who created and sustained the blues in their infancy were African American variations on the famous West African "griot" tradition. The griots were talented musicians and folklorists designated to be the oral carriers of their people's culture. . . . The griots functioned as "the libraries" of West African tribal societies "by supporting among themselves generations of living books." A well-known West African proverb states: "When an old man dies, a library burns to the ground."

> The African American songsters who synthesized the blues from earlier genres of black folk music were descendents of the griots, carrying forward the historical and cultural legacy

of their people even while they were setting a new agenda for social discourse and action.[6]

In his own way, as a theatre artist, August Wilson continues the griot tradition. He has become a storyteller of the African American experience. He tells his stories through dramas rather than songs, although musical rhythms and structures run through his plays. And his characters are storytellers, using myths and personal stories like jazz improvisations to underscore the meanings of the plays. He reaches back to African sources for his mythology and metaphors, and those African traditions and rituals still shine through the evolving African American identity.

THE PLAYWRIGHT'S SOURCES

Bessie Smith and Romare Bearden

In creating his theatrical interpretation of the black experience in America, Wilson has placed himself in a broad tradition of African American culture that includes the blues and visual art. Wilson explains that the songs of Bessie Smith and the paintings and collages of Romare Bearden are of primary importance to him because it was in the work of these two artists that he found himself. In the following excerpt from his foreword to a book about the work of Romare Bearden, Wilson discusses the impact of Smith and Bearden on his own life and art:

> In 1965, as a twenty-year-old poet living in a rooming house in Pittsburgh, I discovered Bessie Smith and the blues. It was a watershed event in my life. It gave me a history. It provided me with a cultural response to the world as well as the knowledge that the text and content of my life were worthy of the highest celebration and occasion of art. . . . The blues gave me a firm and secure ground. It became, and remains, the wellspring of my art.[7]

In 1977, twelve years after he became a student of Bessie Smith and the blues, Wilson was introduced to the art of Romare Bearden. He

Bessie Smith, known as the Queen of the Blues, toured widely and made numerous recordings, becoming one of the most popular singers of the early twentieth century.

describes his response to viewing a collection of Bearden's work called *The Prevalence of Ritual*:

> What for me had been so difficult, Bearden made seem so simple, so easy. What I saw was black life presented on its own terms, on a grand and epic scale, with all its richness and fullness, in a language that was vibrant and which, made attendant to everyday life, ennobled it, affirmed its value, and exalted its presence. It was the art of a large and generous spirit that defined not only the character of black American life, but also its conscience.
>
> I called to my courage and entered the world of Romare Bearden and found a world made in my image. A world of flesh and muscle and blood and bone and fire. A world made of scraps of paper, of line and mass and form and shape and color, and all the melding of grace and

birds and trains and guitars and women bathing and men with huge hands and hearts, pressing on life until it gave back something in kinship. Until it gave back in fragments, in gesture and speech, the colossal remnants of a spirit tested through time and the storm and the lash. A spirit conjured into being, unbroken, unbowed, and past any reason for song—singing an aria of faultless beauty and unbridled hope.[8]

A work of Romare Bearden's appears in this book; the blues, however, must be heard. The text of one of Bessie Smith's most famous recordings, "Nobody Knows You When You're Down and Out," demonstrates the simple eloquence of the blues form. The words printed here are the lyrics written by composer Jimmy Cox. If you listen to the Bessie Smith recording, you will hear her personalized version of the lyrics.

I once lived the life of a millionaire,
Spending my money, I didn't care,
Always taking my friends out for a good time,
Buying champagne, gin and wine.
But just as soon as my dough got low,
I couldn't find a friend, no place I'd go,
If I ever get my hands on a dollar again,
I'm gonna squeeze it and squeeze it—till the
*   eagle grins.*

NOBODY KNOWS YOU WHEN YOU'RE DOWN
*   AND OUT,*
In your pocket, not one penny
And your friends you haven't any.
And soon as you get on your feet again,
Ev'rybody is your long lost friend.
It's mighty strange, without a doubt,
But NOBODY WANTS YOU—WHEN YOU'RE
*   DOWN AND OUT—*
NOBODY WANTS YOU—WHEN YOU'RE
*   DOWN AND OUT.[9]*

Smith sang with all the collective anguish of a people who had survived one of the most wrenching dislocations in human history. The song that first captured Wilson's heart, "Nobody in Town Can Bake a Sweet Jellyroll Like Mine," shows the exuberance and humor of the blues. These songs capture both the history

The paintings and collages of Romare Bearden (1911–1988) represent the African American experience in both a tropical southern landscape and the industrial cities of the North. Bearden had a particular interest in jazz, which he expressed through numerous studies of musicians. The vibrant color of Bearden's works and his eloquent combination of materials are responsible for his growing reputation as one of the great American artists of the twentieth century.

and the consciousness of a people. Bearden added a visual component to that history. Smith and Bearden and Wilson are all connected to what is called the black oral tradition referred to by Anna Deavere Smith in Chapter 1. This black oral tradition is descended from an African culture in which drumming and storytelling were primary means of communicating.

Mill Hand's Lunch Bucket

August Wilson found the central character of *Joe Turner's Come and Gone* in Romare Bearden's *Mill Hand's Lunch Bucket* (1978), one of a series of artworks that Bearden called *Pittsburgh*

Mill Hand's Lunch Bucket *by Romare Bearden provided the inspiration for many of the characters in* Joe Turner's Come and Gone. *This artwork exemplifies Bearden's technique of layering images through collage and painting to give extraordinary life and feeling to the figures he created.*

Memories. Bearden and Wilson share a common geographic history as well as certain artistic concerns. Through collage and painting, Bearden expressed his own interpretation of the historical period that Wilson wanted to write about. Bearden explored images of the life led by black Americans going to work in the steel mills of Pittsburgh, where he himself had grown up.

Mill Hand's Lunch Bucket shows a house that becomes the boardinghouse in *Joe Turner's Come and Gone.* Coming down the stairs in the painting is a young man full of energy, his large hand reaching for the lunch bucket on a small table at the foot of the stairs. He may very well be the model for Jeremy, who works building

roads in Wilson's play. Seated at the dining table at the center of the scene is another man, hunched over and weary. Both men wear the asbestos coats and hats necessary to protect against the heat of the furnaces at the steel mills. The original caption of the collage, "the mills went 24 hours a day with three 8-hour shifts," suggests that what we see in the contrasting figures is one man who is just leaving for his shift and another who has just returned, too exhausted to even remove his heavy asbestos coat. However, August Wilson saw far more than a story of grinding labor in the steel mills. Although the painting takes its title from the strong, extended hand reaching for the lunch bucket, it was the seated man who captured Wilson's attention:

> I began to wonder, who was this figure of the abject man sitting in a posture of defeat. It occurred to me that all the people in the painting were going out, and they were going to leave this man alone just when what he needed most was human contact.[10]

Folk Sources and W. C. Handy

Wilson created a background for the figure who moved him so deeply in the Bearden collage from a folk blues song called "Joe Turner's Come and Gone," which, of course, inspired the play's title:

> *They tell me Joe Turner's come and gone*
> *Ohhh Lordy*
> *They tell me Joe Turner's come and gone*
> *Ohhh Lordy*
> *Got my man and gone*
>
> *Come with forty links of chain*
> *Ohhh Lordy*
> *Come with forty links of chain*
> *Ohhh Lordy*
> *Got my man and gone*[11]

W. C. Handy toured the country as a musician and band leader before becoming a composer, producer, and music historian.

Musician W. C. Handy collected such folk songs and used them as the basis for his own compositions. In 1916 he wrote his own version of the "Joe Turner Blues," which was suggested by several earlier versions of songs about Joe Turner, Joe Turney, or Joe Tunney, as this historical figure was variously called. Joe Turner was notorious for kidnapping black men for work on chain gangs. In his autobiography, *The Father of the Blues*, W. C. Handy tells the story of Joe Turner, who was, in fact, the brother of a Tennessee governor:

> Joe had the responsibility of taking Negro prisoners to the penitentiary at Nashville. Sometimes he took them to the "farms" along the Mississippi. Their crimes, when indeed there were any crimes, were usually very minor, the object of the arrests being to provide needed labor for spots along the river. As usual, the method was to set a stool-pigeon where he could start a game of craps. The bones would roll blissfully til the required number of laborers had been drawn into the circle. At that point the law would fall upon the poor devils, arrest as many as were needed for work, try them for gambling in a kangaroo court and then turn the culprits over to Joe Turner. That night there would be weeping and wailing among the dusky belles. If one of them chanced to ask a neighbor what had become of the sweet good man, she was likely to receive the pat reply, "They tell me Joe Turner's come and gone."[12]

The story that W. C. Handy relates could be the story of Herald Loomis. Drawing inspiration from the songs of Bessie Smith, the collage paintings of Romare Bearden, and stories such as W. C. Handy's, August Wilson has created his own vision of the migration of African American people from the South to the North through the journey of Herald Loomis and his fellow travelers, who arrive at a boardinghouse in Pittsburgh in the early twentieth century.

Joe Turner's Come and Gone

August Wilson

CHARACTERS

SETH HOLLY, *owner of the boardinghouse*
BERTHA HOLLY, *his wife*
BYNUM WALKER, *a rootworker*
RUTHERFORD SELIG, *a peddler*
JEREMY FURLOW, *a resident*
HERALD LOOMIS, *a resident*
ZONIA LOOMIS, *his daughter*
MATTIE CAMPBELL, *a resident*
REUBEN SCOTT, *a boy who lives next door*
MOLLY CUNNINGHAM, *a resident*
MARTHA LOOMIS, *Herald Loomis's wife*

SETTING

August, 1911. A boardinghouse in Pittsburgh. At right is a kitchen. Two doors open off the kitchen. One leads to the outhouse and SETH's workshop. The other to SETH's and BERTHA's bedroom. At left is a parlor. The front door opens into the parlor, which gives access to the stairs leading to the upstairs rooms.

There is a small outside playing area.

THE PLAY

It is August in Pittsburgh, 1911. The sun falls out of heaven like a stone. The fires of the steel mill rage with a combined sense of industry and progress. Barges loaded with coal and iron ore trudge up the river to the mill towns that dot the Monongahela and return with fresh, hard, gleaming steel. The city flexes its muscles. Men throw countless bridges across the rivers, lay roads and carve tunnels through the hills sprouting with houses.

From the deep and the near South the sons and daughters of newly freed African slaves wander into the city. Isolated, cut off from memory, having forgotten the names of the gods and only guessing at their faces, they arrive dazed and stunned, their heart kicking in their chest with a song worth singing. They arrive carrying Bibles and guitars, their pockets lined with dust and fresh hope, marked men and women seeking to scrape from the narrow, crooked cobbles and the fiery blasts of the coke furnace a way of bludgeoning and shaping the malleable parts of themselves into a new identity as free men of definite and sincere worth.

Foreigners in a strange land, they carry as part and parcel of their baggage a long line of separation and dispersement which informs their sensibilities and marks their conduct as they search for ways to reconnect, to reassemble, to give clear and luminous meaning to the song which is both a wail and a whelp of joy.

ACT ONE

Scene One

The lights come up on the kitchen. BERTHA busies herself with breakfast preparations. SETH stands looking out the window at BYNUM in the yard. SETH is in his early fifties. Born of Northern free parents, a skilled craftsman, and owner of the boardinghouse, he has a stability that none of the other characters have. BERTHA is five years his junior. Married for over twenty-five years, she has learned how to negotiate around SETH's apparent orneriness.

SETH: (*at the window, laughing.*) If that ain't the damndest thing I seen. Look here, Bertha.

BERTHA: I done seen Bynum out there with them pigeons before.

SETH: Naw . . . naw . . . look at this. That pigeon flopped out of Bynum's hand and he about to have a fit.

(*BERTHA crosses over to the window.*)

He down there on his hands and knees behind that bush looking all over for that pigeon and it on the other side of the yard. See it over there?

BERTHA: Come on and get your breakfast and leave that man alone.

SETH: Look at him . . . he still looking. He ain't seen it yet. All that old mumbo jumbo nonsense. I don't know why I put up with it.

BERTHA: You don't say nothing when he bless the house.

SETH: I just go along with that 'cause of you. You around here sprinkling salt all over the place . . . got pennies lined up across the threshold . . . all that heebie-jeebie stuff. I just put up with that 'cause of you. I don't pay that kind of stuff no mind. And you going down there to the church and wanna come home and sprinkle salt all over the place.

BERTHA: It don't hurt none. I can't say if it help . . . but it don't hurt none.

SETH: Look at him. He done found that pigeon and now he's talking to it.

BERTHA: These biscuits be ready in a minute.

SETH: He done drew a big circle with that stick and now he's dancing around. I know he'd better not . . .

(*SETH bolts from the window and rushes to the back door.*)

Hey, Bynum! Don't be hopping around stepping in my vegetables.

Hey, Bynum . . . Watch where you stepping!

BERTHA: Seth, leave that man alone.

SETH: (*coming back into the house.*) I don't care how much he be dancing around . . . just don't be stepping in my vegetables. Man got my garden all messed up now . . . planting them weeds out there . . . burying them pigeons and whatnot.

BERTHA: Bynum don't bother nobody. He ain't even thinking about your vegetables.

SETH: I know he ain't! That's why he out there stepping on them.

BERTHA: What Mr. Johnson say down there?

SETH: I told him if I had the tools I could go out here and find me four or five fellows and open up my own shop instead of working for Mr. Olowski. Get me four or five fellows and teach them how to make pots and pans. One man making ten pots is five men making fifty. He told me he'd think about it.

BERTHA: Well, maybe he'll come to see it your way.

SETH: He wanted me to sign over the house to him. You know what I thought of that idea.

BERTHA: He'll come to see you're right.

SETH: I'm going up and talk to Sam Green. There's more than one way to skin a cat. I'm going up and talk to him. See if he got more sense than Mr. Johnson. I can't get nowhere working for Mr. Olowski and selling Selig five or six pots on the side. I'm going up and see Sam Green. See if he loan me the money.

(*SETH crosses back to the window.*)

Now he got that cup. He done killed that pigeon and now he's putting its blood in that little cup. I believe he drink that blood.

BERTHA: Seth Holly, what is wrong with you this morning? Come on and get your breakfast so you can go to bed. You know Bynum don't be drinking no pigeon blood.

SETH: I don't know what he do.

BERTHA: Well, watch him, then. He's gonna dig a little hole and bury that pigeon. Then he's gonna pray over that blood . . . pour it on top . . . mark out his circle and come on into the house.

SETH: That's what he doing . . . he pouring that blood on top.

BERTHA: When they gonna put you back working daytime? Told me two months ago he was gonna put you back working daytime.

SETH: That's what Mr. Olowski told me. I got to wait till he say when. He tell me what to do. I don't tell him. Drive me crazy to speculate on the man's wishes when he don't know what he want to do himself.

BERTHA: Well, I wish he go ahead and put you back working daytime. This working all hours of the night don't make no sense.

SETH: It don't make no sense for that boy to run out of here and get drunk so they lock him up either.

BERTHA: Who? Who they got locked up for being drunk?

SETH: That boy that's staying upstairs . . . Jeremy. I stopped down there on Logan Street on my way home from work and one of the fellows told me about it. Say he seen it when they arrested him.

BERTHA: I was wondering why I ain't seen him this morning.

SETH: You know I don't put up with that. I told him when he came . . .

(*BYNUM enters from the yard carrying some plants. He is a short, round man in his early sixties. A conjure man, or rootworker, he gives the impression of always being in control of everything. Nothing ever bothers him. He seems to be lost in a world of his own making and to swallow any adversity or interference with his grand design.*)

What you doing bringing them weeds in my house? Out there stepping on my vegetables and now wanna carry them weeds in my house.

BYNUM: Morning, Seth. Morning, Sister Bertha.

SETH: Messing up my garden growing them things out there. I ought to go out there and pull up all them weeds.

BERTHA: Some gal was by here to see you this morning, Bynum. You was out there in the yard . . . I told her to come back later.

BYNUM: (*To SETH.*) You look sick. What's the matter, you ain't eating right?

SETH: What if I was sick? You ain't getting near me with none of that stuff.

(*BERTHA sets a plate of biscuits on the table.*)

BYNUM: My . . . my . . . Bertha, your biscuits getting fatter and fatter.

(*BYNUM takes a biscuit and begins to eat.*)

Where Jeremy? I don't see him around this morning. He usually be around riffing and raffing on Saturday morning.

SETH: I know where he at. I know just where he at. They got him down there in the jail. Getting drunk and acting a fool. He down there where he belong with all that foolishness.

BYNUM: Mr. Piney's boys got him, huh? They ain't gonna do nothing but hold on to him for a little while. He's gonna be back here hungrier than a mule directly.

SETH: I don't go for all that carrying on and such. This is a respectable house. I don't have no drunkards or fools around here.

BYNUM: That boy got a lot of country in him. He ain't been up here but two weeks. It's gonna take a while before he can work that country out of him.

SETH: These niggers coming up here with that old backward country style of living. It's hard enough now without all that ignorant kind of acting. Ever since slavery got over with there ain't been nothing but foolish-acting niggers. Word get out they need men to work in the mill and put in these roads . . . and niggers drop everything and head North looking for freedom. They don't know the white fellows looking too. White fellows coming from all over the world. White fellow come over and in six months got more than what I got. But these niggers keep on coming. Walking . . . riding . . . carrying their Bibles. That boy done carried a guitar all the way from North Carolina. What he gonna find out? What he gonna do with that guitar? This the city.

(*There is a knock on the door.*)

Niggers coming up here from the back-woods . . . coming up here from the country carrying Bibles and guitars looking for freedom. They got a rude awakening.

(*SETH goes to answer the door. RUTHERFORD SELIG enters. About SETH's age, he is a thin white man with greasy hair. A peddler, he supplies SETH with the raw materials to make pots and pans which he then peddles door to door in the mill towns along the river. He keeps a list of his customers as they move about and is known in the various communities as the People Finder. He carries squares of sheet metal under his arm.*)

Ho! Forgot you was coming today. Come on in.

BYNUM: If it ain't Rutherford Selig . . . the People Finder himself.

SELIG: What say there, Bynum?

BYNUM: I say about my shiny man. You got to tell me something. I done give you my dollar . . . I'm looking to get a report.

SELIG: I got eight here, Seth.

SETH: (*Taking the sheet metal.*) What is this? What you giving me here? What I'm gonna do with this?

SELIG: I need some dustpans. Everybody asking me about dustpans.

SETH: Gonna cost you fifteen cents apiece. And ten cents to put a handle on them.

SELIG: I'll give you twenty cents apiece with the handles.

SETH: Alright. But I ain't gonna give you but fifteen cents for the sheet metal.

SELIG: It's twenty-five cents apiece for the metal. That's what we agreed on.

SETH: This low-grade sheet metal. They ain't worth but a dime. I'm doing you a favor giving you fifteen cents. You know this metal ain't worth no twenty-five cents. Don't come talking that twenty-five cent stuff to me over no low-grade sheet metal.

SELIG: Alright, fifteen cents apiece. Just make me some dustpans out of them.

(*SETH exits with the sheet metal out the back door.*)

BERTHA: Sit on down there, Selig. Get you a cup of coffee and a biscuit.

BYNUM: Where you coming from this time?

SELIG: I been upriver. All along the Monongahela. Past Rankin and all up around Little Washington.

BYNUM: Did you find anybody?

SELIG: I found Sadie Jackson up in Braddock. Her mother's staying down there in Scotchbottom say she hadn't heard from her and she didn't know where she was at. I found her up in Braddock on Enoch Street. She bought a frying pan from me.

BYNUM: You around here finding everybody how come you ain't found my shiny man?

SELIG: The only shiny man I saw was the Nigras working on the road gang with the sweat glistening on them.

BYNUM: Naw, you'd be able to tell this fellow. He shine like new money.

SELIG: Well, I done told you I can't find nobody without a name.

BERTHA: Here go one of these hot biscuits, Selig.

BYNUM: This fellow don't have no name. I call him John 'cause it was up around Johnstown where I seen him. I ain't even so sure he's one special fellow. That shine could pass on to anybody. He could be anybody shining.

SELIG: Well, what's he look like besides being shiny? There's lots of shiny Nigras.

BYNUM: He's just a man I seen out on the road. He ain't had no special look. Just a man walking toward me on the road. He come up and asked me which way the road went. I told him everything I knew about the road, where it went and all, and he asked me did I have anything to eat 'cause he was hungry. Say he ain't had nothing to eat in three days. Well, I never be out there on the road without a piece of dried meat. Or an orange or an apple. So I give this fellow an orange. He take and eat that orange and told me to come and go along the road a little ways with him, that he had something he wanted to show me. He had a look about him made me wanna go with him, see what he gonna show me.

We walked on a bit and it's getting kind of far from where I met him when it come up on me all of a sudden, we wasn't going the way he had come from, we was going back my way. Since he said he ain't knew nothing about the road, I asked him about this. He say he had a voice inside him telling him which way to go and if I come and go along with him he was gonna show me the Secret of Life. Quite naturally I followed him. A fellow that's gonna show you the Secret of Life ain't to be taken lightly. We get near this bend in the road . . .

(SETH enters with an assortment of pots.)

SETH: I got six here, Selig.
SELIG: Wait a minute, Seth. Bynum's telling me about the secret of life. Go ahead, Bynum. I wanna hear this.

(SETH sets the pots down and exits out the back.)

BYNUM: We get near this bend in the road and he told me to hold out my hands. Then he rubbed them together with his and I looked down and see they got blood on them. Told me to take and rub it all over me . . . say that was a way of cleaning myself. Then we went around the bend in that road. Got around that bend and it seem like all of a sudden we ain't in the same place. Turn around that bend and everything look like it was twice as big as it was. The trees and everything bigger than life! Sparrows big as eagles! I turned around to look at this fellow and he had this light coming out of him. I had to cover up my eyes to keep from being blinded. He shining like new money with that light. He shined until all the light seemed like it seeped out of him and then he was gone and I was by myself in this strange place where everything was bigger than life.

I wandered around there looking for that road, trying to find my way back from this big place . . . and I looked over and seen my daddy standing there. He was the same size he always was, except for his hands and his mouth. He had a great big old mouth that look like it took up his whole face and his hands were as big as hams. Look like they was too big to carry around. My daddy called me to him. Said he had been thinking about me and it grieved him to see me in the world carrying other people's songs and not having one of my own. Told me he was gonna show me how to find my song. Then he carried me further into this big place until we come to this ocean. Then he showed me something I ain't got words to tell you. But if you stand to witness it, you done seen something there. I stayed in that place awhile and my daddy taught me the meaning of this thing that I had seen and showed me how to find my song. I asked him about the shiny man and he told me he was the One Who Goes Before and Shows the Way. Said there was lots of shiny men and if I ever saw one again before I died then I would know that my song had been accepted and worked its full power in the world and I could lay down and die a happy man. A man who done left his mark on life. On the way people cling to each other out of the truth they find in themselves. Then he showed me how to get back to the road. I came out to where everything was its own size and I had my song. I had the Binding Song. I choose that song because that's what I seen most when I was traveling . . . people walking away and leaving one another. So I takes the power of my song and binds them together.

(SETH enters from the yard carrying cabbages and tomatoes.)

Been binding people ever since. That's why they call me Bynum. Just like glue I sticks people together.

SETH: Maybe they ain't supposed to be stuck sometimes. You ever think of that?
BYNUM: Oh, I don't do it lightly. It cost me a piece of myself every time I do. I'm a Binder

of What Clings. You got to find out if they cling first. You can't bind what don't cling.

SELIG: Well, how is that the Secret of Life? I thought you said he was gonna show you the secret of life. That's what I'm waiting to find out.

BYNUM: Oh, he showed me alright. But you still got to figure it out. Can't nobody figure it out for you. You got to come to it on your own. That's why I'm looking for the shiny man.

SELIG: Well, I'll keep my eye out for him. What you got there, Seth?

SETH: Here go some cabbage and tomatoes. I got some green beans coming in real nice. I'm gonna take and start me a grapevine out there next year. Butera says he gonna give me a piece of his vine and I'm gonna start that out there.

SELIG: How many of them pots you got?

SETH: I got six. That's six dollars minus eight on top of fifteen for the sheet metal come to a dollar twenty out the six dollars leave me four dollars and eighty cents.

SELIG: (Counting out the money.) There's four dollars . . . and . . . eighty cents.

SETH: How many of them dustpans you want?

SELIG: As many as you can make out them sheets.

SETH: You can use that many? I get to cutting on them sheets figuring how to make them dustpans . . . ain't no telling how many I'm liable to come up with.

SELIG: I can use them and you can make me some more next time.

SETH: Alright, I'm gonna hold you to that, now.

SELIG: Thanks for the biscuit, Bertha.

BERTHA: You know you welcome anytime, Selig.

SETH: Which way you heading?

SELIG: Going down to Wheeling. All through West Virginia there. I'll be back Saturday. They putting in new roads down that way. Makes traveling easier.

SETH: That's what I hear. All up around here too. Got a fellow staying here working on that road by the Brady Street Bridge.

SELIG: Yeah, it's gonna make traveling real nice. Thanks for the cabbage, Seth. I'll see you on Saturday.

(SELIG exits.)

SETH: (To BYNUM) Why you wanna start all that nonsense talk with that man? All that shiny man nonsense.

BYNUM: You known it ain't no nonsense. Bertha know it ain't no nonsense. I don't know if Selig know or not.

BERTHA: Seth, when you get to making them dustpans make me a coffeepot.

SETH: What's the matter with your coffee? Ain't nothing wrong with your coffee. Don't she make some good coffee, Bynum?

BYNUM: I ain't worried about the coffee. I know she makes some good biscuits.

SETH: I ain't studying no coffeepot, woman. You heard me tell the man I was gonna cut as many dustpans as them sheets will make . . . and all of a sudden you want a coffeepot.

BERTHA: Man, hush up and go on and make me that coffeepot.

(JEREMY enters the front door. About twenty-five, he gives the impression that he has the world in his hand, that he can meet life's challenges head on. He smiles a lot. He is a proficient guitar player, though his spirit has yet to be molded into song.)

BYNUM: I hear Mr. Piney's boys had you.

JEREMY: Fined me two dollars for nothing! Ain't done nothing.

SETH: I told you when you come on here everybody know my house. Know these is respectable quarters. I don't put up with no foolishness. Everybody know Seth Holly keep a good house. Was my daddy's house. This house been a decent house for a long time.

JEREMY: I ain't done nothing, Mr. Seth. I stopped by the Workmen's Club and got me a bottle. Me and Roper Lee from Alabama. Had us a half pint. We was fixing to cut that half in two when they came up on us. Asked us if we was working. We told them we was putting in the road over yonder and that it was our payday. They snatched hold of us to get that two dollars. Me and Roper Lee ain't even had a chance to take a drink when they grabbed us.

SETH: I don't go for all that kind of carrying on.

BERTHA: Leave the boy alone, Seth. You know the police do that. Figure there's too many people out on the street they take some of them off. You know that.

SETH: I ain't gonna have folks talking.

BERTHA: Ain't nobody talking nothing. That's all in your head. You want some grits and biscuits, Jeremy?

JEREMY: Thank you, Miss Bertha. They didn't give us a thing to eat last night. I'll take one of them big bowls if you don't mind.

(*There is a knock at the door. SETH goes to answer it. Enter HERALD LOOMIS and his eleven-year-old daughter, ZONIA. HERALD LOOMIS is thirty-two years old. He is at times possessed. A man driven not by the hellhounds that seemingly bay at his heels, but by his search for a world that speaks to something about himself. He is unable to harmonize the forces that swirl around him, and seeks to recreate the world into one that contains his image. He wears a hat and a long wool coat.*)

LOOMIS: Me and my daughter looking for a place to stay, mister. You got a sign say you got rooms.

(*SETH stares at LOOMIS, sizing him up.*)

Mister, if you ain't got no rooms we can go somewhere else.

SETH: How long you plan on staying?

LOOMIS: Don't know. Two weeks or more maybe.

SETH: It's two dollars a week for the room. We serve meals twice a day. It's two dollars for room and board. Pay up in advance.

(*LOOMIS reaches into his pocket.*)

It's a dollar extra for the girl.

LOOMIS: The girl sleep in the same room.

SETH: Well, do she eat off the same plate? We serve meals twice a day. That's a dollar extra for food.

LOOMIS: Ain't got no extra dollar. I was planning on asking your missus if she could help out with the cooking and cleaning and whatnot.

SETH: Her helping out don't put no food on the table. I need that dollar to buy some food.

LOOMIS: I'll give you fifty cents extra. She don't eat much.

SETH: Okay . . . but fifty cents don't buy but half a portion.

BERTHA: Seth, she can help me out. Let her help me out. I can use some help.

SETH: Well, that's two dollars for the week. Pay up in advance. Saturday to Saturday. You wanna stay on then it's two more come Saturday.

(*LOOMIS pays SETH the money.*)

BERTHA: My name's Bertha. This my husband, Seth. You got Bynum and Jeremy over there.

LOOMIS: Ain't nobody else live here?

BERTHA: They the only ones live here now. People come and go. They the only ones here now. You want a cup of coffee and a biscuit?

LOOMIS: We done ate this morning.

BYNUM: Where you coming from, Mister . . . I didn't get your name.

LOOMIS: Name's Herald Loomis. This my daughter, Zonia.

BYNUM: Where you coming from?

LOOMIS: Come from all over. Whicheverway the road take us that's the way we go.

JEREMY: If you looking for a job, I'm working putting in that road down there by the bridge. They can't get enough mens. Always looking to take somebody on.

LOOMIS: I'm looking for a woman named Martha Loomis. That's my wife. Got married legal with the papers and all.

SETH: I don't know nobody named Loomis. I know some Marthas but I don't know no Loomis.

BYNUM: You got to see Rutherford Selig if you wanna find somebody. Selig's the People Finder. Rutherford Selig's a first-class People Finder.

JEREMY: What she look like? Maybe I seen her.

LOOMIS: She a brownskin woman. Got long pretty hair. About five feet from the ground.

JEREMY: I don't know. I might have seen her.

BYNUM: You got to see Rutherford Selig. You give him one dollar to get her name on his list . . . and after she get her name on his list Rutherford Selig will go right on out there and find her. I got him looking for somebody for me.

LOOMIS: You say he find people. How you find him?

BYNUM: You just missed him. He's gone downriver now. You got to wait till Saturday. He's gone downriver with his pots and pans. He come to see Seth on Saturdays. You got to wait till then.

SETH: Come on, I'll show you to your room.

(*SETH, LOOMIS, and ZONIA exit up the stairs.*)

JEREMY: Miss Bertha, I'll take that biscuit you was gonna give that fellow, if you don't mind. Say, Mr. Bynum, they got somebody like that around here sure enough? Somebody that find people?

BYNUM: Rutherford Selig. He go around selling pots and pans and every house he come to he write down the name and address of whoever lives there. So if you looking for somebody, quite naturally you go and see him . . . 'cause he's the only one who know where everybody live at.

JEREMY: I ought to have him look for this old gal I used to know. It be nice to see her again.

BERTHA: (*Giving JEREMY a biscuit.*) Jeremy, today's the day for you to pull them sheets off the bed and set them outside your door. I'll set you out some clean ones.

BYNUM: Mr. Piney's boys done ruined your good time last night, Jeremy . . . what you planning for tonight?

JEREMY: They got me scared to go out, Mr. Bynum. They might grab me again.

BYNUM: You ought to take your guitar and go down to Seefus. Seefus got a gambling place down there on Wylie Avenue. You ought to take your guitar and go down there. They got a guitar contest down there.

JEREMY: I don't play no contest, Mr. Bynum. Had one of them white fellows cure me of that. I ain't been nowhere near a contest since.

BYNUM: White fellow beat you playing guitar?

JEREMY: Naw, he ain't beat me. I was sitting at home just fixing to sit down and eat when somebody come up to my house and got me. Told me there's a white fellow say he was gonna give a prize to the best guitar player he could find. I take up my guitar and go down there and somebody had gone up and got Bobo Smith and brought him down there. Him and another fellow called Hooter. Old Hooter couldn't play no guitar, he do more hollering than playing, but Bobo could go at it awhile.

This fellow standing there say he the one that was gonna give the prize and me and Bobo started playing for him. Bobo play something and then I'd try to play something better than what he played. Old Hooter, he just holler and bang at the guitar. Man was the worst guitar player I ever seen. So me and Bobo played and after a while I seen where he was getting the attention of this white fellow. He'd play something and while he was playing it he be slapping on the side of the guitar, and that made it sound like he was playing more than he was. So I started doing it too. White fellow ain't knew no difference. He ain't knew as much about guitar playing as Hooter did. After we play awhile, the white fellow called us to him and said he couldn't make up his mind, say all three of us was the best guitar player and we'd have to split the prize between us. Then he give us twenty-five cents. That's eight cents apiece and a penny on the side. That cured me of playing contest to this day.

BYNUM: Seefus ain't like that. Seefus give a whole dollar and a drink of whiskey.

JEREMY: What night they be down there?

BYNUM: Be down there every night. Music don't know no certain night.

BERTHA: You go down to Seefus with them people and you liable to end up in a raid and go to jail sure enough. I don't know why Bynum tell you that.

BYNUM: That's where the music at. That's where the people at. The people down there making music and enjoying themselves. Some things is worth taking the chance going to jail about.

BERTHA: Jeremy ain't got no business going down there.

JEREMY: They got some women down there, Mr. Bynum?

BYNUM: Oh, they got women down there, sure. They got women everywhere. Women be where the men is so they can find each other.

JEREMY: Some of them old gals come out there where we be putting in that road. Hanging around there trying to snatch somebody.

BYNUM: How come some of them ain't snatched hold of you?

JEREMY: I don't want them kind. Them desperate kind. Ain't nothing worse than a desperate woman. Tell them you gonna leave them and they get to crying and carrying on. That just make you want to get away quicker. They get to cutting up your clothes and things trying to keep you staying. Desperate women ain't nothing but trouble for a man.

(*SETH enters from the stairs.*)

SETH: Something ain't setting right with that fellow.

BERTHA: What's wrong with him? What he say?

SETH: I take him up there and try to talk to him and he ain't for no talking. Say he been traveling . . . coming over from Ohio. Say he a deacon in the church. Say he looking for

Martha Pentecost. Talking about that's his wife.

BERTHA: How you know it's the same Martha? Could be talking about anybody. Lots of people named Martha.

SETH: You see that little girl? I didn't hook it up till he said it, but that little girl look just like her. Ask Bynum. (*To BYNUM.*) Bynum. Don't that little girl look just like Martha Pentecost?

BERTHA: I still say he could be talking about anybody.

SETH: The way he described her wasn't no doubt about who he was talking about. Described her right down to her toes.

BERTHA: What did you tell him?

SETH: I ain't told him nothing. The way that fellow look I wasn't gonna tell him nothing. I don't know what he looking for her for.

BERTHA: What else he have to say?

SETH: I told you he wasn't for no talking. I told him where the outhouse was and to keep that gal off the front porch and out of my garden. He asked if you'd mind setting a hot tub for the gal and that was about the gist of it.

BERTHA: Well, I wouldn't let it worry me if I was you. Come on get your sleep.

BYNUM: He says he looking for Martha and he a deacon in the church.

SETH: That's what he say. Do he look like a deacon to you?

BERTHA: He might be, you don't know. Bynum ain't got no special say on whether he a deacon or not.

SETH: Well, if he the deacon I'd sure like to see the preacher.

BERTHA: Come on get your sleep. Jeremy, don't forget to set them sheets outside the door like I told you.

(*BERTHA exits into the bedroom.*)

SETH: Something ain't setting right with that fellow, Bynum. He's one of them mean-looking niggers look like he done killed somebody gambling over a quarter.

BYNUM: He ain't no gambler. Gamblers wear nice shoes. This fellow got on clodhoppers. He been out there walking up and down them roads.

(*ZONIA enters from the stairs and looks around.*)

BYNUM: You looking for the back door, sugar? There it is. You can go out there and play. It's alright.

SETH: (*Showing her the door.*) You can go out there and play. Just don't get in my garden. And don't go messing around in my workshed.

(*SETH exits into the bedroom. There is a knock on the door.*)

JEREMY: Somebody at the door.

(*JEREMY goes to answer the door. Enter MATTIE CAMPBELL. She is a young woman of twenty-six whose attractiveness is hidden under the weight and concerns of a dissatisfied life. She is a woman in an honest search for love and companionship. She had suffered many defeats in her search, and though not always uncompromising, still believes in the possibility of love.*)

MATTIE: I'm looking for a man named Bynum. Lady told me to come back later.

JEREMY: Sure, he here. Mr. Bynum, somebody here to see you.

BYNUM: Come to see me, huh?

MATTIE: Are you the man they call Bynum? The man folks say can fix things?

BYNUM: Depend on what need fixing. I can't make no promises. But I got a powerful song in some matters.

MATTIE: Can you fix it so my man come back to me?

BYNUM: Come on in . . . have a sit down.

MATTIE: You got to help me. I don't know what else to do.

BYNUM: Depend on how all the circumstances of the thing come together. How all the pieces fit.

MATTIE: I done everything I knowed how to do. You got to make him come back to me.

BYNUM: It ain't nothing to make somebody come back. I can fix it so he can't stand to be away from you. I got my roots and powders, I can fix it so wherever he's at this thing will come up on him and he won't be able to sleep for seeing your face. Won't be able to eat for thinking of you.

MATTIE: That's what I want. Make him come back.

BYNUM: The roots is a powerful thing. I can fix it so one day he'll walk out his front door . . . won't be thinking of nothing. He won't know what it is. All he knows is that a powerful dissatisfaction done set in his bones and can't nothing he do make him feel satisfied. He'll set his foot down on the road and the wind in the trees be talking to him and everywhere he step on the road, that road'll give back your name and something will pull him right up to your doorstep. Now, I can do that. I can take my roots and fix that easy. But maybe he ain't supposed to come back. And if he ain't supposed to come back . . . then he'll be in your bed one morning and it'll come up on him that he's in the wrong place. That he's lost outside of time from his place that he's supposed to be in. Then both of you be lost and trapped outside of life and ain't no way for you to get back into it. 'Cause you lost from yourselves and where the places come together, where you're supposed to be alive, your heart kicking in your chest with a song worth singing.

MATTIE: Make him come back to me. Make his feet say my name on the road. I don't care what happens. Make him come back.

BYNUM: What's your man's name?

MATTIE: He go by Jack Carper. He was born in Alabama then he come to West Texas and find me and we come here. Been here three years before he left. Say I had a curse prayer on me and he started walking down the road and ain't never come back. Somebody told me, say you can fix things like that.

BYNUM: He just got up one day, set his feet on the road, and walked away?

MATTIE: You got to make him come back, mister.

BYNUM: Did he say goodbye?

MATTIE: Ain't said nothing. Just started walking. I could see where he disappeared. Didn't look back. Just keep walking. Can't you fix it so he come back? I ain't got no curse prayer on me. I know I ain't.

BYNUM: What made him say you had a curse prayer on you?

MATTIE: 'Cause the babies died. Me and Jack had two babies. Two little babies that ain't lived two months before they died. He say it's because somebody cursed me not to have babies.

BYNUM: He ain't bound to you if the babies died. Look like somebody trying to keep you from being bound up and he's gone on back to whoever it is 'cause he's already bound up to her. Ain't nothing to be done. Somebody else done got a powerful hand in it and ain't nothing to be done to break it. You got to let him go find where he's supposed to be in the world.

MATTIE: Jack done gone off and you telling me to forget about him. All my life I been looking for somebody to stop and stay with me. I done already got too many things to forget about. I take Jack Carper's hand and it feel so rough and strong. Seem like he's the strongest man in the world the way he hold me. Like he's bigger than the whole world and can't nothing bad get to me. Even when he act mean sometimes he still make everything seem okay with the world. Like there's part of it that belongs just to you. Now you telling me to forget about him?

BYNUM: Jack Carper gone off to where he belong. There's somebody searching for your doorstep right now. Ain't no need you fretting over Jack Carper. Right now he's a strong thought in your mind. But every time you catch yourself fretting over Jack Carper you push that thought away. You push it out

your mind and that thought will get weaker and weaker till you wake up one morning and you won't even be able to call him up on your mind.

(*BYNUM gives her a small cloth packet.*)

Take this and sleep with it under your pillow and it'll bring good luck to you. Draw it to you like a magnet. It won't be long before you forget all about Jack Carper.

MATTIE: How much . . . do I owe you?

BYNUM: Whatever you got there . . . that'll be alright.

(*MATTIE hands BYNUM two quarters. She crosses to the door.*)

You sleep with that under your pillow and you'll be alright.

(*MATTIE opens the door to exit and JEREMY crosses over to her. BYNUM overhears the first part of their conversation, then exits out the back.*)

JEREMY: I overheard what you told Mr. Bynum. Had me an old gal did that to me. Woke up one morning and she was gone. Just took off to parts unknown. I woke up that morning and the only thing I could do was look around for my shoes. I woke up and got out of there. Found my shoes and took off. That's the only thing I could think of to do.

MATTIE: She ain't said nothing?

JEREMY: I just looked around for my shoes and got out of there.

MATTIE: Jack ain't said nothing either. He just walked off.

JEREMY: Some mens do that. Womens too. I ain't gone off looking for her. I just let her go. Figure she had a time to come to herself. Wasn't no use of me standing in the way. Where you from?

MATTIE: Texas. I was born in Georgia but I went to Texas with my mama. She dead now. Was picking peaches and fell dead away. I come up here with Jack Carper.

JEREMY: I'm from North Carolina. Down around Raleigh where they got all that tobacco.

Been up here about two weeks. I likes it fine except I still got to find me a woman. You got a nice look to you. Look like you have mens standing in your door. Is you got mens standing in your door to get a look at you?

MATTIE: I ain't got nobody since Jack left.

JEREMY: A woman like you need a man. Maybe you let me be your man. I got a nice way with the women. That's what they tell me.

MATTIE: I don't know. Maybe Jack's coming back.

JEREMY: I'll be your man till he come. A woman can't be by her lonesome. Let me be your man till he come.

MATTIE: I just can't go through life piecing myself out to different mens. I need a man who wants to stay with me.

JEREMY: I can't say what's gonna happen. Maybe I'll be the man. I don't know. You wanna go along the road a little ways with me?

MATTIE: I don't know. Seem like life say it's gonna be one thing and end up being another. I'm tired of going from man to man.

JEREMY: Life is like you got to take a chance. Everybody got to take a chance. Can't nobody say what's gonna be. Come on . . . take a chance with me and see what the year bring. Maybe you let me come and see you. Where you staying?

MATTIE: I got me a room up on Bedford. Me and Jack had a room together.

JEREMY: What's the address? I'll come by and get you tonight and we can go down to Seefus. I'm going down there and play my guitar.

MATTIE: You play guitar?

JEREMY: I play guitar like I'm born to it.

MATTIE: I live at 1727 Bedford Avenue. I'm gonna find out if you can play guitar like you say.

JEREMY: I plays it sugar, and that ain't all I do. I got a ten-pound hammer and I knows how to drive it down. Good god . . . you ought to hear my hammer ring!

MATTIE: Go on with that kind of talk, now. If you gonna come by and get me I got to get home and straighten up for you.

JEREMY: I'll be by at eight o'clock. How's eight o'clock? I'm gonna make you forget all about Jack Carper.

MATTIE: Go on, now. I got to get home and fix up for you.

JEREMY: Eight o'clock, sugar.

(*The lights go down in the parlor and come up on the yard outside. ZONIA is singing and playing a game.*)

ZONIA:

> I went downtown
> To get my grip
> I came back home
> Just a pullin' the skiff
>
> I went upstairs
> To make my bed
> I made a mistake
> And I bumped my head
> Just a pullin' the skiff
>
> I went downstairs
> To milk the cow
> I made a mistake
> And I milked the sow
> Just a pullin' the skiff
>
> Tomorrow, tomorrow
> Tomorrow never comes
> The marrow the marrow
> The marrow in the bone.

(*REUBEN enters.*)

REUBEN: Hi.

ZONIA: Hi.

REUBEN: What's your name?

ZONIA: Zonia.

REUBEN: What kind of name is that?

ZONIA: It's what my daddy named me.

REUBEN: My name's Reuben. You staying in Mr. Seth's house?

ZONIA: Yeah.

REUBEN: That your daddy I seen you with this morning?

ZONIA: I don't know. Who you see me with?

REUBEN: I saw you with some man had on a great big old coat. And you was walking up to Mr. Seth's house. Had on a hat too.

ZONIA: Yeah, that's my daddy.

REUBEN: You like Mr. Seth?

ZONIA: I ain't see him much.

REUBEN: My grandpap say he a great big old windbag. How come you living in Mr. Seth's house? Don't you have no house?

ZONIA: We going to find my mother.

REUBEN: Where she at?

ZONIA: I don't know. We got to find her. We just go all over.

REUBEN: Why you got to find her? What happened to her?

ZONIA: She ran away.

REUBEN: Why she run away?

ZONIA: I don't know. My daddy say some man named Joe Turner did something bad to him once and that made her run away.

REUBEN: Maybe she coming back and you don't have to go looking for her.

ZONIA: We ain't there no more.

REUBEN: She could have come back when you wasn't there.

ZONIA: My daddy said she ran off and left us so we going looking for her.

REUBEN: What he gonna do when he find her?

ZONIA: He didn't say. He just say he got to find her.

REUBEN: Your daddy say how long you staying in Mr. Seth's house?

ZONIA: He don't say much. But we never stay too long nowhere. He say we got to keep moving till we find her.

REUBEN: Ain't no kids hardly live around here. I had me a friend but he died. He was the best friend I ever had. Me and Eugene used to keep secrets. I still got his pigeons. He told me to let them go when he died. He say, "Reuben, promise me when I die you'll let my pigeons go." But I keep them to remember him by. I ain't never gonna let them go.

Even when I get to be grown up. I'm just always gonna have Eugene's pigeons.

(*Pause.*)

Mr. Bynum a conjure man. My grandpap scared of him. He don't like me to come over here too much. I'm scared of him too. My grandpap told me not to let him get close enough to where he can reach out his hand and touch me.

ZONIA: He don't seem scary to me.

REUBEN: He buys pigeons from me . . . and if you get up early in the morning you can see him out in the yard doing something with them pigeons. My grandpap say he kill them. I sold him one yesterday. I don't know what he do with it. I just hope he don't spook me up.

ZONIA: Why you sell him pigeons if he's gonna spook you up?

REUBEN: I just do like Eugene do. He used to sell Mr. Bynum pigeons. That's how he got to collecting them to sell to Mr. Bynum. Sometime he give me a nickel and sometime he give me a whole dime.

(*LOOMIS enters from the house.*)

LOOMIS: Zonia!

ZONIA: Sir?

LOOMIS: What you doing?

ZONIA: Nothing.

LOOMIS: You stay around this house, you hear? I don't want you wandering off nowhere.

ZONIA: I ain't wandering off nowhere.

LOOMIS: Miss Bertha set that hot tub and you getting a good scrubbing. Get scrubbed up good. You ain't been scrubbing.

ZONIA: I been scrubbing.

LOOMIS: Look at you. You growing too fast. Your bones getting bigger everyday. I don't want you getting grown on me. Don't you get grown on me too soon. We gonna find your mamma. She around here somewhere. I can smell her. You stay on around this house now. Don't you go nowhere.

ZONIA: Yes, sir.

(*LOOMIS exits into the house.*)

REUBEN: Wow, your daddy's scary!

ZONIA: He is not! I don't know what you talking about.

REUBEN: He got them mean-looking eyes!

ZONIA: My daddy ain't got no mean-looking eyes!

REUBEN: Aw, girl, I was just messing with you. You wanna go see Eugene's pigeons? Got a great big coop out the back of my house. Come on, I'll show you.

(*REUBEN and ZONIA exit as the lights go down.*)

Scene Two

It is Saturday morning, one week later. The lights come up on the kitchen. BERTHA is at the stove preparing breakfast while SETH sits at the table.

SETH: Something ain't right about that fellow. I been watching him all week. Something ain't right, I'm telling you.

BERTHA: Seth Holly, why don't you hush up about that man this morning?

SETH: I don't like the way he stare at everybody. Don't look at you natural like. He just be staring at you. Like he trying to figure out something about you. Did you see him when he come back in here?

BERTHA: That man ain't thinking about you.

SETH: He don't work nowhere. Just go out and come back. Go out and come back.

BERTHA: As long as you get your boarding money it ain't your cause about what he do. He don't bother nobody.

SETH: Just go out and come back. Going around asking everybody about Martha. Like Henry Allen seen him down at the church last night.

BERTHA: The man's allowed to go to church if he want. He say he a deacon. Ain't nothing wrong about him going to church.

SETH: I ain't talking about him going to church. I'm talking about him hanging around *out-side* the church.

BERTHA: Henry Allen say that?

SETH: Say he be standing around outside the church. Like he be watching it.

BERTHA: What on earth he wanna be watching the church for, I wonder?

SETH: That's what I'm trying to figure out. Looks like he fixing to rob it.

BERTHA: Seth, now do he look like the kind that would rob the church?

SETH: I ain't saying that. I ain't saying how he look. It's how he do. Anybody liable to do anything as far as I'm concerned. I ain't never thought about how no church robbers look . . . but now that you mention it, I don't see where they look no different than how he look.

BERTHA: Herald Loomis ain't the kind of man who would rob no church.

SETH: I ain't even so sure that's his name.

BERTHA: Why the man got to lie about his name?

SETH: Anybody can tell anybody anything about what their name is. That's what you call him . . . Herald Loomis. His name is liable to be anything.

BERTHA: Well, until he tell me different that's what I'm gonna call him. You just getting yourself all worked up about the man for nothing.

SETH: Talking about Loomis: Martha's name wasn't no Loomis nothing. Martha's name is Pentecost.

BERTHA: How you so sure that's her right name? Maybe she changed it.

SETH: Martha's a good Christian woman. This fellow here look like he owe the devil a day's work and he's trying to figure out how he gonna pay him. Martha ain't had a speck of distrust about her the whole time she was living here. They moved the church out there to Rankin and I was sorry to see her go.

BERTHA: That's why he be hanging around the church. He looking for her.

SETH: If he looking for her, why don't he go inside and ask? What he doing hanging around outside the church acting sneaky like?

(*BYNUM enters from the yard.*)

BYNUM: Morning, Seth. Morning, Sister Bertha.

(*BYNUM continues through the kitchen and exits up the stairs.*)

BERTHA: That's who you should be asking the questions. He been out there in that yard all morning. He was out there before the sun come up. He didn't even come in for breakfast. I don't know what he's doing. He had three of them pigeons line up out there. He dance around till he get tired. He sit down awhile then get up and dance some more. He come through here a little while ago looking like he was mad at the world.

SETH: I don't pay Bynum no mind. He don't spook me up with all that stuff.

BERTHA: That's how Martha come to be living here. She come to see Bynum. She come to see him when she first left from down South.

SETH: Martha was living here before Bynum. She ain't come on here when she first left from down there. She come on here after she went back to get her little girl. That's when she come on here.

BERTHA: Well, where was Bynum? He was here when she came.

SETH: Bynum ain't come till after her. That boy Hiram was staying up there in Bynum's room.

BERTHA: Well, how long Bynum been here?

SETH: Bynum ain't been here no longer than three years. That's what I'm trying to tell you. Martha was staying up there and sewing and cleaning for Doc Goldblum when Bynum came. This the longest he ever been in one place.

BERTHA: How you know how long the man been in one place?

SETH: I know Bynum. Bynum ain't no mystery to me. I done seen a hundred niggers like him. He's one of them fellows never could stay in one place. He was wandering all around the country till he got old and settled here. The only thing different about Bynum is he bring all this heebie-jeebie stuff with him.

BERTHA: I still say he was staying here when she came. That's why she came . . . to see him.

SETH: You can say what you want. I know the fact of it. She come on here four years ago all heartbroken 'cause she couldn't find her little girl. And Bynum wasn't nowhere around. She got mixed up in that old heebie-jeebie nonsense with him after he came.

BERTHA: Well, if she came on before Bynum I don't know where she stayed. 'Cause she stayed up there in Hiram's room. Hiram couldn't get along with Bynum and left out of here owing you two dollars. Now, I know you ain't forgot about that!

SETH: Sure did! You know Hiram ain't paid me that two dollars yet. So that's why he be ducking and hiding when he see me down on Logan Street. You right. Martha did come on after Bynum. I forgot that's why Hiram left.

BERTHA: Him and Bynum never could see eye to eye. They always rubbed each other the wrong way. Hiram got to thinking that Bynum was trying to put a fix on him and he moved out. Martha came to see Bynum and ended up taking Hiram's room. Now, I know what I'm talking about. She stayed on here three years till they moved the church.

SETH: She out there in Rankin now. I know where she at. I know where they moved the church to. She right out there in Rankin in that place used to be a shoe store. Used to be Wolf's shoe store. They moved to a bigger place and they put that church in there. I know where she at. I know just where she at.

BERTHA: Why don't you tell the man? You see he looking for her.

SETH: I ain't gonna tell that man where that woman is! What I wanna do that for? I don't know nothing about that man. I don't know why he looking for her. He might wanna do her a harm. I ain't gonna carry that on my hands. He looking for her, he gonna have to find her for himself. I ain't gonna help him. Now, if he had come and presented himself as a gentleman—the way Martha Pentecost's husband would have done—then I would have told him. But I ain't gonna tell this old wild-eyed mean-looking nigger nothing!

BERTHA: Well, why don't you get a ride with Selig and go up there and tell her where he is? See if she wanna see him. If that's her little girl . . . you say Martha was looking for her.

SETH: You know me, Bertha. I don't get mixed up in nobody's business.

(*BYNUM enters from the stairs.*)

BYNUM: Morning, Seth. Morning, Bertha. Can I still get some breakfast? Mr. Loomis been down here this morning?

SETH: He done gone out and come back. He up there now. Left out of here early this morning wearing that coat. Hot as it is, the man wanna walk around wearing a big old heavy coat. He come back in here paid me for another week, sat down there waiting on Selig. Got tired of waiting and went on back upstairs.

BYNUM: Where's the little girl?

SETH: She out there in the front. Had to chase her and that Reuben off the front porch. She out there somewhere.

BYNUM: Look like if Martha was around here he would have found her by now. My guess is she ain't in the city.

SETH: She ain't! I know where she at. I know just where she at. But I ain't gonna tell him. Not the way he look.

BERTHA: Here go your coffee, Bynum.

BYNUM: He says he gonna get Selig to find her for him.

SETH: Selig can't find her. He talk all that . . . but unless he get lucky and knock on her door he can't find her. That's the only way he find anybody. He got to get lucky. But I know just where she at.

BERTHA: Here go some biscuits, Bynum.

BYNUM: What else you got over there, Sister Bertha? You got some grits and gravy over there? I could go for some of that this morning.

BERTHA: (*Sets a bowl on the table.*) Seth, come on and help me turn this mattress over. Come on.

SETH: Something ain't right with that fellow, Bynum. I don't like the way he stare at everybody.

BYNUM: Mr. Loomis alright, Seth. He just a man got something on his mind. He just got a straightforward mind, that's all.

SETH: What's that fellow that they had around here? Moses, that's Moses Houser. Man went crazy and jumped off the Brady Street Bridge. I told you when I seen him something wasn't right about him. And I'm telling you about this fellow now.

(*There is a knock on the door. SETH goes to answer it. Enter RUTHERFORD SELIG.*)

Ho! Come on in, Selig.

BYNUM: If it ain't the People Finder himself.

SELIG: Bynum, before you start . . . I ain't seen no shiny man now.

BYNUM: Who said anything about that? I ain't said nothing about that. I just called you a first-class People Finder.

SELIG: How many dustpans you get out of that sheet metal, Seth?

SETH: You walked by them on your way in. They sitting out there on the porch. Got twenty-eight. Got four out of each sheet and made Bertha a coffeepot out the other one. They a little small but they got nice handles.

SELIG: That was twenty cents apiece, right? That's what we agreed on.

SETH: That's five dollars and sixty cents. Twenty on top of twenty-eight. How many sheets you bring me?

SELIG: I got eight out there. That's a dollar twenty makes me owe you . . .

SETH: Four dollars and forty cents.

SELIG: (*Paying him.*) Go on and make me some dustpans. I can use all you can make.

(*LOOMIS enters from the stairs.*)

LOOMIS: I been watching for you. He say you find people.

BYNUM: Mr. Loomis here wants you to find his wife.

LOOMIS: He say you find people. Find her for me.

SELIG: Well, let see here . . . find somebody, is it?

(SELIG *rummages through his pockets. He has several notebooks and he is searching for the right one.*)

Alright now . . . what's the name?

LOOMIS: Martha Loomis. She my wife. Got married legal with the paper and all.

SELIG: (*Writing.*) Martha . . . Loomis. How tall is she?

LOOMIS: She five feet from the ground.

SELIG: Five feet . . . tall. Young or old?

LOOMIS: She a young woman. Got long pretty hair.

SELIG: Young . . . long . . . pretty . . . hair. Where did you last see her?

LOOMIS: Tennessee. Nearby Memphis.

SELIG: When was that?

LOOMIS: Nineteen hundred and one.

SELIG: Nineteen . . . hundred and one. I'll tell you, mister . . . you better off without them. Now you take me . . . old Rutherford Selig could tell you a thing or two about these women. I ain't met one yet I could understand. Now, you take Sally out there. That's all a man needs is a good horse. I say giddup and she go. Say whoa and she stop. I feed her some oats and she carry me wherever I want to go. Ain't a speck of trouble out of her since I had her. Now, I been married. A long time ago down in Kentucky. I got up one morning and I saw this look on my wife's face. Like way down deep inside her she was wishing I was dead. I walked around that morning and every time I looked at her she had that look on her face. It seem like she knew I could see it on her. Every time I looked at her I got smaller and smaller. Well, I wasn't gonna stay around there and just shrink away. I walked out on the porch and closed the door behind me. When I closed the door she locked it. I went out and bought me a horse. And I ain't been without

one since! Martha Loomis, huh? Well, now I'll do the best I can do. That's one dollar.

LOOMIS: (*Holding out dollar suspiciously.*) How you find her?

SELIG: Well now, it ain't no easy job like you think. You can't just go out there and find them like that. There's a lot of little tricks to it. It's not an easy job keeping up with you Nigras the way you move about so. Now you take this woman you looking for . . . this Martha Loomis. She could be anywhere. Time I find her, if you don't keep your eye on her, she'll be gone off someplace else. You'll be thinking she over here and she'll be over there. But like I say there's a lot of little tricks to it.

LOOMIS: You say you find her.

SELIG: I can't promise anything but we been finders in my family for a long time. Bringers and finders. My great-granddaddy used to bring Nigras across the ocean on ships. That's wasn't no easy job either. Sometimes the winds would blow so hard you'd think the hand of God was set against the sails. But it set him well in pay and he settled in this new land and found him a wife of good Christian charity with a mind for kids and the like and well . . . here I am, Rutherford Selig. You're in good hands, mister. Me and my daddy have found plenty Nigras. My daddy, rest his soul, used to find runaway slaves for the plantation bosses. He was the best there was at it. Jonas B. Selig. Had him a reputation stretched clean across the country. After Abraham Lincoln give you all Nigras your freedom papers and with you all looking all over for each other . . . we started finding Nigras for Nigras. Of course, it don't pay as much. But the People Finding business ain't so bad.

LOOMIS: (*Hands him the dollar.*) Find her. Martha Loomis. Find her for me.

SELIG: Like I say, I can't promise you anything. I'm going back upriver, and if she's around in them parts I'll find her for you. But I can't promise you anything.

LOOMIS: When you coming back?

SELIG: I'll be back on Saturday. I come and see Seth to pick up my order on Saturday.

BYNUM: You going upriver, huh? You going up around my way. I used to go all up through there. Blawknox . . . Clairton. Used to go up to Rankin and take that first righthand road. I wore many a pair of shoes out walking around that way. You'd have thought I was a missionary spreading the gospel the way I wandered all around them parts.

SELIG: Okay, Bynum. See you on Saturday.

SETH: Here, let me walk out with you. Help you with them dustpans.

(*SETH and SELIG exit out the back. BERTHA enters from the stairs carrying a bundle of sheets.*)

BYNUM: Herald Loomis got the People Finder looking for Martha.

BERTHA: You can call him a People Finder if you want to. I know Rutherford Selig carries people away too. He done carried a whole bunch of them away from here. Folks plan on leaving plan by Selig's timing. They wait till he get ready to go, then they hitch a ride on his wagon. Then he charge folks a dollar to tell them where he took them. Now, that's the truth of Rutherford Selig. This old People Finding business is for the birds. He ain't never found nobody he ain't took away. Herald Loomis, you just wasted your dollar.

(*BERTHA exits into the bedroom.*)

LOOMIS: He say he find her. He say he find her by Saturday. I'm gonna wait till Saturday.

(*The lights fade to black.*)

Scene Three

It is Sunday morning, the next day. The lights come up on the kitchen. SETH sits talking to BYNUM. The breakfast dishes have been cleared away.

SETH: They can't see that. Neither one of them can see that. Now, how much sense it take to see that? All you got to do is be able to

count. One man making ten pots is five men making fifty pots. But they can't see that. Asked where I'm gonna get my five men. Hell, I can teach anybody how to make a pot. I can teach you. I can take you out there and get you started right now. Inside of two weeks you'd know how to make a pot. All you got to do is want to do it. I can get five men. I ain't worried about getting no five men.

BERTHA: (*Calls from the bedroom.*) Seth. Come on and get ready now. Reverend Gates ain't gonna be holding up his sermon 'cause you sitting out there talking.

SETH: Now, you take the boy, Jeremy. What he gonna do after he put in that road? He can't do nothing but go put in another one somewhere. Now, if he let me show him how to make some pots and pans . . . then he'd have something can't nobody take away from him. After a while he could get his own tools and go off somewhere and make his own pots and pans. Find him somebody to sell them to. Now, Selig can't make no pots and pans. He can sell them but he can't make them. I get me five men with some tools and we'd make him so many pots and pans he'd have to open up a store somewhere. But they can't see that. Neither Mr. Cohen nor Sam Green.

BERTHA: (*Calls from the bedroom.*) Seth . . . time be wasting. Best be getting on.

SETH: I'm coming, woman! (*To BYNUM.*) Want me to sign over the house to borrow five hundred dollars. I ain't that big a fool. That's all I got. Sign it over to them and then I won't have nothing.

(*JEREMY enters waving a dollar and carrying his guitar.*)

JEREMY: Look here, Mr. Bynum . . . won me another dollar last night down at Seefus! Me and that Mattie Campbell went down there again and I played contest. Ain't no guitar players down there. Wasn't even no contest. Say, Mr. Seth, I asked Mattie Campbell if she wanna come by and have Sunday dinner with us. Get some fried chicken.

SETH: It's gonna cost you twenty-five cents.

JEREMY: That's alright. I got a whole dollar here. Say Mr. Seth . . . me and Mattie Campbell talked it over last night and she gonna move in with me. If that's alright with you.

SETH: Your business is your business . . . but it's gonna cost her a dollar a week for her board. I can't be feeding nobody for free.

JEREMY: Oh, she know that, Mr. Seth. That's what I told her, say she'd have to pay for her meals.

SETH: You say you got a whole dollar there . . . turn loose that twenty-five cents.

JEREMY: Suppose she move in today, then that make seventy-five cents more, so I'll give you the whole dollar for her now till she gets here.

(*SETH pockets the money and exits into the bedroom.*)

BYNUM: So you and that Mattie Campbell gonna take up together?

JEREMY: I told her she don't need to be by her lonesome, Mr. Bynum. Don't make no sense for both of us to be by our lonesome. So she gonna move in with me.

BYNUM: Sometimes you got to be where you supposed to be. Sometimes you can get all mixed up in life and come to the wrong place.

JEREMY: That's just what I told her, Mr. Bynum. It don't make no sense for her to be all mixed up and lonesome. May as well come here and be with me. She a fine woman too. Got them long legs. Knows how to treat a fellow too. Treat you like you wanna be treated.

BYNUM: You just can't look at it like that. You got to look at the whole thing. Now, you take a fellow go out there, grab hold to a woman and think he got something 'cause she sweet and soft to the touch. Alright. Touching's part of life. It's in the world like everything else. Touching's nice. It feels good. But you can lay your hand upside a horse or a cat, and that feels good too. What's the difference? When you grab hold to a woman, you got something there. You got a whole world there. You got a way of life kicking up under your hand. That woman can take and make you feel like something. I ain't just talking about in the way of jumping off into bed together and rolling around with each other. Anybody can do that. When you grab hold to that woman and look at the whole thing and see what you got . . . why, she can take and make something out of you. Your mother was a woman. That's enough right there to show you what a woman is. Enough to show you what she can do. She made something out of you. Taught you converse, and all about how to take care of yourself, how to see where you at and where you going tomorrow, how to look out to see what's coming in the way of eating, and what to do with yourself when you get lonesome. That's a mighty thing she did. But you just can't look at a woman to jump off into bed with her. That's a foolish thing to ignore a woman like that.

JEREMY: Oh, I ain't ignoring her, Mr. Bynum. It's hard to ignore a woman got legs like she got.

BYNUM: Alright. Let's try it this way. Now, you take a ship. Be out there on the water traveling about. You out there on that ship sailing to and from. And then you see some land. Just like you see a woman walking down the street. You see that land and it don't look like nothing but a line out there on the horizon. That's all it is when you first see it. A line that cross your path out there on the horizon. Now, a smart man know when he see that land, it ain't just a line setting out there. He know that if you get off the water to go take a good look . . . why, there's a whole world right there. A whole world with everything imaginable under the sun. Anything you can think of you can find on that land. Same with a woman. A woman is everything a man need. To a smart man she water and berries. And that's all a man need.

That's all he need to live on. You give me
some water and berries and if there ain't
nothing else I can live a hundred years.
See, you just like a man looking at the
horizon from a ship. You just seeing a part
of it. But it's a blessing when you learn to
look at a woman and see in maybe just a
few strands of her hair, the way her cheek
curves . . . to see in that everything there is
out of life to be gotten. It's a blessing to
see that. You know you done right and
proud by your mother to see that. But you
got to learn it. My telling you ain't gonna
mean nothing. You got to learn how to
come to your own time and place with
a woman.

JEREMY: What about your woman, Mr. Bynum?
I know you done had some woman.

BYNUM: Oh, I got them in memory time. That
lasts longer than any of them ever stayed
with me.

JEREMY: I had me an old gal one time . . .

(*There is a knock on the door. JEREMY goes to answer
it. Enter MOLLY CUNNINGHAM. She is about
twenty-six, the kind of woman that "could break in
on a dollar anywhere she goes." She carries a small
cardboard suitcase, and wears a colorful dress of the
fashion of the day. JEREMY's heart jumps out of his
chest when he sees her.*)

MOLLY: You got any rooms here? I'm looking for
a room.

JEREMY: Yeah . . . Mr. Seth got rooms. Sure . . .
wait till I get Mr. Seth. (*Calls.*) Mr. Seth!
Somebody here to see you! (*To MOLLY.*)
Yeah, Mr. Seth got some rooms. Got one
right next to me. This a nice place to stay,
too. My name's Jeremy. What's yours?

(*SETH enters dressed in his Sunday clothes.*)

SETH: Ho!

JEREMY: This here woman looking for a place to
stay. She say you got any rooms.

MOLLY: Mister, you got any rooms? I seen your
sign say you got rooms.

SETH: How long you plan to staying?

MOLLY: I ain't gonna be here long. I ain't looking for no home or nothing. I'd be in Cincin-
nati if I hadn't missed my train.

SETH: Rooms cost two dollars a week.

MOLLY: Two dollars!

SETH: That includes meals. We serve two meals
a day. That's breakfast and dinner.

MOLLY: I hope it ain't on the third floor.

SETH: That's the only one I got. Third floor to
the left. That's pay up in advance week to
week.

MOLLY: (*Going into her bosom.*) I'm gonna pay
you for one week. My name's Molly. Molly
Cunningham.

SETH: I'm Seth Holly. My wife's name is Bertha.
She do the cooking and taking care of
around here. She got sheets on the bed.
Towels twenty-five cents a week extra if you
ain't got none. You get breakfast and dinner.
We got fried chicken on Sundays.

MOLLY: That sounds good. Here's two dollars
and twenty-five cents. Look here,
Mister . . . ?

SETH: Holly. Seth Holly.

MOLLY: Look here, Mr. Holly. I forgot to tell
you. I likes me some company from time to
time. I don't like being by myself.

SETH: Your business is your business. I don't
meddle in nobody's business. But this is a respectable house. I don't have no riffraff
around here. And I don't have no women
hauling no men up to their rooms to be
making their living. As long as we understand each other then we'll be alright with
each other.

MOLLY: Where's the outhouse?

SETH: Straight through the door over yonder.

MOLLY: I get my own key to the front door?

SETH: Everybody get their own key. If you come
in late just don't be making no whole lot of
noise and carrying on. Don't allow no fuss-
ing and fighting around here.

MOLLY: You ain't got to worry about that, mister. Which way you say that outhouse was
again?

SETH: Straight through that door over yonder.

(*MOLLY exits out the back door. JEREMY crosses to watch her.*)

JEREMY: Mr. Bynum, you know what? I think I know what you was talking about now.

(*The lights go down on the scene.*)

Scene Four

The lights come up on the kitchen. It is later the same evening. MATTIE and all the residents of the house, except LOOMIS, sit around the table. They have finished eating and most of the dishes have been cleared.

MOLLY: That sure was some good chicken.

JEREMY: That's what I'm talking about. Miss Bertha, you sure can fry some chicken. I thought my mama could fry some chicken. But she can't do half as good as you.

SETH: I know it. That's why I married her. She don't know that, though. She think I married her for something else.

BERTHA: I ain't studying you, Seth. Did you get your things moved in alright, Mattie?

MATTIE: I ain't had that much. Jeremy helped me with what I did have.

BERTHA: You'll get to know your way around here. If you have any questions about anything just ask me. You and Molly both. I get along with everybody. You'll find I ain't no trouble to get along with.

MATTIE: You need some help with the dishes?

BERTHA: I got me a helper. Ain't I, Zonia? Got me a good helper.

ZONIA: Yes, ma'am.

SETH: Look at Bynum sitting over there with his belly all poked out. Ain't saying nothing. Sitting over there half asleep. Ho, Bynum!

BERTHA: If Bynum ain't saying nothing what you wanna start him up for?

SETH: Ho, Bynum!

BYNUM: What you hollering at me for? I ain't doing nothing.

SETH: Come on, we gonna Juba.

BYNUM: You know me, I'm always ready to Juba.

SETH: Well, come on, then.

(*SETH pulls out a harmonica and blows a few notes.*)

Come on there, Jeremy. Where's your guitar? Go get your guitar. Bynum say he's ready to Juba.

JEREMY: Don't need no guitar to Juba. Ain't you never Juba without a guitar?

(*JEREMY begins to drum on the table.*)

SETH: It ain't that. I ain't never Juba with one! Figured to try it and see how it worked.

BYNUM: (*Drumming on the table.*) You don't need no guitar. Look at Molly sitting over there. She don't know we Juba on Sunday. We gonna show you something tonight. You and Mattie Campbell both. Ain't that right, Seth?

SETH: You said it! Come on, Bertha, leave them dishes be for a while. We gonna Juba.

BYNUM: Alright. Let's Juba down!

(*The Juba is reminiscent of the Ring Shouts of the African slaves. It is a call and response dance. BYNUM sits at the table and drums. He calls the dance as others clap hands, shuffle and stomp around the table. It should be as African as possible, with the performers working themselves up into a near frenzy. The words can be improvised, but should include some mention of the Holy Ghost. In the middle of the dance HERALD LOOMIS enters.*)

LOOMIS: (*In a rage.*) Stop it! Stop!

(*They stop and turn to look at him.*)

You all sitting up here singing about the Holy Ghost. What's so holy about the Holy Ghost? You singing and singing. You think the Holy Ghost coming? You singing for the Holy Ghost to come? What he gonna do, huh? He gonna come with tongues of fire to burn up your woolly heads? You gonna tie onto the Holy Ghost and get burned up? What you got then? Why God got to be so big? Why he got to be bigger than me? How much big is there? How much big do you want?

(*LOOMIS starts to unzip his pants.*)

SETH: Nigger, you crazy!

LOOMIS: How much big you want?

SETH: You done plumb lost your mind!

(*LOOMIS begins to speak in tongues and dance around the kitchen. SETH starts after him.*)

BERTHA: Leave him alone, Seth. He ain't in his right mind.

LOOMIS: (*Stops suddenly.*) You all don't know nothing about me. You don't know what I done seen. Herald Loomis done seen some things he ain't got words to tell you.

(*LOOMIS starts to walk out the front door and is thrown back and collapses, terror-stricken by his vision. BYNUM crawls to him.*)

BYNUM: What you done seen, Herald Loomis?

LOOMIS: I done seen bones rise up out the water. Rise up and walk across the water. Bones walking on top of the water.

BYNUM: Tell me about them bones, Herald Loomis. Tell me what you seen.

LOOMIS: I come to this place . . . to this water that was bigger than the whole world. And I looked out . . . and I seen these bones rise up out the water. Rise up and begin to walk on top of it.

BYNUM: Wasn't nothing but bones and they walking on top of the water.

LOOMIS: Walking without sinking down. Walking on top of the water.

BYNUM: Just marching in a line.

LOOMIS: A whole heap of them. They come up out the water and started marching.

BYNUM: Wasn't nothing but bones and they walking on top of the water.

LOOMIS: One after the other. They just come up out the water and start to walking.

BYNUM: They walking on the water without sinking down. They just walking and walking. And then . . . what happened, Herald Loomis?

LOOMIS: They just walking across the water.

BYNUM: What happened, Herald Loomis? What happened to the bones?

LOOMIS: They just walking across the water . . . and then . . . they sunk down.

BYNUM: The bones sunk into the water. They all sunk down.

LOOMIS: All at one time! They just all fell in the water at one time.

BYNUM: Sunk down like anybody else.

LOOMIS: When they sink down they made a big splash and this here wave come up . . .

BYNUM: A big wave, Herald Loomis. A big wave washed over the land.

LOOMIS: It washed them out of the water and up on the land. Only . . . only . . .

BYNUM: Only they ain't bones no more.

LOOMIS: They got flesh on them! Just like you and me!

BYNUM: Everywhere you look the waves is washing them up on the land right on top of one another.

LOOMIS: They black. Just like you and me. Ain't no difference.

BYNUM: Then what happened, Herald Loomis?

LOOMIS: They ain't moved or nothing. They just laying there.

BYNUM: You just laying there. What you waiting on, Herald Loomis?

LOOMIS: I'm laying there . . . waiting.

BYNUM: What you waiting on, Herald Loomis?

LOOMIS: I'm waiting on the breath to get into my body.

BYNUM: The breath coming into you, Herald Loomis. What you gonna do now?

LOOMIS: The wind's blowing the breath into my body. I can feel it. I'm starting to breathe again.

BYNUM: What you gonna do, Herald Loomis?

LOOMIS: I'm gonna stand up. I got to stand up. I can't lay here no more. All the breath coming into my body and I got to stand up.

BYNUM: Everybody's standing up at the same time.

LOOMIS: The ground's starting to shake. There's a great shaking. The world's busting half in two. The sky's splitting open. I got to stand up.

(LOOMIS attempts to stand up.)

　　My legs . . . my legs won't stand up!
BYNUM: Everybody's standing and walking toward the road. What you gonna do, Herald Loomis?
LOOMIS: My legs won't stand up.
BYNUM: They shaking hands and saying goodbye to each other and walking every whichaway down the road.
LOOMIS: I got to stand up!
BYNUM: They walking around here now. Mens. Just like you and me. Come right up out the water.
LOOMIS: Got to stand up.
BYNUM: They walking, Herald Loomis. They walking around here now.
LOOMIS: I got to stand up. Get up on the road.
BYNUM: Come on, Herald Loomis.

(LOOMIS tries to stand up.)

LOOMIS: My legs won't stand up! My legs won't stand up!

(LOOMIS collapses on the floor as the lights go down to black.)

ACT TWO

Scene One

The lights come up on the kitchen. BERTHA busies herself with breakfast preparations. SETH sits at the table.

SETH: I don't care what his problem is! He's leaving here!
BERTHA: You can't put the man out and he got that little girl. Where they gonna go then?
SETH: I don't care where he go. Let him go back where he was before he come here. I ain't asked him to come here. I knew when I first looked at him something wasn't right with him. Dragging that little girl around with him. Looking like he be sleeping in the woods somewhere. I knew all along he wasn't right.

BERTHA: A fellow get a little drunk he's liable to say or do anything. He ain't done no big harm.
SETH: I just don't have all that carrying on in my house. When he come down here I'm gonna tell him. He got to leave here. My daddy wouldn't stand for it and I ain't gonna stand for it either.
BERTHA: Well, if you put him out you have to put Bynum out too. Bynum right there with him.
SETH: If it wasn't for Bynum ain't no telling what would have happened. Bynum talked to that fellow just as nice and calmed him down. If he wasn't here ain't no telling what would have happened. Bynum ain't done nothing but talk to him and kept him calm. Man acting all crazy with that foolishness. Naw, he's leaving here.
BERTHA: What you gonna tell him? How you gonna tell him to leave?
SETH: I'm gonna tell him straight out. Keep it nice and simple. Mister, you got to leave here!

(MOLLY enters from the stairs.)

MOLLY: Morning.
BERTHA: Did you sleep alright in that bed?
MOLLY: Tired as I was I could have slept anywhere. It's a real nice room, though. This is a nice place.
SETH: I'm sorry you had to put up with all that carrying on last night.
MOLLY: It don't bother me none. I done seen that kind of stuff before.
SETH: You won't have to see it around here no more.

(BYNUM is heard singing offstage.)

　　I don't put up with all that stuff. When that fellow come down here I'm gonna tell him.
BYNUM: *(singing)*
　　Soon my work will all be done
　　Soon my work will all be done
　　Soon my work will all be done
　　I'm going to see the king.

BYNUM: (*Enters.*) Morning, Seth. Morning, Sister Bertha. I see we got Molly Cunningham down here at breakfast.

SETH: Bynum, I wanna thank you for talking to that fellow last night and calming him down. If you hadn't been here ain't no telling what might have happened.

BYNUM: Mr. Loomis alright, Seth. He just got a little excited.

SETH: Well, he can get excited somewhere else 'cause he leaving here.

(*MATTIE enters from the stairs.*)

BYNUM: Well, there's Mattie Campbell.

MATTIE: Good morning.

BERTHA: Sit on down there, Mattie. I got some biscuits be ready in a minute. The coffee's hot.

MATTIE: Jeremy gone already?

BYNUM: Yeah, he leave out of here early. He got to be there when the sun come up. Most working men got to be there when the sun come up. Everybody but Seth. Seth work at night. Mr. Olowski so busy in his shop he got fellows working at night.

(*LOOMIS enters from the stairs.*)

SETH: Mr. Loomis, now . . . I don't want no trouble. I keeps me a respectable house here. I don't have no carrying on like what went on last night. This has been a respectable house for a long time. I'm gonna have to ask you to leave.

LOOMIS: You got my two dollars. That two dollars say we stay till Saturday.

(*LOOMIS and SETH glare at each other.*)

SETH: Alright. Fair enough. You stay till Saturday. But come Saturday you got to leave here.

LOOMIS: (*Continues to glare at SETH. He goes to the door and calls.*) Zonia. You stay around this house, you hear? Don't you go anywhere.

(*LOOMIS exits out the front door.*)

SETH: I knew it when I first seen him. I knew something wasn't right with him.

BERTHA: Seth, leave the people alone to eat their breakfast. They don't want to hear that. Go on out there and make some pots and pans. That's the only time you satisfied is when you out there. Go on out there and make some pots and pans and leave them people alone.

SETH: I ain't bothering anybody. I'm just stating the facts. I told you, Bynum.

(*BERTHA shoos SETH out the back door and exits into the bedroom.*)

MOLLY: (*To BYNUM.*) You one of them voodoo people?

BYNUM: I got a power to bind folks if that what you talking about.

MOLLY: I thought so. The way you talked to that man when he started all that spooky stuff. What you say you had the power to do to people? You ain't the cause of him acting like that, is you?

BYNUM: I binds them together. Sometimes I help them find each other.

MOLLY: How do you do that?

BYNUM: With a song. My daddy taught me how to do it.

MOLLY: That's what they say. Most folks be what they daddy is. I wouldn't want to be like my daddy. Nothing ever set right with him. He tried to make the world over. Carry it around with him everywhere he go. I don't want to be like that. I just take life as it come. I don't be trying to make it over.

(*Pause.*)

Your daddy used to do that too, huh? Make people stay together?

BYNUM: My daddy used to heal people. He had the Healing Song. I got the Binding Song.

MOLLY: My mama used to believe in all that stuff. If she got sick she would have gone and saw your daddy. As long as he didn't make her drink nothing. She wouldn't drink nothing nobody give her. She was always afraid somebody was gonna poison her. How your daddy heal people?

BYNUM: With a song. He healed people by singing over them. I seen him do it. He sung over this little white girl when she was sick. They made a big to-do about it. They carried the girl's bed out in the yard and had all her kinfolk standing around. The little girl laying up there in the bed. Doctors standing around can't do nothing to help her. And they had my daddy come up and sing his song. It didn't sound no different than any other song. It was just somebody singing. But the song was its own thing and it come out and took upon this little girl with its power and it healed her.

MOLLY: That's sure something else. I don't understand that kind of thing. I guess if the doctor couldn't make me well I'd try it. But otherwise I don't wanna be bothered with that kind of thing. It's too spooky.

BYNUM: Well, let me get on out here and get to work.

(*BYNUM gets up and heads out the back door.*)

MOLLY: I ain't meant to offend you or nothing. What's your name . . . Bynum? I ain't meant to say nothing to make you feel bad now.

(*BYNUM exits out the back door.*)

(*To MATTIE.*) I hope he don't feel bad. He's a nice man. I don't wanna hurt nobody's feelings or nothing.

MATTIE: I got to go on up to Doc Goldblum's and finish his ironing.

MOLLY: Now, that's something I don't ever wanna do. Iron no clothes. Especially somebody else's. That's what I believe killed my mama. Always ironing and working, doing somebody's else's work. Not Molly Cunningham.

MATTIE: It's the only job I got. I got to make it someway to fend for myself.

MOLLY: I thought Jeremy was your man. Ain't he working?

MATTIE: We just be keeping company till maybe Jack come back.

MOLLY: I don't trust none of these men. Jack or nobody else. These men liable to do anything. They wait just until they get one woman tied and locked up with them . . . then they look around to see if they can get another one. Molly don't pay them no mind. One's just as good as the other if you ask me. I ain't never met one that meant nobody no good. You got any babies?

MATTIE: I had two for my man, Jack Carper. But they both died.

MOLLY: That be the best. These men make all these babies, then run off and leave you to take care of them. Talking about they wanna see what's on the other side of the hill. I make sure I don't get no babies. My mama taught me how to do that.

MATTIE: Don't make me no mind. That be nice to be a mother.

MOLLY: Yeah? Well, you go on, then. Molly Cunningham ain't gonna be tied down with no babies. Had me a man one time who I thought had some love in him. Come home one day and he was packing his trunk. Told me the time come when even the best of friends must part. Say he was gonna send me a Special Delivery some old day. I watched him out the window when he carried that trunk out and down to the train station. Said if he was gonna send me a Special Delivery I wasn't gonna be there to get it. I done found out the harder you try to hold onto them, the easier it is for some gal to pull them away. Molly done learned that. That's why I don't trust nobody but the good Lord above, and I don't love nobody but my mama.

MATTIE: I got to get on. Doc Goldblum gonna be waiting.

(*MATTIE exits out the front door. SETH enters from his workshop with his apron, gloves, goggles, etc. He carries a bucket and crosses to the sink for water.*)

SETH: Everybody gone but you, huh?

MOLLY: That little shack out there by the outhouse . . . that's where you make them pots and pans and stuff?

SETH: Yeah, that's my workshed. I go out there . . . take these hands and make something out of nothing. Take that metal and bend and twist it whatever way I want. My daddy taught me that. He used to make pots and pans. That's how I learned it.

MOLLY: I never knew nobody made no pots and pans. My uncle used to shoe horses.

(*JEREMY enters at the front door.*)

SETH: I thought you was working? Ain't you working today?

JEREMY: Naw, they fired me. White fellow come by told me to give him fifty cents if I wanted to keep working. Going around to all the colored making them give him fifty cents to keep hold to their jobs. Them other fellows, they was giving it to him. I kept hold to mine and they fired me.

SETH: Boy, what kind of sense that make? What kind of sense it make to get fired from a job where you making eight dollars a week and all it cost you is fifty cents. That's seven dollars and fifty cents profit! This way you ain't got nothing.

JEREMY: It didn't make no sense to me. I don't make but eight dollars. Why I got to give him fifty cents of it? He go around to all the colored and he got ten dollars extra. That's more than I make for a whole week.

SETH: I see you gonna learn the hard way. You just looking at the facts of it. See, right now, without the job, you ain't got nothing. What you gonna do when you can't keep a roof over your head? Right now, come Saturday, unless you come up with another two dollars, you gonna be out there in the streets. Down up under one of them bridges trying to put some food in your belly and wishing you had given that fellow that fifty cents.

JEREMY: Don't make me no difference. There's a big road out there. I can get my guitar and always find me another place to stay. I ain't planning on staying in one place for too long noway.

SETH: We gonna see if you feel like that come Saturday!

(*SETH exits out the back. JEREMY sees MOLLY.*)

JEREMY: Molly Cunningham. How you doing today, sugar?

MOLLY: You can go on back down there tomorrow and go back to work if you want. They won't even know who you is. Won't even know it's you. I had me a fellow did that one time. They just went ahead and signed him up like they never seen him before.

JEREMY: I'm tired of working anyway. I'm glad they fired me. You sure look pretty today.

MOLLY: Don't come telling me all that pretty stuff. Beauty wanna come in and sit down at your table asking to be fed. I ain't hardly got enough for me.

JEREMY: You know you pretty. Ain't no sense in you saying nothing about that. Why don't you come on and go away with me?

MOLLY: You tied up with that Mattie Campbell. Now you talking about running away with me.

JEREMY: I was just keeping her company 'cause she lonely. You ain't the lonely kind. You the kind that know what she want and how to get it. I need a woman like you to travel around with. Don't you wanna travel around and look at some places with Jeremy? With a woman like you beside him, a man can make it nice in the world.

MOLLY: Molly can make it nice by herself too. Molly don't need nobody leave her cold in hand. The world rough enough as it is.

JEREMY: We can make it better together. I got my guitar and I can play. Won me another dollar last night playing guitar. We can go around and I can play at the dances and we can just enjoy life. You can make it by yourself alright, I agrees with that. A woman like you can make it anywhere she go. But you can make it better if you got a man to protect you.

MOLLY: What places you wanna go around and look at?

JEREMY: All of them! I don't want to miss nothing. I wanna go everywhere and do everything there is to be got out of life. With a woman like you it's like having water and berries. A man got everything he need.

MOLLY: You got to be doing more than playing that guitar. A dollar a day ain't hardly what Molly got in mind.

JEREMY: I gambles real good. I got a hand for it.

MOLLY: Molly don't work. And Molly ain't up for sale.

JEREMY: Sure, baby. You ain't got to work with Jeremy.

MOLLY: There's one more thing.

JEREMY: What's that, sugar?

MOLLY: Molly ain't going South.

(*The lights go down on the scene.*)

Scene Two

The lights come up on the parlor. SETH and BYNUM sit playing a game of dominoes. BYNUM sings to himself.

BYNUM: (*Singing.*)
They tell me Joe Turner's come and gone
Ohhh Lordy
They tell me Joe Turner's come and gone
Ohhh Lordy
Got my man and gone

Come with forty links of chain
Ohhh Lordy
Come with forty links of chain
Ohhh Lordy
Got my man and gone

SETH: Come on and play if you gonna play.

BYNUM: I'm gonna play. Soon as I figure out what to do.

SETH: You can't figure out if you wanna play or you wanna sing.

BYNUM: Well sir, I'm gonna do a little bit of both.

(*Playing.*)
There. What you gonna do now?

(*Singing.*)
They tell me Joe Turner's come and gone
Ohhh Lordy
They tell me Joe Turner's come and gone
Ohhh Lordy

SETH: Why don't you hush up that noise.

BYNUM: That's a song the women sing down around Memphis. The women down there made up that song. I picked it up down there about fifteen years ago.

(*LOOMIS enters from the front door.*)

BYNUM: Evening, Mr. Loomis.

SETH: Today's Monday, Mr. Loomis. Come Saturday your time is up. We done ate already. My wife roasted up some yams. She got your plate sitting in there on the table. (*To BYNUM.*) Whose play is it?

BYNUM: Ain't you keeping up with the game? I thought you was a domino player. I just played so it got to be your turn.

(*LOOMIS goes into the kitchen, where a plate of yams is covered and set on the table. He sits down and begins to eat with his hands.*)

SETH: (*Plays.*) Twenty! Give me twenty! You didn't know I had that ace five. You was trying to play around that. You didn't know I had that lying there for you.

BYNUM: You ain't done nothing. I let you have that to get mine.

SETH: Come on and play. You ain't doing nothing but talking. I got a hundred and forty points to your eighty. You ain't doing nothing but talking. Come on and play.

BYNUM: (*Singing.*)
They tell me Joe Turner's come and gone
Ohhh Lordy
They tell me Joe Turner's come and gone
Ohhh Lordy

Got my man and gone
He come with forty links of chain
Ohhh Lordy

LOOMIS: Why you singing that song? Why you singing about Joe Turner?

BYNUM: I'm just singing to entertain myself.

SETH: You trying to distract me. That's what you trying to do.

BYNUM: (*Singing.*)
Come with forty links of chain
Ohhh Lordy
Come with forty links of chain
Ohhh Lordy

LOOMIS: I don't like you singing that song, mister!

SETH: Now, I ain't gonna have no more disturbance around here, Herald Loomis. You start any more disturbance and you leavin' here, Saturday or no Saturday.

BYNUM: The man ain't causing no disturbance, Seth. He just say he don't like the song.

SETH: Well, we all friendly folk. All neighborly like. Don't have no squabbling around here. Don't have no disturbance. You gonna have to take that someplace else.

BYNUM: He just say he don't like the song. I done sung a whole lot of songs people don't like. I respect everybody. He here in the house too. If he don't like the song, I'll sing something else. I know lots of songs. You got "I Belong to the Band," "Don't You Leave Me Here." You got "Praying on the Old Campground," "Keep your Lamp Trimmed and Burning" . . . I know lots of songs.

(*Sings.*)
Boys, I'll be so glad when payday come
Captain, Captain, when payday comes
Gonna catch that Illinois Central
Going to Kankakee

SETH: Why don't you hush up that hollering and come on and play dominoes.

BYNUM: You ever been to Johnstown, Herald Loomis? You look like a fellow I seen around there.

LOOMIS: I don't know no place with that name.

BYNUM: That's around where I seen my shiny man. See, you looking for this woman. I'm looking for a shiny man. Seem like everybody looking for something.

SETH: I'm looking for you to come and play these dominoes. That's what I'm looking for.

BYNUM: You a farming man, Herald Loomis? You look like you done some farming.

LOOMIS: Same as everybody. I done farmed some, yeah.

BYNUM: I used to work at farming . . . picking cotton. I reckon everybody done picked some cotton.

SETH: I ain't! I ain't never picked no cotton. I was born up here in the North. My daddy was a freedman. I ain't never even seen no cotton!

BYNUM: Mr. Loomis done picked some cotton. Ain't you, Herald Loomis? You done picked a bunch of cotton.

LOOMIS: How you know so much about me? How you know what I done? How much cotton I picked?

BYNUM: I can tell from looking at you. My daddy taught me how to do that. Say when you look at a fellow, if you taught yourself to look for it, you can see his song written on him. Tell you what kind of man he is in the world. Now, I can look at you, Mr. Loomis, and see you a man who done forgot his song. Forgot how to sing it. A fellow forget that and he forget who he is. Forget how he's supposed to mark down life. Now, I used to travel all up and down this road and that . . . looking here and there. Searching. Just like you, Mr. Loomis. I didn't know what I was searching for. The only thing I knew was something was keeping me dissatisfied. Something wasn't making my heart smooth and easy. Then one day my daddy gave me a song. That song had a weight to it that was hard to handle. That song was hard to carry. I fought against it. Didn't want to accept that song. I tried to find my daddy to give him back the song. But I found out it wasn't his song. It was my song. It had come from way deep inside me. I looked long back in memory and gathered up pieces and snatches of things to make that song. I was making it up out of myself. And that song helped me on the road. Made it smooth to where my footsteps didn't bite back at me. All the time that song getting bigger and bigger. That song growing with each step of the road. It got so I used all of myself up in the making of that song. Then I was the song in search of itself. That song rattling in my throat and I'm looking for it. See, Mr. Loomis, when a man forgets his song he goes off in search of it . . . till he find out he's got it with him all the time. That's why I can tell you one of Joe Turner's niggers. 'Cause you forgot how to sing your song.

LOOMIS: You lie! How you see that? I got a mark on me? Joe Turner done marked me to where you can see it? You telling me I'm a marked man. What kind of mark you got on you?

(*BYNUM begins singing.*)

BYNUM:
They tell me Joe Turner's come and gone
Ohhh Lordy
They tell me Joe Turner's come and gone
Ohhh Lordy
Got my man and gone

LOOMIS: Had a whole mess of men he catched. Just go out hunting regular like you go out hunting possum. He catch you and go home to his wife and family. Ain't thought about you going home to yours. Joe Turner catched me when my little girl was just born. Wasn't nothing but a little baby sucking on her mama's titty when he catched me. Joe Turner catched me in nineteen hundred and one. Kept me seven years until nineteen hundred and eight. Kept everybody seven years. He'd go out hunting and bring back forty men at a time. And keep them seven years.

I was walking down this road in this little town outside of Memphis. Come up on these fellows gambling. I was a deacon in the Abundant Life Church. I stopped to preach to these fellows to see if maybe I could turn some of them from their sinning when Joe Turner, brother of the Governor of the great sovereign state of Tennessee, swooped down on us and grabbed everybody there. Kept us all seven years.

My wife Martha gone from me after Joe Turner catched me. Got out from under Joe Turner on his birthday. Me and forty other men put in our seven years and he let us go on his birthday. I made it back to Henry Thompson's place where me and Martha was sharecropping and Martha's gone. She taken my little girl and left her with her mama and took off North. We been looking for her ever since. That's been going on four years now we been looking. That's the only thing I know to do. I just wanna see her face so I can get me a starting place in the world. The world got to start somewhere. That's what I been looking for. I been wandering a long time in somebody else's world. When I find my wife that be the making of my own.

BYNUM: Joe Turner tell why he caught you? You ever asked him that?

LOOMIS: I ain't never seen Joe Turner. Seen him to where I could touch him. I asked one of them fellows one time why he catch niggers. Asked him what I got he want? Why don't he keep on to himself? Why he got to catch me going down the road by my lonesome? He told me I was worthless. Worthless is something you throw away. Something you don't bother with. I ain't seen him throw me away. Wouldn't even let me stay away when I was by my lonesome. I ain't tried to catch him when he going down the road. So I must got something he want. What I got?

SETH: He just want you to do his work for him. That's all.

LOOMIS: I can look at him and see where he big and strong enough to do his own work. So it can't be that. He must want something he ain't got.

BYNUM: That ain't hard to figure out. What he wanted was your song. He wanted to have that song to be his. He thought by catching you he could learn that song. Every nigger he catch he's looking for the one he can learn that song from. Now he's got you bound up to where you can't sing your own song. Couldn't sing it them seven years 'cause you was afraid he would snatch it from under you. But you still got it. Your just forgot how to sing it.

LOOMIS: (*To BYNUM.*) I know who you are. You one of them bones people.

(*The lights go down to black.*)

Scene Three

The lights come up on the kitchen. It is the following morning. MATTIE and BYNUM sit at the table. BERTHA busies herself at the stove.

BYNUM: Good luck don't know no special time to come. You sleep with that up under your pillow and good luck can't help but come to you. Sometimes it come and go and you don't even know it's been there.

BERTHA: Bynum, why don't you leave that gal alone? She don't wanna be hearing all that. Why don't you go on and get out the way and leave her alone?

BYNUM: (*Getting up.*) Alright, alright. But you mark what I'm saying. It'll draw it to you just like a magnet.

(*BYNUM exits up the stairs as LOOMIS enters.*)

BERTHA: I got some grits here, Mr. Loomis.

(*BERTHA sets a bowl on the table.*)

If I was you, Mattie, I wouldn't go getting all tied up with Bynum in that stuff. That kind of stuff, even if it do work for a while, it don't last. That just get people more mixed up than they is already. And I wouldn't waste my time fretting over Jeremy either. I seen it coming. I seen it when she first come here. She that kind of woman run off with the first man got a dollar to spend on her.

Jeremy just young. He don't know what he getting into. That gal don't mean him no good. She's just using him to keep from being by herself. That's the worst use of a man you can have. You ought to be glad to wash him out of your hair. I done seen all kind of men. I done seen them come and go through here. Jeremy ain't had enough to him for you. You need a man who's got some understanding and who willing to work with that understanding to come to the best he can. You got your time coming. You just tries too hard and can't understand why it don't work for you. Trying to figure it out don't do nothing but give you a troubled mind. Don't no man want a woman with a troubled mind.

You get all that trouble off your mind and just when it look like you ain't never gonna find what you want . . . you look up and it's standing right there. That's how I met my Seth. You gonna look up one day and find everything you want standing right in front of you. Been twenty-seven years now since that happened to me. But life ain't no happy-go-lucky time where everything be just like you want it. You got your time coming. You watch what Bertha's saying.

(*SETH enters.*)

SETH: Ho!

BERTHA: What you doing come in here so late?

SETH: I was standing down there on Logan Street talking with the fellows. Henry Allen tried to sell me that old piece of horse he got.

(*He sees LOOMIS.*)

Today's Tuesday, Mr. Loomis.

BERTHA: (*Pulling him toward the bedroom.*) Come on in here and leave that man alone to eat his breakfast.

SETH: I ain't bothering nobody. I'm just reminding him what day it is.

(*SETH and BERTHA exit into the bedroom.*)

LOOMIS: That dress got a color to it.

MATTIE: Did you really see them things like you said? Them people come up out the ocean?

LOOMIS: It happened just like that, yeah.

MATTIE: I hope you find your wife. It be good for your little girl for you to find her.

LOOMIS: Got to find her for myself. Find my starting place in the world. Find me a world I can fit in.

MATTIE: I ain't never found no place for me to fit. Seem like all I do is start over. It ain't nothing to find no starting place in the world. You just start from where you find yourself.

LOOMIS: Got to find my wife. That be my starting place.

MATTIE: What if you don't find her? What you gonna do then if you don't find her?

LOOMIS: She out there somewhere. Ain't no such thing as not finding her.

MATTIE: How she got lost from you? Jack just walked away from me.

LOOMIS: Joe Turner split us up. Joe Turner turned the world upside-down. He bound me on to him for seven years.

MATTIE: I hope you find her. It be good for you to find her.

LOOMIS: I been watching you. I been watching you watch me.

MATTIE: I was just trying to figure out if you seen things like you said.

LOOMIS: (*Getting up.*) Come here and let me touch you. I been watching you. You a full woman. A man needs a full woman. Come on and be with me.

MATTIE: I ain't got enough for you. You'd use me up too fast.

LOOMIS: Herald Loomis got a mind seem like you a part of it since I first seen you. It's been a long time since I seen a full woman. I can smell you from here. I know you got Herald Loomis on your mind, can't keep him apart from it. Come on and be with Herald Loomis.

(*LOOMIS has crossed to MATTIE. He touches her awkwardly, gently, tenderly. Inside he howls like a lost wolf pup whose hunger is deep. He goes to touch her but finds he cannot.*)

I done forgot how to touch.

(*The lights fade to black.*)

Scene Four

It is early the next morning. The lights come up on ZONIA and REUBEN in the yard.

REUBEN: Something spookly going on around here. Last night Mr. Bynum was out in the yard singing and talking to the wind . . . and the wind it just be talking back to him. Did you hear it?

ZONIA: I heard it. I was scared to get up and look. I thought it was a storm.

REUBEN: That wasn't no storm. That was Mr. Bynum. First he say something . . . and the wind it say back to him.

ZONIA: I heard it. Was you scared? I was scared.

REUBEN: And then this morning . . . I seen Miss Mabel!

ZONIA: Who Miss Mabel?

REUBEN: Mr. Seth's mother. He got her picture hanging up in the house. She been dead.

ZONIA: How you seen her if she been dead?

REUBEN: Zonia . . . if I tell you something you promise you won't tell anybody?

ZONIA: I promise.

REUBEN: It was early this morning . . . I went out to the coop to feed the pigeons. I was down on the ground like this to open up the door to the coop . . . when all of a sudden I seen some feets in front of me. I look up . . . and there was Miss Mabel standing there.

ZONIA: Reuben, you better stop telling that! You ain't seen nobody!

REUBEN: Naw, it's the truth. I swear! I seen her just like I see you. Look . . . you can see where she hit me with her cane.

ZONIA: Hit you? What she hit you for?

REUBEN: She says, "Didn't you promise Eugene something?" Then she hit me with her cane.

She say, "Let them pigeons go." Then she hit me again. That's what made them marks.

ZONIA: Jeez man . . . get away from me. You done see a haunt!

REUBEN: Shhhh. You promised, Zonia!

ZONIA: You sure it wasn't Miss Bertha come over there and hit you with her hoe?

REUBEN: It wasn't no Miss Bertha. I told you it was Miss Mabel. She was standing right there by the coop. She had this light coming out of her and then she just melted away.

ZONIA: What she had on?

REUBEN: A white dress. Ain't even had no shoes or nothing. Just had on that white dress and them big hands . . . and that cane she hit me with.

ZONIA: How you reckon she knew about the pigeons? You reckon Eugene told her?

REUBEN: I don't know. I sure ain't asked her none. She say Eugene was waiting on them pigeons. Say he couldn't go back home till I let them go. I couldn't get the door to the coop open fast enough.

ZONIA: Maybe she an angel? From the way you say she look with that white dress. Maybe she an angel.

REUBEN: Mean as she was . . . how she gonna be an angel? She used to chase us out her yard and frown up and look evil all the time.

ZONIA: That don't mean she can't be no angel 'cause of how she looked and 'cause she wouldn't let no kids play in her yard. It go by if you got any spots on your heart and if you pray and go to church.

REUBEN: What about she hit me with her cane? An angel wouldn't hit me with her cane.

ZONIA: I don't know. She might. I still say she was an angel.

REUBEN: You reckon Eugene the one who sent old Miss Mabel?

ZONIA: Why he send her? Why he don't come himself?

REUBEN: Figured if he send her maybe that'll make me listen. 'Cause she old.

ZONIA: What you think it feel like?

REUBEN: What?

ZONIA: Being dead.

REUBEN: Like being sleep only you don't know nothing and can't move no more.

ZONIA: If Miss Mabel can come back . . . then maybe Eugene can come back too.

REUBEN: We can go down to the hideout like we used to! He could come back everyday! It be just like he ain't dead.

ZONIA: Maybe that ain't right for him to come back. Feel kinda funny to be playing games with a haunt.

REUBEN: Yeah . . . what if everybody came back? What if Miss Mabel came back just like she ain't dead? Where you and your daddy gonna sleep then?

ZONIA: Maybe they go back at night and don't need no place to sleep.

REUBEN: It still don't seem right. I'm sure gonna miss Eugene. He's the bestest friend anybody ever had.

ZONIA: My daddy say if you miss somebody too much it can kill you. Say he missed me till it liked to killed him.

REUBEN: What if your mama's already dead and all the time you looking for her?

ZONIA: Naw, she ain't dead. My daddy say he can smell her.

REUBEN: You can't smell nobody that ain't here. Maybe he smelling old Miss Bertha. Maybe Miss Bertha your mama?

ZONIA: Naw, she ain't. My mamma got long pretty hair and she five feet from the ground!

REUBEN: Your daddy say when you leaving?

(ZONIA *doesn't respond.*)

Maybe you gonna stay in Mr. Seth's house and don't go looking for your mama no more.

ZONIA: He say we got to leave on Saturday.

REUBEN: Dag! You just only been here for a little while. Don't seem like nothing ever stay the same.

ZONIA: He say he got to find her. Find him a place in the world.

REUBEN: He could find him a place in Mr. Seth's house.

ZONIA: It don't look like we never gonna find her.

REUBEN: Maybe he find her by Saturday then you don't have to go.

ZONIA: I don't know.

REUBEN: You look like a spider!

ZONIA: I ain't no spider!

REUBEN: Got them long skinny arms and legs. You look like one of them Black Widows.

ZONIA: I ain't no Black Widow nothing! My name is Zonia!

REUBEN: That's what I'm gonna call you . . . Spider.

ZONIA: You can call me that, but I don't have to answer.

REUBEN: You know what? I think maybe I be your husband when I grow up.

ZONIA: How you know?

REUBEN: I ask my grandpap how you know and he say when the moon falls into a girl's eyes that how you know.

ZONIA: Did it fall into my eyes?

REUBEN: Not that I can tell. Maybe I ain't old enough. Maybe you ain't old enough.

ZONIA: So there! I don't know why you telling me that lie!

REUBEN: That don't mean nothing 'cause I can't see it. I know it's there. Just the way you look at me sometimes look like the moon might have been in your eyes.

ZONIA: That don't mean nothing if you can't see it. You supposed to see it.

REUBEN: Shucks, I see it good enough for me. You ever let anybody kiss you?

ZONIA: Just my daddy. He kiss me on the cheek.

REUBEN: It's better on the lips. Can I kiss you on the lips?

ZONIA: I don't know. You ever kiss anybody before?

REUBEN: I had a cousin let me kiss her on the lips one time. Can I kiss you?

ZONIA: Okay.

(*REUBEN kisses her and lays his head against her chest.*)

What you doing?

REUBEN: Listening. Your heart singing!

ZONIA: It is not.

REUBEN: Just beating like a drum. Let's kiss again.

(*They kiss again.*)

Now you mine, Spider. You my girl, okay?

ZONIA: Okay.

REUBEN: When I get grown, I come looking for you.

ZONIA: Okay.

(*The lights fade to black.*)

Scene Five

The lights come up on the kitchen. It is Saturday. BYNUM, LOOMIS, and ZONIA sit at the table. BERTHA prepares breakfast. ZONIA has on a white dress.

BYNUM: With all this rain we been having he might have ran into some washed-out roads. If that wagon got stuck in the mud he's liable to be still upriver somewhere. If he's upriver then he ain't coming until tomorrow.

LOOMIS: Today's Saturday. He say he be here on Saturday.

BERTHA: Zonia, you gonna eat your breakfast this morning.

ZONIA: Yes, ma'am.

BERTHA: I don't know how you expect to get any bigger if you don't eat. I ain't never seen a child that didn't eat. You about as skinny as a bean pole.

(*Pause.*)

Mr. Loomis, there's a place down on Wylie. Zeke Mayweather got a house down there. You ought to see if he got any rooms.

(*LOOMIS doesn't respond.*)

Well, you're welcome to some breakfast before you move on.

(*MATTIE enters from the stairs.*)

MATTIE: Good morning.

BERTHA: Morning, Mattie. Sit on down there and get you some breakfast.

BYNUM: Well, Mattie Campbell, you been sleeping with that up under your pillow like I told you?

BERTHA: Bynum, I done told you to leave that gal alone with all that stuff. You around here meddling in other people's lives. She don't want to hear all that. You ain't doing nothing but confusing her with that stuff.

MATTIE: (*To LOOMIS.*) You all fixing to move on?

LOOMIS: Today's Saturday. I'm paid up till Saturday.

MATTIE: Where you going to?

LOOMIS: Gonna find my wife.

MATTIE: You going off to another city?

LOOMIS: We gonna see where the road take us. Ain't no telling where we wind up.

MATTIE: Eleven years is a long time. Your wife . . . she might have taken up with someone else. People do that when they get lost from each other.

LOOMIS: Zonia. Come on, we gonna find your mama.

(*LOOMIS and ZONIA cross to the door.*)

MATTIE: (*To ZONIA.*) Zonia, Mattie got a ribbon here match your dress. Want Mattie to fix your hair with her ribbon?

(*ZONIA nods. MATTIE ties the ribbon in her hair.*)

There . . . it got a color just like your dress. (*To LOOMIS.*) I hope you find her. I hope you be happy.

LOOMIS: A man looking for a woman be lucky to find you. You a good woman, Mattie. Keep a good heart.

(*LOOMIS and ZONIA exit.*)

BERTHA: I been watching that man for two weeks . . . and that's the closest I come to seeing him act civilized. I don't know what's between you all, Mattie . . . but the only thing that man needs is somebody to make him laugh. That's all you need in the world is love and laughter. That's all anybody needs. To have love in one hand and laughter in the other.

(*BERTHA moves about the kitchen as though blessing it and chasing away the huge sadness that seems to envelop it. It is a dance and demonstration of her own magic, her own remedy that is centuries old and to which she is connected by the muscles of her heart and the blood's memory.*)

You hear me, Mattie? I'm talking about laughing. The kind of laugh that comes from way deep inside. To just stand and laugh and let life flow right through you. Just laugh to let yourself know you're alive.

(*She begins to laugh. It is a near-hysterical laughter that is a celebration of life, both its pain and its blessing. MATTIE and BYNUM join in the laughter. SETH enters from the front door.*)

SETH: Well, I see you all having fun.

(*SETH begins to laugh with them.*)

That Loomis fellow standing up there on the corner watching the house. He standing right up there on Manila Street.

BERTHA: Don't you get started on him. The man done left out of here and that's the last I wanna hear of it. You about to drive me crazy with that man.

SETH: I just say he standing up there on the corner. Acting sneaky like he always do. He can stand up there all he want. As long as he don't come back in here.

(*There is a knock on the door. SETH goes to answer it. Enter MARTHA LOOMIS [PENTECOST]. She is a young woman about twenty-eight. She is dressed as befitting a member of an Evangelist church. RUTHERFORD SELIG follows.*)

SETH: Look here, Bertha. It's Martha Pentecost. Come on in, Martha. Who that with you? Oh . . . that's Selig. Come on in, Selig.

BERTHA: Come on in, Martha. It's sure good to see you.

BYNUM: Rutherford Selig, you a sure enough first-class People Finder!

SELIG: She was right out there in Rankin. You take that first righthand road . . . right there

at that church on Wooster Street. I started
to go right past and something told me to
stop at the church and see if they needed
any dustpans.

SETH: Don't she look good, Bertha.

BERTHA: Look all nice and healthy.

MARTHA: Mr. Bynum . . . Selig told me my little
girl was here.

SETH: There's some fellow around here say he
your husband. Say his name is Loomis. Say
you his wife.

MARTHA: Is my little girl with him?

SETH: Yeah, he got a little girl with him. I wasn't
gonna tell him where you was. Not the way
this fellow look. So he got Selig to find you.

MARTHA: Where they at? They upstairs?

SETH: He was standing right up there on Manila
Street. I had to ask him to leave 'cause of
how he was carrying on. He come in here
one night—

(*The door opens and LOOMIS and ZONIA enter.
MARTHA and LOOMIS stare at each other.*)

LOOMIS: Hello, Martha.

MARTHA: Herald . . . Zonia?

LOOMIS: You ain't waited for me, Martha. I got
out the place looking to see your face. Seven
years I waited to see your face.

MARTHA: Herald, I been looking for you. I
wasn't but two months behind you when
you went to my mama's and got Zonia. I
been looking for you ever since.

LOOMIS: Joe Turner let me loose and I felt all
turned around inside. I just wanted to see
your face to know that the world was still
there. Make sure everything still in its place
so I could reconnect myself together. I got
there and you was gone, Martha.

MARTHA: Herald . . .

LOOMIS: Left my little girl motherless in the
world.

MARTHA: I didn't leave her motherless, Herald.
Reverend Tolliver wanted to move the church
up North 'cause of all the trouble the colored folks was having down there. Nobody
knew what was gonna happen traveling

them roads. We didn't even know if we was
gonna make it up here or not. I left her with
my mama so she be safe. That was better
than dragging her out on the road having
to duck and hide from people. Wasn't no
telling what was gonna happen to us. I
didn't leave her motherless in the world.
I been looking for you.

LOOMIS: I come up on Henry Thompson's place
after seven years of living in hell, and all I'm
looking to do is see your face.

MARTHA: Herald, I didn't know if you was ever
coming back. They told me Joe Turner had
you and my whole world split half in two.
My whole life shattered. It was like I had
poured it in a cracked jar and it all leaked
out the bottom. When it go like that there
ain't nothing you can do put it back together. You talking about Henry Thompson's
place like I'm still gonna be working the land
by myself. How I'm gonna do that? You
wasn't gone but two months and Henry
Thompson kicked me off his land and I
ain't had no place to go but to my mama's.
I stayed and waited there for five years before I woke up one morning and decided
that you was dead. Even if you weren't, you
was dead to me. I wasn't gonna carry you
with me no more. So I killed you in my heart.
I buried you. I mourned you. And then I
picked up what was left and went on to
make life without you. I was a young woman
with life at my beckon. I couldn't drag you
behind me like a sack of cotton.

LOOMIS: I just been waiting to look on your face
to say my goodbye. That goodbye got so big
at times, seem like it was gonna swallow me
up. Like Jonah in the whale's belly I sat up in
that goodbye for three years. That goodbye
kept me out on the road searching. Not
looking on women in their houses. It kept
me bound up to the road. All the time that
goodbye swelling up in my chest till I'm
about to bust. Now that I see your face I
can say my goodbye and make my own
world.

(*LOOMIS takes ZONIA's hand and presents her to MARTHA.*)

Martha . . . here go your daughter. I tried to take care of her. See that she had something to eat. See that she was out of the elements. Whatever I know I tried to teach her. Now she need to learn from her mother whatever you got to teach her. That way she won't be no one-sided person.

(*LOOMIS stoops to ZONIA.*)

Zonia, you go live with your mama. She a good woman. You go on with her and listen to her good. You my daughter and I love you like a daughter. I hope to see you again in the world somewhere. I'll never forget you.

ZONIA: (*Throws her arms around LOOMIS in a panic.*) I won't get no bigger! My bones won't get no bigger! They won't! I promise! Take me with you till we keep searching and never finding. I won't get no bigger! I promise!

LOOMIS: Go on and do what I told you now.

MARTHA: (*Goes to ZONIA and comforts her.*) It's alright, baby. Mama's here. Mama's here. Don't worry. Don't cry.

(*MARTHA turns to BYNUM.*)

Mr. Bynum, I don't know how to thank you. God bless you.

LOOMIS: It was you! All the time it was you that bind me up! You bound me to the road!

BYNUM: I ain't bind you, Herald Loomis. You can't bind what don't cling.

LOOMIS: Everywhere I go people wanna bind me up. Joe Turner wanna bind me up! Reverend Tolliver wanna bind me up. You wanna bind me up. Everybody wanna bind me up. Well, Joe Turner's come and gone and Herald Loomis ain't for no binding. I ain't gonna let nobody bind me up!

(*LOOMIS pulls out a knife.*)

BYNUM: It wasn't you, Herald Loomis. I ain't bound you. I bound the little girl to her mother. That's who I bound. You binding yourself. You bound onto your song. All you got to do is stand up and sing it, Herald Loomis. It's right there kicking at your throat. All you got to do is sing it. Then you be free.

MARTHA: Herald . . . look at yourself! Standing there with a knife in your hand. You done gone over to the devil. Come on . . . put down the knife. You got to look to Jesus. Even if you done fell away from the church you can be saved again. The Bible say, "The Lord is my shepherd I shall not want. He maketh me to lie down in green pastures. He leads me beside the still water. He restoreth my soul. He leads me in the path of righteousness for His name's sake. Even though I walk through the shadow of death—"

LOOMIS: That's just where I be walking!

MARTHA: "I shall fear no evil. For Thou art with me. Thy rod and thy staff, they comfort me."

LOOMIS: You can't tell me nothing about no valleys. I done been all across the valleys and the hills and the mountains and the oceans.

MARTHA: "Thou preparest a table for me in the presence of my enemies."

LOOMIS: And all I seen was a bunch of niggers dazed out of their woolly heads. And Mr. Jesus Christ standing there in the middle of them, grinning.

MARTHA: "Thou annointest my head with oil, my cup runneth over."

LOOMIS: He grin that big old grin . . . and niggers wallowing at his feet.

MARTHA: "Surely goodness and mercy shall follow me all the days of my life, and I shall dwell in the house of the Lord forever."

LOOMIS: Great big old white man . . . your Mr. Jesus Christ. Standing there with a whip in one hand and tote board in another, and them niggers swimming in a sea of cotton. And he counting. He tallying up the cotton. "Well, Jeremiah . . . what's the matter, you ain't picked but two hundred pounds of cotton today? Got to put you on half rations." And Jeremiah go back and lay up there on his half rations and talk about what a nice man Mr. Jesus Christ is 'cause he give him salvation after he die. Something wrong here. Something don't fit right!

MARTHA: You got to open up your heart and have faith, Herald. This world is just a trial for the next. Jesus offers you salvation.

LOOMIS: I been wading in the water. I been walking all over the River Jordan. But what it get me, huh? I done been baptized with blood of the lamb and the fire of the Holy Ghost. But what I got, huh? I got salvation? My enemies all around me picking the flesh from my bones. I'm choking on my own blood and all you got to give me is salvation?

MARTHA: You got to be clean, Herald. You got to be washed with the blood of the lamb.

LOOMIS: Blood make you clean? You clean with blood?

MARTHA: Jesus bled for you. He's the Lamb of God who takest away the sins of the world.

LOOMIS: I don't need nobody to bleed for me! I can bleed for myself.

MARTHA: You got to be something, Herald. You just can't be alive. Life don't mean nothing unless it got a meaning.

LOOMIS: What kind of meaning you got? What kind of clean you got, woman? You want blood? Blood make you clean? You clean with blood?

(LOOMIS slashes himself across the chest. He rubs the blood over his face and comes to a realization.)

I'm standing! I'm standing. My legs stood up! I'm standing now!

(Having found his song, the song of self-sufficiency, fully resurrected, cleansed and given breath, free from any encumbrance other than the workings of his own heart and the bonds of the flesh, having accepted the responsibility for his own presence in the world, he is free to soar above the environs that weighed and pushed his spirit into terrifying contractions.)

Goodbye, Martha.

(LOOMIS turns and exits, the knife still in his hands. MATTIE looks about the room and rushes out after him.)

BYNUM: Herald Loomis, you shining! You shining like new money!

The lights go down to BLACK.

THE CONSTRUCTION OF MEANING THROUGH COLLABORATION

Theatre production is a unique process that is unlike the creation of visual art, music, or literature. The creation of a stage production is an **interpretive art** and a **collaborative art.** The beginning point is the playwright's **script.** But a script is not a blueprint with all the details precisely recorded. The playscript essentially expresses a drama through dialogue.

In the case of *Joe Turner's Come and Gone*, in addition to the dialogue, Wilson's script outlines basic stage directions, character entrances and exits and other important movements, and the nature of the physical space. It also provides hints of character description. For example, Wilson tells us that Seth is in his early fifties, a skilled craftsman, and that he has a certain "stability." We also learn from the script that Bertha is slightly younger than Seth and that "she has learned to negotiate around Seth's apparent orneriness." Wilson gives us no details of their appearance or their dress.

The script identifies a boardinghouse as the setting and details the layout of the downstairs rooms and the placement of the doors. Most of the play takes place in the kitchen and the parlor, with two short scenes for the children in the garden. There is no specific description of the architectural style of the house, no indication of painting or wall decor, no discussion of the style or the quantity of furniture, and, perhaps most important, no description of the atmosphere created by the combination of the physical details of place.

The playwright begins a process that must be joined by a director, actors, and designers. Together they will interpret the playwright's work by filling in details of character, action, scenery, costumes, lighting, and sound. All are creative artists in their own right. But in the theatre, no one person's work stands alone. Only when the play is fully realized on the stage with an audience present does theatre actually exist.

Working closely with the **director,** who guides the process, the designers and actors give physical shape, a concrete reality, to the playwright's vision. They study the text closely to grasp the playwright's intentions. And then they use their particular talents as a group to create a theatrical event that expresses their understanding of the truth in the playwright's text. This is an enormously complex task, with many people responsible for different parts of the production, all working under the strictest of deadlines. The curtain must go up on the scheduled day, at the scheduled hour.

In the following pages we explore the process of staging *Joe Turner's Come and Gone* at the Oregon Shakespeare Festival in Ashland, Oregon. We begin to analyze the nature of the work done by the director, the actors, and the designers. We look at the collaborative process, the ways in which people work together, and also at the process of interpretation, how expressive choices are made. An examination of the production process will also give us further insights into the meaning of *Joe Turner's Come and Gone.*

THE OREGON SHAKESPEARE FESTIVAL

Ashland, Oregon, is a small, picturesque town of 30,000 people located in the mountains of southern Oregon. Much of the life of the community revolves around the Oregon Shakespeare Festival, located in the center of the town. The Shakespeare Festival is the largest not-for-profit theatre of its kind in the country. Other theatres that we examine in this book are in the heart of large cities such as New York, Los Angeles, or Seattle. Attending the theatre in Ashland, however, is a quieter, more reflective experience than is going to the theatre in a fast-paced city at the end of a workday or as part of one's daily activities. The actors who perform *Joe Turner's Come and Gone* will have the full attention of their audience as they give life to the world that August Wilson has created.

Although the Festival, which began in 1935, was originally dedicated to the plays of Shakespeare, it now presents the works of many other playwrights as well. Recent seasons have offered a total of eleven plays, with about one third by Shakespeare. For eight months of the year, from late February to October, plays are performed on the Festival's three stages.

Many of the Festival's audience members are Ashland residents or Oregonians from Portland (about four hours away) and closer, smaller communities. But the entire population of Oregon, 2.5 million, would fit into New York City or Los Angeles many times over. It is the out-of-state and even international visitors who enable this large, complex organization to maintain its many enterprises. People come to Ashland from all over the world specifically to go to the theatre. Most people will spend several days and see more than one play. This is why the Festival produces plays in **repertory**—that is, a number of plays are produced at once and then performed on a rotating basis. During the same week, theatregoers might be able to attend performances of *Joe Turner's Come and Gone,* a Shakespearian tragedy, a nineteenth-century French farce, and another new American play. In 1993 the Festival's 600-seat Angus Bowmer Theatre opened the season with *Joe Turner's Come and Gone.*

THE ACTORS AT WORK

Understanding the Play

The actors sit around a large table quietly reading the play to one another. Some of them know each other well. They have worked together for years in this small Oregon town. A few of the actors are new. They have come to Ashland for the first time as part of the *Joe Turner* cast, although they will stay in Ashland to take part in other plays. The director, Clinton Turner Davis, who leads the discussion, has come from New York just to direct this play. Most of the actors are working with Davis for the first time.

During this first phase of the **rehearsal** process, called **table work,** the actors do not get up and start to move around the stage until director Davis feels that they have asked enough questions and explored enough possible answers about the history and motivation of each character. Why does each character make certain choices? What is behind the words they speak? The answers may change a number of times, and more questions will certainly arise. But each actor must have a starting point for the thread that leads him or her from moment to moment during the course of the play.

The discussion shifts to the character of Herald Loomis, and Davis leans toward Derrick Lee Weedon, the actor who is playing Loomis.

Clinton Turner Davis: *What did you feel, what was going through your mind when you went back, when you were released from the chain gang*

J. P. Phillips portrays Seth, "just a regular American guy trying to be decent."

and you went back home and Martha wasn't there? All right now, think of that moment, and nonverbally say the first thing that comes into your mind, nonverbally.[13]

Weedon pauses and then an anguished, choking sound comes from his throat. Davis says softly, "Remember that sound. We'll use that later." What begins as a sound, an inarticulate expression of loss and rage, becomes a point of departure for the passion that drives Herald Loomis through the course of the play.

J. P. Phillips, playing Seth, is intrigued by the connection of Seth to Booker T. Washington, an African American educator who during the 1910s advocated separating the races and focusing on vocational education for African Americans. Phillips strongly believes that Seth is simply a man "searching for the American

---

STARTING POINTS IN THE REHEARSAL PROCESS

1. Careful reading of the play and research into the historical time period
2. Joint reading of the play and discussion of character history and motivation
3. Repetition of and response to the language
4. Physicalization
5. Music

dream and trying to prove his decency. He's just a regular American guy trying to be decent." Davis is eager for the actors to begin the process of building the inner life of their characters as he poses a variety of questions to open up the discussion. But he also welcomes answers of "I don't know."

Clinton Turner Davis: *"I don't know" is sometimes the most empowering answer because it frees the air. And likewise if the actors ask me a question and I don't have an answer, I'll tell them, "I don't know." We have to reveal ourselves to each other and build trust in that revelation.*

As they approach Wilson's characters and the world of the play, Davis and the cast also discuss significant events of the times and background source materials. Sitting around that large table, in the quiet, empty rehearsal hall, the actors spread out pictures of Pittsburgh from the early 1900s. They look at photographs of houses, the clothing of the period, and people at work. They share readings from W. E. B. Dubois's essential work *The Souls of Black Folk*, which explores the political and economic structures of the time and their consequences for black Americans. They read from the work of Zora Neale Hurston to expand their awareness of the language spoken by Wilson's characters and for information on traditional religious practice. Davis shares his studies of the Yoruban culture of western Nigeria, which he feels is the appropriate source for the Juba and for Bynum's incantations. After three days of questions and discussion and reading and rereading the play, the actors know enough about the inside of their characters to get the play "up on its legs." They also know most of their lines.

The Rehearsal Process

The next week and a half is spent working on the **blocking**—that is, all of the actors' movements around the stage that make up the physical action of the performance. Not all directors have lengthy discussions with the actors before they start the blocking rehearsals; some have individual discussions with actors, and some have no discussions at all. But for Davis, it is crucial that the actors arrive at an understanding of the play together and that their understanding be informed by the history and the texture of the times as well as their own emotional and intellectual responses to their characters.

The continuing discussion about the play is one of the ways that the director and the actors collaborate to create meaning. The discussion is also a way of building trust between the members of the company. This way of working depends on shared responsibility rather than on competition or a hierarchical structure. Ultimately, the director must make certain decisions and keep examining the performance to ensure that the playwright's ideas are being communicated. But Davis encourages the actors to take risks, to try out new ideas, to contribute their own thoughts.

Clinton Turner Davis: *When you work with an ensemble, it is essential to have a high degree of trust, and the earlier you can create that, the stronger the working environment will be. I try not to impose my views too early on because I think too often the actors feel that they are just the instrument of the director. An autocratic director will tell the actor what to do, when to do it, where, why, and how. And so the actors spend more time trying to contort and mold themselves into his concept of the characters without totally understanding why. It can be frightening.*

An atmosphere of trust and receptivity gives the actors a freedom that many believe allows them to do their best work.

LeWan Alexander (Bynum):   *The collaborative way that he worked—he encouraged, really demanded, input, not only in what we were doing with our own characters but the shape of the play, how we saw certain scenes develop. It was really a collaborative effort, and that's very rare.*

Tamu Gray (Bertha):   *I was given an opportunity to really concentrate on the craft, to concentrate*

on the art, to be empowered as an actor in the rehearsal hall. We worked in a respectful and truly
collective and community-based way. We walked
into the rehearsal hall with a sense of play and a
desire to play and a willingness to play that I've
not seen anywhere else.

Sometimes when the actors enter the rehearsal room, Davis has music playing.

Clinton Turner Davis: *We listened to gospel
tapes, down home revival, really backwoods revivals where you just had a cappella singing
started by the traditional starter of the church.
They would wail into it and ultimately discover
the communal harmony. And since we had started
rehearsal right after Christmas, we had Quincy
Jones's interpretation of Handel's Messiah—
A Soulful Celebration. Through that recording
Quincy has given a complete history of African
American music. Other times we listened to jazz
or blues. Sometimes we'd have the music playing
to set the mood when the actors would come in in
the morning or when we would take a break.
This would keep us in a specific context.*

Davis sees music as part of the texture of
the play, the connection to the oral tradition
discussed in the first part of this chapter. But he
also recognizes a musical structure in the language itself, a poetry in the rhythm of the
speeches and the telling of the stories. For J. P.
Phillips, who plays Seth, the music has to start
with the language:

J. P. Phillips: *I'm looking for words and minding
the language. You take the playwright's words
and you add breath and bring the words to life
and reveal what the playwright is trying to say.*

BW Gonzalez, who portrays Mattie, also sees
the language as the starting point for building
character:

BW Gonzalez: *What I feel I do as an actor is like
painting. I paint the portrait through the words.
The words create the images that I need to paint
the portrait of the character.*

Physical Characterization

The actors also work to create a specific physical presence for their characters. Although
there are many different approaches to the
physicalization of a character, we look at the
problems faced by the young actor LeWan
Alexander in approaching the much older character of Bynum. In 1993 Alexander was in his
early thirties. The script gives Bynum's age as
early sixties. Not only does that present the actor with a large span of years to bridge physically, but also a significant gap in experience to
bridge emotionally.

LeWan Alexander (Bynum): *Everyone in the
play was already cast before Christmas of last year,
and they were to start rehearsals at the beginning
of January, except for me. I knew I wasn't in the
play. I wasn't cast. They were still looking for*

Bynum (LeWan Alexander) tells Mattie Campbell (BW
Gonzalez) to push thoughts of Jack Carper out of her mind.

Bynum, and I got a call about a week before Christmas to see if I wanted to play Bynum. And I said to Henry Woronicz, the artistic director of the Festival, "Oh thanks, Hank, but I can't do that role. That's just way out of my range." He said, "Well it's either you or someone that we're going to find, so why don't you give yourself a couple of days to think about it?" Well, I didn't sleep that night, and I called him ten hours later and said, "Yeah, I'd like to do it." The main reason that I balked, which is also the reason that I decided to accept, was the fact that not only is he thirty years my senior, but the nature of the man and what he's connected to was very far from my own personal experience. Just the thought of a conjure man, a rootworker, is very foreign to me. It was quite a challenge. I started in the rehearsal process with three things, three physical things. My grandfather died when I was very young, but I remember how he used to sit in a chair. I remember that and the way he used to slump and the way he used to eat, particularly bread. I picked those things up from him. There was a homeless man in Milwaukee that I used to observe a lot. He would never pick up his feet when he walked, and he always walked with his head very low, shoulders slumped. And he had a beard that was very gray, and it was kind of curly around him. The script says that Bynum is very connected to the earth, and I wanted his center of gravity to be very low so that it's easy for him to get down to the ground if he needs to.[14]

The director and the actors work together to create an atmosphere that makes the world of the play gradually come alive for them. They study the play and its times. They explore the specific nature of each character, his or her personal history, objectives, or goals. They begin with individual moments in the stage life of each character and work to build a coherent whole that makes sense of everything the characters say and do. For example, the actor playing Loomis may start with what he has lost and the search for his wife, but ultimately it is himself that he seeks. They focus on the language and the way the rhythms of speech shape character. They listen to music that feeds the work on rhythm and creates a certain atmosphere. They create a physical presence. All of the director's and the actors' preparations are aimed at refining their understanding of the playwright's text and making imaginative choices that will make this understanding clear to an audience.

STAGING THE JUBA

Our summary of the rehearsal process for *Joe Turner's Come and Gone* is far from a complete description of the actors' work. In later chapters we expand our discussion of the nature of acting as we examine other productions and study other actors' work. At this point we pursue the way the director and actors work together to interpret the playwright's text for the audience through staging. We examine the director's blocking of a crucial section of the play to see how the action combines with speech to create meaningful images. For director Davis, the Juba is at the center of the play and leads directly to Herald Loomis's first major revelation: his vision of bones rising up out of the water at the end of act 1. The interruption of the Juba by Loomis's entrance sharply escalates the conflict between the characters and exposes the depth of Loomis's despair. We see in physical terms the crippling of his soul by slavery.

The Juba begins after Sunday dinner with all the boardinghouse characters present except Loomis. Together Seth and Bynum organize the other characters.

SETH: . . . Come on, Bertha, leave them dishes be for a while. We gonna Juba.
BYNUM: Alright. Let's Juba down! (act 1, scene 4)

The stage directions describe the Juba as

reminiscent of the Ring Shouts of the African slaves. It is a call and response dance. BYNUM sits at the

Loomis (Derrick Lee Weedon) destroys the Juba celebration with his vision of the "bones people," which is a symbolic telling of both his personal history and the larger history of a people brought across the sea into slavery.

table and drums. He calls the dance as others clap hands, shuffle and stomp around the table. It should be as African as possible, with the performers working themselves up into a near frenzy. The words can be improvised, but should include some mention of the Holy Ghost. (act 1, scene 4)

Drumming and Dancing

In staging the Juba, Davis begins with the drum. He explains that drumming is at the heart of African communication and language. According to Davis, one of the greatest deprivations in slavery was the loss of the drum. Drumming was forbidden by slaveowners, who couldn't understand but sensed the power of the drum to speak across the distances and carry the voices, the language, of the African captives from plantation to plantation. For Davis, then, the drumming in the Juba is part of reestablishing communication after the end of slavery, a way of developing community.

The stage directions suggest that Bynum use the dining table as his "drum." After discussing with the cast various possibilities for household items that could be used as drums, Davis settles on the table as the "gbedu," a big, deep-timbred royal drum. The table is the hearth, the center of nurturing and community, and is therefore appropiate to serve as the instrument of communication. Davis establishes that Bynum will sit at the table and drum on the tabletop while the others dance in a processional circle around him. The circle is suggested by the descriptions of Bynum's ceremonies at the beginning of the play:

SETH: He done drew a big circle with that stick and now he's dancing around. (act 1, scene 1)

Davis sees power and completeness in the many symbolic associations of the circle that spatially and visually contribute to the harmony he is trying to develop rhythmically.

Once the basic image is established for the cast, Davis works with the actors on African rhythms to be clapped and dance steps that they may use, some of which have African origins and some of which are associated with religious observation in the United States, such as Pentecostal worship. The ceremony represents a merging of African and Christian worship. After Bynum begins his drumming, Davis asks each actor to enter the Juba in order of the age and importance of his or her character to the household. Seth is first as the owner of the house, and Zonia is last as a visiting child. The actors are free to improvise off the basic rhythm and off the basic dance steps to increase the density of sound and movement.

Text and Verbal Improvisation

In addition to the drumming and dancing of the Juba, there is also a whole verbal score to be improvised. Davis asks the cast to approach their words for the Juba section as a kind of personal prayer, a statement of their needs at that particular point in the play. Through a combination of improvised speech, chanting, and song, they call upon the "Spirit" to provide guidance in their lives. Once the actors have begun to develop this verbal text/score for the Juba, Davis adds one more element: he translates some of the actors' improvised words into Dutch, French, Spanish, German, and Portuguese, all languages of the slave traders who carried African people on their ships. The words come out as a kind of genetic memory of the experience of slavery.

The Meaning of the Juba

In this particular production, then, the Juba has a number of structural and thematic functions. In terms of the **plot,** it is an activity that brings the characters together following their Sunday dinner. Even though they come from widely different backgrounds and have very different goals for themselves, they all know the Juba. It is an informal, household religious observation, a ceremony that celebrates an African heritage fused with Christianity and allows for an emotional release following the daily struggle for survival. For the characters it is also a way of focusing their particular search during the course of the play. In addition, the Juba is a symbolic representation of the obstacles the characters have overcome to arrive at this point in their journeys. The languages of the slave traders and the recovery of the drum introduce references to slavery that will become explosive after Herald Loomis's entrance.

The Juba builds a sense of community and harmony that will be broken by Herald Loomis. It also builds all the tensions of act 1 to a high level of intensity, a "frenzy" that essentially launches Herald Loomis into his soul-searing vision. Loomis, who has collapsed to the floor, sees a vision of bones that sink into the ocean and then are washed ashore as black people (Color Plate 7). Bynum, trying to get Loomis to his feet, tells him that the "bones people" have risen and taken to the road. But Loomis is crushed by the vision and cannot rise. Loomis is reexperiencing the Middle Passage, the holocaustic journey of Africans crossing the ocean to become slaves. The Juba establishes a memory of the passage into slavery that sets the context for Loomis's breakdown.

The many levels of meaning that emerge from a piece of staging that lasts only a few minutes demonstrate one of the fundamental aspects of theatrical communication: stage images are constantly built with many layers of expression, some visual, some verbal, some rhythmic, some psychological or emotional.

The audience receives complex information from these images that are so much more than a mere sequence in the storytelling process.

EXPANDING THE STAGE IMAGE: THE WORK OF THE DESIGNERS

The intensity of the actors' movement and language should be riveting for the audience in the sequence that we have been discussing at the end of act 1. All of the actors' skills are engaged at a high level to create a spellbinding moment of revelation. In the Juba the actors create a sense of community, using the whole stage. Then the harmony of the stage picture is destroyed by Herald Loomis's entrance, and the focus narrows until we see only Bynum and Loomis and finally only Loomis. The consequences of slavery come crashing down on us as we see the torment for Herald Loomis when he says, "I got to stand up" and then, "My legs won't stand up! My legs won't stand up!" The primary focus is on the actors, but the work of the designers is essential in supporting and completing the images the actors create.

The Set Design

In the **rendering** of the set designed by Mike Fish (Color Plate 8), we can see the placement of the table center stage and get some idea of its relative size. In developing a **ground plan** for the set (the placement of the furniture, doors, and walls), **scene designer** Fish and director Davis need to create a space that (1) allows the characters a sense of intimacy produced by being in the warmth of Bertha's kitchen and (2) provides a space that is big enough and spacious enough for the characters to eat together at the dining table and then to be able to dance around it in the Juba sequence. The placement of the table center stage gives it primary visual focus and also allows for the character action described in the previous section. The set design must first support the character action and movement required by the play. It must provide spaces that allow the appropriate physical relationships between characters.

As the characters eat their Sunday dinner and then begin the Juba, we in the audience sense the comfort provided by the boarding-house kitchen. The set helps create an atmosphere that is warm and inviting. There is a large fireplace and stove. The colors are reds and browns and antique roses. And precise attention is paid to detail.

Mike Fish: *It was a very large house but at the same time it had to be very, very intimate because this is Bertha's house and it had all her little knickknacks. When I furnished the house I was very careful to put details: the Civil War, little precious mementos, little porcelain figures, a sign above the mantel, "God Bless This Home."*

The set design also reveals the time and place. Fish shapes the space with nineteenth-century architectural details and furnishes it with period antiques that are purchased or are reproduced in the scene shop. The time and place are also strongly reinforced by the use of a painted backdrop that rises above the three-dimensional structure of the house. Behind the house we see the smokestacks of the Pittsburgh steel mills. The backdrop places us in an industrial setting and reminds us that the boarding-house must protect its occupants against the urban factory world (Color Plate 9). Even as we see the family gathering and ritual observation, with its African origins, held in the safety of the kitchen, the reality of Pittsburgh in 1911 looms behind. We see that the characters face an enormous task of integrating experiences and realities.

The Costume Design

The costumes play a very important part in creating a sense of the time period and in defining

---

SUMMARY OF BASIC DESIGN FUNCTIONS

A. Set
1. Reflects time period
2. Gives sense of place
3. Creates appropriate atmosphere
4. Creates space that provides for necessary character action and movement
5. Creates space that allows the appropriate physical relationships between characters

B. Costuming
1. Reflects time period
2. Reveals class and background of characters
3. Demonstrates individuality of characters
4. Highlights contrasts between characters

C. Lighting
1. Creates visibility
2. Creates atmosphere
3. Works with pacing and rhythms of actors to establish overall rhythm of the play

All build visual metaphors.

---

the class and individuality of the characters. As the characters gather for their Sunday dinner and then the Juba, we see them in their "good" clothes, which are nicer but well-worn versions of their work clothes. These are proud people who have to work extremely hard for everything they have. The goal of the **costume designer,** Candice Cain, is to create the effect of real clothing.

Candice Cain: *I didn't want them to be "costumes." I called them clothes the whole time. There was a lot of work to do after the clothing was built and fit. We even ill-fitted some of the clothing, so it didn't look perfect. We worked with sandpaper, we worked with paint, we worked with washing and dying. You know when they washed their clothes, they used washboards. A lot of the petticoats were actually real petticoats from the period. And I chose some style lines earlier than when the play is set because these people had these clothes for a long period of time.*

One of the major design issues for the costume designer in *Joe Turner's Come and Gone* is establishing a strong contrast between Herald Loomis and all of the other characters. He destroys the harmony of the Juba with his entrance just as he has unbalanced the household since his first appearance. The character is in a fury, and his visual presence is a critical part of his disruptive force.

Candice Cain: *When Loomis walked into that room, I wanted him to suck up everybody's energy, every bit of energy that was in there. The playwright says he comes in a black coat, but you have to find out why that is. All those layers that he wears. There's almost an ecclesiastical feel, and his coat is so solid and so dark and so mysterious. And then that hat with the five-inch brim.*

Loomis is the only character in black, whereas the other characters wear a variety of lighter and brighter colors—blues, greens, and browns (Color Plate 10). Loomis is wearing large, heavy pieces of clothing that hide the outline of his body. His shape is that of the huge coat and the broad hat. The clothing of the other characters is much more formfitting, suggesting that these are ordinary human beings. They also have much more visible details on their clothes—ruffles, buttons, suspenders—giving them a smaller-scale presence. Nothing breaks the line of Loomis's silhouette. Visually, when Loomis is not onstage, all the other characters emerge as individuals. When Loomis enters, the other characters become a group.

The Lighting Design

The **lighting designer,** Jim Sale, had much to do with creating the atmosphere for the Juba sequence. Slowly, as the characters start to dance and shout, the lights change from the warm, realistic light of the kitchen to a strange, moody light, casting strong shadows. The lights for the Juba build gradually so that the audience becomes aware of the shifting mood

Costume designer Candice Cain begins her work by sketching ideas for the costumes of the characters. The silhouette of each character emerges from the sketches. The top costume sketches are for Jeremy Furlow (left) and Herald Loomis (right). Following discussions with the director and the other designers, sketches are developed into detailed color renderings, accompanied by fabric swatches that indicate the texture and pattern of the different fabrics that will make up each costume (bottom; see also Color Plate 10).

but not the mechanics. But then, on Loomis's entrance, the lights shift instantly to the bright, realistic light.

Jim Sale: *It's almost like he came in and flipped on a light switch, his energy came in so strong.*

The designers work continuously with the director and the actors to create a coherent interpretation of the playwright's work. They create images in space, using materials that add layers of meaning to the images created by the actors. Their work goes far beyond illustrating time and place. All the design areas contribute

This photograph of the first entrance of Herald Loomis demonstrates the way the heavy, severe costume contributes to the power of the character's appearance.

CONCLUSION: HISTORY AND MEANING IN *JOE TURNER'S COME AND GONE*

At the beginning of the chapter we introduced August Wilson as a dramatic historian. In examining Wilson's sources, we outlined the history of African Americans that forms the background for the play, a history that includes forced labor and migration. Within the play itself, however, Wilson presents an understanding of history that goes beyond the facts of the chain gang and the movement of African Americans to the urban areas of the North. That history is built from the actions of all the characters, as each searches for what is most precious in life and what has been lost. Multiple stories are told, and so what we might call a multidimensional view of history emerges from the play. This multidimensional vision of history begun in the text by Wilson is given physical shape in production by the imaginative work of the actors, director, and designers.

The Quest for Self

The central action of the play is Herald Loomis's search for himself, which is connected to Bynum's search for the "shiny man." In fact, what they seek is the same. By the end of the play, Loomis becomes what his name suggests. He becomes the "luminous," shiny man of Bynum's vision from act 1. Together, the quests of Loomis and Bynum can be seen to represent a large movement from slavery to freedom that suggests both the hundreds of years of American slavery and the internal journey of the individual. Herald Loomis cannot begin his life until he finds a way to cut the ties that bind him, to cleanse himself of the pollution of slavery. This he does symbolically by cutting himself with a knife at the end of the play and bleeding for himself. He has regained the song of himself, a "song of self-sufficiency."

Bynum cannot die "a happy man, a man who done left his mark on life" until he helps

to visual metaphors that define the world of the play. The warmth of Bertha's kitchen juxtaposed with the imposing Pittsburgh skyline of factory smokestacks sets the stage for the struggles of the characters to find a place for themselves. Shadows contrast with the light as Herald Loomis emerges from the dark clothes—in which he hides himself and which weigh him down—to embrace a reborn, expansive sense of himself.

bring about the liberation of Herald Loomis that transforms him into the shiny man. A celebration of freedom echoes in the final line of the play, which is spoken by Bynum: "Herald Loomis, you shining! You shining like new money!"

Family and Inheritance: The Way from the Past to the Future

This movement toward freedom and affirmation is the overarching history that the play expresses. But this history of the journey out of slavery is framed by the views of Seth, the northern African American born in freedom, and of the People Finder, Rutherford Selig, who is the descendant of slave traders. The house where the play takes place belongs to Seth, a man born free, unburdened by the baggage of slavery. His history is tied to a father who could leave him the inheritance of a house and a strong sense of himself, in spite of the fact that he is still unable to start his own business.

Seth fears the decency of his house, his history, will be compromised by the turmoil that Loomis brings with him. He rejects Loomis even though he and Bertha have committed their dwelling as a home for people who have nowhere else to go. Because Seth and Bertha have no children of their own, in a symbolic way, they become the parents of the children of slavery, creating a family out of the separated individuals who come to stay at the boardinghouse. In the making of this hybrid family, two different histories of life in America confront each other, and the conflict is strongest in the struggle between Seth and Loomis.

Seth and Bertha represent the only coherent sense of family in the play. One of Wilson's major concerns in *Joe Turner's Come and Gone* is the breakdown of the family under slavery and under the various forms of oppression that followed slavery. The destruction of the Loomis family is central to the events of the play, but most of the other characters are also alone and seeking some form of family. Mattie Campbell is particularly poignant in her search for Jack Carper, the father of her two babies who died as infants. The characters are cut off from the future until they can resolve issues of family, particularly in terms of building relationships that will sustain children.

Under these circumstances, the inheritance from parents takes on tremendous importance. Seth's inheritance of a house from his father has literally given him a place in the world. Bynum has inherited wisdom from his father, even though it comes to him in a vision. And Mattie Campbell, for all her loneliness, is sustained by the memory of her mother. The question of family and inheritance finally focuses on Zonia. Herald Loomis has been desperate to find his wife so that he can regain his bearings. But he cannot begin anew for himself until he secures Zonia's proper inheritance, which is to know both of her parents.

The nature of inheritance for the African American characters contrasts uneasily with the inheritance of the Selig family. They too are searchers, but the search has been connected to the enslavement of Africans. The legacy of searching passed from father to son in this family began with the transportation of slaves, progressed to the hunting of runaway slaves, and ends with Rutherford Selig, who charges for reuniting the very people his family has worked for generations to tear apart. However, in the end, even Rutherford Selig becomes part of the circumstances that finally allow the play's title to be true for Herald Loomis. Joe Turner indeed has come, and at last he is gone.

SUMMARY

The American playwright August Wilson is chronicling African American history by writing a play for each decade of the twentieth century. Inspired by the blues songs of Bessie Smith and the paintings and collages of Romare

Bearden, Wilson sees his plays as part of an oral tradition. In the production of Wilson's play *Joe Turner's Come and Gone*, produced by the Oregon Shakespeare Festival, the vision of the playwright was expressed by the interpretive work of other theatre artists.

Joe Turner's Come and Gone focuses on the migration of African Americans to the North shortly after the turn of the century. The journey of migration is both an actual and a metaphoric search for a better way of life following emancipation. Part of that search involves the process of separation and re-creation of families that touches all of the characters' lives. For Herald Loomis, the journey of migration becomes a way of reclaiming himself after having been enslaved physically and spiritually on the chain gang.

Theatre production is a collaborative process in which theatre practitioners work closely together to interpret the playwright's script. Director, actors, and designers study the play and its context and then make imaginative contributions to shaping the production onstage. The production of the play at the Oregon Shakespeare Festival demonstrated the way meaning is constructed through theatrical communication. The scene designer created an environment that would support the action of the play and locate the characters first in the comfortable atmosphere of the boardinghouse and second against the much harsher background of industrial Pittsburgh. The costume designer gave the characters a sense of time, social class, and individuality through the garments she designed; she also used color and silhouette to separate Herald Loomis from the other characters. The lighting designer shifted the mood onstage through color and shadow to reinforce the qualities expressed by the characters. The director and the actors worked together to shape characters and character interactions that would give life to the stories that Wilson weaves together, ultimately focusing on the stories of Loomis and Bynum as they merge into one "song" of freedom.

TOPICS FOR DISCUSSION AND WRITING

1. What is meant by the oral tradition? Can music, painting, and drama all be part of an oral tradition? Is it a contradiction to consider a play with a written text to be part of an oral tradition? What aspects of *Joe Turner's Come and Gone* support its placement in an oral tradition?

2. What is the effect of including the long stories in the text of *Joe Turner's Come and Gone?* How do the stories affect the rhythm of the play and the audience's or reader's response? Choose one of the stories, and write a short essay that includes your responses to the following questions: (a) What do we come to learn about the character from the story? (b) What images in the story make the strongest impression on you? (c) How does the story relate to the events of the play and the play's meaning?

3. What is the relationship of the play to Christianity? Many of the characters are Christian. Herald Loomis is a deacon of the church, and yet he makes a very strong statement about slave labor, associating the gang boss with Jesus Christ. How are we to understand his outburst? Is the attack on religion or hypocrisy?

NOTES

1. August Wilson, preface to *Three Plays* (Pittsburgh: University of Pittsburgh Press, 1991), viii.

2. Richard Bernstein, "August Wilson's Voices from the Past," *New York Times*, 27 March 1988, sec. 2, p. 1.

3. Wilson, preface to *Three Plays*, viii.

4. Wilson, preface to *Three Plays*, ix.

5. Imamu Amira Baraka [LeRoi Jones], *Blues People* (New York: Morrow, 1963), 61.

6. William Barlow, *Looking Up at Down* (Philadelphia: Temple University Press, 1989), 7–8.

7. August Wilson, foreword to Myron Schwartzman, *Romare Bearden: His Life and Art* (New York: Harry N. Abrams, 1990), 8.

8. Wilson, foreword to *Romare Bearden*, 9.

9. To hear Bessie Smith's version, listen to Bessie Smith, "Nobody Knows You When You're Down and Out," *The Complete Recordings, Vol. 4*, Columbia, 1993.

10. Bernstein, sec. 2, p. 1.

11. August Wilson, *Joe Turner's Come and Gone* (New York: New American Library, 1988), 67.

12. W. C. Handy, *The Father of the Blues* (New York: Collier, 1941), 146.

13. All quotations in the production analysis are from the author's interviews.

14. The untimely death of LeWan Alexander is a loss to the nation's theatre community.

SUGGESTIONS FOR FURTHER READING

Barlow, William. *Looking Up at Dawn: The Emergence of Blues Culture*. Philadelphia: Temple University Press, 1989.

A study of the blues from its origins in the rural South to its development in urban areas. Barlow explores the social context as a constant background to the musical analysis; he examines the blues' origins, the history of movements and individual artists, and the themes and analysis of individual blues songs.

Berlin, Ira. *Generations of Captivity: A History of African-American Slaves*. Cambridge: The Belknap Press/Harvard University Press, 2003.

A major new study of the history of slavery in the United States from the seventeenth century until the Civil War. This landmark study analyzes the social consequences of slavery for those held captive and the place of slavery in the economy of the South.

DuBois, W. E. B. *The Souls of Black Folk*. 1903. Reprint Mineola, NY: Dover, 1994.

The classic portrait of African American culture at the turn of the twentieth century.

Fulop, Timothy E., and Raboteau, Albert J., eds. *African American Religion: Interpretive Essays in History and Culture*. New York: Routledge, 1997.

An informative collection of essays that addresses a number of the questions raised in *Joe Turner's Come and Gone* about Christianity and traditional African religions.

Harrison, Alferdteen, ed. *Black Exodus: The Great Migration from the American South*. Jackson: University Press of Mississippi, 1991.

An analysis of the causes of African American migration from South to North and the resulting social changes.

Hay, Samuel. *African American Theatre*. Cambridge: University of Cambridge Press, 1994.

An analysis of African American theatre from 1898 to the present, offering a social and political critique of the position of black plays and performers in the United States. The theories of Alain Locke and W. E. B. DuBois form the foundation of the discussion.

Nadel, Alan, ed. *May All Your Fences Have Gates: Essays on the Drama of August Wilson*. Iowa City: University of Iowa Press, 1994.

A very helpful collection of essays exploring various aspects of Wilson's plays, including an extensive annotated bibliography of Wilson's writing, interviews, and critical responses to his work.

Savran, David. *In Their Own Words: Contemporary American Playwrights*. New York: Theatre Communications Group, 1998.

A compilation of interviews with contemporary American playwrights, including August Wilson, Anna Deavere Smith, José Rivera, Ntozake Shange, and Luis Valdez.

Schwartzman, Myron. *Romare Bearden: His Life and Art*. With a foreword by August Wilson. New York: Harry N. Abrams, Inc., 1990.

A thorough exploration of Bearden's development as an artist, the forms of his work, and his inspirations and influences; includes outstanding reproductions of all Bearden's major paintings, including *Mill Hand's Lunch Bucket* and *The Piano Lesson*.

Turner, Elizabeth Hutton, ed. *Jacob Lawrence: The Migration Series*. With an introductory essay by Henry Louis Gates, Jr. Washington, DC: Rappahannock Press, 1993.

The story of African American migration told visually through sixty paintings. The hardships and courage of Lawrence's subjects are expressed through bold colors and striking compositions in this extraordinarily moving work of American art. The paintings are supported by insightful essays about social issues, as well as many photographs of the artist and the times.

Wilson, August. *Three Plays*. Pittsburgh: University of Pittsburgh Press, 1991.

An anthology that includes *Ma Rainey's Black Bottom, Fences*, and *Joe Turner's Come and Gone*, with an eloquent introduction by August Wilson and a concluding essay—"August Wilson's Blues Poetics"—by Paul Carter Harrison.

CHAPTER 4

The Art of the Actor

In Chapter 3 we studied the collaboration between playwright, director, actors, and designers in producing *Joe Turner's Come and Gone*. We began with the work of the playwright, August Wilson, but, in fact, at the center of the theatre is the work of the actor. If everything that was not absolutely necessary to the theatre were stripped away, we would be left with the actor, a simple playing space, and the audience. The impulse to perform, discussed at the beginning of this book, is the essential force of the theatre. The work of all of the other theatre practitioners builds on the impulse to perform: the creation of stories for the actor to play; costumes to enhance or define the actor's body; scenery and light to provide an environment for the action; music and sound to build atmosphere, mood, and energy.

THE PRESENCE OF THE ACTOR

In Chapter 1 we examined the transformation of the Hopi when they are inhabited by the kachina spirits, and in Chapter 2 we considered the transformation of the Greek actor through the mask. Whether or not an idea of the supernatural or a mask is part of the process, the

Here a wary and watchful Tartuffe anticipates his seduction of Elmire, his benefactor's wife. In the 2001 Theatre de la Jeune Lune production, directed by Dominique Serrand, Stephen Epp plays Tartuffe with cunning and calculation. His face and his body language convey the predator, ready to strike. Tartuffe, originally written by Molière in 1664, has inspired new interpretations by leading actors of every succeeding generation.

In a production of Ibsen's A Doll's House, *Janet McTeer riveted audiences with her charismatic interpretation of Nora. The sensual, high-energy portrayal of a nineteenth-century woman who leaves her husband and children caused audiences to rethink a character that for some had become predictable.*

actor always undergoes a transformation when appearing onstage in front of an audience. The actor becomes more than an ordinary person going about daily life. The actor in performance becomes a presence charged with energy and vitality who transmits a heightened sense of life to the audience. As the actor opens up to greater emotional and sensory awareness, the audience members also experience a heightened awareness. The actor is able to project a sense of character life across the stage space and the auditorium space to reach the audience. The actor

invents a world onstage that audience members may also inhabit through their imaginations.

David Warrilow, an actor known for his adventurous work in the plays of Samuel Beckett and in exploratory theatre forms, sees the actor-audience relationship as a matter of trust:

> If I as an actor invest myself to the best of my ability in the work I have chosen to present—if I give it my best energy—then there's a chance that the audience can trust what is going on on stage. If I hold back, if I sit in judgment on myself or the material or the audience, then there is less chance that the audience is going to be justified in trusting and therefore joining the experience. If the actor is willing to go through some kind of transmutation, then the audience can, too.[1]

Frequently the actor's presence is described as a kind of double or triple existence. On the stage the actor is always present in his or her own person. In addition to this elemental self, the actor creates a character who has his or her own boundaries separate from those of the actor's own person. The performer projects a double representation of self and character. A third layer of the actor's presence might be considered a critical facility that the actor uses to step back from the performance and view it from the audience's perspective, making adjustments and modifications as necessary. BW Gonzalez, who played Mattie Campbell in *Joe Turner's Come and Gone*, describes the actor's state of mind as one of "hyper-awareness."[2] Stephen Spinella, who played Prior in *Angels in America* at the Eureka Theatre, at the Mark Taper Forum, and on Broadway, discussed in Chapter 11, says that he is always aware of his own presence on the stage and the presence of the audience:

> I am absolutely, completely conscious of the audience. I feel what they are doing. I'm completely conscious of what's going on in my body. It's the height of reality. I actually feel as though I'm suspended above myself or in back of myself and my body. Everything is moving and doing exactly what it should be doing. And I'm saying to myself, "Now do this," making little tiny artistic choices.[3]

The actor commands the attention of the audience by bringing concentrated and explosive energy onto the stage. The actor brings the stage space to life and sweeps the audience up in the vitality of the performance. This energy is part of the actor's charisma. In this respect, the actor is like an athlete or a rock and roll performer. For the actor, the energy may be less overtly displayed than for a football receiver leaping to make a catch or a popular singer dancing in front of the microphone. But high-voltage energy is present nonetheless, and the audience senses the electricity generated by the actor's presence.

Because of the unique nature of live performance—with the very real connection between performer and audience—the actor receives energy from the audience just as the audience is energized by the actor's presence. For BW Gonzalez, the energy generated by the audience contributes directly to her readiness to begin the play.

> Before I say my first line, once I feel the energy of the audience, I feel perfectly at home on the stage.[4]

Stephen Spinella sees the audience energy as a major catalyst for his performance:

> The theatrical event requires the overwhelming focus of the audience. The actors, who have acquired that attention through control of the space and the moment, have power, and if the muse is with them, that power makes them soar.[5]

James Earl Jones also uses the analogy of flight to describe the propulsion that the audience brings to the performance:

> All acting, at its best, is about entering the stage and, spiritually, going to the edge of that cliff that is the proscenium, acknowledging there is an energy there, and like a sky-diver, pushing yourself off. You trust the thermal waves of energy that the audience is and you soar.[6]

SUMMARY OF THE ACTOR'S RESPONSIBILITIES

- To study the text
- To memorize lines and blocking quickly
- To bring new ideas to the rehearsal process on a daily basis
- To work openly with the director and other actors
- To be creative in rehearsal
- To constantly refine and adjust character development
- To work with consistent high energy
- To maintain the health and flexibility of voice and body
- To sustain freshness in performance and execute repeated performances at a consistent level of quality

Karen Ryker works with students on breath control and vocal production in her voice class at the University of Wisconsin-Madison. Voice studies frequently involve exercises designed to free the voice from bad habits of speech and shallow breathing acquired over a lifetime. We learn to inhibit our voices in response to social pressures or expectations. To open or liberate the voice involves work to enhance awareness of vocal production as well as to eliminate the restrictions we place on our own voices.

Phillip B. Zarrilli, the former director of the Asian/Experimental Theatre Program at the University of Wisconsin-Madison, is shown here working with a student on movement training. The training is designed to increase body awareness, to facilitate breath control, and to allow for the development of heightened concentration and focus. Zarrilli describes the acting approach as "psychophysiological," emphasizing the connections between the mind and the body.

THE ACTOR'S CRAFT

The vitality and talent of the actor are contained and shaped through the development of technique. We expect musicians to study and practice for many years to perfect skills on the piano, the cello, or the saxophone and to acquire subtleties of musicianship. Dancers, too, commit to a training schedule of many hours a day to develop their physical abilities and artistry. In the same way, technique is essential to the actor working on the stage.

We can easily summarize the skills that most actors work to achieve and maintain. The vocal technique of the actor involves the ability to control and project the voice, to speak with richness of tone and nuance of expression, to enunciate with clarity at all times, to use dialects and accents with authenticity, to maintain a healthy voice that doesn't succumb to overuse, to give the language of Shakespeare or August Wilson its own style and rhythm, to speak for the characters and the playwright with authority and imagination. Physical technique allows the actor to move with grace; to command the stage space; to change posture, gestures, and body rhythms to create a range of characters; to present a sense of period style; to perform at a high level of intensity on a daily basis; to achieve the appropriate degree of relaxation and freedom from tension; to dance or juggle or walk on stilts.

However, performance skills alone do not make an actor. The words *alchemy* and *magic* are frequently used to describe the way the actor animates the skills of performance and gives life to dramatic text or situation. Analogy is often used to describe acting because it is difficult to define the actor's process with precision. In the first place, many forces intervene: the text, the director, the other actors, the rehearsal structure and duration, the playing space. In the second place, acting is such a personal and individual endeavor that it can be impossible to identify with certainty what has taken place internally to produce the result that the audience sees. Some choices are conscious; some the result of intuitive responses to the text or the rehearsal situation. To investigate the components of the actor's work, we begin with the stages the actor goes through before arriving at a performance in front of an audience: the audition, individual preparation for the role, and the rehearsal.

THE WORK OF THE ACTOR

Competing for Roles: The Audition

One of the harshest and must grueling aspects of the actor's profession is the **audition.** Acting is a highly competitive business. There are many more actors and aspiring actors than there are acting opportunities at every level of theatre and film production, in part because of the passion that actors feel about their work and in part because of the large rewards for the few "stars." To enter the competition for roles or places in training programs, actors must participate in auditions.

The audition allows directors and casting directors to see how different actors may fill a certain role or to see which actors complement each other as a group to make an **ensemble.** Because auditions are usually set up to screen a large number of people, the actors are allotted very little time to convince those making the casting decisions of their "rightness" for the part and the depth of their talent. For example, the Yale School of Drama auditions 900 aspiring actors for its graduate training program. Of those 900, only 16 students are offered places. Likewise, hundreds of dancers and singers may audition for the roles in the chorus of a Broadway musical, and smaller theatres attract scores of actors to their auditions. Furthermore, auditions may call for unique combinations of talents. Susan Stroman auditioned actors for both the recent revival of *Oklahoma* (1999) and the new production of *The Producers* (2001). For *Oklahoma*, the actors had to sing and dance and then do an American monologue. For *The Producers* they also had to be able to tell jokes.

Directors pride themselves on being able to recognize the qualities that they seek for a certain role almost instantly. Gordon Davidson, artistic director of the Mark Taper Forum, says, "I have a feeling within a minute of the audition that you know whether you're in the presence of talent or not."[7] Composer and lyricist Stephen Sondheim can judge singing ability in sixteen measures, or even in eight or four bars of a song.[8] This tendency toward immediate judgment puts enormous pressure on the actor in the audition to deliver a knockout performance. Actors, in fact, study auditioning techniques as part of their career preparation and constantly work to hone their auditioning skills.

Some auditions may involve the presentation of set pieces that the actors have had a chance to study and prepare in detail in advance of the audition. Actors perform monologues or songs of their own choosing for graduate training programs, repertory theatre, or summer stock opportunities—all situations that require actors to take multiple roles. Actors try to choose material from well-respected plays and musicals, but also material that directors may not have already seen hundreds of times. Independent casting director Joseph Albado cautions actors that "Right now, *Les Miz* is very

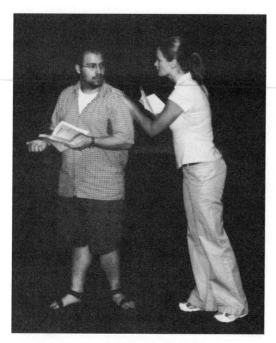

Here student actors Zack Ross and Fauna Doyle audition for a play by reading a scene with scripts in hand.

ability to take direction is one of the single most important factors that directors try to ascertain in the audition:

> Most directors are pretty insecure themselves. They want to come away from an audition knowing that they're going to be able to work with the actor, and that the actor is imaginative enough and well-trained enough to handle different directions. They also need to get a feel for what the actor will be like to work with for an extended period of time.[10]

Some auditions focus on cold readings of scenes from the play that is going into production. In this situation, with minimal preparation, actors must read from the script, often with a stage manager or other production staff member who is not an actor as their scene partner. Producer Stuart Ostrow believes that although the cold reading is "the best of a worst lot," its benefits outweigh the drawbacks:

> What it does first and foremost is tell you about the intelligence quotient of the actor. And I would always opt for an intelligent actor, even though he may be wrong for the part. In the creation of a play, that cold reading leads to an understanding about the actor's capacity for imagination and creativity.[11]

popular, as is *Phantom*. It doesn't bother me, but a lot of directors will refuse to hear them."[9] The pieces also need to be well suited to the actor and show the range of the actor's abilities.

A dramatic audition consisting of two contrasting monologues is frequently limited to four minutes. A singing audition may be limited to thirty-two measures of music. In that scant period of time, actors must show their understanding of the text, their speech or singing skills, their energy, and their ability to reach an audience. The actor must jump into the heart of the character and the play and deliver the lines or the song with all the passion and intensity of a performance, usually without the help of the supporting cast, set, or costumes. The audition also reveals how much training the actors have, their stage presence, and their openness. Jack Bowdan, who casts for Broadway and television, emphasizes that the

If the actor gets through the initial phase of the audition and is called back for further readings, then the process opens up in interesting ways, depending on the type of production and the producing company. Interviews, group improvisations, and extended readings with other potential cast members may all be part of the "callback." But first actors must show that they have enough talent, skill, flexibility, and commitment to stand out from the crowd. No matter how stressful or disappointing the audition process may be, all actors must struggle through the ordeal of auditioning if they are to work. Tamu Gray, who played Bertha in *Joe Turner's Come and Gone*, summarizes the feelings of many actors when she says, "You must raise an amazing amount of courage to go out and audition, but that makes you even stronger because you do it."[12]

James Earl Jones transformed his physical appearance to play boxer Jack Jefferson in The Great White Hope *at the Arena Stage in Washington, D.C. The physical training involved in preparing for the role of a boxer also provided psychological insight into the character. James Earl Jones and Jane Alexander, shown here, also re-created their stage roles for the film version of Howard Sackler's play.*

Preparing for the Role

When a part has been secured, actors may go to extraordinary lengths to prepare for their roles. They might read histories and biographies or study real-life situations, or they might immerse themselves in the actual circumstances of characters' lives before they try to re-create or interpret those circumstances on the stage or in front of the camera. Sometimes actors transform themselves physically, losing or gaining weight or participating in intense physical training to reshape their bodies or learn difficult physical skills.

James Earl Jones is an actor known for his distinguished performances in the plays of Shakespeare, South African Athol Fugard, and August Wilson, as well as for his film work, including the famous voice of Darth Vader in *Star*

Wars. To play the role of Jack Jefferson, a boxer, in *The Great White Hope*, by Howard Sackler, Jones undertook the training of a fighter:

> I didn't have the bulk of a fighter but I had the sinewy-ness, the flexibility. In Washington D.C., when we were at the Arena Stage, I had a trainer named Bill Terry who was a former fighter. He took me through the life of a boxer-in-training. Every morning you get up, you run a certain number of miles, you go to the gymnasium, you consume certain kinds of liquids and foods that are good for strength and endurance.

Jones then shaved his beard and his head as part of his mental and physical preparation:

> At this point the physical training I had been doing came into focus and I was a different person. By then I had learned, with the

THE NECESSARY SKILLS AND TALENTS OF THE ACTOR

- Interest in human nature
- Keen observation skills
- A good memory
- Concentration
- Imagination
- The drive to appear on the stage in front of an audience
- The ability to create characters and interpret dramatic situations
- A strong, expressive voice
- An expressive face and body
- High energy and physical stamina
- The ability to work openly as part of a group process
- Discipline

Kathleen Chalfant is seen here as Vivian Bearing, a character dying of cancer in Wit, the Pulitzer Prize-winning play by Margaret Edson.

director Ed Sherin's encouragement, to walk and behave physically, unconsciously like an athlete, which I'm not. By the time I finished the run of the play and the film, I hated the training. I was not good at diets and I wanted to be free to eat what I thought my body was crying out for in terms of sustenance.[13]

The Rehearsal Process

In the preceding chapter, we reviewed the work of the actors as they rehearsed *Joe Turner's Come and Gone*. We saw them studying the text, memorizing lines, seeking character motivation, developing character relationships, rehearsing blocking patterns, and finding the speech rhythms that would give authenticity to their characters and bring passion and eloquence to the playwright's words.

Interaction with the Director   What happens in rehearsal is a very intricate process of give-and-take between the actors and the director. For a production to have vitality and originality, the rehearsal must be a time of exploration. Discoveries must be made about characters and character relationships. Staging ideas are tested and discarded. Rhythms and pacing are built and adjusted.

Acting is extraordinarily hard work. It is a physical and mental process that requires great physical stamina and high energy. Actors must be able to remember their lines, work creatively, and be open and receptive to one another and the director. They must come to rehearsal well rested and fully alert, able to concentrate intensely on the work at hand, whether it is repeating a sword fight many times or discovering the intimate rhythms of a love scene. At each rehearsal, actors must be prepared to try out new approaches to line readings and blocking or to make refinements of choices that have already been made. Rehearsals demand as much or more from the actors as performances; and, for some, rehearsals are the most satisfying part of the production process.

Kathleen Chalfant, who played multiple roles in *Angels in America*, including the part of Ethel Rosenberg, describes rehearsals as a way of pulling a role or a text apart in order to put it back together again:

> In order to learn to act you must take apart something that happens faster than thought, break it into its component parts, and then put it back together. That's also what rehearsal is, breaking down a speech or a reaction, and then getting it close to the speed at which a human being actually does it. Quite often, plays are just a little slower than life because you've

In this scene, Geoff Hoyle, playing Berenger, must convince the audience through his reactions that his friend Jean, played by Jarion Monroe, has just turned into a rhinoceros in the 2002 production of Rhinoceros *by Eugene Ionesco at Berkeley Repertory Theatre, directed by Barbara Damashek.*

added a step, the breaking down. The trick is to act as quickly as you think, which is not necessarily a function of speed. When you're doing it properly, it often feels as though you have all the time in the world. Then you can allow yourself to be entirely taken, with no conscious control. That's what being in the moment means. In order to be prepared to give yourself over to the moment, you have to have done all the work beforehand: knowing the words backwards and forwards, knowing where you're supposed to stand, and more importantly, knowing what the character is doing at every turn and why she does it.[14]

Action and Reaction   In rehearsal, actors discover their actions and their reactions. Much of their work depends on playing actions that communicate a passionate expression of life's defining moments. The action may be contained in a speech such as Hamlet's "to be, or not to be, that is the question," or Bynum's story of the "shiny man." The action may be physicalized through gesture—for example, when the actor playing Herald Loomis cuts himself with the knife or when the actor playing Juliet drinks the sleeping potion.

But as important as the actors' actions are the actors' reactions. Much of what actors create

comes through reaction, through response, through seeing and believing. Actors bring a sense of the environment onto the stage; they feel the weather—the cold wind blowing through the cracks of a dilapidated house or the stifling heat of an urban summer. They experience the weariness of the passing of time, see the opulence of a ballroom or the emptiness of a Beckett landscape. Most of all, through reaction, actors give reality to the characters of the other actors onstage. They make them believable for the audience by the way that they watch and register the truth of what they have seen. They recognize loss, and they recognize triumph. They feel a threat and respond to an invitation. The art of acting has to do with creative expression and with the construction of belief.

Frances McDormand, whose work as a stage and film actor we discussed in Chapter 1, speaks about the help she received from her fellow actors in creating the role of Josie in Eugene O'Neill's *A Moon for the Misbegotten*. Josie is written to be a large, physically powerful, and, at times, threatening woman:

> In order for the audience to sustain that belief for three hours, the other actors had to help support the illusion. When I hit my brother,

In South African playwright Athol Fugard's most recent play, Sorrows and Rejoicings, *actors Cynthia Martells and John Glover re-create their characters' love for each other, even though the character played by Glover has recently died. The actors must create a sense of the present and the past simultaneously. They must bring the intimacy of their relationship to life for the audience, which for one character is a memory and for the other the reason for his presence.* Sorrows and Rejoicings *was directed by the playwright Athol Fugard for the Mark Taper Forum in 2002.*

he falls down. When I put my hand on Jamie Tyrone's shoulder to push him down on the step, he goes down on the step. When I go towards my father, he steps back. They create the reality as much as I do.[15]

Improvisation Improvisation is a useful rehearsal method for enhancing belief and creating imaginative actions. It is used with increasing frequency in many different kinds of production situations. Improvisation can be defined as spontaneous invention that goes beyond the scripted material to explore aspects of character or situation. Actors may do group improvisations at the beginning of rehearsals as a warm-up. They may also use improvisation to solve acting problems or to generate staging ideas. Improvisation is also an important method for establishing creative rapport between actors. Most acting students now have considerable exposure to improvisation as a fundamental part of their training.

One of the most common improvisations involves playing a scene in the actors' own words instead of the playwright's scripted words. This technique allows actors to work through scene content and to explore areas of character relationship. For example, there may

be an argument between two characters that lasts a couple minutes or less in the actual play. The two actors involved might then improvise a much longer argument to explore the sources of the tension between their characters. Their improvisation might even involve extreme physical interactions to help shape the verbal exchange. The scripted argument might be set at a dining room table or a court of law, where restrained behavior is expected, but to get to the strong feelings underlying the situation, the two actors might improvise some physical interaction while saying their lines. They might begin a tug-of-war or shoving match to heighten their responses to each other. The actors then use the intensity generated by the physicalization of the conflict in their verbal exchanges when they play the argument as scripted in the more confined situation.

Improvisation can also take the form of a game. Actors often invent situations in which, for example, the weather, the age of the characters, or the nature of the relationships keep changing. Actors also improvise stories in which one person begins with a single word or a sentence and then the other actors add pieces to the developing narration. Improvisation can also involve invented languages in which the actors communicate for long periods of time through made-up words. Susan Stroman, whose work as a director and choreographer is discussed in Chapter 7 on musical theatre, has dancers who have no lines to speak create what she calls "back stories" to give each of them more character detail and a sense of individual development when they dance their roles.

Improvisation is a liberating technique for actors that encourages spontaneity and quickness and can deepen relationships with the other actors in a production. Most of all, by immersing themselves completely in the given circumstances, actors use improvisation to increase their commitment to the truth of the situation.

The Rehearsal Schedule In **equity theatres** (theatres with more than one hundred seats in which all actors are paid according to a union contract), rehearsals last eight hours a day. At the Oregon Shakespeare Festival, which must rehearse several plays at once because actors perform in repertory, rehearsals are held in four-hour units. Actors may rehearse two different plays in one day or rehearse for one play during the day and perform a different play during the evening. In **equity waiver theatres** (theatres with fewer than one hundred seats that are not governed by union regulations), rehearsals may last several hours each evening after actors finish their other jobs.

The standard rehearsal process for a play begins with the reading aloud of the script by the company. Sometimes the actors read their parts; sometimes the director reads to the actors. The objective of the reading is for all the actors to hear the words as a starting point for their work. The actors are neither expected nor encouraged to have defined their characters at the first reading. Decisions made too early in the process may impede the work to be done. First readings are not meant to be performances and can sometimes seem very flat.

The work done after the first reading is usually referred to as "table work," which in-

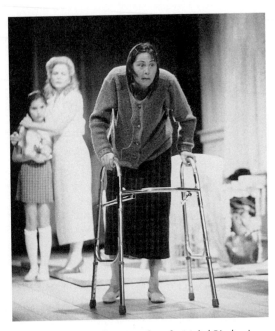

Cherry Jones creates the sense of age for Mabel Bigelow in Tina Howe's play Pride's Crossing *through posture, movement, and facial expression rather than through elaborate makeup. The shapeless clothing and the walker help both the actor and the audience imagine the character's ninety-one years.*

volves the kind of discussion, questioning, and rereading of the play that we observed in the early rehearsals of *Joe Turner's Come and Gone*. During the table work, the director might present the actors with background materials as well as establish the directorial concept or interpretation of the play that will be pursued.

Collaboration with the Designers Sometimes the designers participate at this stage by showing the actors a model of the set and costume sketches, or "renderings." The participation of the designers helps the actors to imagine the world of the play being constructed and contributes to their own work on their characters. The physical interpretation of a character in terms of silhouette, color, weight and texture of fabric, and accessories has enormous implications for the actors' own work in defining character. The presentation of the designers' work gives the actors a sense of the visual style of the production and makes clear the physical realities and practical requirements of the set and costumes: how many steps they will have to negotiate, how long a skirt will be, what colors their character will wear. Joe Mantello, who played the role of Louis in *Angels in America*, found costume choices to be an important part of the foundation for his character work:

> Louis is always looking to be judged. Tony Kushner, the playwright, and I always saw Louis wearing oversized boy clothes that he could disappear into when things got hard, when he was being judged. . . . Louis is swimming in his clothes. They make him look like he just wouldn't grow up. . . . In rehearsal I always wore an overcoat or a scarf that I made sure was too big for me.[16]

Early on in the rehearsal process, the actors will start wearing **rehearsal costumes.** Doing so allows them to practice with the limitations created by their particular costume pieces and also to experience the feelings generated by wearing particular items of clothing and undergarments. The difference between wearing a baseball cap and a bowler hat or between a cotton bandana or a velvet hat with feathers is enormous. Likewise, a change in shoes from cowboy boots to wing tips or from tennis shoes to high heels makes a huge difference not only to posture and style of walking but most significantly to how the actor feels. The designers' input feeds the actors' creative process. BW Gonzalez recently played Lady Macbeth in *Macbeth*, written by William Shakespeare. She began the rehearsal process wearing boots but found that the boots made her "too masculine." They "stopped her energy and blocked the sensuality" she and the director had determined were central to the character. Ultimately she wore sandals for most of the play and was barefoot in the famous sleepwalking scene.[17]

Richard Thomas, an actor with a youthful appearance, was working on a production of *The Count of Monte Cristo* with director Peter Sellars at the American National Theatre at the Kennedy Center in Washington, D.C. The role called for Thomas to go through major changes when he is sent to prison as a young man and emerges years later as the "mysterious Count":

> At one point during rehearsals I said, Peter, how am I going to do this? I can't age enough for the character. He said, "Oh, I ought to apologize. I should have told you that you're gonna be in all this makeup. There's gonna be wigs . . . you're gonna be red in this act and blue here . . . nobody's even going to know who you are." I thought, "Thank God. The production will be doing some of the work for me."[18]

APPROACHES TO ACTING

Actors take many different approaches to their work on a role. Frequently, for the same production, actors work in different ways and use a combination of techniques they find useful. Ultimately, the style of acting throughout the production must be consistent. That is, the audience must perceive that all of the actors are in the same play.

The Internal Approach

In a simplified overview of approaches to acting, we can distinguish between a psychological, internal approach and a technical, external approach. The **internal acting approach** involves identifying as closely as possible with the character to be played. This internal approach is associated with the acting innovations developed by Constantin Stanislavsky (see Chapter 8). Actors using a psychological method look for areas of the character's life that somehow correspond to their own experiences. They draw on their own personal histories and reactions to contribute to the life they create for the

Actors may achieve their greatest power in moments of stillness. Here Gary Sinise and Lois Smith are seen in a quiet, reflective moment in The Grapes of Wrath, *produced by Steppenwolf Theatre (Chicago). The Grapes of Wrath was written and directed by Frank Galati, who adapted the material from the John Steinbeck novel.*

character. Actors working internally view the character as having a life beyond what is contained in the play text; they may develop an autobiography that provides them with a sense of the character's past. They investigate character motivation in great depth to discover what the character wants from the other characters at any given moment in the play. They fill in the "subtext"—that is, what thoughts occur behind or between the character's lines but go unspoken. The subtext is translated into a stream of consciousness called the "inner monologue" that becomes the actor's silent text. The subtext is not expressed verbally but is communicated through vocal tone, gesture, or facial expression. The actors work to feel the emotions of the character's situation as if they were in the character's place. They are constantly asking why, constantly seeking the source or cause of behavior. Physical choices follow from psychological exploration, and it is that physicalization that reflects the character's state of mind.

The External Approach

In contrast to the internal approach, some actors work technically to give characterization a clear, external shape. Much of our discussion of acting thus far has centered on actor identification with character. When actors seek ways of linking their inner lives with the inner life of the character, they are in the realm of psychological acting. Because so much of American theatre and American actor training depends on an internal, psychological approach, it is harder for us to understand the nature and validity of external, technical approaches to acting.

The **external acting approach** has more to do with conscious choices about how language is to be spoken, which physical details to emphasize, and how emotional content is to be expressed. The actor creates a structure for character through imagination and analysis but not through psychological identification. Under such circumstances, character emotion may be created through the manipulation of the actor's expressive abilities rather than through the actor's actual emotional response. For actors who begin with an external approach, the speaking of the text is frequently the foundation for their work. Character emerges from the investigation of the language, the content and sounds of the words, the rhythm and phrasing. Anna Deavere Smith's imitation and repetition of the speeches from her interviews is one form of an external approach to acting. Bill Irwin begins by creating an oversized physical reality for the character. But actors who work externally can also be conscious of the needs and goals of their character, what we have called objectives or motivation; although Irwin takes a physical approach to characterization, he acknowledges that he is always aware of what his character wants. An external choice often unlocks a strong emotional response.

Acting Cordelia in King Lear

To further explore the concepts of internal and external acting approaches we consider here the possible approaches to the role of Cordelia in Shakespeare's *King Lear*. In the opening scene of the play, Lear's youngest daughter, Cordelia, faces the most difficult decision of her life. Her father, King Lear, has decided to give up his throne and divide his kingdom between his three daughters. He has assembled his daughters and the entire court to make a public ceremony out of his abdication of the throne. But he is looking for a show of adulation from his children in exchange for his apparent generosity in giving them a share of the lands and property. The king insists that his three daughters respond to his demand, "Which of you shall we say doth love us most." In responding to this manipulative ploy, Cordelia must either compromise her own beliefs to satisfy her father's vanity, or she must disappoint him publicly to maintain her own integrity. Her two sisters, Goneril and Regan, make elaborate declarations of love, and Lear rewards them each with a third of his kingdom. But although Cordelia loves her father far more than do her sisters, she cannot offer the kind of false praise her father seeks.

In the following two speeches, Cordelia tries to explain her position. She loves her father as a devoted and faithful daughter, but she knows that human beings have multiple loyalties and multiple claims on their affections. Because she is about to be married herself, she is acutely aware that her love must be divided.

CORDELIA: Unhappy that I am, I cannot heave
   My heart into my mouth. I love your Majesty
   According to my bond, no more nor less.

.   .   .   .

                    Good my lord,
You have begot me, bred me, loved me. I

Return those duties back as are right fit,
Obey you, love you, and most honor you.
Why have my sisters husbands if they say
They love you all? Haply when I shall wed,
That lord whose hand must take my plight shall carry
Half my love with him, half my care and
   duty.
Sure I shall never marry like my sisters,
To love my father all.[19]

An actor playing Cordelia who works internally might carefully consider and construct a family history, particularly focusing on Cordelia's relationship to her father. She might invent situations in which Cordelia has acquiesced to her father in the past, encouraging him in his belief that she will follow his desires in this scene. The actor might even imagine situations in which Lear and Cordelia have clashed before in order to explore the dynamic of the power struggle between them. The nature of the relationship might be worked out together by the actors playing Lear and Cordelia. Then when Cordelia speaks to Lear, the actor can use this history as a reference point; she can work to project a sense of what has already passed between them.

As part of an internal process, the actor might also look for her own emotional connections to the situation in two different ways. She might imagine what it would be like to be faced with such a dilemma. By making the pressures of Lear's demands seem real, feelings of her own might surface. The actor might also go back through her own personal history to a time when she faced a difficult choice or defied an authority figure with whom she had a close relationship, such as her own father or mother. This process is called "substitution"—the actor uses feelings she recalls from her own experiences as the foundation for the character responses in the play.

The actor might also work on the character's thought process to create a flow of ideas and responses that we have identified as the inner monologue. She might create a stream-of-consciousness dialogue with herself and the other characters. An example of a brief inner monologue might come before the line "Unhappy that I am." The actor might think but not speak, "his moment of glory . . . that look on his face . . . he will never forgive me for this." She might even improvise parts of the inner monologue aloud during some rehearsals.

The actor who approaches the role of Cordelia externally might begin with the language, the rhythm and sounds of the words. For example, the line "I cannot heave my heart into my mouth" expresses the essence of Cordelia's anguished situation. The words *heave*, *heart*, and *mouth* have long vowel sounds and soft consonants, giving the words weight and emotional depth as the starting point for the presentation of the character. The phrasing of the line "you have begot me, bred me, loved me" is answered by the rhythm in "I . . . obey you, love you and most honor you." The repeated "me" of the first line is linked to the repeated "you" of the second line, tying Cordelia's life to her father's. The insertion of "and most" before the third verb in the sequence adds emphasis to Cordelia's expression of respect for her father. Cordelia's straightforward declaration of her position in short, patterned syllables is followed by a question, "Why have my sisters husbands . . . ?" which offers a distinct contrast to the tone of the preceding three lines, challenging her sisters' sincerity. Careful analysis of the linguistic structure and the meaning of the words—as well as intuitive responses to the sounds and patterning of the words—yields a character foundation that emerges from Shakespeare's language rather than from an analysis of situation and character psychology.

In either case, before an actor can play Cordelia, there are many questions to be answered. How much control is the character consciously exerting over her own emotions? Are the two speeches played directly to Lear, or is part of the longer speech played to the two sisters? Is Cordelia challenging her father's authority, or is she warning her father of the consequences of taking her sisters' speeches for the truth? Is Cordelia trying to plead her case or prove her point? Is the longer speech a passionate accusation directed at the hypocrisy of Regan and Goneril or a restrained defense of principle? Does she want to expose her sisters as liars or force Lear to see his own vanity? In order to play these few short lines, the actor has many choices to make, whether she uses internal or external techniques for creating character.

Gestural Acting

Today is an explosive time for the actor. Method acting, associated with Stanislavsky and American realism, is being attacked from many sides. Experimental theatre companies, performers, and directors are exploring intriguing alternatives to or variations on method acting. Acting programs now offer remarkably eclectic courses of study that include dance, Asian theatre, improvisation, games, circus techniques, singing, and speech as well as character analysis and development. The actor has various sources to draw on, some of which strongly reject psychological motivation as part of character development.

In the production of *And the Soul Shall Dance* at East West Players, discussed in Chapter 9, hooded figures dressed in black who are identified by the Japanese term **kuroko** act in a style that does not have a psychological base. Although a primary function of the kurokos is to change the scenery, these actors are far more than stagehands. Their performance is choreographed; their expressive language is based on movement, not words. They embody forces such as the wind rather than detailed human characters. The technique they use in production is based on dance training and the disciplines of Asian theatre.

Asian theatre forms and acting techniques have had a growing influence on many Western theatres and theatre artists, not just on theatres with an Asian cultural base such as East West

The acting style of the Omaha Magic Theatre depends on the actors' skillful movement and gesture as they use abstracted props and costume pieces to create images that comment on contradictions in American life. To develop such complicated imagery, productions are usually in rehearsal for six months. Shown here is a scene from Sound Fields, *created by Megan Terry, Jo Ann Schmidman, and Sora Kimberlain.*

Players. Some actor training programs teach forms of Asian martial arts in combination with a movement vocabulary influenced by the kabuki or nō theatres of Japan, the Beijing Opera, or Indian kathakali. Eastern approaches to performance may be combined with Western dramatic literature—for example, in kabuki productions of Shakespeare.

Another Asian influence on Western performance technique comes from the work of contemporary Japanese director Tadashi Suzuki. Drawing on traditional Japanese forms, Suzuki has evolved a foundation for training and performance that is based on the actor's moving body and its relationship to the stage floor. He has designed a sequence of movements to "eradicate the ordinary, everyday sense of the body." Using these movements, actors focus on the rhythmical stamping of their feet while developing a sense of stillness in their upper body:

> The gesture of stamping on the ground, whether performed by Europeans or Japanese, gives the actor a sense of the strength inherent in his own body. It is a gesture that can lead to the creation of a fictional space, perhaps even a ritual space, in which the actor's body can achieve a transformation from the personal to the universal.[20]

Suzuki believes that spiritual energy is derived from the stamping movements that then infuse the actors' expressions.

Two actors from very different backgrounds have worked recently with directors stressing a **gestural acting approach** rather than an approach based on psychological motivation. Richard Thomas, whose parents were ballet dancers, learned his first acting skills as a child working with actors trained in method acting. He then went on to play John-Boy in the popular television series *The Waltons*. Television, particularly, draws on details associated with everyday behavior as the source for character. Another actor, David Warrilow, acted from 1970 to 1979 with the experimental theatre Mabou Mines and also performed in dance works by Mary Overlie. Both Thomas and Warrilow were in Peter Sellars's production of *The Count of Monte Cristo*. Commenting on this production, Thomas said:

> Working with Peter was my first contact with a directorial style that I could identify as being

Alyssa Bresnahan, playing Thetis in Tantalus, *uses stylized gesture in combination with the flowing lines of her costume and the fixed expression of her mask to create a larger-than-life mythical figure in the compilation of Greek tragedies produced by the Denver Center for the Performing Arts.*

related to the choreographic work I had seen my parents do. In rehearsals for *Monte Cristo,* I saw that it wasn't going to be a naturalistic production—we were going to be given very specific movements which would be used in relation to an overall vision. And I knew that I could accomplish those things without sacrificing my inner nature as an actor. . . . I could take very rigorous and formal physical work and get a lot of life into it.[21]

In preparation for his role as Old Dantes, Warrilow used his studies of t'ai chi ch'uan and the work of Tadashi Suzuki. Warrilow consciously chose a slightly bent posture, a "gliding" slow motion walk, and a few stylized hand gestures that would communicate the essence of the character:[22]

The character was, over a long period of time, dying of starvation. I knew that it would not be satisfying to me to place a hand over the stomach, which would be one's normal relationship to something like starvation. . . . I then was drawn to think about the heart area because of the emotional nature of the relationship to the son, Edmond Dantes, who was to be in the scene with me. That, however, could look like a heart condition and be misleading. So I placed the hand just on the bottom of the rib cage on the left side and instead of laying it flat against the body as if to hold in pain, I let the hand open gently and slightly curved so that to

David Warrilow created the essence of his character Old Dantes in The Count of Monte Cristo, *directed by Peter Sellars, through carefully selected and highly concentrated details. By drawing on dance and Asian and Western theatre traditions, Warrilow achieves remarkable intensity as an actor.*

me inside it felt like an acknowledgement of hurt, but a willingness to accept.[23]

Thomas and Warrilow have also acted recently in pieces directed by Robert Wilson (see Chapter 10), although not together in the same production. Thomas sees close connections between the formal composition of ballet choreography and the precise movement patterns composed by director Robert Wilson (Color Plate 11). Thomas describes his experience in rehearsal for *Danton's Death:*

> Bob has what he calls the visual book, which is set before the dialogue is rehearsed. What he does is plan every movement and give each a number, and you learn the numbers before you start to work on the text. He'll say, "Okay, Richard, put your right hand on top of your head and turn upstage. . . ." You do the moves and the numbers—"One, two three, four. . . ." When you start on the text, you get in your first position and as you read the dialogue, he calls the numbers and you make the corresponding moves. It's the strangest experience you've ever had, because you're trying to remember numbers and moves which may or may not have anything to do with the text. Sometimes it's amazing how the two *do* come together. That's the alchemy the actor creates. . . . He's not interested in your subtext, he's not interested in your inner life, he doesn't care how you get what you need, . . . but he wants you vigilant, listening, looking.[24]

When David Warrilow acted in Wilson's production of *The Golden Windows*, he had one five-minute sequence when he sat still with his head bowed. He explains that what he did during that five-minute period was simply to count in order to complete exactly five minutes in his position.[25] The audience might read many different interpretations into his sitting or create their own associations, but Warrilow was not motivating the action of sitting. An actor working from a psychological perspective might play that the man was waiting for someone, that he was too tired or burdened to get up, or that he was deep in thought about important matters.

The actor's process is both highly individual and subject to fluctuation. Actors usually combine various techniques in their work, and there may be many subtle shifts in the degree of actual emotional engagement in the role at various

Marisol, by José Riviera, takes the characters through a nightmare landscape of contemporary urban America. Here Karina Arroyave as Marisol and V. Craig Heidenreich as her assailant create a subway scene with simple, suggestive properties in the production of Marisol *by the Actors Theatre of Louisville. The location and atmosphere are created through the actors' belief.*

stages of the rehearsal and performance process. Actors constantly integrate various sources of information and inspiration into their creation of role. All of the work focuses on the creation of stage life that is original and truthful and that the actor can play with maximum conviction. No matter what the approach, good actors achieve complete concentration on the moment being played.

THE PERFORMANCE

The purpose of all of the actor's training and all of the work in rehearsal is to provide the foundation for performance. A well-rehearsed play provides the actor with the control and confidence to give a fully energized and completely detailed performance, to be open to audience responses and to make adjustments for the unexpected that always occurs with live performance. Sometimes the run of a play lasts a few weeks or a few months. Sometimes an actor may appear in the same play for years. The final, crucial element of the actor's work is finding ways to sustain the performance over the entire run no matter how long that may be (Color Plate 12).

THEATRE AND FILM

Far more than other theatre practitioners, actors working in the United States today frequently alternate between the theatre and film work. Bill Irwin and Anna Deavere Smith focus most of their energies on the theatre. But Irwin has been in films such as *Hot Shots* and *My Blue Heaven*, and Smith acted in *Philadelphia* and *The American President*. Frances McDormand divides her time between theatre and film, Richard Thomas between theatre and television. Other prominent film actors have been closely associated with the plays discussed in

this text. Angela Bassett, known for her work in *Waiting to Exhale*, *What's Love Got to Do with It*, and *Boyz N the Hood*, began her professional acting career playing Martha Pentecost in the Broadway production of *Joe Turner's Come and Gone*. Elizabeth Peña, who played the role of Jesse in *Dog Lady* discussed in Chapter 14, has been seen on television in *Resurrection Blvd.*, *Law & Order*, and *Hill Street Blues* and in films such as *Lone Star*, *La Bamba*, and *Down and Out in Beverly Hills*.

The difference between acting in the theatre and acting on film is usually described in terms of scale. In film acting, the camera comes to the actor. Actors then work to open their responses but not to enlarge them. In the theatre, the actor crosses a distance to reach the audience. The size of the performance must respond to the size of the stage and the auditorium. Stage actors need to contain their instincts to be expansive when they are working on a film, and film actors must increase their energy and the breadth of their response when they appear on the stage.

The film actor is aware at all times of the camera lens, both the width of the shot and the focus. Acting must be concentrated in the body parts seen by the camera—the face or a hand,

Elizabeth Peña trained as a stage actor before embarking on a career in television and film. Peña is shown here with Chris Cooper in a scene from the film Lone Star.

for example, in a close-up. Film actors compose their actions and reactions in synchronization with the size and movement of the lens. Like so many other aspects of the actor's craft, working with the camera is a technical skill to be learned and practiced.

Some actors find the financial rewards and the exposure of film acting to be more attractive than the work itself. For actors, film work usually involves more waiting than acting. Setups for stunts or special effects require an extraordinary amount of preparation. Sometimes the waiting depends on the weather or the light. Sometimes huge numbers of extras must be organized. Although the work of the actor is usually the most visible expression of the medium, the actor's work is scheduled around the needs of an elaborate technical process.

Films are frequently shot out of sequence. Actors may have to play a climactic moment at the end of the story before they have filmed the incidents that lead up to that point. The film actor learns only the lines that are necessary to the scene currently being filmed. There is no need to learn all the lines at once or to retain lines from scenes that have been completed. The film editor is responsible for organizing and making sense of the pieces of film that have been shot. The editor constructs what the viewer sees of the plot and the actor's progression.

Although the amount of rehearsal time for films varies widely, there is never as much rehearsal time as there is for most plays, and sometimes there is no rehearsal time at all. Sarah Jessica Parker, acting in *Once Upon a Mattress* in New York, says, "In the theatre, everything you do is about acting. In the movies, it's about a fifth, or an eighth."[26] The theatre's rehearsal process has great appeal for Amy Irving, who interrupted her film career to appear in a 1997 production of *The Three Sisters*, by Anton Chekhov:

> The interchange with the director and the other actors, the chance to come up with something you couldn't come up with by yourself. You don't get that in film. You can do a film

and never meet your colleagues, and you're at the opening and it's, "Hey, nice to meet you."[27]

BECOMING AN ACTOR

There are many different paths to becoming an actor, although all require talent and the acquisition of technique. Both Elizabeth Peña and Richard Thomas came from theatrical families and acted in many productions as children before pursuing theatre and film careers as adults. Peña studied dance, mime, and clowning and then attended the High School of the Performing Arts in New York City. Thomas was studying Chinese art and literature at Columbia University when he was cast in *The Waltons*. Angela Bassett and Frances McDormand acted in high school and went on to earn their master's of fine arts in acting from the Yale School of Drama. Bill Irwin studied theatre at Oberlin College and then spent years studying circus techniques and clowning before developing his own theatre pieces and acting in plays and films. Elizabeth Peña is adamant, as are most actors, about the amount of work necessary to become an actor. "I studied for ten years. I didn't go in and get a photo resume and call myself an actress. Every job I've gotten has come out because I broke my tush trying to get it."[28]

SUMMARY

The art of the actor is the primary force of the theatre. For theatre to exist, in its essential form, only an actor, a playing space, and an audience are required. When actors appear on the stage, they undergo a transformation. Because actors convey concentrated energy and heightened awareness, they seem larger than life. Through their charismatic presence, they inspire the audience's belief in the stage action.

Years of demanding training in voice, movement, textual analysis, character development, and improvisation lay the foundation for performance in front of an audience. Beyond the challenges of actor training, the opportunity to work in the theatre depends on successfully competing for roles in the audition process. Once an actor has been cast, pre-rehearsal preparation may involve physical training or body reshaping in addition to research and study of the text. Actors immerse themselves in their roles during the rehearsal period.

The rehearsal is a collaborative process of discovery guided by the director. Approaches to character development during rehearsals may include improvisation as well as psychological, method acting techniques and/or external acting techniques. Improvisation involves the spontaneous creation of character, action, and dialogue. Improvisation may be used as a way to explore the playwright's text, to develop rapport between actors, or to generate staging ideas. The goal of internal, method acting is identification with the character that grows out of the actor's own personal experience as well as the actor's imaginative placement of himself or herself in the character's situation. External technique refers to the shaping of character through the manipulation of language and the construction of physical details of posture, movement, and appearance. Gestural acting, a more stylized form of acting that uses abstracted movements to capture the essence of character, reflects the growing influence of Asian performance styles on American theatre.

Many actors today work in both theatre and film. Acting in the theatre demands a more expansive presentation that is scaled to the size of the theatre. In contrast, acting on film emphasizes subtleties and nuances, which the camera can capture close-up. Acting in the theatre involves an integrated, sequential process of rehearsal and performance. Film acting, on the other hand, is a more fragmented process in which action is often shot out of sequence. Actors working on the same film may never meet. On the stage, the actor organizes the details of the performance; in film, the editor has considerable control over how the actor's performance will ultimately be seen.

TOPICS FOR DISCUSSION AND WRITING

1. What is meant by the actor's presence? How would you describe your own response to performances you have witnessed that you would call charismatic?

2. Attend a theatre performance at your university or college. Where do you notice the actors' creativity in creating belief through their reactions? What do they help you to see or be aware of? Look for reactions to both physical circumstances and to the actions of the other characters.

3. Choose one of these short scenes from *Joe Turner's Come and Gone:* Seth and Bertha (page 76) or Molly and Jeremy (page 100). Explore the subtext in the scene you have chosen. What thoughts may be behind the lines that the characters do not verbalize? Choose a section of lines and write an inner monologue that an actor might think as he or she plays the lines. How might the inner monologue affect the way the lines themselves are spoken?

NOTES

1. David Warrilow, quoted in Laurie Lassiter, "David Warrilow: Creating Symbol and Cypher," in *Acting (Re)Considered,* ed. Phillip B. Zarrilli (London: Routledge, 1995), 321.

2. BW Gonzalez, interview with the author, 17 July 2002.

3. Stephen Spinella, quoted in Janet Sonenberg, *The Actor Speaks* (New York: Random House, 1996), 252.

4. Gonzalez interview.

5. Spinella, quoted in Sonenberg, 278.

6. James Earl Jones, quoted in Holly Hill, *Actors' Lives: On and off the American Stage, Interviews by Holly Hill* (New York: Theatre Communications Group, 1993), 19.

7. Gordon Davidson, quoted in Gordon Hunt, *How to Audition* (New York: HarperCollins, 1995), 203.

8. Hunt, 184.

9. Joseph Albado, quoted in Heltie Lynee Hurtes, *The Back Stage Guide to Casting Directors* (New York: Watson-Guptill, 1992), 3.

10. Jack Bowdan, quoted in Hurtes, 15.

11. Stuart Ostrow, quoted in Hunt, 168.

12. Tamu Gray, interview with the author, 24 March 1993.

13. James Earl Jones, quoted in Hill, 9–10.

14. Kathleen Chalfant, quoted in Sonenberg, 102–103.

15. Frances McDormand, quoted in Sonenberg, 255.

16. Joe Mantello, quoted in Sonenberg, 141–42.

17. Gonzalez interview.

18. Richard Thomas, quoted in Hill, 343.

19. *King Lear*, in *The Complete Works of Shakespeare*, ed. David Bevington (New York: HarperCollins, 1992), 1173 (I, i).

20. Tadashi Suzuki, *The Way of Acting*, trans. J. Thomas Rimer (New York: Theatre Communications Group, 1986), 11–12.

21. Thomas, quoted in Hill, 342.

22. Lassiter, 375.

23. Warrilow, quoted in Lassiter, 375.

24. Thomas, quoted in Hill, 349–50.

25. Laurence Shyer, *Robert Wilson and His Collaborators* (New York: Theatre Communications Group, 1989), 18.

26. Sarah Jessica Parker, quoted in Bruce Weber, "The Starry 'Three Sisters' Cast Reveals a Trend," *New York Times*, 9 February 1997, 31.

27. Amy Irving, quoted in Weber, 31.

28. "Elizabeth Peña—Untapped," *Hollywood Reporter Magazine*, September 1987.

SUGGESTIONS FOR FURTHER READING

Cole, Toby, and Helen Krich Chinoy, eds. *Actors on Acting*. New York: Crown, 1970.

A collection of statements on the nature of acting in the Western tradition by theatre practitioners and philosophers from the time of the ancient Greek theatre up to the mid-twentieth century in Europe and the United States.

Hagen, Uta. *A Challenge for the Actor*. New York: Scribner, 1991.

An impassioned discussion of acting by a devoted proponent of internal, psychological acting; includes a personal appraisal of the development of the American theatre as well as an analysis of roles and an explanation of acting method.

Hill, Holly. *Actors' Lives: On and off the American Stage*. New York: Theatre Communications Group, 1993.

A collection of interviews with a wide range of American actors including Olympia Dukakis, Cherry Jones, James Earl Jones, and Richard Thomas; interweaves personal and professional materials.

Olivier, Laurence. *Laurence Oliver On Acting*. New York: Simon and Shuster, 1986.

Observations by one of the great English actors on his approach to roles and the work of other actors. The book begins with the comment, "For me acting is a technical problem." Olivier explores extensively, but not exclusively, the external approach to acting.

Seham, Amy E. *Whose Improv Is It Anyway: Beyond Second City*. Jackson: University of Mississippi Press, 2001.

An examination of the evolution of improvisational comedy in the United States during the latter part of the twentieth century. The author considers both the nature of improvisational performance and the way issues of gender, race, and power affect improvisational companies.

Sonenberg, Janet. *The Actor Speaks*. New York: Random House, 1996.

A collection of interviews regarding the craft of acting and actors' approaches to their roles; includes interviews with American actors Frances McDormand and Joe Mantello.

Spolin, Viola. *Improvisation for the Theatre*. Evanston: Northwestern University Press, 1963.

A rich collection of exercises structured to build skill and confidence in improvisation with a clear theoretical foundation. A good source for actors, directors, and teachers doing drama in school situations.

Stanislavski, Constantin. *An Actor Prepares*. With an introduction by Sir John Gielgud. New York: Theatre Arts Books, 1984.

One of the essential books on acting. This text introduces Stanislavsky's "method," the most famous approach to internal psychological acting. (Stanislavsky's name is spelled differently—ending with an *i* or a *y*—depending on the particular translation from Russian.) First published in the United States in 1936, the book addresses such areas as concentration, relaxation, the uses of the imagination, the separation and organization of a role into units, and the technique of drawing on one's own emotional resources. Stanislavsky's theories on acting are made accessible by showing them in practice as a supposedly fictional director works with a group of student actors.

Suzuki, Tadashi. *The Way of Acting*. Translated by J. Thomas Rimer. New York: Theatre Communications Group, 1986.

A presentation of a philosophy of performance in relation to society. In an examination of the nō theatre of Japan, Suzuki explores the way the modern international theatre may draw upon earlier Japanese traditions.

Wilson, Garff B. *A History of Acting*. Bloomington: Indiana University Press, 1966.

A chronicle of acting styles in the early American theatre from the nineteenth to the first part of the twentieth century.

CHAPTER 5

The Director

The actor brings the playwright's characters to life and secures the vital connection to the audience. The designers create an environment for the actor's presence. Uniting all of the elements of the performance—script, acting, set, costumes, lights, music, and sound—into a meaningful whole is the business and the art of the director. Director Libby Appel says, "it is the director's job to illuminate the play for the audience."[1] The director creates a theatrical language, a language of space and movement and sound that coherently communicates the ideas of the production to the audience. Director and critic Harold Clurman, one of the founders of the Group Theatre (the 1930s American theatre dedicated to new realistic plays) and a major force in the American theatre for fifty years, calls the director the "author" of the stage action:

> That action speaks louder than words is the first principle of the stage; the director, I repeat, is the "author" of the stage action. Gestures and movements, which are the visible manifestations of action, have a different specific gravity from the writer's disembodied ideas. Theatrical action is virtually a new medium, a different language from that which the playwright uses, although the playwright hopes that his words will suggest the kind of action

that ought to be employed. The director must be a master of theatrical action, as the dramatist is the master of the written concept of his play.[2]

THE HISTORY OF
THE DIRECTOR

The actor and the playwright are as old as the theatre itself. The designer, in the form of a stage machinist, mask maker, or costumer, is also connected to ancient traditions in the theatre. But the position of the director is a relatively recent addition to the process of theatre production. In earlier times the playwright or a leading actor was responsible for coordinating the production and placing the actors on the stage. In the Greek, medieval, Elizabethan, and Chinese theatres, traditions and conventions were firmly established, and therefore questions of stylistic interpretation were not an issue. Productions did not strive for historical authenticity in representing earlier periods, nor was there an array of acting approaches to choose from.

The Director and
the Development of Realism

The position of the director came into being in the Western theatre during the nineteenth century in response to certain shifts in the nature of the theatre. The director filled needs created by (1) an interest in a more detailed representation of place and character history—the movement called realism, which attempted to put a sense of daily life on the stage—and (2) the profusion of theatre styles that arose in response to realism.

As playwrights such as Ibsen and Chekhov began to write realistic plays in which environment deeply affected character feeling and action, the authenticity of the environment became very important. Exact details of costume were also necessary to place the characters accurately in their situations. Actors couldn't simply go to their own wardrobes and choose

costumes they thought would be suitable or glamorous. And the psychological motivation and subtext implied by the plays needed careful development by an ensemble of actors, not a presentation by individuals each eager to draw attention to their own particular expertise. Someone was needed to coordinate the production elements of the realistic stage, and this is where the director first appeared.

The Duke of Saxe-Meiningen   George II, Duke of Saxe-Meiningen (1826–1914), the leader of a small duchy in what would become Germany, contributed considerable resources and energy to the development of the Meiningen court theatre. Taking on the role of director himself, he was determined to reclaim the theatre from haphazard production practices and the excesses of actors indulged by a star system in which all elements of a production were dedicated to showing off the talents of popular, leading actors. In collaboration with Ludwig Chronegk, who functioned as codirector, and the duke's third wife, Ellen Franz, an actor, he built his company on principles that became influential throughout Europe. The actors were hired to be part of an ensemble; an actor who played a leading role in one production might be part of the crowd in the next. Costumes and settings were carefully researched and constructed with great attention to period detail. All of the elements of the production were coordinated in a unified presentation. Between 1874 and 1890, the company toured from England to Russia, eventually presenting forty-one plays. European theatre practitioners who subsequently pursued the nuances and subtleties of realism in acting and staging had the integrated productions of the Meininger Players as a foundation for their efforts.

Constantin Stanislavsky   The most famous and influential director of this early realistic period was Constantin Stanislavsky. As we observed in our discussion of the internal approach to acting in Chapter 4, Stanislavsky's psychological approach to character development

Stanislavsky's production of The Seagull *for the Moscow Art Theatre demonstrates the profusion of details in early realism. Rooms were fully structured with walls, doors, and windows. Furnishings and accessories defined character background and also provided many opportunities for naturalistic character action. Stanislavsky maintained that the settings were as important for the actors as for the audience in providing a sense of the environment.*

asked actors to behave onstage as if they were living the circumstances of the characters' lives. Stanislavsky defined himself as a director in 1898, when he and his partner Vladimir Nemirovich-Danchenko undertook the direction of Anton Chekhov's first major play, *The Seagull,* at their theatre, the Moscow Art Theatre.

The Seagull had failed in its first production at another theatre because no one had recognized that changes in production methods were necessary to make a success of Chekhov's play. In its initial production, Chekhov's delicate play, which involves the struggles of a small group of characters to be recognized as artists while they also seek to resolve failed love relationships, was performed at the footlights with speeches played melodramatically out to the audience. Stanislavsky recognized the need to turn the characters toward each other. Stanislavsky saw that building an ensemble of the actors would help to create the links between the characters' lives so crucial to Chekhov's dramatic intent. An ensemble could create the essential rhythms of character action and speech that together would build a rhythmic structure for the play and draw the audience into its rising and falling breath. Stanislavsky believed that ensemble

acting would give the lives of all of the characters equal weight and interest rather than having the dramatic material be dominated by the performance of a star.

Stanislavsky also worked to physicalize in small, realistic details the inner, spiritual lives of the characters and to create an atmosphere of setting and sounds that would give the appearance of reality and provide a believable environment for the character action. Here he was very concerned about the objects handled by the actors, such as cigarettes and walking sticks, as well as sound effects such as bird calls and cricket chirps.

Stanislavsky built a recognizable world for the play through a profusion of details taken from daily life. But to make sense of the physical details and the realistic character action, Stanislavsky recognized the need to discover or identify what he called the **spine** of the play—that is, the central action or central idea that draws together all of the smaller plot incidents and character actions.

As a young director, Stanislavsky followed a method of preparation that some directors today still use. He made copious notes of character actions and business, diagrams of the actors' placement onstage, sketches of settings, and lists

Anton Chekhov (center) reads The Seagull *to the actors of the Moscow Art Theatre. Director Constantin Stanislavsky sits immediately to Chekhov's right. Poor health curtailed Chekhov's participation in the development of these famous first productions of his plays. Much of his interaction with the company was reduced to correspondence.*

of sound effects and properties. He determined the details and the shape of the production in advance of the rehearsal period with the idea that the actors would be told or taught what to do. The process of discovery was his alone. Later in his directing career, however, Stanislavsky came to see the need for the actors to assume more responsibility for the creative work of building characters. Stanislavsky's revised view of the discovery process is one that many directors adhere to today. Although most contemporary directors immerse themselves in a process of preparation for months or even years before they begin rehearsals, they view the rehearsal process as a journey of discovery that is embarked upon in a spirit of partnership between the actors and the director. British

director Peter Brook, known for his bold interpretation of classical works and highly original new pieces, stresses the importance of spontaneity in the rehearsal process:

> I make hundreds of sketches of the scenery and the movements. But I do this merely as an exercise, knowing that none of it is to be taken seriously the next day. . . . If I were to ask actors to apply the sketches that I did three days or three months earlier, I would kill everything that can come to life at the moment in rehearsal.[3]

The Director and the Determination of Style

Although the position of director emerged in response to developments of realism, the role

The plot of Twelfth Night *by William Shakespeare revolves around mistaken identities. Viola, played here by Opal Alladin, assumes the disguise of a man, causing Olivia, Kathryn Meisle, to fall in love with her. Joe Dowling directed this production at the Guthrie Theatre in 2000, moving the play from its original Elizabethan time period to the early twentieth century to allow audiences to see the material from a new perspective.*

frankly acknowledges the presence of the audience, or it can use the convention of the "fourth wall" (an imaginary barrier between the actors and the audience across the front of the stage) to seal the characters in their own world. A director can choose to emphasize the central character's philosophical questioning or the struggles of power politics (Color Plates 13 and 14). In the words of Brook:

> Many years ago it used to be claimed that one must "perform the play as Shakespeare wrote it." Today the absurdity of this is more or less recognized: nobody knows what scenic form he had in mind. All that one knows is that he wrote a chain of words that have in them the possibility of giving birth to forms that are constantly renewed. There is no limit to the virtual forms that are present in a great text.[4]

And the plays of Anton Chekhov, for whom Stanislavsky created intricately realistic productions full of detailed properties and sound effects, could be interpreted with abstract settings that emphasize the symbolic content of the plays. Although some, including the playwright himself, have disagreed with Stanislavsky's interpretations of Chekhov's plays, Stanislavsky understood the position of the director as one who interprets the playwright's creation. Other directors have moved beyond the idea of collaboration with a playwright to view themselves as the primary creators of the theatrical event.

The Visionary Director: Jerzy Grotowski

In 1959, sixty years after Stanislavsky began his work on *The Seagull,* Jerzy Grotowski, a Polish director, began an experimental theatre in Opole, Poland. Six years later, in 1965, Grotowski's Laboratory Theatre moved to the larger city of Wroclaw, Poland. Throughout its existence, the experimental Laboratory Theatre would be subsidized through state and city resources. Although the subsidy was hardly lavish, it did provide a level of basic support that such an experimental company could not expect

of the director as a theatre artist who gives a production a clear stylistic point of view that integrates all of the elements of the performance became fundamental to the multiplicity of styles that followed realism. It is the director who decides how a play is to be interpreted, whether it is a classic play from an earlier era or a new play. For example, a director can choose to set *Hamlet* in twelfth-century Denmark, in seventeenth-century England, in a contemporary time frame, or in the future. A production can follow Elizabethan staging practice that

Peter Brook has recently done his own adaptation of Hamlet, *in collaboration with Marie-Helene Estienne, in which he has cut and rearranged the text. The entire play is performed by only eight actors, without intermission. In the Brook production, the play becomes even more tightly focused on Hamlet himself, played by Adrian Lester. The stage is defined only by an orange carpet with a few large stools and cushions moved around by the actors to provide a sense of the change of scenes.*

Andrei Serban directed The Cherry Orchard *in 1977 at Lincoln Center, New York. Although the actors are dressed in period costumes, Serban and designer Santo Loquasto dispensed with the walls and most of the furnishings of realism that are evident in Stanislavsky's late-nineteenth-century production of another Chekhov play,* The Seagull, *shown on page 151. The house in which the characters live is suggested by a white rug and only a few pieces of furniture. Serban creates the idea that the characters' lives are suspended. The cherry orchard that defines the history of the family estate becomes a symbolic environment for the play's action.*

in the United States. The following discussion of Grotowski's theatre practice is based on his career in Poland, before he shifted the site of his work to the United States and then to Italy.

Like Stanislavsky, Grotowski was devoted to reforming actor training. But instead of employing Stanislavsky's internal acting system, aimed at producing the most naturalistic performance, Grotowski sought an approach to acting that would maximize the expressive power of the actor's total instrument. Grotowski wanted to train actors to use their voices and bodies in astonishing ways to communicate a heightened expression of human experience:

> At a moment of psychic shock, a moment of terror, of mortal danger or tremendous joy, a man does not behave "naturally." A man in an elevated spiritual state uses rhythmically articulated signs, begins to dance, to sing.[5]

Grotowski's rigorous and athletic program of actor training was based on his own studies of both Western acting styles and methods, including Stanislavsky's, and Eastern theatres, including the Beijing Opera, the Indian kathakali, and the Japanese nō theatre. Although the training depended on stretching vocal and physical capacity to extraordinary limits, the goal was not simply technical brilliance. Grotowski encouraged a process that would allow actors to reveal themselves, to strip away the "life-masks" that they use to protect themselves, so that the spectators would be encouraged to look deeply into themselves as well.

The actor training was essential to Grotowski's own work as a director, which involved staging plays with an entirely different emphasis from that used in the realistic theatre. Grotowski was interested in creating theatre performances that explored myths and archetypal characters as they confronted or illuminated the experiences of the members of his theatre company and the experiences of his audiences, the people of Poland:

> I am very fond of texts which belong to a great tradition. For me, these are like the voices of my ancestors and those voices which come to us from the sources of our European culture.[6]

He was particularly concerned, for example, about the legacy of World War II for Poland and about the presence of Nazi concentration camps such as Auschwitz on Polish land and their effect on the collective Polish psyche. For one of his plays, *Akropolis*, Grotowski arranged a text—based on the play by Stanislaw Wyspianski—that brought together mythical figures from throughout Western history who, in the production, became inmates in a concentration camp. During the course of the production, the characters constructed a crematorium that they all entered at the end of the performance. Ludwik Flaszen, who was the literary adviser of the Laboratory Theatre, writes that the production of *Akropolis* asked the question, "What happens to human nature when it faces total violence?"[7]

As a director, Grotowski believed that the text should be part of the production but not necessarily the dominating force. He believed that a director should be able to reshape a text or bring several texts together and create a collage of pieces of plays. With this approach, the director goes beyond being the partner of the playwright in developing the production of a play. The director essentially becomes the author. It is the director's imagination that creates the foundation for what happens on the stage.

Grotowski believed that the director should also shape the stage space, the actor-audience relationship, as he shapes the text and the actors' work. In his attempt to bring the actors and audience as close together as possible, Grotowski created a new spatial arrangement for each of the productions of the Polish Laboratory Theatre. For a production of *Doctor Faustus*, the audience sat at long tables while the actors moved around the tables and even performed on top of them. The tables were to suggest the Last Supper. For *The Constant Prince*, the audience looked down from their seats, raised slightly behind a fence, as if they were at a bull fight or in a surgical operating theatre. The fence was used

Time Rocker, *designed and directed by Robert Wilson with music by Lou Reed and based on H.G. Wells's* Time Machine, *is the last piece of a trilogy of rock operas. Wilson produces his work more frequently in Europe than in the United States, and* Time Rocker *was created in Hamburg, Germany, before being produced at the Théâtre de l'Odeon in Paris.*

to suggest that the audience was looking at something "forbidden."[8]

Through the Laboratory Theatre, Grotowski was able to control all of the elements of the performance to realize his vision of the theatre. Like the spatial arrangement of the actor-audience placement that we have just discussed, all of the physical elements of set, costumes, and properties had an abstract and symbolic quality. Grotowski believed that the theatre should leave lavish and high-tech production values to the film industry and focus instead on the most stripped-down, basic materials that could support the actors' work. Found objects, reworked fabrics or clothes, and bare lights served the design elements of his **poor theatre.** Only those objects or costume pieces that served the actor were incorporated. Nothing was used merely for the purposes of decoration, mood, or background.

Although few directors follow Grotowski's particular path of the poor theatre, the model that he presented at the Polish Laboratory Theatre of the director as the primary creative artist of the theatre has been adopted by other directors throughout the twentieth century. Early in the century, Vsevolod Meyerhold, the director whose murder by Soviet authorities we

discussed in Chapter 2, identified himself as the "author of the spectacle."[9] In our own time, Robert Wilson, a director who embraces the most elaborate scenic, costume, and lighting effects, creates theatre that reflects his vision of subject and spectacle (Color Plate 15). Although the majority of contemporary directors participate in a more traditional process of collaboration in which the playwright's work is the starting point for the rest of the theatre practitioners, the director as visionary has been instrumental in bringing new possibilities to the theatre.

APPROACHES TO DIRECTING

The role of the director is still in flux, and there is much disagreement about how much a director should impose on a production and how much should emerge from collaboration. Declan Donnellan directed the London production of *Angels in America: Millennium Approaches* by Tony Kushner, which preceded the play's Los Angeles and New York productions. (*Angels in America* is presented in Chapter 11.) Playwright Tony Kushner participated in the rehearsal process in London, and his presence led to considerable tension between director and playwright. Donnellan reports that he and Kushner "almost killed each other," in part over a disagreement about the role of the director:

> I was much freer with the actors than Tony expected. There was one great row when Tony asked why a certain actor was standing to say a line when it was very clear from the written line that she should be sitting down. I said that I hadn't even noticed that she was standing up because the scene varied from day to day, and Tony couldn't believe that I wouldn't control whether an actor should stand or sit. He thought this showed a terrible lack of respect for detail. But I told him that on the whole it was for the actor to make the detail, it's up to me to make sure that the actors know what they are doing, which is very different from telling them to stand or sit.[10]

The director Bertolt Brecht was outspoken about his theories of epic theatre as they applied to acting methods and scenic presentation. But in rehearsal he was famous for sitting quietly while the actors worked and making only brief suggestions when they had finished.

Describing the process the director uses is even more difficult than pinning down the process and methods that actors use to create roles and give performances. Directing is studied and discussed less than acting is. Far fewer people are involved as directors than as actors, and the path of the director is a highly individual one. We can identify only the kinds of tasks that a director must accomplish, and we can form an overview of the directing process by describing the approaches used by some prominent directors. Frequently, the views and the methods used by one director contradict those of another director.

There are four models of directorial approach that summarize the current status of the directing profession. The first two refer to approaches we have already discussed. The first model, the director who works in partnership with the playwright and the actors, was established by the Duke of Saxe-Meiningen and Stanislavsky and is exemplified by the production of *Joe Turner's Come and Gone* studied in Chapter 3. Directors who follow the second model, using the text to support their own visions, include Grotowski and Robert Wilson. Wilson extends his own personal control over the performance by formulating the patterns and movements the actors are expected to follow.

Two additional models demonstrate further possibilities for the director. In the third model, the director guides the work of a theatre collective. For example, Elizabeth LeCompte is a founding member and director of the Wooster Group, an experimental theatre company. The performances of the Wooster Group interweave materials from many sources, including play texts, autobiographies, poetry, letters, personal biographical contributions from the actors, and group improvisation. This theatre company creates its own material, but through a group process rather than through the view of a single director. Although the material is generated collectively, LeCompte exerts authority in shaping the performance:

> I like to run a tight ship. I like to have the final say, not so much because I want the power of it, but because otherwise I lose my way. These workers bring this material to me, and I sift and siphon through it. It isn't that some material is "better than other material." I use it when it links up to something very particular with me, when it extends my vision.[11]

The fourth model is a return to the earliest tradition of the theatre: playwrights who direct their own works. Emily Mann is both a prominent playwright and a director who directs her own works as well as those of other playwrights. Mann's plays include *Still Life, Execution of Justice, Having Our Say,* and *Greensboro: A Requiem.* Mann's work as a playwright is unique because she arranges the actual language of real people to focus on traumatic, historical events and their impact on people's lives. Her characters function as witnesses to history, and

The original production of Emily Mann's Execution of Justice *was coproduced by the Berkeley Repertory Theatre and the Eureka Theatre. In this scene, Ralph Marchetti plays a police officer who is a rabid supporter of Dan White, the confessed killer of Mayor George Moscone and Supervisor Harvey Milk. The play uses the actual statements of the people involved in this historic situation to dramatize the polarization of the San Francisco community.*

> **SUMMARY OF THE DIRECTOR'S RESPONSIBILITIES**
>
> - To choose the play
> - To study the play and the historical context, possibly in collaboration with a dramaturg
> - To develop a "concept" for the production in collaboration with the designers
> - To audition and cast the actors
> - To guide the work of the actors:
>   To establish an acting style
>   To block the play
>   To clarify the character development and relationships
>   To build the play's rhythm to maximize audience involvement
> - To maintain an atmosphere that is conducive to the creative work of all involved
> - To guide the work of all participants to a timely and coherent readiness for performance

as a director she works with actors to present a documentary style of theatre.

THE DIRECTOR AT WORK

Choosing the Play

Directors usually have some choice about what they are going to direct, and they tend to choose plays they care deeply about. They choose plays that connect to their understanding of the world, plays that make sense to them. A play that is a good choice for one director may not work for another. A director may admire and enjoy a particular play and yet lack an inner understanding of the work that would lead to a successful production. Although some directors are hired for a theatre season for which the plays have already been selected, most theatre practitioners and producers recognize the importance of the connection between the director and the script. If the director is to interpret the world of the play for an audience, then the playwright's vision must appeal to the director's imagination and understanding of human nature.

JoAnne Akalaitis, a member of the experimental Mabou Mines for many years and a director in regional theatres, looks for an imagistic response to new material (Color Plate 16):

> If I don't see a picture in my mind when I read a script, I know that play is not for me. The first images are the most important. When I first read *Leonce and Lena*, I saw a road, a colored sky, the sun and I heard Terry Allen's music. As far as content goes, I'm interested in

history and social and political issues. I feel I have a responsibility to work in these areas.[12]

Peter Sellars, who moves back and forth between directing theatre and opera, is concerned about the opportunity for discovery:

> It seems to me that drama is about the search for the unknown. . . . If somebody sends me a play and I understand it, I will never do it. Why spend six weeks in rehearsal? I can understand it just reading it. You need a play that you can't figure out and have to rehearse in order to discover it. I only embark on material that I feel is wide open at the end, when I don't know where the journey will end, don't know what the final production will look or feel like.[13]

Lloyd Richards, who has directed the original productions of many of August Wilson's plays, found that the beliefs articulated by Wilson's characters coincided with his own understanding of human nature. Richards says of reading the plays for the first time:

> There were characters in the play that were well delineated. And the things that they were talking about, I believed. So the playwright, in a sense, was speaking for me as well as to me.[14]

Richards is drawn to Wilson's artistry in expressing a moral position: "He has a very deep sense of social responsibility. He is a repository of unlimited stories which reveal human experience."[15] And the rhythmic structure of the plays inspired Richards's directorial approach: "August Wilson is music. I directed all of his pieces as if they were music."[16]

When directors have a feel for certain material, they sometimes direct a play more than once. Libby Appel, who first directed *Macbeth* in 1987, felt compelled to return to this play at the Oregon Shakespeare Festival in 2002 because she had come to a new understanding of this work.

> I've always wanted to do it differently, in a way that would focus on the psychology of

the event. I wanted to take it out of the spectacular epic and put it in a smaller space to concentrate on the thought processes of the characters.

Since directing *Joe Turner's Come and Gone* at the Oregon Shakespeare Festival, Clinton Turner Davis has directed Wilson's play for the Milwaukee Repertory Theatre and the New Federal Theatre in New York City. Tisa Chang, the artistic director of the Pan Asian Repertory Theatre in New York, directed *And the Soul Shall Dance*, discussed in Chapter 9, twice and produced a third production over a period of fifteen years. She says that she is drawn to Yamauchi's work because of the truth she recognizes in the characters:

> *And the Soul Shall Dance* is so special because it has very strong women's roles. Emiko is a woman who is utterly unfulfilled, unsatisfied, but has great yearnings, intellectual yearnings, artistic yearnings, and very deep feelings, emotional and sensual. There's nothing false, the sexuality, the brutality. Yamauchi really is the central figure and she was writing about issues that were very daring. *And the Soul Shall Dance* is also remarkable because it seems to speak to so many different people at once. We've had audiences, Italian, Jewish, all say, "this is my story."
>
> The play is an actor's paradise. These roles are so meaty. And until then most of the roles for Asian actors on the American stage were abysmally stereotypical images.[17]

The Director's Initial Response to the Play

Just as actors go through a process of discovering the essence or inner life of the characters they will play, so directors go through their own process of discovering the essence or inner life of the play. They build their own understanding of the world of the play before they attempt to communicate their responses to other members of the production team. Directors use many approaches for exploring a play's images, textures, rhythms, characters, and possible meanings. Directors analyze character motivation, but they also listen to music and look at paintings. They study thematic developments, and they also read history. They travel to cities and even foreign countries in search of landscapes or ways of life or performance traditions that may serve the needs of the production. The directorial process is analytical, but it is also intuitive and imaginative.

Creating Metaphors

As a director approaches a play, he or she begins a process of discovering a metaphor, or image, that will translate the ideas of the play into a stage language. The metaphor is a way of expressing the most compelling ideas of the play in a concentrated form that will become a guide for the work of all of the theatre artists involved in the production. A metaphor is an analogy, or comparison, a symbolic way of expressing the action of the play. The founding director of the American Conservatory Theatre in San Francisco, William Ball, emphasizes the need for a single, strong metaphor to guide the work on the production:

> I have learned from my own experiences and from my observations of the work of other directors that the more clear and striking the metaphor, the more unified and powerful the production.[18]

The formulation of a metaphor is a process initiated by the director but very much dependent on the collaboration between the director and the designers. Exactly who will define the nature of the stage imagery and at what point in the process a central metaphor can be determined varies from production to production and depends on the working dynamics of the production team.

For a new production, the process of formulating a metaphor, involving the director and the designers, is usually begun well in advance of the work involving the actors. However, in certain situations when the production process takes months or even years, the designers may work in rehearsal with the actors and make design decisions and changes as the production evolves. Theatrical metaphors must be strong enough to provide a physical shape to a production and open-ended enough that they will engage the imaginations of the theatre artists and the audience members.

Directorial images have a visual component that is crucial to the designers, and the images usually include a sense of the stage action as well that will guide the director in the movement work with the actors. At the Oregon Shakespeare Festival, the director and designers for the 2002 production of *Macbeth* looked for a simple, concentrated image around which to build their work. Shakespeare's *Macbeth* is about the ambition of the title character to become king and then to keep the crown at any cost. This ambition transforms Macbeth from a heroic soldier into a bloody murderer who strikes king and servant, friend and foe, woman and child in a desperate course of spiraling violence. The first key decision made by director Libby Appel was to do the play in the round with the audience surrounding the stage (see page 178).

> I knew that I wanted an empty space and that it was just about the actors telling the story. I wanted the audience to be as "cabined, cribbed, confined" as Macbeth is—so that they would feel the claustrophobia of the small space with Macbeth. There's no escape.

Aware that only minimal visual effects would be possible, the director and the designers turned to the language of the play, the many references to blood, summed up in the following lines spoken by Macbeth, as the source for the production's guiding metaphor.

Will all great Neptune's ocean wash this blood
Clean from my hand? No. This my hand will rather
The multitudinous seas incarnadine,
Making the green one red.[19]

First they decided that a bucket or pool of blood would be placed center stage around which all the action would revolve.

> It grew into this pool of blood that became the cauldron, "fire burn and cauldron bubble." And the whole of the round, the theatre, is the cauldron. And we're all in this cauldron together.

Once the idea of placing a pool of blood onstage was established, the costume designer, Deborah Dryden, concluded that the costumes should be white in order to show the blood (see Color Plate 17), which then evolved into the idea that the "blood should be accumulated all the way through the play with every bloody deed multiplied." The costumes became a canvas that would be painted with the murderous actions of the characters. Finally, the movement director, John Sipes, responsible for staging the fight sequences, saw that the onstage pool of blood should govern the fight choreography. Rather than fighting with swords, the fighting was stylized with the characters dipping into the pool and marking each other with blood where a blow would have opened a wound.

WORKING WITH THE ACTORS

Casting

The first crucial contact the director has with the actors comes during the auditions. Choosing actors wisely is imperative to the success of the entire enterprise. Sometimes actors will be chosen from the kind of open auditions discussed in Chapter 4. Sometimes actors are invited to read for a play, and sometimes actors whom the director has worked with before are simply asked to take a part. Actors in a repertory situation such as the Oregon Shakespeare Festival are cast in several parts for different plays, all at the beginning of the season.

The director must choose actors who are suited to the roles in the play, who have good work habits, and who will work well in the particular configuration of the cast. The right balance and chemistry among the cast members are as important as the talents of individual actors. **Typecasting,** the selection of certain actors because they have a certain type of physical appearance and personality, is still entrenched in some areas of the American theatre, particularly in musicals and summer stock. Although a presence that makes the character believable is essential, more and more directors seek actors who will bring insight and creativity to a role rather than a preconceived physical appearance.

Nontraditional Casting

A recent development in the American theatre involves a rethinking of approaches to casting in terms of race. This shift has resulted in part from the increased participation in the theatre of actors and directors from diverse ethnic groups as well as increased social awareness on the part of theatre producers and directors.

Contemporary productions frequently combine actors from different racial backgrounds—even when playing members of the same family. Such casting is currently referred to as "nontraditional" or "color-blind casting." The director assumes in this kind of casting that the best actor should be cast for the role and that the audience will respond to the group of characters, not to the racial difference of the actors. In some productions, characters are cast specifically with race in mind to bring out certain ideas in the text. As we reevaluate where we are as a nation in terms of race, casting in the theatre will serve as a way of expressing and addressing the diversity of the U.S. population.

The Work Environment

At the heart of the director's responsibilities in the production of a play is his or her work with the actors. This process begins with the audition and continues through the rehearsal period and the first performances. From the beginning of the auditions, the director is responsible for

Director Tony Taccone works with Carl Lumbly, who is playing Macbeth, during a dress rehearsal at the Berkeley Repertory Theatre. Tony Taccone was the codirector of Angels in America *at the Mark Taper Forum.*

creating an atmosphere that is conducive to the creative work of all involved, that ensures respectful consideration of the actors' efforts, and that recognizes the vulnerability inherent in the acting process. Because the actors' progress during the rehearsal period depends on their making open and honest responses, the director must be protective of the working environment. Rehearsals are usually closed to outside observers who might make inappropriate commentary or inhibit the actors' work by making them feel that they are "performing" before they have completed their foundation work. The actors must trust the director, otherwise the process is imperiled. The director who shouts or humiliates an actor immediately shuts down the lines of communication.

The rehearsal should be a time when risks are taken and discoveries are made about the characters' deepest feelings and most compelling motivations. Hidden desires, buried secrets, burdens of the past, ambitions for the future must be teased out during the rehearsal process. The actors must be open not only to the director and themselves but also, perhaps most of all, to each other. The connections between the actors drive a play forward and create a sense of an imagined world come to life. And it is the responsibility of the director to encourage the bonding of the actors and to guide them in making sense of the character relationships.

We have already discussed a number of directorial approaches in our discussion of the production process at different theatres and in the chapter on acting. Although the director usually has a planned structure for the rehearsal process, involving table work, blocking, and character development, the creativity and spontaneity of the director in rehearsals is as important as the creativity of the actors. The director must respond in the moment to the contributions and questions of the actors and the progress of the work. The director may stop a scene that is problematic to set up an improvisation in an attempt to get at deeper, more committed responses from the actors. Or the director may make suggestions for stage business that will physicalize a character's motivation.

The director always functions as the actor's audience to confirm what is being clearly communicated and to help clarify moments when the actor's intention is unclear. The director must maintain the company's focus and do whatever is necessary to inspire a continuous high level of energy and creativity. Although the director may be watching the action quietly, in fact she or he must match and encompass the energy of everyone on the stage.

Ti Jean Blues is an adaptation of the writings of Jack Kerouac by director JoAnne Akalaitis. Staged by Akalaitis for the Humana Festival at Actors Theatre of Louisville, the production emphasizes Kerouac's connection to jazz through the actors' vocal rhythms. Akalaitis drew on the Kathakali theatre of India in working with the actors to develop their gestural expression.

Improvisation

Zelda Fichandler, the founder of the Arena Stage in Washington, D.C., and the director of the graduate theatre program at New York University, uses improvisation as a fundamental part of her rehearsal process. Her improvisation, which tends to be related to a realistic approach to acting, begins immediately after reading and discussing the play. She may have the actors improvise the text of the play in their own words or go back to crucial past events in the characters' lives, such as a wedding anniversary or a car accident.[20] Fichandler also uses improvisation to facilitate the transition from table work to blocking. She sets out props and furniture pieces around the stage and encourages the actors to begin experimenting with character actions. A play that she was directing, *The Ascent of Mount Fuji*, began with a picnic:

> I just had a box of stuff: picnic baskets, jars, hard-boiled eggs, cucumbers, tomatoes, bread. The actors just gathered the stuff up as if they were buying it. We didn't talk about it. We'd already shown slides and pictures of Central Asians and what they ate. So the actors made up their own business and before you knew it, the picnic looked as if it had been worked on for six months. Someone was slicing the cucumbers, someone was peeling apples and somebody else was making tea.[21]

Other directors use improvisational techniques that purposely lead away from a realistic base. JoAnne Akalaitis uses slow-motion improvisations of scenes to increase the actors' awareness of their bodies in space and their physical relationships. She also has the actors experiment with creating gestures to music.[22]

Early in the rehearsals for his production of *The Cherry Orchard*, director Andrei Serban had the actors, who included Irene Worth, play their roles in silence while others read their lines to enable them to investigate character interactions unimpeded by holding a script or searching for lines. Serban also had them do animal improvisations. Irene Worth chose a swan for her character, Madame Ranevskaya, a graceful and elegant woman who has made disastrous choices in her personal life: "I felt that Ranevskaya was a swan. She's very beautiful and she just sails the water in this rather enigmatic, not neurotic way."[23] Serban observed that through the improvisation Worth discovered a ferocious side to the character, "vicious, very fierce, that she could bite."[24] Late in the play, the character loses her usual control and has a brief but intense quarrel with another character. In that quarrel, Worth used the material generated by the improvisation and, in fact, even made a sharp hissing sound that viscerally communicated the character's deep distress.

STAGING THE PLAY

The director's own particular eloquence is expressed through the staging of the play. The director must arrange the actors in the theatrical space and develop sequences of actions that account for the necessary actions required by the script. But this staging of action through spatial relationships goes far beyond serving the practical needs of the script. Like designers, directors should be spatial artists. They compose in space and time with the actors and the scenic elements to interpret the ideas of the play.

The director arranges what is called the **stage picture,** the arrangements of actors onstage to communicate character relationships.

> **THE NECESSARY SKILLS AND TALENTS OF THE DIRECTOR**
>
> - A visual sense
> - A rhythmic sense
> - The ability to analyze dramatic structure
> - The ability to interpret through image and metaphor
> - The ability to work with actors
> - The ability to compose stage action
> - Strong managerial skills
> - Physical stamina
> - Discipline

But unlike a photograph, the stage picture cannot remain static and still hold the audience's attention. Characters cannot appear like posed statues. The stage picture must be dynamic, ever changing. And the composition of the stage picture must direct the audience's attention to the important character or characters while also making clear the relationships among the group of characters. Blocking a play is far more complicated and subtle than merely getting the actors on and off the stage and getting them to do interesting things.

Focus

One of the most important components of directorial composition is focus. By the arrangement of the actors' bodies in the theatrical space the director must guide the audience's attention to a specific actor or to the point on the stage where key actions, reactions, or line deliveries will take place. A film director uses the camera to focus the spectator's attention. With a close-up shot, the camera singles out the significant actor and makes sure that the slightest response is registered clearly for the audience's appreciation. A long shot is used to give a view of the whole scene and then, through editing, the film cuts from actor to actor as the director wishes the spectator's attention to shift from character to character.

Focus is achieved in this scene from Sorrows and Rejoicings *through the placement of the actors and the direction of their attention to the daughter, Rebecca, played by Brienin Nequa Bryant. The three older characters hope that she will accept her father (to her right), which she refuses to do. The play, written and directed by Athol Fugard, explores the difficulties of race relations in South Africa. Rebecca, who is the interracial child of a white father and a black mother, now denies the father whom she was not allowed to acknowledge when she was a child. The production from the Mark Taper Forum also features John Glover, Cynthia Martells, and Judith Light.*

Stage directors, however, cannot employ such editing techniques. The audience views the full stage space continuously and remains at a constant distance from the stage. The director achieves focus through the placement of characters in relation to one another on the stage. Contrast in the visual presentation of the characters is one of the director's most important compositional tools. A character dressed differently from all of the other characters and placed prominently attracts focus. A character separated from a group of characters becomes the focal point (Color Plate 18). Contrast can also be achieved by elevating or lowering the position of the actors onstage. A character who stands while everyone else sits receives focus, and as long as the character is plainly visible, a character who sits or even falls to the floor while everyone else stands receives the focus. A character raised up higher yet on stairs or an elevated platform will receive the focus if the other characters onstage are on a lower level. The focus of the actors will also direct the focus of the audience. If all of the actors are looking at one character, audience attention will follow. Actors may also lean their bodies toward a particular character, or they may hold objects that direct the audience to look in a particular

The Adding Machine, written in 1923 by Elmer Rice, is considered one of the major works of American expressionism. Mr. Zero loses his job after spending twenty-five years in mind-numbing routine. Here his wife Mrs. Zero becomes the focus of the scene through the arrangement of the actors and the use of light and scenic devices in the production at the Actors Theatre of Louisville, directed by Anne Bogart.

direction. The photograph of Herald Loomis on the floor at the end of act 1 of *Joe Turner's Come and Gone* demonstrates several of the principles of stage focus (see page 116).

Spatial Composition and Character Development

In addition to focus, another major function of directorial composition is the communication of character relationships and character development. William Ball compares his spatial work with actors to choreography:

> Picturization is similar to choreography in that the body positions reveal the relationships, independent of the words. My productions usually bear a slight resemblance to ballets, because I tend to picturize as intensely as possible. For example in my production, when the script calls for two people seated on opposite

sides of a table, the one who is winning is usually climbing over the table, and the one who is losing is sliding under the other side.[25]

By expressing the essence of character relationships and individual character development spatially, the director provides a visual telling of a play's story or a visual score just as the playwright's script provides a verbal score. The audience reads the nature of relationships or changes in relationships by the placement of the characters in space and their physical interactions. How close together or far apart are the characters? Do they face each other, or do they face away? Do they touch each other or avoid physical contact? Do the play's events bring the characters together, or do they push the characters apart? Does one character dominate the space while the other shrinks into a less important or a restricted part of the space? Does one character move freely through the space while the other is hesitant? Does one character lead while the other follows? The **progression,** the evolution of the spatial placements, is crucial in defining the progression of the character relationships or character development. Does an independent character who has kept herself apart come to depend on the character she has avoided? Does a character who has moved aggressively through the whole stage space come to occupy a smaller and smaller part of the stage as his power is stripped away?

Plays frequently have strong spatial implications built into their structure that give directors the starting point for their work. A battle for the stage space occurs in a number of plays. The confrontation between the Angel and Prior in act 2, scene 2 of *Perestroika* is a fight for Prior's soul that is realized in physical terms. In *Joe Turner's Come and Gone,* Seth wants to force Loomis out of his house while Loomis is determined to keep his place. In contrast, the sharing of the stage space is central to the supportive character relationships of a play such as *And the Soul Shall Dance.*

Rhythm and Pacing

A play progresses through character development and conflict, through visual imagery, and through rhythm. The rhythmic development and pacing of a play is another of the director's responsibilities. A play has a number of rhythmic components. Each actor's speeches have a certain rhythm as do each actor's movements. Rhythm is in fact an important part of character development. Character rhythms feed into the overall rhythm and pace of the play. Pace is simply the speed at which the production moves. The pace of the play must be slow enough for the audience to comprehend the information they are receiving but fast enough to maintain a sense of forward drive and excitement. Plays frequently accelerate in pace to build the intensity of character conflict or certain moments of revelation. Or the pace may be slowed considerably to allow the characters and the audience

to reflect on some catastrophic event. Pacing that is relentlessly fast is exhausting for an audience, just as pacing that is too slow drains away the audience's energy. The pacing of a play is a crucial way of drawing the audience into the drama unfolding before them.

PREPARING THE PLAY FOR PERFORMANCE

The goal of all the work on a production is always performance. The rehearsal process has its own accelerated pacing as the production moves toward opening night. According to schedule, rehearsals shift from exploration to a tentative shape, from changing and adding details to a completed form. "Run-throughs" of acts and then the whole play take the place of minute work on character and scenes. Rehearsals during which the actors may call for their lines are replaced by rehearsals without interruptions or lapses of concentration. The director brings the play to a point where the actors have confident control of their material and pacing just in advance of the "technical rehearsals."

During the **technical rehearsals** the actors' work receives less focus as the director's attention shifts to the lighting **cues,** the final appearance of the costumes, and the look and movement of the set. It is during the technical rehearsals that all of the details of the production, so long in the planning and development stages, are brought together to create the effect that the director has envisioned. Lighting cues may need to be adjusted and set changes rehearsed until they take an acceptably brief amount of time. The director's capacity to attend to myriad details while moving toward performance is most severely tested at this stage of the process.

After the technical rehearsals and dress rehearsals, **preview** performances are given to allow the actors to finish their work on the play in the presence of an audience. (The preview audience consists of invited individuals or those

Directors actively involve themselves in all aspects of the production. Here, director Gary Sinise consults with lighting designer Rob Milburn during rehearsals for Buried Child, *by Sam Shepard, produced by Steppenwolf Theatre Company, while cast members Leo Burmester and James Gammon wait for their scene to resume. Recognized for his directorial work on the plays of Sam Shepard, Gary Sinise is also a well-known stage and film actor.*

who have bought tickets at reduced prices.) The director continues to work closely with the actors during the preview performances to refine pacing and timing and to make sure that clarity has been achieved. This is the final stage of the director's involvement. When the play officially opens—the moment that all the director's energies have been focused on—the production belongs to the actors, who will continue to draw on the foundation built during the rehearsal process. The director's work is finished.

THE DIRECTOR'S TRAINING

Becoming a director is not unlike training to become an orchestra conductor. Conductors usually study several musical instruments for years before they take on the responsibility for a whole group of musicians. Similarly, directors must have expertise in several areas of theatre before they assume responsibility for coordinating an entire production. Sometimes directors begin their work in the theatre as actors, and their preparation then includes their own work in performance as well as their observation of the methods of the different directors they have worked with. Sometimes directors begin as stage managers, obtaining a foundation in the organization of production details as well as production oversight. Some directors start as scene designers, gaining experience that gives them a strong visual sense. And there are also examples of successful directors who begin as dancers and choreographers. Choreographic skills are extremely important in the placement of actors on the stage and in the development of spatial relationships. Many directors also have strong musical backgrounds, either as practicing musicians or as scholars of many periods and styles of music. Whatever the director's starting point, the successful director must develop skills in all of the areas mentioned.

In addition to those directors who work their way up through theatre companies, there are directors who receive their training from undergraduate and graduate theatre programs. Graduate study in directing usually focuses on the M.F.A. degree, although there are Ph.D. programs that also have a directing component. Frequently, graduate schools expect students to have worked in the theatre as directors before entering their programs. In graduate school, directing students study the analysis of plays and directing methods and often scene design, costume design, and lighting design. Studying the design areas not only builds visual skills but also provides a vocabulary and point of view that facilitates the crucial dialogue between directors and designers. Graduate programs in directing usually involve a minimum of three years of study.

SUMMARY

The director is the "author" of the stage action, the theatre practitioner who unifies all of the elements of performance. Sometimes the director functions as the primary interpreter of the playwright's work, and sometimes the director composes both the drama and the theatrical presentation of the drama.

The modern history of the director began in the late nineteenth century with George II, Duke of Saxe-Meiningen. Directing numerous productions that were influential throughout Europe, the duke emphasized the integration of the elements of spectacle and the authenticity of period costumes and settings. At the turn of the century, Constantin Stanislavsky developed his directorial approach in his work with the plays of Anton Chekhov, which Stanislavsky believed required an ensemble of actors and a more "natural" acting style than had been used previously. Stanislavsky began as a dictatorial director but gradually involved the actors in a more creative partnership.

During the 1960s, Jerzy Grotowski developed the Laboratory Theatre in Wroclaw, Poland. Grotowski was as influential on the theatre of the latter part of the twentieth century as Stanislavsky was on theatre earlier in the century. Grotowski used the texts of playwrights as a springboard for his own ideas and frequently combined more than one source. He was committed to what he called the "poor theatre," using only the simplest, roughest materials for sets and costumes. The actors trained by Grotowski practiced a physical form of acting heavily influenced by Asian performance techniques.

Today, directors take widely differing approaches to staging plays and working with actors. Directors such as Clinton Turner Davis work to interpret the playwright's text. Robert Wilson structures a visual presentation of an idea to which he adds text. Elizabeth LeCompte directs the productions of the Wooster Group in which all participants contribute to the shape of the text and the interpretation of that text. Emily Mann is a playwright who frequently directs her own plays. Many directors rely on the creative contributions of the actors, although some expect the actors to follow their (the directors') expressive choices.

Many directors have the freedom to choose plays that they find inspiring. Through a collaborative process, the director and the designers evolve a metaphor, or image, that guides the work on the production. The director selects actors who are suited to the roles of the play and the style of the production. The director is responsible for creating a rehearsal atmosphere that encourages the actors to be open with one another and to take creative risks.

In rehearsal, the director faces two major tasks: to guide the interpretive work of the actors and to stage the play's action. Through the arrangement of the actors on the stage, the director clarifies the character relationships and the plot elements. The director pays close attention to the expression of the play's rhythms through the actors' speeches, movements, entrances and exits, and the pacing of their interactions. During the technical rehearsals and preview performances, the director works with the designers, the technical staff, and the crews to finalize all details of the production.

TOPICS FOR DISCUSSION AND WRITING

1. Review the principles of directorial composition related to focus. Find photographs and paintings of groups of people in which the composition is arranged to focus on one or only a few people. Use magazines, newspapers, collections of photographs, or books on painters, but do *not* use photographs of theatre productions. Bring five pictures to class that clearly establish focus, each through a different element of composition and contrast. Examine the pictures together to see the range of possibilities for spatial composition assembled by the class. What kinds of statements about relationships do the photographs convey? If space and time permit, select some of the most striking compositions and re-create the relationships between the people in the photographs using members of the class.

2. Observe people in different situations and environments to see how they respond to each other in terms of space. Choose one situation that involves a significant negotiation over space, and write a short paper in which you describe the nature of the interaction. For example, you might observe someone trying to maneuver someone else to get the largest share of the space or the most comfortable chair. Someone conducting a job interview might dominate the space while the interviewee takes up as little space as possible. People involved in an argument might try to assert themselves by expanding their physical position. Find a spatial interaction that you think communicates strong motivations, and write a detailed description of approximately one page.

NOTES

1. All comments by Libby Appel in Chapter 5 are from an interview with the author, 17 July 2002.

2. Harold Clurman, "In a Different Language," in *Directors on Directing*, ed. Toby Cole and Helen Krich Chinoy (New York: Bobbs-Merrill, 1963), 275.

3. Peter Brook, *There Are No Secrets: Thoughts on Acting and Theatre* (London: Methuen, 1993), 25.

4. Brook, 52–53.

5. Jerzy Grotowski, "Towards a Poor Theatre," in *Towards a Poor Theatre*, ed. Jerzy Grotowski (New York: Simon and Schuster, 1968), 17.

6. Jerzy Grotowski, quoted in Naim Kattan, "Theatre Is an Encounter: An Interview with Jerzy Grotowski," in Grotowski, 58.

7. Ludwik Flaszen, "*Akropolis:* Treatment of the Text," in Grotowski, 62.

8. Grotowski, 164.

9. Vsevolod Meyerhold, quoted in Helen Krich Chinoy, "The Emergence of the Director," in Cole and Chinoy, 55.

10. Declan Donellan, quoted in Maria M. Delgado and Paul Heritage, *In Contact with the Gods? Directors*

Talk Theatre (Manchester: Manchester University Press, 1996), 89.

11. Elizabeth LeCompte, quoted in David Savran, *The Wooster Group, 1975–1985: Breaking the Rules* (Ann Arbor: Books on Demand, 1986), 115–16.

12. JoAnne Akalaitis, quoted in Arthur Bartow, *The Director's Voice* (New York: Theatre Communications Group, 1988), 4.

13. Peter Sellars, quoted in Bartow, 276.

14. Lloyd Richards, quoted in April Austin, "Lloyd Richards and August Wilson: A Winning Partnership Plays On," *Christian Science Monitor,* 18 September 1995, 13.

15. Lloyd Richards, quoted in "Theater-Maker at Yale," *Fairpress* (Norwalk, Conn., 21 June 1990), F3.

16. Richards, quoted in "Theater-Maker at Yale," F3.

17. Tisa Chang, interview with the author, 23 June 1995.

18. William Ball, *A Sense of Direction* (New York: Drama Book Publishers, 1984), 36.

19. Shakespeare, William, *Macbeth* (New York: Applause, 1996), 46.

20. Bartow, 118.

21. Zelda Fichandler, quoted in Bartow, 119.

22. Bartow, 5–6.

23. Irene Worth, quoted in Lally Weymouth, "In Order to Achieve Real Wings in Chekhov You Just Live It," *New York Times,* 6 March 1977, 24.

24. Andrei Serban, quoted in Richard Eder, "Andrei Serban," *New York Times,* 13 February 1977, sec. 6, p. 53.

25. Ball, 111.

SUGGESTIONS FOR FURTHER READING

Ball, William. *A Sense of Direction.* New York: Drama Book Publishers, 1984.

> An accessible discussion of the art of directing that is particularly strong in analyzing the relationship between directors and actors.

Bogart, Anne. *A Director Prepares: Seven Essays on Art and Theatre.* New York: Routledge, 2001.

> An investigation of the creative process from the perspective of the director, Bogart explores artistic choices through thoughtful responses to her own work and the work of other directors and artists.

Brecht, Bertolt. *Brecht on Theatre.* New York: Hill and Wang, 1964.

> A collection of Brecht's writings on the theatre in which he presents detailed examples of putting theory into practice, explaining epic theatre and alienation in acting, music, and directing. Brecht discusses his own plays, the influence of the Chinese theatre, and his responses to Stanislavsky.

Cole, Toby, and Helen Krich Chinoy, eds. *Directors on Directing.* New York: Bobbs-Merrill, 1963.

> A book that begins with a good history of directing, starting with developments in the nineteenth century; includes statements on directing by a number of prominent directors working from about 1850 to 1960 as well as directorial notes and plans from famous productions.

Delgado, Maria, and Paul Heritage. *In Contact with the Gods? Directors Talk Theatre.* New York: Manchester University Press, 1996.

> A collection of interviews with an international group of the most prominent directors working today; includes an introduction to the career of each director.

Diamond, David, and Terry Berliner, eds. *Stage Directors Handbook: Opportunities for Directors and Choreographers.* New York: Theatre Communications Group, 1998.

> A resource book for aspiring directors that details training programs, theatre opportunities, the acquisition of agents and managers, and helpful books and periodicals; includes discussions by young directors on how they started their own theatre companies.

Grotowski, Jerzy. *Towards a Poor Theatre.* New York: Simon and Schuster, 1968.

> A detailed discussion of the theory and practice of Grotowski's Laboratory Theatre in Poland; includes photographs and acting exercises that help to clarify Grotowski's highly stylized theatre, which focused almost exclusively on the art of the actor.

Shyer, Lawrence. *Robert Wilson and His Collaborators.* New York: Theatre Communications Group, 1989.

> An exploration of the ways in which Robert Wilson approaches performance and his methods of collaborating with actors, writers, designers, and musicians.

Taymor, Julie, and Eileen Blumenthal. *Playing with Fire.* New York: Harry N. Abrams, 1995.

> A history and exploration of the career of Julie Taymor, who combines her work as a director and designer to create visually arresting productions

that draw particularly on international influences and puppet and mask traditions; includes many reproductions of design and production photos.

Williams, David. *Peter Brook: A Theatrical Casebook.* London: Methuen, 1988.

A compilation of rehearsal descriptions, interviews, and reviews that document Brook's directorial approach and his aesthetic and social concerns. Peter Brook is one of the most influential directors of the second half of the twentieth century and is known for a number of groundbreaking productions.

CHAPTER 6

The Designers

Stage design—the work of the scene designer, the costume designer, the lighting designer, and the sound designer—is an essential part of what makes the audience experience in the theatre a magical one. Stage design, together with the presence of the actor, creates a world apart from the life outside of the theatre's boundaries. The designers create a poetry of space, visual and aural, that brings the stage to life with startling images and creates an eloquent foundation for the actor's work.

On the cover of this book is a photograph of a scene from *Metamorphoses*, a play about transformations directed and adapted by Mary Zimmerman. Taken from Greek myths about life and death, love and rebirth, the text of *Metamorphoses* offers a collection of beloved stories that distill essences of human experience. To tell these ancient stories in today's theatre, designers Daniel Ostling (set), Mara Blumenfeld (costumes), and TJ Gerckens (lights) joined images of the past and present to create a place that seems to float in the imagination. A huge golden door provides the entrance to the playing space; clouds on a panel of blue make a home for the gods; a crystal chandelier hangs above, suggesting the many possibilities of light; and a large pool of water provides the stage for much of the action where humans and gods meet and

For The Master and Margarita *produced by Seattle's Theater Simple, Paul Bohlke faced the challenge of creating a set that could suggest many locations and be completely portable for touring to spaces with widely differing stages. Bohlke designed a group of white rolling screens that could be quickly reconfigured by the cast and lit from behind to create a variety of images with shadows.*

struggle with life's mysteries. The costumes mingle flowing robes and gowns reminiscent of Greek dress with elements of contemporary style. Modern theatre lights focused from above are augmented by lanterns and candles handled by the actors. Tying all of the design elements together is the large pool of water. The water reinforces the movements of the actors, becoming playful or highly dramatic. And the water is full of metaphoric significance as it suggests many of life's passages.

The stage speaks with color and shape, with light and shadow, with music and sound. The flight of an angel, a boardinghouse seen against a city skyline, a rolling piece of tumbleweed, the haunting sound of a shakuhachi flute, the lyrics of a blues song—these images from productions discussed in this book appeal to the senses. The designers engage the audience with sensory information to locate the actor physically and psychologically and to support the ideas of the text.

STAGECRAFT AND THE THEATRE

The actor and the director are artists who are made for the theatre. Their skills and talents are wholly claimed by the theatre itself. Designers,

on the other hand, have skills and talents that they share with other visual artists, sound artists, and craftspeople. Scene designers have drafting and construction skills. Costume designers work with fabrics and have cutting, sewing, and dyeing skills. Many scene and costume designers also have extensive training in drawing, painting, sculpture, and/or architecture. Lighting designers create with a broad range of electrical instruments and control boards. Sound designers work with music, sound effects, recording equipment, and amplifiers. If designers do not sew or do carpentry or work with electricity themselves, they must clearly understand the properties of the materials they incorporate in their designs. But no matter how many overlapping abilities designers share with visual artists or craftspeople, like actors and directors they are interpretive artists whose creativity must be used to shape the world of the play or the theatre piece. A designer's work of art does not stand alone onstage as an individual creation but interprets the ideas of the play with materials just as the actors shape ideas with their voices and bodies.

Much of our discussion of the theatre has to do with the serious interpretation of serious subjects. But whether the material is comedy or tragedy, spontaneity and playfulness are crucial to theatre work and part of the theatre's great appeal to its participants. The possibility for creative problem solving, for tackling curious challenges that most people never have the opportunity to take on, is part of the basic work of the stage designers and technicians. The following examples demonstrate some of the intriguing problems designers are called on to address.

- For the New York production of *Angels in America*, the staff faced the problem of flying the angel in such a way that she could perform her aerial gymnastics without catching her wires in her very elaborate costume.

- In *Fool Moon*, Bill Irwin and David Shiner make a surprising and eloquent exit at the end of their mime play on a moon (see Color Plate 2). The inner glow that gave the moon its charm posed a difficult problem for lighting designer Nancy Schertler, who had to create a light strong enough to be dazzling without revealing the twenty-four lighting instruments inside the structure responsible for the effect.

- For a production of Wagner's *Ring* at the San Francisco Opera, lighting designer Tom Munn experimented with an effect of fog hovering a few feet off the ground—fog that he hoped would stay in place for twenty minutes.

- For the production of *Macbeth* discussed in Chapter 6, costume designer Deborah Dryden needed to find white fabric for the costumes that could be stained with "blood" at each performance and then washed and dried for the next performance, sometimes on the same day when there was a matinee and an evening show.

Bodies need to disappear and ghosts walk the earth; costumes and sets must be changed in a matter of seconds; ships must sail across the sea; or a mountain must give the appearance of snow and ice. Theatrical design requires continuous imaginative thinking, first to visualize the image in response to the needs of the play and then to come up with the technological solution that will make it possible.

THE THEATRICAL SPACE

The first condition that governs the work of all the designers is the nature of the theatrical space, the relationship between the audience and the stage. The size and atmosphere of theatres in the United States vary widely, from the traditional elegance of Broadway to the modern comfort of large regional theatres such as the Oregon Shakespeare Festival and the Mark Taper Forum to the small and sometimes cramped spaces of equity waiver theatres such as East West Players (Chapter 9) and the Eureka Theatre (Chapter 11).

The common denominator for all theatre spaces is their three-dimensionality. In contrast, movie audiences sit in front of a large flat screen on which filmed images give the impression of dimensional space, but that sense of depth is in fact an illusion created by the camera. In the theatre, the dimensionality of the stage space is actual. For this reason, the audience space and the stage space can be arranged in different configurations. The audience relationship to the screen at the movies, however, always remains the same.

The Proscenium Theatre

In many large theatres, such as the Oregon Shakespeare Festival's Bowmer Theatre and Broadway theatres, the audience sits opposite the stage, facing what is called the **proscenium** (Color Plate 19). A proscenium theatre refers to a theatre constructed in a rectangular form with the stage at one end of the rectangle. The stage opening follows the rectangular form of the space as if the audience were looking through one end of a box. The audience's view is shaped by a framing device that defines the

The proscenium stage began its evolution in the Italian Court Theatre of the sixteenth century; painted scenery and lavish special effects became an increasingly important part of stage spectacle. A framing device, the proscenium arch, was placed around the scenic spectacle to define the boundaries of the picture and to hide the backstage activity. Eventually, the rectangular proscenium theatre became a home to realism. The proscenium theatre is also distinguished by the separation that it creates between actors and audience, thereby reinforcing the completeness of the stage illusion. Represented here is a modern proscenium stage with a set designed by Cliff Faulkner for Blithe Spirit *at South Coast Repertory Theatre.*

rectangular opening called the **proscenium arch.** The proscenium arch is like a picture frame. The stage frame of the proscenium masks the mechanics of the backstage operations and creates a clearly defined theatrical space that is particularly suited to realism. The opening of the proscenium arch can be covered by a curtain, which also functions as a masking device to allow scene changes out of the view of the audience. Today, however, many styles of theatre other than realism are presented on proscenium stages, and rectangular stages that lack a curtain or even a defined frame are referred to as proscenium stages.

Thrust, Arena, and Black Box Stages

In contrast to the seating arrangement in a proscenium theatre, some theatres are designed to allow the audience to sit on three sides of the stage, which may be rectangular or rounded in its shape. The three-sided arrangement is called a **thrust stage.** The thrust stage extends into the audience, and different sections of seating look across to other seating areas. The audience members in a thrust situation are much more aware of the presence of other audience members than they would be in a proscenium arrangement and are therefore more likely to be conscious of their own presence in a theatre watching a play. When the audience sits surrounding the entire stage space, the configuration is referred to as **arena staging,** or **theatre in the round,** whether the stage space is an actual circle or a square with the audience on four distinct sides.

Theatre architecture is frequently permanent; that is, a theatre building is constructed so

The thrust stage is historically connected to the Greek and Shakespearian theatres, where the audience was placed around three sides of the stage. A thrust stage allows for a close relationship between actors and audience members. Theatre historians speculate that the soliloquies of Shakespearian characters such as Hamlet would have been played in very close proximity to the audience so that overhearing the character's thoughts would have seemed very natural. Actors working on thrust stages frequently make entrances through the auditorium, reinforcing the integration of the audience space and the stage space. In this scene from Damn Yankees, *produced on a thrust stage at Pacific Conservatory of the Performing Arts, the scenic units are placed at the back of the stage, and the actors are angled to play to audience members seated on three sides. The scene design is by R. Eric Stone.*

that the actor-audience relationship always remains the same. Sometimes a theatre plant will have more than one stage, as the Oregon Shakespeare Festival does; this arrangement allows the staging of plays in different kinds of spaces. Sometimes a theatre space will be constructed specifically so that the stage space itself can be flexible. Small theatres and colleges frequently have what are called **black box** spaces that can be arranged differently depending on

The arena stage is surrounded on all sides by audience seating. The arena stage emerged from performance traditions in which ceremonial plays were performed in community plazas. The morality plays of medieval times, at which audience members sat on the hillsides of a natural amphitheatre, are one of the best-known historical uses of arena staging. Today the arena stage provides an intimate relationship between actors and audience members. Scenic elements must be carefully scaled and arranged to protect the audience view. The emphasis in the performance is on the actors. The Oregon Shakespeare Festival has recently opened a new theatre with an arena stage, shown here for the 2002 production of Macbeth. *The pool of blood in the center was the only constant scenic element beyond the structure of the stage itself. Two chairs were brought on for the banquet scene to suggest the thrones of the Macbeths.*

the needs of the specific production. A found space can also function as a flexible theatre. The Omaha Magic Theatre performed in an old department store. The audience members sat in swivel chairs that allowed them to turn to any part of the space. The store elevator and staircases provided intriguing entrances and additional playing spaces.

The Implications of Theatre Architecture for Designers

Thrust and arena stages have neither the masking of the proscenium arch nor curtains that can

block the stage from the audience's view. Therefore, all set changes must be done in view of the audience. In the production of *And the Soul Shall Dance* at East West Players, the set changes were performed by costumed actors, kurokos, whose choreographed movements were an integral part of the play that was important for the audience to see. In *Angels in America*, the actors themselves changed the set, but during scene changes they projected a neutral persona rather than portraying one of their characters from the play. In other productions, the lights are dimmed for the set changes, which are performed by stagehands in dark clothes who move quickly and quietly across the stage space, changing or rearranging the set as efficiently as possible. In theatres with sophisticated physical plants and large budgets, scenic units may be moved mechanically across the stage or on a revolving platform, or they may be flown in from above. The movement of scenery in musicals is frequently choreographed to the music and becomes part of the visual spectacle.

Each spatial configuration makes different kinds of demands on the designers. In a proscenium arrangement, the audience cannot see the back of set pieces, which therefore do not have to be finished; in theatre in the round, however, every object on the stage has to be completely finished because it can be seen from all angles. Towering set pieces or backgrounds can be used on proscenium stages or at the back of a thrust stage, whereas set pieces on an arena stage must be designed not to block the view of anyone in the audience. All kinds of ingenious solutions have been developed for arena stages to allow the audience to look over or through stage objects. Costumes and properties become the design focus in arena or thrust staging. The size of the stage and the size of the audience area are also important factors in determining the scale of the scenery and the detail of the sets and costumes.

Three-Dimensional Space

Although the shape of each stage configuration presents unique problems and opportunities, the basic notion of three-dimensional space remains the same. The director and the designers are composing in space. The costume designer and the lighting designer are particularly concerned with shaping the body of the actor. The costume designer creates a silhouette; the lighting designer molds that silhouette. The scene designer creates the physical environment that contains and defines the figures shaped by the costume designer and the lighting designer. The director creates meaningful relationships between the figures of the actors within the space defined by the set designer. Ultimately, the lighting designer unifies all of the stage elements, including the figure of the actor.

MEETINGS AND INTERACTIONS

Once rehearsals begin, the actors and the director become a tight unit and do almost all of their work on the play together, developing their ideas about the play as an ensemble. The designers spend as much time in rehearsal as possible to see the blocking, to get a sense of character development and relationships, to monitor how a costume piece, a prop, a lighting choice will work. But much of their work is done before the rehearsal process begins, and much is done away from the process going on in the rehearsal hall. To illustrate how theatre design evolves, we examine the unique collaborative processes of two productions: we return to the Oregon Shakespeare Festival's production of *Joe Turner's Come and Gone* and then shift our attention to the Public Theatre's (New York) production of the musical *Bring in da Noise Bring in da Funk*.

Because *Joe Turner's Come and Gone* was to open in Ashland in February, the director, Clinton Turner Davis, began meeting with the designers in October. Conflicting work schedules necessitated design meetings in New York, Los Angeles, and Ashland in restaurants and hotel rooms as well as at the theatre. Usually only two or three of the four central production staff members could be present at any one time. This is typical of the American professional theatre. Most directors and designers work for more than one theatre, and frequent travel is not an unusual part of their lives. Geography becomes part of the design process.

At the design meetings, the discussions shifted back and forth between highly practical matters and more abstract images and feelings. The scene and costume designers brought in examples of their initial research. Scene designer Mike Fish studied photographs and

SUMMARY OF THE DESIGNERS' RESPONSIBILITIES

- *Costume and scene designers*—prepare sketches and then color renderings of sets and costumes to provide visual definition of designs; develop complete designs that meet the needs of the production, the theatre, and the budget
- *Lighting designer*—prepare a light plot that indicates the position and angle of all lighting instruments; arrange for any additional instruments or materials for special effects
- *Sound designer*—identify cues and collect or compose sounds or musical pieces

All designers:
- Read the play carefully and research possible sources
- Collaborate with the director and the other designers to arrive at a production concept
- Prepare appropriate breakdown of design elements (blueprints, elevations, hook-ups) to allow support technicians to construct sets and costumes and to hang lights and prepare cues
- Attend rehearsals to monitor necessary changes in designs
- Maintain a dialogue with other designers and the director
- Supervise the construction of sets and costumes, and where appropriate, execute the most difficult processes such as painting and dyeing
- Work through the period of technical and dress rehearsals to make all necessary adjustments

engravings of Pittsburgh at the turn of the century as well as period wallpapers and furniture found in old Sears Roebuck catalogues. He found a very useful book, *Blast Furnaces*, that contained photographs of steel mills from places around the world, including Pittsburgh. The photographs of the steel mills in Pittsburgh

eventually were influential in the backdrop that Mike Fish designed for the space behind the boardinghouse.

Photographs were also a very important research source for costume designer Candice Cain, who used the picture collection at the New York City Public Library extensively. She was also able to bring her own collection of photographs to the meetings; these were period pictures of African American families in posed groups and at picnics that had been preserved by an African American photographer. The photographs offered valuable details of dress and accessories as well as more intangible evidence of attitude and bearing. Early on in the design meetings, an image was settled upon that had a major impact on all the designers. For Clinton Turner Davis, seeing the play in historical terms was essential, but he saw it as a memory. Consequently, the decision was made to use the idea of an old sepia photograph as a visual guide for the look of the production.

Other considerations affect the organization of the design work in general at Ashland. Because the company performs in repertory, the scene shop must build several sets at once, and the light plot needs to accommodate four productions at once. The **light plot** designates the placement of all the lighting instruments hung at various positions in the theatre. Neither the positions nor the angle of the lights can be changed between performances of different plays in Ashland, although some color changes are possible. The intricate scheduling problems generated by a repertory system demand maximum efficiency in organization as well as a fundamental cooperation between all the members of the production staff and the actors. As such, the basic designs for *Joe Turner's Come and Gone* were well under way before rehearsals began.

For the musical *Bring in da Noise Bring in da Funk*, the design process was quite different from the advanced planning done at Ashland. The idea for the musical grew out of discussions between George C. Wolfe, the director of the Public Theatre in New York, and Savion

Glover, a young but remarkably experienced choreographer and tap dancer. They began with a concept, not a written script. The show, which took the form of a series of thematically related scenes built around music and dance, developed in an improvisational workshop process at the Public Theatre (Color Plate 20).

A group of dancers and musicians began working with Wolfe at the Public Theatre in August 1995. Even without a script, large amounts of research—in American history and black dance—accompanied and supported the explorations of the performers. A month and a half before the opening, the designers put aside any preconceived notions they had about the material and began sitting in on the rehearsals.[1] Scene designer Riccardo Hernandez, lighting designers Jules Fisher and Peggy Eisenhauer, projection specialist Robin Silvestri, and costume designer Paul Tazewell created their designs in response to the evolving musical numbers, the intense rhythm of the drumming and tap dancing, and the emotional content of the scenes. The designers were as inspired as the dancers and the director by the creative freedom of working without a script. The designs continued to grow and change when the production moved from the 299-seat Newman Theatre at the Public to the 1,000-seat Ambassador Theatre on Broadway. We will return to *Bring in da Noise Bring in da Funk* in Chapter 7.

THE HISTORY
OF SCENE DESIGN

The history of scene design moves back and forth between periods featuring open theatre spaces with little scenic definition and periods when the scenic environment is of utmost importance to the presentation of the drama. The Greek theatre in the fifth century B.C.E., the Elizabethan theatre, and the Chinese theatre are all examples of theatres that used neutral playing spaces defined through character action, language, or minimal use of properties.

The Roman and the medieval theatres began to show considerable interest in scenic effect. But it was in the court theatres of the Renaissance and Baroque periods throughout Europe that stage design generated great enthusiasm and remarkable ingenuity. Some of the leading inventors and artists of the time—including Leonardo da Vinci—contributed their skills to the theatre.

To imagine the energy and resources that went into the effects of the Renaissance theatre, the contemporary film industry provides a useful comparison. Film studios spend tens of millions of dollars on intergalactic special effects, stunts, models of cities or space ships, hundreds or thousands of elaborate costumes, and the most advanced technology in cameras and sound. This was the kind of fascination that swept the court and later the public theatres. During the Renaissance not only was perspective scenery painted lavishly with palatial interiors or mythical lands, but stunning special effects were also executed with dazzling results. Fifty angels at a time could rise to the heavens on cloud units called **glories.** The stage floor could be made to resemble the ocean, with dolphins and whales diving through the waves. Mythical figures flew across the stage on the backs of animals or birds. Buildings collapsed, and actors appeared in the midst of flames. Stupendous costumes matched the scenic invention.

In the nineteenth century, the introduction of scenic realism was a continuation of the Renaissance ideal of an integrated scenic background or environment for the drama. But the realistic stage focused on the limitations of human existence rather than on the fantasies dramatized in earlier centuries. And in the hands of American directors and designers of the late nineteenth and early twentieth centuries, such as Steele McKay and David Belasco, realism turned into a spectacle of its own, with rivers running across the stage and fifteen-minute sunsets.

Design for the contemporary theatre includes the aesthetics of both the open, neutral

Paul Clay's set design for Rent *uses ladders and scaffolding to provide multiple levels and playing spaces. With only minimal changes in the placement of furniture, the space can become the interior of an old factory divided into makeshift apartments, a restaurant, the street, or a church. Folding tables and chairs, garbage cans, and materials scrounged from a junkyard create an environment for lives lived in poverty and under improvised circumstances. Objects are used in practical and symbolic ways. A paper Japanese lantern is both a light and the moon. A metal sculpture serves as a Christmas tree, a wood stove, and a church steeple. Integrated with a few realistic details, the design provides a complex terrain for the play's action.*

playing space and some form of elaborate scenic background. Broadway musicals usually use very elaborate scenic effects as do the productions of Robert Wilson, although with different goals and a different impact on the audience. Contemporary productions of Shakespeare are frequently, although not exclusively, produced on some kind of open stage, relying on the talents of the actors and the language they speak to express the essence of the world of the play. And elements of the two approaches can be combined in different ways. In both types of staging, the work of the costume and lighting

designers has a great deal to do with completing the visual statement of the production. On an open stage, however, the costumes and lights take on particular expressive significance.

At the beginning of the twentieth century, when a fusion of realism and spectacular effects dominated the European and American theatres, a quiet Swiss scene designer, Adolphe Appia (1862–1928), proposed a radical change in scene design. Appia was an idealist searching for a way to merge music, acting, scenery, and light into an integrated expression of the drama. Appia's research in the theatre was aimed at

In the scene design by R. Eric Stone for Julius Caesar *in an arena configuration at the Pacific Conservatory of the Performing Arts, the floor was created as a terrain, providing levels for the actors that would allow for effective staging without blocking the audience view. The actors entered the stage from the audience area, and scaffolds were placed above the aisles to allow for additional playing spaces that took the action farther into the auditorium.*

various levels that would help shape the movement of the actor. Through a combination of ramps, steps, and playing areas of different heights, Appia designed a **terrain** for the action of the drama that would have rhythmic implications as well as visual ones.

A multileveled stage provides many expressive possibilities for arranging groups of actors. The stage picture formulated by the director is greatly facilitated when the possible positions for the actors are increased vertically as well as horizontally. Steps and ramps also provide for movement patterns and in fact dictate a rhythm of movement through the number of steps and the distances that may be measured in the actors' movements. Appia was interested in supporting the moving figure of the actor as the focus of the performance. He believed in stripping away unnecessary details of spectacle because they detracted from a focus on the actor.

He encouraged the use of light instead to bring color to the stage and create mood and atmosphere through the creative use of shadows. Foremost in his writings on the theatre were his observations on the way that light can define and reveal the moving figure of the actor. Experimentation with the expressive possibilities of light was in its infancy. Appia understood the potential of light as a transformative element in theatre design that would take on a new partnership with both the drama and the actor.

finding the most eloquent way to stage the operas of Richard Wagner. His conclusions about the possibilities of the stage space in combination with new uses of lighting had a lasting effect on the development of scenic and lighting practices throughout the twentieth century.

Appia advocated a return to the idea of the open playing space and the elimination of painted scenery and all realistic objects. However, rather than the flat platform of the Elizabethan or Chinese stages, Appia thought that the stage floor should be broken up into

SCENE DESIGN TODAY

Designing The Grapes of Wrath

Scene design today may emphasize an elaborate scenic background or an architectural shaping of space. The scenic elements may be realistic or abstract; they may be constructed of simple or highly finished materials. The design may acknowledge the architectural definitions of the theatre or attempt to disguise or transform the space. To explore some of the concepts of theatre architecture and scene design that have been introduced thus far, we turn to the scene

The setting for the Hartford Stage Company's production of Romeo and Juliet, *designed by Michael Yeargan, recalls the architectural simplicity suggested by Adolphe Appia. The characters are set in sharp relief against the few basic scenic structures as Juliet (Calista Flockhart) and her mother, Lady Capulet (Mary Layne), confront each other over whom Juliet is to marry; the Nurse (Roberta Maxwell) looks on.*

design for a specific production at the Pacific Conservatory of the Performing Arts.[2]

R. Eric Stone was the resident scene designer at the Pacific Conservatory of the Performing Arts in Santa Maria, California. In 1997 he designed the scenery for a production of *The Grapes of Wrath*, a play by Frank Galati adapted from the novel by John Steinbeck. The play chronicles the geographical and emotional journey of Tom Joad and his family as they search for a new beginning following the loss of their farm to the dust bowl and the Great Depression. In designing *The Grapes of Wrath*, Stone faced a number of challenges—interpretive, logistical, and technological—as he worked to create a visual expression of the conditions governing the characters' lives. The theatre at Santa Maria has a thrust stage, and so

the design needed to accommodate the sight lines of an audience seated on three sides of the playing space. Furthermore, the play itself is written as a journey with multiple scenes and locations. The play also calls for several specific scenic effects: a truck capable of movement that carries thirteen characters, a river in which a number of characters immerse themselves, and falling rain.

Stone designed three major scenic units—a barn door, the truck, and a suspended, sculptural construction—that together formed the visual interpretation of the world inhabited by the characters. The set pieces were designed to provide spatial definition for the stage without compromising any audience member's view. All three scenic structures were composed of rough materials.

The model of the set for The Grapes of Wrath *shows two of the three basic scenic units: the barn door and the abstract sculptural unit rising above it. Such scale models of set designs provide a three-dimensional representation of the stage that is of great value to the director and the actors as well as to the technical staff.*

Together, the three units gave the environment a weathered, fragile, and decaying appearance; separately, each unit had a different function in the production. The scenic unit we refer to as the "barn door" was used to indicate the different structures associated with the characters' journey. It was moved to different locations on the stage to suggest new places. In the first scene only one edge was visible, enough to create an impression of the Joad house; in a later scene it represented a railroad boxcar; in another scene it became an actual barn. As the placement of the door changed, the entire stage was transformed according to the new location implied by this simple piece of scenery. In the tradition of the medieval theatre, a small symbolic scenic unit defined the entire playing space. This device provided the flexibility needed for the multiple scenes of the play within the limitations of a thrust stage. It also provided a physical dwelling or building to frame the character action, and it expressed thematic content through its frayed surface.

The battered old truck was constructed with far more realistic detail than the other set pieces, adding visual texture to the stage. The truck was a concentrated symbol of the journey, a dilapidated, jerry-built mode of transportation, requiring continuous ingenuity to keep it running until it, too, was lost. The truck also functioned in a practical way to carry the actors and to allow staging opportunities through the placement of actors on and around the vehicle.

The sculptural unit at the back of the stage was abstract in comparison to the other scenic pieces. Elevated about ten feet above the stage floor and extending up to a height of twenty-four feet, the vertical construction was made from the same slats of wood as the barn door. It created a looming presence, ominous and oppressive. Streaks of red paint at the top suggested the blood and bitterness of the characters' lives. The appearance of the sculptural unit, however, could be changed dramatically through the contribution of lighting designer Michael Peterson. Amber light on the weathered wood created a sense of warmth on the stage; blue light created a colder atmosphere. **Gobos,** stenciled cutouts placed inside lighting instruments to produce a patterned effect, were also projected onto the structure to give additional texture to its surface through slashes of color or through more realistic leaf patterns. The set piece could be lit from behind to outline its shapes in silhouette and cast shadows on the stage floor. When a scene change placed the characters on the desert at night, tiny lights, called "grains of wheat," were used to shine through the open spaces of the structure to create the impression of stars. And finally, by eliminating all light on the structure, the set piece could be made to disappear.

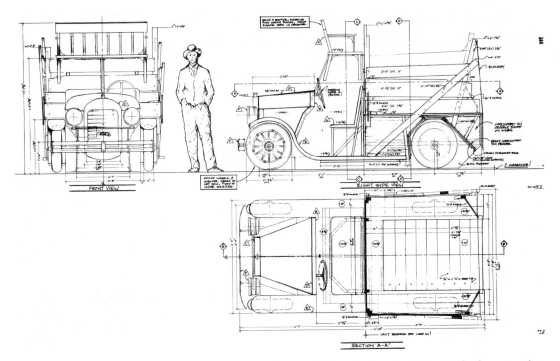

The scene designer provides technical drawings of the scenic elements as blueprints for the construction of each unit.

The truck is the most detailed scenic element in the design for The Grapes of Wrath, *providing a visual statement of the journey and the condition of the characters' lives.*

The scene design also included the construction of the stage floor. Traps were built into the floor to allow for fire effects created through light and for the burial of one of the characters who dies on the way. And around the outer edge of the stage a trough was constructed to hold enough water to make the river. Panels of the stage floor covered the river and could be folded back to reveal the water. The river then formed another level, with the actors in the water fully visible below the actors standing or sitting on the stage. The placement of the river also allowed for the parallel placement of a pipe above the stage that could release rain that would fall into the river, keeping the stage floor dry. For about twelve minutes, the actors were seen through a curtain of rain.

The scene design for *The Grapes of Wrath* demonstrates a combined use of realistic and abstract design elements created for a thrust stage. The design elements for this production shaped the stage space, placed the play geographically and temporally, and reflected the hardships faced by the characters. The design was realized through a minimal amount of scenery in keeping with the imaginative structure of the play and the impoverished lives of the

The full cast of The Grapes of Wrath *appears in the scenic environment designed for the thrust stage at the Pacific Conservatory of the Performing Arts.*

characters (Color Plate 21). We now turn to two additional productions—*Blithe Spirit* and *Belches on Couches*—that demonstrate other approaches to design in the contemporary American theatre.

Realism and Blithe Spirit

A fully realistic design involves a much more detailed rendering of the environmental circumstances of the characters' lives than the suggestive design elements in *The Grapes of Wrath*. *Blithe Spirit*, by English playwright Noel Coward, is a ghost story in which the spirit of the title, Elvira, comes back to haunt her husband, Charles, and his second wife, Ruth. For a production of *Blithe Spirit* at South Coast Repertory, shown on page 176, scenic designer Cliff Faulkner created a mostly realistic set. The realism of the design was deliberately undercut by an image of the playwright placed above the set to make clear from the

outset that this was a comedy and that one must expect the unexpected. Eventually, the set took an active part in the comic mishaps that befall the haunted characters. At the beginning of the play, however, the set presented an environment of grace and breeding for wealthy, upper-class characters. The set, a fully furnished interior with upholstered furniture, draperies, carpets, piano, food, and drink, provided a profusion of information about the life contained within its walls. The many objects incorporated into the set functioned as artifacts of the characters' lives, pinpointing time, place, status, occupation, and concerns. Because the play was done on a proscenium stage, a large, densely detailed scenic environment was possible.

Abstraction and Belches on Couches

Abstraction in scene design involves a stylized and symbolic visual expression of the play. Abstract design uses concentrated images in

A trough was constructed around the perimeter of the set to create the river in The Grapes of Wrath. *All audience members were able to see part, if not all, of the river.*

which ideas are reduced to their essence. The sculptural construction in *The Grapes of Wrath* is one example of abstraction in scene design. But abstraction can take many forms. The experimental Omaha Magic Theatre used provocative, abstract design elements as a central part of the performance. Found objects were used in surprising ways. Because the creative partners who directed the theatre, Megan Terry and JoAnn Schmidman, shared writing and design responsibilities, text and design were developed simultaneously. Each element was a completely interdependent part of the whole.

The Omaha Magic Theatre's production of *Belches on Couches* was about the "evolutionary possibilities of the couch potato."[3] The performance was concerned with the effects of the media on American life. The scene design for the production was based on the idea of a disinte-

grating couch in the midst of media presentations. Oversized metal springs were placed around the stage to suggest the ruptured couch. The springs came from wrecked automobiles and were then air brushed. The characters were shown sitting in plastic bubbles—a testimony to their sedentary life in front of the television. The plastic semicircles were actually skylights, which had multiple uses in the production. Thematically they were used to suggest broadcasting devices that could send and receive media signals. Practically they functioned to distort the voices of the actors, and they also created lighting effects when held overhead to reflect light. Actors also carried lights during the production to light themselves and each other.

The floor was covered with scatterings of unraveled videotape. Playing throughout the production was a video collage of edited

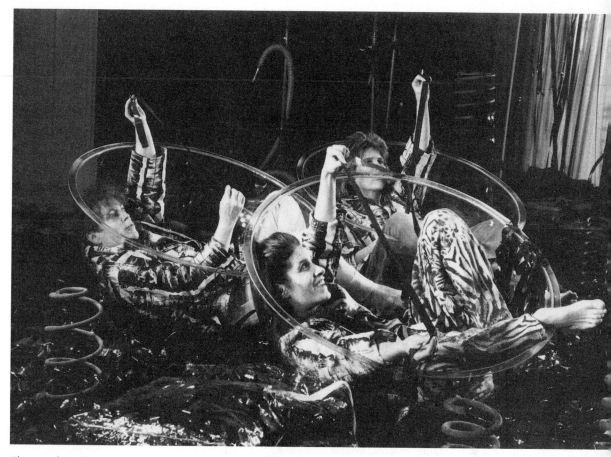

The scene design for Belches on Couches *at the Omaha Magic Theatre used found objects to create larger-than-life images of the effects of the media on modern American life. The central metaphor for the production played with the idea of a couch that has finally disintegrated into its component parts. The abstract and symbolic design elements contrast with the realistic design elements of a production such as* Blithe Spirit.

television images, including the first walk on the moon, Nixon resigning the presidency, and clips from *I Love Lucy* and *The Jackie Gleason Show*. Sometimes the video played images and no sound, sometimes sound and no images. The videotape was started in a new place for each performance so that the sound or image accompanying the live action of the actors occurred by chance.

For a production such as *Belches on Couches,* the audience members must participate with their imaginations fully engaged to organize, integrate, and make sense of the images created onstage.

COSTUME DESIGN

The costume designer creates through fabric, color, and texture. The materials used range from sumptuous brocades and hand-painted fabrics to clothing found in thrift shops, from delicate laces to metal. Hats, wigs, feathers, and jewelry are just some of the many accessories

Imago Theatre of Portland, Oregon, is known for its remarkable blend of actor movement with costuming to create surprising and delightful effects. Here, codesigners and directors Jerry Mouawad and Carol Triffle have created masks and costumes that transform the actors into lizards.

that add detail and style to a character's presentation. Distortion of the actor's body may be achieved through padded costume pieces, masks, or makeup as illustrated by the very theatrical lizards shown here. (See also Color Plates 22 and 23.) Costumes may present a dazzling vision of a fairy-tale world or show poverty and deprivation. The costumes may place the characters in terms of time, place, and social status, or the costumes may be symbolic rather than realistic.

Costume designer Angela Wendt begins her work by asking herself questions:

> Who are these people and what do the clothes mean to them? How do they decide to put on a particular piece of clothing? What does it say about their attitude toward other people and the world? Even though I do research beforehand, I always leave myself the freedom to wait until I've seen the actors themselves, gotten to know them a little bit, so I can pick costumes that support their artistic choices.[4]

Stylistic Unity

Whatever period and style is established for the costumes in a play, the costume designer must approach the characters as a group. Costumes usually have a coherent sense of style as a unit and clearly express visual relationships between the characters in terms of color, line, shape, and texture. Within the group, individual identities are established through contrast and variations in the style lines, colors, and materials. Together a group of costumes can be "read" to reveal hierarchical relationships based on wealth or power, differences in age and background, and relationships between smaller units of characters, such as families.

The Psychology of Character

The costume designer has a most interesting responsibility in helping the actor to define what could be called the psychology of character. The clothes we wear have a great deal to say about how we see ourselves and about how we wish to be seen or perceived by others. Joe Mantello, who played Louis in *Angels in America*, imagined his character choosing clothes that were too big for him, clothes that the character "could disappear into when things got bad." On the other hand, Molly Cunningham in *Joe Turner's Come and Gone* is a character who wants to be noticed. The other characters comment on the appeal of her appearance, but she is also careful not to go too far with the impression that creates. She says of herself, "Molly don't work. And Molly ain't up for sale." The image she presents of herself through the

Costume designer Ann Bruice's use of contrasting costumes to establish the clashing of characters from different backgrounds and with different personalities is apparent in this scene from Blithe Spirit *at South Coast Repertory. Charles and Ruth Condomine wear the conservative clothes of the upper middle class. Madame Arcati, the medium (played by Jean Stapleton), is dressed in many layers of varying textures; her odd hat and fingerless gloves create a picture of unself-conscious eccentricity. And behind Madame Arcati, and invisible to the other characters, is Elvira, the ghost of Charles Condomine's first wife. With her seductive gown and free-flowing hair, Elvira offers a strong contrast to the much more staid appearance of Charles's second wife, Ruth.*

choices the costume designer makes is quite different from the costume image for Mattie Campbell, who is filled with self-doubt, even though the two characters are both young women who come from very similar socioeconomic backgrounds.

There are people who gain security by carefully following social conventions. Dressing "correctly" in the most acceptable manner, therefore, could be an important character statement. For a rebellious character, choosing the way the character breaks the rules in terms

of clothing becomes an interesting challenge for the costume designer. For example, Hamlet continues to wear mourning attire out of respect for his father after the rest of the court, particularly his mother and his uncle-stepfather, have returned to their everyday clothes. His solemn clothes become a point of contention between the uncle, Claudius, and Hamlet, and their disagreement is a very important issue for the costume designer. In consultation with the director, the costume designer must connect the individuation of the characters to internal character considerations as well as external ones.

Deborah Dryden, the resident costume designer for the Oregon Shakespeare Festival, who also designs for many of the other major theatres on the West Coast, points out that a further psychological issue is expressed through clothing chosen by one character for another character. Dryden designed an adaptation of Ibsen's play, *A Doll's House*, by Ingmar Bergman, the Swedish film director. In the play, the conservative husband, Torvald, has purchased an "Italian peasant girl dress" for his wife, Nora, to wear as part of a masquerade in which she is to dance the tarantella. The dress is far from her usual, tasteful, nineteenth-century Norwegian dress. But the peasant dress is not Nora's choice; it is Torvald's and therefore must be designed from his perspective. Dryden says first of all "it is 'costumey' as opposed to 'clothing.'" The dress needs to be "a highly provocative garment that fulfills his fantasy, not hers. At this moment, Nora is at her most doll-like, his sexual toy."[5]

The Costume Designer and the Actor

The character definition expressed through costume must support rather than impede the actor's work. A character grows and changes during the course of a play. The audience should be surprised by revelations as the play progresses. The costume designer must allow room for character development rather than make such an obvious statement that the actor's choices are limited or entirely predictable. The definition of character becomes a collaboration between the designer and the actor, with the designer's work enhancing and focusing the creativity of the actor. In the musical *Contact*, the lead dancer wears a yellow dress that was redesigned and constructed nine times during the last two weeks of rehearsal to make sure the fabric and the cut of the dress would accommodate the actor's movement (Color Plate 30).

For the musical *A Chorus Line*, which is about dancer-actors, costume designer Theoni

Aldredge based her designs on what the cast wore to rehearsal. She attended many rehearsals where she both sketched and photographed the actors' own clothes. When the designs were completed, numerous adjustments were made for both appearance and the comfort of the dancers. Aldredge maintained a continuing dialogue with the actors about their costumes and also consulted with replacement actors as they joined this long-running show. At one point an actor with red hair, Petra Siniawski, was cast in the role of Cassie. The character Cassie, originated by Donna McKechnie, wore a signature red dress, a well-known feature of the musical. But because of the new actor's coloring, Aldredge redesigned the character's dress in blue.

Deborah Dryden says she spends as much time in rehearsal as possible, which is one of her favorite parts of the work:

> Sitting in rehearsal is exceedingly useful. That's one reason I like to work in a resident theatre. I've built up a relationship with some of these actors over the years. We already have a common language, and there's a mutual trust as well. And not just being part of rehearsals—being involved with the actors in the fitting room—is a very extensive, intimate form of actor-designer collaboration. I enjoy working with actors who are willing to explore the character in terms of clothing.

Deborah Dryden collaborated with actor BW Gonzalez during rehearsals for *Macbeth* in making decisions about Lady Macbeth's costume (Color Plate 17). Dryden had already developed a basic idea for a sensuous, off-the-shoulder dress to support the character concept arrived at by director Libby Appel and Gonzalez, who was playing the role. In rehearsal, Dryden and Gonzalez talked about ways of exposing more of the character's body. Dryden also saw the flexibility Gonzalez needed to be able to kneel and then easily rise back to standing, so she added slits to the costume's skirt. Dryden and Gonzalez also talked about the character's volatility, and together they worked toward an idea of using asymmetrical, diagonal lines as a reflection of the character's state of mind. The skirt was also given a train that extended the actor's range of movement and heightened the drama of her silhouette. The movement of the character, sexually charged and dynamic, was essential for the actor in expressing her understanding of Lady Macbeth's state of mind. The costume became the actor's partner in building the role.

Dryden also draws on a kind of improvisation in the fitting room to explore the possibilities of costume pieces for actors and their characters.

> One of my favorite moments in the fitting room was with Bill Irwin, the incredible actor-vaudevillian. He was working on a piece at La Jolla Playhouse, *The Three Cuckolds.* We had had many conversations about what his clothes might look like, and we had mocked up some examples. And he was doing one particular sequence of the ages of man, where he literally transformed himself from a child to an old person in a matter of moments before your eyes.
>
> I had prepared things for him to try on. As he did, he brought so much of his own physicality and his own ideas. He would throw out ideas and play with the garment I had put on him. I would chime in with my ideas, and we wouldn't know where my idea left off and his began. It allowed both of us to enter into the fray with great trust and humor and good fun.

LIGHTING DESIGN

Light is one of the most powerful influences on human existence. The rhythm of our lives is guided by the cycles of day and night and the lengthening and shortening of days as the seasons change. Summer light is different in intensity from winter light. Light that is filtered by trees and leaves is different from uninterrupted light that glares off water or sand or snow. The light of dawn is often seen as a promise, a beginning; the light of dusk may be seen as a closing or a fading. The beauty of sunrise and sun-

In The Master and Margarita *directed by Rachel Katz Carey, an ingenious cordless lamppost functioned as both a lighting instrument and a prop with many uses, held here as a torch by Amy Augustine playing Margarita.*

set offers unending variation and inspiration. Moonlight suggests romance, while a shadow across the moon may seem ominous (Color Plate 24). We gather around candles and fires because they break the darkness. Light is one of the most expressive tools available to the theatre, and audience members carry with them thousands of impressions and associations with light.

Light has always been a central metaphor in the drama because the effects of light are deeply embedded in the human psyche. Blanche DuBois in Tennessee Williams's *A Streetcar Named Desire* is frightened by the light. She needs to cover the light bulb to soften the marks of age on her face but also to hide the signs of fear. Ibsen's characters are strongly affected by the Norwegian light; the short winter days of a northern country made gloomier yet by constant rain coming off the fjords play a significant part in the characters' outlook and the mood of the plays. *The Oresteia*, by Aeschylus, begins with the flare of a beacon that signals the end of the Trojan War. The metaphor that guides the entire trilogy is that of light coming out of the darkness. Romeo is drawn to the light in Juliet's window. For him, she becomes the sun and the "envious moon" grows "pale with grief."

The History of Light in the Theatre

It is easy to divide the history of light in the theatre into three periods. Early theatres were located outdoors and relied on natural light. Beginning in the Renaissance there were indoor theatres, which were lit by candles and eventually by gaslight. The modern era of theatre can be dated from the introduction of electric lighting on the stage. With the auditorium darkened and intense light focused on the stage, the realm of the audience became separated from the realm of the actors. And the nature of theatre spectacle was completely transformed by the ability of light to isolate, to create contrasts of light and shadow, to mold the body of the actor, to project a dimensional sense of color rather than the flat color of painted scenery.

However, expressive uses of light surely predated the modern theatre. There is some speculation that in ancient Greece *The Oresteia* would have been staged early in the morning to allow the natural dawn to express the daybreak that begins the play. The earliest versions of the Christian mystery plays were sung as part of church services and therefore would have been dimly lit by candles and the filtered light coming through windows, thus creating a mood of mystery and reverence far different from the mood set by the late spring light that would have shone brightly on the more exuberant outdoor productions. Lanterns and torches have

THE NECESSARY SKILLS AND TALENTS OF DESIGNERS
■ Interest in a collaborative process
■ Fascination with dramatic literature and the work of actors
■ Strong imagination
■ Curiosity
■ Flexibility
■ Stamina and discipline
■ Openness to varied materials and approaches
■ Advanced artistic abilities
■ Advanced technical abilities

been used throughout the history of the theatre. But the lighting technology that began in the nineteenth century and has advanced exponentially since then has given light in the theatre an entirely new expressive capacity.

The Lighting Designer's Materials

The lighting designer works with electrical instruments of different shapes and sizes that are placed at various angles to create a design through light. Side light shapes the actors' bodies. Front light illuminates their faces. Followspots are used, particularly in musicals, to highlight and isolate an individual character.

Colored gels are placed across the lighting instruments to change the mood of the light and to interact appropriately with the color choices of the scene designer and the costume designer. Blue is usually considered a cool color, and yellow and straw, warmer more cheerful colors. A choice from hundreds of gel colors allows the lighting designer to achieve very subtle gradations of color effect. Patterned stencils, or gobos, can also be placed inside lighting instruments to fragment the light and create special effects on the floor or other flat surfaces. Back lighting of actors behind scrims can create a dance of shadows. And projections can be used on various surfaces to provide moving imagery.

Copenhagen, *by Michael Frayn, presents an encounter between two scientists on opposite sides during World War II whose research on atomic physics has made them both friends and enemies. The three characters in the play, based on figures from history—Niels Bohr, his wife Margrethe, and Werner Heisenberg—meet after their deaths to try to establish the truth underlying their actions. Here the lighting by Mark Henderson and Michael Lincoln for the 2000 New York production directed by Michael Blakemore suspends the three characters in a world of their own as they struggle to resolve the uncertainties of their relationships to each other and the significance of the choices they made. The actors are Philip Bosco, Blair Brown, and Michael Cumpsty.*

Conceptualizing with Light

Directors and lighting designers approach their creations imagistically and metaphorically, just as scene and costume designers do. For example, in developing the lighting for the musical *A Chorus Line*, lighting designer Tharon Musser and director Michael Bennett used the geometric paintings of Mondrian as part of their conceptualization process:

> Michael and I always worked from art books. Lighting is such an intangible thing, you can't do sketches. Art books are a great way to demonstrate to a director the kind of color or texture you're thinking about.[6]

Jim Sale, the lighting designer for *Joe Turner's Come and Gone*, used character as the key to his lighting concept:

> Who is the light force, who is the energy of the play at any one time? When Seth is in there, there is an openness, there's a comfort.

He knows people need to eat, people need to sleep. When Loomis comes in, he creates a shadow. He demands attention even when he doesn't want it. So the light that was left around him and the rest of the room got darker and more menacing. I started creating places to hide.[7]

The Light Plot and Light Cues

The lighting designer is responsible for creating a light plot, which charts the placement of lighting instruments to meet the needs of the production. Following the completion of the light plot, the lighting designer works closely with the director in developing a sequence of light cues for the production. Each change in light during the course of a production is recorded as a separate cue. In a realistic production, lights may change to indicate changes in the time of day or the weather or to reflect changes in onstage light sources such as candles or chandeliers. Lights also change to reflect mood, to shift focus to different parts of the stage, to emphasize an important entrance, or to create a special effect. Lighting cues provide the audience with very important information in addition to setting the mood of the production. Some plays have a hundred light cues or more. The execution of light cues must be timed exactly and is now done with computer programs.

To develop effective and responsive lighting cues, the lighting designer spends as much time as possible observing rehearsals. During the technical and dress rehearsals, the lighting designer and the light board operators make continuous adjustments in the level of light and the timing of the cues. Light is choreographed in response to the stage action as if it were a dance. Lighting for the theatre is another form of expressive movement on the stage.

Visibility

Although the lighting design is the last piece of the production puzzle to be fitted into place, it is by no means less important than the work of the scene and costume designers. The light unifies the stage space and the figures of the actors. The visibility of the actors, particularly their faces, depends on the proper use of light. Sometimes lighting designers and directors are drawn to moody, dimly lit effects. But audiences cannot appreciate what they cannot see, and eye strain rapidly increases general fatigue, making otherwise attentive and involved audience members restless.

For Bill Irwin's *Fool Moon*, lighting designer Nancy Schertler acknowledges that the most important issue was visibility.[8] *Fool Moon* was performed entirely without words. Although there was music throughout much of the piece, all of the content was visual. Faces and bodies needed to be sharply defined for the audience to understand the character development and to follow the continuous visual jokes. Furthermore, this need for visual clarity applied not only to the stage but to parts of the audience area as well. Irwin and his partner, David Shiner, played some of their most inspired moments in the auditorium, climbing over audience members, stealing cameras and clothing from individuals, and inviting audience members to join them on the stage. The two actors silently coached the amateurs through improvisations, which were also played without words. The lighting of the action in the auditorium had to be contained enough to allow the actors to stand out and at the same time not blind any of the audience members seated in the lit areas. Only after Schertler had solved the various visibility issues could she begin to play with light in response to the antics of the performance.

Focus

The lighting designer and the director work closely together to guide the audience members' focus. The lighting designer reinforces the director's arrangement of the actors to highlight crucial characters or stage locations. A musical comedy star about to start her song is lit by a spotlight. A doorway receives a special light in anticipation of an important character's entrance. The central figure in a group is picked out with light. As important as the presence of light in establishing focus is the absence of light. Lowering lights on one area of the stage and bringing them up on a new area redirects the audience's focus (Color Plate 25).

In the production photo of *Jitney* (shown in Color Plate 19), we see how the use of light establishes focus, in combination with the director's placement of the actors. The characters onstage have just returned from the funeral of the central figure in the play, Becker. The overall atmosphere of the lighting reflects the somber mood of the funeral. Becker's son, Booster, receives the most intense light as he stands center at the telephone. Father and son have been locked in a battle throughout the play over their relationship and the son's future. The telephone call represents a point of

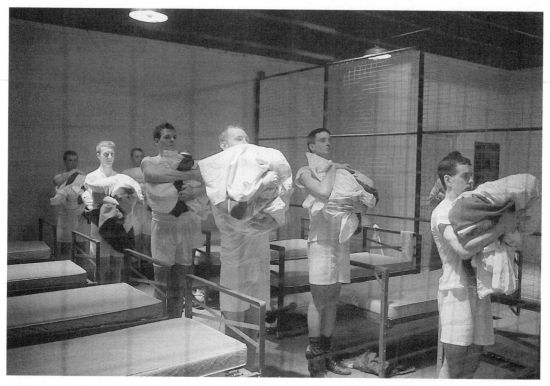

For The Brig, *a play about the brutal indoctrination of soldiers, the light must seem to come from the "practical" sources onstage which give a harsh, institutional glare. Lighting designer Joan Arhelger reinforces the intensity of the practicals with separate, hidden theatrical lights that mimic the angle and color of the onstage units. The production was staged at the University of Wisconsin, Madison.*

reconciliation between them even though it comes after the father's death. The other characters' faces are highlighted as they turn to watch Booster, anxiously waiting to see how he will respond to the telephone call. The background elements of the set glow with just enough light to reinforce the history that has led to this moment.

Mood and Atmosphere

In addition to visibility and focus, light is crucial to the visual expression of mood (Color Plate 15). Through a change in the lights, the stage atmosphere can be transformed to reflect the characters' state of mind or the external forces with which they must contend. In *And the Soul Shall Dance*, the playwright specifically calls for an important light cue when Emiko comes to the Murata house to try to sell her kimonos. The play indicates that Emiko and Hana sit in silence together, and then Yamauchi writes, "Emiko's depression pervades the atmosphere. . . . At the moment, light grows dim on the two lonely figures." How to interpret the playwright's stage directions is up to the director and the lighting designer. The lighting of the scene could suspend and isolate the figures or cast them in shadows that suggest the hopelessness of the situation through the momentary loss of daylight.

The photograph in Color Plate 20 captures one of the lighting images created by Jules Fisher and Peggy Eisenhauer for *Bring in da*

Noise Bring in da Funk. The dancers have become part of the machinery that is industrializing America. The angular, scenic structure and the dancers' bodies are revealed in a cold, harsh light that expresses the dominance of the machine. Furthermore, the rhythm of the lighting cues accentuates the mechanical quality of the dancers' movements.

The Rhythm of Light

Lighting designer Joan Arhelger says that the lighting designer makes a large contribution to building the rhythm of a play, musical, or opera.

> The light breathes. Without movement of the light, the stage and the piece, itself, become static. Our eyes expect change. Every piece has a rhythm to it like music. Is it a love song? Do things flow like a gentle rain or like lightning or thunder? Where are the stepping stones in the telling of the story? Which ones need a memorable visual moment? The lighting designer must be concerned with how fast things change, the length of the builds and the timing of the climactic moments.[9]

The lighting for *A Chorus Line* was shaped in response to the dancing and the music. All of the 128 cues were called (initiated) by the stage manager in time to the music. Rather than following a verbal script or cueing the lights off lines spoken by the actors, the stage manager followed the music score and called the cues so that the change in lights would coincide with changes in the music or moments in the dance. The timing of the light cues is a critical aspect of performance and is as carefully set and rehearsed as anything that happens on the stage.

Light usually has a rhythmic function in the theatre even for plays that are not musicals. The rhythm of the lights is created not only through the timing of the changes in the lights but also through the length of time taken for each cue. Light cues are done on timed counts, and the pace of the counting must respond to the pacing of the performance. Sometimes a light cue will be executed rapidly to give visual punch to the moment being played. In contrast, fading up the light on a ten count or longer gives an entirely different effect. Robert Wilson is known for the very slow, meditative movement in his productions. Extremely long, meticulously counted light cues are an enormously important part of his aesthetic.

THE GROWING PROMINENCE OF SOUND DESIGN

The sound designer is the most recent addition to the theatre production process. Music and sound effects have always been fundamental to theatre performance. Musical accompaniment or onstage orchestras are associated with almost all theatre traditions. Simple but ingenious solutions to sound effects can be traced to the earliest performances. A storm effect was created by snapping or shaking a metal thunder sheet; rolling wooden balls simulated approaching horse hoofs; a slapstick accompanied the mock violence of comedy. These are all faithful elements of backstage equipment from centuries past. However, the technological advances in electronic recording equipment—first records and tape recorders and then compact discs and computerized sound applications, in addition to amplifiers and mixers—have completely revolutionized the way sound is produced and used in the theatre. The sound designer now creates a sound score for a performance just as a lighting designer creates a light plot and a sequence of lighting cues.

The Integration of Sound into the Production Process

Sound design is still very much in evolution as a design area, and not all theatre companies or directors accept the contributions of sound designers as readily as others. For logistical and expressive reasons, sound is most effectively integrated into a production when the sound

A specialized sound application is employed by Wild Swan Theatre in making its productions accessible to children who are blind or sight-impaired. The children are provided with receivers through which they listen to a live description of the action of the play at appropriate moments throughout the production. Children with visual impairments are invited to the theatre an hour before the production begins to meet the actors and become acquainted with the sound of their voices so that they can identify the characters more easily during the performance. They are also given the opportunity to climb on parts of the set and to feel the costumes so that they have a kinesthetic and tactile awareness of production components that are communicated visually to other audience members. With the help of the audio description the children can integrate the information they receive from the actors' spoken words during the play with the impressions of set and costumes that they experienced before the performance began. In the photograph, a small boy becomes accustomed to the audio transmitter as he sits on the lap of Noonie Anderson, who played the Czarina in The Firebird, *directed by Hilary Cohen.*

designer is included in the earliest stages of the planning process. Speakers or microphones may need to be hidden by the set, an issue of obvious urgency. Disguising sound equipment after the set is built is a poor use of precious time and energy and may have detrimental effects on the scene design, the sound design, or both. Elizabeth LeCompte, director of the Wooster Group, sees sound as a crucial element of production: "I wouldn't do a show without sound—that would be like losing one of the performers."[10]

The Sound Designer's Materials

Sound design frequently involves a combination of live sound and recorded sound, as well as musical cues, which can be live or recorded. For example, in Chapter 9 we will read about a production of *And the Soul Shall Dance* staged at East West Players, which used a complex combination of live music and recorded sound designed by Yuki Nakamura. The director and the sound designer decided to use sound to express several key factors about the play: to reference the Japanese ancestry of the characters, to create the atmosphere of the vast and isolated Imperial Valley of California where the play is placed, and to provide evidence of the events in the characters' lives. Sound sources were blended for effect or overlapped to facilitate the transition from stylization to realism. Live music performed on Japanese wind and percussion instruments placed the play not only culturally but also environmentally, with musical sounds that suggested the wind blowing across a huge, lonely space. Recorded sound indicated realistic occurrences that contributed to the movement of the plot. The crackling of fire suggested the bathhouse burning; the noise of a car engine approaching and stopping indicated the arrival of Oka and his daughter, Kiyoko. And there was a very important onstage sound source—a Victrola used to play Japanese records. The sound score offered an aural presentation of the world of the play that paralleled the visual presentation through the scenic and costume elements.

Environmental Sound and Sound Reinforcement

Sound design falls into two distinct areas: (1) creating **environmental sound** cues that become part of the production's expressive language and (2) reinforcing the speaking or singing of the actors or musicians—that is, **amplification.** Environmental sound refers to the use of sound that we have just discussed in *And the Soul Shall Dance.* Amplification, or **sound reinforcement,** refers to augmentation of the words and music of a production to make sure that the voices carry to all parts of the theatre. Reinforcement was introduced to the theatre in the 1940s but was not widely used until the 1960s. Today, amplification is a fact of life in many theatres, particularly for musicals, a situation that some sound designers, among other theatre practitioners, regret because when the actors' voices are miked, it makes the speech or song sound recorded instead of live. Sound designer Tom Mardikes is concerned about the "alienation" of the audience through the use of wireless microphones, which he calls instruments of "acoustical death." Because the performers become separated from the source of their voices, Mardikes observes that "a lot of shows on Broadway and on tour might as well be on tape."[11]

For years, hiding the wireless microphones has been a chore for actors, hair and wig designers, and costume designers. However, most recently, in some contemporary productions such as the musical *Rent*, the actors all wear head mikes in view of the audience. The attitude suggests that we are all well aware of such technology today and we accept it as part of life. The open appearance of the mikes is also part of what engineer Kurt Fischer calls "the rock-and-roll aesthetic" of the play.[12] Another interesting use of the wireless mike takes place in the musical *Bring in da Noise Bring in da Funk*, which features the sensational tap dancing of Savion Glover. Because the dancing of Glover and four other actors is a critical part of the production's sound, the dancers wear microphones on their ankles to amplify the rhythm of their tapping.

SUMMARY

Stage designers communicate the essence of a play through visual and aural forms. Although designers share skills with visual artists, craftspeople, and musicians, the goal of the stage designer is to provide a foundation for the actor, not to create art that exists for its own sake. Designers are highly imaginative in their selection of materials and their uses of technology. They may use advanced electronic and computer technologies and sophisticated methods for forming plastic or metal. They may engage in time-consuming sequences of painting, dyeing, distressing, or otherwise transforming fabric or wood. They may scavenge old material or objects from secondhand sources. Designers must combine a capacity for creating eloquent images with a capacity for practical, technological applications. They are inventors as well as artists.

The designer's work is heavily influenced by the nature of the theatrical space. The proscenium theatre is constructed in a rectangular form with the stage at one end of the rectangle. The proscenium arrangement provides the greatest degree of separation between audience and actor. In a thrust theatre the audience sits on three sides of the stage, and an arena stage has audience members on four sides of a square or completely surrounding a circular stage space. A black box theatre is a flexible space that can be arranged in any of the preceding configurations. Large pieces of scenery and complicated scenic effects are appropriate on a proscenium stage. For thrust and arena stages, scenery must be designed so that it will not block the view of audience members. The back of scenery for a proscenium stage need not be finished. In contrast, a scenic piece on an arena stage must be finished because it will be seen from all angles.

The scene designer may provide a detailed, complete environment for a play, such as the realistic set for *Blithe Spirit*. Scenery may also be suggestive, as in the design of *The Grapes of Wrath*, or abstract, using symbolic imagery to convey a concentrated idea of the play's meaning, as in the design of *Belches on Couches*. The scene design for a play may also consist of an architectural shaping of the stage space rather than a realistic or abstract background.

The costume designer is concerned with establishing the period and background of the characters through silhouette and the textures of the fabrics. The costume designer establishes the individuality of characters as well as the relationships between groups of characters. He or she enhances the actor's presence without restricting the possibilities for character development.

The lighting designer unifies all of the visual elements of the performance, bringing together the costumed figure of the actor and the scenic environment. The lighting designer is concerned with visibility, atmosphere, focus, and rhythm. Lighting contributes to the movement of the performance in time and also shapes stage space.

Because of rapidly advancing technology, sound design is becoming an increasingly important part of theatre production. Sound design includes the expressive area of environmental sound, such as music and sound effects, and the area of reinforcement, which involves the amplification of the actors' voices.

Stage designers work closely together to develop a coherent production in which the design elements complement each other in terms of style, color, scale, degree of detail, and mood. The designers interpret the world of the play through visual and aural images that communicate to the audience members' senses and intellects. The stage design may be dazzling and opulent or simple and suggestive. Theatre production depends on the imagination of the designers to transform the stage space into a magical world that reveals the play in physical terms and that enhances the actors' potential.

TOPICS FOR DISCUSSION AND WRITING

1. *Costume:* The following writing assignment explores the concept of the psychology of character used by costume designers. Begin by observing the clothing choices made by people in different locations and situations. Consider the impressions created by the clothing choices that you observe, and consider what you perceive to be the intended impressions. For example, one person may choose clothes to create an impression of power but instead project a sense of uncertainty, yet another person may be very effective in creating an aura of power. Choose three people who have made distinct clothing and style choices that project a strong sense of character. Describe the choices in detail. Include your own interpretation of what is communicated to you about each person by the construction of his or her appearance. Write a one-half-to one-page description of each observation.

2. *Light:* Bring notes to class for discussion on the following: (a) Choose an interesting outdoor location. Observe the light at three different times during the day and, if possible, under different weather conditions. (b) Choose three interior locations—such as a store, restaurant, house, or classroom—with distinctly different lighting. What kind of lighting is used in each location? Are the light sources natural or artificial? How bright is the light? Is the light soft or harsh? How does the lighting affect the appearance and mood of each space?

3. *Sound:* (a) Over the course of several days, keep a log of sounds that you hear. How

many sounds did you hear that you are not normally aware of? How did the various sounds affect your mood? What kinds of qualities do you associate with the different sounds? What sounds are soothing? What sounds are irritating? What kinds of emotional characteristics does a specific sound convey? For example, what emotion does a loud automobile horn in a traffic jam convey? Make a list of sounds that seem to have an emotional component. Include some that involve the human voice and some that do not. (b) Creating a soundscape: Work in groups of four or five. Bring interesting soundmakers to class. Using the soundmakers, as well as vocal sounds and hand sounds, compose a "soundscape" that suggests a specific location, such as a harbor, an amusement park, or a bar. Your soundscape may have individual words in it but no descriptive phrases. Think of your composition as a collage in which sounds will be layered. Some will repeat; some will fade in and out. Each soundscape should last thirty seconds. While performing the soundscapes for class members, have them close their eyes. (c) Creating a sound story: After warming up with the soundscape, create a short dramatic story with a beginning, middle, and end, using only sound. The sound stories can be performed live or taped. Use dialogue sparingly or not at all. For example, the subject of a sound story could be a burglary that begins with the sound of cautious footsteps, followed by the rattling of a doorknob, the prying of a lock, and/or the breaking of glass. Other sounds might include drawers being opened and closed, papers being shuffled, and coins clinking. Breathing and muttered voices might also be used. The story could conclude with a police siren, running footsteps, and shouting. Experiment with different soundmakers to create the most interesting and vivid sounds, keeping in mind that the actual object being represented

may not make the most convincing sound effect. The sound story should last from thirty to ninety seconds. Length, however, is not as important as creating an intriguing sequence of sounds.

NOTES

1. Elizabeth Kendall, "'Bring in da Noise' Steps Uptown, Feet First," *New York Times*, 21 April 1996, 7.

2. Material on *The Grapes of Wrath* is derived from Eric Stone, interviews with the author, June 1997.

3. JoAnn Schmidman, interview with the author, 1 July 1997.

4. Angela Wendt, quoted in Evelyn McDonnell and Katherine Silberger, *Rent: Book, Music, and Lyrics by Jonathan Larson* (New York: William Morrow, 1997), 153.

5. Deborah Dryden's comments in this chapter are from an interview with the author, 30 May 1997.

6. Tharon Musser, quoted in Gary Stevens and Alan George, *The Longest Line: Broadway's Most Singular Sensation: A Chorus Line* (New York: Applause, 1995), 66.

7. Jim Sale, interview with the author, April 1994.

8. E. L. Greaux, "Light Up the Moon," *TCI*, May 1993, 8.

9. Author's interview with Joan Arhelger, 5 August 2002.

10. Elizabeth LeCompte, quoted in Michael Sommers, "Why Do You Need Sound Anyway?" *Theatre Crafts*, August/September 1991, 36.

11. Tom Mardikes, quoted in Steve Winn, "Tom Mardikes," *Theatre Crafts*, October 1991, 30.

12. Kurt Fischer, quoted in McDonnell and Silberger, 60.

SUGGESTIONS FOR FURTHER READING

Appia, Adolphe. *Adolphe Appia: Essays, Scenarios, and Designs.* Translated by Walter Volbach. Edited with notes and commentary by Richard C. Beacham. Ann Arbor/London: UMI Research Press, 1989.

A collection of writings on theatre by scene designer Adolphe Appia; covers his ideas about the significance of art, the relationship between theatre and music, the nature of acting, and his approaches to design. The introduction and commentary provide a good overview of Appia's career in the theatre and his significance as a theatre artist. The book also includes some reproductions of major scene designs.

Aronson, Arnold. *American Set Design.* New York: Theatre Communications Group, 1985.

A discussion of the creative process of major American scene designers such as Ralph Funicello, Ming Cho Lee, Santo Loquasto, and Robin Wagner, with numerous illustrations of their designs.

Dryden, Deborah M. *Fabric Painting and Dyeing for the Theatre.* New York: Drama Book Specialists, 1981.

A detailed description of various techniques for creating imaginative fabrics to expand the range of what may be expressed with costumes on the stage; carefully discusses the painting, dyeing, printing, aging, and distressing processes and equipment in the creation of costumes from glorious gowns for royalty to armor to masks. The book also discusses the place of the dyer-painter in theatre companies and the relationship between the dyer and the designer.

Jones, Robert Edmond. *The Dramatic Imagination.* New York: Theatre Arts Books, 1941.

Robert Edmond Jones was one of the most innovative American designers during the first half of the twentieth century. In this small book he offers wisdom that has withstood the test of time about the relationship between designers and the theatre. His insights about the "suspense" of settings, the "surprise and adventure" of costumes, and the "livingness of light" are an inspiring starting point for all theatre practitioners.

Kaye, Deena, and James Lebrecht. *Sound and Music for the Theatre.* New York: Back Stage Books, 1992.

Hands-on instruction on how to develop and execute sound design for the theatre; introduces vocabulary, equipment, and procedures and discusses the place of the sound designer in the development of the production.

Pecktal, Lynn. *Costume Design.* New York: Back Stage Books, 1993.

A collection of interviews with major costume designers, such as Theoni Aldredge, Ann Hould-Ward, Willa Kim, Santo Loquasto, Tony Walton, and Patricia Zipprodt; includes many color plates of costume designs.

Rich, Frank, with Lisa Aronson. *The Theatre Art of Boris Aronson.* New York: Alfred A. Knopf, 1987.

A comprehensive study of one of the foremost American designers of the twentieth century by one of the finest American writers on theatre and culture. The exceptional collection of photographs is particularly helpful in understanding the creative process of the scene designer.

Rosenthal, Jean, and Lael Wertenbaker. *The Magic of Light.* Boston: Little, Brown, 1972.

A personal approach to lighting design by Jean Rosenthal, one of the great twentieth-century lighting designers; combines a theoretical foundation with a hands-on approach in considering the lighting for plays, musicals, opera, and dance, with many supporting illustrations.

Russell, Douglas A. *Stage Costume Design: Theory, Technique and Style.* Englewood Cliffs: Prentice-Hall, 1973.

A book that defines the role of the costume designer; addresses the costume designer's training and responsibilities and principles of characterization and design. The book also reviews a number of style issues related to period plays from ancient Greece to the mid-twentieth century.

Smith, Ronn. *American Set Design 2.* New York: Theatre Communications Group, 1991.

An assessment of work in American scene design told through interviews with designers such as Loy Arcenas, Robert Israel, Heidi Landesman, and Charles McClennahan; includes a number of production photographs.

Svoboda, Josef. *The Secret of Theatrical Space.* Edited and translated by J. M. Burian. New York: Applause Theatre Books, 1993.

A compilation of insights from one of the great contemporary scene designers. Svoboda shares his work experiences in the theatre and the sources of his inspiration. The book traces Svoboda's career in his native Czechoslovakia, before that country divided, as well as his work for the international theatre. It also provides an eloquent visual presentation of Svoboda's designs.

CHAPTER 7

The Musical Theatre

Music and dance are forms of human expression that respond to some of life's most intensely felt moments, when it is neither enough to speak or to remain silent. Through rhythmic movement or by lifting our voices in song, we express joy or heartache. The blues, Celtic ballads, country music, work songs, rap, and reggae are all connected to essential life experiences.

Music and dance mark our observations of life's defining occasions. At weddings we celebrate through music. Music and dance accompany courtship, from the prom to the nightclub, from rock and roll concerts to moonlight serenades. Fight songs inspire battles and sporting events. The Maori of New Zealand still dance the ferocious *haka* that once motivated their warriors. Most religious worship includes musical expression, from the solemnity of a restrained hymn to the exuberance of gospel. Ecstatic dancing that liberates the spirit is also associated with religious observation throughout the world. We mourn the dead through music as well, in the form of a solemn requiem or the livelier music of a wake or the spontaneous keening and wailing of individual mourners.

Much of our musical expression is formalized in its association with particular events, from worship services to sporting events. We also organize musical participation through orchestras, bands, and choirs. However, spontaneous musical expression is one of life's great pleasures, whether it is the hip-hop danced on street corners or the singing of a lullaby to a child. If music and dance were eliminated from our lives, we would find human existence greatly diminished.

Music and dance have been fundamental to many of the world's great theatre traditions: the Greek choruses danced and sang; bands played before and during the medieval mystery cycles; and Elizabethan theatres had a special place built for musicians. Most forms of Asian theatre involve onstage musicians who play throughout the performances, and many of the actors' lines are sung. The theatre has always recognized the emotional and dramatic expressiveness of music. No matter what the theatre form, when the band strikes up, the audience comes to attention. The music announces that something special is about to begin. Music provides an air of festival or celebration. Music builds the energy and pulls the audience into the rhythm of the performance.

ORIGINS OF MUSICAL THEATRE IN AMERICA

The immigrant groups that made up the U.S. population of the nineteenth and early twentieth centuries brought many music and dance traditions with them. Musical entertainment of all kinds grew out of the free-swirling mixture of cultures. For example, tap dancing developed in part because of the incorporation of Irish clog dancing into the developing black tradition of dance.[1] The young nation enjoyed entertainments in which song and dance routines were laced with comedy, in which novelty acts brought together the latest in musical styles and dance steps. Minstrel shows and then musical revues and vaudeville eventually led to the development of a **musical theatre** form that presented the popular dancing and singing in a dramatic plot with characters who played out a

complete story. A collection of loosely connected routines or variety acts gave way to an integration of spoken text, singing, and dance that developed a dramatic idea. The evolving musical theatre drew on diverse talents and diverse backgrounds. Entertainers from the world of jazz and vaudeville eventually intersected with ballet choreographers and classically trained composers and musicians to create the American musical theatre.

The term *musical comedy* was used for years to describe this theatre form because most of the early works followed the pattern of a troubled love relationship that was accompanied by comic variations and that ended with reconciliation and celebration. In fact, musical comedy in this version fits nicely into the definition of comedy discussed in Chapter 13. However, the musical theatre form has grown and expanded beyond the formulaic romance to include a variety of subjects and situations that do not always lead to reconciliation. We use the term *musical theatre* to include the most open definition of this form.

THE BROADWAY THEATRE

Our discussion of musical theatre focuses on Broadway, which continues to be the heart of musical theatre production. For much of the twentieth century, most musicals originated on Broadway. Over time, however, the musical theatre too has been affected by the decentralization of the American theatre. New musicals today are often developed in regional theatres and then move to Broadway, or they may develop in not-for-profit theatres or workshops before achieving a Broadway production. Nonetheless, the goal in most musical theatre is still a Broadway engagement.

Broadway is composed of a group of large, elegant theatres located on or close to Broadway and Times Square in New York City. Most of the theatres are found between 41st Street and 50th Street. Broadway theatres usually seat more than a thousand audience members in an orchestra and two balconies and are equipped with state-of-the-art technology. The price of a ticket for a Broadway musical at $75 and higher makes attendance at this "popular" form of theatre a very expensive proposition. Half-price tickets can be purchased on the day of performance at the TKTS booth in Times Square, and some musicals reserve a number of lower-priced seats for students.

As we examine some of the most celebrated musicals of the American theatre, we focus primarily on the original productions. There we can see the work of the composer, lyricist, and librettist joined to the work of the director and choreographer. In contemporary American theatre, the choreographer has become a major theatre practitioner, contributing significant new ideas to the staging of the drama.

Oklahoma!

Opening on Broadway in 1943, *Oklahoma!* was a musical about farmers and cowboys that reinforced traditional American values at a time when the nation was in the middle of its participation in World War II. The musical tells a simple love story set against the progression of Oklahoma toward statehood. *Oklahoma!* represented a nostalgia for the past at a time when war made for an anxious and uncertain present. Songs such as "O What a Beautiful Morning," "The Surrey with the Fringe on Top," and the title song, "Oklahoma!" created an onstage sense of optimism and faith in rural American life. *Oklahoma!* was a retreat from the sophisticated subject matter of earlier musical theatre but an advance in the integration of theatrical materials. Each song in *Oklahoma!* contributed to the development of the plot or the emotional state of a character.

Known for its enduring musical score, *Oklahoma!* also established new possibilities for the use of dance in the musical theatre form. Instead of serving as a break in the action to provide variety and show off the skills of talented performers, dance was used to develop character and express ideas nonverbally. Cowboy posture and movement that derived from actions such as horseback riding and roping were combined with square dancing to give the choreography and the play a distinctive flavor. Significantly, the dance went beyond filling the stage with charming western idioms to accompany the songs. In the most innovative use of dance, a prolonged choreographic sequence was used for psychological development. The central character, Laurey, has foolishly encouraged the attention of Jud Fry, to provoke the hero, Curly. Jud is a hostile, threatening figure, and Laurey's fear of him is played out in an elaborate dream ballet. Curly and Jud fight, and Curly is killed. Laurey is carried off by Jud to live in his sleazy world of violence and used-up dancehall girls.

Oklahoma! was the first creation of the partnership of Richard Rodgers, who composed the music, and Oscar Hammerstein II, who wrote the **book** (script) and lyrics. Together, Rodgers and Hammerstein later created such popular musicals as *Carousel, South Pacific, The King and I,* and *The Sound of Music.* All of the Rodgers and Hammerstein collaborations are known for their use of music to define character and to contribute to the structure of the plot. Each of their musicals tells the story of characters, usually in love, who overcome conflicts and obstacles to reach a triumphant ending. Sentimental but inspired melodies and good-humored characters carry the Rodgers and Hammerstein musicals.

For *Oklahoma!* Agnes de Mille joined the Rodgers and Hammerstein team as choreographer. She brought her considerable ballet background into the musical theatre but also drew on tap and folk dance forms. De Mille continued to choreograph Rodgers and Hammerstein productions and became one of the first choreographer-directors. Her approach to the integration of choreography into the musical opened the way for the brilliant innovations in the musical theatre to come. It is interesting to note that choreographer Susan Stroman, whose

The dream ballet from Oklahoma! *features the "Post Card Girls," who suggest another side of life on* *the American frontier in the choreography by Agnes de Mille.*

work is discussed later in the chapter, has recently restaged Agnes de Mille's original dances for *Oklahoma!* in a new Broadway production that opened in 2001.

West Side Story

Oklahoma! reflected the sensibility of a nation engaged in war abroad that looked to the stage for a comforting, rural view of the home front. In 1957 a new musical, *West Side Story*, would take on our own urban warfare. Based on the feuding families that doomed the love of Romeo and Juliet, *West Side Story* dramatizes the gang conflict between Puerto Rican and Anglo youths in an impoverished New York City neighborhood. Choreographer-director Jerome Robbins originated the idea for the production and invited the collaboration of composer and conductor Leonard Bernstein. Robbins and Bernstein had already worked together successfully on a ballet, "Fancy Free,"

that became a Broadway musical and then a film, *On the Town*. Each had extensive experience in the musical theatre in addition to Robbins's work in the ballet and Bernstein's contributions to the world of classical music. They were both at the top of their professions and were able to merge their formidable talents to create one of the great American works of the modern theatre. Playwright Arthur Laurents adapted Shakespeare's *Romeo and Juliet*, and a young songwriter, Stephen Sondheim, wrote the lyrics. Sondheim would go on to become one of the foremost composers and lyricists of the musical theatre, creating such works as *Company*, *Sweeney Todd*, and *Sunday in the Park with George*.

The young lovers in the 1950s version of Shakespeare's play are Maria and Tony, on opposite sides of the gang conflict. Tony is a former member of the Jets, the gang made up of the sons of European immigrants; Maria is the sister of Bernardo, leader of the Sharks, the

Jerome Robbins's explosive choreography distinguished West Side Story *and brought the musical the-atre to a new level in the integration of drama and movement. In the "Dance at the Gym," the Jets and the Sharks continue their rivalry on the dance floor.*

Puerto Rican gang. As in its Shakespearian source, hostilities and misunderstandings lead to the deaths of several young men. Yet in the musical version Maria lives. As with much contemporary gang violence, the woman is left to face the consequences of the fighting alone. The entire play focuses on the young people involved: the limitations of their circumstances, their reliance on one another, their alienation from the larger society, their aspirations, and their love.

West Side Story has very little dialogue. Almost the entire story is told through songs and dances, with dance playing a much more important part than it had previously in the American musical theatre. The Bernstein score has an edgy, urban dissonance influenced by jazz and Latin rhythms. Some of the most memorable love songs of the musical theatre come from *West Side Story*, such as "Maria,"

"Tonight," and "Somewhere." The score is also notable for its use of counterpoint. For example, a love theme is introduced and then returns to be played against the theme of the impending gang fight. The score is percussive, with a drive and urgency that would be adopted by many later musicals.

Matching the intensity of the music, the choreography had the actors flying across the stage and at each other for much of the production. The characters were in constant motion, cruising the streets, looking for fights, dancing at the gym. Intricately choreographed sequences defined character and dramatized the action of the play. Robbins combined a ballet base with a heavy use of jazz and gymnastics to create a tough, jagged street-smart choreography for the gang sequences and a sexy, competitive choreography for the men and women.

Henry Higgins (Rex Harrison), Eliza Doolittle (Julie Andrews), and Colonel Pickering (Robert Coote) celebrate Eliza's newly achieved mastery of proper pronunciation in "The Rain in Spain" from My Fair Lady, *with choreography by Hanya Holm and stage direction by Moss Hart.*

Latin dance styles were integrated into the movement of the Puerto Rican characters in the "Dance at the Gym" and "America" to physicalize the difference between the backgrounds of the two groups of characters. The raw dancing of the gang members and their girlfriends formed a contrasting background for the softer, lyrical duets of Tony and Maria. Robbins's position as director and choreographer ensured the complete integration of all of the staging elements, with dance becoming the central force around which the rest of the production was built.

My Fair Lady

In the mid-1950s, two musicals based on classics of drama from different eras—*Romeo and Juliet*, by Shakespeare, and *Pygmalion*, by George Bernard Shaw—brought the musical theatre to a new level of artistry. *West Side Story* fulfilled the dance possibilities suggested by *Oklahoma!*, and *My Fair Lady* introduced brilliant language to the musical stage. Both used the unique advantages of the musical theatre to create dramas of substance and style.

My Fair Lady (1956) represents the collaborative efforts of another well-known Broadway team, Alan Lerner and Frederick Loewe. Their third collaborator, the English playwright George Bernard Shaw, is sometimes overlooked as one of the creators of this most witty of all Broadway musicals. In *West Side Story*, although the situation resembles *Romeo and Juliet* and some of the plot incidents coincide, the language and terms of expression are entirely reworked. In contrast, much of the strength of *My Fair Lady* derives from the characters and the language written by Shaw.

My Fair Lady tells the story of the transformation of Eliza Doolittle, who sells flowers in Covent Garden, from a "guttersnipe" and "a squashed cabbage leaf" into a young woman of such distinction that she can be passed off as a princess at a royal ball. Her two mentors in this unlikely venture are both noted linguists: the abrasive Professor Henry Higgins and the milder Colonel Pickering. Their project to reinvent Eliza grows out of a bet over how much work it will take to eliminate Eliza's cockney speech patterns and instill in her instead the speech of a lady.

As the lessons proceed, Eliza and Henry engage in a battle of wills and wits that creates one of the more original female-male relationships in the musical theatre. Their verbal sparring is expanded to include the contributions of Eliza's father, the opportunistic Alfred Doolittle, a dustman, and Henry's eminently sensible mother, Mrs. Higgins. The score, which includes the popular favorites "I Could Have Danced All Night" and "The Street Where You Live," also has a series of brilliant character songs that are as engaging musically as they are dramatically. Higgins and Eliza carry their skirmishes into musical attacks that are filled with humor and bite.

The casting of Rex Harrison and Julie Andrews in the lead roles became one of the celebrated partnerships of the musical theatre. The director, Moss Hart, who was an exceptional comic playwright himself, staged the play with a sophistication that matched the brilliance of the material. Another major dance figure of the mid-twentieth century, Hanya Holm, did the choreography. The choreography complemented the clever staging by Moss Hart. But it was the music and language that carried *My Fair Lady* to the heights of the musical form.

Cabaret

The 1960s saw major changes in the U.S. political scene and in the theatre. The divisiveness of the Vietnam War and student protests marked the decade, as did new theatre companies concerned with both political issues and new forms of expression. *Cabaret*, a musical first produced in 1966, expressed some of the anxieties of the times and the upheaval in traditional forms while turning back to an earlier era for its subject.

Cabaret draws on *The Berlin Stories* of Christopher Isherwood and the play *I Am a Camera*, by John Van Druten, based on the Isherwood material. *Cabaret* presents a sleazy picture of Berlin in the late 1920s, just preceding the Nazis' and Hitler's rise to power in Germany. The musical is set in a trashy nightclub, the Kit Kat Club, inhabited by tacky dance girls dressed in skimpy torn stockings and underwear. These women go through the motions of nightclub routines under the control of the bizarre Master of Ceremonies, a bitterly flamboyant character who directs the false gaeity of all the proceedings. At the Kit Kat Club we come to meet a young American writer, Clifford Bradshaw, who is at first attracted to the decadence that pervades Berlin, symbolized by the Kit Kat Club, and then repelled by it as he realizes that the Nazis are gathering power while careless people indulge their jaded appetites. The world of the musical is seen through Bradshaw's eyes as he becomes involved with a young English expatriate, Sally Bowles, a singer at the Kit Kat Club. When Bowles becomes pregnant, Bradshaw offers to marry her and move with her to the United States, but Bowles chooses an abortion and the chance to go on being part of the Kit Kat Club. The fate of the Jews is particularly focused in the subplot of a Jewish grocer who insists in the face of increasingly violent antisemitism that normalcy will return to Germany.

The book for *Cabaret* was written by Joe Masterhoff, the music by John Kander, and the lyrics by Fred Ebb. But rather than telling a straightforward story in the style of *Oklahoma!* or *My Fair Lady*—musicals that are designated as **book musicals** because of their reliance on traditional dramatic plotting—*Cabaret* created a new style for expressing its content. In collab-

Alan Cummings, as the Master of Ceremonies, is surrounded by the jaded dance girls of the Kit Kat Club in the 1998 revival of Cabaret *directed by Sam Mendes at the Henry Miller Theatre in New York City, which was turned into a nightclub for the production.*

oration with the director, Harold Prince, the writers created what is called a **concept musical**—a musical that emphasizes a theme in which scenic and performance elements are of greater significance than the plot. This innovation is not unlike the emphasis on imagery in German expressionism and the theatre of the absurd discussed in Chapter 10. In the case of this play, the idea of the world defined as a cabaret shaped the basic concept. And the jangling cabaret music, recalling the jarring music composed by Kurt Weill for Brecht's early plays, became the framing structure for the drama itself rather than a device to complement or fill out the play's dialogue. In the *New York Times* review of the original production, Walter Kerr wrote:

> Instead of telling a little story about the decadence of Berlin just before Hitler came to

power into which casual musical numbers can be sandwiched whenever politeness permits, *Cabaret* lunges forward to insist on music as mediator between audience and characters, as lord and master of the revels, as mocking conferencier without whose ministrations we should have no show at all. We are inside the music looking out, tapping our feet to establish a cocky rhythm and a satanically grinning style to which the transient people of the narrative must accommodate themselves, through which—in irony and after the fact—they can be known.[2]

The play's tone established by the music was continued in Ronald Field's choreographed sequences set in the Kit Kat Club, which were vulgar and suggestive and backed by a large mirror in which audience members could watch themselves watching the show. Under Harold Prince's direction, the staging shifted the audience's sense of being detached from the action to becoming part of the audience in the Kit Kat Club itself. In the 1998 Broadway revival of *Cabaret*, the audience involvement was heightened by turning the entire seating area of the audience into an extension of the nightclub with tables and chairs, red lamps on the tables, and food and drink served and consumed by audience members during the performance. The atmosphere in the recent production emphasized the cheap, harsh sexual exchange that underscores all of the action and the bleak, abusive world of the Kit Kat Club. With *Cabaret*, the musical left the romance of the form far behind.

Among the actors in the original production, Joel Grey created a sensation as the Master of Ceremonies and went on to re-create the role in the highly regarded film, which starred Grey and Liza Minelli. Lotte Lenya, who began her career acting with Bertolt Brecht, played the role of Fräulein Schneider, who runs the boardinghouse in which Bowles and Bradshaw live and who ultimately rejects her Jewish suitor when the Nazi presence becomes too ominous. In the 1997 revival, Alan Cumming was scintillating as the Master of Ceremonies, with a more vicious quality yet than that of Joel Grey, a reflection perhaps of our own times. And Natasha Richardson gave the most complete interpretation of Sally Bowles since the musical was first produced (Color Plate 26). The revival was directed by Sam Mendes, following a production of the same play, which he directed in London in 1993.

Stephen Sondheim

The contributions of Stephen Sondheim to the musical theatre cannot be represented by a single defining work. From his earliest effort as a composer of both music and lyrics in *A Funny Thing Happened on the Way to the Forum*, the works of Stephen Sondheim have followed no formula or pattern. Rather, he is known for his experimentation with subject and form, for being adventurous in a field that has tended to favor predictability. During his time as theatre critic for the *New York Times*, Frank Rich observed that Sondheim was "persistent" in trying "to transform the Broadway musical" and considered him "as adventurous and as accomplished an author, playwrights included, as Broadway has produced over the last two decades."[3] Sondheim has spent his career in the musical theatre, from 1957 to the present, exploring new ways of creating musical dramas.

Stephen Sondheim was a committed student of music composition at Williams College, which he followed with three years of study with the avant-garde composer Milton Babitt. He wrote his first musicals in high school and was always focused on the goal of composing for the musical stage. As a family friend of Oscar Hammerstein II, he had the unique opportunity of being mentored by the author of some of the most compelling and successful song lyrics in the musical theatre. Sondheim learned much from Hammerstein, but Hammerstein wrote optimistic lyrics about overcoming adversity, the "golden sky and the sweet silver song of a lark" that followed the storm (*Carousel*), and the sustaining power of love, "younger than springtime am I with you" (*South Pacific*). Sondheim would move in a very different direction.

Steeped in musical theatre tradition, Stephen Sondheim began his professional career as lyricist first for *West Side Story* and then for *Gypsy*, collaborating with other major figures in the musical theatre such as Jerome Robbins, Jules Styne, and Harold Prince. When he began to write his own complete scores as well as the lyrics, Sondheim placed increasing responsibility on the music and lyrics as the driving force in the creation of the drama. The book that in earlier musicals told a story through dialogue augmented by songs was replaced by the score itself. Building his works around a theme or an idea rather than a highly structured plot, Sondheim was a major influence in the development of the concept musical.

The subjects of the Sondheim musicals are challenging for audiences: examining the stresses and disappointments of urban life, the difficulties in building satisfactory relationships, the painful and sometimes bitter path to maturity, and the contradictory nature of American values. Whereas many musicals are written and produced to provide audiences with a form of escape from their concerns, Sondheim musicals ask audiences to participate in a thoughtful process. For example, *Pacific Overtures* explores the forced opening of Japan in the nineteenth century to Western commerce and the consequences for Japanese society as it underwent enormous social change. *Sunday in the Park with George* considers the nature of artistic creation, and *Assassins* takes on the disturbing subject of violence in American public life. Music and lyrics in combination are used as social commentary, as narrative, and as reflection or debate as well as the expression of a character's state of mind. In *Pacific Overtures* traditional Japanese instruments create a texture of life in sound whose rhythms are interrupted and distorted by the demands of outside forces. In *Assassins* the style of folk ballads usually associated with a positive sense of American character is employed as a departure point for the confusion expressed by those trying to rewrite U.S. history through murder.

The work of Stephen Sondheim demonstrates particularly the way song lyrics can be seen as poetry set to music. The lyrics are a condensed and eloquent expression of a significant moment in a character's life. The lyrics contain the particularity of the character's voice as well as an intricate verbalization of the changing or developing circumstances of the drama. The sung lyrics must be listened to as carefully or more carefully than any of the spoken dialogue, and the audience cannot simply lose themselves in the melody or the staging of a song.

> You try to make the language dance, not only to your own tune, which is a metaphor, but to the actual tune that's there. You try to make the words sit on music, to rhyme them, to make jokes land, to use literary techniques. It's technical, like poetry or any creative art is

technical. But, because lyric writing makes you deal with so few words and the language is not so elastic when sung . . . it becomes very crossword puzzle-like.[4]

Here is the final section of the song "Four Black Dragons" from the 1976 musical *Pacific Overtures* in which the local people and the narrator, the Reciter, sing of their terror at the arrival of U.S. warships off the coast of Japan.

> (*Townspeople*)
> *Four black dragons*
> *Spitting fire!*
> (*Reciter*)
> *Then the hooves clattered*
> *And the warriors were there,*
> *Diving quickly through the panic*
> *Like the gulls.*
> *Hai! Hai!*
> *And the swords were things of beauty*
> *As they glided through the air—*
> *Hai!*
> *Like the gulls.*
> *Hai!*
> (*Townspeople*)
> *Hai! Hai!*
> *Four black dragons,*
> *Spitting fire!*
> (*Thief and Company*)
> *And the sun darkened*
> *And the sea bubbled,*
> *And the earth trembled,*
> *And the sky cracked,*
> *And I thought it was the end*
> *Of the world!*
> (*Reciter*)
> *And it was.*[5]

Through the lyrics Sondheim furthers the drama in a number of ways. He creates the action of the arrival of the ships, the "four black dragons." He captures the fear of the community as they record this invasion of their private world. He creates explosive visual imagery of the upheaval that it represents, and he foreshadows the transformation to come.

When Pacific Overtures, *by Stephen Sondheim and John Weidman, was first produced in 1976, director Harold Prince and scenic designer Boris Aronson drew on the Japanese theatre tradition of Kabuki in shaping the acting style and visual presentation. The most recent production of the play (2001), represented in this photograph, is by a Japanese company, the New National Theatre of Tokyo, that has gone further yet than Western companies in using parody and the grotesque to underline the clash between cultures. Here the representatives of the United States, Holland, France, and Russia—who are demanding the use of Japanese ports to advance their national interests—are presented as huge and distorted figures. The Japanese production, directed by Amon Miyamoto, also includes images of Japan's aggression in World War II as well as the bombing of Hiroshima, which were not part of the original production.*

Sondheim songs have not had nearly the success of the work of other composers as popular songs performed outside of their plays because of the deep connection of the words to the ongoing drama. And Sondheim works can be hard to appreciate without their proper instrumentation because of the close integration between the lyrics and the score. In spite of the fact that the music and lyrics dominate Sondheim musicals, Sondheim has chosen not to write the spoken dialogue of his plays, relying instead on a series of collaborators. Some of his work has suffered as a result of dramatic construction that lacks the sophistication and skill of the score.

But there is no doubt that Sondheim has created a body of work that is a major force in shaping the musical theatre at the beginning of the twenty-first century. Recent productions of Sondheim musical theatre pieces reflect his continuing importance for the American theatre. In 2002 Sondheim was represented on Broadway by a well-received revival of *Into the Woods* (see Color Plate 27), and *Pacific Overtures* was presented at the Lincoln Center summer festival in a new production by the New National Theatre of Tokyo. At the same time, a major retrospective of six Sondheim musicals was produced at the Kennedy Center in Washington, D.C. And in June 2003, the Goodman Theatre in Chicago premiered Sondheim's newest work, *Gold*, which returns to U.S. history to look at the lives of the Mizner brothers, trying to grasp the opportunities available to the adventurous as they travel from Alaska to Florida at the beginning of the twentieth century.

A Chorus Line

Before *West Side Story*, musicals relied on a chorus of singers and dancers to dress the stage and carry the choreographic responsibility of the big production numbers. There was a clear delineation between principals and chorus members, and the groups even rehearsed separately. In *West Side Story*, Jerome Robbins essentially eliminated the chorus by making all the roles singing and dancing characters, thereby assigning importance to all the performers. For the first time, the musical cast became an ensemble.

In his musical *A Chorus Line* (1975), with music by Marvin Hamlisch and lyrics by Edward Kleban, Michael Bennett made the chorus the subject of the play. The premise of this musical is based on the endless auditioning required of performers seeking employment as chorus members. Bennett created a musical that told the stories of young singers and dancers desperately hoping for their big break. In a time-honored tradition, the theatrical performance was about the theatre.

Bennett began dancing as a child and served his apprenticeship dancing in the choruses of musicals before becoming a choreographer. Always focused on a theatrical career, he dropped out of high school to become one of the Jets in the international touring company of *West Side Story* and to learn from the master, Jerome Robbins. Bennett's theatre education and training took place in the musical theatre. In 1970, he joined Stephen Sondheim and Harold Prince as the choreographer of *Company* and then became the choreographer and codirector of *Follies*. When he turned to the lives of dancers as the subject for a new musical, he was able to draw on his own experiences from many productions as well as those of a group of dancers he invited to brainstorm with him in a workshop at the Public Theatre, then under the direction of Joseph Papp.

In creating *A Chorus Line*, Bennett reduced the musical form to its essence, in the words of one of its famous songs, "the music and the mirror, and the chance to dance." Gone were the sets that had become increasingly lavish for musical theatre production; gone were the elaborate costumes and the cast of "thousands." A group of young characters stood in a line at the front of the stage wearing a combination of leotards, tights, jeans, and T-shirts. One at a time, they told the stories that had brought them into the theatre, beginning with spoken words that segued into song and then into dance. Because the play took the form of a fictional audition, the stories were addressed to the character of the director, who was placed at the back of the auditorium behind the audience seats, allowing the actors to speak out directly to the audience.

A Chorus Line has a very thin plot, involving a relationship between the dancer, Cassie, and the director, Zach. Like *Cabaret*, *A Chorus Line* is a concept musical. But the heart of the piece is in the characters' stories and their quest for approval and for a chance to show their worth and to follow their dreams. *A Chorus Line* became a metaphor for a new era of life in the United States (Color Plate 28).

NEW DIRECTIONS FOR THE MUSICAL THEATRE

Four musicals have once again turned the musical theatre in new directions at a time when some critics were suggesting that the form had exhausted its possibilities. *Bring in da Noise Bring in da Funk* (1995) explores historical and contemporary perspectives in black American life through tap dancing. *Rent* (1995) chronicles the lives of artists and their impoverished friends living in the East Village in New York City. *The Lion King* (1997) introduces a style of integrating puppets and moving sculpture into a musical production that makes the director-designer the principal author of the story told onstage. And lastly, *Contact* (1999) features the

Savion Glover and his fellow dancers bring the choreography of Bring in da Noise Bring in da Funk *into the present. The dancers and drummers celebrate one of the musical's fundamental themes, "In the beginning there was . . . da beat!"*

work of the director-choreographer who composes the entire piece through dance and music with spoken dialogue but without songs. Both *Bring in da Noise Bring in da Funk* and *Rent* deal with serious, sensitive, and controversial issues: oppression and self-determination in *Bring in da Noise Bring in da Funk* and drug addiction and AIDS in *Rent*. *The Lion King* and *Contact* are recognized more for innovations in style than subject matter. But all four musicals are noted for their high spirits and originality. They were created by young authors and feature very young cast members, some without traditional theatre backgrounds. Although the sound and style of these productions are completely contemporary, these new musicals are tied to musical theatre traditions that are clearly still evolving.

Savion Glover and Bring in da Noise Bring in da Funk

Savion Glover grew up in Newark, New Jersey, but in the shadow of Broadway. By the time he was twelve years old, he was already recognized as a dance prodigy. He tap-danced his way through *The Tap Dance Kid*, *Black and Blue*, and *Jelly's Last Jam* before he was eighteen years old. Dancing with Gregory Hines, Honi Cole, and Jimmy Slyde provided Glover with an education in American tap styles that he merged with his own sense of rap and reggae to create a new approach, called "the beat."

Savion Glover performs with a style of dance distinctly different from the light and graceful approach frequently associated with African American tap dancers. Glover's dancing is forceful and appears self-involved. He drives his feet into the floor and uses the whole foot in new ways. He dances on his toes and on the sides of his feet. The focus of the dance is in his legs and feet; his head is often down, and he doesn't use his torso or his arms to extend the range of movement. The dancing is very athletic and includes gymnastic and break-dancing elements. This is dance that can express anger and sorrow as well as joy and freedom. Savion Glover represents the tap dancing of a new generation.

George C. Wolfe, the director of the Public Theatre, was the creator and director of *Jelly's Last Jam*, whose premier production featured

Glover as the young Jelly. After this production Wolfe began to consider the significance of African American tap dance as a folk form and its possibilities for expressing the African American experience. He proposed a collaboration with Glover in the development of a performance without a script. Glover brought to the developmental process at the Public Theatre four young men with whom he had danced (the oldest among them was twenty-six) and two drummers. They were joined by Ann Duquesnay, an actor and singer who would collaborate on and eventually perform the songs for the show, and Reg Gaines, a poet who was working on the text. Together they evolved a series of scenes, focused in dance, that each addressed a different aspect of black life in the United States.

In *Bring in da Noise Bring in da Funk*, tap dance is used to depict a lynching, the post-slavery migration to the North, and even the attempts of black men to flag a cab in New York City. *Bring in da Noise Bring in da Funk* has an episodic organization of scenes related to a theme rather than a traditional plot made up of connected incidents. Like *A Chorus Line*, the show is about the dancers themselves. But in *A Chorus Line* the dancers are always in character, even though much of the content of their characters' lives may be close to their own. In *Bring in da Noise Bring in da Funk* the dancers speak for themselves. Their taped voices describing the place of dance in their lives accompany one sequence of their dancing. The actual lives of the actor-dancers are seen as the final movement of history that the play presents.

The black musical was a significant part of the early history of musical theatre in the United States. Musicals such as *Ain't Misbehavin'* and *Jelly's Last Jam* have reinterpreted a tradition that has deep roots in the American theatre. *Bring in da Noise Bring in da Funk* makes a place for young dancers in the musical theatre and brings an entirely new sensibility to a choreographed, dramatic form. At age twenty-three, Savion Glover joins Jerome Robbins and Michael Bennett as creators of modern, choreographically authored musical theatre pieces at the same time that he reaches back to the traditions of African American dance and musical theatre.

Jonathan Larson and Rent

Like *Bring in da Noise Bring in da Funk*, *Rent* grew out of a workshop production, in this case at New York Theatre Workshop, and then moved to the Nederlander Theatre on what is considered the outer perimeter of Broadway. *Bring in da Noise Bring in da Funk* was the work of young creators and performers but had the very experienced and well-connected hand of George C. Wolfe guiding the process. *Rent* was sustained by the energy and commitment of its creator, Jonathan Larson.

Larson studied acting and musical composition in college, and with encouragement from Stephen Sondheim, he committed himself to a career of writing for the musical theatre. It took fifteen years of living the life represented by the characters in *Rent* to bring his vision of a new musical to the stage. Larson sought to merge the tradition of the musical theatre with 1990s music and the sensibility of young people raised with MTV, film technology, and rapidly changing social values. He wanted to place the heart of rock-and-roll culture on the musical stage in order to tell the story of young people struggling to make sense of life in the midst of poverty and the AIDS epidemic.

Larson found the starting point for what would become *Rent* in a nineteenth-century opera, *La Bohème* (1895), by Puccini, and in the novel *Scenes de la Vie Bohème*, by Henri Murger, on which *La Bohème* was based. From *La Bohème* he took the situation of a group of artists struggling with poverty and illness but sustaining themselves through their friendships and their faith in life. Many of the plot incidents and the characters are suggested by the opera; an example is Mimi, who in the opera dies of tuberculosis and in *Rent* is dying of drug addiction and AIDS.

But *Rent* is definitely a late-twentieth-century creation: a rock band is placed on the stage; the characters all wear head mikes; one of the characters records everything on a video camera; and drug addiction underscores the troubled lives of the characters. The music reflects the mix of pop music culture, all with a rock-and-roll beat. Instead of the slickness and polished finish of most musical theatre productions, Larson sought a roughness and rawness in the performance, in terms of both the singing and the visual presentation. The set appears to be made from found pieces of junk; the costumes are a grungy compilation of worn and frayed castoff garments or the cheapest of the new. The staging has an improvisational feel. Where there is choreography, there is a sense of looseness and invention in the moment rather than the highly crafted dance structures of Jerome Robbins, Michael Bennett, or Savion Glover (Color Plate 29).

The story behind the creation of *Rent* is as dramatic as what occurs on the stage. The night before the production's final dress rehearsal, thirty-five-year-old Jonathan Larson died suddenly of an aortic aneurysm. The grief-stricken cast "went on with the show," which has met with great success. But the success is mixed with sadness for the young playwright and composer who didn't live to see his music and lyrics lighting up Broadway.

Julie Taymor and The Lion King

In 1997 a new musical opened on Broadway that once again took the form in a major new direction. *The Lion King* was adapted from the extraordinarily popular Walt Disney film of the same name and followed the Disney re-creation of *Beauty and the Beast* as a stage musical. The stage version of *Beauty and the Beast* was guided by the cartoon imagery of the film, but the stage production of *The Lion King* broke new ground in the musical theatre. Avant-garde director and designer Julie Taymor was invited by Walt Disney Theatrical Productions to interpret the story of *The Lion King* in her own way. Impressed by Taymor's previous intercultural work using astounding sculpted puppets and cinematic design effects, the Disney organization provided the opportunity for highly imaginative exploration in a commercial context. *The Lion King* continues the tradition of Broadway musicals that rely on lavish sets and costumes but integrates these elements into the telling of a story in a significantly new way. The designer-director becomes the driving force behind the expressive elements of the production.

Taymor became a serious student of theatre as a child and expanded her awareness of non-Western theatre traditions when she traveled to India and Sri Lanka during high school. During college she was part of the same experimental theatre company as Bill Irwin at Oberlin College. She also studied mime in Paris, improvisational acting in New York, and puppetry with the Bread and Puppet Theatre. Taymor was always concerned with the anthropological origins of theatre and with mythical subjects. She also showed talent early on as a painter and sculptor as well as a performer, talents that she continued to nurture as she apprenticed with different theatre companies and traditions.

After graduating from college, Taymor spent four years in Indonesia studying its brilliant movement theatre and observing the cultural conditions out of which it emerged. In Indonesia she became part of the Bengkel Theatre, which encouraged her to create a production with the company actors. Her first major work, *Way of Snow*, began her lifelong experimentation with theatre expressed through masks, puppets, live actors, and startling visual effects drawing on myth and ritual to probe the human condition. And she continued to build her design and construction skills in the areas of scene, costume, and puppet design at the same time that she refined her vision as a director. Taymor worked for twenty years directing and designing original works, Shakespeare, and opera before being invited to bring her imaginative approach to *The Lion King*.

The masks for the lionesses in The Lion King *are made like urns to sit on the actors' heads so that both the actors' faces and the masks are visible at all times. Each lioness costume has variations in design, but all of the costumes billow during dance sequences to increase character size. The masks have white ribbons stored behind the eyes, which are pulled down for tears when the lionesses are in mourning.*

Director Taymor first worked with the original screenwriters of the film to expand and strengthen the narrative of the young lion, Simba, who must undertake a complicated journey to earn his place as king. She became a collaborator on the script itself at the same time that she began to envision the form that the characters should be given and a staging concept that would allow for the extremely adventurous nature of the action. The music from the film also required considerable augmentation, with particular attention paid to its African sources. Elton John and Tim Rice, the original composers who had worked with South African performer Lebo M, wrote two additional pop-style character songs; Lebo M, Hans Zimmer, and Mark Mancina filled out the score, drawing

on Zulu chanting and African rhythms and musical instruments. Just as Taymor's production style would draw on international sources and performance traditions, so the score would be an eclectic blend of American, European, and African styles. But as important as the music and the script were to the production, the greatest excitement would come from the visual presentation.

Taymor determined that various forms of puppets inhabited by actors would bring the animal characters to life and give her the flexibility to create magical action sequences, such as stampeding wildebeests or characters who could fly. The actors were not to be hidden by the puppet forms but rather to exist in puppet form and human form at the same time. The faces of the actors would always be seen. The actors playing lions would wear large masks placed above their own faces and be dressed in gowns of African-inspired fabrics rather than animal bodies. The hippopotamus was designed in full animal form for two actors whose bodies would be inside the large animal but whose heads would appear above the huge puppet. The character of Zazu, the comic bird, was designed as a fully realized rod puppet to be worn on the head of the actor who would sing and dance the role but who would be dressed in a suit that suggested the attitude of the bird character rather than in any kind of costume representing a bird. Human figures were designed into costumes representing plants, vines, and grass. Contraptions were invented such as the Gazelle Wheel, which would allow an actor to push across stage a wheeled vehicle that provided the momentum for the seven leaping figures of gazelle that were attached to it. Other "corporate" puppet forms were designed to enable one actor to present other groups of animals such as a flock of birds. Taymor explains her reasons for keeping the actor-puppeteers visible.

> When we see a person actually manipulating an inanimate object like a puppet and making it come alive, the duality moves us. Hidden special effects lack humanity, but when the

human spirit visibly animates an object, we experience a special, almost life giving connection. We become engaged by both the method of story telling as well as by the story itself.[6]

Taymor also conceptualized a method of changing scale that would help develop the sense of movement across vast spaces. Characters would be represented by small puppets when they were meant to be seen at a distance, what she calls a "long shot," and then would be played by human actors when they had traveled far enough to be seen in a "close-up." For the wildebeest stampede, the first image seen by the audience is created by painted figures on cloth being turned on rollers at the back of the stage. As the stampede approaches the audience, larger and larger masks are used to create the sense that the animals are coming closer and closer.

Developing this visually stupendous musical involved the creative collaboration of many theatre artists. Michael Curry coauthored the puppet designs and was responsible for engineering and constructing the puppets, and Taymor was responsible for sculpture and aesthetics. Richard Hudson created the actual scene design after Taymor developed the basic staging concept. Seven of the actors who ultimately appeared in the production were involved in experimentation with puppets and masks throughout the development process to see what would work and what would communicate effectively. In fact, Taymor incorporated puppets in the audition process:

> I also brought puppets to auditions to see how performers would look in relation to specific puppets and how they would respond when asked to animate an inanimate object. And though performers would not be totally immersed within the puppets nor hidden behind the masks, they would have to be willing to accept that the audience is not going to be looking at them alone. Attitude is a very important part of my casting decision. I want an actor who is going to enjoy the challenge and not view it as a burden. Rather than expressly

hiring puppeteers, I look for inventive actors who move well. A strong actor gives an idiosyncratic performance, because he infuses the puppet characters with his own personality instead of relying on generic puppetry technique. The thrill of working with a good actor who is new to this medium, is that he will take the form further than I ever imagined.[7]

Designers have frequently created spectacular environments for musicals in the past with astonishing special effects. However, in *The Lion King*, Julie Taymor has investigated ways in which the work of the actor may be extended through her puppet and mask creations. She has returned to ancient theatre traditions and brought them into contemporary performance to challenge the imaginations of both actors and audiences.

Susan Stroman and Contact

Susan Stroman called her 1999 theatre piece *Contact* a "dance play" because the essential medium for storytelling in this work was choreographic. Despite the facts that there was no actual singing in *Contact* and that the music for the dancing was recorded rather than played live, the Broadway community chose to extend the term *musical* to include this performance of three loosely related stories, each in its own way based on the central human need for emotional and physical connection to other people. In *Contact* the work of the choreographer, which had become a major force in earlier American musicals such as *West Side Story*, *A Chorus Line*, and *Bring in da Noise Bring in da Funk*, replaced the work of both the playwright-librettist and the lyricist. Although John Weidman collaborated with Stroman to provide the actor-dancers with small segments of spoken dialogue, it was dance that shaped the characters, the character relationships, and the actions of their stories.

In 1997 Andre Bishop, who was the artistic director of Lincoln Center Theater, invited Susan Stroman to create an original piece for his theatre because he admired the excitement and energy her choreography had brought to more traditional musicals such as *Crazy for You* (1992) and the revival of *Showboat* (1994). Bishop provided rehearsal space and resources to enable Stroman to develop material of her own choosing. *Contact* was inspired by Stroman's own experience in a late-night swing club in which she observed the magnetism of a stunning dancer in a yellow dress. From this seductive image evolved a story of a man who has lost the will to live until he dances with the woman in the yellow dress. Writer John Weidman explains that dance became salvation for a man betrayed by the failure of words: "The character came from a world that was all about language and language was something that failed him. He was going to have to escape from language to get saved."[8]

The story is danced out in the man's lonely apartment, which, in a dreamlike way, keeps changing into the swing club where he first watches from a distance and then finally, overcoming his inhibitions, dances with the woman in the yellow dress (Color Plate 30). Much of the piece consists of high-voltage swing dancing by characters who have discovered a world of dance that the alienated man is unable to enter. Because the story is set in a dance club, Stroman chose to use recorded jazz and swing music to reinforce the atmosphere of being in a club. When the work was expanded to include two additional stories, Stroman decided to use recorded music for all three vignettes.

The choreography of Susan Stroman is distinguished by invention and by the way dance movement creates character. For example, the first vignette of *Contact*, entitled "Swinging," consists of a playful and exuberant romantic encounter between lovers on a swing. The young man first pushes the woman on the swing and then joins her, sometimes sharing the seat and sometimes doing gymnastics on the ropes holding the swing. As the swing sails back and forth suspended high above the stage, the lovers find myriad ways of using the swing as part of their romance.

Stroman's ability to develop character through dance is exemplified by the second of the three *Contact* pieces, "Did You Move?" The essence of composing dance drama depends on conceptualizing the needs of the characters and the conflicts between them as physical problems. In this piece the central conflict is between a man trying to control his wife by imprisoning her in stillness while she tries to take back her freedom through movement. The woman begins the short story seated opposite her surly, gangsterlike husband in an Italian restaurant. Hunched over his food, he discourages her attempts at conversation, and when he leaves the table to get more food from the buffet, he barks at her, "don't move." The woman overcomes the paralyzing effect of his threats, and during each of her husband's absences she dances out her fantasies with increasing abandon. Gradually she engages all of the other people in the restaurant, diners and waiters, in a wild celebration of human connection. Full of humor, the dance evolves into a broad conspiracy involving actor-dancers and food and serving trays to confuse and outwit the joyless, thuggish husband.

Since the success of *Contact*, Susan Stroman has gone on to work as the director-choreographer first of a revival of *The Music Man* and then most notably of *The Producers* (2001). Starring Nathan Lane and Matthew Broderick, *The Producers* was adapted by the comedian Mel Brooks from his film of the same name and is a comedy about the theatre itself. *The Producers* tells a simple story of a down-on-his-luck theatre producer who hits on an outrageous scheme to make money. He persuades a large number of older women, foolishly susceptible to his charms, to invest in his next show, selling each of them a half interest or more, percentages that are clearly too large to be paid back. Then he guarantees that the show will be a catastrophic failure by choosing the most offensive and tasteless material possible, a cheerful musical about Nazi Germany. He is certain the show will close after one night, and he will be able to keep his elderly investors' money.

However, audiences believe the show must be a satire and find it so amusing that it becomes a huge success. This success, of course, means that the producer, Max Bialystock, is exposed as a fraud, dashing his fortunes but not his survival instincts. *The Producers* enjoyed a notable success in the months after September 11, 2001, providing audiences with the much needed release of laughter during disturbing times.

SUMMARY

Works of musical theatre integrate singing, spoken text, and dance to communicate the drama. The musical theatre is a unique development of the American theatre that has had widespread influence throughout the world. The musical theatre grew out of the minstrel shows, revues, and vaudeville of the nineteenth century, which drew heavily on the various immigrant groups that made up the U.S. population.

Oklahoma! made major advances in drawing together the expressive elements of musical theatre. All of the songs in *Oklahoma!* were necessary to the development of plot or character, and dance was also used in a new way to further the ideas of the work. In *West Side Story*, based on William Shakespeare's *Romeo and Juliet*, Jerome Robbins made the choreography of equal importance to the singing. *My Fair Lady* drew on its source, *Pygmalion*, by George Bernard Shaw, to bring brilliant language to the musical stage. *Cabaret* turned the musical theatre away from the carefully plotted book musicals represented by *Oklahoma!*, *West Side Story*, and *My Fair Lady* to a new form, the concept musical, in which theme expressed through scenic and performance elements is of greater importance than the plot. Stephen Sondheim contributed major innovations in subject matter and dramatic construction and set new standards for the writing of lyrics. *A Chorus Line* continued the evolution of the concept musical with its prominent use of dance to tell the stories

of actors auditioning for a musical. New directions in theme and style have been provided by recent musicals such as *Bring in da Noise Bring in da Funk*, *Rent*, *The Lion King*, and *Contact*.

The use of popular music to convey dramatic ideas and to build character and the centrality of dance in telling a story distinguish the musical theatre form. The popular music of each era has been embraced by the musical theatre, including, most recently, hip-hop and rock and roll. The choreographer-director has emerged as a new theatre creator, as exemplified by Jerome Robbins, Michael Bennett, and Susan Stroman. In *The Lion King*, it was the designer-director, Julie Taymor, who contributed a startling new vision for musical theatre by extending the actors' expressive possibilities through puppets and masks.

TOPICS FOR DISCUSSION AND WRITING

1. Discuss the ways that music is an integral part of student life today. When and what kinds of music do you listen to or participate in creating? In addition to concerts, where music is the focus of the event, what events that are significant to you have some kind of musical association? What experiences in your life involve some kind of musical expression?

2. How does experiencing musical theatre differ from experiencing the spoken text of a nonmusical play. Draw on the musicals seen by members of the class, whether on the stage or on film, to discuss the way music changes the nature of theatrical expression and the audience response. What kinds of material is music especially suited to?

3. What subject material and style of music in a musical production would appeal to an audience of your peers?

NOTES

1. Richard A. Long, *The Black Tradition in Dance* (New York: Rizzoli, 1990), 11.

2. Walter Kerr, *New York Times*, 4 December 1966, 5.

3. Frank Rich, "A Musical Theatre Breakthrough," *New York Times*, 21 October 1984, sec. 6, 53.

4. Stephen Sondheim quoted in Linda Winer, "Sondheim in His Own Words," *American Theatre*, II, no. 2 (May 1985): 12.

5. Stephen Sondheim and John Weidman, *Pacific Overtures* (New York: Theatre Communications Group, 1991), 20–21.

6. Julie Taymor, *The Lion King: Pride Rock on Broadway* (New York: Hyperion, 1999), 28.

7. Taymor, 136.

8. John Weidman quoted in Robin Pogrebin, "Making 'Contact' Without Conflict," *New York Times*, 18 October 1999, E3.

SUGGESTIONS FOR FURTHER READING

Alpert, Hollis. *The Life and Times of Porgy and Bess*. New York: Alfred A. Knopf, 1990.

A history of the popular opera *Porgy and Bess*, written by George Gershwin and first performed in 1935; offers a fascinating study of the condition of American musical theatre in the 1930s and the evolution of attitudes toward a celebrated but controversial theatre work by a white composer about the lives of African Americans.

Citron, Stephen. *The Musical Theatre from the Inside Out*. Chicago: I. R. Dee, 1992.

An examination of the way musicals are created and produced; describes the responsibilities of the librettist, lyricist, composer, director, and producer and discusses various forms of musical theatre and the specific approaches that have led to success.

Easton, Carol. *No Intermissions: The Life of Agnes de Mille*. Boston: Little, Brown, 1996.

A biography of the choreographer of *Oklahoma!*; provides insight into the merging of the dance world and the theatre world in the musical. De Mille, a major figure in dance in the twentieth century, began her career as a ballet dancer before becoming a highly innovative choreographer in both the ballet and the musical theatre. De Mille

choreographed such musicals as *Oklahoma!*, *Carousel*, *Brigadoon*, and *Paint Your Wagon;* among her ballets are *Rodeo*, *Three Virgins and a Devil*, and *Fall River Legend*, about Lizzie Borden. De Mille also choreographed for film and television.

Flinn, Denny Martin. *Musical: The Rise, Glory and Fall of an American Institution*. New York: Schirmer Books, 1997.

A detailed and lively history of the American musical theatre that begins with an overview of musical theatre in earlier periods, including ancient Greek, medieval, and Renaissance theatres. This book is not as lavishly illustrated as *Red, Hot, and Blue* (see following entry), and the photographs are in black and white, but it covers different subjects such as rock musicals and offers more of a critical appraisal of the strengths and weaknesses of the musical form.

Henderson, Amy, and Dwight Blocker Bowers. *Red, Hot, and Blue: A Smithsonian Salute to the American Musical Theatre*. Washington: Smithsonian Institution Press, 1996.

A beautifully illustrated history of musical theatre and film, from nineteenth-century vaudeville to the 1980s, includes photographs of posters, set and costume designs, individual composers, writers, directors, and choreographers, as well as a terrific collection of memorable production shots.

Lees, Gene. *Inventing Champagne: The Worlds of Lerner and Loewe*. New York: St. Martin's Press, 1990.

An investigation of the collaboration of Alan Lerner and Frederick Loewe, who wrote *Brigadoon*, *An American in Paris*, *Camelot*, and most memorably, *My Fair Lady;* contains many anecdotes that reveal the difficult nature of collaboration and intriguing details about the composition, casting, and performances of their celebrated musicals.

Schlebera, Jurgen. *Kurt Weill*. Translated by Caroline Murphy. New Haven: Yale University Press, 1995.

A biography of Kurt Weill, whose career crossed a number of musical theatre movements in the twentieth century. Weill began as a composer in Germany and collaborated with Bertolt Brecht on Brecht's most famous musical work, *The Threepenny Opera*, before coming to the United States, where he worked first with the Group Theatre and then for the Broadway musical stage.

Taymor, Julie. *The Lion King: Pride Rock on Broadway*. New York: Hyperion, 1999.

A photo essay with supporting text of how the film of *The Lion King* was made into a Broadway musical; includes color photographs of the puppet design and construction process as well as of the production choreography.

Woll, Allen. *Black Musical Theatre: From Coontown to Dreamgirls.* New York: Da Capo Press, 1989.

An insightful account of African American participation in musical theatre from 1890 to the present; explains the relationship between black musical theatre and the minstrel show and identifies the many significant and original contributions of black composers and performers, with rarely seen photographs from the early period of black musical theatre.

The Nature of Style
Realism and Theatricalism

The play is central to the expression of ideas in the theatre. Through stylistic choices playwrights give shape to their particular understanding of the human condition. The play's vocabulary, the arrangement of the words, the rhythm of the speeches, the details of the characters' lives and actions, all contribute to the way a story is told or what we call the style of the play. In creating their dramas, playwrights draw on their own life experiences as well as traditions from both the American drama and the dramas of other nations. In Part Three we approach the examination of style by studying the history of two major dramatic traditions: realism and theatricalism. Then we consider the works of two additional playwrights: Wakako Yamauchi and Tony Kushner. We focus on the style of the expressive elements in their plays and the way those elements are arranged to create meaning, expanding the discussion of American playwriting begun with the study of *Joe Turner's Come and Gone*.

After examining the work of the playwright, we study the way the play's meaning is further defined throughout the production process. We see that the choices of directors, actors, and designers also have stylistic significance and shape the ideas communicated to the audience. We look at Wakako Yamauchi's play *And the Soul Shall Dance*, in production at East West Players and Northwest Asian American Theatre, and Tony Kushner's play *Angels in America*, in production at the Eureka Theatre. Through play text and performance we examine issues of self-determination and self-knowledge, family, social equality, American politics and history, race, and gender. We see the assumptions that are challenged through the plays and the contributions the plays make to social change.

CHAPTER 8

Understanding Style: Realism

In theatrical communication, the distinctive manner in which a playwright chooses to describe, express, interpret, or present her or his worldview is referred to as **style.** A playwright makes stylistic choices, as do the theatre practitioners who mount productions. Many plays are written in one style; others, however, are written in mixed styles. Furthermore, although the goal in much theatre production is to stage a play according to the style indicated by the script, some productions seek to interpret or reinterpret material by staging a play in a different style.

Since the early twentieth century, American theatre has been dominated by the style known as **realism.** Realistic plays explore social and economic problems, psychological issues, and the personal struggles of ordinary people. Realistic productions attempt to give the audience members a sense that they are watching real life rather than a theatrical event. It is as if a "fourth wall" has been removed and the audience members are looking in at actual events. Realism is a style we frequently see on television and in movies. It is, however, only one of numerous styles seen in the American theatre.

This chapter focuses on the characteristics of realism and the realistic theatre. We begin by identifying realistic elements in *Joe Turner's*

Come and Gone and considering the use of realism in film. We then examine the historical context for the development of realism and some of the most important European and American playwrights and theatre practitioners of the realistic school.

INTRODUCTION TO REALISM

Most forms of theatre are an exploration of some truth about human existence. Realism seeks to construct truth through an accumulation of surface detail. Realists are guided by the supposition that if we understand enough of the "facts," if we see enough of the details, we will be able to make sense of the situation. And if we see the details of the environment in which characters live or the psychological forces that affect them, we will understand why they behave as they do.

In realistic plays, audience members forget that they are in a darkened auditorium and feel transported to the locale of the play: a restaurant, a home, or a business. Functional furniture, sinks with running water, stoves that cook real food, and working radios and televisions all help to create the "illusion" that what the audience sees and hears are the occurrences of daily life.

This illusion is heightened by the fact that the actors perform their actions, play their parts, as if the audience were not present. They do not look directly at audience members or speak to them. They address each other as if no one else were present to overhear them. If the actors do look out to where the audience is seated, they may create the impression that they are looking out a window into a garden or onto railroad tracks or into another part of the defined space. In strict realism, the actors do not acknowledge the audience's presence.

The language in realistic plays echoes the language of daily life. Characters use language that seems to come from the streets, the corner bar, or the workplace—what we can call the vernacular. Realistic plays are also frequently concerned with the way the past shapes the present. For some playwrights, heredity is an important element in the characters' identity; often, past secrets are of primary significance in understanding the characters' present. For other playwrights, environment is the crucial factor.

Realistic Elements in Joe Turner's Come and Gone

For August Wilson's *Joe Turner's Come and Gone*, realism is clearly a useful means of expression. The past is a crucial factor in this play, particularly the past of slavery and the chain gang. Herald Loomis's past is buried in his flesh and bones; it is a bitter secret that must be revealed before he can move into the present and then the future as a free man.

Heredity is also important. Seth inherited property and values from his father, an inheritance that puts him in a unique position. Bynum has a different kind of inheritance from his father. He has inherited a song, a way of being in the world, a vision of life's possibility. Seth contrasts sharply with most of the other characters, who have been disinherited by slavery and the political upheavals in the American South. They are cut off from the past as they try to find the basics of making a living and some sense of family or companionship.

The world that *Joe Turner's Come and Gone* presents is one of daily struggle for survival. The play's environment is life as it is lived day to day in the boardinghouse. Food is prepared and eaten. Bertha's biscuits and coffee are what keep everyone going. Seth makes dustpans for Selig and works in his own garden. Money and sheets of metal change hands. Seth's conversations with his tenants also focus on money and the rules of the house. The basics of living arrangements and work arrangements give the play its underlying rhythm. The clatter of life—cooking, tools against metal, dishes on the table—blends with the earthy language of the characters, as Wilson employs the speech patterns and expressions of characters from a particular time and place.

A tone of sensuality also contributes to the vital atmosphere of the boardinghouse in all of the male-female relationships, most noticeably in the interactions between Jeremy and Mollie, who exude sexual energy. August Wilson constructs his play with an earthy realism to give us a tangible view of African American life at a turning point in American history. Although our focus at this point is on realism, we must not fail to recognize other stylistic elements in *Joe Turner's Come and Gone*, such as the mythic background that Bynum establishes with his story of the shiny man and the larger-than-life, symbolic struggle that Herald Loomis goes through to gain control of his own destiny.

Realism in Film

Realism has found its most receptive medium in film. A brief discussion of realism and film will help to further define the nature of realism. Film can create the appearance of reality far more completely than most theatre productions can. The camera, in fact, is frequently positioned at what would be the fourth wall. It becomes the silent witness that carries the audience into the most private or intimate of circumstances.

Because a film audience cannot interrupt film actors, cannot alter what is fixed on the screen, the illusion is never broken. During the course of a film, actors cannot forget their lines, because scenes are reshot to achieve a perfection that is neither possible nor even desirable in the theatre. Enormous amounts of money and energy go into building elaborate sets full of intricate, concrete details that simulate "real" spaces, whether they are homes or western towns or space stations. Alternatively, the actors and film crew often go on location and use actual places; they take over houses, public buildings, and city streets to create a realistic effect. A whole city may form the set for a car chase. Real vehicles are blown up to create the effect of

car crashes. Mangled bodies and disturbing amounts of stage blood are carefully arranged to create the illusion of death and destruction. Of course, we are also aware that films can overload the senses with such an excess of spectacular realism that they lose any feeling of actuality.

The perfectability of realism in film is one of the reasons theatre practitioners do not try to create completely realistic productions. In the early part of the century, when film was in its infancy, entire restaurants or rivers with flowing water were created onstage, but rarely do we see this kind of elaborate attempt at realism in today's theatre.

By presenting an accumulation of externally observed details of human action and environment, realism gives us one view of human existence. Other styles of theatrical communication (such as expressionism; see Chapter 10) might move inside the characters' psyches and present a world shaped by distortion and exaggeration, or they might focus on large symbolic actions rather than minute details, or they might emphasize the political context of human action rather than an in-depth exploration of individual characters' lives. Today, theatrical performances are unlikely to follow only one style or another; styles tend to be mixed, reflecting the sense that we experience the world around us in different ways at the same time.

ORIGINS OF REALISM

During the nineteenth century the theatre underwent profound changes, in both the subjects that playwrights chose for their plays and the style in which plays were written and performed. Before that time, as we discussed earlier in the book, serious dramas were written about royal or noble families or about religious figures. The histories or conflicts involving kings and gods were considered representative of the concerns of the entire society. Only **comedies** focused on the lives of average citizens or those who were disenfranchised, and then the focus was on human weakness.

In the nineteenth century, however, a movement began that was aimed at making the lives of middle-class and poor characters the focus of serious drama. The world inhabited by these characters was made more tangible by the use of language that seemed to come from overheard daily conversations.

In earlier styles, environment was indicated by suggestion or theatrical conventions, or backgrounds were created for the actors' presentations by a kind of generalized decoration. In the Greek theatre, for example, the scene building suggested the palace of whatever royal family was the subject of the play, and new characters were indicated by changes in masks. In the Elizabethan theatre, the throne room of the king was indicated by bringing on a chair, or a battlefield was created by the entrance of soldiers carrying banners. The audience's imagination was crucial to completing the stage image.

Decorative backgrounds became popular after the introduction of **perspective** painting by the Italians in the early seventeenth century. They were used in opera, court masques, or pageants, and then in the romantic drama of the eighteenth and early nineteenth centuries. Images of gardens or palaces were painted on flat scenic pieces that were arranged **upstage** (the area of the stage farthest away from the audience) to create a pictorial background for the actors.

But as the drama began to consider the struggles of working people, the theatre shifted in its style of presentation in order to place those struggles in actual three-dimensional environments rather than on bare stages or in front of painted backgrounds. The material environment became a crucial factor in character development. The lives of characters living in harsh circumstances, speaking the informal language of the workplace and the home, presented in seemingly real environments also generated the development of a new acting style. Actors and directors sought a more natural style of acting

that would make sense of the changes playwrights were bringing to the drama. No longer could actors be expected to stand at the front edge of the stage and declaim their lines with grand gestures directly to the audience. Actors had to move upstage to give the appearance that they lived in the onstage furnishings and speak to each other conversationally as if the audience were not there. This new fusion of subject matter and performance became the basis for the realistic style of theatre. A working definition of *realism* might be theatre that seeks to give the appearance of everyday reality.

THE SOCIAL BACKGROUND OF REALISM

Realism occurred at a particular point in human history and served as an artistic crossroads, as a representation of the intersection of various developments in philosophical, social, and scientific thought. It is no coincidence that dramas began to portray the "common" man or woman at the same time democratic governments began to replace kings ruling by "divine right." Nor is it surprising that as advances in science and technology fueled the industrial revolution, the theatre would include more evidence of the material world. The study of human psychology also had its counterpart in the theatre, as playwrights, directors, and actors probed the sources of human behavior and looked to heredity and environment to explain why human beings act as they do. And as social reformers began to consider the inequitable distribution of wealth and the consequences of poverty, the impact of social circumstances on the development of character became an important consideration in the theatre as well.

Realism became a dominant force in the theatre as society became interested in questions of how individuals are defined by or overcome the limitations placed on them by the circumstances of their history, their environment, their social positions, and their relationships. In examining realism, however, it is always crucial to remember that although realistic plays are constructed to give the appearance of reality, realism is a theatrical style involving artistic choices; it is not life itself.

EUROPEAN REALISM

Henrik Ibsen

Norwegian playwright Henrik Ibsen (1828–1906) profoundly changed the nature of the European theatre when he wrote a group of plays during the latter part of the nineteenth century that focused on social problems and the struggle of individuals to resist the social, religious, and familial restrictions of a tightly structured, hierarchical society. Writing about surprisingly contemporary subjects such as pollution, venereal disease, and women's rights, Ibsen brought problems and concerns onto the stage that shifted the emphasis of theatrical content. In *An Enemy of the People* (1882), for example, a town furiously turns on the doctor who exposes the pollution in the community water system because the citizens fear that their lucrative spa business will be ruined. In *A Doll's House* (1879), a woman chooses to leave her husband and children rather than go on living the charade of a doll wife in a doll's house (Color Plate 31).

Ibsen looked at the daily lives of middle-class characters as they dealt with the need to earn a living, to provide properly for their children, to find meaningful work, to establish satisfying relationships. And he placed his characters in the environment of the middle class, replacing flat, painted scenery with the three-dimensional furnishings of detailed houses. The settings became metaphors for the characters' lives: warm but stifling rooms filled with wood stoves, rocking chairs, and needlework or colder spaces furnished with thick, heavy couches and draperies, the windows looking out on endless rain or withered leaves.

August Strindberg

Whereas Ibsen focused on the struggle between individual self-determination and social restrictions, his fellow Scandinavian, August

One of the early realistic plays was An Enemy of the People *by Norwegian playwright Henrik Ibsen. Shown here is a 1998 production directed by Trevor Nunn. Ian McKellan portrays Dr. Stockmann, a character trying to persuade his fellow citizens that the mineral baths on which the town depends for revenue must be shut down because the water is polluted.*

Before being recognized as one of the leading playwrights of the late nineteenth century, Henrik Ibsen worked in almost every capacity in the theatre, directing plays, building scenery, and selling tickets. In addition to writing twelve plays that provided the foundation for realism in the theatre, Ibsen wrote verse plays such as Peer Gynt *and symbolic plays such as* The Wild Duck.

August Strindberg's early plays were known for their combination of detailed naturalism and emotional explosiveness. He later focused on the inner journeys of his characters, whom he placed in strange, symbolic circumstances.

Strindberg (1849–1912), from Sweden, laid bare the highly charged emotions of couples caught in love-hate relationships. Strindberg's characters tear at each other using words as weapons to wound or destroy each other in what frequently becomes a fight to the death. American critic Ruby Cohn has called these verbal battles "dialogues of cruelty."[1]

In Strindberg's play *The Father* (1887), the Captain is tormented by his own unfounded doubts about his daughter's paternity. A power struggle with his wife, Laura, over the direction of their daughter's education and upbringing turns into a nightmarish conflict of manipulation and attack. Laura's cleverness in outmaneuvering her husband sends him into a violent rage that becomes her proof that he is unfit to remain in the household.

Strindberg's play *Miss Julie* (1888) adds class conflict to sexual conflict. The aristocratic mistress of a wealthy house, Miss Julie, is seduced by the valet, Jean. Their struggle for domination in the relationship results in her suicide. This brief and intense relationship unleashes bitter, insulting denunciations from both characters that alternate with painful admissions of dependency. Strindberg's pessimistic examination of male–female relationships was in part meant to answer Ibsen's apparent championship of women's rights.

Miss Julie is torn between her desires and the need to maintain her social position as the daughter of a count. She commits suicide rather than face the consequences of her affair with a servant. Hope Chernov plays Miss Julie in the 1998 Pearl Theatre production of Miss Julie *by August Strindberg, directed by Christopher Martin.*

Anton Chekhov

The third major playwright in the development of European realism was the Russian Anton Chekhov (1860–1904). Chekhov finished his medical degree and supported himself and his family as a writer during his student days, before he turned to writing as his primary occupation. He wrote numerous short stories and sketches, and at the end of his career and his short life he wrote the four plays that established his unique place in the theatre.

Chekhov's plays contain neither the complicated plots of Ibsen nor the emotional fireworks of Strindberg. In fact, very little seems to happen in Chekhov's plays. The characters barely hear each other, so absorbed are they by their own concerns. In *The Cherry Orchard* (1904), for example, a group of characters gather at the family estate supposedly to prevent the sale of their beloved cherry trees. But while they gossip and give sad little parties and fret endlessly over their own failures, the cherry orchard slips away, sold to a developer who will cut down the trees for summer cottages. The developer was once a peasant on the very land that he has purchased. As a friend of the family members, he has tried to advise them on ways to save the cherry orchard, but they are incapable of hearing him. Chekhov's characters speak passionately about love, but lasting relationships prove to be as elusive for them as their ability to save the cherry orchard.

Although much in Chekhov's plays is very painful, the plays are actually full of humor. By juxtaposing incongruous incidents and exposing the foolishness of characters who take themselves too seriously, the Chekhovian world shifts constantly between evoking sympathy and evoking laughter. Chekhov concentrated on the small details of his characters' lives and wrote dialogue that frequently goes unanswered because the characters are more interested in what they have to say than in listening to each other. Although Chekhov chose each

Anton Chekhov's medical training and his own health problems with tuberculosis seemed to make him an especially acute observer of human interactions. He approached his characters with an objectivity that revealed human weakness in all of them. He was sympathetic to his characters yet gently exposed their hypocrisy and vanity.

In The Three Sisters, *Chekhov presents the gradual wearing away of the characters' hopes and dreams for the future. In the first act of* The Three Sisters *at Lewis and Clark College, directed by Stephanie K. Arnold, most of the characters still share an optimism about the future. Masha (far left) already seems to sense the disappointments to come. Heidi Van Schoonhoven plays Masha; Christine Calfas plays Irina.*

Color Plate 1   *This mask represents another ceremonial performance tradition, that of the Northwest Coast Native Americans. Ritual dramas were enacted as part of the potlatch, a ceremony lasting for days that was both a social occasion involving the immediate community and many invited guests and a means of expressing changes in the social order. Rites of passage for the young, marriages, and mourning cycles were all observed through the potlatch. Dramatic performances were a highlight of these gatherings and included elaborately carved masks, spectacular costumes, and astonishing special effects. The mask in the photograph is used in performances open to the public at Tillicum Village on Blake Island, Washington.*

Color Plate 2 Bill Irwin and David Shine, the creators of Fool Moon, *performed the entire piece without speaking, relying on broad physical characterization and audience participation to build comic sketches that are based on the anxieties of modern life. Their exit, sailing away on the moon at the end of the performance, created a moment of glowing theatre magic.*

Color Plate 3 Iphigeneia in Tauris *returns to the story of Agamemnon and his children but focuses on a time long after the deaths of Agamemnon and Clytaemnestra. This version of the events explains that Iphigeneia survived her ordeal at Aulis when the goddess Artemis substituted a deer as the sacrificial victim and secretly brought Iphigeneia away to serve as her temple priestess. As shown in this 1997 production entitled* Iphigeneia Cycle *at the Court Theatre, directed by JoAnne Akalaitis, Iphigeneia is now responsible, herself, for human sacrifices. Here the chorus cleans the blood off the stairs of the temple to Artemis where these sacrifices take place as Iphigeneia tells her bitter story.*

Color Plate 4 Jonathan Epstein is seen here as Shakespeare's villainous Richard III caught in a trap of his own making in a 1999 production directed by Tina Packer for Shakespeare & Company (Lenox, Massachusetts).

Color Plate 5 The heroine prepares for battle in this scene from The Peony Pavilion, which demonstrates the way the intensity of the gestural acting style combined with brilliant costumes and elaborate makeup provides the visual expression of Chinese Opera without the use of any scenic background.

Color Plate 6 *Under the direction of Lloyd Richards, the premiere production of* Joe Turner's Come and Gone *featured Delroy Lindo as Herald Loomis and Angela Bassett as Martha Pentecost; their dramatic meeting takes place with the boardinghouse residents as witnesses.*

Color Plate 7 *Herald Loomis (Derrick Lee Weedon) describes his paralyzing vision of bones rising from the water to Bynum (LeWan Alexander) in the Oregon Shakespeare Festival production of* Joe Turner's Come and Gone.

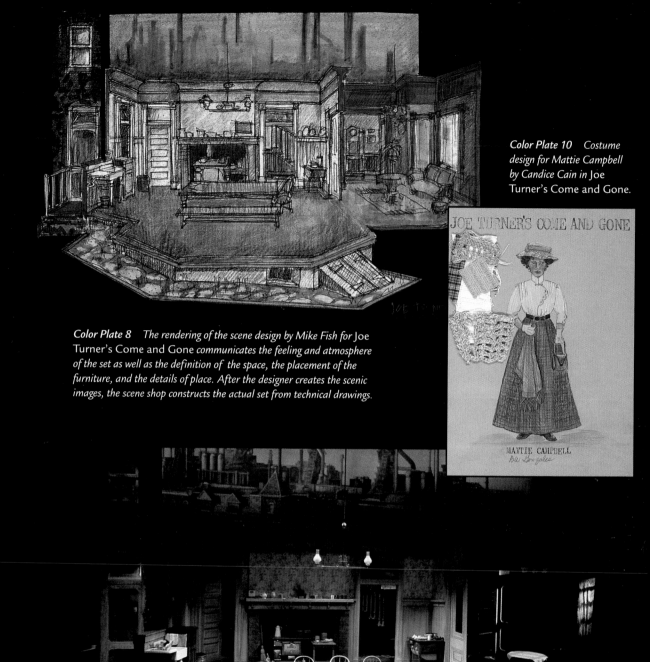

Color Plate 10 Costume design for Mattie Campbell by Candice Cain in Joe Turner's Come and Gone.

JOE TURNER'S COME AND GONE

MATTIE CAMPBELL

Color Plate 8 The rendering of the scene design by Mike Fish for Joe Turner's Come and Gone *communicates the feeling and atmosphere of the set as well as the definition of the space, the placement of the furniture, and the details of place. After the designer creates the scenic images, the scene shop constructs the actual set from technical drawings.*

Color Plate 9 The scene design is transformed into the actual setting for Joe Turner's Come and Gone. *The warmth of the kitchen is placed against the smokestacks of industrial Pittsburgh. The table offers a gathering place for the characters and becomes the center of the play's action.*

Color Plate 11 *In Robert Wilson's production of* Danton's Death *at the Alley Theatre in Houston, the actors achieved a sculptural quality through their own movements, their placement on the stage, and the use of light. Richard Thomas, playing Danton, was given detailed instructions by director Wilson for all of his movements. He relied on his more traditional training in the realistic theatre to fill out his character internally.*

Color Plate 12 *Mary-Louise Parker, seen here in* Proof *with Ben Shenkman, emphasizes that process is the way actors sustain the freshness of their work when doing a long run. "The idea that I've got a role completely doesn't fit in with my philosophy. It's never something to be fully arrived at. It's just something to experience, to just keep flexing and testing and to grow with, rather than to fully find" (Mary-Louise Parker quoted in Mervyn Rothstein, "Getting* Proof *to Work Is a Delicate Equation,"* New York Times, *3 June 2001, 7).*

Color Plate 13   Randall Duk Kim as Hamlet contemplates the fleeting nature of human mortality in this scene from Hamlet. The American Players Theatre of Spring Green, Wisconsin, chose a traditional period setting for this production staged outdoors in a large amphitheatre.

Color Plate 14 In her 1999 production of Richard III for Shakespeare & Company, director Tina Packer focused on Richard as a character determined to win at any cost. Here, Richard (Jonathan Epstein) seduces Lady Anne (Elizabeth Aspenlieder) over the coffin of her husband, whom Richard has murdered. Richard persuades Lady Anne of his devotion to her by offering her the chance to kill him. To establish Richard's ferocity in the Shakespeare & Company production, even the crutches that he used to compensate for his physical deformity became weapons armed with their own array of daggers and ax heads.

Color Plate 15 Robert Wilson creates a vivid and horrifying image of violence using the actors' body positions and the light to convey the intensity of the moment in his 2002 production of Woyzeck, produced in collaboration with the Betty Nansen Teatret of Denmark, with music by Kathleen Brennan and Tom Waits.

Color Plate 16 *For a play written by Friedrich Schiller in 1800, director JoAnne Akalaitis uses bold stage images to express character situation and relationships in her 2001 production of* Mary Stuart *at the Court Theatre. The title character, played by Jenny Bacon, bids farewell to her ladies-in-waiting before being executed.*

Color Plate 17 *BW Gonzalez is seen here as Lady Macbeth in the sleepwalking scene wearing the white costume designed by Deborah Dryden to show the bloody misdeeds committed by the Macbeths during the course of the play. The production was directed by Libby Appel at the Oregon Shakespeare Festival in 2002.*

Color Plate 18 *The principles of directorial focus are clearly demonstrated in this scene from* The Adding Machine, *directed by Anne Bogart in 1995 for the Actors Theatre of Louisville. The choreographed appearance of the actors' positions was achieved using a directorial approach called the viewpoints, in which the actors are encouraged to develop expressive gestures and spatial relationships that interpret the situations of the characters metaphorically. The stage picture results from the collaborative efforts of the director and the actors rather than through the director's positioning of the actors. The director, Anne Bogart, divides her time between the Actors Theatre of Louisville, the Saratoga Theatre Institute which she codirects with Tadashi Suzuki, and teaching responsibilities at Columbia University.*

Color Plate 23   *In 1988 Julie Taymor adapted a short story by Horacio Quiroga into a musical puppet theatre piece entitled* Juan Darien: A Carnival Mass. *Like* The Lion King, *the play used a combination of actors, masked dancers, and various forms of puppets. The photograph shows the character of the teacher, who was nine feet tall and whose hair was an open book with pages that moved when he was angry.*

Color Plate 24   Opera is frequently staged on a large scale with striking visual effects. The design elements must support the emotional intensity expressed in the music. Lighting design for opera may emphasize the mood of the music through a heightened use of color and strong contrasts of light and shadow. In the San Francisco Opera production of Abduction *by Mozart, lighting designer Joan Arhelger creates a moonlit night that offers the hope of reconciliation but also the threat of discovery. The set design is by Thomas Lynch; the stage director is Stephen Wadsworth.*

detail carefully, his plays lack the obvious buildup of increasing tension and the exciting plot development that shape the dramas of Ibsen and Strindberg. But because of the seeming randomness of the actions and dialogue, Chekhov's plays may be the most realistic, the most like life. And yet the construction of the worldview through carefully selected objects and actions gives a heightened sense of life that takes on a poetic quality.

AMERICAN REALISM

Realism was the dominant style of American theatre in the first half of the twentieth century. Lillian Hellman (1905–1984), Arthur Miller (1915–), and Tennessee Williams (1911–1983) consolidated and shaped the foundation of American realism during the 1930s and 1940s. Hellman and Miller were particularly concerned with the moral positions of their characters, whereas Williams wrote about highly sensitive characters struggling to reconcile personal longing with the harsh and judgmental society surrounding them. Hellman and Williams also brought issues of gay and lesbian sexuality onto the stage, startling their audiences, given the taboos concerning such subjects at the time.

Lillian Hellman

Lillian Hellman's first major play, *The Children's Hour*, was produced in New York in 1934. The play is the story of two young women teachers whose lives are ruined by a lie told by a restless student looking for attention. In both *The Children's Hour* and *The Little Foxes* (1939), which looks at the greed and exploitation inherent in American capitalism, Hellman was concerned with characters who are aware of a wrong being perpetrated but who do not step forward, thereby leaving a void that is quickly filled by slander and manipulation. The kind of realism used by Hellman in her plays is reminiscent of Ibsen, with an emphasis on the concrete details

Lillian Hellman is known for the fervent moral concerns of her plays, including Watch on the Rhine *and* The Searching Wind. *Later in her writing career she turned to the memoir in* An Unfinished Woman *and* Pentimento.

of the characters' lives and a plot in which one incident causes the next.

Poetic Realism: Arthur Miller and Tennessee Williams

Arthur Miller and Tennessee Williams transformed the realism of Hellman's work by focusing on a psychological exploration that places the characters' memories and fantasies onstage. Williams's *A Streetcar Named Desire* (1947) and Miller's *Death of a Salesman* (1949) begin in what seem to be realistic family situations but then change the point of view by moving inside the minds of characters who are beginning to slip away from reality. The plays shift back and forth between the present and the past, and it

Arthur Miller continues to be a force in American theatre and film. A highly regarded revival of Death of a Salesman, *with Brian Dennehy playing Willy Loman, was produced on Broadway in 1999 followed by a new production of* The Crucible, *about the Salem witch trials, in 2002 with Liam Neeson and Laura Linney (see Color Plate 32). Miller has also participated in the adaptation of his play* A View from the Bridge *into an opera, which premiered in 1999 and continues to be produced at opera houses around the country. And most recently he has written a new play,* Resurrection Blues, *produced in 2002 at the Guthrie Theatre in Minneapolis, which in Miller's words is about "the commercialization of everything."*

Tennessee Williams achieved recognition as a playwright with The Glass Menagerie (1944), *which drew on Williams's own family history. Later plays, such as* Cat on a Hot Tin Roof *and* Suddenly Last Summer, *are charged with sexual tensions that frequently erupt in violence.*

becomes impossible to know if what the characters remember is truth or illusion.

In *Death of a Salesman* the walls actually dissolve, allowing the space to become as flexible as the character's mind. In *A Streetcar Named Desire* symbolic characters enter the seemingly realistic stage space. The imagery and structure of Miller's and Williams's plays inspired memorable productions directed by Elia Kazan and designed by Jo Mielziner in a style that came to be known as **poetic realism.** For decades, this style was considered the most eloquent representation of American drama.

Arthur Miller's first play, *All My Sons* (1947), is a traditional, realistic, family drama that concerns the corrosive effect of greed on the human spirit and the need for individuals to take responsibility, both for the larger society and for their families. In this play, the father, Joe Keller, has sold flawed aircraft parts to the government during World War II. His partner, a less forceful man, goes to prison when this fraud is exposed. Although Keller continues to proclaim his innocence, his own son, a pilot in the war, disappears in combat, unable to live with the knowledge of his father's crime against

Biff (John Malkovich) tries to convince his father, Willy (Dustin Hoffman), that neither of them was meant to be a leader of men in Arthur Miller's most famous play, Death of a Salesman.

all the young pilots destined to fly unsafe equipment.

Miller took the essence of the family drama from *All My Sons*, the conflict between fathers and sons, and expanded its dimensions in his play *Death of a Salesman*. In this play, the father, Willy Loman, is driven to suicide by the fear that he has failed his son, Biff. Biff, who was full of promise until his senior year in high school, has spent his adult life drifting from job to job, including a stint in prison for stealing. Through flashbacks we see Willy's obsession with Biff's youth and Willy's attempt to defend the lesson that he repeatedly taught him: to create an image for yourself in a world in which everything is for sale rather than build a base of accomplishment.

Although the play critiques the notion of success in the United States as measured by dollar signs, it also looks again to the theme of re-sponsibility for one's children and the children of the nation. Here Miller presents a character cut off from his roots, cut off from his heritage, who consequently does not know what to teach his own children.

Tennessee Williams came to prominence as a playwright with his 1944 play *The Glass Menagerie*. The central character, Tom, ultimately abandons his domineering mother and fragile sister in order to make a life for himself. The mother, Amanda, lives through exaggerated memories of her own youth as a much sought after Southern belle, while the sister, Laura, lives in an imaginary world she shares with her glass figurines. Laura is too mentally unstable to cope with life beyond the shabby family apartment, a complete contradiction of her mother's fantasy that a gentleman caller will appear to marry her and transform all their lives.

Marlon Brando and Jessica Tandy created the original interpretations of Tennessee Williams's famous characters, Stanley and Blanche, in A Streetcar Named Desire, *directed by Elia Kazan.*

In *A Streetcar Named Desire*, Williams explores the disintegration of a young woman, Blanche Dubois, who retreats further and further into a world of illusions to block out her own failures and the failures of those around her to live up to a code of gentility from a bygone era. When her reduced circumstances force her to move in with her sister, Stella, and brother-in-law, Stanley, the tensions between the characters explode in Stanley's sexual assault on Blanche and her final collapse.

CONSTANTIN STANISLAVSKY AND REALISTIC ACTING

The new realistic dramas of the nineteenth century prompted actors to rethink the nature of their craft. The most influential figure in the development of a new approach to acting was Constantin Stanislavsky (1863–1938), an actor who became a prominent stage director and teacher as cofounder and artistic director of the Moscow Art Theatre. Stanislavsky directed the initial productions of all of Chekhov's plays. It was in part from his work with Chekhov that Stanislavsky evolved his approach to acting—one appropriate to the subtlety and introspection of Chekhov's characters. This approach has become a mainstay of realistic theatre and film.

The ideas suggested by Stanislavsky have come to be organized into something of a system that is frequently referred to as **method acting.** In his own time, however, Stanislavsky was continuously reviewing and adjusting his approach. Stanislavsky believed that the actor should look for ways to identify as closely as possible with his or her character, to undergo a transformation in which the actor would disappear and the character would emerge in his or her place. He proposed an internal rather than an external approach to character development.

From Stanislavsky's work has come the idea that one of the major sources for character development should be the life of the actor. That is, the actor should draw on personal experiences and relationships to provide the foundation for the character's inner life. The actor should also study the role closely to discover a network of objectives—motivations that can then carry the actor from moment to moment. At all times the actor must know what the character's intention is. The actor may then invent strategies or tactics to achieve the objective. Each objective, together with the actions and words involved in playing that objective, is considered a **beat.** A role is composed of a sequence of beats that together form a coherent **throughline** for the character. The character's dominant motive, or the **superobjective,** will make sense of all the smaller objectives that feed into the particular focus of the character.

In developing this internal acting approach, Stanislavsky was particularly concerned with keeping actors in an alert and creative frame of

Constantin Stanislavsky, who was a cofounder of the Moscow Art Theatre in 1898, used this most famous realistic theatre to explore new ideas in both playwriting and staging.

mind to offset the numbness that he believed resulted from the endless repetitions of the same lines and actions in rehearsals and performances. Stanislavsky also looked to maximize actors' concentration so they could focus on their creative work rather than on the distractions of playing in front of an audience.

In the United States in the 1930s, theatre practitioners associated with the Group Theatre (a company dedicated to the production of works by new playwrights and to the development of a new acting style) became interested in Stanislavsky's work, which they adapted for the American theatre. Lee Strasberg, Stella Adler, and Morris Carnovsky contributed their interpretations of an internal approach to acting, and their modifications of Stanislavsky's work became the basis for much American acting both on the stage and in film.

SUMMARY

The theatrical style called realism refers to elements of both playwriting and production. Realistic plays are concerned with social problems and the struggles that characters undergo to overcome difficulties of circumstance. The relationship of the present to the past is important, as is the connection between cause and effect. Realistic plays present incidents, characters, and language that appear to come from daily life. The truth of a situation is expressed through observable, external details of character and situation.

Among the European playwrights whose work formed the foundation of the realistic style are Henrik Ibsen, August Strindberg, and Anton Chekhov; American playwrights who developed a realistic theatre in this country include Lillian Hellman, Arthur Miller, and Tennessee Williams. In the work of Miller and Williams we see an evolution of a style based on realism that becomes more poetic in its expression. Constantin Stanislavsky's work on an internal approach to acting, which emphasized actor identification with the character's psychological motivation, provided the basis for much American acting on the stage and in films today.

TOPICS FOR DISCUSSION AND WRITING

1. What is meant by the term *realism?* What are examples of realistic elements in *Joe Turner's Come and Gone?* What is the most realistic play or film that you have seen recently?

2. Anton Chekhov writes dialogue in which the characters do not listen to each other and frequently respond by saying things unrelated to the subject of the first speaker. Listen to several different groups of people talking together under different circumstances. Where do you see examples of Chekhov's observation that people are so

absorbed by their own problems and concerns that they fail to hear the concerns of others?

3. If Ibsen were to write social problem plays today, what kinds of social problems might he address?

NOTE

1. Ruby Cohn, *Currents in Contemporary Drama* (Bloomington: Indiana University Press, 1969), 54–55.

SUGGESTIONS FOR FURTHER READING

Adler, Stella. *Stella Adler on Ibsen, Strindberg and Chekhov.* Edited by Barry Paris. New York: Alfred A. Knopf, 1999.

An informal analysis of the plays of Ibsen, Strindberg, and Chekhov from the perspective of a great American actor who studied with Stanislavsky and was a founding member of the Group Theatre.

Clurman, Harold. *The Fervent Years: The Group Theatre and the Thirties.* New York: Da Capo Press, 1983.

An examination of the period from 1931 to 1941, when some of the most innovative theatre practitioners in the United States joined together to form a company called the Group Theatre. Much of the work done by members of the Group Theatre contributed to the foundations of American realism. The book is a fascinating account of this period in American theatre history and social history.

Hellman, Lillian. *An Unfinished Woman.* 1969. Reprint, with a foreword by Wendy Wasserstein, Boston: Little, Brown, 1999.

This edition has a foreword by Pulitzer Prize–winning playwright Wendy Wasserstein. Hellman looks back on her childhood in New Orleans, on her early work in publishing and her adventures in Hollywood in the 1930s, on her surreal journeys through Europe on the brink of World War II, on her relationship with American writer Dashiell Hammett, and above all on her life as a writer. Wasserstein comments, "I can think of few more candid memoirs of the working writing life and most particularly the writing life of a female playwright."

Kindelan, Nancy. *Shadows of Realism.* Westport, CT: Greenwood Press, 1996.

A history of the development of realism, including contemporary commentary by theatre practitioners about how to produce the plays of the realistic period in the theatre of today.

Leverich, Lyle. *Tom: The Unknown Tennessee Williams.* New York: Crown, 1995.

A deeply personal evaluation of the connections between Williams's family relationships and the writing of his plays.

Marker, Frederick J., and Lise-Lone Marker. *Ibsen's Lively Art: A Performance Study of the Major Plays.* Cambridge: Cambridge University Press, 1989.

A history of Ibsen's own work in the theatre as a director and the changing interpretations of his plays. This book brings Ibsen's work to life and reveals the great interest and excitement generated by the plays.

Miller, Arthur. *The Theatre Essays of Arthur Miller.* Edited by Robert Martin. New York: Viking Press, 1978.

A series of essays in which Miller addresses the writing of his own plays and the nature of the American theatre. The essays touch on tragedy, realism, the family in drama, and political conflict in relation to the arts.

Stanislavsky, Constantin. *My Life in Art.* Translated by J. J. Robbins. Boston: Little, Brown, 1938.

Stanislavsky's memoirs of his development first as an actor and then as a director, with insights into his evolving philosophy of theatre and stories of his encounters with the major theatre artists of his time.

Strindberg, August. *Pre-Inferno Plays.* Translated by Walter Johnson. Seattle: University of Washington Press, 1970.

A collection of Strindberg's plays, including *The Father* and *Lady Julie (Miss Julie)*, that demonstrate Strindberg's contribution to psychological realism before he turned to expressionism. Also included is Strindberg's preface to *Miss Julie*, which served as a cornerstone of realistic theory.

CHAPTER 9

Expressing a Worldview Through Realism

Looking at And the Soul Shall Dance by Wakako Yamauchi

Wakako Yamauchi is another contemporary American playwright working in the realistic style. Yamauchi's plays have been compared to those of Anton Chekhov because of the small but precisely chosen details with which she renders her characters' lives and the quiet anguish that the characters express. Her plays also focus on a group of characters rather than on a central individual. And like Tennessee Williams, whom she acknowledges as a major influence, Yamauchi creates plays with a heightened, lyrical quality.

We turn now to an exploration of the play *And the Soul Shall Dance*, by Wakako Yamauchi, with a focus on its realistic elements. Following the text of the play we analyze two different productions, one at East West Players in Los Angeles and the other at Northwest Asian American Theatre in Seattle. In our analysis of these productions, we take a close look at the development of performance techniques used in realistic staging.

Like August Wilson's *Joe Turner's Come and Gone*, Wakako Yamauchi's *And the Soul Shall Dance* gives us a detailed view of a particular time and place in the United States. The play examines a brief passage of time in the life of an eleven-year-old girl, Masako, through what seems to be a memory of childhood. As Masako returns to this critical moment in her formative years, we experience with her the life of Japanese immigrants to the United States in the 1930s.

On the surface the play presents the harsh realities of immigrant life, of lives circumscribed by U.S. laws that preclude citizenship and land ownership, of a people who have left their homeland and find themselves out of place in their new circumstances. Underneath the story of survival is another story of longing for a life that is more than mere drudgery. For the adult characters, the longing is to return to Japan. For the child, Masako, the longing concerns a desire to create her own identity, to find her own place in the culture that is so alien to her parents.

And the Soul Shall Dance juxtaposes the contrasting experiences of two Japanese immigrant families farming the Imperial Valley in California during the 1930s. Each family suffers hardships. One carries on with grace and humor because the family relationships are intact; the warm regard of the parents for each other and their daughter creates a refuge from the economic struggle and the cultural isolation. The other family builds a closed world of alcoholism and abuse that deepens their dislocation.

PLOT AND CHARACTERS

And the Soul Shall Dance has a simple plot that follows the encounters of the two families over a period of about one year. The Muratas and the Okas are brought together when the Murata bathhouse burns down because of Masako's

The Muratas (Sharon Omi and Nelson Mashita) face the hardships of immigrant life by relying on each other's strength and will to endure in the production staged by East West Players, directed by Jim Ishida.

carelessness. When the Muratas are invited to use the Oka bathhouse, the bitter secrets of the Oka family begin to emerge.

Mr. Oka has a daughter, Kiyoko, in Japan whom he has not seen for years. Kiyoko feels abandoned by Oka, and he is desperate for money to bring her to the United States. Kiyoko is the daughter of a previous, happier marriage. As a young man, Oka was married to his current wife's sister, who died after her husband had emigrated to the United States in search of a better life for his small family. The dead woman's sister, Emiko, left Japan under mysterious circumstances. She was married to Oka by proxy after her sister's death and sent to the United States by her parents. The second Oka marriage has degenerated into hostility and recrimination.

Emiko Oka emerges as a most surprising character. She is an alcoholic who drinks and smokes openly. She flaunts all traditional standards of Japanese decorum. At the same time, she is devoted to the traditional Japanese arts of dance and music. The arranged marriage is a disaster for both husband and wife. Emiko is already on the edge of madness at the beginning of the play. The arrival of the daughter, Kiyoko, leads directly to catastrophe for her stepmother-aunt, Emiko.

PERSONAL, CULTURAL, AND HISTORICAL CONTEXTS OF THE PLAY

The Play as Memory

Although the play is obviously about the contrasting lives of the two families, the point of view is that of Masako, the Murata daughter. The play consists of events that would have made a significant impression on an adolescent girl and that still seem worth telling by the adult that Masako has become. At the end of the play, Masako's mother, Hana, points to this memory when she says,

> Maybe someday when you're grown up, gone away, you'll . . . remember yourself as this little girl . . . remember this old house, the ranch, and . . . your old mama . . .
> (act 2, scene 5)

And the Soul Shall Dance takes the playwright back to her earliest memories of her own family history, to a time when her sense of herself as an artist began to unfold. As an artist, Yamauchi aspired to transcend the limitations of the first-generation Japanese immigrants in America, known as *Issei*. Yamauchi originally wrote *And the Soul Shall Dance* as a short story but later adapted it to drama. The original short story makes the point of view of memory very clear in its opening words:

> It's all right to talk about it now. Most of the principals are dead, except, of course, me and my younger brother, and possibly Kiyoko Oka, who might be near forty-five now because, yes, I'm sure of it, she was fourteen then. I was

nine, and my brother about four, so he hardly counts. Kiyoko's mother is dead, my father is dead, my mother is dead, and her father could not have lasted all these years with his tremendous appetite for alcohol and pickled chiles—those little yellow ones, so hot they could make your mouth hurt—he'd eat them like peanuts and tears would surge from his bulging thyroid eyes in great waves and stream down the coarse terrain of his face.[1]

The play approaches the issue of memory through Masako's position in the structure of the scenes. She is the only character who appears in almost every scene, and frequently we see her as she is watching the other characters. The play, then, is about the startling entrance of the Oka family into Masako's consciousness and her assessment of their strangeness in relation to the accepted "normalcy" of her own family. Masako, who seeks a wider view of life than can be imagined or accommodated in the safety of her own home, finds tantalizing possibilities in the aberrant behavior of the elusive neighbor, Emiko. The importance of the memory lies in the way Emiko's rebellion and her life as an artist, as eccentric as it may be, serves to open up possibilities for Masako. The memory is the beginning of Masako's consciousness of herself as an artist.

The play builds layers of feeling as Masako's memory intersects with the memories of Emiko and Masako's mother, Hana. The empathetic child is able to enter these other memories and consider what they may mean for her future. Emiko's memory is of beauty and grace. She lives in her memory of herself dancing and singing, studying the arts of Japanese high culture. And, most significantly, this memory of classical training allows her to sustain a memory of love and desire. She lives for the man she would have chosen for herself if her family had not intervened because he was unacceptable to them.

Hana is also sustained by her memories. She too longs to return to Japan. But instead of indulging in the past, she suppresses her memories in order to function in the present. She consciously chooses practical solutions, even

In Context

LEGISLATION RESTRICTING ASIAN IMMIGRATION

Date	Act
1790	Naturalization Law: declared only whites eligible to become naturalized citizens of the United States.
1882	Chinese Exclusion Act: barred immigration of Chinese nationals.
1913	First Alien Land Law (California): declared Japanese immigrants could lease land for a period of no more than three years; barred purchase of land by Japanese immigrants.
1920	Second Alien Land Law (California): barred lease or purchase of land by individual Japanese nationals or corporations.
1922	U.S. Supreme Court decision in the *Ozawa* case: decided that a Japanese national whom the Court deemed qualified in every other way for citizenship could be denied citizenship because he was not white.
1924	National Origins Act (Immigration Act of 1924): barred immigration of aliens ineligible for citizenship—that is, barred nonwhites; aimed particularly at Japanese, who were consequently barred from immigration to the United States for the next twenty-eight years, until 1952; excluded all Asian immigrants except Filipinos.
1934	Tydings-McDuffie Act: limited Filipino immigration to the United States to fifty people per year.
1942	Executive Order 9066, President Franklin D. Roosevelt: ordered incarceration of all West Coast people of Japanese heritage; of the 120,000, two thirds were American citizens by birth.[2]

Masako (Roxanne Chang) watches Emiko, Dawn A. Saito, dance by herself in the desert, living in her memories, in a production of And the Soul Shall Dance *at Pan Asian Repertory Theatre in New York directed by Tisa Chang.*

though we see that under other circumstances she would have cultivated her imagination for more than survival.

Personal History

Both the short stories and the plays of Wakako Yamauchi are largely autobiographical. Yamauchi was born in 1924 in Westmoreland, California. Both of her parents were Issei. The playwright is, in fact, Masako, the child whose memory forms the basis for the play. Yamauchi's childhood was spent moving from one shabby rented farm to another as her parents struggled with the precariousness of being part of an unwelcome immigrant community.

Yamauchi's mother was eighteen or nineteen in 1920, when she came to the United States. Her father, thirteen years older than her mother, was thirty-two. Theirs was an arranged marriage that resulted from financial developments. Yamauchi's mother came from the merchant class, as did her father. Her maternal grandfather was a tea packer. Her paternal grandfather made fish cakes. Yamauchi's maternal grandfather had many daughters but no son to inherit the family business and carry forth the family name. Therefore, the grandfather "adopted" a son-in-law and gave him his name (much like the character Oka in *And the Soul Shall Dance* who tells the story of giving up his own name for that of his father-in-law).

But then a son was born to Yamauchi's grandfather and his second wife. For the son-in-law, seeing his inheritance slip away to the new baby was too much to bear, and he embezzled the family money, leaving the business bankrupt. So Yamauchi's mother had no financial prospects to offer potential suitors, and the grandfather accepted the one proposal that she received from a young man who had returned to Japan to marry and then take his new wife to California.

The young couple had neither the skills nor the background that would prepare them for the life they would face in California. Nor

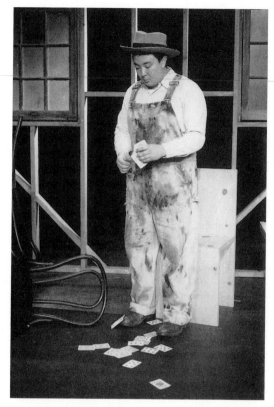

Wakako Yamauchi wrote about the incarceration of Japanese Americans during World War II in her play 12-1-A. The title refers to the barracks in which the central characters live at the "camp" in Poston, Arizona. In a 1999 production directed by Stephanie Arnold, Harry (Brian Kameoka) is left alone to try to pick up the pieces of his life following the release of the internees. Autobiographical details of Yamauchi's own internment experiences form the foundation of the play.

did they have relatives to turn to. Everything would depend on their own ingenuity and hard work. Their lives were governed by laws such as the California Alien Land Law, which barred Japanese immigrants from buying property, and the naturalization statutes and Supreme Court decisions that specifically excluded Asian immigrants from becoming American citizens. Because they could not own their own land and were forced to move every two or three years, many of the Japanese immigrant farmers had to grow annual crops such as carrots, which were

Why does anyone write? To record a time, maybe; to get things right.[3]

• • •

My mother died and I felt I had to put something down for my daughter to remember me because mothers don't tell their kids everything; but at least if she read my stories, my plays, she'd know what kind of person I am . . . or was.[4]

—WAKAKO YAMAUCHI

particularly vulnerable to drought and rain, rather than planting more stable nursery stock such as fruit trees.

Prejudice, Discrimination, and Internment

Prejudice against Asians in the United States was encouraged by a combination of business and union interests, the political maneuvering of state and national legislators, and powerful media interests such as the Hearst newspapers. The precarious position of Asian immigrants was forged by contradictions in the workings of the nation. The country was eager for Asian labor to build the railroads and to work in the canneries and the fields. Although the nation would prosper from the backbreaking labor of Asian nationals and the farming techniques they introduced to irrigate the dry valleys of California, it was unwilling to treat Asian workers equally under the laws or to provide them the opportunities enjoyed by "white" residents. Comparisons to current debates about immigration, particularly with respect to Latin American immigrants, are unavoidable.

An extremely prejudicial attitude toward Japanese and Chinese people was well established on the West Coast long before the Japanese bombed Pearl Harbor in 1941 and the U.S. government incarcerated all West Coast Japanese nationals and Japanese Americans in detention camps. The internment of the "Japanese," fully two thirds of whom were American

citizens by birth, remains one of the travesties of American democracy. Among the many disturbing aspects of this infamous episode in American race relations are two that reveal the prevailing American attitude toward Asian immigrants at this time. One is that many West Coast Americans profited from the acquisition of possessions of Japanese Americans who were incarcerated. The other is that Americans of German (European) descent were not treated as enemies of the nation (see Color Plate 33).

The Play as Social Document

Like the writing of August Wilson, the plays and short stories of Wakako Yamauchi have great value as social documents as well as works of art. They record the experiences and events that shaped the lives of a group of people whose history has gone largely unrecorded. Whereas some historians write about the events they experience firsthand in journals or diaries, Yamauchi has recorded her history in short stories, plays, and, more recently, memoirs.

Yamauchi's work as a writer is both historical and personal. She explores her own evolving consciouness as an artist and as a woman at the same time that she explores the family and community life for Japanese immigrants and Japanese Americans at different stages of their American history. Yamauchi is particularly concerned with gender issues, as the men and women in her stories and plays make awkward and frequently unsuccessful attempts to adapt their relationships from Japanese expectations to the demands and shifting cultural perspectives of their new circumstances. The plays and stories are full of misunderstood and unfulfilled sexual longing. Male and female characters frequently fail to understand each other's aspirations and stifle rather than nurture individual development, particularly of an artistic or intellectual nature. For the women characters this stifling of ambitions is part of a pattern in which they are forced to assume the responsibility for their families' survival while the men abandon the struggle.

EVOKING A WORLD THROUGH DETAIL

And the Soul Shall Dance presents characters caught between cultures whose memories of the past constantly seep into the present. Yamauchi has chosen the small moments of her characters' lives as the most revealing reflections of the deep disturbance caused by this cultural collision. Through a realistic approach to the material world, the playwright gives us concrete details that bring to life the two cultures that exert such strong pulls on the characters.

The plot of *And the Soul Shall Dance* revolves around key objects. The bathhouse burns to the ground. Oka must sell his horse to raise money for Kiyoko's boat passage from Japan. The families listen to memory-laden records on the Victrola. Oka takes the money that Emiko has been saving to return to Japan and spends it on Americanizing and pampering his daughter with clothes, trips to the hairdresser, and movies. The realistic plotting of the play concludes with Emiko's painful attempts to sell her kimonos to Hana and Masako.

The focus on these objects defines the world of the play very carefully. The period, the culture of the characters, and their economic circumstances are quickly established. Motives and values are also defined in relation to this presentation of the material world. Oka,

Distraught, Emiko (Dawn A. Saito) holds an empty can that no longer contains her savings. The money that she hoped would take her back to Japan has been spent by her husband, Oka, to "Americanize" his daughter. This production is from the Pan Asian Repertory Theatre.

desperate for affection, does for his daughter what he cannot do for his wife. He surrounds her with American "luxuries"; he tries to overcome his cultural isolation by creating the appearance that he and Kiyoko are part of America, that they fit in. Emiko will sell her most treasured possessions, her kimonos, before she will give up her dream of recovering the sense of herself that she projects onto Japan.

Another characteristic of realism is that the objects used in the play and the material concerns, such as crop failure and financial worries, not only ground the lives of the characters in a particular time and place and form an integral part of the plot structure but also have symbolic significance. *And the Soul Shall Dance* is dense with objects that communicate layers of meaning. For example, the food and drink—the sake, chiles, and tea—that Hana puts on the table are signs of a functioning home, of warmth and nourishment. In contrast, Emiko refuses to make tea. The absence of food at the Oka's house symbolizes the emptiness of the dwelling; the family members fail to nurture each other. The illegal liquor they brew and the cigarettes Emiko smokes are poisonous substitutes for the missing food. The parents' addictions are part of the profound dysfunction of the family. At the same time that the cigarettes indicate a self-destructive attitude, they are also an important symbol of Emiko's rebellion against her husband and the accepted Japanese social structure.

Even the hairstyles of the two daughters have extremely important symbolic value. Kiyoko is transformed by a permanent wave in act 2 of the play. The processed curly hair says a great deal about the father-daughter relationship and the movement of Oka and Kiyoko toward an image of assimilation. The permanent wave suggests the fabrication of a value system to cover the confusion brought on by their dislocation. The permanent wave is also a weapon in the war between husband and wife. Oka revenges himself on Emiko by spending on Kiyoko the money that Emiko has hoarded to return to Japan. Additionally, the permanent wave provides a way of acknowledging the firm foundation of the Murata family. Hana shows her love and regard for her daughter and also her own strength and stability when she says simply to Masako at the end of the play, "your hair is so black and straight . . . nice."

The use of objects to develop the symbolic meaning of the play leads to one final conclusion about realism. The careful selection of lifelike details highlights the characters' experiences. Realism, in fact, has its own poetic quality. A movement of the spirit is expressed in the precisely chosen actions and objects that contain the essence of the characters' lives. The appearance of reality becomes a concentrated view of a particular way of life. In *And the Soul Shall Dance*, the simplicity of the play's structure, delicately rendered like Japanese brush painting, presents an almost lyrical impression of memory and longing.

And the Soul Shall Dance
Wakako Yamauchi

CHARACTERS

MURATA, 40, *Issei farmer*
HANA, 35, *Issei wife of Murata*
MASAKO, 11, *Nisei daughter of the Muratas*
OKA, 45, *Issei farmer*
EMIKO, 30, *wife of Oka*
KIYOKO, 14, *Oka's daughter*

Kokoro Ga Odoru	*And the Soul Shall Dance*
Akai kuchibiru	Red lips
Kappu ni yosete	Press against a glass
Aoi sake nomya	Drink the green wine
Kokoro ga odoru	And the soul shall dance
Kurai yoru no yume	In the dark night
Setsu nasa yo	Dreams are unbearable
Aoi sake nomya	Drink the green wine
Yume ga odoru	And the dreams will dance
Asa no munashisa	The morning's truth
Yume wo chirasu	Scatter the dreams
Sora to kokoro wa	Sky and soul
Sake shidai	Are suspended by wine
Futari wakare no	In the separation
Samishisa yo	The desolation
Hitori sake nomya	Drink the wine
Kokoro ga odoru	And the soul shall dance

ACT ONE

Scene 1

Summer afternoon, 1935. Interior of the Murata house. The set is spare. There are a kitchen table, four chairs, a bed, and on the wall, a calendar indicating the year and month: June 1935. A doorway leads to the other room. Props are: a bottle of sake, two cups, a dish of chiles, a phonograph, and two towels hanging on pegs on the wall. A wide wooden bench is outside.

The bathhouse has just burned to the ground due to MASAKO's carelessness. Offstage there are sounds of MURATA putting out the fire.

Inside, HANA MURATA, in a drab housedress, confronts MASAKO (in summer dress). MASAKO is sullen and defiant.

HANA: How could you be so careless, Masako? You know you should be extra careful with fire. How often have I told you? Now the whole bathhouse is gone. I told you time and again—when you stoke a fire, you must see that everything is swept into the fireplace.

(MURATA enters. He is in old work clothes. He suffers from heat and exhaustion.)

MURATA: *(coughing)* Shack went up like a matchbox. This kind of weather dries everything . . . just takes a spark to make a bonfire out of that dry timber.
HANA: Did you save any of it?
MURATA: No. Couldn't.
HANA: *(to MASAKO)* How many times have I told you . . .

(MASAKO moves nervously.)

MURATA: No use crying about it now. *Shikata ga nai.* It's gone now. No more bathhouse. That's all.
HANA: But you've got to tell her. Otherwise she'll make the same mistake. You'll be building a bathhouse every year.

249

(*MURATA removes his shirt and wipes off his face. He throws his shirt on a chair and sits at the table.*)

MURATA: *Baka!* Ridiculous!

MASAKO: I didn't do it on purpose.

(*MASAKO goes to the bed. She opens a book. HANA follows her.*)

HANA: I know that, but you know what this means? It means we bathe in a bucket . . . inside the house. Carry water in from the pond, heat it on the stove . . . we'll use more kerosene.

MURATA: Tub's still there. And the fireplace. We can still build a fire under the tub.

HANA: (*shocked*) But no walls! Everyone in the country can see us!

MURATA: Wait till dark then. Wait till dark.

HANA: We'll be using a lantern. They'll still see us.

MURATA: Angh! Who? Who'll see us? You think everyone in the country waits to watch us take a bath? Hunh! You know how stupid you sound? Who cares about a couple of farmers taking a bath at night?

HANA: (*defensively*) It'll be inconvenient.

(*HANA is saved by a rap on the door. OKA enters. He is short and stout. He wears faded work clothes.*)

OKA: Hello! Hello! *Oi!* What's going on here? Hey! Was there some kind of fire?

(*HANA rushes to the door to let OKA in. He stamps the dust from his shoes and enters.*)

HANA: Oka-san! You just wouldn't believe . . . We had a terrible thing happen.

OKA: Yeah. Saw the smoke from down the road. Thought it was your house. Came rushing over. Is the fire out?

(*MURATA half rises and sits back again. He's exhausted.*)

MURATA: (*gesturing*) Oi, oi. Come in. Sit down. No big problem. It was just our bathhouse.

OKA: Just the *furoba*, eh?

MURATA: Just the bath.

HANA: Our Masako was careless, and the *furoba* caught fire. There's nothing left but the tub.

(*MASAKO looks up from her book, pained. She makes a small sound.*)

OKA: Long as the tub's there, no problem. I'll help you with it.

(*He starts to roll up his sleeves.*)

MURATA: What . . . now? Now?

OKA: (*heh-heh*) Long as I'm here.

HANA: Oh, Papa. Aren't we lucky to have such friends?

MURATA: (*to HANA*) We can't work on it now. The ashes are still hot. I just now put the damned fire out. Let me rest a while. (*to OKA*) Oi, how about a little sake? (*gesturing to HANA*) Make sake for Oka-san.

(*OKA sits at the table. HANA goes to prepare the sake. She heats it, gets out the cups, and pours it for the men.*)

MURATA: (*continuing*) I'm tired . . . I am *tired*.

HANA: Oka-san has so generously offered his help . . .

(*OKA is uncomfortable. He looks around and sees MASAKO sitting on the bed.*)

OKA: Hello, there, Masako-chan. You studying?

MASAKO: No, it's summer vacation.

MURATA: (*sucking in his breath*) Kids nowadays . . . no manners.

HANA: She's sulking because I had to scold her.

(*MASAKO makes a small moan.*)

MURATA: Drink, Oka-san.

OKA: (*sipping*) Ahhhh . . . That's good.

MURATA: Eh, you not working today?

OKA: No-no. I took the afternoon off today. I was driving over to Nagata-san's when I saw this big black cloud of smoke coming from your yard.

HANA: It went up so fast.

MURATA: What's up at Nagata-kun's? (*to HANA*) Get out the chiles. Oka-san loves chiles.

(*HANA opens a jar of chiles and puts them on a plate. She serves them and gets out her mending basket and walks to MASAKO. MASAKO makes room for her.*)

OKA: (*helping himself*) Ah, chiles.

(*MURATA waits for an answer.*)

OKA: (*continuing*) Well, I want to see him about my horse. I'm thinking of selling my horse.

MURATA: Sell your horse?

OKA: (*scratching his head*) The fact is, I need some money. Nagata-san's the only one around made money this year, and I'm thinking he might want another horse.

MURATA: Yeah, he made a little this year. And he's talking big . . . big! Says he's leasing twenty more acres this fall.

OKA: Twenty acres?

MURATA: Yeah. He might want another horse.

OKA: Twenty acres, eh?

MURATA: That's what he says. But you know his old woman makes all the decisions at that house.

(*OKA scratches his head.*)

HANA: They're doing all right.

MURATA: Heh. Nagata-kun's so henpecked, it's pathetic. Peko-peko. (*He makes henpecking motions.*)

OKA: (*feeling the strain*) I better get over there.

MURATA: Why the hell you selling your horse?

OKA: Well . . . a . . . I need cash.

MURATA: Oh yeah. I could use some too. Seems like everyone's getting out of the depression but the poor farmers. Nothing changes for us. We go on and on planting our tomatoes and summer squash and eating them. Well, at least it's healthy.

HANA: Papa, do you have lumber?

MURATA: Lumber? For what?

HANA: The bath . . .

MURATA: (*impatiently*) Don't worry about that. We need more sake now.

(*HANA rises wearily.*)

OKA: You sure Nagata-kun's working twenty more?

MURATA: Last I heard. What the hell, if you need a few bucks, I can loan (you) . . .

OKA: A few hundred. I need a few hundred dollars.

MURATA: Oh, a few hundred. But what the hell you going to do without a horse? Out here a man's horse is as important as his wife.

OKA: (*seriously*) I don't think Nagata will buy my wife.

(*The men laugh, but HANA doesn't find it so funny. MURATA glances at her. She fills the cups again. OKA makes a half-hearted gesture to stop her. MASAKO watches the pantomime carefully. OKA finishes his drink.*)

OKA: (*continuing*) I better get moving.

MURATA: What's the big hurry?

OKA: Like to get the horse business done.

MURATA: Eh . . . relax. Do it tomorrow. He's not going to die, is he?

OKA: (*laughing*) Hey, he's a good horse. I want to get it settled today. If Nagata-kun won't buy, I got to find someone else.

OKA: (*continuing*) You think maybe Kawaguchi-kun . . . ?

MURATA: No-no. Not Kawaguchi. Maybe Yamamoto.

HANA: What is all the money for, Oka-san? Does Emiko-san need an operation?

OKA: No-no. Nothing like that.

HANA: Sounds very mysterious.

OKA: No mystery, Missus. No mystery. No sale, no money, no story.

MURATA: (*laughing*) That's a good one. "No sale, no money, no . . ." Eh, Mama . . . (*He points to the empty cups.*)

HANA: (*filling the cups, muttering*) I see we won't be getting any work done today. (*to MASAKO*) Are you reading again? Maybe we'd still have a bath if you . . .

MASAKO: I didn't do it on purpose.

MURATA: (*loudly*) I sure hope you know what you're doing, Oka-kun. What'd you do without a horse?

OKA: I was hoping you'd lend me yours now and then. (*He looks at HANA.*) I'll pay for some of the feed.

MURATA: Sure! Sure!

OKA: The fact is, I need that money. I got a daughter in Japan, and I just got to send for her this year.

(*HANA leaves her mending and sits at the table.*)

HANA: A daughter? You have a daughter in Japan? Why, I didn't know you had children. Emiko-san and you . . . I thought you were childless.

OKA: (*scratching his head*) We are. I was married before.

MURATA: You son-of-a-gun!

HANA: (*overlapping*) Is that so? How old is your daughter?

OKA: Kiyoko must be . . . fifteen now. Yeah, fifteen.

HANA: Fifteen! Oh, that *would* be too old for Emiko-san's child. Is Kiyoko's-san living with relatives in Japan?

OKA: (*reluctantly*) With grandparents. Shizue's parents. (*pause*) Well, the fact is, Shizue— that's my first wife—Shizue and Emiko were sisters. They come from a family with no sons. I was a boy when I went to work for them . . . as an apprentice. They're black-smiths. Later I married Shizue and took on the family name—you know, *yoshi*—because they had no sons. My real name is Sakakihara.

MURATA: Sakakihara! That's a great name!

HANA: A magnificent name!

OKA: No one knows me by that here.

MURATA: Should have kept that—Sakakihara.

OKA: (*muttering*) I don't even know myself by that name.

HANA: And Shizue-san passed away and you married Emiko-san?

OKA: Oh. Well, Shizue and I lived with the family for a while, and we had the baby— you know, Kiyoko. (*He gets looser with the liquor.*) Well, while I was serving apprentice with the family, they always looked down

their noses at me. After I married, it got worse.

HANA: (*distressed*) Worse!

OKA: That old man . . . (*unnnnh!*) Always push-ing me around, making me look bad in front of my wife and kid. That old man was the meanest . . . ugliest . . .

MURATA: Yeah, I heard about that apprentice work—*detchi-boko*. Heard it was damned humiliating.

OKA: That's the God's truth!

MURATA: Never had to do it myself. I came to America instead. They say *detchi-boko* is blood work.

OKA: The work's all right. I'm not afraid of work. It's the humiliation! I hated them! Pushing me around like I was still a boy. Me, a grown man! And married to their daughter!

(*MURATA and HANA groan in sympathy.*)

OKA: (*continuing*) Well, Shizue and I talked it over, and we decided the best thing was to get away. We thought if I came to America and made some money . . . you know, send her money until we had enough, and I'd go back and we'd leave the family . . . you know, move to another province . . . start a small business, maybe in the city . . . a noodle shop or something.

MURATA: That's everyone's dream. Make money, go home, and live like a king.

OKA: I worked like a dog. Sent every penny to Shizue. And then she dies. She died on me!

(*HANA and MURATA observe a moment of silence in respect for OKA's anguish.*)

HANA: And you married Emiko-san.

OKA: I didn't marry her. They married her to me! Right after Shizue died.

HANA: But Oka-san, you were lu(cky) . . .

OKA: Before the body was cold! No respect. By proxy. The old man wrote me that they were arranging a marriage by proxy for me and Emiko. They said she'd grown to be a beau-tiful woman and would serve me well.

HANA: Emiko-san *is* a beautiful woman.

OKA: And they sent her to me. Took care of everything! Immigration, fare, everything.

HANA: But she's your sister-in-law. Kiyoko's aunt. It's good to keep the family together.

OKA: That's what I thought. But hear this: Emiko was the favored one. Shizue was not so pretty, not so smart. They were grooming Emiko for a rich man—his name was Yamato—lived in a grand house in the village. They sent her to schools; you know, the culture thing: the dance, tea ceremony, you know, all that. They didn't even like me, and suddenly they married her to me.

MURATA: Yeah. You don't need all that formal training to make it over here. Just a strong back.

HANA: And a strong will.

OKA: It was all arranged. I couldn't do anything about it.

HANA: It'll be all right. With Kiyoko-san coming . . .

OKA: (*dubiously*) I hope so. (*pause*) I never knew human beings could be so cruel. You know how they mistreated my daughter? After Emiko came here, things got from bad to worse, and I *never* had enough money to send to Kiyoko and . . .

MURATA: They don't know what it's like here. They think money's picked off the ground here.

OKA: And they treated Kiyoko so bad. They told her I forgot about her. They told her I didn't care . . . said I abandoned her. Well, she knew better. She wrote to me all the time, and I always told her I'd send for her . . . as soon as I got the money. (*He shakes his head.*) I just got to do something this year.

HANA: She'll be happier here. She'll know her father cares.

OKA: Kids tormented her for being an orphan.

MURATA: Kids are cruel.

HANA: Masako will help her. She'll help her get started at school. She'll make friends. She'll be all right.

OKA: I hope so. She'll need friends. (*He tries to convince himself he's making the right decision.*) What could I say to her? Stay there? It's not what you think over here? I can't help her? I just have to do this thing. I just have to do this one thing for her.

MURATA: Sure.

HANA: Don't worry. It'll work out fine.

(*MURATA gestures to HANA. She gets the sake.*)

MURATA: You talk about selling your horse, I thought you were pulling out.

OKA: I wish I could. But there's nothing else I can do.

MURATA: Without money, yeah.

OKA: You can go into some kind of business with money, but a man like me . . . no education . . . there's no kind of job I can do. I'd starve in the city.

MURATA: Dishwashing, maybe. Janitor.

OKA: At least here we can eat. Carrots, maybe, but we can eat.

(*They laugh. HANA starts to pour more wine.*)

OKA: I better not drink anymore. Got to drive to Nagata-san's yet. (*He walks over to MASAKO.*) You study hard, don't you? You'll teach Kiyoko English, eh? When she gets here . . . ?

HANA: Oh, yes, she will.

MURATA: Kiyoko-san could probably teach her a thing or two.

OKA: She won't know about American ways.

MASAKO: I'll help her.

HANA: Don't worry, Oka-san. She'll have a good friend in our Masako.

(*They move to the door.*)

OKA: Well, thanks for the sake. I guess I talk too much when I drink. (*He scratches his head and laughs.*) Oh. I'm sorry about the fire. By the way, come to my house for your bath . . . until you build yours again.

HANA: Oh, a . . . thank you. I don't know if . . .

MURATA: Good, good! I need a good hot bath tonight.

OKA: Tonight, then.

MURATA: We'll be there.

HANA: (*bowing*) Thank you very much. *Sayonara.*

OKA: (*nodding*) See you tonight.

(*OKA leaves. HANA faces MURATA as soon as the door closes.*)

HANA: Papa, I don't know about going over there.

MURATA: (*surprised*) Why?

HANA: Well, Emiko-san . . .

MURATA: (*irritated*) What's the matter with you? We need a bath and Oka's invited us over.

HANA: (*to MASAKO*) Help me clear the table.

(*MASAKO reluctantly leaves her book.*)

HANA: (*continuing*) Papa, you know we've been neighbors already three, four years, and Emiko-san's never been very hospitable.

MURATA: She's shy, that's all.

HANA: Not just shy. She's strange. I feel like she's pushing me off. She makes me feel like—I don't know—like I'm prying or something.

MURATA: Maybe you are.

HANA: And never puts out a cup of tea . . . If she had all that training in the graces . . . why, a cup of tea . . .

MURATA: So if you want tea, ask for it.

HANA: I can't do that, Papa. (*pause*) She's strange. . . . I don't know . . . (*to MASAKO*) When we go there, be very careful not to say anything wrong.

MASAKO: I never say anything anyway.

HANA: (*thoughtfully*) Would you believe the story Oka-san just told? Why, I never knew . . .

MURATA: There're lots of things you don't know. Just because a man don't . . . don't talk about them, don't mean he don't feel . . . don't think about . . .

HANA: (*looking around*) We'll have to take something. There's nothing to take. Papa, maybe you can dig up some carrots.

MURATA: God, Mama, be sensible. They got carrots. Everybody's got carrots.

HANA: Something . . . Maybe I should make something.

MURATA: Hell, they're not expecting anything.

HANA: It's not good manners to go empty-handed.

MURATA: We'll take the sake.

(*HANA grimaces. MASAKO sees the phonograph.*)

MASAKO: I know, Mama. We can take the Victrola! We can play records for Mrs. Oka. Then nobody has to talk.

(*MURATA laughs.*)

Scene 2

That evening. The exterior wall of the Okas' weathered house. There is a workable screen door and a large screened window. Outside there is a wide wooden bench that can accommodate three or four people. There is one separate chair, and a lantern stands against the house.

The last rays of the sun light the area in a soft golden glow. This light grows gray as the scene progresses, and it is quite dark by the end of the scene.

Through the screened window, EMIKO can be seen walking erratically back and forth. She wears drab cotton but her grace and femininity come through. Her hair is bunned back in the style of the Issei women of the era.

OKA sits cross-legged on the bench. He wears a Japanese summer robe (yukata) and fans himself with a round Japanese fan.

The MURATAS enter. MURATA carries towels and a bottle of sake. HANA carries the Victrola, and MASAKO, a package containing their yukata.

OKA: (*standing to greet the MURATAS*) Oh, you've come. Welcome!

MURATA: *Yah* . . . Good of you to ask us.

HANA: (*bowing*) Yes, thank you very much. (*to MASAKO*) Say hello, Masako.

MASAKO: Hello.

HANA: And thank you.

MASAKO: Thank you.

(*OKA makes motions of protest. EMIKO stops her pacing and watches from the window.*)

HANA: (*glancing briefly at the window*) And how is Emiko-san this evening?

OKA: (*turning to the house*) Emi! Emiko!

HANA: That's all right. Don't call her out. She must be busy.

OKA: Emiko!

(*EMIKO comes to the door. HANA starts a bow toward the house.*)

MURATA: *Konbanwa!* (Good evening)

HANA: *Konbanwa,* Emiko-san. I feel so badly about this intrusion. (*pause*) Your husband has told you our bathhouse was destroyed by fire, and he graciously invited us to come use yours.

(*EMIKO shakes her head.*)

OKA: I didn't have a chance to . . .

(*HANA recovers and nudges MASAKO.*)

HANA: Say hello to Mrs. Oka.

MASAKO: Hello, Mrs. Oka.

(*HANA lowers the Victrola to the bench.*)

OKA: What's this? You brought a phonograph?

MASAKO: It's a Victrola.

HANA: (*laughing indulgently*) Yes. Masako wanted to bring this over and play some records.

MURATA: (*extending the wine*) Brought a little sake too.

OKA: (*taking the bottle*) Ah, now that I like. Emiko, bring out the cups.

(*OKA waves at his wife, but she doesn't move. He starts to ask again but decides to get them himself. He enters the house and returns with two cups.*)

(*EMIKO seats herself on the single chair. The MURATAS unload their paraphernalia; OKA pours the wine, the men drink, HANA chatters and sorts the records. MASAKO stands by helping her.*)

HANA: Yes, our Masako loves to play records. I like records too, and Papa, he . . .

MURATA: (*watching EMIKO*) They take me back home. The only way I can get there. In my mind.

HANA: Do you like music, Emiko-san?

(*EMIKO looks vague, but smiles.*)

HANA: (*continuing*) Oka-san, you like them, don't you?

OKA: Yeah. But I don't have a player. No chance to hear them.

MURATA: I had to get this for them. They wouldn't leave me alone until I got it. Well . . . a phonograph . . . what the hell; they got to have *some* fun.

HANA: We don't have to play them, if you'd rather not.

OKA: Play. Play them.

HANA: I thought we could listen to them and relax. (*She extends some records to EMIKO.*) Would you like to look through these, Emiko-san?

(*EMIKO doesn't respond. She pulls out a sack of Bull Durham and begins to roll a cigarette. HANA pushes MASAKO to her.*)

HANA: (*continuing*) Take these to her.

(*MASAKO goes to EMIKO with the records. She stands watching her as EMIKO lights a cigarette.*)

HANA: (*continuing*) Some of these are very old. You might know them, Emiko-san. (*She sees MASAKO watching EMIKO.*) Masako, bring those over here. (*She laughs uncomfortably.*) You might like this one, Emiko-san. (*She starts the player.*) Do you know it?

(*The record whines out "Kago No Tori." EMIKO listens with her head cocked.*)

(*She smokes her cigarette. She is wrapped in nostalgia and memories of the past. MASAKO watches her carefully.*)

MASAKO: (*whispering*) Mama, she's crying.

(*Startled, HANA and MURATA look toward EMIKO.*)

HANA: (*pinching MASAKO*) Shhh. The smoke is in her eyes.

MURATA: Did you bring the record I like, Mama?

(*EMIKO rises abruptly and enters the house.*)

MASAKO: They're tears, Mama.

HANA: From yawning, Masako. (*regretfully to OKA*) I'm afraid we offended her.

OKA: (*unaware*) Hunh? Aw . . . no . . . pay no attention. No offense.

(*MASAKO looks toward the window. EMIKO stands forlornly and slowly drifts into a dance.*)

HANA: I'm very sorry. Children, you know . . . they'll say anything. Anything that's on their minds.

(*MURATA notices MASAKO looking through the window and tries to divert her attention.*)

MURATA: The needles. Masako, where're the needles?

MASAKO: (*still watching*) I forgot them.

(*HANA sees what's going on. OKA is unaware.*)

HANA: Masako, go take your bath now. Masako . . .

(*MASAKO reluctantly takes her towel and leaves.*)

OKA: Yeah, yeah. Take your bath, Masako-chan.

MURATA: (*sees EMIKO still dancing*) Change the record, Mama.

OKA: (*still unaware*) That's kind of sad.

MURATA: No use to get sick over a record. We're supposed to enjoy.

(*HANA stops the record. EMIKO disappears from the window. HANA selects a lively* ondo ["Tokyo Ondo"].)

HANA: We'll find something more fun.

(*The three tap to the music.*)

HANA: (*continuing*) Can't you just see the festival? The dancers, the bright kimonos, the paper lanterns bobbing in the wind, the fireflies . . . How nostalgic. Oh, how nostalgic.

(*EMIKO appears from the side of the house. Her hair is down; she wears an old straw hat. She dances in front of the MURATAS. They are startled.*)

(*After the first shock, they watch with frozen smiles. They try to join EMIKO's mood, but something is missing. OKA is grieved. He finally stands as though he's had enough. EMIKO, now close to the door, ducks into the house.*)

HANA: That was pretty. Very nice.

(*OKA settles down and grunts. MURATA clears his throat, and MASAKO returns from her bath.*)

MURATA: You're done already? (*He's glad to see her.*)

MASAKO: I wasn't very dirty. The water was too hot.

MURATA: Good! Just the way I like it.

HANA: Not dirty?

MURATA: (*picking up his towel*) Come on, Mama . . . scrub my back.

HANA: (*laughing with embarrassment*) Oh, oh . . . well . . . (*She stops the player.*) Masako, now don't forget. Crank the machine and change the needle now and then.

MASAKO: I didn't bring them.

HANA: Oh. Oh . . . all right. I'll be back soon. Don't forget . . . Crank. (*She leaves with her husband.*)

(*OKA and MASAKO are alone. OKA is awkward and falsely hearty.*)

OKA: So! So you don't like hot baths, eh?

MASAKO: Not too hot.

OKA: (*laughing*) I thought you like it real hot. Hot enough to burn the house down.

(*MASAKO doesn't laugh.*)

OKA: (*continuing*) That's a little joke.

(*MASAKO busies herself to conceal her annoyance.*)

OKA: (*continuing*) I hear you're real good in school. Always top of the class.

MASAKO: It's a small class. Only two of us.

OKA: When Kiyoko comes, you'll help her in school, yeah? You'll take care of her . . . a favor for me, eh?

MASAKO: Okay.

OKA: You'll be her friend, eh?

MASAKO: Okay.

OKA: That's good. That's good. You'll like her. She's a nice girl too.

(*OKA stands, yawns, and stretches.*)

OKA: (*continuing*) I'll go for a little walk now. (*He touches his crotch to indicate his purpose.*)

(*MASAKO turns her attention to the records and selects one, "And the Soul Shall Dance," and begins to sway with the music. The song draws EMIKO from the house. She looks out the window, sees MASAKO is alone, and slips into a dance.*)

EMIKO: Do you like that song, Masa-chan?

(*MASAKO is startled. She remembers her mother's warning. She doesn't know what to do. She nods.*)

EMIKO: (*continuing*) That's one of my favorite songs. I remember in Japan I used to sing it so often. My favorite song. (*She sings along with the record.*) *Akai kuchibiru / Kappu ni yosete / Aoi sake nomya / Kokoro ga odoru.* Do you know what that means, Masa-chan?

MASAKO: I think so. The soul will dance?

EMIKO: Yes, yes, that's right. The soul shall dance. Red lips against a glass, drink the green . . .

MASAKO: Wine?

EMIKO: (*nodding*) Drink the green wine . . .

MASAKO: Green? I thought wine was purple.

EMIKO: Wine is purple, but this is a green liqueur.

(*EMIKO holds up one of the cups as though it were crystal and looks at the light that would shine through the green liquid.*)

EMIKO: (*continuing*) It's good. It warms your heart.

MASAKO: And the soul dances.

EMIKO: Yes . . .

MASAKO: What does it taste like? The green wine?

EMIKO: Oh, it's like . . . it's like . . .

(*The second verse starts:* Kurai yoru no yume / Setsu nasa yo / Aoi sake nomya / Yume ga odoru.)

MASAKO: In the dark night . . .

EMIKO: Dreams are unbearable . . .

MASAKO: Drink the . . .

EMIKO: Drink the green wine . . .

MASAKO: And the dreams will dance.

EMIKO: (*softly*) I'll be going back one day.

MASAKO: Where?

EMIKO: My home. Japan. My real home. I'm going back one day.

MASAKO: By yourself?

EMIKO: Oh, yes. It's a secret. You can keep a secret?

MASAKO: Un-hunh. I have lots of secrets. All my own.

(*The music stops. EMIKO sees OKA approaching and disappears into the house. MASAKO attends to the record and does not know EMIKO is gone.*)

MASAKO: (*continuing*) Secrets I never tell any-one . . .

OKA: Secrets? What kind of secrets? What did she say?

MASAKO: (*startled*) Oh! Nothing.

OKA: What did you talk about?

MASAKO: Nothing. Mrs. Oka was talking about the song. She was telling me what it meant . . . about the soul.

OKA: (*scoffing*) Heh! What does she know about soul? (*calming down*) Ehhh . . . Some people don't have them—souls.

MASAKO: (*timidly*) I thought . . . I thought everyone has a soul. I read in a book . . .

OKA: (*laughing*) Maybe . . . maybe you're right. I'm not an educated man, you know. I don't know too much about books. When Kiyoko comes you can talk to her about it. Kiyoko is very . . .

(*From inside the house, we hear EMIKO begin to sing loudly at the name KIYOKO as though trying to drown it out. OKA stops talking, then resumes.*)

OKA: (*continuing*) Kiyoko is very smart. You'll have a good time with her. She'll learn your language fast. How old did you say you are?

MASAKO: Almost twelve.

(*By this time OKA and MASAKO are shouting to be heard above EMIKO's singing.*)

OKA: Kiyoko is fifteen. Kiyoko . . .

(*OKA is exasperated. He rushes into the house seething. MASAKO hears OKA's muffled rage. "Behave yourself" and "Kitchigai" come through. MASAKO slinks to the window and looks in. OKA slaps EMIKO around. MASAKO reacts to the violence. OKA comes out. MASAKO returns to the bench in time. He pulls his fingers through his hair and sits next to MASAKO. She draws away.*)

OKA: Want me to light a lantern?
MASAKO: (*shaken*) No . . . ye . . . okay.
OKA: We'll get a little light here.

(*He lights the lantern as the MURATAS return from their bath. They are in good spirits.*)

MURATA: Ahhh . . . Nothing like a good hot bath.
HANA: So refreshing.
MURATA: A bath should be taken hot and slow. Don't know how Masako gets through so fast.
HANA: She probably doesn't get in the tub.
MASAKO: I do.

(*Everyone laughs.*)

MASAKO: (*continuing*) Well, I do.

(*EMIKO comes out. She has a large purple welt on her face. She sits on the separate chair, hands folded, quietly watching the MURATAS. They look at her with alarm. OKA engages himself with his fan.*)

HANA: Oh! Emiko-san . . . what . . . a . . . a . . . whaa . . . (*She draws a deep breath.*) What a nice bath we had. Such a lovely bath. We do appreciate your hos . . . pitality. Thank you so much.
EMIKO: Lovely evening, isn't it?
HANA: Very lovely. Very. Ah, a little warm, but nice. Did you get a chance to hear the records? (*turning to MASAKO*) Did you play the records for Mrs. Oka?
MASAKO: Ye . . . no. The needle was . . .

EMIKO: Yes, she did. We played the records together.
MURATA: Oh, you played the songs together?
EMIKO: Yes . . . yes.
MURATA: That's nice. Masako can understand pretty good, eh?
EMIKO: She understands everything. Everything I say.
MURATA: (*withdrawing*) Oh, yeah? Eh, Mama, we ought to be going. (*He closes the player.*) Hate to bathe and run but . . .
HANA: Yes, yes. Tomorrow is a busy day. Come, Masako.
EMIKO: Please . . . stay a little longer.
MURATA: Eh, well, we got to be going.
HANA: Why, thank you, but . . .
EMIKO: It's still quite early.
OKA: (*ready to say good-bye*) Enjoyed the music. And the sake.
EMIKO: The records are very nice. Makes me remember Japan. I sang those songs . . . those very songs . . . Did you know I used to sing?
HANA: (*politely*) Why, no. No. I didn't know that. You must have a very lovely voice.
EMIKO: Yes.
HANA: No, I didn't know that. That's very nice.
EMIKO: Yes, I sang. My parents were very strict. They didn't like it. They said it was frivolous. Imagine?
HANA: Yes, I can imagine. Things were like that . . . in those days singing was not considered proper for nice . . . I mean, only for women in the profess . . .
MURATA: We better get home, Mama.
HANA: Yes, yes. What a shame you couldn't continue with it.
EMIKO: In the city I did do some classics: the dance, and the koto, and the flower, and of course, the tea. (*She makes the gestures for the disciplines.*) All those. Even some singing. Classics, of course.
HANA: (*politely*) Of course.
EMIKO: All of it is so disciplined . . . so disciplined. I was almost a *natori*.
HANA: How nice!
EMIKO: But everything changed.

HANA: Oh!

EMIKO: I was sent here to America. (*She glares at OKA.*)

HANA: Oh, too bad. I mean, too bad about your *natori*.

MURATA: (*loudly to OKA*) So did you see Nagata-san today?

OKA: Oh, yeah, yeah.

MURATA: What did he say? Is he interested?

OKA: Yeah. Yeah. He's interested.

MURATA: He likes the horse, eh?

OKA: Ah . . . yeah.

MURATA: I knew he'd like him. I'd buy him myself if I had the money.

OKA: Well, I have to take him over tomorrow. He'll decide then.

MURATA: He'll buy. He'll buy. You'd better go straight over to the ticket agent and get that ticket. Before you (*ha-ha*) spend the money.

OKA: (*ha-ha*) Yeah.

HANA: It'll be so nice when Kiyoko-san comes to join you. I know you're looking forward to it.

EMIKO: (*confused*) Oh . . . oh . . .

HANA: Masako is so happy. It'll be good for her too.

EMIKO: I had more freedom in the city. I lived with an aunt and she let me . . . she wasn't so strict.

(*MURATA and MASAKO have their gear together and are ready to leave.*)

MURATA: Good luck on the horse tomorrow.

OKA: Yeah.

HANA: (*bowing*) Many, many thanks.

OKA: Thanks for the sake.

HANA: (*bowing again*) Good night, Emiko-san. We'll see you again soon. We'll bring the records too.

EMIKO: (*softly*) Those songs. Those very songs.

MURATA: Let's go, Mama.

(*The MURATAS pull away. Light follows them and grows dark on the OKAS. The MURATAS begin walking home.*)

HANA: That was uncomfortable.

MASAKO: What's the matter with . . .

HANA: Shhh!

MURATA: I guess Oka has his problems.

MASAKO: Is she really *kitchigai*?

HANA: Of course not. She's not crazy. Don't say that word.

MASAKO: I heard Mr. Oka call her that.

HANA: He called her that?

MASAKO: I . . . I think so.

HANA: You heard wrong, Masako. Emiko-san isn't crazy. She just likes her drinks. She had too much to drink tonight.

MASAKO: Oh.

HANA: She can't adjust to this life. She can't get over the good times she had in Japan. Well, it's not easy. But one has to know when to bend . . . like the bamboo. When the winds blow, bamboo bends. You bend or crack. Remember that, Masako.

MURATA: (*wryly*) Bend, eh? Remember that, Mama.

HANA: (*softly*) You don't know. It isn't ever easy.

MASAKO: Do you want to go back to Japan, Mama?

HANA: Everyone does.

MASAKO: Do you, Papa?

MURATA: I'll have to make some money first.

MASAKO: I don't. Not me. Not Kiyoko.

HANA: After Kiyoko-san comes, Emiko will have company and things will straighten out. She has nothing to live on but memories. She doesn't have any friends. At least I have my friends at church. At least I have that. She must get awful lonely. . . .

MASAKO: I know that. She tried to make friends with me.

HANA: She did? What did she say?

MASAKO: Well, sort of . . .

HANA: What did she say?

MASAKO: She didn't say anything. I just felt it. Maybe you should be her friend, Mama.

MURATA: Poor woman. We could have stayed longer.

HANA: But you wanted to leave. I tried to be friendly. You saw that. It's not easy to talk to Emiko. She either closes up, you can't pry a word from her, or else she goes on and on. All that . . . that . . . about the koto and tea and the flower . . . I mean, what am I supposed to say? She's so unpredictable. And the drinking . . .

MURATA: All right, all right, Mama.

MASAKO: Did you see her black eye?

HANA: (*calming down*) She probably hurt herself. She wasn't very steady.

MASAKO: Oh, no. Mr. Oka hit her.

HANA: I don't think so.

MASAKO: He hit her. I saw him.

HANA: You saw? Papa, do you hear that? She saw them. That does it. We're not going there again.

MURATA: Aw . . . Oka wouldn't do that. Not in front of a kid.

MASAKO: Well, they didn't do it in front of me. They were in the house.

MURATA: You see?

HANA: That's all right. You just have to fix the bathhouse. Either that or we're going to bathe at home . . . in a bucket, if we have to. We're not going . . . we'll bathe at home.

(*MURATA mutters to himself.*)

HANA: What?

MURATA: I said all right, it's the bucket then. I'll get to it when I can.

(*HANA passes MURATA and walks ahead.*)

Scene 3

The same evening. The exterior of the Oka house. The MURATAS have just left. EMIKO sits on the bench, her back to OKA. OKA, still standing, looks at her contemptuously as she pours herself a drink.

OKA: Nothing more disgusting than a drunk woman.

(*EMIKO ignores him.*)

OKA: (*continuing*) You made a fool of yourself. You made a fool of *me!*

EMIKO: One can only make a fool of one's self.

OKA: You learn that in the fancy schools, eh?

(*EMIKO examines the pattern of her cup.*)

OKA: (*continuing*) Eh? Ehhh? (*pause*) Answer me!

(*EMIKO ignores him.*)

OKA: (*continuing*) I'm talking to you. Answer me! (*threatening*) You don't get away with that. You think you're so fine. . . .

(*EMIKO looks off at the horizon. OKA roughly turns her around.*)

OKA: (*continuing*) When I talk, you listen!

(*EMIKO turns away again. OKA pulls the cup from her hand.*)

OKA: (*continuing*) Goddammit! What'd you think my friends think of you? What kind of ass they think I am?

(*He grabs her shoulders.*)

EMIKO: Don't touch me. Don't touch (me) . . .

OKA: Who the hell you think you are? "Don't touch me, don't touch me." Who the hell! High and mighty, eh? Too good for me, eh? Don't put on the act for me. I know who you are.

EMIKO: Tell me who I am, Mister Smart Peasant.

OKA: Shut your fool mouth, goddammit! Sure. I'll tell you. I know all about you. Shizue told me. The whole village knows.

EMIKO: Shizue!

OKA: Yeah, Shizue. Embarrassed the hell out of her, your own sister.

EMIKO: Embarrassed? I have nothing to be ashamed of. I don't know what you're talking about.

OKA: (*derisively*) You don't know what I'm talking about. I know. The whole village knows. They're all laughing at you. At me! Stupid Oka got stuck with a secondhand woman. I didn't say anything because . . .

EMIKO: I'm not secondhand!

OKA: Who you trying to fool? I know. Knew long time ago. Shizue wrote me all about your . . . your affairs in Tokyo. The men you were mess(ing) . . .

EMIKO: Affairs? Men?

OKA: That man you were messing with. I knew all along. I didn't say anything because you . . . I . . .

EMIKO: I'm not ashamed of it.

OKA: You're not ashamed! What the hell! Your father thought he was pulling a fast one on me . . . thought I didn't know nothing . . . thought I was some kind of dumb ass . . . I didn't say nothing because Shizue's dead. Shizue's dead. I was willing to give you a chance.

EMIKO: (*laughing*) A chance? Give me a chance?

OKA: Yeah. A chance! Laugh! Give a *joro* another chance. Sure, I'm stupid . . . dumb.

EMIKO: I'm not a whore. I'm true. He knows I'm true.

OKA: True! (*Hah!*)

EMIKO: You think I'm untrue just because I let . . . let you . . . There's only one man for me.

OKA: Let me (*obscene gesture*)? I can do what I want with you. Your father palmed you off on me—like a dog or cat—animal. Couldn't do nothing with you. Even the rich dumb Yamato wouldn't have you. Your father—greedy father—so proud . . . making big plans for you . . . for himself. (*Humh!*) the whole village laughing at him.

(*EMIKO hangs her head.*)

OKA: (*continuing*) Shizue told me. And she was working like a dog . . . trying to keep your goddam father happy . . . doing my work and yours.

EMIKO: My work?

OKA: Yeah, your work too! She killed herself working. She killed herself. (*He has tender memories of his uncomplaining wife.*) Up in the morning getting the fires started, working the bellows, cleaning the furnace, cooking, and late at night working with the sewing . . . tending the baby. (*He mutters.*) The goddam family killed her. And you . . . you out there in Tokyo with the fancy clothes, doing the (*sneering*) dance, the tea, the flower, the (*obscene gesture*) . . .

EMIKO: (*hurting*) Ahhhhh . . .

OKA: Did you have fun? Did you have fun on your sister's blood?

(*EMIKO doesn't answer.*)

OKA: (*continuing*) Did you? He must have been a son-of-a-bitch. What would make that goddam greedy old man send his prize mare to a plow horse like me? What kind of bum was he that your father would . . .

EMIKO: He's not a bum. He's not a bum.

OKA: Was he Korean? Was he *Etta?* That's the only thing I could figure.

EMIKO: I'm true to him. Only him.

OKA: True? You think he's true to you? You think he waits for you? Remembers you? *Aho!* Think he cares?

EMIKO: He does.

OKA: And waits ten years? *Baka!* Go back to Japan and see. You'll find out. Go back to Japan. *Kaire!*

EMIKO: In time.

OKA: In time. How about now?

EMIKO: I can't now.

OKA: (*Hah!*) Now! Go now! Who needs you? Who needs you? You think a man waits ten years for a woman? You think you're some kind of . . . of diamond . . . treasure . . . he's going to wait his life for you? Go to him. He's probably married with ten kids. Go to him. Get out! Goddam *joro*. Go! Go!

(*OKA sweeps EMIKO off the bench.*)

EMIKO: Ahhh! I . . . I don't have the money. Give me money to . . .

OKA: If I had money I would give it to you ten years ago. You think I been eating this *kuso* for ten years because I like it?

EMIKO: You're selling the horse. Give me the (*money*) . . .

OKA: (*scoffing*) That's for Kiyoko. I owe you nothing.

EMIKO: Ten years, you owe me.

OKA: Ten years of what? Misery? You gave me nothing. I give you nothing. You want to go, pack your bag and start walking. Try cross the desert. When you get dry and hungry, think about me.

EMIKO: I'd die out there.

OKA: Die? You think I didn't die here?

EMIKO: I didn't do anything to you.

OKA: No, no, you didn't. All I wanted was a little comfort and you . . . no, you didn't. No. So you die. We all die. Shizue died. If she was here, she wouldn't treat me like this. Ah, I should have brought her with me. She'd be alive now. We'd be poor but happy like . . . like Murata and his wife . . . and the kid.

EMIKO: I wish she were alive too. I'm not to blame for her dying. I didn't know. I was away. I loved her. I didn't want her to die. I . . .

OKA: (*softening*) I know that. I'm not blaming you for that. And it's not my fault what happened to you either.

(*OKA is encouraged by EMIKO's silence which he mistakes for a change of attitude.*)

OKA: (*continuing*) You understand that, eh? I didn't ask for you. It's not my fault you're here in this desert with . . . with me.

(*EMIKO weeps. OKA reaches out.*)

OKA: (*continuing*) I know I'm too old for you. It's hard for me too. But this is the way it is. I just ask you be kinder . . . understand it wasn't my fault. Try make it easier for me. For yourself too.

(*OKA touches her and she shrinks from his hand.*)

EMIKO: Ach!

OKA: (*humiliated again*) Goddam it! I didn't ask for you! *Aho!* If you was smart, you'da done as your father said . . . cut out that *saru shibai* with the *Etta* . . . married the rich Yamato. Then you'd still be in Japan. Not here to make my life so miserable.

(*EMIKO is silent.*)

OKA: (*continuing*) And you can have your *Etta* . . . or anyone else you want. Take them all on.

(*OKA is worn out. It's hopeless.*)

OKA: (*continuing*) God, why do we do this all the time? Fighting all the time. There must be a better way to live. There must be another way.

(*OKA waits for a response, gives up, and enters the house. EMIKO watches him leave and pours another drink. The storm has passed, the alcohol takes over.*)

EMIKO: I must keep the dream alive. The dream is all I live for. I am only in exile now. If I give in, all I've lived before will mean nothing . . . will be for nothing. Nothing. If I let you make me believe this is all there is to my life, the dream would die. I would die.

(*She pours another drink and feels warm and good.*)

ACT TWO

Scene 1

Mid-September afternoon. Muratas' kitchen. The calendar reads September. MASAKO is at the kitchen table with several books. She thumbs through a Japanese magazine. HANA is with her sewing.

MASAKO: Do they always wear kimonos in Japan, Mama?

HANA: Most of the time.

MASAKO: I wonder if Kiyoko will be wearing a kimono like this.

HANA: (*looking at the magazine*) They don't dress like that. Not for every day.

MASAKO: I wonder what she's like.

HANA: Probably a lot like you. What do you think she's like?

MASAKO: She's probably taller.

HANA: Mr. Oka isn't tall.

MASAKO: And pretty.

HANA: (*laughing*) Mr. Oka . . . Well, I don't suppose she'll look like her father.

MASAKO: Mrs. Oka is pretty.

HANA: She isn't Kiyoko-san's real mother, remember?

MASAKO: Oh, that's right.

HANA: But they are related. Well, we'll soon see.

MASAKO: I thought she was coming in September. It's already September.

HANA: Papa said Oka-san went to San Pedro a few days ago. He should be back soon with Kiyoko-san.

MASAKO: Didn't Mrs. Oka go too?

HANA: (*glancing toward the Oka house*) I don't think so. I see lights in their house at night.

MASAKO: Will they bring Kiyoko over to see us?

HANA: Of course. First thing, probably. You'll be very nice to her, won't you?

(*MASAKO finds another book.*)

MASAKO: Sure. I'm glad I'm going to have a friend. I hope she likes me.

HANA: She'll like you. Japanese girls are very polite, you know.

MASAKO: We have to be or our mamas get mad at us.

HANA: Then I should be getting mad at you more often.

MASAKO: It's often enough already, Mama. (*She opens the book.*) Look at this, Mama. I'm going to show her this book.

HANA: She won't be able to read at first.

MASAKO: I love this story. Mama, this is about people like us—settlers—it's about the prairie. We live in a prairie, don't we?

HANA: Prairie? Does that mean desert?

MASAKO: I think so.

HANA: (*looking at the bleak landscape*) We live in a prairie.

MASAKO: It's about the hardships and the floods and droughts and how they have nothing but each other.

HANA: We have nothing but each other. But these people . . . they're white people.

MASAKO: Sure, Mama. They come from the east. Just like you and Papa came from Japan.

HANA: We come from the far far east. That's different. White people are different from us.

MASAKO: I know that.

HANA: White people among white people . . . that's different from Japanese among white people. You know what I'm saying?

MASAKO: I know that. How come they don't write books about us . . . about Japanese people?

HANA: Because we're nobodies here.

MASAKO: If I didn't read these, there'd be nothing for me.

HANA: Some of the things you read, you're never going to know.

MASAKO: I can dream though.

HANA: (*sighing*) Sometimes the dreaming makes the living harder. Better to keep your head out of the clouds.

MASAKO: That's not much fun.

HANA: You'll have fun when Kiyoko-san comes. You can study together, you can sew, and sometime you can try some of those fancy American recipes.

MASAKO: Oh, Mama. You have to have chocolate and cream and things like that.

HANA: We'll get them.

(*We hear the sound of Oka's old car. MASAKO and HANA pause and listen. MASAKO runs to the window.*)

MASAKO: I think it's them!

HANA: Oka-san?

MASAKO: It's them! It's them!

(*HANA stands and looks out. She removes her apron and puts away her sewing.*)

HANA: Two of them. Emiko-san isn't with them. (*pause*) Let's go outside.

(*OKA and KIYOKO enter. OKA is wearing his going-out clothes: a sweater, white shirt, dark pants, but no tie. KIYOKO walks behind him.*)

(*KIYOKO is short, broad-chested, and very self-conscious. Her hair is straight and banded into two shucks. She wears a conservative cotton dress, white socks, and two-inch heels.*)

(*OKA is proud. He struts in, his chest puffed out.*)

OKA: Hello, hello! We're here. We made it! (*He pushes KIYOKO forward.*) This my daughter, Kiyoko. (*to KIYOKO*) Murata-san. Remember, I was talking about? My friends . . .

KIYOKO: (*bowing deeply*) *Hajime mashite yoroshiku onegai shimasu.*

HANA: (*also bowing deeply*) I hope your journey was pleasant.

OKA: (*pushing KIYOKO to MASAKO while she still bows*) This is Masako-chan; I told you about her.

(*MASAKO is shocked at KIYOKO's appearance. The girl she expected is already a woman. She stands with her mouth agape and withdraws noticeably. HANA rushes in to fill the awkwardness.*)

HANA: Say hello, Masako. My goodness, where are your manners? (*She laughs apologetically.*) In this country they don't make much to-do about manners. (*She stands back to examine KIYOKO.*) My, my, I didn't picture you so grown up. My, my . . . Tell me, how was your trip?

OKA: (*proudly*) We just drove in from Los Angeles this morning. We spent the night in San Pedro, and the next two days we spent in Los Angeles . . . you know, Japanese town.

HANA: How nice!

OKA: Kiyoko was so excited. Twisting her head this way and that—couldn't see enough with her big eyes. (*He imitates her fondly.*) She's from the country, you know . . . just a big country girl. Got all excited about the Chinese dinner—we had a Chinese dinner. She never ate it before.

(*KIYOKO covers her mouth and giggles.*)

HANA: Chinese dinner!

OKA: Oh, yeah. Duck, *pakkai,* chow mein, sea-weed soup . . . the works!

HANA: A feast!

OKA: Oh, yeah. Like a holiday. Two holidays. Two holidays in one.

(*HANA pushes MASAKO forward.*)

HANA: Two holidays in one! Kiyoko-san, our Masako has been looking forward to meeting you.

KIYOKO: (*bowing again*) *Hajime mashite . . .*

HANA: She's been planning all sorts of things she'll do with you: sewing, cooking . . .

MASAKO: Oh, Mama . . .

(*KIYOKO covers her mouth and giggles.*)

HANA: It's true, Kiyoko-san. She's been looking forward to having a best friend.

(*KIYOKO giggles and MASAKO pulls away.*)

OKA: Kiyoko, you shouldn't be so shy. The Muratas are my good friends, and you should feel free with them. Ask anything, say anything. Right?

HANA: Of course, of course. (*She is annoyed with MASAKO.*) Masako, go in and start the tea.

(*MASAKO enters the house.*)

HANA: (*continuing*) I'll call Papa. He's in the yard. Papa! Oka-san is here! (*to KIYOKO*) Now tell me, how was your trip? Did you get seasick?

KIYOKO: (*bowing and nodding*) Eh (*affirmative*). A little.

OKA: Tell her. Tell her how sick you got.

(*KIYOKO covers her mouth and giggles.*)

HANA: Oh, I know, I know. I was too. That was a long time ago. I'm sure things are improved now. Tell me about Japan. What is it like now? They say it's so changed . . . modern.

OKA: Kiyoko comes from the country . . . backwoods. Nothing changes much there from century to century.

HANA: Ah! That's true. That's why I love Japan. And you wanted to leave. It's unbelievable. To come here!

OKA: She always dreamed about it.

HANA: Well, it's not really that bad.

OKA: No, it's not that bad. Depends on what you make of it.

HANA: That's right. What you make of it. I was just telling Masako today . . .

(*MURATA enters. He rubs his hands to remove the soil and comes in grinning. He shakes OKA's hand.*)

MURATA: *Oi, oi . . .*

OKA: *Yah . . .* I'm back. This is my daughter.

MURATA: No! She's beautiful!

OKA: Finally made it. Finally got her here.

MURATA: (*to KIYOKO*) Your father hasn't stopped talking about you all summer.

HANA: And Masako too.

KIYOKO: (*bowing*) *Hajime mashite . . .*

MURATA: (*with a short bow*) *Yah.* How'd you like the trip?

OKA: I was just telling your wife . . . had a good time in Los Angeles. Had a couple of great dinners, took in the cinema—Japanese pictures, bought her some American clothes . . .

HANA: Oh, you bought that in Los Angeles.

MURATA: Got a good price for your horse, eh? Lots of money, eh?

OKA: Nagata-kun's a shrewd bargainer. Heh. It don't take much money to make her happy. She's a country girl.

MURATA: That's all right. Country's all right. Country girl's the best.

OKA: Had trouble on the way back.

MURATA: Yeah?

OKA: Fan belt broke.

MURATA: That'll happen with these old cars.

OKA: Lucky I was near a gasoline station. We were in the mountains. Waited in a restaurant while it was getting fixed.

HANA: Oh, that was good.

OKA: Guess they don't see Japanese much. Stare? Terrible! Took them a long time to wait on us. Dumb waitress practically threw the food at us. Kiyoko felt bad.

HANA: Ah! That's too bad . . . too bad. That's why I always pack a lunch when we take trips.

MURATA: They'll spoil the day for you . . . those barbarians!

OKA: Terrible food too. Kiyoko couldn't swallow the dry bread and bologna.

HANA: That's the food they eat!

MURATA: Let's go in . . . have a little wine. Mama, we got wine? This is a celebration.

HANA: I think so. A little.

(*They enter the house talking. MASAKO has made tea and HANA serves the wine.*)

HANA: (*continuing*) How is your mother? Was she happy to see you?

KIYOKO: Oh, she . . . yes.

HANA: I just know she was surprised to see you so grown up. Of course, you remember her from Japan, don't you?

KIYOKO: (*nodding*) *Eh* (affirmative). I can barely remember. I was very young.

HANA: Of course. But you do, don't you?

KIYOKO: She was gone most of the time . . . at school in Tokyo. She was very pretty, I remember that.

HANA: She's still very pretty.

KIYOKO: Yes. She was always laughing. She was much younger then.

HANA: Oh, now, it hasn't been that long ago.

(*MASAKO goes outside. The following dialogue continues muted as the light goes dim in the house and focuses on MASAKO. EMIKO enters, is drawn to the Murata window, and listens.*)

OKA: We stayed at an inn on East First Street. *Shizuokaya.* Whole inn filled with Shizuoka people . . . talking the old dialect. Thought I was in Japan again.

MURATA: That right?

OKA: Felt good. Like I was in Japan again.

HANA: (*to KIYOKO*) Did you enjoy Los Angeles?

KIYOKO: Yes.

OKA: That's as close as I'll get to Japan.

MURATA: *Mattakuna!* That's for sure. Not in this life.

(*Outside MASAKO is aware of EMIKO.*)

MASAKO: Why don't you go in?

EMIKO: Oh. Oh. Why don't you?

MASAKO: They're all grown-ups in there. I'm not grown up.

EMIKO: (*softly*) All grown-ups. Maybe I'm not either. (*Her mood changes.*) Masa-chan, do you have a boyfriend?

MASAKO: I don't like boys. They don't like me.

EMIKO: Oh, that will change. You will change. I was like that too.

MASAKO: Besides, there's none around here . . . Japanese boys. There are some at school, but they don't like girls.

HANA: (*calling from the kitchen*) Masako . . .

(*MASAKO doesn't answer.*)

EMIKO: Your mother is calling you.

MASAKO: (*to her mother*) *Nani?* (What?)

HANA: (*from the kitchen*) Come inside now.

EMIKO: You'll have a boyfriend one day.

MASAKO: Not me.

EMIKO: You'll fall in love one day. Someone will make the inside of you light up, and you'll know you're in love. Your life will change . . . grow beautiful. It's good, Masa-chan. And this feeling you'll remember the rest of your life . . . will come back to you . . . haunt you . . . keep you alive . . . five, ten years . . . no matter what happens. Keep you alive.

HANA: (*from the house*) Masako . . . Come inside now.

(*MASAKO turns aside to answer and EMIKO slips away.*)

MASAKO: What, Mama?

(*HANA comes out.*)

HANA: Come inside. Don't be so unsociable. Kiyoko wants to talk to you.

MASAKO: (*watching EMIKO leave*) She doesn't want to talk to me. You're only saying that.

HANA: What's the matter with you? Don't you want to make friends with her?

MASAKO: She's not my friend. She's your friend.

HANA: Don't be silly. She's only fourteen.

MASAKO: Fifteen. They said fifteen. She's your friend. She's an old lady.

HANA: Don't say that.

MASAKO: I don't like her.

HANA: Shhh! Don't say that.

MASAKO: She doesn't like me either.

HANA: Ma-chan. Remember your promise to Mr. Oka? You're going to take her to school,

teach her the language, teach her the ways of Americans.

MASAKO: She can do it herself. You did.

HANA: That's not nice, Ma-chan.

MASAKO: I don't like the way she laughs. (*She imitates KIYOKO holding her hand to her mouth and giggling and bowing.*)

HANA: Oh, how awful! Stop that. That's the way the girls do in Japan. Maybe she doesn't like your ways either. That's only a difference in manners. What you're doing now is considered very bad manners. (*She changes her tone.*) Ma-chan, just wait: when she learns to read and speak, you'll have so much to say to each other. Come on, be a good girl and come inside.

MASAKO: It's just old people in there, Mama. I don't want to go in.

(*HANA calls to KIYOKO inside.*)

HANA: Kiyoko-san, please come here a minute. Maybe it's better for you to talk to Masako alone.

(*KIYOKO dutifully goes outside.*)

HANA: (*continuing*) Masako has a lot of things to tell you . . . about what to expect in school and . . . things.

MURATA: (*calling from the table*) Mama, put out something . . . chiles—for Oka-san.

(*HANA enters the house. KIYOKO and MASAKO stand awkwardly facing each other, KIYOKO glancing shyly at MASAKO.*)

MASAKO: Do you like it here?

KIYOKO: (*nodding*) *Eh* (affirmative).

(*There is an uncomfortable pause.*)

MASAKO: School will be starting next week.

KIYOKO: (*nodding*) *Eh.*

MASAKO: Do you want to walk to school with me?

KIYOKO: (*nodding*) *Hai.*

(*MASAKO rolls her eyes and tries again.*)

MASAKO: I leave at 7:30.

KIYOKO: *Eh.*

(*There's a long pause. MASAKO gives up and moves offstage.*)

MASAKO: I have to do something.

(*KIYOKO watches her leave and uncertainly moves back to the house. HANA looks up at KIYOKO coming in alone, sighs, and quietly pulls out a chair for her.*)

Scene 2

November night. Interior of the Murata home. Lamps are lit. The family is at the kitchen table. HANA sews, MASAKO does her homework, MURATA reads the paper. They're dressed in warm robes and are having tea.

Outside, thunder rolls in the distance and lightning flashes.

HANA: It'll be *ohigan* (autumn festival) soon.
MURATA: Something to look forward to.
HANA: We'll need sweet rice for *omochi* (rice cakes).
MURATA: I'll order it next time I go to town.
HANA: (*to MASAKO*) How is school? Getting a little harder?
MASAKO: Not that much. Sometimes the arithmetic is hard.
HANA: How is Kiyoko-san doing? Is she getting along all right?
MASAKO: She's good in arithmetic. She skipped a grade already.
HANA: Already? That's good news. Only November and she skipped a grade! At this rate she'll be through before you.
MASAKO: Well, she's older.
MURATA: Sure, she's older, Mama.
HANA: Has she made any friends?
MASAKO: No. She follows me around all day. She understands okay, but she doesn't talk. She talks like, you know . . . she says "ranchi" for lunch and "ranchi" for ranch too, and like that. Kids laugh and copy behind her back. It's hard to understand her.
HANA: You understand her, don't you?
MASAKO: I'm used to it.

HANA: You should tell the kids not to laugh. After all, she's trying. Maybe you should help her practice those words . . . show her what she's doing wrong.
MASAKO: I already do. Our teacher told me to do that.
MURATA: (*looking up from his paper*) You ought to help her all you can.
HANA: And remember, when you started school, you couldn't speak English either.
MASAKO: I help her.

(*MURATA goes to the window. The night is cold. Lightning flashes and the wind whistles.*)

MURATA: Looks like a storm coming up. Hope we don't have a freeze.
HANA: If it freezes, we'll have another bad year. Maybe we ought to start the smudge pots.
MURATA: (*listening*) It's starting to rain. Nothing to do now but pray.
HANA: If praying is the answer, we'd be in Japan now. Rich.
MURATA: (*wryly*) We're not dead yet. We still have a chance.

(*HANA glares at the small joke.*)

MURATA: (*continuing*) Guess I'll turn in.
HANA: Go to bed, go to bed. I'll sit up and worry.
MURATA: If worrying was the answer, we'd be around the world twice and in Japan. Come on, Mama. Let's go to bed. It's too cold tonight to be mad.

(*There's an urgent knock on the door. The MURATAS react.*)

MURATA: (*continuing*) *Dareh da!* (Who is it?)

(*MURATA goes to the door and hesitates.*)

MURATA: (*continuing*) Who is it!
KIYOKO: (*weakly*) It's me . . . help me . . .

(*MURATA opens the door and KIYOKO stumbles in. She wears a kimono with a shawl thrown over. Her legs are bare except for a pair of straw zori. Her hair is wet and stringy, and she trembles uncontrollably.*)

MURATA: My God! Kiyoko-san! What's the matter?

HANA: (*overlapping*) Kiyoko-san! What is it?

MURATA: What happened?

KIYOKO: They're fighting, they're fighting!

MURATA: Oh, don't worry. Those things happen. No cause to worry. Mama, make tea for her. Sit down and catch your breath. Don't worry. I'll take you home when you're ready.

HANA: Papa, I'll take care of it.

MURATA: Let me know when you're ready to go home.

HANA: It must be freezing out there. Try to get warm. Try to calm yourself.

MURATA: Kiyoko-san, don't worry. (*He puts his robe around her.*)

(*HANA waves MASAKO and MURATA off. MURATA leaves. MASAKO goes to her bed in the kitchen.*)

HANA: Papa, I'll take care of it.

KIYOKO: (*looking at MURATA'S retreating form*) But I came to ask your help. . . .

HANA: You ran down here without a lantern? You could have fallen and hurt yourself.

KIYOKO: I don't care . . . I don't care . . .

HANA: You don't know, Kiyoko-san. It's treacherous out there—snakes, spiders . . .

KIYOKO: I must go back! I . . . I . . . you . . . please come with me. . . .

HANA: First, first we must get you warm. Drink your tea.

KIYOKO: But they'll kill each other. They're fighting like animals. Help me stop them!

(*HANA warms a pot of soup.*)

HANA: (*calmly*) I cannot interfere in a family quarrel.

KIYOKO: It's not a quarrel. It's a . . . a . . .

HANA: That's all it is. A family squabble. You'll see. Tomorrow . . .

(*KIYOKO pulls at HANA's arm.*)

KIYOKO: Not just a squabble! Please . . . please . . .

(*KIYOKO starts toward the door, but HANA stops her.*)

HANA: Now listen. Listen to me, Kiyoko-san. I've known your father and mother a little while now. I suspect it's been like this for years. Every family has some kind of trouble.

KIYOKO: Not like this, not like this.

HANA: Some have it better, some worse. When you get married, you'll understand. Don't worry. Nothing will happen. (*She takes a towel and dries KIYOKO's hair.*) You're chilled to the bone. You'll catch your death.

KIYOKO: I don't care. . . . I want to die.

HANA: Don't be silly. It's not that bad.

KIYOKO: It is! They started drinking early in the afternoon. They make some kind of brew and hide it somewhere in the desert.

HANA: It's illegal to make it. That's why they hide it. That home brew is poison to the body. The mind too.

KIYOKO: It makes them crazy. They drink it all the time and quarrel constantly. I was in the other room studying. I try so hard to keep up with school.

HANA: We were talking about you just this evening. Masako says you're doing so well. You skipped a grade?

KIYOKO: It's hard . . . hard. I'm too old for the class and the children . . .

(*She remembers all her problems and starts crying again.*)

HANA: It's always hard in a new country.

KIYOKO: They were bickering and quarreling all afternoon. Then something happened. All of a sudden they were on the floor . . . hitting and . . . and . . . He was hitting her in the stomach, the face . . . I tried to stop them, but they were so . . . drunk.

HANA: There, there. It's probably all over now.

KIYOKO: Why does it happen like this? Nothing is right. Everywhere I go. Masa-chan is so lucky. I wish my life was like hers. I can hardly remember my real mother.

HANA: Emiko-san is almost a real mother to you. She's blood kin.

KIYOKO: She hates me. She never speaks to me. She's so cold. I want to love her, but she won't let me. She hates me.

HANA: I don't think so, Kiyoko-san.

KIYOKO: She does! She hates me.

HANA: No. I don't think you have anything to do with it. It's this place. She hates it. This place is so lonely and alien.

KIYOKO: Then why didn't she go back? Why did they stay here?

HANA: You don't know. It's not so simple. Sometimes I think . . .

KIYOKO: Then why don't they make the best of it here? Like you?

HANA: That isn't easy either. Believe me. (*She leaves KIYOKO to stir the soup.*) Sometimes . . . sometimes the longing for home . . . the longing fills me with despair. Will I never return again? Will I never see my mother, my father, my sisters again? But what can one do? There are responsibilities here . . . children . . . (*pause*) And another day passes . . . another month . . . another year. (*She takes the soup to KIYOKO.*) Did you have supper tonight?

KIYOKO: (*bowing*) Ah. When my . . . my aunt gets like this, she doesn't cook. No one eats. I don't get hungry anymore.

HANA: Cook for yourself. It's important to keep your health.

KIYOKO: I left Japan for a better life.

HANA: It isn't easy for you, is it? But you must remember your filial duty.

KIYOKO: It's so hard.

HANA: But you can make the best of it here, Kiyoko-san. And take care of yourself. You owe that to yourself. Eat. Keep well. It'll be better, you'll see. And sometimes it'll seem worse. But you'll survive. We do, you know.

HANA: (*continuing*) It's getting late.

KIYOKO: (*apprehensively*) I don't want to go back.

HANA: You can sleep with Masako tonight. Tomorrow you'll go back. And you'll remember what I told you. (*She puts her arm around KIYOKO.*) Life is never easy, Kiyoko-san. Endure. Endure. Soon you'll be marrying and going away. Things will not always be this way. And you'll look back on this . . . this night and you'll . . .

(*There is a rap on the door. HANA exchanges glances with KIYOKO and opens the door a crack.*)

(*OKA has come looking for KIYOKO. He wears an overcoat and holds a wet newspaper over his head.*)

OKA: Ah! I'm sorry to bother you so late at night—the fact is . . .

HANA: Oka-san.

OKA: (*jovially*) Good evening, good evening. (*He sees KIYOKO.*) Oh, there you are. Did you have a nice visit?

HANA: (*irritated*) Yes, she's here.

OKA: (*still cheerful*) Thought she might be. Ready to come home now?

HANA: She came in the rain.

OKA: (*ignoring HANA's tone*) That's foolish of you, Kiyoko. You might catch cold.

HANA: She was frightened by your quarreling. She came for help.

OKA: (*laughing with embarrassment*) Oh! Kiyoko, that's nothing to worry about. It's just we had some disagreement.

HANA: That's what I told her, but she was frightened just the same.

OKA: Children are . . .

HANA: Not children, Oka-san. Kiyoko. Kiyoko was terrified. I think that was a terrible thing to do to her.

OKA: (*rubbing his head*) Oh, I . . . I . . .

HANA: If you had seen her a few minutes ago . . . hysterical . . . shaking . . . crying . . . wet and cold to the bone . . . out of her mind with worry.

OKA: (*rubbing his head*) Oh, I don't know what she was so worried about.

HANA: You. You and Emiko fighting like you were going to kill each other.

OKA: (*lowering his head in penitence*) Aaaaaaahhh-hhhhh . . .

HANA: I know I shouldn't tell you this, but there's one or two things I have to say: You sent for Kiyoko-san, and now she's here. You said yourself she had a bad time in Japan, and now she's having a worse time. It's not easy for her in a strange country; the least you can do is try to keep from worrying her . . . especially about yourselves. I think it's terrible what you're doing to her . . . terrible!

OKA: (*bowing in deep humility*) I am ashamed.

HANA: I think she deserves better. I think you should think about that.

OKA: (*still bowing*) I thank you for this reminder. It will never happen again. I promise.

HANA: I don't need that promise. Make it to Kiyoko-san.

OKA: Come with Papa now. He did a bad thing. He'll be a good Papa from now. He won't worry his little girl again. All right?

(*They move toward the door. KIYOKO tries to return Murata's robe.*)

KIYOKO: Thank you so much.

OKA: Thank you again.

HANA: (*to KIYOKO*) That's all right. You can bring it back tomorrow. Remember . . . remember what we talked about. (*loudly*) Good night, Oka-san.

(*They leave. HANA goes to MASAKO, who pretends to sleep. She covers her. MURATA appears from the bedroom. He's heard it all. He and HANA exchange a quick glance and together they retire to their room.*)

Scene 3

The next morning. The Murata house and yard. HANA and MURATA have already left the house to examine the rain damage in the fields.

MASAKO prepares to go to school. She puts on a coat and gets her books and lunch bag. Meanwhile, KIYOKO slips quietly into the yard. She wears a coat and carries Murata's robe and sets it on the outside bench.

MASAKO walks out and is surprised to see KIYOKO.

MASAKO: Hi. I thought you'd be . . . sick today.

KIYOKO: Oh. I woke up late.

MASAKO: (*scrutinizing KIYOKO's face*) Your eyes are red.

KIYOKO: (*averting her face*) Oh. I . . . got . . . sand in it. Yes.

MASAKO: Do you want eye drops? We have eye drops in the house.

KIYOKO: Oh, no. That's all right.

MASAKO: That's what's called bloodshot.

KIYOKO: Oh.

MASAKO: My father gets it a lot. When he drinks too much.

KIYOKO: Oh.

(*MASAKO notices KIYOKO doesn't carry a lunch.*)

MASAKO: Where's your lunch bag?

KIYOKO: I . . . forgot it.

MASAKO: Did you make your lunch today?

KIYOKO: Yes. Yes, I did. But I forgot it.

MASAKO: Do you want to go back and get it?

KIYOKO: No. (*pause*) We will be late.

MASAKO: Do you want to practice your words?

KIYOKO: (*thoughtfully*) Oh . . .

MASAKO: Say, "My."

KIYOKO: My?

MASAKO: Eyes . . .

KIYOKO: Eyes.

MASAKO: Are . . .

KIYOKO: Are.

MASAKO: Red.

KIYOKO: Red.

MASAKO: Your eyes are red.

(*KIYOKO will not repeat it.*)

MASAKO: (*continuing*) I . . .

(*KIYOKO doesn't cooperate.*)

MASAKO: (*continuing*) Say, "I."

KIYOKO: I.

MASAKO: Got . . .

KIYOKO: Got.

MASAKO: Sand . . .

(*KIYOKO balks.*)

MASAKO: (*continuing*) Say, "I."

KIYOKO: (*sighing*) I.

MASAKO: Reft . . .

KIYOKO: Reft.

MASAKO: My . . .

KIYOKO: My.

MASAKO: Runch.

KIYOKO: Run . . . Lunch. (*pause*) Masako-san, you are mean. You are hurting me.

MASAKO: It's a joke! I was just trying to make you laugh!

KIYOKO: I cannot laugh today.

MASAKO: Sure you can. You can laugh. Laugh! Like this! (*She makes a hearty laugh.*)

KIYOKO: I cannot laugh when you make fun of me.

MASAKO: Okay, I'm sorry. We'll practice some other words then, okay?

(*KIYOKO doesn't answer.*)

MASAKO: (*continuing*) Say, "Okay."

KIYOKO: (*reluctantly*) Okay.

MASAKO: Okay, then . . . um . . . um . . . Say . . . um . . . (*rapidly*) "She sells seashells by the seashore."

(*KIYOKO turns away indignantly.*)

MASAKO: (*continuing*) Aw, come on, Kiyoko! It's just a joke. Laugh!

KIYOKO: (*sarcastically*) Ha-ha-ha. Now you say, "*Kono kyaku wa yoku kaki ku kyaku da!*"

MASAKO: Sure I can say it. *Kono kyaku waki ku kyoku kaku . . .*

KIYOKO: That's not right.

MASAKO: *Koki kuki kya . . .*

KIYOKO: No. No-no-no.

MASAKO: Okay, then. You say, "Sea sells she shells . . . shu . . . sh."

(*They both laugh, KIYOKO with her hands over her mouth. MASAKO takes KIYOKO's hands away.*)

MASAKO: Not like that. Like this! (*She makes a big laugh.*)

KIYOKO: Like this? (*She imitates MASAKO.*)

MASAKO: Yeah, that's right! (*pause*) You're not mad anymore?

KIYOKO: I'm not mad anymore.

MASAKO: Okay. You can share my lunch because we're . . .

KIYOKO: "Flends?"

(*MASAKO looks at KIYOKO. They giggle and move on.*)

(*HANA and MURATA come in from assessing the storm's damage. They are dressed warmly. HANA is depressed. MURATA tries to be cheerful.*)

MURATA: It's not so bad, Mama.

HANA: Half the ranch is flooded. At least half.

MURATA: No-no. Quarter, maybe. It's sunny today. It'll dry.

HANA: The seedlings will rot.

MURATA: No-no. It'll dry. It's all right. Better than I expected.

HANA: If we have another bad year, no one will lend us money for the next crop.

MURATA: Don't worry. If it doesn't drain by tomorrow, I'll replant the worst places. We still have some seed left. Yeah, I'll replant.

HANA: More work.

MURATA: Don't worry, Mama. It'll be all right.

HANA: (*quietly*) Papa, where will it end? Will we always be like this—always at the mercy of the weather . . . prices . . . always at the mercy of the Gods?

MURATA: (*patting HANA's back*) Things will change. Wait and see. We'll be back in Japan by . . . in two years. Guarantee. Maybe sooner.

HANA: (*dubiously*) Two years . . .

MURATA: (*finding the robe on the bench*) Ah, look, Mama. Kiyoko-san brought back my robe.

HANA: (*sighing*) Kiyoko-san . . . poor Kiyoko-san. And Emiko-san . . .

MURATA: Ah, Mama. We're lucky. We're lucky, Mama.

Scene 4

The following spring afternoon. Exterior of the Oka house. OKA is dressed to go out. He wears a sweater, long-sleeved white shirt, dark pants, no tie. He puts his foot to the bench to wipe off his shoe with the palm of his hand. He straightens his sleeve, removes a bit of lint, and runs his fingers through his hair. He hums softly.

KIYOKO comes from the house. Her hair is frizzled in a permanent wave, she wears a gaudy new dress and a pair of new shoes. She carries a movie magazine.

OKA: (*appreciatively*) Pretty. Pretty.
KIYOKO: (*turning for him*) It's not too *hadeh*? I feel strange in colors.
OKA: Oh, no. Young girls should wear bright colors. Time enough to wear gray when you get old. Old-lady colors.

(*KIYOKO giggles.*)

OKA: (*continuing*) Sure you want to go to the picture show? It's such a nice day . . . shame to waste in a dark hall.
KIYOKO: Where else can we go?
OKA: We can go to Murata-san's.
KIYOKO: All dressed up?
OKA: Or Nagata-san's. I'll show him what I got for my horse.
KIYOKO: I love the pictures.
OKA: We don't have many nice spring days like this. Here the season is short. Summer comes in like a dragon . . . right behind . . . breathing fire . . . like a dragon. You don't know the summers here. They'll scare you.

(*He tousles KIYOKO's hair and pulls a lock of it. It springs back. He shakes his head in wonder.*)

OKA: (*continuing*) Goddam. Curly hair. Never thought curly hair could make you so happy.
KIYOKO: (*giggling*) All the American girls have curly hair.
OKA: Your friend Masako like it?
KIYOKO: (*nodding*) She says her mother will never let her get a permanent wave.
OKA: She said that, eh? Bet she's wanting one.
KIYOKO: I don't know about that.
OKA: Bet she's wanting some of your pretty dresses too.
KIYOKO: Her mother makes all her clothes.
OKA: Buying is just as good. Buying is better. No trouble that way.

KIYOKO: Masako's not interested in clothes. She loves the pictures, but her mother won't let her go. Someday, can we take Masako with us?
OKA: If her mother lets her come. Her mother's got a mind of her own. Stiff back.
KIYOKO: But she's nice.
OKA: (*dubiously*) Oh, yeah. Can't be perfect, I guess. Kiyoko, after the harvest I'll have money, and I'll buy you the prettiest dress in town. I'm going to be lucky this year. I feel it.
KIYOKO: You're already too good to me . . . dresses, shoes, permanent wave . . . movies . . .
OKA: That's nothing. After the harvest, just wait . . .
KIYOKO: . . . magazines. You do enough. I'm happy already.
OKA: You make me happy too, Kiyoko. You make me feel good . . . like a man again. (*That bothers him.*) One day you're going to make a young man happy.

(*KIYOKO giggles.*)

OKA: (*continuing*) Someday we going to move from here.
KIYOKO: But we have good friends here, Papa.
OKA: Next year our lease will be up and we got to move.
KIYOKO: The ranch is not ours?
OKA: No. In America Japanese cannot own land. We lease and move every two to three years. Next year we going go someplace where there's young fellows. There's none good enough for you here. Yeah. You going to make a good wife. Already a good cook. I like your cooking.
KIYOKO: (*a little embarrassed*) Shall we go now?
OKA: Yeah. Put the magazine away.
KIYOKO: I want to take it with me.
OKA: Take it with you?
KIYOKO: Last time, after we came back, I found all my magazines torn in half. Even the new ones.
OKA: (*looking toward the house*) Torn?

KIYOKO: This is the only one I have left.
OKA: All right, all right.

(*The two prepare to leave when EMIKO lurches through the door. Her hair is unkempt—she looks wild. She holds an empty can in one hand, the lid in the other.*)

EMIKO: Where is it?

(*OKA tries to make a hasty departure.*)

KIYOKO: Where is what?

(*OKA pushes KIYOKO ahead of him, still trying to make a getaway.*)

EMIKO: Where is it? Where is it? What did you do with it?

(*EMIKO moves toward OKA.*)

OKA: (*with false unconcern to KIYOKO*) Why don't you walk on ahead to Murata-san's.
KIYOKO: We're not going to the pictures?
OKA: We'll go. First you walk to Murata-san's. Show them your new dress. I'll meet you there.

(*KIYOKO enters the house, pushing past EMIKO, emerges with a small package, and exits, looking worriedly back at OKA and EMIKO. OKA sighs and shakes his head.*)

EMIKO: (*shaking the can*) Where is it? What did you do with it?
OKA: (*feigning surprise*) With what?
EMIKO: You know what. You stole it. You stole my money.
OKA: *Your* money?
EMIKO: I've been saving that money.
OKA: Yeah? Well, where'd you get it? Where'd you get it, eh? You stole it from me! Dollar by dollar! You stole it from me! Out of my pocket!
EMIKO: I saved it!
OKA: From *my* pocket!
EMIKO: It's mine! I saved for a long time. Some of it I brought from Japan.
OKA: *Bakayuna!* What'd you bring from Japan? Nothing but some useless kimonos.

(*OKA tries to leave, but EMIKO hangs on to him.*)

EMIKO: Give back my money! Thief!

(*OKA swings around and balls his fists but doesn't strike.*)

OKA: Goddam! Get off me!
EMIKO: (*now pleading*) Please give it back . . . please . . . please . . .

(*EMIKO strokes his legs, but OKA pulls her hands away and pushes her from him.*)

EMIKO: (*continuing*) Oni!
OKA: (*seething*) Oni? What does that make you? *Oni-baba?* Yeah, that's what you are . . . a devil!
EMIKO: It's mine! Give it back!
OKA: The hell! You think you can live off me and steal my money too? How stupid you think I am?
EMIKO: (*tearfully*) But I've paid. I've paid . . .
OKA: With what?
EMIKO: You know I've paid.
OKA: (*scoffing*) You call that paying?
EMIKO: What did you do with it?
OKA: I don't have it.
EMIKO: It's gone? It's gone?
OKA: Yeah! It's gone. I spent it. The hell! Every last cent.
EMIKO: The new clothes . . . the curls . . . restaurants . . . pictures . . . shoes . . . My money. My going-home money.
OKA: You through?
EMIKO: What will I do? What (will) . . .
OKA: I don't care what you do. Walk. Use your feet. Swim to Japan. I don't care. I give you no more than you gave me. Now I don't want anything. I don't care what you do. (*He walks away.*)

(*EMIKO still holds the empty can. Offstage we hear OKA's car start off. Accustomed to crying alone, she doesn't utter a sound. Her shoulders shake, her dry soundless sobs turn to a silent laugh. She wipes the dust gently from the can as though comforting a friend. Her movements grow sensuous, her hands move to her own body, around her throat, over her breasts, to her hips, caressing, soothing, reminding her of her lover's hands.*)

Scene 5

Same day, late afternoon. Exterior of the Murata house. The light is soft. HANA sweeps the yard; MASAKO hangs a glass wind chime on the wall.

HANA: (*directing MASAKO*) There. There. That's a good place.

MASAKO: Here?

HANA: (*nodding*) It must catch the slightest breeze. (*sighing and listening*) It brings back so much. That's the reason I never hung one before. I guess it doesn't matter much anymore.

MASAKO: I thought you liked to think about Japan.

HANA: (*laughing softly*) I didn't want to hear that sound too often . . . get too used to it. Sometimes you hear something too often, after a while you don't hear it anymore. I didn't want that to happen. The same thing happens to feelings too, I guess. After a while, you don't feel anymore. You're too young to understand that yet.

MASAKO: I understand, Mama.

HANA: Wasn't it nice of Kiyoko-san to give you the *furin*?

MASAKO: I love it. I don't know anything about Japan, but it makes me feel something too.

HANA: Maybe someday when you're grown up, gone away, you'll hear it and remember yourself as this little girl . . . remember this old house, the ranch, and . . . your old mama.

MASAKO: That's kind of scary.

(*EMIKO enters unsteadily. She carries a bundle wrapped in a colorful scarf* (furoshiki). *In the package are two beautiful kimonos.*)

HANA: Emiko-san! What a pleasant surprise! Please sit down. We were just hanging the wind chime. It was so sweet of Kiyoko-san to give it to Masako. She loves it.

(*EMIKO looks mildly interested. She acts as normal as she can throughout the scene, but at times drops the facade, revealing her desperation.*)

EMIKO: Thank you. (*She sets the bundle on the bench but keeps her hand on it.*)

HANA: Your family was here earlier.

(*EMIKO smiles vaguely.*)

HANA: (*continuing*) On their way to the pictures, I think. Make tea for us, Ma-chan.

EMIKO: Please don't.

HANA: Kiyoko-san was looking so nice . . . her hair all curly. Of course, in our day, straight black hair was desirable. Of course, times change.

EMIKO: Yes . . .

HANA: But she did look fine. My, my, a colorful new dress, new shoes, a permanent wave—looked like a regular American girl. Did you choose her dress?

EMIKO: No . . . I didn't go.

HANA: You know, I didn't think so. Very pretty though. I liked it very much. Of course, I sew all Masako's clothes. It saves money. It'll be nice for you to make things for Kiyoko-san too. She'd be so pleased. I know she'd be pleased.

(*While HANA talks, EMIKO plucks nervously at the package. She waits for HANA to stop.*)

HANA: (*continuing*) Emiko-san, is everything all right?

EMIKO: (*smiling nervously*) Yes.

HANA: Masako, please go make tea for us. See if there aren't any more of those crackers left. Or did you finish them? (*to EMIKO*) We can't keep anything in this house. She eats everything as soon as Papa brings it home. You'd never know it, she's so skinny. We never have anything left for company.

MASAKO: We hardly ever have company anyway.

(*HANA gives MASAKO a strong look before MASAKO leaves. EMIKO is lost in her own thoughts.*)

HANA: Is there something you . . . I can help you with? (*very gently*) Emiko-san?

EMIKO: (*suddenly frightened*) Oh, no. I was thinking . . . Now that . . . now that . . . Masa-chan is growing up . . . older . . .

HANA: Oh, yes.

EMIKO: I was thinking . . .

(*She stops, puts the package on her lap, and is lost again.*)

HANA: Yes, she is growing. Time goes so fast. I think she'll be taller than me soon. (*She laughs weakly but looks puzzled.*)

EMIKO: Yes . . .

(*EMIKO's depression pervades the atmosphere. HANA is affected by it. The two women sit in silence. A small breeze moves the wind chimes. At the moment, light grows dim on the two lonely figures.*)

(*MASAKO brings the tray of tea. The light returns to normal.*)

HANA: (*gently*) You're a good girl.

(*MASAKO looks first to EMIKO, then to her mother. She sets the tray on the bench and stands near EMIKO. EMIKO seems to notice her for the first time.*)

EMIKO: How are you?

(*HANA pours the tea.*)

HANA: Emiko-san, is there something I can do for you?

EMIKO: There's . . . I was . . . I . . . Masa-chan will be a young lady soon. . . .

HANA: Well, I don't know about "lady."

EMIKO: Maybe she would like a nice . . . nice . . . (*She unwraps the package.*) I have kimonos I wore in Japan for dancing. Maybe she can . . . if you like, I mean. They'll be nice on her. She's so slim.

(*EMIKO shakes out a robe. HANA and MASAKO are impressed.*)

HANA: Ohhh! Beautiful!

MASAKO: Oh, Mama! Pretty!

(*They touch the material.*)

MASAKO: (*continuing*) Gold threads, Mama.

HANA: Brocade!

EMIKO: Maybe Masa-chan would like them. I mean for her school programs . . . Japanese school.

HANA: Oh, no! Too good for country. People will be envious of us . . . wonder where we got them.

EMIKO: I mean for festivals. *Obon, Hana Matsuri* . . .

HANA: Oh, but you have Kiyoko-san now. You should give them to her. Has she seen them?

EMIKO: Oh. No.

HANA: She'll love them. You should give them to her—not our Masako.

EMIKO: I thought . . . I mean, I was thinking of . . . if you could give me a little . . . if you could pay . . . manage to give me something for . . .

HANA: But these gowns, Emiko-san—they're worth hundreds.

EMIKO: I know, but I'm not asking for that. Whatever you can give. Only as much as you can give.

MASAKO: Mama?

HANA: Masako, Papa doesn't have that kind of money.

EMIKO: Anything you can give. Anything . . .

MASAKO: Ask Papa.

HANA: There's no use asking. I *know* he can't afford it.

EMIKO: (*looking at MASAKO*) A little at a time . . .

MASAKO: Mama?

HANA: (*firmly*) No, Masako. This is a luxury.

(*HANA folds the gowns and puts them away. EMIKO is decimated. HANA sees this and tries to find a way to help.*)

HANA: (*continuing*) Emiko-san, I hope you understand.

(*EMIKO is silent, trying to gather her resources.*)

HANA: (*continuing*) I know you can sell them and get the full price somewhere. Let's see . . . a family with lots of growing daughters . . . someone who did well last year. Nagata-san has no girls. Umeda-san has girls but no money. Well, let's see . . . Maybe not here in this country town. Ah . . . you can take them to the city—Los Angeles—and sell them to a store. Or Terminal Island. Lots of wealthy fishermen there. Yes, that would be the place. Why, it's no problem, Emiko-san. Have your husband take them there. I know you'll get your money. He'll find a buyer. I know he will.

EMIKO: Yes . . . (*She ties the bundle and sits quietly.*)
HANA: Please have your tea. I'm sorry. I really would like to take them for Masako, but it just isn't possible. You understand, don't you?

(*EMIKO nods.*)

HANA: (*continuing*) Please don't feel so . . . so bad. It's not really a matter of life or death, is it? Emiko-san?

(*EMIKO nods again. HANA sips her tea.*)

MASAKO: Mama? If you could ask Papa . . .
HANA: Oh, the tea is cold. Masako, could you heat the kettle?
EMIKO: No more. I must be going. (*She picks up her package and rises slowly.*)
HANA: (*helplessly*) So soon? Emiko-san, please stay.

(*EMIKO starts to go.*)

HANA: (*continuing*) Masako will walk with you. (*She pushes MASAKO forward.*)
EMIKO: It's not far.
HANA: Emiko-san? You'll be all right?
EMIKO: Yes . . . yes . . . yes . . .
HANA: (*calling after EMIKO*) I'm sorry, Emiko-san.
EMIKO: Yes.

(*MASAKO and HANA watch as EMIKO leaves. The light grows dim as though a cloud passed over. HANA strokes MASAKO's hair.*)

HANA: Your hair is so black and straight . . . nice.

(*They stand close. The wind chimes tinkle; light grows dim. Light returns to normal.*)

(*MURATA enters. He sees the tableau of mother and child and is puzzled.*)

MURATA: What's going on here?

(*The women part.*)

HANA: Oh . . . nothing. Nothing.
MASAKO: Mrs. Oka was here. She had two kimo(nos) . . .
HANA: (*putting her hand on MASAKO's shoulder*) It was nothing.
MURATA: Eh? What'd she want?
HANA: Later, Papa. Right now, I'd better fix supper.
MURATA: (*looking at the sky*) Strange how that sun comes and goes. Maybe I didn't need to irrigate . . . looks like rain. (*He remembers.*) Ach! I forgot to shut the water!
MASAKO: I'll do it, Papa.
HANA: Masako, that gate's too heavy for you.
MURATA: She can handle it. Take out the pin and let the gate fall all the way down. All the way. And put the pin back. Don't forget to put the pin back.
HANA: And be careful. Don't fall in the canal.

(*MASAKO leaves.*)

MURATA: What's the matter with that girl?
HANA: Nothing. Why?
MURATA: Usually have to *beg* her to (do) . . .
HANA: She's growing up.
MURATA: Must be that time of the month.
HANA: Oh, Papa, she's too young for that yet.
MURATA: (*genially as they enter the house*) Got to start sometime. Looks like I'll be outnumbered soon. I'm outnumbered already.

(*HANA glances at him and quietly begins preparations for supper. MURATA removes his shirt and picks up a paper. Light fades slowly.*)

Scene 6

Same evening. Exterior, desert. There is at least one shrub, a tumbleweed maybe. MASAKO walks slowly.

From a distance we hear EMIKO singing the song, "And the Soul Shall Dance." MASAKO looks around, sees the shrub, and crouches by it. EMIKO appears. She wears her beautiful kimono tied loosely at her waist. She carries a branch of sage. Her hair is loose.

EMIKO: *Akai kuchibiru / Kappu ni yosete / Aoi sake nomya / Kokoro ga odoru / Kurai yoru no yume / Setsu nasa yo. . . .*

(EMIKO breaks into a dance, laughs mysteriously, turns round and round acting out a fantasy. MASAKO stirs uncomfortably. EMIKO senses a presence. She stops, drops her branch, empties out her sleeve of imaginary flowers at MASAKO, and exits singing.)

EMIKO: *(continuing) Aoi sake nomya / Yume ga odoru. . . .*

(MASAKO watches as EMIKO leaves. She rises slowly and picks up the branch EMIKO has left. She moves forward a step and looks off to the point where EMIKO disappeared.)

Light slowly fades on MASAKO, and the image of her forlorn form remains etched on the retina.

PRODUCING *AND THE SOUL SHALL DANCE*

INTRODUCTION TO EAST WEST PLAYERS

The Oregon Shakespeare Festival, discussed in Chapter 3, is firmly rooted in the English (European) theatre tradition. The next producing company we discuss, East West Players, represents another tradition and community altogether. The primary focus of East West Players is presenting the voices of Asian/Pacific Americans as writers, actors, and producers. The repertory of East West Players emphasizes American plays that reflect the experiences of Asian/Pacific Americans.

The theatre's early productions most frequently featured plays by Americans of Japanese, Chinese, and Korean heritage; more recently, performances have expanded to include the work of Southeast Asians and Pacific Islanders. Although there is an international influence, that influence is first Asian and then European. And when European plays are performed, they are acted by Asian American or multiracial casts. An East West Players production of Ibsen's *Hedda Gabler*, for example, was set in Japan rather than Norway, and the roles were played by Asian American actors. The name East West Players reflects this theatre's goal of serving as a cultural bridge between the East and the West.

History of East West Players

In 1965 a group of Japanese American, Chinese American, and Korean American actors came together in Los Angeles to form East West Players, the first Asian American theatre company in the United States. Tired of the demeaning and frequently ridiculous, stereotypical roles they were playing in films and theatre, such as subservient "house boys," exotic and treacherous women, or sinister villains, these actors were determined to create a theatre in their own image, where they could choose how they were represented on the stage.

As with so many other struggling young theatre groups, the first performances of East West Players took place in a church basement. In 1968, however, they made the triumphant move to their own space. At first the Asian American casts performed plays written by Europeans and non-Asian Americans; actors at long last had the opportunity to play major, complex roles rather than one-dimensional characters.

The group also supported the development of new plays by Asian American playwrights. These plays recorded the experiences of Asian

In the late 1990s, East West Players moved from the renovated garment factory to a larger and more graceful theatre space housed in the centrally located Union Center for the Arts, which is also home to Visual Communication and L.A. Art Core, two other arts organizations. The David Henry Hwang Theatre provides expanded seating, including a balcony, and sophisticated technical support for lights, sound, and scenery.

To inaugurate East West Players' new theatre, the company staged Pacific Overtures, *the musical by Stephen Sondheim and John Weidman that brings together a Western theatre form, the musical, with Eastern performance traditions. Michael K. Lee and Orville Mendoza are directed by Tim Dang.*

immigrants to the United States and their Asian American children, histories that had not been recorded elsewhere. They were stories of farming California's agricultural valleys in the 1930s, of struggling for survival in the internment camps in the 1940s, of creating new families when American soldiers returned from World War II with Japanese "war brides." They were about dislocation, the clash of cultures, and the struggle for identity. These stories were dramatized for audiences made up largely of Asian Americans who recognized themselves and the stories of their own lives in the plays.

Location and Physical Space

And the Soul Shall Dance was produced by East West Players in 1996, when they still performed in their long-standing home, a renovated garment factory on a rundown section of Santa Monica Boulevard in Los Angeles. With only 99 seats, East West Players was at that time an equity waiver theatre—a professional theatre that because of its limited seating was exempt from certain regulations of the Actors Equity union.

To get to the theatre, audiences had to drive past factories and industrial yards cluttered with trucks, pipes, and metal fittings. There were few shops or restaurants within walking distance of the theatre. The external ambience of East West Players was light-years away from the slow pace and charm of Ashland, Oregon, with its quiet streets, cafes, and parks.

Since the 1996 production of *And the Soul Shall Dance*, East West Players, having more than outgrown its space on Santa Monica Boulevard, moved to the Union Center for the Arts in the Little Tokyo area of downtown Los Angeles. The company now has a 236-seat theatre, expanded rehearsal and classroom spaces, sophisticated technology, and comfortable parking for staff and audiences. But the creativity that was generated in the cramped old space, the careers that were launched, and the barriers that were broken all reflected a wealth of talent and commitment not dependent on an impressive physical plant. In fact, for many theatre practitioners, the satisfaction is greater in a theatre of limited resources, where gold seems to be spun out of straw.

For our production analysis, we return to the experience of the performance at the garment factory where East West Players spent its first thirty years. Inside the theatre, the audience steps away from the grubby Los Angeles street into a tiny but lively and congenial lobby crowded with photographs and posters from previous productions. The audience is drawn largely from the Asian American community, and for this play, *And the Soul Shall Dance*, most noticeably from the Japanese American community. Many audience members know each other and exchange friendly greetings over coffee and cookies. Older members of the audience recall the original production of the play, staged eighteen years ago. Younger members of the audience seeing the play for the first time are prepared to be introduced to one of the classics of the Asian American theatre.

STAGING THE PLAY

The Director's Prologue

The small stage (measuring 20 by 30 feet) of East West Players is completely empty except for a muslin scrim (curtain) that hangs around the upstage perimeter of the playing space. A small, elevated platform juts out over the audience at one side. On the platform are Japanese wind and percussion instruments, including shakuhachi (bamboo) flutes of various lengths, taiko drums of different sizes, Tibetan cymbals, and Japanese wind chimes. While the house lights are still up, a light comes up on the platform, where a musician (either George Abe or Masakazu Yoshizawa) in a Japanese *yukata* (a loose tunic) and *hakama* (wide-cut pants) appears. He begins to beat the large taiko drum, sending sharp reverberations through the small theatre, announcing the beginning of the play. At the end of the short drum overture, the lights go down on both the audience and the stage space.

The sound of the wind comes over the theatre's speakers, and the musician begins to play long, mournful notes on the largest shakuhachi flute. A dim light illuminates a single shape on the stage. The shape is a piece of tumbleweed. A **kuroko**—a hooded actor dressed completely in black—who seems to blend in with the darkness of the stage, rolls and lifts the tumbleweed

The set design for And the Soul Shall Dance, *by Yuki Nakamura, featured two small rolling house units that ingeniously were unfolded in view of the audience. The walls were either cut down or covered with transparent material to allow the audience a full view of the interiors.*

through the air as if it is being blown by the wind.

With these simple elements—the sounds of the wind, the haunting notes of the flute, and the single piece of blowing, rolling tumbleweed—the production creates the sense of a vast, open, lonely space. Suddenly a sharp clicking sound is heard, and two more hooded figures dressed in black rush silently onto the stage and sweep aside half of the curtain hanging at the back. Using highly stylized, choreographed movement, the three kurokos roll forward and unfold what will become the walls of the Muratas' house. As the simple frame of the house takes shape, one of the kurokos whirls in first with a table and then with chairs. All of the movement suggests that it is the wind that is blowing the small dwelling and its simple furnishings onto the stage. The walls of the house are suggestive rather than complete. They are cut low to allow the audience to see all the action inside. A table and chairs, a bed, a stove, a sink, and dishes give the sense of a functional but spartan household.

The drumming that has accompanied the scene shift gives way to the sound of fire. The actors playing the Murata family enter, dismayed over the loss of the bathhouse, and the play as it is written in the script begins: the realistic story of a child who has been careless, an anxious, scolding mother, and a weary father. But in the few minutes that precede their entrance, a vivid atmosphere has been created for their story. With a few strokes of sound and stage imagery, like the brush strokes of Japanese calligraphy, the characters have been placed spatially and emotionally in the emptiness and desolation of the Imperial Valley.

The Influence of Asian Theatre

The presence of the kurokos, in combination with the sounds of the musical instruments, also introduces the cultural background of the characters. They are clearly tied to Asia. The director of the production, Jim Ishida, says, "No matter how long the Issei, first generation, are here, there is still that connection to their cultural heritage."[5] Through the references to Asian theatre, the director, in collaboration with scene designer Yuki Nakamura, who has also designed the sound, establishes the production's theatrical style. Realism is combined with a simple, concentrated, poetic expression to take us into the daily lives of the characters and beyond, into their "souls."

Jim Ishida: *I wanted to incorporate as much of Eastern theatre technique as I possibly could. So therefore we thought of kabuki and the use of kurokos and the cycs (**cyclorama**—cloth that forms the background for the action) rising and everything coming out in a big flurry. I like actors to be very physical. I like the actors to be part of the wind, bringing the tumbleweed in, creating the nothing space into something.*

The kurokos are based on figures from the traditional kabuki theatre of Japan. In kabuki the kuroko changes the scenery, helps actors make onstage costume changes, and brings in props. The role of the kuroko has its own history in Japanese theatre tradition. Just as acting certain parts was handed down from father to son, so the position of kuroko was passed down through certain families.

In the production of *And the Soul Shall Dance*, the kurokos serve a double purpose. They serve first to change the scenery and the props. But the movement of the kurokos is also meaningful choreographically. As they whirl about the stage, they suggest the feeling of the wind; the audience accepts the notion that the kurokos are invisible. The kurokos allow for a certain kind of theatrical magic that does not depend on highly complex and expensive technical equipment. The actors playing the kurokos have prepared for their roles by studying dance and the stylized movement of the Japanese theatre. In contrast, the actors playing Yamauchi's characters must create a physically and psychologically believable rendering of Japanese American life in the 1930s.

Through the stylized movement of the kurokos and the realistic acting of the characters, the production blends the poetic and concrete elements of the play. Another example of blending is the mixture of expressive musical accompaniment with realistic sound effects. The production is a fusion of lyricism and realism.

Staging a Period Play: The Work of the Director and the Actors

In rehearsing the actions of the characters, in constructing the realistic life of poor families struggling with hardship, Jim Ishida finds the starting point in "Japanese behavior." The characters' manners, their posture and gestures, and their speech rhythms must echo the conduct of Japanese immigrants to the United States in the early part of the twentieth century.

Jim Ishida: *That was the hardest work, the physical work, the dance and the behavior. To eliminate the actors' Western colloquialisms, their Western behavior. They've lived their lives as Westerners. In a short period of time they've had to find Japanese behavior. The way they bow, the way farmers hold their hands, the way they drink.*

Acquiring such specialized mannerisms is a highly complex task. The actors, third- and fourth-generation descendents of immigrant families, must learn from the outside what was a way of life for their grandparents and great-grandparents.

Denise Iketani (Emiko):   *We are so American. The culture has changed. I'm fourth generation. In terms of how we talk to our parents and how our parents talked to their parents and how their parents talked to their parents, each generation is completely different.*

Period Style   In the American theatre, specialists typically coach actors in what is called **period style,** the deportment, manners, attitudes, and gestures of times past. Frequently, actors take classes in various aspects of period behavior, particularly combat and dance, which are excellent sources of posture and gesture in addition to being useful for their own sake when a fight must be staged or movement sequences choreographed. Dance styles and the martial arts codify physical attitudes in forms that can be passed down through generations. Paintings and, more recently, photographs and films offer additional sources for details of period behavior.

Another essential source for understanding the movement and posture of other eras is period clothing. If a character must wear a garment that binds the body in various ways—a military uniform or a kimono, for example—the garment structure determines how the character will stand and walk to a large degree. Although the period of *And the Soul Shall Dance*, the 1930s, does not seem that long ago, in fact the cultural circumstances of that time pose a geographic and temporal distance that cannot be bridged without assistance.

Movement and Gesture   Ishida and the actors turn to a variety of sources for the period information they need. Ishida draws on his memory of the actions and attitudes of his grandparents, as well as observations made during recent travels to Japan. The actors watch Japanese films and observe the interactions of senior members of the community. In this production Ishida takes responsibility for coaching the men, and Mary Tamaki is invited to join the production staff to coach the women's movement and to choreograph Emiko's dance sequences. Mary Tamaki has spent years studying the classical dance of Japan and is designated *natori*, the level of achievement that the character Emiko had aspired to.

For this production, the director has another special consultant—the playwright, Wakako Yamauchi. Playwrights are frequently unavailable for consultation after the original production of a play, and theatre companies feel honored if the playwrights come to see their particular productions. But in this case, Wakako Yamauchi attends rehearsals and makes suggestions to Ishida. The play, of course, represents her own experience, the times that she lived through as a child.

During the early rehearsals, Jim Ishida and Mary Tamaki coach the actors on the basics of movement and social interaction—how to walk and stand, how to bow, how to greet each other. Although ultimately Ishida will give the actors much freedom to experiment and make choices,

this beginning work is all done through imitation and drill, with endless precise corrections.

For example, the male characters, Murata and Oka, meet twice in the two opening scenes and drink sake. The greeting between them is far from a contemporary American handshake or slap on the back. They make repeated shallow, sharp bows to each other and greet each other heartily, with a guttural, barking kind of laughter. In the first scene they sit together to drink—as if it is understood that the privilege of the sake and the table is theirs—while Hana as dutiful wife waits on them. They drink their sake quickly, with short bursts of energy. When the chiles are called for, Hana serves them, head down, using chopsticks to take them out of the jar. The men punctuate their speech with Japanese rather than American exclamations. After eating the chiles, both men pick their teeth and cover their mouths while continuing their conversation.

The movement work for the women is very difficult. American women have a freedom of movement and a lift in their walk that is incompatible with the style necessary to give authenticity to the production.

Mary Tamaki: *The women must learn to walk with the center of gravity lower, which is the more traditional Japanese style, shuffling the feet. Japanese women do not pick up their feet. They shuffle, wearing the zoris (Japanese sandals). They must be demure. There's no loud laughing, and they must cover their mouths when they want to smile.*

Mary Tamaki brings kimonos to rehearsals to facilitate the learning of the necessary body positions and walking style, even though the actors will not wear kimonos in the production.

Mary Tamaki: *These are not natural movements . . . to walk with your knees slightly bent, to shuffle along taking tiny steps. It is a style that you learn. It is not part of our Western nature to be so humble. When you're in kimonos the movements become so much more natural. You are slightly*

Oka (Benjamin Lum) and Murata (Nelson Mashita) share painful memories as Hana (Sharon Omi) and Masako (Anna Quirino) look on.

bound in them, so your movements of course are restricted. The way you walk is definitely restricted by the kimono.

Denise Iketani (Emiko): *Having to wear the kimono completely changes the way you move. When you put on a kimono it's very tight. It's even hard to breathe sometimes. That just affects what you can and cannot do.*

Anna Quirino (Masako): *When you wear the kimono, it can't flap open at the bottom. Once you see the flap you know you're walking wrong. It has to be like a cylinder walking, so the steps are very small and pigeon-toed.*

In rehearsal under Mary Tamaki's guidance, the women practice entering a room, bowing and greeting each other. They learn the correct way to pour tea and to sit down.

Mary Tamaki: *I walked for them. Then I would remind them to bend their knees more. Don't bounce. Shuffle along. Keep your hands to your side.*

Dance Mary Tamaki also works separately with Denise Iketani on the dances that come from Emiko's past. Tamaki choreographs a dance of two minutes that is based on five basic movements from the classical Japanese dance. One minute of this dance will be used when Emiko dances inside her house and first captivates Masako. Denise Iketani will use the full two-minute piece as the basis for the improvised movements she does outside at other points in the play. Mary Tamaki and Denise Iketani rehearse the two-minute dance sequence for ten hours during different rehearsals. Tamaki feels the pressure of the time limit. In her own dance studies, a ten-minute dance would be rehearsed for over a year. However, in the theatre, time is always measured. In a concentrated period of time, choreography that serves the needs of the production must be created and learned.

The period movement that Jim Ishida, Mary Tamaki, and the actors have worked hard to achieve gives the play a certain authenticity, a texture of the times. It establishes the cultural

Denise Iketani (Emiko) and Anna Quirino (Masako) rehearse the sequence that uses the choreography developed by Mary Tamaki. Quirino uses a kimono for rehearsal although she will not wear one in the play.

background that makes clear the standards of propriety, what is expected of or acceptable for men and for women.

Mary Tamaki: *As far as the women's role at that time, the women were second to the men. They had no large gestures. They were not usually able to express themselves in public in front of the men. The wife was able to express herself inside the home but not outside of the home.*

But most importantly, the period movement provides the starting point for the development of character. In Jim Ishida's words, "emotionality must come out of the Japanese behavior." What begin as general standards of deportment and social interaction evolve into highly individuated characters.

Speech Rhythms   Another element Yamauchi uses to create a realistic atmosphere for her play

is the suggestion that the adult characters are all speaking Japanese. She includes a number of Japanese words in the text, but it is the rhythm of the speeches that is most important and that also poses another significant task for the actors. They must learn their lines in English, of course, but with Japanese inflection and intonation. In addition to the physical work they must do to develop the character's behavior, they must study and acquire Japanese speech rhythms. Speech and dialect coaching plays a regular part in the American theatre, preparing actors to speak with foreign or regional accents.

Only the actor playing Masako speaks an Americanized English. The Americanization of Masako's speech rhythms and the freedom of her movement obviously set her apart from the other characters. She is of a new generation, without her parents' ties to Japan. Whereas her parents maintain their identities through observing Japanese traditions and long to return to Japan, Masako looks to the future. She seeks a wider view of the world and her place in it.

Building Character Relationships

To further examine the way realism and lyricism are combined to shape character and to establish crucial character relationships, we consider now the staging of act 1, scene 2 of *And the Soul Shall Dance* at East West Players. Following scene 1, the kurokos roll away the Murata house, and the other half of the curtain is pulled back to allow the unfolding of a second small house on the right side of the stage. The shakuhachi flute is heard again as the Oka house appears.

The sweeping aside of the curtains to reveal each little house is an actual and figurative expression of the opening of memory. What the audience sees is what Masako remembers. When the curtain is brushed aside and the Murata house appears in scene 1, we go back with Masako to the day she burned down the bathhouse. The significance of the burning of the bathhouse becomes clear as the curtain draws back on scene 2, the memory of the Oka house. It is through this small catastrophe that Masako encounters the elusive and withdrawn Emiko.

As act 1, scene 2 begins, Oka, Murata, and Hana sit amicably together on a bench by the door to the Oka house while Masako kneels in front of them with the Victrola. At Oka's insistence, Emiko finally, but reluctantly, comes outside and moves to the other side of the door, where she sits in a chair with her face turned partly away. As the script is written, Emiko does not speak until she is alone with Masako. This means that in the first part of the scene, everything that Emiko communicates must be expressed physically.

As the other characters uneasily make cheerful but forced small talk about the records and the Victrola, Emiko begins to roll herself a cigarette. The rolling of the cigarette is clearly called for in the stage directions: "She pulls out

Masako's (Emily Keiko Pruiksma) attitude contrasts with that of her parents, Murata and Hana (Ken Chin and Kathy Hsieh) in the production of And the Soul Shall Dance at Northwest Asian American Theatre in Seattle, directed by Judi Nihei.

a sack of Bull Durham and begins to roll a cigarette." The playwright has chosen this detail very carefully. Emiko does not speak. She does not greet her guests or offer to serve them tea. But she does roll herself a cigarette. This single action speaks volumes about Emiko's attitude. She is rebellious and defiant; she does not care to be seen as a proper, traditional Japanese woman.

Hana attempts to break the tension of this moment by sending Masako to Emiko with a stack of records. As Masako timidly approaches Emiko with her arms folded around the record albums, Emiko finishes rolling her cigarette. Then holding the cigarette in one hand and the pouch of tobacco in the other, Emiko inclines her head and pulls the string to close the bag of tobacco sharply with her teeth. This tough, masculine gesture secures Masako's attention.

In the Northwest Asian American Theatre production, Emiko (Sherryl Ray) attracts Masako's attention with her cigarette and her mysterious attitude.

Emiko then turns her head to look at Masako for the first time. She has the cigarette in her mouth and a defiant look on her face, an attitude that makes a large impression on an eleven-year-old girl raised by a very proper mother.

Anna Quirino (Masako):   *When she pulls out the cigarette . . . that's the big thing for me. Wow! Who is this woman? Because my mother is so traditional. She wants me to be polite. Hana would never do this. She's very strong, especially against my father. She can speak up. But here is Emiko who is very quiet in her corner. But what she's doing! My character is so fascinated by her, scared too in the beginning. At first I just don't want to be there. But the taking out of the cigarette. I've never seen a woman do that before.*

The second sequence of actions that draws Masako to Emiko begins when Emiko reenters the house after they begin to play the Japanese records on the Victrola. Emiko dances by herself inside the house, and the audience can see her because the walls are partially cut away or constructed in places with transparent mesh. The adult characters outside are unaware of the dancing, but Masako, on her way to the bath, stops at the window and stares in at Emiko dancing. She is now captivated by the strangeness and wonder of a Japanese woman who drinks and smokes and is also trained in classical movement.

Masako's relationship to Emiko continues to grow when the other adults exit and Masako is left alone on the stage. She puts "And the Soul Shall Dance" on the Victrola and becomes lost in the music. When Emiko returns and sees Masako with a distant expression on her face, she recognizes some kinship between them.

Denise Iketani (Emiko):   *The song, of course. "And the Soul Shall Dance" Kokoro ga odoru. The fact that Masako plays this song that was Emiko's favorite song and that she understands—that's the instant connection. The whole world that she lives in right now is just so horrible. This one little thing that Masako does—it amazes her that Masako does understand. She knows that she's found some sort of bonding, a kinship, with this person even though she is a child. She sees this child who understands what it is about your soul dancing.*

Emiko begins to sing with the voice on the record, and after a moment Masako sings too. With a warmth growing between them, Emiko crosses to Masako, and the two seem bound in the same spell. They kneel together by the Victrola, and Emiko speaks for the first time: "Do you like that song, Masa-chan?" Their intimacy deepens, and Emiko rises to dance again, now easily and fluidly. The woman and the child speak the words of the song together while Emiko dances. She seems to be dancing out the feeling of the green wine as Masako watches, enchanted.

EMIKO: Drink the green wine . . .
MASAKO: Green? I thought wine was purple.
EMIKO: Wine is purple, but this is a green liqueur. It's good. It warms your heart.

MASAKO: And the soul dances.

EMIKO: Yes . . .

MASAKO: What does it taste like? The green wine?

EMIKO: Oh, it's like . . . it's like . . .

MASAKO: In the dark night . . .

EMIKO: Dreams are unbearable . . .

MASAKO: Drink the . . .

EMIKO: Drink the green wine . . .

MASAKO: And the dreams will dance.

(act 1, scene 2)

The two actors speak the words as if together they understand a special language that lifts them out of the present. The song provides a vocabulary, a rhythm, a melody, and an atmosphere that allows for a shift in consciousness. Emiko's soul emerges through the grace of the dance, and Masako's spirit seems to join in the dance of the soul with her. It is a transcendent moment.

All too quickly the moment is interrupted by Oka's return. In this scene Masako is exposed to abuse, the battery of Emiko by her husband, and she sees a drunk Japanese woman smoking a cigarette. But she also experiences Emiko's passion for music and dance. She catches a glimpse of a way of life not limited by the unending cycle of protecting seedlings from freezes, irrigating fragile crops, and paying bills.

Anna Quirino (Masako):   *Masako has dreams that go way beyond the ranch. That's why her books are so important to her. And Masako has a rebellious streak. Watching Emiko being able to break away from tradition. She's almost a hero. She sees in Emiko this whole other world.*

CONTRASTING PRODUCTIONS: EAST WEST PLAYERS AND NORTHWEST ASIAN AMERICAN THEATRE

To deepen our understanding of *And the Soul Shall Dance*, we examine now three points of contrast between the 1996 production at East West Players and a 1994 production of the play at Northwest Asian American Theatre in Seattle. Different productions of the same play may offer strikingly different interpretations of the playwright's material, or through more subtle distinctions they may turn the audience's attention to one idea instead of another.

Scene Design and the Physical Space

A tangible difference that is relatively easy to assess is the arrangement of the physical space. Northwest Asian American Theatre is located in the basement space under the Wing Luke Asian Museum in the International District of Seattle. Like East West Players when they were located in the renovated factory, Northwest Asian American Theatre has a small stage space and little technical support for elaborate scenic effects. But given similar stage limitations, the two productions take entirely different approaches to staging.

In the play the two small houses are isolated and set apart in the desert landscape. The script simply calls for an alternation between the Murata kitchen and yard and the Oka yard. At East West Players, a design was created by Yuki Nakamura to keep the space as open and empty as possible through the use of the rolling and unfolding house units. Only one house appears on the stage at a time, suggesting that each exists in a completely separate space.

In the design of the Seattle production by Jan Tominaga, both houses are permanent structures on the stage, placed immediately next to each other. To suggest the distance between the two locations, the actors move though the aisles of the audience area. This approach to staging highlights certain meanings in the play. The proximity of the houses reinforces the contrast between the responses of the two families to the hostile environment in which they find themselves. The Muratas create a home that will sustain them and nurture Masako's aspirations. The Okas engage in a mutually destructive relationship fed by alcohol and despair. One house is a home that may be entered; the other features only a window that reveals fragments of the misery inside. The physical presentation of the houses symbolizes the life of those who live within.

There are two key differences in the visual images presented by these companies. First, in contrast to the Seattle production, the Los Angeles production emphasizes the sense of isolation, of two tiny houses in the vast, dusty Imperial Valley, widely separated from neighbors and community. The physical isolation speaks eloquently of the spiritual isolation. The wind-blown effect of the scene shifts heightens the idea of lives at the mercy of the elements. Second, in contrast to the Los Angeles production, the Seattle production features dissimilar house exteriors to comment on the health or dysfunction of the families. In the Los Angeles production, each family has essentially the same physical environment; the difference is the response to that environment.

Interpreting Family Relationships

In addition to the differences in scene design, the two productions approach relationship issues differently. For example, after Emiko exits with her kimonos, the play describes a moment of closeness between Hana and Masako.

Masako and Hana watch as Emiko leaves. The light grows dim as though a cloud passed over. Hana strokes Masako's hair.

HANA: Your hair is so black and straight . . . nice.

They stand close. The wind chimes tinkle; light grows dim. Light returns to normal. Murata enters. He sees the tableau of mother and child and is puzzled. (act 2, scene 5)

Hana's line is an understated way of expressing her love for her daughter. At this painful moment when she recognizes Emiko's desperation and Masako's longing, Hana pulls Masako to her with this gentle remark about straight hair,

which so obviously contrasts with the loss of identity represented by Kiyoko's curly permanent. Hana underlines the health of their relationship and her determination to protect her daughter's childhood and her heritage. The stage directions imply that the father, Murata, is outside of this intimacy between mother and daughter and that he is "puzzled" by it, although he recognizes the growing bond between them.

The production at Northwest Asian American Theatre accentuates the father's distance at this particular moment. However, the East West Players' production opens up this moment to reinforce the family bond. The stage directions indicate that "the wind chimes tinkle." At East West Players, it is Murata who sounds the chimes. As he enters, the actor playing Murata responds with delight to the newly hung *furin* (wind chimes) and brushes his hand across them, sharing his obvious pleasure at their sound with Masako. The smile that the father and daughter share creates a sense of family that builds on the moment shared by Hana and Masako. Director Jim Ishida said he saw the foundation for his interpretation of the play in the short story: "the beautiful little thing . . . the Murata family . . . this combination of people makes life bearable." The emphasis at the end of the play is on the shared responsibility of the parents and the strength that each shares with their daughter.

The production at Northwest Asian American Theatre focuses instead on the inner lives of Emiko and Hana and on their isolation. Director Judi Nihei looks for moments where that isolation might be broken. For example, Nihei sees in Hana and Masako a reinvention of the mother-daughter relationship that responds to their unique environment and the difficulties and opportunities that it presents.

Judi Nihei: *Masako gets away with murder. If I had spoken to my mother the way Masako speaks to her mother, I wouldn't be sitting here today. I always take the writer at their word. So if this is who Wakako Yamauchi was writing about, then there is obviously something more going on here than what we might assume to be a typical mother-daughter relationship. So that says something to me about Hana and how she sees her daughter in her life.*

The director and the actor playing Hana, Kathy Hsieh, together develop an approach to this character that depends not on the certainty of an experienced mother who is confident of what is best for her child but on a continuous process of discovery. Kathy Hsieh is actually younger than her character; her youth immediately reminds the audience of the enormity of facing life in a hostile country without the benefit of family and social structure. She has no mother or sisters to turn to for advice. Her only support comes from the women she knows at church.

Hsieh's age and performance choices clarify the struggle of the character to invent solutions to the challenges of dislocation and racism. There is no ready-made wisdom that can be transferred easily from her Japanese background to the circumstances of raising a Japanese American daughter caught between cultures. Each challenge from her daughter leads to introspection and experimentation. We see her puzzling out each decision. The answers do not come from the past but from an attempt to imagine the future. Although there is a very special bond between mother and daughter, the very spirit of openness and shared discovery that distinguishes the relationship will eventually lead to separation.

Kathy Hsieh (Hana):   *She wants her daughter to have those dreams, but she doesn't want her to be disappointed at things that don't come true. She wants her daughter to study and learn, but the things that she is learning and the language that she is studying are all about American people, white people, and English, not Japanese. There are more and more things that her daughter is learning about that Hana will never be able to understand because she doesn't read English. She knows Masako is learning a whole different*

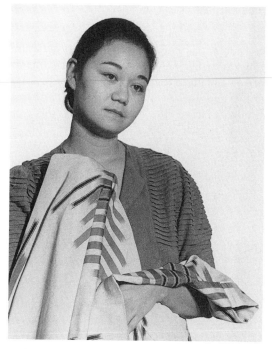

In the Northwest Asian American Theatre production of And the Soul Shall Dance, *Hana holds the kimonos that she knows she cannot accept for her daughter. She recognizes Emiko's desperation and Masako's longing. The kimonos also bring back her own memories of life in Japan.*

world than the world Hana knows. And she realizes that that is creating distance between her and her daughter.

Nihei and Hsieh also look for connections between Hana and Emiko that may be discovered in the subtext rather than in their guarded conversations.

Judi Nihei: *I really wanted to make more of a relationship between Emiko and Hana even though they don't really have one scene seriously together. To have Hana not be judgmental of Emiko but have much more sympathy for her, just not have a venue in which to express it. And that's a cultural conflict and a cultural imposition on a woman that even if you'd want to align yourself with your sex in support, you may not have that opportunity.*

Sexuality and Gender

An aspect of Emiko's character that receives considerable attention in the Seattle production is her sexuality. More powerful than her memory of dancing and singing in her kimonos is her immersion in her memory of desire. When Emiko is alone, the actress playing the role touches herself as her lover may have touched her. She expresses herself as a sensual woman who defines herself at least in part through her own sexual response. What she seeks is control of her own body. All of her acts of defiance are related to this claiming of herself.

By contrast, in the Los Angeles production, Emiko's character is built through withdrawal, defiance, and escape into a dream world of dance and music. But her state of mind does not lead to overt expression of sexual desire. In fact, her life with Oka seems to have robbed her of connections to the world around her and even to herself. Denise Iketani's (East West Players) dancing is ethereal and leads the character away from earthly or bodily concerns. For Sherryl Ray (Northwest Asian American Theatre), her own body and the comfort of sexual response is a primary focus of the characterization.

In Japan, Emiko's point of contention with her parents was her sexuality and ownership of her body. They saw her as a commodity to be traded to the "rich Yamato." Yamato is the name of the older, wealthy merchant to whom Emiko's parents had expected to marry her, but it is also a name that refers to all of Japan. Thus, it contains a suggestion of the position of women in the social hierarchy of Japan. In the eyes of Emiko's father, when she had engaged in a sexual relationship of her own choosing, she had become damaged goods, no longer of value in the marriage market. For this reason, Emiko was married by proxy to Oka against her wishes and sent to the United States.

Oka has been dispossessed by both the Japanese and the American economic and social structures. In Japan he gave up his name and self-respect as an apprentice to his father-in-law. In the United States he is an alien ineligible for citizenship, unable to purchase land and make a home for his family. But he is still in a position to regard Emiko as his property.

The confrontation between Emiko and Oka in act 1, scene 3 results largely from her challenge to his authority. He sees her drunkenness as a personal affront to him: "You made a fool of *me*!" Infuriated that she will not speak to him, he attacks her physically. When Emiko asserts her autonomy—"Don't touch me. Don't touch me"—he is outraged: "Who the hell you think you are? . . . Too good for me?" And when Emiko answers his accusations of promiscuity by assuming ownership of her body—"Just because I let . . . let you . . ."—he responds, "Let me (obscene gesture)? I can do what I want with you. Your father palmed you off on me—like a dog or cat—animal." While Oka struggles to maintain the patriarchal view of a woman as property, Emiko, for all of her self-destructive actions, is set on self-determination. Emiko's rebellion against the traditional social structures is all the more striking when possession of her own sexuality is joined with her sense of herself as an artist.

Theatre production is an interpretive art. The three points of contrast identified here—the design of the houses and the arrangement of the physical space, the handling of the wind chimes scene, and the treatment of Emiko's sexuality—underscore the kinds of choices that may be made in different productions of the same play. The directors, actors, and designers all add layers of meaning to the words written by the playwright.

SUMMARY

In *And the Soul Shall Dance*, the playwright presents the harsh lives of immigrant farmers eking out a living in the Imperial Valley in the 1930s. The past, the characters' Japanese background, is an important factor in shaping the present, as is the hostile attitude of Americans toward Asian immigrants. The playwright tells

her story through small, domestic incidents such as the bathhouse burning down. Although the details seem to come from ordinary circumstances, they are selected to express the characters' spirits. Emiko's longing to return to Japan is bound up in her kimonos. Masako's search for inspiration draws her to Emiko's music and dance.

In the East West Players' performance of *And the Soul Shall Dance*, realistic style was mixed with the more abstract style of the kabuki theatre. Scenes were performed with attention to period authenticity in speech, in characters' attitudes and manners, and in dress. But the scenery was made up of unfolding houses that were whirled around by dancing figures dressed in black, and Japanese percussion and wind instruments were used to create a musical background for the characters' lives. Realism is frequently modified by more abstract elements.

Another production of *And the Soul Shall Dance* at Northwest Asian American Theatre in Seattle demonstrates ways in which two productions of the same play may differ. The scene design in Seattle focused on the contrast between the homes of the Okas and the Muratas, whereas the scene design of the Los Angeles production emphasized the isolation of all the characters. The Seattle production explored gender conflict, while the Los Angeles production was concerned with family connections that are sustaining.

TOPICS FOR DISCUSSION AND WRITING

1. Early in *And the Soul Shall Dance*, the neighbor Oka is finally able to bring his daughter Kiyoko from Japan. What are the different aspects of Oka's history that contribute to his determination to make Kiyoko feel successful in the United States?

2. Director Judi Nihei of Northwest Asian American Theatre observes that "Masako gets away with murder" in her behavior toward her mother. What is the nature of their relationship? How does Masako challenge her mother, and in what ways does Hana allow her extra freedom? What does the mother want for her daughter?

3. Is Emiko's memory of her former life in Japan real or imagined?

NOTES

1. Wakako Yamauchi, "And the Soul Shall Dance," in *Songs My Mother Taught Me: Stories, Plays, and Memoir*, ed. Garrett Hongo (New York: Feminist Press, 1994).

2. Sources are Roger Daniels, *The Politics of Prejudice: The Anti-Japanese Movement in California and the Struggle for Japanese Exclusion* (New York: Atheneum, 1977), 63, 88; Ronald Takaki, *Strangers from a Different Shore: A History of Asian Americans* (Boston: Little, Brown, 1989), 180, 203–209; and the Wing Luke Asian Museum, Seattle.

3. Wakako Yamauchi, quoted in preface to *Songs My Mother Taught Me*, ed. Garrett Hongo (New York: Feminist Press, 1994), vii.

4. Wakako Yamauchi, quoted in Stephanie Arnold, "Dissolving the Half Shadows," in *Making a Spectacle*, ed. Lynda Hart (Ann Arbor: University of Michigan Press, 1988), 181–82.

5. All quotes in the production analysis are from the author's interviews.

SUGGESTIONS FOR FURTHER READING

Berson, Misha, ed. *Between Worlds: Contemporary Asian-American Plays*. New York: Theatre Communications Group, 1990.

An anthology of plays, including those by Philip Kan Gotanda, Jessica Hagedorn, David Henry Hwang, Ping Chong, and Wakako Yamauchi, with introductions to the playwrights. The anthology comprises a mix of realistic and nonrealistic plays.

Burton, Jeffrey F., Mary M. Farrell, Florence B. Lord, and Richard W. Lord. *Confinement and Ethnicity: Japanese American Relocation Sites*. Seattle: University of Washington Press, 2002.

This book documents the internment of Japanese Americans through historical overviews of each camp including photographs, diagrams, and discussion of camp life and major incidents.

Harth, Erica, ed. *Last Witnesses: Reflections on the Wartime Internment of Japanese Americans.* New York: Palgrave, 2001.

Last Witnesses emphasizes personal responses to internment with essays written by people who experienced the incarceration or were deeply affected by it. A concluding set of essays offers historical and sociological analysis. The book is beautifully written and achieves a remarkable depth in probing the experience and consequences of internment. Among the many topics covered are the internment of artist Isamu Noguchi, theatrical responses to internment, and the legacy of the all–Japanese American 442nd Regimental Combat Team.

Houston, Velina Hasu, ed. *The Politics of Life: Four Plays by Asian American Women.* Philadelphia: Temple University Press, 1993.

An anthology that includes two additional plays by Wakako Yamauchi: *12-1-A*, about the internment of Japanese Americans, and *The Chairman's Wife*, about Chiang Ching, the wife of Mao Zedong. Also included are the plays *Paper Angels* by Genny Lim and *Asa Ga Kimashita* (*Morning Has Broken*) by Velina Hasu Houston.

Nelson, Brian, ed. *Asian American Drama: 9 Plays from the Multiethnic Landscape.* New York: Applause, 1997.

A collection of plays showcasing evolving styles and issues in the Asian American theatre as well as the changing nature of the Asian American community. The plays are drawn from theatres with a specific Asian American focus as well as from regional theatres across the country. Playwrights include Philip Kan Kotanda, Amy Hill, David Henry Hwang, Lane Nishikawa, and Denise Uyehara.

Shimakawa, Karen. *National Abjection: The Asian American Body Onstage.* Durham, NC: Duke University Press, 2002.

A complex exploration of the way the work of Asian American theatre companies and plays by Asian American playwrights challenge stereotypical or abject portrayals of Asian Americans. Shimakawa begins with a detailed discussion of the musical *Miss Saigon* and then focuses on the Asian American theatre community. The work of Wakako Yamauchi is prominently featured with additional interview material from the playwright.

Takaki, Ronald. *Issei and Nisei: The Settling of Japanese America.* Adapted by Rebecca Stefoff from *Strangers from a Different Shore.* New York: Chelsea House, 1994.

An account of Japanese immigration to the United States that provides a very useful background to *And the Soul Shall Dance*. The book addresses the working conditions and social circumstances for Japanese immigrants and their children and discusses the legislative restrictions they faced. It also includes personal responses, anecdotes, and photographs.

Yamauchi, Wakako. *Songs My Mother Taught Me: Stories, Plays, and Memoir.* Edited by Garrett Hongo. New York: Feminist Press at the City University of New York, 1994.

A collection of plays and short stories by playwright Wakako Yamauchi. The short story on which the play *And the Soul Shall Dance* is based is included, as well as another play, *The Music Lessons*.

CHAPTER 10

Understanding Style: Theatricalism

The two plays we have examined in depth—*Joe Turner's Come and Gone* and *And the Soul Shall Dance*—are largely realistic plays, both in their dramatic construction and in their staging. Although realism has had a prominent position in twentieth-century theatre and film, another style of theatre, nonrealistic theatre, has provided a different way of expressing many of the tensions and uncertainties of modern life. Nonrealistic theatre takes a variety of startling forms that continue to be invented. Audacity and challenge are fundamental to the highly theatrical expression of **nonrealism,** which theatre practitioners and audiences alike find energizing and compelling, as well as sometimes puzzling and disturbing.

As we discussed in Chapter 8, the period of realism in the theatre began with the work of European playwrights and theatre practitioners in the second half of the nineteenth century. Realism continues to be a popular style today, particularly in Western theatre and film and also in many non-Western nations. Realists have sought to focus on the social problems engulfing ordinary people by examining psychologically coherent characters placed in detailed environments.

Shortly after the advent of realism, however, some theatre practitioners rejected the

idea that constructing an illusion of reality was the most revealing way to examine the human condition. Other styles arose in the arts and in the theatre that were inspired both by the limitations of the realistic theatre and by the tremendous changes in social organization and in scientific and philosophical thought. The Industrial Revolution, for example, drastically changed the nature of human labor and threatened individual identity. The increasingly destructive weaponry of World War I and World War II brought the human community closer to annihilation. Religious skepticism increased in the face of the meaningless slaughter of millions. Changing views of the nature of the universe, such as that provided by Einstein's general theory of relativity, contributed to growing uncertainty about the existence of absolute truths. All of these developments prompted the emergence of new styles in the theatre.

These new theatre styles have been referred to collectively as "nonrealistic theatre" or "antirealism" because of their specific reaction against realism. However, they have more in common than just their opposition to realism. If the realistic theatre depends on carefully chosen surface details, then the nonrealistic theatre seeks ways of going beneath the surface to identify something essential about human existence and then to express that essence through theatrical imagery. The theatrical image is an abstraction of or a poetic metaphor for some aspect of life. In the next play we read, *Angels in America* (Chapter 11), an angel appears on the stage. The angel is not presented as part of an actual event in the lives of the characters but as a fantastic creature in both appearance and behavior who symbolizes the characters' struggle to change. The angel is an imagistic way of expressing a complex structure of ideas about religion, psychology, and politics. Although the styles that make up the nonrealistic theatre take many forms, most of these forms rely on bold **theatricalism** that interprets the human condition in concentrated images. Theatricalism expands the concept of

nonrealism by indicating a theatre composed of images. For our purposes, we use the terms *nonrealism* and *theatricalism* interchangeably.

Plays that use the style of theatricalism are concerned with expressing the interior journeys of their characters. Frequently the point of view is expressed subjectively; that is, we see the world as the character sees it. Distortion, grotesque images, and nightmare visions are projected onto the stage from the character's mind. In contrast to the realistic concrete world of work, home, and everyday activities in which the characters are viewed objectively by the playwright, the subjective landscape is often bizarre and highly personal. In *Angels in America*, one of the characters is seen largely through her hallucinations; she places herself in a frozen landscape of ice to avoid confronting fears that threaten to destroy her.

Theatricalism also often involves poetic or extravagant language, which frequently blends with the visual imagery to heighten the play's expressiveness. Many twentieth-century nonrealistic plays that focus on the failure of human beings to communicate with each other use fragmented or even nonsensical speech to explore the absence of meaning in human interactions.

EXPOSING THE MECHANICS OF THE THEATRE

In addition to concentrated imagery, the subjective point of view, and exaggerated speech, theatricalism changes the actor-audience relationship that is the goal of realism. Although we as audience members always know at the deepest level that we are in the theatre, the realistic theatre tries to make us forget where we are, whereas the nonrealistic theatre tends to remind us that what we are watching is a theatrical creation. In the realistic theatre, the tricks of the theatre are hidden. We do not watch the set changes or the costume changes. Certainly, the East West Players' production

added nonrealistic elements of kabuki theatre to the scene changes of an otherwise realistic production of *And the Soul Shall Dance*. But in the Oregon Shakespeare Festival's production of *Joe Turner's Come and Gone*, the backstage areas were blocked off or masked so the audience would not be distracted by what was going on in the wings. The audience's awareness of such activity would have broken the illusion that was being carefully constructed onstage.

Additionally, in realistic staging the actors consciously remain in character the entire time they are onstage. Sometimes offstage sound effects are used in realistic theatre to suggest that the characters' fictional lives continue even when they have exited the stage. We can then imagine them in conversations or actions that continue their stage life when they are no longer in view. The intrusion of the mechanics of the theatre into the realistic illusion onstage would be like watching a film in which a microphone hanging above the actors is accidentally shown on camera. We are instantly taken out of the fictional world of the film and reminded of the devices used to construct the illusion.

In the nonrealistic theatre, the mechanics of the theatre are frequently exposed or the stage effects are so obviously executed that they call attention to themselves as theatrical gestures rather than as subtle elements of a realistic whole. In the nonrealistic theatre we may see the ropes that support the scenery or the movements of the stagehands. In *Angels in America*, the actors themselves change the scenery in view of the audience. A scenic effect such as moonlight, which might be handled in the realistic theatre by a soft light coming through a window, might be presented in the nonrealistic theatre as a cardboard cutout of a moon attached to a stick.

The words *representational* and *presentational* are used to identify the distinction between realistic and nonrealistic theatre. **Representational staging** refers to the creation of a completely realistic illusion, and **presentational staging** refers to staging that recognizes the audience's awareness of theatrical manipulation. Presentational staging demands more of the audience's imagination than does representational staging, in which all of the details have already been filled in. The presentational, nonrealistic theatre frequently uses bold images, and abstract ideas or concepts are given symbolic expression through character, character action, and design as well as through language.

EXPRESSIONISM

In the early part of the twentieth century, a loosely knit group of theatre artists and visual artists experimented with a form that would become known as **German Expressionism.** Although the movement of German expressionism itself lasted from 1905 to 1922, the influences of the German expressionists extend until the present. For example, a contemporary experimental Japanese form, *butoh*, was inspired by the work of the German Expressionists.

The word **expressionism** is also frequently used in a more general way to indicate the various developments in Western painting, sculpture, architecture, dance, film, and theatre that were concerned with the abstraction of form. The painters Pablo Picasso and Marc Chagall, composer Igor Stravinsky, and choreographer Martha Graham are all included in a long list of expressionist artists. The playwright August Strindberg, whose work is discussed in Chapter 8, turned to a more subjective, abstracted form of theatre in his plays *The Ghost Sonata* and *The Dream Play*, which broke ground for the later expressionists. Early on in his career, Bertolt Brecht was part of the German expressionist movement. The innovations and concerns of the expressionists can still be seen in a play such as *Angels in America*.

German Expressionism

German expressionist theatre was infused with a sense of anguish. It has even been called the theatre of the shriek or the cry; its aim was to

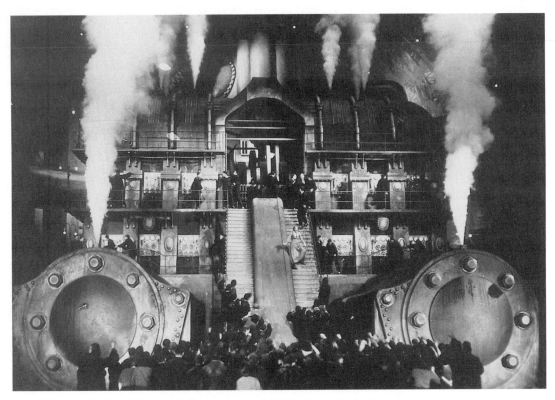

The film Metropolis, *by Fritz Lang, drew on many of the techniques developed in the German expressionist theatre to create the bitter mechanical world inhabited by oppressed workers. The style and scale of the images in the film were influential throughout the twentieth century.*

put into theatrical terms the feeling that was expressed in Edvard Munch's then highly influential painting *The Scream*. The German expressionists were horrified by the arms buildup in Germany and the militarization of their country. Their theatre performances were a cry for humanitarianism to replace the brutality they saw around them. The expressionists, of course, proved to be prophetic. Many of them fled Germany during Hitler's rise in the 1930s, but those who didn't died in the concentration camps.

The silent film *Metropolis*, by the great German filmmaker Fritz Lang, uses many of the techniques developed in the German expressionist theatre. At this point we briefly examine the techniques used in *Metropolis* because

this classic film is readily accessible on video and provides an excellent opportunity to experience the fundamental principles and themes of the German expressionist movement.

The plot of *Metropolis* focuses on the attempt of an industrialist's son to stop the manufacture of poison gas in his father's chemical plant. The film is dominated by striking visual images of the gleaming modern city aboveground, inhabited by the unthinking rich, and the brutal factory below, where the workers live out their hopeless days. The workers have become dehumanized cogs in the operation of the vast factory. Almost lifeless, dressed in identical clothes like prisoners, they go through choreographed sequences that integrate their stylized, repetitive, robotlike movements with the work-

Willem Dafoe and Kate Valk appeared in a new production (1997) of Eugene O'Neill's The Hairy Ape, *produced by the Wooster Group and directed by Elizabeth LeCompte.*

ings of the wheels and pulleys of the machinery and the giant hands of a huge, regulatory clock. The enormous scenic images of the factory below and the skyscrapers above dwarf the tiny human characters, who have become insignificant in the world of relentless machines.

The scenes are presented as a sequence of episodes enacted by characters without names who are meant to be types rather than individuals and who speak (in subtitles) in abbreviated bursts of dialogue. The actors' stylized movements and the visual images are as important as the spoken language—or even more important. Although some of the acting is humorous by today's standards because of the exaggerated facial expressions and body language, the power of the workers' segments is undiminished by time.

American Expressionism: Eugene O'Neill

Early in the twentieth century, a number of American playwrights were drawn to expressionism as a style suited to exploring the contradictions and anxieties of American life. Elmer Rice wrote about the dehumanization of the machine world in *The Adding Machine*; Sophie Treadwell explored gender conflicts in *Machinal* (1927); and Eugene O'Neill used expressionistic elements in a number of his plays. Of these playwrights O'Neill has had the most lasting influence.

Eugene O'Neill (1888–1953) grew up in an Irish American family dominated by his father, James O'Neill, a well-known actor. James O'Neill played the lead in *The Count of Monte*

Kevin Spacey plays Hickey in a 1999 Broadway revival of Eugene O'Neill's The Iceman Cometh. *Here, Hickey tries to force the alcoholic inhabitants of Harry Hope's saloon to face their failures and resume their former lives.*

Cristo for years, unable to give up the role for fear of financial failure. Thus, Eugene O'Neill's youth was steeped in nineteenth-century melodrama. O'Neill remains a seminal figure in the American theatre because of his attempt to lift the level of the medium above nineteenth-century melodrama and spectacle and find an authentic American voice in playwriting that would approach the eloquence of the Europeans Ibsen and Strindberg.

No established form of serious American drama existed when O'Neill began writing one-act plays for the Provincetown Players in 1915. O'Neill's career as a playwright was marked by his experimentation with form, as he searched for the language and dramatic structures that

would express his understanding of the American experience. He was concerned with the way human beings deceive themselves with illusions of success or love and then become paralyzed when those illusions are shattered.

Early in his career, in his plays *The Emperor Jones* (1920) and *The Hairy Ape* (1922), O'Neill used expressionism to present the distorted, nightmarish worlds of his characters. Borrowing a convention of the ancient Greek theatre, O'Neill used masks in *The Great God Brown* (1925). And in *Strange Interlude* (1928), which took many hours to perform, he had the characters speak their **inner monologues** and **subtext** aloud. He turned in yet another direction when he wrote *Mourning Becomes Electra* (1931), a trilogy modeled on Greek tragedy. Set during and after the Civil War, the three plays explore the destructive passions of the Mannon family.

O'Neill finally came to a bitter kind of realism in his last and most successful plays, *The Iceman Cometh* (produced posthumously in 1956), *Hughie*, *A Moon for the Misbegotten* (1947), and *Long Day's Journey into Night* (produced posthumously in 1957). The Irish American personages of his youth figure prominently in O'Neill's work, and in the last two plays, he turns to the searing history of his own family, destroyed by alcoholism and drug addiction. *Hughie*, a long two-character, one-act play about a gambler and his only companion, the night clerk in a cheap hotel, received a successful new production (1996) in New York, starring Al Pacino as the lonely gambler.

EPIC THEATRE: BERTOLT BRECHT

Bertolt Brecht (1898–1956) was a prolific playwright and director who began his work in the theatre as part of the German expressionist movement. Brecht envisioned a new theatre experience to replace what he perceived as the failings of the realistic theatre. Brecht's **epic theatre** has achieved an influence on the development of the modern theatre equal to the influence of Stanislavsky's method acting on the development of contemporary psychological acting. Following World War II, Brecht moved to East Berlin. There he founded the famous Berliner Ensemble theatre, where he directed highly regarded performances of his plays. We investigate Brecht's theories of theatre here at some length because of their importance to the twentieth-century theatre and because of their influence on the major playwright we study in Chapter 11, Tony Kushner.

Brecht believed that there was a danger in the audience's becoming too deeply engrossed or lost in the story of a play. For Brecht,

Bertolt Brecht, who began his theatre work in Germany, sought exile in the United States during World War II. The repressive political climate in the United States following the war encouraged Brecht to return to East Germany, where he founded the Berliner Ensemble, which became one of the most distinguished theatres of the century.

the goal of realism—to make the audience members forget that they were in the theatre—made the theatre into a kind of anesthetic. He wanted to find ways to make the audience step back from the drama in order to encourage analysis rather than empathy or identification. He wanted to provoke questioning so that audiences would maintain an active, internal dialogue with the performance. From Brecht comes the idea, then, of interruption, of breaking the narrative to snap the audience out of what Brecht saw as a hypnotic state.

Brecht also did not want the experience of the play to be completed within the time and space of the performance. Rather, he saw theatre as a call to action. He hoped the performance would be a beginning point or part of a process in which audience members and actors would become engaged in social action. Therefore, Brecht did not look to provide the audience with the kind of experience that involves empathy and then the emotional release often referred to as **catharsis.** Brecht wrote:

> The spectator was no longer in any way allowed to submit to an experience uncritically (and without practical consequences) by means of simple empathy with the characters in a play. . . .
>
> The dramatic [realist] theatre's spectator says: Yes, I have felt like that too—Just like me—It's only natural—It'll never change— The sufferings of this man appall me, because they are inescapable—That's great art; it all seems the most obvious thing in the world— I weep when they weep, I laugh when they laugh.
>
> The epic theatre's spectator says: I'd never have thought it—That's not the way—That's extraordinary, hardly believable—It's got to stop—The sufferings of this man appall me, because they are unnecessary—That's great art: nothing obvious in it—I laugh when they weep, I weep when they laugh.[1]

Brecht's Concept of Alienation

To bring the audience to this receptive or alert mental state, Brecht employed techniques to achieve an **alienation effect,** or, in German, the *verfremdungseffekt (V-effekt)*. In Brecht's vocabulary, *alienation* did not mean "withdrawal"; rather, it meant "to make strange." He saw this strangeness as a way of interrupting audience involvement in the fiction created onstage.

As a director and a playwright, Brecht used a number of theatrical devices to create the alienation effect. The mechanics of the theatre were exposed to destroy any sense of magic or illusion. Set pieces and props were simple and suggestive. Titles posted at the beginning of each new scene told the audience in advance what would happen to interrupt the development of suspense. Slide projections and films were introduced to provide information that clarified or contradicted the situations of the characters. In Brecht's conception, epic theatre encourages spectators to question why the characters make the choices that they do.

Brecht also used music to interrupt the action and to comment on the situation. Rather than heighten the emotional mood of scenes as songs do in British and American musicals, songs in Brecht's plays change the mood and demand the audience's attention. Brecht's goal was to separate the music from the other elements of the drama, whereas in musical or lyrical theatre the goal is to integrate the music into the drama. According to Tony Kushner, the music in Brecht's plays provokes thought rather than provides a mental break:

> When it's good, [Brecht's music is] harder to listen to than the dialogue. It's more upsetting and more difficult. Which sort of reverses the traditional notion of musical theatre, at least American musical theatre, where the music is sort of your rest from thinking. And I think that really great composers for Brecht respond to the lyrics by writing something ugly and hard and difficult.[2]

Brecht's Approach to Acting

Brecht's approach to acting was one of his most intriguing and challenging ideas about changing the nature of the theatre. Brecht was opposed to Stanislavsky's idea of complete identification with the character. Brecht suggested a new approach to performance in which the actor would comment on the character, that is, stand both inside and outside of the character—as if the actor were describing his or her conduct and in some way engaging in a dialogue with the audience about the character. This technique is sometimes referred to as **acting in quotes.** In Brecht's words:

> The actor does not allow himself to become completely transformed on the stage into the character he is portraying. He is not Lear, Harpagon, Schweik; he shows them.[3]

Brecht is very clear in his writings that he did not mean that the actor should not be emotionally invested in the characterization or that the emotions of the audience should remain disengaged. Instead, he wanted both the actor and the audience to bring a critical attitude to their participation in the theatre event so that they could consider what was possible under the circumstances:

> Human behavior is shown as alterable; man himself as dependent on certain political and economic factors and at the same time as capable of altering them. . . . The idea is that the spectator should be put in a position where he can make comparisons about everything that influences the way in which human beings behave.[4]

Brecht focused his plays on characters forced to make difficult choices. The plays are written in long sequences of short scenes that reveal the various forces affecting the characters' decision-making process. Brecht also presented a comprehensive history of the situation rather than entering the storyline at a late point, as did Ibsen, whose plays begin just before the characters' major crises. *Mother Courage*, written in a collaboration with Margarete Steffin, for example, takes place during the Thirty Years' War of the seventeenth century. Concerned with the devastation of war, Brecht and Steffin created some historical distance so that the audience could consider the effect of all wars. The central character is a peddler who crosses back and forth over the battlefields, selling her wares to both sides in the conflict. She is a pragmatist who is committed to her own survival. But during the many years of the war, she ends up losing her own children because of decisions she makes about the family's economic welfare (Color Plate 34). Brecht's play *Galileo* demonstrates the influences on the central character Galileo as he first proposes his notion that the earth revolves around the sun and then recants his position after being threatened by the Catholic Church.

THEATRE OF THE ABSURD

In the 1950s another dramatic style evolved in response to the devastation of modern warfare, this time World War II. Based more on philosophical or metaphysical explorations than was the overtly political German expressionist theatre, the **theatre of the absurd** was created by a group of international playwrights who all lived and wrote in Paris: the Irish Samuel Beckett; the Romanian Eugène Ionesco; the Russian Arthur Adamov; and the French Jean Genet, who began writing in a prison cell.

In the face of the horrendous slaughter of World War II and the complicity of various segments of European society in the extermination of huge groups of innocent people, the playwrights of the absurd found traditional value systems bankrupt. They wrote about the meaninglessness of human existence and the inability of language to communicate in an effective way. The ultimate isolation of human beings shaped the images of futility that emerged from the absurdist movement. In his definitional study on absurdism, Martin Esslin writes:

> The Theatre of the Absurd . . . tends toward a radical devaluation of language, toward a poetry that is to emerge from the concrete and objectified images of the stage itself. The element of language still plays an important part in this conception, but what happens on the stage transcends and often contradicts the words spoken by the characters.[5]

The most famous play of the theatre of the absurd is Samuel Beckett's *Waiting for Godot.* Two tramps wait by the side of the road, essentially a physical "void" interrupted only by the presence of a shriveled tree. In the play the two characters wait for another character named Godot who never comes. While they wait, they struggle to fill the empty time with patter and activity reminiscent of clowning routines from vaudeville. But each attempt at interaction is more futile than the last. Long silences

In this Seattle Repertory Theatre production of Waiting for Godot, *Bill Irwin and Stephen Spinella play Vladimir and Estragon, Beckett's tramps, as they wait by the side of the road for their appointment with Mr. Godot. The dialogue and actions of the characters are frequently funny but become painful as the audience recognizes the characters' isolation and desperation.*

surround and break their speeches. The tree is the only visual detail that breaks the bleakness of the physical space, just as their meaningless chatter may be seen as only a brief interruption of the vast silence of the universe.

Although the two characters speak of parting from each other, they don't. They speak of leaving, yet they are unable to exit from the stage. They simply go on waiting. The nature of Godot is never defined; he is a puzzle that has led to intense speculation about what he may represent. Interpreted simply, Godot represents a reason for the characters to go on waiting, and that must suffice. Beckett constructs a powerful and disturbing image of life itself in his play: life

is reduced to the act of waiting for something that never comes. Beckett's plays are extremely dark in spite of their humor (Color Plate 35).

Eugène Ionesco also wrote about the uselessness of human activity but sometimes in a more playful way than Beckett. Ionesco delighted in creating situations in plays, such as *The Bald Soprano*, in which characters speak to each other at length in various forms of nonsense. Ionesco was particularly concerned with the failure of language to provide us with a means of reaching one another, as is Tony Kushner, whose *Angels in America* includes a scene in which an assembly of angels blather empty phrases simultaneously.

A REVOLUTION IN MOVEMENT: MARTHA GRAHAM

The expressionists and the absurdists made major changes in the use of language, in plot structure, in characterization, and in the nature of stage action. It would require an artist of a different sensibility to contribute a way of approaching stage movement to match the other innovations of expressionism and absurdism. Martha Graham (1893–1991) stands out as one of the most innovative and influential artists of the twentieth century, comparable to Picasso in visual art and James Joyce in literature. Her work has changed the way we understand the expressive possibilities of the human figure in space and the interactions of the figure with objects and costumes. Although Graham's contributions are most evident in modern dance and theatre, her influence, like that of other seminal artists and thinkers, spreads across many disciplines.

Martha Graham was a dancer, choreographer, actress, and playwright. Dance was her language, but her compositions took the form of drama. Graham was an actor who communicated through her body her own versions of Greek and American myths. She began her independent work as a choreographer in the early 1930s and continued to compose dramatic dance works until her death in 1991. The enormous output of this visionary artist spanned the twentieth century.

A New Dance Vocabulary

All of the innovators of modern theatre in the West, from the realists to the expressionists to Brecht to the absurdists, sought new styles of acting that would fully engage the body of the actor as well as the voice, to make performance more than posed figures declaiming speeches. Many of these theatre practitioners were inspired by the brilliance of the moving actor in the Asian theatre but frustrated by the lack of a comparable movement tradition in the West.

Graham revolutionized what was possible in movement on the stage. Strongly influenced by Asian forms, Graham developed a movement system that contributed to both the technique and the climate that would enable Western experimentation with Eastern forms.

Until the early part of the twentieth century, the available dance vocabulary came from the ballet. In Graham's work, the bare, flexed foot replaced the pointed foot in ballet toe shoes. Angular, asymmetrical movement contrasted sharply with the symmetrical elegance of ballet. The pelvis and abdomen became a primary center for movement so the body could contract and then release rather than always maintain a vertical line. And fundamental to the movement of both women and men was the expression of the body's weight. The floor became a partner in this exploration of the substance of the human body rather than a springboard. The fall, the pull of gravity, was central to Graham's movement system; dancers pressed up from the floor, using their visible power to oppose gravity. Graham herself was a virtuoso performer with an astounding technique and a riveting dramatic presence. She opened the way for much of what would follow in the twentieth-century experimental theatre.

Costume and Set as Partners in Dance

Graham also approached scenic and costume elements as partners to the dancers rather than as decorations or representations of period, although they also served both of these functions. Sewing her own costumes and working with designers such as Isamu Noguchi, who created sculptures for her settings, Graham used design elements to give further definition to the dancing figure and to provide for the development of character through movement. In an early piece entitled *Lamentation*, the dancer is cloaked and hooded by a piece of draped fabric. In this dance of grief, the dancer pushes against the fabric that surrounds her with angular, stretching gestures. The tension of the dance and its

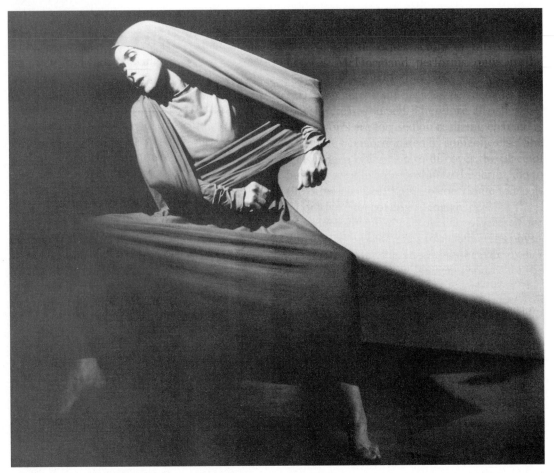

Early in her career, Martha Graham choreographed and performed Lamentation, *a dance of grief that recalls images of the German expressionists.*

emotional content are generated by the way the fabric resists the efforts of the dancer to displace or break through its binding force.

An example of a sculptural set piece by Noguchi is a free-form, metal frame bed that he created for a dance about Jocasta, the mother and wife of Oedipus, in Graham's work entitled *Night Journey*. The bed has a strong symbolic presence. It serves first as the place where Jocasta gave birth to Oedipus, second as the site of their incestuous relationship; and third as the funeral bier that carries Jocasta's body to her grave. The bed has physical importance as well. It is central to the movement of

Jocasta and Oedipus as they dance out their relationship on its slanted surface. The hard, metal frame supports the dancers' bodies and sets in relief the strength and the vulnerability of their characters: Oedipus, who will lose his eyes, and Jocasta, who will lose her life.

TOTAL THEATRE: ROBERT WILSON

Another American theatre artist, Robert Wilson (1941–), has become one of the dominant figures in shaping today's theatre of images.

Wilson's theatrical style is connected to a movement in theatre called **total theatre,** a form that stretches back to the mid-nineteenth century and the operas of Richard Wagner. Since Wagner's time, many theatre artists have been drawn to a vision of theatre that fuses music, dance, language, scenic image, and light; this is exactly what Wilson aims at. He creates works on a very large scale: in terms of (1) the numbers of performers and collaborators involved, sometimes more than one hundred and fifty; (2) the duration of the performances, which can last up to twelve hours; and (3) the size and complexity of the images he constructs. Wilson begins his theatre pieces with scenic images and with music and dance. Language is frequently used, but text is neither the starting point nor the foundation of what is communicated (Color Plate 15).

Wilson's expectation of the audience experience is very different from that of most of the other theatre artists we have discussed so far. Wilson is not attempting to build a visible and coherent structure of ideas or to interpret character psychology, nor is he offering a social critique. He seeks to trigger associations in the minds of audience members. Rather than consciously constructing work that interprets themes, Wilson and his collaborators present loosely related images that the audience members must then organize and interpret according to their individual responses. Wilson creates stage images that seem to come from the world of dreams and hallucinations.

Wilson's Experience

Robert Wilson brings to his work a unique combination of training and personal experience. A brief consideration of his background is helpful in understanding his point of view and his approaches to his theatre pieces. Wilson studied painting in Paris before he returned to the United States to earn an undergraduate degree in architecture. He experimented with various visual art forms, including large out-

door installations. His first involvement in the New York theatre was as a scene designer. Wilson is a visual thinker; he develops scenes through long sequences of drawings rather than dialogue.

Another profound influence on Wilson's life is dance. As a child Wilson had a pronounced stutter, which inhibited his ability to communicate verbally. At seventeen he began to study dance with a remarkable seventy-year-old teacher, Bird Hoffman. Through controlled movement and relaxation, Wilson was able to overcome his stutter. His studies with Hoffman inspired Wilson's work with disabled children and adults, in which he encouraged creative responses, in part through the use of slow, controlled repetitions of patterned movement. Eventually he incorporated this approach to movement into his theatre performances. He also invited the participation of some of the children he worked with and used their contributions onstage. Wilson frequently communicates nonverbally with the performers in his pieces; there is none of the discussion of character or motivation that is so important to the realistic theatre.

The Interior Landscape

Wilson's work includes *The Life and Times of Joseph Stalin, A Letter to Queen Victoria, Einstein on the Beach,* and *The Life and Times of Sigmund Freud.* As the titles suggest, Wilson uses large subjects that can be interpreted in many different ways. He frequently focuses on a major historical figure whose influence has been felt across generations and continents; he builds collages of images in response to the impact of the central figure. The images relate to each other thematically, often in a very loose sense. Critic John Rockwell summarizes Wilson's approach to these subjects:

> What Wilson really is concerned with is deeper questions of authority, terror, fear and hope and the smaller (deeper?) human quirks of such seemingly overpowering figures.[6]

In Einstein on the Beach, *Robert Wilson explores themes of time and space suggested by the life and work of Albert Einstein through scenic image, dance movement, and text that have associational rather than logical relationships.*

In Wilson's work one image slowly dissolves to the next: immense architectural backgrounds; enormous figures; characters in elaborate costumes from different periods; dancers; animals such as bears, elephants, and fish; suspended objects and people; burning houses. Various pieces of text are read or spoken, sometimes in several different languages. Exploratory work that was done for a production of *King Lear* involved a complete reordering of Shakespeare's text, spoken sometimes in English and sometimes in German, with an early Russian film version of *King Lear* playing in the background. Music also plays a prominent role in Wilson's work. Some of his work has featured the compositions of avant-garde musicians Philip Glass and Laurie Anderson and the voice of opera singer Jessye Norman. Through the intersection of abstract scenic imagery, hauntingly strange music, hypnotic dance, and pedestrian and poetic fragments of text, Wilson pushes back the boundaries of theatrical expression to reveal, in Martha Graham's words, "the interior landscape."

SUMMARY

In response to what many saw as realism's failure to completely reveal the human condition, new theatre styles arose in the early twentieth century. These theatrical forms communicated through overtly theatrical images, through stylized movement and poetic language, through the abstract rather than the concrete, through a concentration of expression rather than through the accumulation of detail. Although these theatre styles are often grouped under the category of nonrealism, or theatricalism, no single term adequately defines the many forms of theatre in the twentieth century that have sought to express the inner life of human beings.

During the twentieth century, many playwrights, choreographers, and directors took a number of different approaches to theatrical expression. In the theatre of the German expressionists, plays often took the form of protest against war, industrialization, and inhumanity. Characters and language were reduced to their essence and supported by stylized movement and distorted scenic images to produce an effect of anguish. American playwright Eugene O'Neill used expressionism in much of his early work. Bertolt Brecht sought an alienation effect to interrupt the audience's emotional involvement in the drama in order to encourage analysis of the dramatic event. Absurdist playwrights such as Samuel Beckett and Eugène Ionesco used theatrical imagery to explore philosophical rather than social issues.

Other theatre artists have created unique styles through the use of movement, music, and scenic image rather than language. Martha Graham invented a movement vocabulary to explore the passions of archetypal characters engaged in mythic dramas. Robert Wilson creates a dreamlike total theatre in which enormous scenic images, evocative music, and dancing figures suggest mysterious relationships.

TOPICS FOR DISCUSSION AND WRITING

1. Research the work of such artists as Edvard Munch, Pablo Picasso, Salvador Dalí, and Käthe Kollwitz that distort and fracture the represented figures, landscapes, or

environments. What kinds of commentary about the human condition do these paintings make? How do they diverge from more realistic image making?

2. What changes in the nature of the actor-audience relationship were proposed by Bertolt Brecht? How do Brecht's ideas about acting contrast with those of Stanislavsky outlined in Chapter 8? We frequently see evidence of Stanislavsky's approach to acting in theatre and film today. Cite some examples of Brecht's approach to acting, in which actors call attention to themselves as actors.

3. Compare the plot of *Waiting for Godot* with that of *Joe Turner's Come and Gone* or *And the Soul Shall Dance*. What is the difference in the kinds of actions performed by the characters, and what is the significance of those actions? What is the difference in the endings and what we imagine will happen to the characters after the plays have ended?

NOTES

1. Bertolt Brecht, *Brecht on Theatre*, ed. and trans. John Willett (New York: Hill and Wang, 1964), 71.
2. Wendy Arons, "Preaching to the Converted: An Interview with Tony Kushner," *Communications from the International Brecht Society*, 23, no. 2 (1994): 59.
3. Brecht, 137–38.
4. Brecht, 86.
5. Martin Esslin, *The Theatre of the Absurd* (London: Penguin, 1988), 26.
6. John Rockwell, *Robert Wilson: The Theatre of Images* (New York: Harper and Row, 1984), 27.

SUGGESTIONS FOR FURTHER READING

Artaud, Antonin. *The Theatre and Its Double.* Translated by Mary Caroline Richards. New York: Grove Press, 1958.

One of the most influential books on theatre in the twentieth century. Deeply moved by the

Balinese theatre of dance and music, Artaud sought to free the Western theatre from an over-reliance on language and psychology.

Eisner, Lotte H. *The Haunted Screen: Expressionism in the German Cinema*. Berkeley: University of California Press, 1969.

A discussion of a number of influential films that contributed to the German expressionist movement including *Metropolis*. This book contains excellent photographs and discussions that draw comparisons between theatre and film in the areas of acting, design, lighting, and composition.

Esslin, Martin. *The Theatre of the Absurd*. London: Penguin Books, 1983.

A definitive work that identifies the characteristics of the theatre of the absurd; includes essays on Beckett, Ionesco, Adamov, and Genet.

Kirby, E. T., ed. *Total Theatre*. New York: E. P. Dutton, 1969.

An anthology of essays exploring the work of key European theatre artists of the late nineteenth and early twentieth centuries who worked in symbolic, imagistic, gestural theatre, such as Richard Wagner, Edward Gordon Craig, Vsevolod Meyerhold, and Max Reinhardt; also includes a brief article on the impact of the Chinese theatre on the development of gestural theatre.

Mews, Siegfried. *A Bertolt Brecht Reference Companion*. Westport, CT: Greenwood Press, 1997.

An exceptional collection of essays that examines Brecht's work from a number of perspectives; includes an overview of Brecht's life and career. The book addresses Brecht's plays, his theories of performance, his perspectives on film and music, his position as a Marxist, and his influence in the United States, Latin America, and Asia.

Morgan, Barbara. *Martha Graham: Sixteen Dances in Photographs*. Dobbs Ferry, NY: Morgan & Morgan, 1980.

A chronicle of Graham's career through photographs; provides beautiful visual documentation of a number of Graham's choreographed works, including *Frontier, Lamentation, Every Soul Is a Circus,* and *Letter to the World*.

Rockwell, John. *Robert Wilson: The Theatre of Images*. New York: Harper & Row, 1984.

An examination of Wilson's approach to theatre through essays, fine production photographs, and reproductions of Wilson's preliminary sketches, which demonstrate Wilson's visual thought process.

Shank, Theodore. *American Alternative Theatre*. New York: Grove Press, 1982.

An examination of recent experimental work in the American theatre, emerging from two "energizing forces—the moral energy of social causes and the spirit of artistic exploration"; includes discussions of social activist theatre, such as El Teatro Campesino and the San Francisco Mime Troup, and formalist theatre concerned with challenging perception, such as the work of Robert Wilson and the Wooster Group.

Sokel, Walter, ed. *Anthology of German Expressionism: Ist Drama*. Rev. and Abr. ed. Ithaca: Cornell Paperbacks, 1984.

An anthology of German expressionist drama, with an introduction that clearly outlines the characteristics of expressionist drama and theatre and places it in relation to absurdism, realism, and American expressionism.

Willett, John. *Expressionism*. New York: McGraw-Hill, 1970.

An excellent introduction to the aesthetics of and the connections between expressionism in painting and in the theatre; contains numerous illustrations. This book covers the development of expressionism throughout Europe and the United States.

CHAPTER 11

Expressing a Worldview Through Theatricalism

Looking at Angels in America: Millennium Approaches *by* Tony Kushner

Tony Kushner was born in New York in 1956 but grew up in Lake Charles, Louisiana. Both of his parents were professional musicians, and Kushner was raised in an artistic world rich with music and theatre. Although he was raised in a close-knit and supportive Jewish family, life was a struggle for a politically concerned teenager coming to terms with his identity as a gay man. Kushner chose to attend college at Columbia University in the hope that New York City would provide a more hospitable social and political environment than he found in Louisiana. At Columbia, Kushner discovered that his interests in political activism and theatre complemented each other. Through his studies of Bertolt Brecht, Kushner began to envision an idea of theatre that would address the social inequities that he saw damaging the fabric of American life. Kushner pursued his theatre studies further at New York University, where he received a master of fine arts in directing, before turning his energies to playwriting.

Kushner had completed only one major play, *A Bright Room Called Day*, before he began work on *Angels in America*, which would become one of the most celebrated plays of the 1990s and, for some, one of the most important American plays of the twentieth century. Since

Louis (Michael Ornstein, *left*) *and Joe (Michael Scott Ryan)* *begin their friendship in* Angels in America: Millennium Approaches, *produced at the Eureka Theatre under the direction of David Esbjornson.*

writing *Angels in America,* Kushner has written a play set against the experience of Soviet repression, *Slavs!,* as well as adaptations of major works from different historical periods, including *Stella,* by the German romantic playwright Johann Wolfgang von Goethe; *The Illusion,* by the seventeenth-century playwright Pierre Corneille; *The Good Woman of Sezuan,* by Bertolt Brecht; and *The Dybbuk,* a play from the Yiddish Theatre early in the twentieth century by Solomon Ansky. His most recent work is *Homebody/Kabul* about the political turmoil in Afghanistan discussed in Chapter 2.

Angels in America is a brilliant example of the kind of experimentation with form that is characteristic of the nonrealistic theatre. In constructing his play, Tony Kushner draws on elements of expressionism, absurdism, and epic theatre, as well as realism. *Angels in America,* in fact, is not one play but two: *Millennium Approaches* and *Perestroika.* Each play lasts about three and a half hours; the two plays are sometimes presented on alternate days or in marathon sessions beginning in the afternoon, breaking for dinner, and then going on until late into the night. The presentation of *Angels in America* was considered a major theatrical event because of the scale of the undertaking, the sheer theatricality of the work, and the themes and issues that the two plays address.

Our study focuses on the first play, *Millennium Approaches,* with a more limited discussion of *Perestroika.* In the production analysis following the playscript, we examine the development of the play itself in relation to its production at the Eureka Theatre, a small theatre in San Francisco, and at the Mark Taper Forum in Los Angeles. In both the introduction to the play and the production analysis, we consider the ways Kushner juxtaposes realistic and theatricalized elements to create his vision of life in the United States in the late-twentieth century.

Angels in America comprises a complicated mix of characters, plot incidents, and ideas. The playwright, Tony Kushner, tells a broad sweep of a story that involves love and betrayal, politics and religion. Subtitled, "A Gay Fantasia on National Themes," *Angels in America* examines American life in the 1980s from a gay male point of view that is heavily influenced by the AIDS epidemic.

PLOT AND CHARACTERS: A WORLD IN SPIRITUAL COLLAPSE

The plot of *Angels in America: Millennium Approaches* focuses on two troubled couples living in New York City. Louis and Prior are gay lovers who have been together for four years

I believe that the playwright should be a kind of public intellectual, even if only a crackpot public intellectual: someone who asks her or his thoughts to get up before crowds, on platforms, and entertain, challenge, instruct, annoy, provoke, appall. I'm amused and horrified when I realize that, on occasion, I'm being taken seriously. But of course being taken seriously is my ambition, semi-secretly-and-very-ambivalently held. I enjoy the tension between responsibility and frivolity; it's where my best work comes from.[1]

— Tony Kushner

when Prior is diagnosed with AIDS. Unable to cope with the grim realities of the disease and the ever present threat of death, Louis abandons Prior. Harper and Joe Pitt are a young, married Mormon couple who have moved from Utah so that Joe, an ambitious lawyer, can take a job clerking for a federal judge. Joe is struggling with his own closeted homosexuality or bisexuality and eventually abandons Harper, although emotionally he has been absent for some time already. Harper is a frightened young woman, addicted to Valium, who hallucinates about a man attacking her with knives and despairs about the depletion of the earth's ozone layer (Color Plate 36). Louis, a passionately liberal Jew, and Joe, a conservative Republican, become lovers in spite of the apparent conflicts in their political and religious backgrounds.

This personal drama of abandonment and self-gratification is intricately connected to Kushner's larger social and political concerns. The play takes place in the 1980s during Ronald Reagan's presidency. Both Louis and Joe work for the federal government, and their personal behavior clearly mirrors Kushner's interpretation of the Reagan administration's attitude toward those in need. Louis and Joe both have strong political and religious affiliations, yet neither traditional politics nor religion provides a moral or spiritual guide for the times in which they find themselves. They have become what Louis calls "Reagan's children. Selfish and greedy and loveless and blind."[2]

The two characters whom Louis and Joe abandon each embody the cancers of the body and soul spreading through the country. Prior struggles with the ravages brought on by HIV infection. Harper is obsessed with the damage to the earth's atmosphere. The health crisis of the gay community links to the environmental crisis of the planet.

The Role of Roy Cohn

Kushner introduces one more major character who also serves to expand the play's frame of reference beyond the domestic drama of the two couples. This character, lawyer Roy Cohn, is an extreme representative of the moral decay of the country. The character of Cohn is based on a real person who, in fact, moved in the upper echelons of Republican power circles and died of AIDS in 1986, never having publicly acknowledged his homosexuality.

In the play, Joe Pitt, the ambitious young lawyer, turns to Roy Cohn as a kind of mentor, and Cohn eagerly looks to exploit the younger man in his own illegal schemes and power struggles. With the obscene and self-serving character of Cohn serving as background to the rest of the action, Kushner presents us with a nation in physical, moral, and spiritual collapse. Under such circumstances, Kushner asks, how do we restore compassion to our lives? Faced with such enormous obstacles, where do we find the will to change?

The Shifting Point of View

Like August Wilson and Wakako Yamauchi, Kushner is concerned with the impact of historical and sociological issues on his characters' lives. For Wilson and Yamauchi, social and economic injustice—racism, prejudice, slavery, anti-immigration policies—are a basic part of the environment, the fabric against which we see the characters' lives take shape. Kushner also addresses social and economic issues—the deeply ingrained homophobia of American society and the greed and lack of compassion that he perceives were represented by national policies in the 1980s.

But Kushner's approach to his material is different in essential ways from that of Wilson and Yamauchi. Wilson and Yamauchi focus on the interior movement of the characters' psyches, a progression of struggle, recognition, and awareness. As members of the audience, we are aware of the social background, but our principal concern is the story of the characters. Kushner changes this focus; he asks the audience for analysis as much as for empathy.

Wilson and Yamauchi draw us deeper and deeper into a created world that remains constant. We see their characters from a consistent point of view. Kushner, however, keeps shifting the perspective, alternating between domestic intimacy and spectacle, between a realistic representation of relationships and a surrealistic presentation of dreams and hallucinations. The nature of the created world changes abruptly, going through wild swings of imagery and point of view. Sometimes we see the characters objectively from the outside, sometimes subjectively from the inside. We move inside the characters' minds and see distorted views of experience that have been brought on by illness or addiction. Sometimes the characters enter each other's dreams, and the view of reality seems to be objective and subjective at the same time. And sometimes the play becomes fantasy, with the entrance of historical characters into the present or the appearance of supernatural characters.

INFLUENCES ON KUSHNER AS PLAYWRIGHT: BERTOLT BRECHT AND CARYL CHURCHILL

As we discussed in Chapter 10, the work of Bertolt Brecht has had a significant influence on Tony Kushner. Epic theatre, whose ideas come largely from Brecht's plays and productions as they evolved from the 1930s to the 1950s, has also shaped the playwriting of another source of inspiration for Kushner: the British playwright Caryl Churchill (1938–). Churchill has refined the Brechtian approach to respond to such contemporary concerns as race, gender, class, and economics. She has developed her own vocabulary of alienation devices. For example, in her play *Cloud 9*, Churchill uses **cross-gender casting** and **nontraditional casting;** that is, some of the female roles are played by men, some of the male roles are played by women, and a white actor plays the role of a black character. The purpose of such casting is to raise questions about how attitudes toward gender and race have originated. This casting calls attention to the idea that much human behavior is the result of social conditioning—that the way we perceive other people is the result of social expectations. These theatrical strategies challenge stereotypical thinking and ask us to question the social values regarding race and gender that limit human potential. In *Angels in America*, Tony Kushner employs this particular strategy of Churchill's by specifying in the script that some of the male roles be played by women actors.

Churchill develops her Brechtian approach further by creating a panorama that juxtaposes contemporary characters with historical figures who comment on the situations of the contemporary characters. She essentially widens the frame surrounding her characters to expose more than their daily lives and their physical and psychological environments. Into the frame she places historical figures whose presence connects the characters' situations to larger economic and political concerns. In her play

Caryl Churchill's Top Girls *begins with a scene in which a contemporary business executive, Marlene (Deborah Kassner), meets extraordinary women from earlier centuries. This scene from the Lewis and Clark College production, directed by Stephanie Arnold, shows Lady Nijo (Sakiko Taoka), a thirteenth-century Buddhist nun; Dull Gret (Christine Calfas), a figure from a Breughel painting; and Pope Joan (Heidi Van Schoonhoven), a pope from the eighth century who was discovered to be a woman when she gave birth to a child.*

Top Girls, the difficult lives of ordinary, contemporary English women and their children are placed against a background of remarkable women from different periods in history. Dialogues occur between characters from different centuries and between historical and fictional characters.

Brecht and Churchill are among the most influential theatre practitioners of their respective times. Much of the political theatre that exploded in the United States in the 1960s and afterward was heavily influenced by Brecht. And Caryl Churchill has had a similar impact on American theatrical expression since the 1980s. Although Tony Kushner is generally

associated with the Brechtian tradition, his dramatic structure is very specifically shaped by Churchill's influence. She has provided him with a method of bringing together the private and public aspects of his vision and then of placing the contemporary situation in a historical framework.

THE HISTORICAL FRAMEWORK OF *ANGELS IN AMERICA*

An obvious example of a historical framework in *Millennium Approaches* is the appearance of two ghostlike characters, both named Prior

Roy Cohn (*John Bellucci*, center) *seeks to persuade Joe Pitt (Michael Scott Ryan) to become a "Roy-boy" in the premiere production of* Angels in America *at the Eureka Theatre. The part of Martin Heller* (left) *is played by a woman, Anne Darragh.*

Walter, in act 3, scene 1. Prior Walter is also the name of the central character of *Angels in America* who becomes a representative of the gay community and the larger American community through his suffering with AIDS and then his transcendence of both illness and despair. Prior 1 and Prior 2 are the English ancestors of the twentieth-century Prior: Prior 1 from the thirteenth century and Prior 2 from the seventeenth century. Prior 1 and Prior 2 visit the contemporary Prior while he is in bed one night to warn him of the coming of the Angel (a character who makes a spectacular appearance at the end of *Millennium Approaches*), much like the ghosts who appear to Scrooge in Dickens's *Christmas Carol*. Prior 1 and Prior 2 were both victims of the plague, the thirteenth century's "spotty monster" and the seventeenth

century's "Black Jack." The presence of these plague victims puts the AIDS epidemic in historical perspective; the Prior ancestors place the twentieth-century Prior in a long line of descendents that can be seen as the human family. We see outbreaks of plague as illnesses that affected entire societies, not as historically unique events or as punishments visited on any one group of people for their sins.

The Character Roy Cohn as a Historical Figure

Kushner's most complex and original development of Churchill's historical framework comes in the character Roy Cohn. Cohn is central to Kushner's dramatic vision and his commentary on history and politics.

In Context

THE LIFE AND TIMES OF ROY COHN

Date	Event
1927	Birth of Roy Cohn.
1938	Formation of the House Committee on Un-American Activities (HUAC). The committee focuses on subversive, communist activity, contributing to the climate of suspicion that would prepare the way for the unfounded accusations of Joe McCarthy and Roy Cohn.
1946	Joseph McCarthy is elected to the U.S. Senate as a Republican from Wisconsin.
1947	Bertolt Brecht is called to testify before the HUAC. Scrutiny of artists and intellectuals expands.
1951	Espionage trial of Julius and Ethel Rosenberg begins. Roy Cohn is appointed assistant to the prosecutor, Irving Saypol. The Rosenbergs are convicted of stealing atomic secrets for the Soviet Union, although the case against Ethel Rosenberg indicates minimal involvement. Judge Irving Kaufman sentences both Rosenbergs to die in the electric chair against even the recommendation of the FBI. Roy Cohn claims that he personally influenced the judge on the sentencing.
1952	Joseph McCarthy is reelected to the U.S. Senate in a campaign that focuses on the communist menace. He accuses the Democratic administrations of Franklin Roosevelt and Harry Truman of "twenty years of treason." McCarthy receives the chairmanship of the Senate's Government Operations Committee, which gives him a platform for attacking individuals in the Eisenhower administration, in public life, and in the Senate. Eisenhower tolerates such attacks no matter how outrageous and damaging to individuals and to the atmosphere in the nation as long as they seem to benefit the Republican Party.
1953	Following Roy Cohn's successful participation in the Rosenberg trial, McCarthy appoints him as the chief counsel for his Senate committee.
1953	Execution of Julius and Ethel Rosenberg.
1954	Army-McCarthy hearings, in which the tactics and "above the law" attitude of McCarthy and Cohn are exposed on television.
1954	Cohn resigns as McCarthy's chief counsel. McCarthy is "condemned" by the Senate. Cohn begins his career as lawyer to the wealthy. He cultivates connections and trades favors with the powerful in business and government.
1956	Arthur Miller is called to testify before the HUAC.
1957	McCarthy dies, apparently of acute alcoholism.
1986	Roy Cohn dies of AIDS. He never publicly acknowledges his homosexuality.

Born in 1927, Roy Cohn first achieved national prominence during the cold war of the late 1940s and 1950s. He served as an assistant to the prosecutor in the trial of Julius and Ethel Rosenberg, who in 1951 were found guilty of selling atomic secrets to the Soviet Union and in 1953 were executed in the electric chair. Cohn claimed that he personally influenced the judge to sentence the Rosenbergs to death.

Cohn then became counsel and sidekick to Senator Joseph McCarthy, who launched the anticommunist "witch hunts" of the early 1950s that destroyed the lives and careers of many American writers, artists, and intellectuals. McCarthy died in 1957, discredited and censured, but Cohn lived on, finding new allies in right-wing politics and new opportunities as a lawyer to the wealthy. He died of AIDS in 1986.

Roy Cohn is pictured here (right) *as assistant to Joseph McCarthy during the Army-McCarthy hearings.*

Because of Roy Cohn's position in U.S. history, the character Roy Cohn brings onstage with him a long trail of historical baggage. His appearance evokes the excesses of the cold war and especially the execution of the Rosenbergs. But he is also a contemporary reference, with his connections to the Reagan administration and his death from AIDS.

A study in contradictions, Cohn is a homophobic homosexual; a Jew whose harshest judgments were made against other Jews; a lawyer who twisted the law for his own enrichment, self-gratification, and aggrandizement. Condensed in the Cohn character is a large share of the contradictions in American life that are the subjects of Kushner's play. Cohn, real and fictionalized, historical and contemporary, is placed in the center of Kushner's plot structure as a background to the rest of the action.

Roy Cohn and the Plot of Angels in America

Kushner brings Cohn into the construction of *Angels in America: Millennium Approaches* through two different subplots. In the first subplot, Cohn faces disbarment proceedings because of his shady dealings as a lawyer. He is

therefore searching for an attractive, loyal, young Republican man to place in the Justice Department in a desperate attempt to outmaneuver the disbarment. The young lawyer on whom Cohn fixes his attention and hopes for salvation is Joe Pitt, the Mormon husband at a crossroads in his own life.

The second subplot is when Cohn's health deteriorates and he becomes part of the AIDS community inhabited by Prior and his close friend and nurse, Belize. Of course, these tangled interactions at crucial points are calculated. There is no pretense here that all of these characters' paths would intersect in such convenient ways in the natural course of events, as there would be in a realistic play. Kushner wants us to see these lives in contrast with each other; he cleverly and boldly arranges the circumstances to enable such encounters.

Roy Cohn and Ethel Rosenberg

Toward the end of *Millennium Approaches*, Kushner expands the focus on Cohn as a historical figure by providing him with a disturbing companion. He creates a fictional version of Ethel Rosenberg as she might have appeared had she lived to be an older woman. The associ-

Prior (Stephen Spinella) is comforted by Belize (Harry Waters, Jr.) in the Eureka Theatre production of Angels in America.

Political activists Julius and Ethel Rosenberg were convicted of stealing atomic secrets for the Soviet Union in 1951 and executed for treason in 1953.

ation of Cohn with the execution of Ethel Rosenberg (1953) is the most heinous of the various crimes against humanity that Kushner draws on in his construction of the Cohn character.

Although few historians continue to argue that Julius Rosenberg was framed by the government, the degree of Ethel Rosenberg's involvement as a spy is uncertain. Some conclude

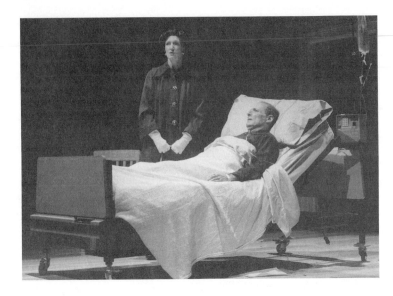

Ethel Rosenberg (Kathleen Chalfant) approaches the bedside of the dying Roy Cohn (Ron Liebman) in Angels in America: Perestroika, *produced at the Mark Taper Forum under the direction of Oskar Eustis and Tony Taccone.*

that she provided her husband a minimal amount of support; others maintain that her only crime was knowledge of Julius Rosenberg's treason. Government documents released in 1980 make clear that the execution of this young mother of two children was a ploy to gain information from her husband. It was also part of the government's anticommunist propaganda campaign. Above all, the execution of Ethel Rosenberg was far in excess of any reasonable sentence for her limited participation in espionage. For people who lived through the repressive climate of the 1950s in the United States, the appearance of Ethel Rosenberg on the stage in *Angels in America* is shocking.

The character that Kushner creates for Ethel Rosenberg bears little resemblance to the historical woman, at least as she has been interpreted by historians. A young woman when she died, she now appears as a comfortable Jewish grandmother with a toughness beneath the recognizable stereotypical role. In keeping with Kushner's outrageous approach to his material, Cohn and Rosenberg banter and bicker as if they are old friends rather than mortal enemies.

Like the figure of Cohn, the character of Ethel Rosenberg is loaded with complex significance. She seems to represent the angel of death, coming for Cohn at the end of his life. She is an accusation and a reminder. But perhaps most startling, there is also forgiveness in this character, a character who would have less reason than anyone in the United States to forgive Roy Cohn and his colleagues for their transgressions.

Angels in America: Millennium Approaches

Tony Kushner

THE CHARACTERS

ROY M. COHN, *a successful New York lawyer and unofficial power broker.*

JOSEPH PORTER PITT, *chief clerk for Justice Theodore Wilson of the Federal Court of Appeals, Second Circuit.*

HARPER AMATY PITT, *Joe's wife, an agoraphobic with a mild Valium addiction.*

LOUIS IRONSON, *a word processor working for the Second Circuit Court of Appeals.*

PRIOR WALTER, *Louis's boyfriend. Occasionally works as a club designer or caterer, otherwise lives very modestly but with great style off a small trust fund.*

HANNAH PORTER PITT, *Joe's mother, currently residing in Salt Lake City, living off her deceased husband's army pension.*

BELIZE, *a former drag queen and former lover of Prior's. A registered nurse. Belize's name was originally Norman Arriaga; Belize is a drag name that stuck.*

THE ANGEL, *four divine emanations, Fluor, Phosphor, Lumen and Candle; manifest in One: the Continental Principality of America. She has magnificent steel-gray wings.*

Other Characters in Part One

RABBI ISIDOR CHEMELWITZ, *an orthodox Jewish rabbi, played by the actor playing Hannah.*

MR. LIES, *Harper's imaginary friend, a travel agent, who in style of dress and speech suggests a jazz musician; he always wears a large lapel badge emblazoned "IOTA" (The International Order of Travel Agents). He is played by the actor playing Belize.*

THE MAN IN THE PARK, *played by the actor playing Prior.*

THE VOICE, *the voice of The Angel.*

HENRY, *Roy's doctor, played by the actor playing Hannah.*

EMILY, *a nurse, played by the actor playing The Angel.*

MARTIN HELLER, *a Reagan Administration Justice Department flackman, played by the actor playing Harper.*

SISTER ELLA CHAPTER, *a Salt Lake City real-estate saleswoman, played by the actor playing The Angel.*

PRIOR 1, *the ghost of a dead Prior Walter from the 13th century, played by the actor playing Joe. He is a blunt, gloomy medieval farmer with a guttural Yorkshire accent.*

PRIOR 2, *the ghost of a dead Prior Walter from the 17th century, played by the actor playing Roy. He is a Londoner, sophisticated, with a High British accent.*

THE ESKIMO, *played by the actor playing Joe.*

THE WOMAN IN THE SOUTH BRONX, *played by the actor playing The Angel.*

ETHEL ROSENBERG, *played by the actor playing Hannah.*

PLAYWRIGHT'S NOTES

A Disclaimer

Roy M. Cohn, the character, is based on the late Roy M. Cohn (1927–1986), who was all too real; for the most part the acts attributed to the character Roy, such as his illegal conferences with Judge Kaufmann during the trial of Ethel Rosenberg, are to be found in the historical record. But this Roy is a work of dramatic fiction; his words are my invention, and liberties have been taken.

A Note About the Staging

The play benefits from a pared-down style of presentation, with minimal scenery and scene shifts done rapidly (no blackouts!), employing the cast as well as stagehands—which makes for an actor-driven event, as this must be. The moments of magic—the appearance and disappearance of Mr. Lies and the ghosts, the Book hallucination, and the ending—are to be fully realized, as bits of wonderful *theatrical* illusion—which means it's OK if the wires show, and maybe it's good that they do, but the magic should at the same time be thoroughly amazing.

> In a murderous time
> the heart breaks and breaks
> and lives by breaking.
> —Stanley Kunitz
> "The Testing-Tree"

ACT ONE

Bad News
October–November 1985

Scene 1

The last days of October. Rabbi Isidor Chemelwitz alone onstage with a small coffin. It is a rough pine box with two wooden pegs, one at the foot and one at the head, holding the lid in place. A prayer shawl embroidered with a Star of David is draped over the lid, and by the head a yarzheit candle is burning.

RABBI ISIDOR CHEMELWITZ (*He speaks sonorously, with a heavy Eastern European accent, unapologetically consulting a sheet of notes for the family names*): Hello and good morning. I am Rabbi Isidor Chemelwitz of the Bronx Home for Aged Hebrews. We are here this morning to pay respects at the passing of Sarah Ironson, devoted wife of Benjamin Ironson, also

deceased, loving and caring mother of her sons Morris, Abraham, and Samuel, and her daughters Esther and Rachel; beloved grandmother of Max, Mark, Louis, Lisa, Maria . . . uh . . . Lesley, Angela, Doris, Luke and Eric. (*Looks more closely at paper*) Eric? This is a Jewish name? (*Shrugs*) Eric. A large and loving family. We assemble that we may mourn collectively this good and righteous woman.

(*He looks at the coffin*)

This woman. I did not know this woman. I cannot accurately describe her attributes, nor do justice to her dimensions. She was. . . . Well, in the Bronx Home of Aged Hebrews are many like this, the old, and to many I speak but not to be frank with this one. She preferred silence. So I do not know her and yet I know her. She was . . .

(*He touches the coffin*)

. . . not a person but a whole kind of person, the ones who crossed the ocean, who brought with us to America the villages of Russia and Lithuania—and how we struggled, and how we fought, for the family, for the Jewish home, so that you would not grow up *here*, in this strange place, in the melting pot where nothing melted. Descendants of this immigrant woman, you do not grow up in America, you and your children and their children with the goyische names. You do not live in America. No such place exists. Your clay is the clay of some Litvak shtetl, your air the air of the steppes—because she carried the old world on her back across the ocean, in a boat, and she put it down on Grand Concourse Avenue, or in Flatbush, and she worked that earth into your bones, and you pass it to your children, this ancient, ancient culture and home.

(*Little pause*)

You can never make that crossing that she made, for such Great Voyages in this world do not any more exist. But every day of your

lives the miles that voyage between that place and this one you cross. Every day. You understand me? In you that journey is. So . . .
She was the last of the Mohicans, this one was. Pretty soon . . . all the old will be dead.

Scene 2

Same day. Roy and Joe in Roy's office. Roy at an impressive desk, bare except for a very elaborate phone system, rows and rows of flashing buttons which bleep and beep and whistle incessantly, making chaotic music underneath Roy's conversations. Joe is sitting, waiting. Roy conducts business with great energy, impatience and sensual abandon: gesticulating, shouting, cajoling, crooning, playing the phone, receiver and hold button with virtuosity and love.

ROY (*Hitting a button*): Hold. (*To Joe*) I wish I was an octopus, a fucking octopus. Eight loving arms and all those suckers. Know what I mean?

JOE: No, I . . .

ROY (*Gesturing to a deli platter of little sandwiches on his desk*): You want lunch?

JOE: No, that's OK really I just . . .

ROY (*Hitting a button*): Ailene? Roy Cohn. Now what kind of a greeting is. . . . I thought we were friends, Ai. . . . Look Mrs. Soffer you don't have to get. . . . You're upset. You're yelling. You'll aggravate your condition, you shouldn't yell, you'll pop little blood vessels in your face if you yell. . . . No that was a joke, Mrs. Soffer, I was joking. . . . I already apologized sixteen times for that, Mrs. Soffer, you . . . (*While she's fulminating, Roy covers the mouthpiece with his hand and talks to Joe*) This'll take a minute, *eat* already, what is this tasty sandwich here it's—(*He takes a bite of a sandwich*) Mmmmm, liver or some. . . . Here.

(*He pitches the sandwich to Joe, who catches it and returns it to the platter.*)

ROY (*Back to Mrs. Soffer*): Uh huh, uh, huh. . . . No, I already told you, it wasn't a vacation, it was business, Mrs. Soffer, I have clients in

Haiti, Mrs. Soffer, I. . . . Listen, Ailene, YOU THINK I'M THE ONLY GODDAM LAWYER IN HISTORY EVER MISSED A COURT DATE? Don't make such a big fucking. . . . Hold. (*He hits the hold button*) You HAG!

JOE: If this is a bad time . . .

ROY: *Bad* time? This is a *good* time! (*Button*) Baby doll, get me. . . . Oh fuck, wait . . . (*Button, button*) Hello? Yah. Sorry to keep you holding, Judge Hollins, I. . . . Oh *Mrs.* Hollins, sorry dear deep voice you got. Enjoying your visit? (*Hand over mouthpiece again, to Joe*) She sounds like a truckdriver and he sounds like Kate Smith, very confusing. Nixon appointed him, all the geeks are Nixon appointees . . . (*To Mrs. Hollins*) Yeah yeah right good so how many tickets dear? Seven. For what, *Cats, 42nd Street,* what? No you wouldn't like *La Cage,* trust me, I know. Oh for godsake. . . . Hold. (*Button, button*) Baby doll, seven for *Cats* or something, anything hard to get, I don't give a fuck what and neither will they. (*Button; to Joe*) You see *La Cage?*

JOE: No, I . . .

ROY: Fabulous. Best thing on Broadway. Maybe ever. (*Button*) Who? Aw, Jesus H. Christ, Harry, *no,* Harry, Judge John Francis Grimes, Manhattan Family Court. Do I have to do every goddam thing myself? *Touch* the bastard, Harry, and don't call me on this line again, I told you not to . . .

JOE (*Starting to get up*): Roy, uh, should I wait outside or . . .

ROY (*To Joe*): Oh sit. (*To Harry*) You hold. I pay you to hold fuck you Harry you jerk. (*Button*) Half-wit dick-brain. (*Instantly philosophical*) I see the universe, Joe, as a kind of sandstorm in outer space with winds of megahurricane velocity, but instead of grains of sand it's shards and splinters of glass. You ever feel that way? Ever have one of those days?

JOE: I'm not sure I . . .

ROY: So how's life in Appeals? How's the Judge?

JOE: He sends his best.

ROY: He's a good man. Loyal. Not the brightest man on the bench, but he has manners. And a nice head of silver hair.

JOE: He gives me a lot of responsibility.

ROY: Yeah, like writing his decisions and signing his name.

JOE: Well . . .

ROY: He's a nice guy. And you cover admirably.

JOE: Well, thanks, Roy, I . . .

ROY (*Button*): Yah? Who is *this*? Well who the fuck are *you*? Hold—(*Button*) Harry? Eighty-seven grand, something like that. Fuck him. Eat me. New Jersey, chain of porno film stores in, uh, Weehawken. That's—Harry, that's the beauty of the law. (*Button*) So, baby doll, what? *Cats?* Bleah. (*Button*) *Cats!* It's about cats. Singing cats, you'll love it. Eight o'clock, the theatre's always at eight. (*Button*) Fucking tourists. (*Button, then to Joe*) Oh live a little, Joe, *eat* something for Christ sake—

JOE: Um, Roy, could you . . .

ROY: What? (*To Harry*) Hold a minute. (*Button*) Mrs. Soffer? Mrs. . . . (*Button*) God-fucking-dammit to hell, where is . . .

JOE (*Overlapping*): Roy, I'd really appreciate it if . . .

ROY (*Overlapping*): Well she was here a minute ago, baby doll, see if . . .

(*The phone starts making three different beeping sounds, all at once.*)

ROY (*Smashing buttons*): Jesus fuck this goddam thing . . .

JOE (*Overlapping*): I really wish you wouldn't . . .

ROY (*Overlapping*): Baby doll? Ring the *Post* get me Suzy see if . . .

(*The phone starts whistling loudly.*)

ROY: CHRIST!

JOE: *Roy.*

ROY (*Into receiver*): Hold. (*Button; to Joe*) What?

JOE: Could you please not take the Lord's name in vain?

(*Pause*)

I'm sorry. But please. At least while I'm . . .

ROY (*Laughs, then*): Right. Sorry. Fuck.

Only in America. (*Punches a button*) Baby doll, tell 'em all to fuck off. Tell 'em I died. You handle Mrs. Soffer. Tell her it's on the way. Tell her I'm schtupping the judge. I'll call her back. I *will* call her. I *know* how much I borrowed. She's got four hundred times that stuffed up her. . . . Yeah, tell her I said that. (*Button. The phone is silent*)
So, Joe.

JOE: I'm sorry Roy, I just . . .

ROY: No no no no, principles count, I respect principles, I'm not religious but I like God and God likes me. Baptist, Catholic?

JOE: Mormon.

ROY: Mormon. Delectable. Absolutely. Only in America. So, Joe. Whattya think?

JOE: It's . . . well . . .

ROY: Crazy life.

JOE: Chaotic.

ROY: Well but God bless chaos. Right?

JOE: Ummm . . .

ROY: Huh. Mormons. I knew Mormons, in, um, Nevada.

JOE: Utah, mostly.

ROY: No, these Mormons were in Vegas.
So. So, how'd you like to go to Washington and work for the Justice Department?

JOE: Sorry?

ROY: How'd you like to go to Washington and work for the Justice Department? All I gotta do is pick up the phone, talk to Ed, and you're in.

JOE: In . . . what, exactly?

ROY: Associate Assistant Something Big. Internal Affairs, heart of the woods, something nice with clout.

JOE: Ed . . . ?

ROY: Meese. The Attorney General.

JOE: Oh.

ROY: I just have to pick up the phone . . .

JOE: I have to think.

ROY: Of course.

(*Pause*)

It's a great time to be in Washington, Joe.

JOE: Roy, it's incredibly exciting . . .

ROY: And it would mean something to me. You understand?

(*Little pause.*)

JOE: I . . . can't say how much I appreciate this Roy, I'm sort of . . . well, stunned, I mean. . . . Thanks, Roy. But I have to give it some thought. I have to ask my wife.

ROY: Your wife. Of course.

JOE: But I really appreciate . . .

ROY: Of course. Talk to your wife.

Scene 3

Later that day. Harper at home, alone. She is listening to the radio and talking to herself, as she often does. She speaks to the audience.

HARPER: People who are lonely, people left alone, sit talking nonsense to the air, imagining . . . beautiful systems dying, old fixed orders spiraling apart . . .

When you look at the ozone layer, from outside, from a spaceship, it looks like a pale blue halo, a gentle, shimmering aureole encircling the atmosphere encircling the earth. Thirty miles above our heads, a thin layer of three-atom oxygen molecules, product of photosynthesis, which explains the fussy vegetable preference for visible light, its rejection of darker rays and emanations. Danger from without. It's a kind of gift, from God, the crowning touch to the creation of the world: guardian angels, hands linked, make a spherical net, a blue-green nesting orb, a shell of safety for life itself. But everywhere, things are collapsing, lies surfacing, systems of defense giving way. . . . This is why, Joe, this is why I shouldn't be left alone.

(*Little pause*)

I'd like to go traveling. Leave you behind to worry. I'll send postcards with strange stamps and tantalizing messages on the back. "Later maybe." "Nevermore . . ."

(*Mr. Lies, a travel agent, appears.*)

HARPER: Oh! You startled me!

MR. LIES: Cash, check or credit card?

HARPER: I remember you. You're from Salt Lake. You sold us the plane tickets when we flew here. What are you doing in Brooklyn?

MR. LIES: You said you wanted to travel . . .

HARPER: And here you are. How thoughtful.

MR. LIES: Mr. Lies. Of the International Order of Travel Agents. We mobilize the globe, we set people adrift, we stir the populace and send nomads eddying across the planet. We are adepts of motion, acolytes of the flux. Cash, check or credit card. Name your destination.

HARPER: Antarctica, maybe. I want to see the hole in the ozone. I heard on the radio . . .

MR. LIES (*He has a computer terminal in his briefcase*): I can arrange a guided tour. Now?

HARPER: Soon. Maybe soon. I'm not safe here you see. Things aren't right with me. Weird stuff happens . . .

MR. LIES: Like?

HARPER: Well, like you, for instance. Just appearing. Or last week . . . well never mind.

People are like planets, you need a thick skin. Things get to me, Joe stays away and now. . . . Well look. My dreams are talking back to me.

MR. LIES: It's the price of rootlessness. Motion sickness. The only cure: to keep moving.

HARPER: I'm undecided. I feel . . . that something's going to give. It's 1985. Fifteen years till the third millennium. Maybe Christ will come again. Maybe seeds will be planted, maybe there'll be harvests then, maybe early figs to eat, maybe new life, maybe fresh blood, maybe companionship and love and protection, safety from what's outside, maybe the door will hold, or maybe . . . maybe the troubles will come, and the end will come, and the sky will collapse and there will be terrible rains and showers of poison light, or maybe my life is really fine, maybe Joe loves me and I'm only crazy thinking otherwise, or maybe not, maybe it's even worse than I know, maybe . . . I want to know, maybe I don't. The suspense, Mr. Lies, it's killing me.

MR. LIES: I suggest a vacation.

HARPER (*Hearing something*): That was the elevator. Oh God, I should fix myself up, I. . . . You have to go, you shouldn't be here . . . you aren't even real.

MR. LIES: Call me when you decide . . .

HARPER: Go!

(*The Travel Agent vanishes as Joe enters.*)

JOE: Buddy?
    Buddy? Sorry I'm late. I was just . . . out. Walking. Are you mad?

HARPER: I got a little anxious.

JOE: Buddy kiss.

(*They kiss.*)

JOE: Nothing to get anxious about.
    So. So how'd you like to move to Washington?

Scene 4

Same day. Louis and Prior outside the funeral home, sitting on a bench, both dressed in funeral finery, talking. The funeral service for Sarah Ironson has just concluded and Louis is about to leave for the cemetery.

LOUIS: My grandmother actually saw Emma Goldman speak. In Yiddish. But all Grandma could remember was that she spoke well and wore a hat.
    What a weird service. That rabbi . . .

PRIOR: A definite find. Get his number when you go to the graveyard. I want him to bury me.

LOUIS: Better head out there. Everyone gets to put dirt on the coffin once it's lowered in.

PRIOR: Oooh. Cemetery fun. Don't want to miss that.

LOUIS: It's an old Jewish custom to express love. Here, Grandma, have a shovelful. Latecomers run the risk of finding the grave completely filled.
    She was pretty crazy. She was up there in that home for ten years, talking to herself.

I never visited. She looked too much like my mother.

PRIOR (*Hugs him*): Poor Louis. I'm sorry your grandma is dead.

LOUIS: Tiny little coffin, huh?
    Sorry I didn't introduce you to. . . . I always get so closety at these family things.

PRIOR: Butch. You get butch. (*Imitating*) "Hi Cousin Doris, you don't remember me I'm Lou, Rachel's boy." Lou not Louis, because if you say Louis they'll hear the sibilant S.

LOUIS: I don't have a . . .

PRIOR: I don't blame you, hiding. Bloodlines. Jewish curses are the worst. I personally would dissolve if anyone ever looked me in the eye and said "Feh." Fortunately WASPs don't say "Feh." Oh and by the way, darling, cousin Doris is a dyke.

LOUIS: No.
    Really?

PRIOR: You don't notice anything. If I hadn't spent the last four years fellating you I'd swear you were straight.

LOUIS: You're in a pissy mood. Cat still missing?

(*Little pause.*)

PRIOR: Not a furball in sight. It's your fault.

LOUIS: It is?

PRIOR: I warned you, Louis. Names are important. Call an animal "Little Sheba" and you can't expect it to stick around. Besides, it's a dog's name.

LOUIS: I wanted a dog in the first place, not a cat. He sprayed my books.

PRIOR: He was a female cat.

LOUIS: Cats are stupid, high-strung predators. Babylonians sealed them up in bricks. Dogs have brains.

PRIOR: Cats have intuition.

LOUIS: A sharp dog is as smart as a really dull two-year-old child.

PRIOR: Cats know when something's wrong.

LOUIS: Only if you stop feeding them.

PRIOR: They know. That's why Sheba left, because she knew.

LOUIS: Knew what?

(*Pause.*)

PRIOR: I did my best Shirley Booth this morning, floppy slippers, housecoat, curlers, can of Little Friskies; "Come back, Little Sheba, come back. . . ." To no avail. Le chat, elle ne reviendra jamais, jamais . . .

(*He removes his jacket, rolls up his sleeve, shows Louis a dark-purple spot on the underside of his arm near the shoulder*)

See.

LOUIS: That's just a burst blood vessel.

PRIOR: Not according to the best medical authorities.

LOUIS: What?

(*Pause*)

Tell me.

PRIOR: K.S., baby. Lesion number one. Lookit. The wine-dark kiss of the angel of death.

LOUIS (*Very softly, holding Prior's arm*): Oh please . . .

PRIOR: I'm a lesionnaire. The Foreign Lesion. The American Lesion. Lesionnaire's disease.

LOUIS: Stop.

PRIOR: My troubles are lesion.

LOUIS: Will you *stop.*

PRIOR: Don't you think I'm handling this well? I'm going to die.

LOUIS: Bullshit.

PRIOR: Let go of my arm.

LOUIS: No.

PRIOR: Let go.

LOUIS (*Grabbing Prior, embracing him ferociously*): No.

PRIOR: I can't find a way to spare you baby. No wall like the wall of hard scientific fact. K.S. Wham. Bang your head on that.

LOUIS: Fuck you. (*Letting go*) Fuck you fuck you fuck you.

PRIOR: Now that's what I like to hear. A mature reaction.

Let's go see if the cat's come home. Louis?

LOUIS: When did you find this?

PRIOR: I couldn't tell you.

LOUIS: Why?

PRIOR: I was scared, Lou.

LOUIS: Of what?

PRIOR: That you'll leave me.

LOUIS: Oh.

(*Little pause.*)

PRIOR: Bad timing, funeral and all, but I figured as long as we're on the subject of death . . .

LOUIS: I have to go bury my grandma.

PRIOR: Lou?

(*Pause*)

Then you'll come home?

LOUIS: Then I'll come home.

Scene 5

Same day, later on. Split scene: Joe and Harper at home; Louis at the cemetery with Rabbi Isidor Chemelwitz and the little coffin.

HARPER: Washington?

JOE: It's an incredible honor, buddy, and . . .

HARPER: I have to think.

JOE: Of course.

HARPER: Say no.

JOE: You said you were going to think about it.

HARPER: I don't want to move to Washington.

JOE: Well I do.

HARPER: It's a giant cemetery, huge white graves and mausoleums everywhere.

JOE: We could live in Maryland. Or George-town.

HARPER: We're happy here.

JOE: That's not really true, buddy, we . . .

HARPER: Well happy enough! Pretend-happy. That's better than nothing.

JOE: It's time to make some changes, Harper.

HARPER: No changes. Why?

JOE: I've been chief clerk for four years. I make twenty-nine thousand dollars a year. That's ridiculous. I graduated fourth in my class and I make less than anyone I know. And I'm . . . I'm tired of being a clerk, I want to go where something good is happening.

HARPER: Nothing good happens in Washington. We'll forget church teachings and buy furniture at . . . at *Conran's* and become yuppies. I have too much to do here.

JOE: Like what?

HARPER: I *do* have things . . .

JOE: What things?

HARPER: I have to finish painting the bedroom.

JOE: You've been painting in there for over a year.

HARPER: I know, I. . . . It just isn't done because I never get time to finish it.

JOE: Oh that's . . . that doesn't make sense. You have all the time in the world. You could finish it when I'm at work.

HARPER: I'm afraid to go in there alone.

JOE: Afraid of what?

HARPER: I heard someone in there. Metal scraping on the wall. A man with a knife, maybe.

JOE: There's no one in the bedroom, Harper.

HARPER: Not now.

JOE: Not this morning either.

HARPER: How do you know? You were at work this morning. There's something creepy about this place. Remember *Rosemary's Baby?*

JOE: *Rosemary's Baby?*

HARPER: Our apartment looks like that one. Wasn't that apartment in Brooklyn?

JOE: No, it was . . .

HARPER: Well, it looked like this. It did.

JOE: Then let's move.

HARPER: Georgetown's worse. *The Exorcist* was in Georgetown.

JOE: The devil, everywhere you turn, huh, buddy?

HARPER: Yeah. Everywhere.

JOE: How many pills today, buddy?

HARPER: None. One. Three. Only three.

LOUIS (*Pointing at the coffin*): Why are there just two little wooden pegs holding the lid down?

RABBI ISIDOR CHEMELWITZ: So she can get out easier if she wants to.

LOUIS: I hope she stays put.

I pretended for years that she was already dead. When they called to say she had died it was a surprise. I abandoned her.

RABBI ISIDOR CHEMELWITZ: "Sharfer vi di tson fun a shlang iz an umdankbar kind!"

LOUIS: I don't speak Yiddish.

RABBI ISIDOR CHEMELWITZ: Sharper than the serpent's tooth is the ingratitude of children. Shakespeare. *Kenig Lear.*

LOUIS: Rabbi, what does the Holy Writ say about someone who abandons someone he loves at a time of great need?

RABBI ISIDOR CHEMELWITZ: Why would a person do such a thing?

LOUIS: Because he has to.

Maybe because this person's sense of the world, that it will change for the better with struggle, maybe a person who has this neo-Hegelian positivist sense of constant historical progress towards happiness or perfection or something, who feels very powerful because he feels connected to these forces, moving uphill all the time . . . maybe that person can't, um, incorporate sickness into his sense of how things are supposed to go. Maybe vomit . . . and sores and disease . . . really frighten him, maybe . . . he isn't so good with death.

RABBI ISIDOR CHEMELWITZ: The Holy Scriptures have nothing to say about such a person.

LOUIS: Rabbi, I'm afraid of the crimes I may commit.

RABBI ISIDOR CHEMELWITZ: Please, mister. I'm a sick old rabbi facing a long drive home to the Bronx. You want to confess, better you should find a priest.

LOUIS: But I'm not a Catholic, I'm a Jew.

RABBI ISIDOR CHEMELWITZ: Worse luck for you, bubbulah. Catholics believe in forgiveness. Jews believe in Guilt. (*He pats the coffin tenderly*)

LOUIS: You just make sure those pegs are in good and tight.

RABBI ISIDOR CHEMELWITZ: Don't worry, mister. The life she had, she'll stay put. She's better off.

JOE: Look, I know this is scary for you. But try to understand what it means to me. Will you try?

HARPER: Yes.

JOE: Good. Really try.

I think things are starting to change in the world.

HARPER: But I don't want . . .

JOE: Wait. For the good. Change for the good. America has rediscovered itself. Its sacred position among nations. And people aren't ashamed of that like they used to be. This is a great thing. The truth restored. Law restored. That's what President Reagan's done, Harper. He says "Truth exists and can be spoken proudly." And the country responds to him. We become better. More good. I need to be a part of that, I need something big to lift me up. I mean, six years ago the world seemed in decline, horrible, hopeless, full of unsolvable problems and crime and confusion and hunger and . . .

HARPER: But it still seems that way. More now than before. They say the ozone layer is . . .

JOE: Harper . . .

HARPER: And today out the window on Atlantic Avenue there was a schizophrenic traffic cop who was making these . . .

JOE: Stop it! I'm trying to make a point.

HARPER: So am I.

JOE: You aren't even making sense, you . . .

HARPER: My point is the world seems just as . . .

JOE: It only seems that way to you because you never go out in the world, Harper, and you have emotional problems.

HARPER: I do so get out in the world.

JOE: You don't. You stay in all day, fretting about imaginary . . .

HARPER: I get out. I do. You don't know what I do.

JOE: You don't stay in all day.

HARPER: No.

JOE: Well. . . . Yes you do.

HARPER: That's what you think.

JOE: Where do you go?

HARPER: Where *you* go? When you walk. (*Pause, then angrily*) And I DO NOT have emotional problems.

JOE: I'm sorry.

HARPER: And if I do have emotional problems it's from living with you. Or . . .

JOE: I'm sorry buddy, I didn't mean to . . .

HARPER: Or if you do think I do then you should never have married me. You have all these secrets and lies.

JOE: I want to be married to you, Harper.

HARPER: You shouldn't. You never should.

(*Pause*)

Hey buddy. Hey buddy.

JOE: Buddy kiss . . .

(*They kiss.*)

HARPER: I heard on the radio how to give a blowjob.

JOE: What?

HARPER: You want to try?

JOE: You really shouldn't listen to stuff like that.

HARPER: Mormons can give blowjobs.

JOE: *Harper.*

HARPER (*Imitating his tone*): *Joe.*

It was a little Jewish lady with a German accent.

This is a good time. For me to make a baby.

(*Little pause. Joe turns away.*)

HARPER: Then they went on to a program about holes in the ozone layer. Over Antarctica. Skin burns, birds go blind, icebergs melt. The world's coming to an end.

Scene 6

First week of November. In the men's room of the offices of the Brooklyn Federal Court of Appeals; Louis is crying over the sink; Joe enters.

JOE: Oh, um. . . . Morning.

LOUIS: Good morning, counselor.

JOE (*He watches Louis cry*): Sorry, I . . . I don't know your name.

LOUIS: Don't bother. Word processor. The lowest of the low.

JOE (*Holding out hand*): Joe Pitt. I'm with Justice
   Wilson . . .

LOUIS: Oh, I know that. Counselor Pitt. Chief
   Clerk.

JOE: Were you . . . are you OK?

LOUIS: Oh, yeah. Thanks. What a nice man.

JOE: Not so nice.

LOUIS: What?

JOE: Not so nice. Nothing. You sure you're . . .

LOUIS: Life sucks shit. Life . . . just sucks shit.

JOE: What's wrong?

LOUIS: Run in my nylons.

JOE: Sorry . . . ?

LOUIS: Forget it. Look, thanks for asking.

JOE: Well . . .

LOUIS: I mean it really is nice of you.

(*He starts crying again*)

   Sorry, sorry, sick friend . . .

JOE: Oh, I'm sorry.

LOUIS: Yeah, yeah, well, that's sweet.
   Three of your colleagues have preceded
   you to this baleful sight and you're the first
   one to ask. The others just opened the door,
   saw me, and fled. I hope they had to pee
   real bad.

JOE (*Handing him a wad of toilet paper*): They just
   didn't want to intrude.

LOUIS: Hah. Reaganite heartless macho asshole
   lawyers.

JOE: Oh, that's unfair.

LOUIS: What is? Heartless? Macho? Reaganite?
   Lawyer?

JOE: I voted for Reagan.

LOUIS: You did?

JOE: Twice.

LOUIS: Twice? Well, oh boy. A Gay Republican.

JOE: Excuse me?

LOUIS: Nothing.

JOE: I'm not . . .
   Forget it.

LOUIS: Republican? Not Republican? Or . . .

JOE: What?

LOUIS: What?

JOE: Not gay. I'm not gay.

LOUIS: Oh. Sorry.

(*Blows his nose loudly*) It's just . . .

JOE: Yes?

LOUIS: Well, sometimes you can tell from the
   way a person sounds that . . . I mean you
   sound like a . . .

JOE: No I don't. Like what?

LOUIS: Like a Republican.

(*Little pause. Joe knows he's being teased; Louis knows
he knows. Joe decides to be a little brave.*)

JOE (*Making sure no one else is around*): Do I?
   Sound like a . . . ?

LOUIS: What? Like a . . .? Republican, or . . . ?
   Do *I*?

JOE: Do you what?

LOUIS: Sound like a . . . ?

JOE: Like a . . . ?
   I'm . . . confused.

LOUIS: Yes.
   My name is Louis. But all my friends
   call me Louise. I work in Word Processing.
   Thanks for the toilet paper.

(*Louis offers Joe his hand, Joe reaches, Louis feints and
pecks Joe on the cheek, then exits.*)

Scene 7

*A week later. Mutual dream scene. Prior is at a fan-
tastic makeup table, having a dream, applying the face.
Harper is having a pill-induced hallucination. She has
these from time to time. For some reason, Prior has
appeared in this one. Or Harper has appeared in
Prior's dream. It is bewildering.*

PRIOR (*Alone, putting on makeup, then examining the
   results in the mirror; to the audience*): "I'm ready
   for my closeup, Mr. DeMille."
   One wants to move through life with elegance and grace, blossoming infrequently
   but with exquisite taste, and perfect timing,
   like a rare bloom, a zebra orchid. . . . One
   wants. . . . But one so seldom gets what one
   wants, does one? No. One does not. One
   gets fucked. Over. One . . . dies at thirty,
   robbed of . . . decades of majesty.
   Fuck this shit. Fuck this shit.

(*He almost crumbles; he pulls himself together; he studies his handiwork in the mirror*)

I look like a corpse. A corpsette. Oh my queen; you know you've hit rock-bottom when even drag is a drag.

(*Harper appears.*)

HARPER: Are you. . . . Who are you?

PRIOR: Who are you?

HARPER: What are you doing in my hallucination?

PRIOR: I'm not in your hallucination. You're in my dream.

HARPER: You're wearing makeup.

PRIOR: So are you.

HARPER: But you're a man.

PRIOR (*Feigning dismay, shock, he mimes slashing his throat with his lipstick and dies, fabulously tragic. Then*): The hands and feet give it away.

HARPER: There must be some mistake here. I don't recognize you. You're not. . . . Are you my . . . some sort of imaginary friend?

PRIOR: No. Aren't you too old to have imaginary friends?

HARPER: I have emotional problems. I took too many pills. Why are you wearing makeup?

PRIOR: I was in the process of applying the face, trying to make myself feel better—I swiped the new fall colors at the Clinique counter at Macy's. (*Showing her*)

HARPER: You stole these?

PRIOR: I was out of cash; it was an emotional emergency!

HARPER: Joe will be so angry. I promised him. No more pills.

PRIOR: These pills you keep alluding to?

HARPER: Valium. I take Valium. Lots of Valium.

PRIOR: And you're dancing as fast as you can.

HARPER: I'm not *addicted*. I don't believe in addiction, and I never . . . well, I *never* drink. And I *never* take drugs.

PRIOR: Well, smell *you*, Nancy Drew.

HARPER: Except Valium.

PRIOR: Except Valium; in wee fistfuls.

HARPER: It's terrible. Mormons are not supposed to be addicted to anything. I'm a Mormon.

PRIOR: I'm a homosexual.

HARPER: Oh! In my church we don't believe in homosexuals.

PRIOR: In my church we don't believe in Mormons.

HARPER: What church do . . . oh! (*She laughs*) I get it.

I don't understand this. If I didn't ever see you before and I don't think I did then I don't think you should be here, in this hallucination, because in my experience the mind, which is where hallucinations come from, shouldn't be able to make up anything that wasn't there to start with, that didn't enter it from experience, from the real world. Imagination can't create anything new, can it? It only recycles bits and pieces from the world and reassembles them into visions. . . . Am I making sense right now?

PRIOR: Given the circumstances, yes.

HARPER: So when we think we've escaped the unbearable ordinariness and, well, untruthfulness of our lives, it's really only the same old ordinariness and falseness rearranged into the appearance of novelty and truth. Nothing unknown is knowable. Don't you think it's depressing?

PRIOR: The limitations of the imagination?

HARPER: Yes.

PRIOR: It's something you learn after your second theme party: It's All Been Done Before.

HARPER: The world. Finite. Terribly, terribly. . . . Well . . .

This is the most depressing hallucination I've ever had.

PRIOR: Apologies. I do try to be amusing.

HARPER: Oh, well, don't apologize, you. . . . I can't expect someone who's really sick to entertain me.

PRIOR: How on earth did you know . . .

HARPER: Oh that happens. This is the very threshhold of revelation sometimes. You can see things . . . how sick you are. Do you see anything about me?

PRIOR: Yes.

HARPER: What?

PRIOR: You are amazingly unhappy.

HARPER: Oh big deal. You meet a Valium addict and you figure out she's unhappy. That doesn't count. Of course I. . . . Something else. Something surprising.

PRIOR: Something surprising.

HARPER: Yes.

PRIOR: Your husband's a homo.

(*Pause.*)

HARPER: Oh, ridiculous.

    (*Pause, then very quietly*)

    Really?

PRIOR (*Shrugs*): Threshhold of revelation.

HARPER: Well I don't like your revelations. I don't think you intuit well at all. Joe's a very normal man, he . . .

    Oh God. Oh God. He. . . . Do homos take, like, lots of long walks?

PRIOR: Yes. We do. In stretch pants with lavender coifs. I just looked at you, and there was . . .

HARPER: A sort of blue streak of recognition.

PRIOR: Yes.

HARPER: Like you knew me incredibly well.

PRIOR: Yes.

HARPER: Yes.

    I have to go now, get back, something just . . . fell apart.

    Oh God, I feel so sad . . .

PRIOR: I . . . I'm sorry. I usually say, "Fuck the truth," but mostly, the truth fucks you.

HARPER: I see something else about you . . .

PRIOR: Oh?

HARPER: Deep inside you, there's a part of you, the most inner part, entirely free of disease. I can see that.

PRIOR: Is that. . . . That isn't true.

HARPER: Threshhold of revelation.

Home . . .

(*She vanishes.*)

PRIOR: People come and go so quickly here . . .

(*To himself in the mirror*) I don't think there's any uninfected part of me. My heart is pumping polluted blood. I feel dirty.

(*He begins to wipe makeup off with his hands, smearing it around. A large gray feather falls from up above. Prior stops smearing the makeup and looks at the feather. He goes to it and picks it up.*)

A VOICE (*It is an incredibly beautiful voice*): Look up!

PRIOR (*Looking up, not seeing anyone*): Hello?

A VOICE: Look up!

PRIOR: Who is that?

A VOICE: Prepare the way!

PRIOR: I don't see any . . .

(*There is a dramatic change in lighting, from above.*)

A VOICE:
    Look up, look up,
    prepare the way
    the infinite descent
    A breath in air
    floating down
    Glory to . . .

(*Silence.*)

PRIOR: Hello? Is that it? Helloooo!
    What the fuck . . . ? (*He holds himself*)
    Poor me. Poor poor me. Why me? Why poor poor me? Oh I don't feel good right now. I really don't.

Scene 8

That night. Split scene: Harper and Joe at home; Prior and Louis in bed.

HARPER: Where were you?

JOE: Out.

HARPER: Where?

JOE: Just out. Thinking.

HARPER: It's late.

JOE: I had a lot to think about.

HARPER: I burned dinner.

JOE: Sorry.

HARPER: Not my dinner. My dinner was fine. Your dinner. I put it back in the oven and turned everything up as high as it could go and I watched till it burned black. It's still hot. Very hot. Want it?

JOE: You didn't have to do that.

HARPER: I know. It just seemed like the kind of thing a mentally deranged sex-starved pill-popping housewife would do.

JOE: Uh huh.

HARPER: So I did it. Who knows anymore what I have to do?

JOE: How many pills?

HARPER: A bunch. Don't change the subject.

JOE: I won't talk to you when you . . .

HARPER: No. No. Don't do that! I'm . . . I'm fine, pills are not the problem, not our problem, I WANT TO KNOW WHERE YOU'VE BEEN! I WANT TO KNOW WHAT'S GOING ON!

JOE: Going on with what? The job?

HARPER: Not the job.

JOE: I said I need more time.

HARPER: Not the job!

JOE: Mr. Cohn, I talked to him on the phone, he said I had to hurry . . .

HARPER: Not the . . .

JOE: But I can't get you to talk sensibly about anything so . . .

HARPER: SHUT UP!

JOE: Then what?

HARPER: Stick to the subject.

JOE: I don't know what that is. You have something you want to ask me? Ask me. Go.

HARPER: I . . . can't. I'm scared of you.

JOE: I'm tired, I'm going to bed.

HARPER: Tell me without making me ask. Please.

JOE: This is crazy, I'm not . . .

HARPER: When you come through the door at night your face is never exactly the way I remembered it. I get surprised by something . . . mean and hard about the way you look. Even the weight of you in the bed at night, the way you breathe in your sleep seems unfamiliar.

You terrify me.

JOE (Cold): I know who you are.

HARPER: Yes. I'm the enemy. That's easy. That doesn't change.

You think you're the only one who hates sex; I do; I hate it with you; I do. I dream that you batter away at me till all my joints come apart, like wax, and I fall into pieces. It's like a punishment. It was wrong of me to marry you. I knew you . . . (She stops herself) It's a sin, and it's killing us both.

JOE: I can always tell when you've taken pills because it makes you red-faced and sweaty and frankly that's very often why I don't want to . . .

HARPER: Because . . .

JOE: Well, you aren't pretty. Not like this.

HARPER: I have something to ask you.

JOE: Then ASK! ASK! What in hell are you . . .

HARPER: Are you a homo?

(Pause)

Are you? If you try to walk out right now I'll put your dinner back in the oven and turn it up so high the whole building will fill with smoke and everyone in it will asphyxiate. So help me God I will.

Now answer the question.

JOE: What if I . . .

(Small pause.)

HARPER: Then tell me, please. And we'll see.

JOE: No. I'm not.

I don't see what difference it makes.

LOUIS: Jews don't have any clear textual guide to the afterlife; even that it exists. I don't think much about it. I see it as a perpetual rainy Thursday afternoon in March. Dead leaves.

PRIOR: Eeeugh. Very Greco-Roman.

LOUIS: Well for us it's not the verdict that counts, it's the act of judgment. That's why I could never be a lawyer. In court all that matters is the verdict.

PRIOR: You could never be a lawyer because you are oversexed. You're too distracted.

LOUIS: Not distracted; *abstracted*. I'm trying to make a point:

PRIOR: Namely:

LOUIS: It's the judge in his or her chambers, weighing, books open, pondering the evidence, ranging freely over categories: good, evil, innocent, guilty; the judge in the chamber of circumspection, not the judge on the bench with the gavel. The shaping of the law, not its execution.

PRIOR: The point, dear, the point . . .

LOUIS: That it should be the questions and shape of a life, its total complexity gathered, arranged and considered, which matters in the end, not some stamp of salvation or damnation which disperses all the complexity in some unsatisfying little decision—the balancing of the scales . . .

PRIOR: I like this; very zen; it's . . . reassuringly incomprehensible and useless. We who are about to die thank you.

LOUIS: You are not about to die.

PRIOR: It's not going well, really . . . two new lesions. My leg hurts. There's protein in my urine, the doctor says, but who knows what the fuck that portends. Anyway it shouldn't be there, the protein. My butt is chapped from diarrhea and yesterday I shat blood.

LOUIS: I really hate this. You don't tell me . . .

PRIOR: You get too upset, I wind up comforting you. It's easier . . .

LOUIS: Oh thanks.

PRIOR: If it's bad I'll tell you.

LOUIS: Shitting blood sounds bad to me.

PRIOR: And I'm telling you.

LOUIS: And I'm handling it.

PRIOR: Tell me some more about justice.

LOUIS: I *am* handling it.

PRIOR: Well Louis you win Trooper of the Month.

(*Louis starts to cry.*)

PRIOR: I take it back. You aren't Trooper of the Month.

This isn't working . . .
Tell me some more about justice.

LOUIS: You are not about to die.

PRIOR: Justice . . .

LOUIS: . . . is an immensity, a confusing vastness. Justice is God.
Prior?

PRIOR: Hmmm?

LOUIS: You love me.

PRIOR: Yes.

LOUIS: What if I walked out on this?
Would you hate me forever?

(*Prior kisses Louis on the forehead.*)

PRIOR: Yes.

JOE: I think we ought to pray. Ask God for help. Ask him together . . .

HARPER: God won't talk to me. I have to make up people to talk to me.

JOE: You have to keep asking.

HARPER: I forgot the question.
Oh yeah. God, is my husband a . . .

JOE (*Scary*): Stop it. Stop it. I'm warning you. Does it make any difference? That I might be one thing deep within, no matter how wrong or ugly that thing is, so long as I have fought, with everything I have, to kill it. What do you want from me? What do you want from me, Harper? More than that? For God's sake, there's nothing left, I'm a shell. There's nothing left to kill.
As long as my behavior is what I know it has to be. Decent. Correct. That alone in the eyes of God.

HARPER: No, no, not that, that's Utah talk, Mormon talk, I hate it, Joe, tell me, say it . . .

JOE: All I will say is that I am a very good man who has worked very hard to become good and you want to destroy that. You want to destroy me, but I am not going to let you do that.

(*Pause.*)

HARPER: I'm going to have a baby.

JOE: Liar.

HARPER: You liar.

A baby born addicted to pills. A baby who does not dream but who hallucinates, who stares up at us with big mirror eyes and who does not know who we are.

(*Pause.*)

JOE: Are you really . . .

HARPER: No. Yes. No. Yes. Get away from me. Now we both have a secret.

PRIOR: One of my ancestors was a ship's captain who made money bringing whale oil to Europe and returning with immigrants—Irish mostly, packed in tight, so many dollars per head. The last ship he captained foundered off the coast of Nova Scotia in a winter tempest and sank to the bottom. He went down with the ship—la Grande Geste—but his crew took seventy women and kids in the ship's only longboat, this big, open rowboat, and when the weather got too rough, and they thought the boat was overcrowded, the crew started lifting people up and hurling them into the sea. Until they got the ballast right. They walked up and down the longboat, eyes to the waterline, and when the boat rode low in the water they'd grab the nearest passenger and throw them into the sea. The boat was leaky, see; seventy people; they arrived in Halifax with nine people on board.

LOUIS: Jesus.

PRIOR: I think about that story a lot now. People in a boat, waiting, terrified, while implacable, unsmiling men, irresistibly strong, seize . . . maybe the person next to you, maybe you, and with no warning at all, with time only for a quick intake of air you are pitched into freezing, turbulent water and salt and darkness to drown.

I like your cosmology, baby. While time is running out I find myself drawn to anything that's suspended, that lacks an ending—but it seems to me that it lets you off scot-free.

LOUIS: What do you mean?

PRIOR: No judgment, no guilt or responsibility.

LOUIS: For me.

PRIOR: For anyone. It was an editorial "you."

LOUIS: Please get better. Please. Please don't get any sicker.

Scene 9

Third week in November. Roy and Henry, his doctor, in Henry's office.

HENRY: Nobody knows what causes it. And nobody knows how to cure it. The best theory is that we blame a retrovirus, the Human Immunodeficiency Virus. Its presence is made known to us by the useless antibodies which appear in reaction to its entrance into the bloodstream through a cut, or an orifice. The antibodies are powerless to protect the body against it. Why, we don't know. The body's immune system ceases to function. Sometimes the body even attacks itself. At any rate it's left open to a whole horror house of infections from microbes which it usually defends against.

Like Kaposi's sarcomas. These lesions. Or your throat problem. Or the glands.

We think it may also be able to slip past the blood-brain barrier into the brain. Which is of course very bad news.

And it's fatal in we don't know what percent of people with suppressed immune responses.

(*Pause.*)

ROY: This is very interesting, Mr. Wizard, but why the fuck are you telling me this?

(*Pause.*)

HENRY: Well, I have just removed one of three lesions which biopsy results will probably tell us is a Kaposi's sarcoma lesion. And you have a pronounced swelling of glands in your neck, groin, and armpits—lymphadenopathy is another sign. And you have oral candidiasis and maybe a little more fungus under the fingernails of two digits on your right hand. So that's why . . .

ROY: This disease . . .

HENRY: Syndrome.

ROY: Whatever. It afflicts mostly homosexuals and drug addicts.

HENRY: Mostly. Hemophiliacs are also at risk.

ROY: Homosexuals and drug addicts. So why are you implying that I . . .

(*Pause*)

What are you implying, Henry?

HENRY: I don't . . .

ROY: I'm not a drug addict.

HENRY: Oh come on Roy.

ROY: What, what, come on Roy what? Do you think I'm a junkie, Henry, do you see tracks?

HENRY: This is absurd.

ROY: Say it.

HENRY: Say what?

ROY: Say, "Roy Cohn, you are a . . ."

HENRY: Roy.

ROY: "You are a. . . ." Go on. Not "Roy Cohn you are a drug fiend." "Roy Marcus Cohn, you are a . . ."

Go on, Henry, it starts with an "H."

HENRY: Oh I'm not going to . . .

ROY: *With an "H,"* Henry, and it isn't "Hemophiliac." Come on . . .

HENRY: What are you doing, Roy?

ROY: No, say it. I mean it. Say: "Roy Cohn, you are a homosexual."

(*Pause*)

And I will proceed, systematically, to destroy your reputation and your practice and your career in New York State, Henry. Which you know I can do.

(*Pause.*)

HENRY: Roy, you have been seeing me since 1958. Apart from the facelifts I have treated you for everything from syphilis . . .

ROY: From a whore in Dallas.

HENRY: From syphilis to venereal warts. In your rectum. Which you may have gotten from a whore in Dallas, but it wasn't a female whore.

(*Pause.*)

ROY: So say it.

HENRY: Roy Cohn, you are . . .

You have had sex with men, many many times, Roy, and one of them, or any number of them, has made you very sick. You have AIDS.

ROY: AIDS.

Your problem, Henry, is that you are hung up on words, on labels, that you believe they mean what they seem to mean. AIDS. Homosexual. Gay. Lesbian. You think these are names that tell you who someone sleeps with, but they don't tell you that.

HENRY: No?

ROY: No. Like all labels they tell you one thing and one thing only: where does an individual so identified fit in the food chain, in the pecking order? Not ideology, or sexual taste, but something much simpler: clout. Not who I fuck or who fucks me, but who will pick up the phone when I call, who owes me favors. This is what a label refers to. Now to someone who does not understand this, homosexual is what I am because I have sex with men. But really this is wrong. Homosexuals are not men who sleep with other men. Homosexuals are men who in fifteen years of trying cannot get a pissant antidiscrimination bill through City Council. Homosexuals are men who know nobody and who nobody knows. Who have zero clout. Does this sound like me, Henry?

HENRY: No.

ROY: No. I have clout. A lot. I can pick up this phone, punch fifteen numbers, and you know who will be on the other end in under five minutes, Henry?

HENRY: The President.

ROY: Even better, Henry. His wife.

HENRY: I'm impressed.

ROY: I don't want you to be impressed. I want you to understand. This is not sophistry. And this is not hypocrisy. This is reality. I have sex with men. But unlike nearly every other man of whom this is true, I bring the guy I'm screwing to the White House and President Reagan smiles at us and shakes his hand. Because *what* I am is defined entirely by *who* I am. Roy Cohn is not a homosexual. Roy Cohn is a heterosexual man, Henry, who fucks around with guys.

HENRY: OK, Roy.

ROY: And what is my diagnosis, Henry?

HENRY: You have AIDS, Roy.

ROY: No, Henry, no. AIDS is what homosexuals have. I have liver cancer.

(*Pause.*)

HENRY: Well, whatever the fuck you have, Roy, it's very serious, and I haven't got a damn thing for you. The NIH in Bethesda has a new drug called AZT with a two-year waiting list that not even I can get you onto. So get on the phone, Roy, and dial the fifteen numbers, and tell the First Lady you need in on an experimental treatment for liver cancer, because you can call it any damn thing you want, Roy, but what it boils down to is very bad news.

ACT TWO

In Vitro
December 1985–January 1986

Scene 1

Night, the third week in December. Prior alone on the floor of his bedroom; he is much worse.

PRIOR: Louis, Louis, please wake up, oh God.

(*Louis runs in.*)

PRIOR: I think something horrible is wrong with me I can't breathe . . .

LOUIS (*Starting to exit*): I'm calling the ambulance.

PRIOR: No, wait, I . . .

LOUIS: *Wait?* Are you fucking crazy? Oh God you're on fire, your head is on fire.

PRIOR: It hurts, it hurts . . .

LOUIS: I'm calling the ambulance.

PRIOR: I don't want to go to the hospital, I don't want to go to the hospital please let me lie here, just . . .

LOUIS: No, no, God, Prior, stand up . . .

PRIOR: DON'T TOUCH MY LEG!

LOUIS: We have to . . . oh God this is so crazy.

PRIOR: I'll be OK if I just lie here Lou, really, if I can only sleep a little . . .

(*Louis exits.*)

PRIOR: Louis?
  NO! NO! Don't call, you'll send me there and I won't come back, please, please Louis I'm begging, baby, please . . .
  (Screams) LOUIS!!

LOUIS (*From off, hysterical*): WILL YOU SHUT THE FUCK UP!

PRIOR (*Trying to stand*): Aaaah. I have . . . to go to the bathroom. Wait. Wait, just . . . oh. Oh God. (*He shits himself*)

LOUIS (*Entering*): Prior? They'll be here in . . . Oh my God.

PRIOR: I'm sorry, I'm sorry.

LOUIS: What did . . . ? What?

PRIOR: I had an accident.

(*Louis goes to him.*)

LOUIS: This is blood.

PRIOR: Maybe you shouldn't touch it . . . me. . . . I . . . (*He faints*)

LOUIS (*Quietly*): Oh help. Oh help. Oh God oh God oh God help me I can't I can't I can't.

Scene 2

Same night. Harper is sitting at home, all alone, with no lights on. We can barely see her. Joe enters, but he doesn't turn on the lights.

JOE: Why are you sitting in the dark? Turn on the light.

HARPER: *No.* I heard the sounds in the bedroom again. I know someone was in there.

JOE: No one was.

HARPER: Maybe actually in the bed, under the covers with a knife.

Oh, boy. Joe. I, um, I'm thinking of going away. By which I mean: I think I'm going off again. You . . . you know what I mean?

JOE: Please don't. Stay. We can fix it. I pray for that. This is my fault, but I can correct it. You have to try too . . .

(*He turns on the light. She turns it off again.*)

HARPER: When you pray, what do you pray for?

JOE: I pray for God to crush me, break me up into little pieces and start all over again.

HARPER: Oh. Please. Don't pray for that.

JOE: I had a book of Bible stories when I was a kid. There was a picture I'd look at twenty times every day: Jacob wrestles with the angel. I don't really remember the story, or why the wrestling—just the picture. Jacob is young and very strong. The angel is . . . a beautiful man, with golden hair and wings, of course. I still dream about it. Many nights. I'm. . . . It's me. In that struggle. Fierce, and unfair. The angel is not human, and it holds nothing back, so how could anyone human win, what kind of a fight is that? It's not just. Losing means your soul thrown down in the dust, your heart torn out from God's. But you can't not lose.

HARPER: In the whole entire world, you are the only person, the only person I love or have ever loved. And I love you terribly. Terribly. That's what's so awfully, irreducibly real. I can make up anything but I can't dream that away.

JOE: Are you . . . are you really going to have a baby?

HARPER: It's my time, and there's no blood. I don't really know. I suppose it wouldn't be a great thing. Maybe I'm just not bleeding because I take too many pills. Maybe I'll give birth to a pill. That would give a new meaning to pill-popping, huh?

I think you should go to Washington. Alone. Change, like you said.

JOE: I'm not going to leave you, Harper.

HARPER: Well maybe not. But I'm going to leave you.

Scene 3

One AM, the next morning. Louis and a nurse, Emily, are sitting in Prior's room in the hospital.

EMILY: He'll be all right now.

LOUIS: No he won't.

EMILY: No. I guess not. I gave him something that makes him sleep.

LOUIS: Deep asleep?

EMILY: Orbiting the moons of Jupiter.

LOUIS: A good place to be.

EMILY: Anyplace better than here. You his . . . uh?

LOUIS: Yes. I'm his uh.

EMILY: This must be hell for you.

LOUIS: It is. Hell. The After Life. Which is not at all like a rainy afternoon in March, by the way, Prior. A lot more vivid than I'd expected. Dead leaves, but the crunchy kind. Sharp, dry air. The kind of long, luxurious dying feeling that breaks your heart.

EMILY: Yeah, well we all get to break our hearts on this one.

He seems like a nice guy. Cute.

LOUIS: Not like this.

Yes, he is. Was. Whatever.

EMILY: Weird name. Prior Walter. Like, "The Walter before this one."

LOUIS: Lots of Walters before this one. Prior is an old old family name in an old old family. The Walters go back to the Mayflower and beyond. Back to the Norman Conquest. He says there's a Prior Walter stitched into the Bayeux tapestry.

EMILY: Is that impressive?

LOUIS: Well, it's old. Very old. Which in some circles equals impressive.

EMILY: Not in my circle. What's the name of the tapestry?

LOUIS: The Bayeux tapestry. Embroidered by La Reine Mathilde.

EMILY: I'll tell my mother. She embroiders. Drives me nuts.

LOUIS: Manual therapy for anxious hands.

EMILY: Maybe you should try it.

LOUIS: Mathilde stitched while William the Conqueror was off to war. She was capable of . . . more than loyalty. Devotion.

She waited for him, she stitched for years. And if he had come back broken and defeated from war, she would have loved him even more. And if he had returned mutilated, ugly, full of infection and horror, she would still have loved him; fed by pity, by a sharing of pain, she would love him even more, and even more, and she would never, never have prayed to God, please let him die if he can't return to me whole and healthy and able to live a normal life. . . . If he had died, she would have buried her heart with him.

So what the fuck is the matter with me?

(*Little pause*)

Will he sleep through the night?

EMILY: At least.

LOUIS: I'm going.

EMILY: It's one AM. Where do you have to go at . . .

LOUIS: I know what time it is. A walk. Night air, good for the. . . . The park.

EMILY: Be careful.

LOUIS: Yeah. Danger.

Tell him, if he wakes up and you're still on, tell him goodbye, tell him I had to go.

Scene 4

An hour later. Split scene: Joe and Roy in a fancy (straight) bar; Louis and a Man in the Rambles in Central Park. Joe and Roy are sitting at the bar; the place is brightly lit. Joe has a plate of food in front of him but he isn't eating. Roy occasionally reaches over the table and forks small bites off Joe's plate. Roy is drinking heavily, Joe not at all. Louis and the Man are eyeing each other, each alternating interest and indifference.

JOE: The pills were something she started when she miscarried or . . . no, she took some before that. She had a really bad time at home, when she was a kid, her home was really bad. I think a lot of drinking and physical stuff. She doesn't talk about that, instead she talks about . . . the sky falling down, people with knives hiding under sofas. Monsters. Mormons. Everyone thinks Mormons don't come from homes like that, we aren't supposed to behave that way, but we do. It's not lying, or being two-faced. Everyone tries very hard to live up to God's strictures, which are very . . . um . . .

ROY: Strict.

JOE: I shouldn't be bothering you with this.

ROY: No, please. Heart to heart. Want another. . . . What is that, seltzer?

JOE: The failure to measure up hits people very hard. From such a strong desire to be good they feel very far from goodness when they fail.

What scares me is that maybe what I really love in her is the part of her that's farthest from the light, from God's love; maybe I was drawn to that in the first place. And I'm keeping it alive because I need it.

ROY: Why would you need it?

JOE: There are things. . . . I don't know how well we know ourselves. I mean, what if? I know I married her because she . . . because I loved it that she was always wrong, always doing something wrong, like one step out of step. In Salt Lake City that stands out. I never stood out, on the outside, but inside, it was hard for me. To pass.

ROY: Pass?

JOE: Yeah.

ROY: Pass as what?

JOE: Oh. Well. . . . As someone cheerful and strong. Those who love God with an open heart unclouded by secrets and struggles are cheerful; God's easy simple love for them shows in how strong and happy they are. The saints.

ROY: But you had secrets? Secret struggles . . .

JOE: I wanted to be one of the elect, one of the Blessed. You feel you ought to be, that the blemishes are yours by choice, which of course they aren't. Harper's sorrow, that really deep sorrow, she didn't choose that. But it's there.

ROY: You didn't put it there.

JOE: No.

ROY: You sound like you think you did.

JOE: I am responsible for her.

ROY: Because she's your wife.

JOE: That. And I do love her.

ROY: Whatever. She's your wife. And so there are obligations. To her. But also to yourself.

JOE: She'd fall apart in Washington.

ROY: Then let her stay here.

JOE: She'll fall apart if I leave her.

ROY: Then bring her to Washington.

JOE: I just can't, Roy. She needs me.

ROY: Listen, Joe. I'm the best divorce lawyer in the business.

(*Little pause.*)

JOE: Can't Washington wait?

ROY: You do what you need to do, Joe. What *you* need. *You.* Let her life go where it wants to go. You'll both be better for that. *Somebody* should get what they want.

MAN: What do you want?

LOUIS: I want you to fuck me, hurt me, make be bleed.

MAN: I want to.

LOUIS: Yeah?

MAN: I want to hurt you.

LOUIS: Fuck me.

MAN: Yeah?

LOUIS: Hard.

MAN: Yeah? You been a bad boy?

(*Pause. Louis laughs, softly.*)

LOUIS: Very bad. Very bad.

MAN: You need to be punished, boy?

LOUIS: Yes. I do.

MAN: Yes what?

(*Little pause.*)

LOUIS: Um, I . . .

MAN: Yes *what,* boy?

LOUIS: Oh. Yes sir.

MAN: I want you to take me to your place, boy.

LOUIS: No, I can't do that.

MAN: No *what?*

LOUIS: No sir, I can't, I . . .
  I don't live alone, sir.

MAN: Your lover know you're out with a man tonight, boy?

LOUIS: No sir, he . . .
  My lover doesn't know.

MAN: Your lover know you . . .

LOUIS: Let's change the subject, OK? Can we go to your place?

MAN: I live with my parents.

LOUIS: Oh.

ROY: Everyone who makes it in this world makes it because somebody older and more powerful takes an interest. The most precious asset in life, I think, is the ability to be a good son. You have that, Joe. Somebody who can be a good son to a father who pushes them farther than they would otherwise go. I've had many fathers, I owe my life to them, powerful, powerful men. Walter Winchell, Edgar Hoover. Joe McCarthy most of all. He valued me because I am a good lawyer, but he loved me because I was and am a good son. He was a very difficult man, very guarded and cagey; I brought out something tender in him. He would have died for me. And me for him. Does this embarrass you?

JOE: I had a hard time with my father.

ROY: Well sometimes that's the way. Then you have to find other fathers, substitutes, I don't know. The father-son relationship is central to life. Women are for birth, beginning, but the father is continuance. The son offers the father his life as a vessel for carrying forth his father's dream. Your father's living?

JOE: Um, dead.

ROY: He was . . . what? A difficult man?

JOE: He was in the military. He could be very unfair. And cold.

ROY: But he loved you.

JOE: I don't know.

ROY: No, no, Joe, he did, I know this. Sometimes a father's love has to be very, very hard, unfair even, cold to make his son grow strong in a world like this. This isn't a good world.

MAN: Here, then.

LOUIS: I. . . . Do you have a rubber?

MAN: I don't use rubbers.

LOUIS: You should. (*He takes one from his coat pocket*) Here.

MAN: I don't use them.

LOUIS: Forget it, then. (*He starts to leave*)

MAN: No, wait.
   Put it on me. Boy.

LOUIS: Forget it, I have to get back. Home. I must be going crazy.

MAN: Oh come on please he won't find out.

LOUIS: It's cold. Too cold.

MAN: It's never too cold, let me warm you up. Please?

(*They begin to fuck.*)

MAN: Relax.

LOUIS (*A small laugh*): Not a chance.

MAN: It . . .

LOUIS: What?

MAN: I think it broke. The rubber. You want me to keep going? (*Little pause*) Pull out? Should I . . .

LOUIS: Keep going.
   Infect me.
   I don't care. I don't care.

(*Pause. The Man pulls out.*)

MAN: I . . . um, look, I'm sorry, but I think I want to go.

LOUIS: Yeah.
   Give my best to mom and dad.

(*The Man slaps him.*)

LOUIS: Ow!

(*They stare at each other.*)

LOUIS: It was a joke.

(*The Man leaves.*)

ROY: How long have we known each other?

JOE: Since 1980.

ROY: Right. A long time. I feel close to you, Joe. Do I advise you well?

JOE: You've been an incredible friend, Roy, I . . .

ROY: I want to be family. Familia, as my Italian friends call it. La Familia. A lovely word. It's important for me to help you, like I was helped.

JOE: I owe practically everything to you, Roy.

ROY: I'm dying, Joe. Cancer.

JOE: Oh my God.

ROY: Please. Let me finish.
   Few people know this and I'm telling you this only because. . . . I'm not afraid of death. What can death bring that I haven't faced? I've lived; life is the worst. (*Gently mocking himself*) Listen to me, I'm a philosopher.
   Joe. You must do this. You must must must. Love; that's a trap. Responsibility; that's a trap too. Like a father to a son I tell you this: Life is full of horror; nobody escapes, nobody; save yourself. Whatever pulls on you, whatever needs from you, threatens you. Don't be afraid; people are so afraid; don't be afraid to live in the raw wind, naked, alone. . . . Learn at least this: What you are capable of. Let nothing stand in your way.

Scene 5

Three days later. Prior and Belize in Prior's hospital room. Prior is very sick but improving. Belize has just arrived.

PRIOR: Miss Thing.

BELIZE: Ma cherie bichette.

PRIOR: Stella.

BELIZE: Stella for star. Let me see. (*Scrutinizing Prior*) You look like shit, why yes indeed you do, comme la merde!

PRIOR: Merci.

BELIZE (*Taking little plastic bottles from his bag, handing them to Prior*): Not to despair, Belle Reeve. Lookie! Magic goop!

PRIOR (*Opening a bottle, sniffing*): Pooh! What kinda crap is that?

BELIZE: Beats me. Let's rub it on your poor blistered body and see what it does.

PRIOR: This is not Western medicine, these bottles . . .

BELIZE: Voodoo cream. From the botanica 'round the block.

PRIOR: And you a registered nurse.

BELIZE (*Sniffing it*): Beeswax and cheap perfume. Cut with Jergen's Lotion. Full of good vibes and love from some little black Cubana witch in Miami.

PRIOR: Get that trash away from me, I am immune-suppressed.

BELIZE: I *am* a health professional. I *know* what I'm doing.

PRIOR: It stinks. Any word from Louis?

(*Pause. Belize starts giving Prior a gentle massage.*)

PRIOR: Gone.

BELIZE: He'll be back. I know the type. Likes to keep a girl on edge.

PRIOR: It's been . . .

(*Pause.*)

BELIZE (*Trying to jog his memory*): How long?

PRIOR: I don't remember.

BELIZE: How long have you been here?

PRIOR (*Getting suddenly upset*): I don't remember, I don't give a fuck. I want Louis. I want my fucking boyfriend, where the fuck is he? I'm dying, I'm dying, where's Louis?

BELIZE: Shhhh, shhh . . .

PRIOR: This is a very strange drug, this drug. Emotional lability, for starters.

BELIZE: Save a tab or two for me.

PRIOR: Oh no, not this drug, ce n'est pas pour la joyeux noël et la bonne année, this drug she is serious poisonous chemistry, ma pauvre bichette.

And not just disorienting. I hear things. Voices.

BELIZE: Voices.

PRIOR: A voice.

BELIZE: Saying what?

(*Pause.*)

PRIOR: I'm not supposed to tell.

BELIZE: You better tell the doctor. Or I will.

PRIOR: No no don't. Please. I want the voice; it's wonderful. It's all that's keeping me alive. I don't want to talk to some intern about it.
You know what happens? When I hear it, I get hard.

BELIZE: Oh my.

PRIOR: Comme ça. (*He uses his arm to demonstrate*) And you know I am slow to rise.

BELIZE: My jaw aches at the memory.

PRIOR: And would you deny me this little solace—betray my concupiscence to Florence Nightingale's storm troopers?

BELIZE: Perish the thought, ma bébé.

PRIOR: They'd change the drug just to spoil the fun.

BELIZE: You and your boner can depend on me.

PRIOR: Je t'adore, ma belle nègre.

BELIZE: All this girl-talk shit is politically incorrect, you know. We should have dropped it back when we gave up drag.

PRIOR: I'm sick, I get to be politically incorrect if it makes me feel better. You sound like Lou.

(*Little pause*)

Well, at least I have the satisfaction of knowing he's in anguish somewhere. I loved his anguish. Watching him stick his head up his asshole and eat his guts out over some relatively minor moral conundrum—it was the best show in town. But Mother warned me: if they get overwhelmed by the little things . . .

BELIZE: They'll be belly-up bustville when something big comes along.

PRIOR: Mother warned me.

BELIZE: And they do come along.

PRIOR: But I didn't listen.

BELIZE: No. (*Doing Hepburn*) Men are beasts.

PRIOR (*Also Hepburn*): The absolute lowest.

BELIZE: I have to go. If I want to spend my whole lonely life looking after white people I can get underpaid to do it.

PRIOR: You're just a Christian martyr.

BELIZE: Whatever happens, baby, I will be here for you.

PRIOR: Je t'aime.

BELIZE: Je t'aime. Don't go crazy on me, girl-friend, I already got enough crazy queens for one lifetime. For two. I can't be bothering with dementia.

PRIOR: I promise.

BELIZE (*Touching him; softly*): Ouch.

PRIOR: Ouch. Indeed.

BELIZE: Why'd they have to pick on you?
     And eat more, girlfriend, you really do look like shit.

(*Belize leaves.*)

PRIOR (*After waiting a beat*): He's gone.
     Are you still . . .

VOICE: I can't stay. I will return.

PRIOR: Are you one of those "Follow me to the other side" voices?

VOICE: No. I am no nightbird. I am a messenger . . .

PRIOR: You have a beautiful voice, it sounds . . . like a viola, like a perfectly tuned, tight string, balanced, the truth. . . . Stay with me.

VOICE: Not now. Soon I will return, I will reveal myself to you; I am glorious, glorious; my heart, my countenance and my message. You must prepare.

PRIOR: For what? I don't want to . . .

VOICE: No death, no:
     A marvelous work and a wonder we undertake, an edifice awry we sink plumb and straighten, a great Lie we abolish, a great error correct, with the rule, sword and broom of Truth!

PRIOR: What are you talking about, I . . .

VOICE:
     I am on my way; when I am manifest, our
        Work begins:
     Prepare for the parting of the air,
     The breath, the ascent,
     Glory to . . .

Scene 6

The second week of January. Martin, Roy and Joe in a fancy Manhattan restaurant.

MARTIN: It's a revolution in Washington, Joe. We have a new agenda and finally a real leader. They got back the Senate but we have the courts. By the nineties the Supreme Court will be block-solid Republican appointees, and the Federal bench—Republican judges like land mines, everywhere, everywhere they turn. Affirmative action? Take it to court. Boom! Land mine. And we'll get our way on just about everything: abortion, defense, Central America, family values, a live investment climate. We have the White House locked till the year 2000. And beyond. A permanent fix on the Oval Office? It's possible. By '92 we'll get the Senate back, and in ten years the South is going to give us the House. It's really the end of Liberalism. The end of New Deal Socialism. The end of ipso facto secular humanism. The dawning of a genuinely American political personality. Modeled on Ronald Wilson Reagan.

JOE: It sounds great, Mr. Heller.

MARTIN: Martin. And Justice is the hub. Especially since Ed Meese took over. He doesn't specialize in Fine Points of the Law. He's a flatfoot, a cop. He reminds me of Teddy Roosevelt.

JOE: I can't wait to meet him.

MARTIN: Too bad, Joe, he's been dead for sixty years!

(*There is a little awkwardness. Joe doesn't respond.*)

MARTIN: Teddy Roosevelt. You said you wanted to. . . . Little joke. It reminds me of the story about the . . .

ROY (*Smiling, but nasty*): Aw shut the fuck up Martin.
     (*To Joe*) You see that? Mr. Heller here is one of the mighty, Joseph, in D.C. he sitteth on the right hand of the man who sitteth on the right hand of The Man. And yet I can say "shut the fuck up" and he will take no offense. Loyalty. He . . .
     Martin?

MARTIN: Yes, Roy?

ROY: Rub my back.

MARTIN: Roy . . .

ROY: No no really, a sore spot, I get them all the time now, these. . . . Rub it for me darling, would you do that for me?

(*Martin rubs Roy's back. They both look at Joe.*)

ROY (*To Joe*): How do you think a handful of Bolsheviks turned St. Petersburg into Leningrad in one afternoon? *Comrades.* Who do for each other. Marx and Engels. Lenin and Trotsky. Josef Stalin and Franklin Delano Roosevelt.

(*Martin laughs.*)

ROY: *Comrades,* right Martin?

MARTIN: This man, Joe, is a Saint of the Right.

JOE: I know, Mr. Heller, I . . .

ROY: And you see what I mean, Martin? He's special, right?

MARTIN: Don't embarrass him, Roy.

ROY: Gravity, decency, smarts! His strength is as the strength of ten because his heart is pure! *And* he's a Royboy, one hundred percent.

MARTIN: We're on the move, Joe. On the move.

ROY: Mr. Heller, I . . .

MARTIN (*Ending backrub*): We can't wait any longer for an answer.

(*Little pause.*)

JOE: Oh. Um, I . . .

ROY: Joe's a married man, Martin.

MARTIN: Aha.

ROY: With a wife. She doesn't care to go to D.C., and so Joe cannot go. And keeps us dangling. We've seen that kind of thing before, haven't we? These men and their wives.

MARTIN: Oh yes. Beware.

JOE: I really can't discuss this under . . .

MARTIN: Then *don't* discuss. Say yes, Joe.

ROY: Now.

MARTIN: Say yes I will.

ROY: Now.

        Now. I'll hold my breath till you do, I'm turning blue waiting. . . . *Now,* goddammit!

MARTIN: Roy, calm down, it's not . . .

ROY: Aw, fuck it. (*He takes a letter from his jacket pocket, hands it to Joe*)
        Read. Came today.

(*Joe reads the first paragraph, then looks up.*)

JOE: Roy. This is . . . Roy, this is terrible.

ROY: You're telling me.
        A letter from the New York State Bar Association, Martin.
        They're gonna try and disbar me.

MARTIN: Oh my.

JOE: Why?

ROY: Why, Martin?

MARTIN: Revenge.

ROY: The whole Establishment. Their little rules. Because I know no rules. Because I don't see the Law as a dead and arbitrary collection of antiquated dictums, thou shall, thou shalt not, because, because I know the Law's a pliable, breathing, sweating . . . *organ,* because, because . . .

MARTIN: Because he borrowed half a million from one of his clients.

ROY: Yeah, well, there's that.

MARTIN: *And* he forgot to *return* it.

JOE: Roy, that's. . . . You borrowed money from a client?

ROY: I'm deeply ashamed.

(*Little pause.*)

JOE (*Very sympathetic*): Roy, you know how much I admire you. Well I mean I know you have unorthodox ways, but I'm sure you only did what you thought at the time you needed to do. And I have faith that . . .

ROY: Not so damp, please. I'll deny it was a loan. She's got no paperwork. Can't prove a fucking thing.

(*Little pause. Martin studies the menu.*)

JOE (*Handing back the letter, more official in tone*): Roy I really appreciate your telling me this, and I'll do whatever I can to help.

ROY (*Holding up a hand, then, carefully*): I'll tell you what you can do.
        I'm about to be tried, Joe, by a jury that is not a jury of my peers. The disbarment committee: genteel gentleman Brahmin lawyers, country-club men. I offend them, to these men . . . I'm what, Martin, some sort of filthy little Jewish troll?

MARTIN: Oh well, I wouldn't go so far as . . .
ROY: Oh well I would.

Very fancy lawyers, these disbarment committee lawyers, fancy lawyers with fancy corporate clients and complicated cases. Antitrust suits. Deregulation. Environmental control. Complex cases like these need Justice Department cooperation like flowers need the sun. Wouldn't you say that's an accurate assessment, Martin?

MARTIN: I'm not here, Roy. I'm not hearing any of this.
ROY: No. Of course not.

Without the light of the sun, Joe, these cases, and the fancy lawyers who represent them, will wither and die.

A well-placed friend, someone in the Justice Department, say, can turn off the sun. Cast a deep shadow on my behalf. Make them shiver in the cold. If they overstep. They would fear that.

(*Pause.*)

JOE: Roy. I don't understand.
ROY: You do.

(*Pause.*)

JOE: You're not asking me to . . .
ROY: Sssshhhh. Careful.
JOE (*A beat, then*): Even if I said yes to the job, it would be illegal to interfere. With the hearings. It's unethical. No. I can't.
ROY: Un-ethical.

Would you excuse us, Martin?
MARTIN: Excuse you?
ROY: Take a walk, Martin. For real.

(*Martin leaves.*)

ROY: Un-ethical. Are you trying to embarrass me in front of my friend?
JOE: Well it is unethical, I can't . . .
ROY: Boy, you are really something. What the fuck do you think this is, Sunday School?
JOE: No, but Roy this is . . .
ROY: This is . . . this is gastric juices churning, this is enzymes and acids, this is intestinal is

what this is, bowel movement and blood-red meat—this stinks, this is *politics*, Joe, the game of being alive. And you think you're. . . . What? Above that? Above alive is what? Dead! In the clouds! You're on earth, goddammit! Plant a foot, stay a while.

I'm sick. They smell I'm weak. They want blood this time. I must have eyes in Justice. In Justice you will protect me.
JOE: Why can't Mr. Heller . . .
ROY: Grow up, Joe. The administration can't get involved.
JOE: But I'd be part of the administration. The same as him.
ROY: Not the same. Martin's Ed's man. And Ed's Reagan's man. So Martin's Reagan's man. And you're mine.

(*Little pause. He holds up the letter*)

This will never be. Understand me?

(*He tears the letter up*)

I'm gonna be a lawyer, Joe, I'm gonna be a lawyer, Joe, I'm gonna be a goddam motherfucking legally licensed member of the bar lawyer, just like my daddy was, till my last bitter day on earth, Joseph, until the day I die.

(*Martin returns.*)

ROY: Ah, Martin's back.
MARTIN: So are we agreed?
ROY: Joe?

(*Little pause.*)

JOE: I will think about it.
    (*To Roy*) I will.
ROY: Huh.
MARTIN: It's the fear of what comes after the doing that makes the doing hard to do.
ROY: Amen.
MARTIN: But you can almost always live with the consequences.

Scene 7

That afternoon. On the granite steps outside the Hall of Justice, Brooklyn. It is cold and sunny. A Sabrett wagon is selling hot dogs. Louis, in a shabby overcoat, is sitting on the steps contemplatively eating one. Joe enters with three hot dogs and a can of Coke.

JOE: Can I . . . ?

LOUIS: Oh sure. Sure. Crazy cold sun.

JOE (*Sitting*): Have to make the best of it. How's your friend?

LOUIS: My . . . ? Oh. He's worse. My friend is worse.

JOE: I'm sorry.

LOUIS: Yeah, well. Thanks for asking. It's nice. You're nice. I can't believe you voted for Reagan.

JOE: I hope he gets better.

LOUIS: Reagan?

JOE: Your friend.

LOUIS: He won't. Neither will Reagan.

JOE: Let's not talk politics, OK?

LOUIS (*Pointing to Joe's lunch*): You're eating *three* of those?

JOE: Well . . . I'm . . . hungry.

LOUIS: They're really terrible for you. Full of rat-poo and beetle legs and wood shavings 'n' shit.

JOE: Huh.

LOUIS: And . . . um . . . irridium, I think. Something toxic.

JOE: You're eating one.

LOUIS: Yeah, well, the shape, I can't help myself, plus I'm *trying* to commit suicide, what's your excuse?

JOE: I don't have an excuse. I just have Pepto-Bismol.

(*Joe takes a bottle of Pepto-Bismol and chugs it. Louis shudders audibly.*)

JOE: Yeah I know but then I wash it down with Coke.

(*He does this. Louis mimes barfing in Joe's lap. Joe pushes Louis's head away.*)

JOE: Are you *always* like this?

LOUIS: I've been worrying a lot about his kids.

JOE: Whose?

LOUIS: Reagan's. Maureen and Mike and little orphan Patti and Miss Ron Reagan Jr., the

you-should-pardon-the-expression heterosexual.

JOE: Ron Reagan Jr. is *not*. . . . You shouldn't just make these assumptions about people. How do you know? About him? What he is? You don't know.

LOUIS (*Doing Tallulah*): Well darling he never sucked *my* cock but . . .

JOE: Look, if you're going to get vulgar . . .

LOUIS: No no really I mean. . . . What's it like to be the child of the Zeitgeist? To have the American Animus as your dad? It's not really a *family*, the Reagans, I read *People,* there aren't any connections there, no love, they don't ever even speak to each other except through their agents. So what's it like to be Reagan's kid? Enquiring minds want to know.

JOE: You can't believe everything you . . .

LOUIS (*Looking away*): But . . . I think we all know what that's like. Nowadays. No connections. No responsibilities. All of us . . . falling through the cracks that separate what we owe to our selves and . . . and what we owe to love.

JOE: You just. . . . Whatever you feel like saying or doing, you don't care, you just . . . do it.

LOUIS: Do what?

JOE: It. Whatever. Whatever it is you want to do.

LOUIS: Are you trying to tell me something?

(*Little pause, sexual. They stare at each other. Joe looks away.*)

JOE: No, I'm just observing that you . . .

LOUIS: Impulsive.

JOE: Yes, I mean it must be scary, you . . .

LOUIS (*Shrugs*): Land of the free. Home of the brave. Call me irresponsible.

JOE: It's kind of terrifying.

LOUIS: Yeah, well, freedom is. Heartless, too.

JOE: Oh you're not heartless.

LOUIS: You don't know. Finish your weenie.

(*He pats Joe on the knee, starts to leave.*)

JOE: Um . . .

(*Louis turns, looks at him. Joe searches for something to say.*)

JOE: Yesterday was Sunday but I've been a little unfocused recently and I thought it was Monday. So I came here like I was going to work. And the whole place was empty. And at first I couldn't figure out why, and I had this moment of incredible . . . fear and also. . . . It just flashed through my mind: The whole Hall of Justice, it's empty, it's deserted, it's gone out of business. Forever. The people that make it run have up and abandoned it.

LOUIS (*Looking at the building*): Creepy.

JOE: Well yes but. I felt that I was going to scream. Not because it was creepy, but because the emptiness felt so *fast*.

And . . . well, good. A . . . happy scream.

I just wondered what a thing it would be . . . if overnight everything you owe anything to, justice, or love, had really gone away. Free.

It would be . . . heartless terror. Yes. Terrible, and . . .

Very great. To shed your skin, every old skin, one by one and then walk away, unencumbered, into the morning.

(*Little pause. He looks at the building*)

I can't go in there today.

LOUIS: Then don't.

JOE (*Not really hearing Louis*): I can't go in, I need . . .

(*He looks for what he needs. He takes a swig of Pepto-Bismol*)

I can't *be* this anymore. I need . . . a change, I should just . . .

LOUIS (*Not a come-on, necessarily; he doesn't want to be alone*): Want some company? For whatever?

(*Pause. Joe looks at Louis and looks away, afraid. Louis shrugs.*)

LOUIS: Sometimes, even if it scares you to death, you have to be willing to break the law. Know what I mean?

(*Another little pause.*)

JOE: Yes.

(*Another little pause.*)

LOUIS: I moved out. I moved out on my . . . I haven't been sleeping well.

JOE: Me neither.

(*Louis goes up to Joe, licks his napkin and dabs at Joe's mouth.*)

LOUIS: Antacid moustache.

(*Points to the building*) Maybe the court won't convene. Ever again. Maybe we are free. To do whatever.

Children of the new morning, criminal minds. Selfish and greedy and loveless and blind. Reagan's children.

You're scared. So am I. Everybody is in the land of the free. God help us all.

Scene 8

Late that night. Joe at a payphone phoning Hannah at home in Salt Lake City.

JOE: Mom?

HANNAH: Joe?

JOE: Hi.

HANNAH: You're calling from the street. It's . . . it must be four in the morning. What's happened?

JOE: Nothing, nothing, I . . .

HANNAH: It's Harper. Is Harper. . . . Joe? Joe?

JOE: Yeah, hi. No, Harper's fine. Well, no, she's . . . not fine. How are you, Mom?

HANNAH: What's happened?

JOE: I just wanted to talk to you. I, uh, wanted to try something out on you.

HANNAH: Joe, you haven't . . . have you been drinking, Joe?

JOE: Yes ma'am. I'm drunk.

HANNAH: That isn't like you.

JOE: No. I mean, who's to say?

HANNAH: Why are you out on the street at four AM? In that crazy city. It's dangerous.

JOE: Actually, Mom, I'm not on the street. I'm near the boathouse in the park.

HANNAH: What park?

JOE: Central Park.

HANNAH: CENTRAL PARK! Oh my Lord. What on earth are you doing in Central Park at this time of night? Are you . . .

Joe, I think you ought to go home right now. Call me from home.

(*Little pause*)

Joe?

JOE: I come here to watch, Mom. Sometimes. Just to watch.

HANNAH: Watch what? What's there to watch at four in the . . .

JOE: Mom, did Dad love me?

HANNAH: What?

JOE: Did he?

HANNAH: You ought to go home and call from there.

JOE: Answer.

HANNAH: Oh now really. This is maudlin. I don't like this conversation.

JOE: Yeah, well, it gets worse from here on.

(*Pause.*)

HANNAH: Joe?

JOE: Mom. Momma. I'm a homosexual, Momma.

Boy, did that come out awkward.

(*Pause*)

Hello? Hello?
I'm a homosexual.

(*Pause*)

Please, Momma. Say something.

HANNAH: You're old enough to understand that your father didn't love you without being ridiculous about it.

JOE: What?

HANNAH: You're ridiculous. You're being ridiculous.

JOE: I'm . . .
What?

HANNAH: You really ought to go home now to your wife. I need to go to bed. This phone call. . . . We will just forget this phone call.

JOE: Mom.

HANNAH: No more talk. Tonight. This . . . (*Suddenly very angry*) Drinking is a sin! A sin! I raised you better than that. (*She hangs up*)

Scene 9

The following morning, early. Split scene: Harper and Joe at home; Louis and Prior in Prior's hospital room. Joe and Louis have just entered. This should be fast and obviously furious; overlapping is fine; the proceedings may be a little confusing but not the final results.

HARPER: Oh God. Home. The moment of truth has arrived.

JOE: Harper.

LOUIS: I'm going to move out.

PRIOR: The fuck you are.

JOE: Harper. Please listen. I still love you very much. You're still my best buddy; I'm not going to leave you.

HARPER: No, I don't like the sound of this. I'm leaving.

LOUIS: I'm leaving.
I already have.

JOE: Please listen. Stay. This is really hard. We have to talk.

HARPER: We are talking. Aren't we? Now please shut up. OK?

PRIOR: Bastard. Sneaking off while I'm flat out here, that's low. If I could get up now I'd beat the holy shit out of you.

JOE: Did you take pills? How many?

HARPER: No pills. Bad for the . . . (*Pats stomach*)

JOE: You aren't pregnant. I called your gynecologist.

HARPER: I'm seeing a new gynecologist.

PRIOR: You have no right to do this.

LOUIS: Oh, that's ridiculous.

PRIOR: No right. It's criminal.

JOE: Forget about that. Just listen. You want the truth. This is the truth.

I knew this when I married you. I've known this I guess for as long as I've known anything, but . . . I don't know, I thought maybe that with enough effort and will I could change myself . . . but I can't . . .

PRIOR: Criminal.

LOUIS: There oughta be a law.

PRIOR: There is a law. You'll see.

JOE: I'm losing ground here, I go walking, you want to know where I walk, I . . . go to the park, or up and down 53rd Street, or places where. . . . And I keep swearing I won't go walking again, but I just can't.

LOUIS: I need some privacy.

PRIOR: That's new.

LOUIS: Everything's new, Prior.

JOE: I try to tighten my heart into a knot, a snarl, I try to learn to live dead, just numb, but then I see someone I want, and it's like a nail, like a hot spike right through my chest, and I know I'm losing.

PRIOR: Apartment too small for three? Louis and Prior comfy but not Louis and Prior and Prior's disease?

LOUIS: Something like that.

I won't be judged by you. This isn't a crime, just—the inevitable consequence of people who run out of—whose limitations . . .

PRIOR: Bang bang bang. The court will come to order.

LOUIS: I mean let's talk practicalities, schedules; I'll come over if you want, spend nights with you when I can, I can . . .

PRIOR: Has the jury reached a verdict?

LOUIS: I'm doing the best I can.

PRIOR: Pathetic. Who cares?

JOE: My whole life has conspired to bring me to this place, and I can't despise my whole life. I think I believed when I met you I could save you, you at least if not myself, but . . .

I don't have any sexual feelings for you, Harper. And I don't think I ever did.

(*Little pause.*)

HARPER: I think you should go.

JOE: Where?

HARPER: Washington. Doesn't matter.

JOE: What are you talking about?

HARPER: Without me.

Without me, Joe. Isn't that what you want to hear?

(*Little pause.*)

JOE: Yes.

LOUIS: You can love someone and fail them. You can love someone and not be able to . . .

PRIOR: You *can*, theoretically, yes. A person can, maybe an editorial "you" can love, Louis, but not *you*, specifically you, I don't know, I think you are excluded from that general category.

HARPER: You were going to save me, but the whole time you were spinning a lie. I just don't understand that.

PRIOR: A person could theoretically love and maybe many do but we both know now you can't.

LOUIS: I do.

PRIOR: You can't even say it.

LOUIS: I love you, Prior.

PRIOR: I repeat. Who cares?

HARPER: This is so scary, I want this to stop, to go back . . .

PRIOR: We have reached a verdict, your honor. This man's heart is deficient. He loves, but his love is worth nothing.

JOE: Harper . . .

HARPER: Mr. Lies, I want to get away from here. Far away. Right now. Before he starts talking again. Please, please . . .

JOE: As long as I've known you Harper you've been afraid of . . . of men hiding under the bed, men hiding under the sofa, men with knives.

PRIOR (*Shattered; almost pleading; trying to reach him*): I'm dying! You stupid fuck! Do you know what that is! Love! Do you know what love means? We lived together four-and-a-half years, you animal, you idiot.

LOUIS: I have to find some way to save myself.

JOE: Who are these men? I never understood it. Now I know.

HARPER: What?

JOE: It's me.

HARPER: It is?

PRIOR: GET OUT OF MY ROOM!

JOE: I'm the man with the knives.

HARPER: You are?

PRIOR: If I could get up now I'd kill you. I would. Go away. Go away or I'll scream.

HARPER: Oh God . . .

JOE: I'm sorry . . .

HARPER: It is you.

LOUIS: Please don't scream.

PRIOR: Go.

HARPER: I recognize you now.

LOUIS: Please . . .

JOE: Oh. Wait, I. . . . Oh!

(*He covers his mouth with his hand, gags, and removes his hand, red with blood*)

I'm bleeding.

(*Prior screams.*)

HARPER: Mr. Lies.

MR. LIES (*Appearing, dressed in antarctic explorer's apparel*): Right here.

HARPER: I want to go away. I can't see him anymore.

MR. LIES: Where?

HARPER: Anywhere. Far away.

MR. LIES: Absolutamento.

(*Harper and Mr. Lies vanish. Joe looks up, sees that she's gone.*)

PRIOR (*Closing his eyes*): When I open my eyes you'll be gone.

(*Louis leaves.*)

JOE: Harper?

PRIOR (*Opening his eyes*): Huh. It worked.

JOE (*Calling*): Harper?

PRIOR: I hurt all over. I wish I was dead.

Scene 10

The same day, sunset. Hannah and Sister Ella Chapter, a real-estate saleswoman, Hannah Pitt's closest friend, in front of Hannah's house in Salt Lake City.

SISTER ELLA CHAPTER: Look at that view! A view of heaven. Like the living city of heaven, isn't it, it just fairly glimmers in the sun.

HANNAH: Glimmers.

SISTER ELLA CHAPTER: Even the stone and brick it just glimmers and glitters like heaven in the sunshine. Such a nice view you get, perched up on a canyon rim. Some kind of beautiful place.

HANNAH: It's just Salt Lake, and you're selling the house *for* me, not *to* me.

SISTER ELLA CHAPTER: I like to work up an enthusiasm for my properties.

HANNAH: Just get me a good price.

SISTER ELLA CHAPTER: Well, the market's off.

HANNAH: At least fifty.

SISTER ELLA CHAPTER: Forty'd be more like it.

HANNAH: Fifty.

SISTER ELLA CHAPTER: Wish you'd wait a bit.

HANNAH: Well I can't.

SISTER ELLA CHAPTER: Wish you would. You're about the only friend I got.

HANNAH: Oh well now.

SISTER ELLA CHAPTER: Know why I decided to like you? I decided to like you 'cause you're the only unfriendly Mormon I ever met.

HANNAH: Your wig is crooked.

SISTER ELLA CHAPTER: Fix it.

(*Hannah straightens Sister Ella's wig.*)

SISTER ELLA CHAPTER: New York City. All they got there is tiny rooms.

I always thought: People ought to stay put. That's why I got my license to sell real estate. It's a way of saying: Have a house! Stay put! It's a way of saying traveling's no good. Plus I needed the cash. (*She takes a pack of cigarettes out of her purse, lights one, offers pack to Hannah*)

HANNAH: Not out here, anyone could come by. There's been days I've stood at this ledge and thought about stepping over.

It's a hard place, Salt Lake: baked dry. Abundant energy; not much intelligence. That's a combination that can wear a body out. No harm looking someplace else. I don't need much room.

My sister-in-law Libby thinks there's radon gas in the basement.

SISTER ELLA CHAPTER: Is there gas in the . . .

HANNAH: Of course not. Libby's a fool.

SISTER ELLA CHAPTER: 'Cause I'd have to include that in the description.

HANNAH: There's no gas, Ella. (*Little pause*) Give a puff. (*She takes a furtive drag of Ella's cigarette*) Put it away now.

SISTER ELLA CHAPTER: So I guess it's good-bye.

HANNAH: You'll be all right, Ella, I wasn't ever much of a friend.

SISTER ELLA CHAPTER: I'll say something but don't laugh, OK?

This is the home of saints, the godliest place on earth, they say, and I think they're right. That mean there's no evil here? No. Evil's everywhere. Sin's everywhere. But this . . . is the spring of sweet water in the desert, the desert flower. Every step a Believer takes away from here is a step fraught with peril. I fear for you, Hannah Pitt, because you are my friend. Stay put. This is the right home of saints.

HANNAH: Latter-day saints.

SISTER ELLA CHAPTER: Only kind left.

HANNAH: But still. Late in the day . . . for saints and everyone. That's all. That's all.

Fifty thousand dollars for the house, Sister Ella Chapter; don't undersell. It's an impressive view.

ACT THREE

Not-Yet-Conscious, Forward Dawning
January 1986

Scene 1

Late night, three days after the end of Act Two. The stage is completely dark. Prior is in bed in his apartment, having a nightmare. He wakes up, sits up and switches on a nightlight. He looks at his clock. Seated by the table near the bed is a man dressed in the clothing of a 13th-century British squire.

PRIOR (*Terrified*): Who are you?

PRIOR 1: My name is Prior Walter.

(*Pause.*)

PRIOR: My name is Prior Walter.

PRIOR 1: I know that.

PRIOR: Explain.

PRIOR 1: You're alive. I'm not. We have the same name. What do you want me to explain?

PRIOR: A ghost?

PRIOR 1: An ancestor.

PRIOR: Not *the* Prior Walter? The Bayeux tapestry Prior Walter?

PRIOR 1: His great-great grandson. The fifth of the name.

PRIOR: I'm the thirty-fourth, I think.

PRIOR 1: Actually the thirty-second.

PRIOR: Not according to Mother.

PRIOR 1: She's including the two bastards, then; I say leave them out. I say no room for bastards. The little things you swallow . . .

PRIOR: Pills.

PRIOR 1: Pills. For the pestilence. I too . . .

PRIOR: Pestilence. . . . You too what?

PRIOR 1: The pestilence in my time was much worse than now. Whole villages of empty houses. You could look outdoors and see Death walking in the morning, dew dampening the ragged hem of his black robe. Plain as I see you now.

PRIOR: You died of the plague.

PRIOR 1: The spotty monster. Like you, alone.

PRIOR: I'm not alone.

PRIOR 1: You have no wife, no children.

PRIOR: I'm gay.

PRIOR 1: So? Be gay, dance in your altogether for all I care, what's that to do with not having children?

PRIOR: Gay homosexual, not bonny, blithe and . . . never mind.

PRIOR 1: I had twelve. When I died.

(*The second ghost appears, this one dressed in the clothing of an elegant 17th-century Londoner.*)

PRIOR 1 (*Pointing to Prior 2*): And I was three years younger than him.

(*Prior sees the new ghost, screams.*)

PRIOR: Oh God another one.

PRIOR 2: Prior Walter. Prior to you by some seventeen others.

PRIOR 1: He's counting the bastards.

PRIOR: Are we having a convention?

PRIOR 2: We've been sent to declare her fabulous incipience. They love a well-paved entrance with lots of heralds, and . . .

PRIOR 1: The messenger come. Prepare the way. The infinite descent, a breath in air . . .

PRIOR 2: They chose us, I suspect, because of the mortal affinities. In a family as long-descended as the Walters there are bound to be a few carried off by plague.

PRIOR 1: The spotty monster.

PRIOR 2: Black Jack. Came from a water pump, half the city of London, can you imagine? His came from fleas. Yours, I understand, is the lamentable consequence of venery . . .

PRIOR 1: Fleas on rats, but who knew that?

PRIOR: Am I going to die?

PRIOR 2: We aren't allowed to discuss . . .

PRIOR 1: When you do, you don't get ancestors to help you through it. You may be surrounded by children but you die alone.

PRIOR: I'm afraid.

PRIOR 1: You should be. There aren't even torches, and the path's rocky, dark and steep.

PRIOR 2: Don't alarm him. There's good news before there's bad.

We two come to strew rose petal and palm leaf before the triumphal procession. Prophet. Seer. Revelator. It's a great honor for the family.

PRIOR 1: He hasn't got a family.

PRIOR 2: I meant for the Walters, for the family in the larger sense.

PRIOR (*Singing*):
All I want is a room somewhere,
Far away from the cold night air . . .

PRIOR 2 (*Putting a hand on Prior's forehead*): Calm, calm, this is no brain fever . . .

(*Prior calms down, but keeps his eyes closed. The lights begin to change. Distant Glorious Music.*)

PRIOR 1 (*Low chant*):
Adonai, Adonai,
Olam ha-yichud,
Zefirot, Zazahot,
Ha-adam, ha-gadol
Daughter of Light,
Daughter of Splendors,
Fluor! Phosphor!
Lumen! Candle!

PRIOR 2 (*Simultaneously*):
Even now,
From the mirror-bright halls of heaven,
Across the cold and lifeless infinity of space,
The Messenger comes
Trailing orbs of light,
Fabulous, incipient,
Oh Prophet,
To you . . .

PRIOR 1 and PRIOR 2:
Prepare, prepare,
The Infinite Descent,
A breath, a feather,
Glory to . . .

(*They vanish.*)

Scene 2

The next day. Split scene: Louis and Belize in a coffee shop. Prior is at the outpatient clinic at the hospital with Emily, the nurse; she has him on a pentamidine IV drip.

LOUIS: Why has democracy succeeded in America? Of course by succeeded I mean comparatively, not literally, not in the present, but what makes for the prospect of some sort of radical democracy spreading outward and growing up? Why does the power that was once so carefully preserved at the top of the pyramid by the original framers of the Constitution seem drawn inexorably downward and outward in spite of the best effort of the Right to stop this? I mean it's the really hard thing about being Left in this country, the American Left can't help but trip over all these petrified little fetishes: freedom, that's the worst; you know, *Jeane Kirkpatrick* for God's sake will go on and on about freedom and so what does that mean, the word freedom, when she talks about it, or human rights; you have Bush talking about human rights, and so what are these people talking about, they might as well be talking about the mating habits of Venusians, these people don't begin to know what, ontologically, freedom is or human rights, like they see these bourgeois property-based Rights-of-Man-type rights but that's not enfranchisement, not democracy, not what's implicit, what's potential within the idea, not the idea with blood in it. That's just liberalism, the worst kind of liberalism, really, bourgeois tolerance, and what I think is that what AIDS shows us is the limits of tolerance, that it's not enough to be tolerated, because when the shit hits the fan you find out how much tolerance is worth. Nothing. And underneath all the tolerance is intense, passionate hatred.

BELIZE: Uh huh.

LOUIS: Well don't you think that's true?

BELIZE: Uh huh. It is.

LOUIS: *Power* is the object, not being tolerated. Fuck assimilation. But I mean in spite of all this the thing about America, I think, is that ultimately we're different from every other nation on earth, in that, with people here of every race, we can't. . . . Ultimately what defines us isn't race, but politics. Not like any European country where there's an in-surmountable fact of a kind of racial, or ethnic, monopoly, or monolith, like all Dutchmen, I mean Dutch people, are well, Dutch, and the Jews of Europe were never Europeans, just a small problem. Facing the monolith. But here there are so many small problems, it's really just a collection of small problems, the monolith is missing. Oh, I mean, of course I suppose there's the

monolith of White America. White Straight Male America.

BELIZE: Which is not unimpressive, even among monoliths.

LOUIS: Well, no, but when the race thing gets taken care of, and I don't mean to minimalize how major it is, I mean I know it is, this is a really, really incredibly racist country but it's like, well, the British. I mean, all these blue-eyed pink people. And it's just weird, you know, I mean I'm not all that Jewish-looking, or . . . well, maybe I am but, you know, in New York, everyone is . . . well, not everyone, but so many are but so but in England, in London I walk into bars and I feel like Sid the Yid, you know I mean like Woody Allen in *Annie Hall,* with the payess and the gabardine coat, like never, never anywhere so much—I mean, not actively despised, not like they're Germans, who I think are still terribly anti-Semitic, and racist too, I mean black-racist, they pretend otherwise but, anyway, in London, there's just . . . and at one point I met this black gay guy from Jamaica who talked with a lilt but he said his family'd been living in London since before the Civil War—the American one—and how the English never let him forget for a minute that he wasn't blue-eyed and pink and I said yeah, me too, these people are anti-Semites and he said yeah but the British Jews have the clothing business all sewed up and blacks there can't get a foothold. And it was an incredibly awkward moment of just. . . . I mean here we were, in this bar that was gay but it was a *pub,* you know, the beams and the plaster and those horrible little, like, two-day-old fish and egg sandwiches—and just so British, so *old,* and I felt, well, there's no way out of this because both of us are, right now, too much immersed in this history, hope is dissolved in the sheer age of this place, where race is what counts and there's no real hope of change—it's the racial destiny of the Brits that matters to them, not their political destiny, whereas in America . . .

BELIZE: Here in America race doesn't count.

LOUIS: No, no, that's not. . . . I mean you *can't* be hearing that . . .

BELIZE: I . . .

LOUIS: It's—look, race, yes, but ultimately race here is a political question, right? Racists just try to use race here as a tool in a political struggle. It's not really about race. Like the spiritualists try to use that stuff, are you enlightened, are you centered, channeled, whatever, this reaching out for a spiritual past in a country where no indigenous spirits exist—only the Indians, I mean Native American spirits and we killed them off so now, there are no gods here, no ghosts and spirits in America, there are no angels in America, no spiritual past, no racial past, there's only the political, and the decoys and the ploys to maneuver around the inescapable battle of politics, the shifting downwards and outwards of political power to the people . . .

BELIZE: POWER to the People! AMEN! (*Looking at his watch*) *OH MY GOODNESS!* Will you look at the time, I gotta . . .

LOUIS: Do you. . . . You think this is, what, racist or naive or something?

BELIZE: Well it's certainly *something*. Look, I just remembered I have an appointment . . .

LOUIS: What? I mean I really don't want to, like, speak from some position of privilege and . . .

BELIZE: I'm sitting here, thinking, eventually he's *got* to run out of steam, so I let you rattle on and on saying about maybe seven or eight things I find really offensive.

LOUIS: What?

BELIZE: But I know you, Louis, and I know the guilt fueling this peculiar tirade is obviously already swollen bigger than your hemorrhoids.

LOUIS: I don't have hemorrhoids.

BELIZE: I hear different. May I finish?

LOUIS: Yes, but I don't have hemorrhoids.

BELIZE: So finally, when I . . .

LOUIS: Prior told you, he's an asshole, he shouldn't have . . .

BELIZE: You promised, Louis. Prior is not a subject.

LOUIS: You brought him up.

BELIZE: I brought up hemorrhoids.

LOUIS: So it's indirect. Passive-aggressive.

BELIZE: Unlike, I suppose, banging me over the head with your theory that America doesn't have a race problem.

LOUIS: Oh be fair I never said that.

BELIZE: Not exactly, but . . .

LOUIS: I said . . .

BELIZE: . . . but it was close enough, because if it'd been that blunt I'd've just walked out and . . .

LOUIS: You deliberately misinterpreted! I . . .

BELIZE: Stop interrupting! I haven't been able to . . .

LOUIS: Just let me . . .

BELIZE: NO! What, *talk?* You've been running your mouth nonstop since I got here, yad-dadda yaddadda blah blah blah, up the hill, down the hill, playing with your MONOLITH . . .

LOUIS (*Overlapping*): Well, you could have joined in at any time instead of . . .

BELIZE (*Continuing over Louis*): . . . and gir!friend it is truly an *awesome* spectacle but I got better things to do with my time than sit here listening to this racist bullshit just because I feel sorry for you that . . .

LOUIS: I am not a racist!

BELIZE: Oh come on . . .

LOUIS: So maybe I am a racist but . . .

BELIZE: Oh I really hate that! It's no fun picking on you Louis; you're so guilty, it's like throwing darts at a glob of jello, there's no satisfying hits, just quivering, the darts just blop in and vanish.

LOUIS: I just think when you are discussing lines of oppression it gets very complicated and . . .

BELIZE: Oh is that a fact? You know, we black drag queens have a rather intimate knowledge of the complexity of the lines of . . .

LOUIS: *Ex*-black drag queen.

BELIZE: Actually ex-ex.

LOUIS: You're doing drag again?

BELIZE: I don't. . . . Maybe. I don't have to tell you. Maybe.

LOUIS: I think it's sexist.

BELIZE: I didn't ask you.

LOUIS: Well it is. The gay community, I think, has to adopt the same attitude towards drag as black women have to take towards black women blues singers.

BELIZE: Oh my we *are* walking dangerous tonight.

LOUIS: Well, it's all internalized oppression, right, I mean the masochism, the stereotypes, the . . .

BELIZE: Louis, are you deliberately trying to make me hate you?

LOUIS: No, I . . .

BELIZE: I mean, are you deliberately transforming yourself into an arrogant, sexual-political Stalinist-slash-racist flag-waving thug for my benefit?

(*Pause.*)

LOUIS: You know what I think?

BELIZE: What?

LOUIS: You hate me because I'm a Jew.

BELIZE: I'm leaving.

LOUIS: It's true.

BELIZE: You have no basis except your . . .

Louis, it's good to know you haven't changed; you are still an honorary citizen of the Twilight Zone, and after your pale, pale white polemics on behalf of racial insensitivity you have a flaming *fuck* of a lot of nerve calling me an anti-Semite. Now I really gotta go.

LOUIS: You called me Lou the Jew.

BELIZE: That was a joke.

LOUIS: I didn't think it was funny. It was hostile.

BELIZE: It was three years ago.

LOUIS: So?

BELIZE: You just called yourself Sid the Yid.

LOUIS: That's not the same thing.

BELIZE: Sid the Yid is different from Lou the Jew.

LOUIS: Yes.

BELIZE: Someday you'll have to explain that to me, but right now . . .

You hate me because you hate black people.

LOUIS: I do not. But I do think most black people are anti-Semitic.

BELIZE: "Most black people." *That's* racist, Louis, and *I* think most Jews . . .

LOUIS: Louis Farrakhan.

BELIZE: Ed Koch.

LOUIS: Jesse Jackson.

BELIZE: Jackson. Oh really, Louis, this is . . .

LOUIS: Hymietown! Hymietown!

BELIZE: Louis, you voted for Jesse Jackson. You send checks to the Rainbow Coalition.

LOUIS: I'm ambivalent. The checks bounced.

BELIZE: All your checks bounce, Louis; you're ambivalent about everything.

LOUIS: What's that supposed to mean?

BELIZE: You may be dumber than shit but I refuse to believe you can't figure it out. Try.

LOUIS: I was never ambivalent about Prior. I love him. I do. I really do.

BELIZE: Nobody said different.

LOUIS: Love and ambivalence are. . . . Real love isn't ambivalent.

BELIZE: "Real love isn't ambivalent." I'd swear that's a line from my favorite bestselling paperback novel, *In Love with the Night Mysterious,* except I don't think you ever read it.

(*Pause.*)

LOUIS: I never read it, no.

BELIZE: You ought to. Instead of spending the rest of your life trying to get through *Democracy in America*. It's about this white woman whose Daddy owns a plantation in the Deep South in the years before the Civil War—the American one—and her name is Margaret, and she's in love with her Daddy's number-one slave, and his name is Thaddeus, and she's married but her white slave-owner husband has AIDS: Antebellum Insufficiently Developed Sexorgans. And there's a lot of hot stuff going down when Margaret and Thaddeus can catch a spare torrid ten under the cotton-picking moon, and then of course the Yankees come, and they set the slaves free, and the slaves string up old Daddy, and so on. Historical fiction. Somewhere in there I recall Margaret and Thaddeus find the time to discuss the nature of love; her face is reflecting the flames of the burning plantation—you know, the way white people do—and his black face is dark in the night and she says to him, "Thaddeus, real love isn't ever ambivalent."

(*Little pause. Emily enters and turns off IV drip.*)

BELIZE: Thaddeus looks at her; he's contemplating her thesis; and he isn't sure he agrees.

EMILY (*Removing IV drip from Prior's arm*): Treatment number . . . (*Consulting chart*) four.

PRIOR: Pharmaceutical miracle. Lazarus breathes again.

LOUIS: Is he. . . . How bad is he?

BELIZE: You want the laundry list?

EMILY: Shirt off, let's check the . . .

(*Prior takes his shirt off. She examines his lesions.*)

BELIZE: There's the weight problem and the shit problem and the morale problem.

EMILY: Only six. That's good. Pants.

(*He drops his pants. He's naked. She examines.*)

BELIZE: And. He thinks he's going crazy.

EMILY: Looking good. What else?

PRIOR: Ankles sore and swollen, but the leg's better. The nausea's mostly gone with the little orange pills. BM's pure liquid but not bloody anymore, for now, my eye doctor says everything's OK, for now, my dentist says "Yuck!" when he sees my fuzzy tongue, and now he wears little condoms on his thumb and forefinger. And a mask. So what? My dermatologist is in Hawaii and my mother . . . well leave my mother out of it. Which is usually where my mother is, out of it. My glands are like walnuts, my weight's holding steady for week two, and a friend

died two days ago of bird tuberculosis; bird tuberculosis; that scared me and I didn't go to the funeral today because he was an Irish Catholic and it's probably open casket and I'm afraid of . . . something, the bird TB or seeing him or. . . . So I guess I'm doing OK. Except for of course I'm going nuts.

EMILY: We ran the toxoplasmosis series and there's no indication . . .

PRIOR: I know, I know, but I feel like something terrifying is on its way, you know, like a missile from outer space, and it's plummeting down towards the earth, and I'm ground zero, and . . . I am generally known where I am known as one cool, collected queen. And I am ruffled.

EMILY: There's really nothing to worry about. I think that shochen bamromim hamtzeh menucho nechono al kanfey haschino.

PRIOR: What?

EMILY: Everything's fine. Bemaalos k'doshim ut'horim kezohar horokeea mazhirim . . .

PRIOR: Oh I don't understand what you're . . .

EMILY: Es nishmas Prior sheholoch leolomoh, baavur shenodvoo z'dokoh b'ad hazkoras nishmosoh.

PRIOR: Why are you doing that? Stop it! Stop it!

EMILY: Stop what?

PRIOR: You were just . . . weren't you just speaking in Hebrew or something.

EMILY: *Hebrew?* (*Laughs*) I'm basically Italian-American. No. I didn't speak in Hebrew.

PRIOR: Oh no, oh God please I really think I . . .

EMILY: Look, I'm sorry, I have a waiting room full of. . . . I think you're one of the lucky ones, you'll live for years, probably—you're pretty healthy for someone with no immune system. Are you seeing someone? Loneliness is a danger. A therapist?

PRIOR: No, I don't need to see anyone, I just . . .

EMILY: Well think about it. You aren't going crazy. You're just under a lot of stress. No wonder . . . (*She starts to write in his chart*)

(*Suddenly there is an astonishing blaze of light, a huge chord sounded by a gigantic choir, and a great book with steel pages mounted atop a molten-red pillar pops up from the stage floor. The book opens; there is a large Aleph inscribed on its pages, which bursts into flames. Immediately the book slams shut and disappears instantly under the floor as the lights become normal again. Emily notices none of this, writing. Prior is agog.*)

EMILY (*Laughing, exiting*): Hebrew . . .

(*Prior flees.*)

LOUIS: Help me.

BELIZE: I beg your pardon?

LOUIS: You're a nurse, give me something, I . . . don't know what to do anymore, I. . . . Last week at work I screwed up the Xerox machine like permanently and so I . . . then I tripped on the subway steps and my glasses broke and I cut my forehead, here, see, and now I can't see much and my forehead . . . it's like the Mark of Cain, stupid, right, but it won't heal and every morning I see it and I think, Biblical things, Mark of Cain, Judas Iscariot and his silver and his noose, people who . . . in betraying what they love betray what's truest in themselves, I feel . . . nothing but cold for myself, just cold, and every night I miss him, I miss him so much but then . . . those sores, and the smell and . . . where I thought it was going. . . . I could be . . . I could be sick too, maybe I'm sick too. I don't know.

Belize. Tell him I love him. Can you do that?

BELIZE: I've thought about it for a very long time, and I still don't understand what love is. Justice is simple. Democracy is simple. Those things are unambivalent. But love is very hard. And it goes bad for you if you violate the hard law of love.

LOUIS: I'm dying.

BELIZE: He's dying. You just wish you were.

Oh cheer up, Louis. Look at that heavy sky out there.

LOUIS: Purple.

BELIZE: *Purple?* Boy, what kind of a homosexual are you, anyway? That's not purple, Mary, that color up there is (*Very grand*) mauve.

All day today it's felt like Thanksgiving. Soon, this . . . ruination will be blanketed white. You can smell it—can you smell it?

LOUIS: Smell what?

BELIZE: Softness, compliance, forgiveness, grace.

LOUIS: No . . .

BELIZE: I can't help you learn that. I can't help you, Louis. You're not my business. (*He exits*)

(*Louis puts his head in his hands, inadvertently touching his cut forehead.*)

LOUIS: Ow FUCK! (*He stands slowly, looks towards where Belize exited*) Smell what?
(*He looks both ways to be sure no one is watching, then inhales deeply, and is surprised*) Huh. Snow.

Scene 3

Same day. Harper in a very white, cold place, with a brilliant blue sky above; a delicate snowfall. She is dressed in a beautiful snowsuit. The sound of the sea, faint.

HARPER: Snow! Ice! Mountains of ice! Where am I? I . . .
I feel better, I do, I . . . feel better. There are ice crystals in my lungs, wonderful and sharp. And the snow smells like cold, crushed peaches. And there's something . . . some current of blood in the wind, how strange, it has that iron taste.

MR. LIES: Ozone.

HARPER: Ozone! Wow! Where am I?

MR. LIES: The Kingdom of Ice, the bottommost part of the world.

HARPER (*Looking around, then realizing*): Antarctica. This is Antarctica!

MR. LIES: Cold shelter for the shattered. No sorrow here, tears freeze.

HARPER: Antarctica, Antarctica, oh boy oh boy, LOOK at this, I. . . . Wow, I must've really snapped the tether, huh?

MR. LIES: Apparently . . .

HARPER: That's great. I want to stay here forever. Set up camp. Build things. Build a city, an enormous city made up of frontier forts, dark wood and green roofs and high gates made of pointed logs and bonfires burning on every street corner. I should build by a river. Where are the forests?

MR. LIES: No timber here. Too cold. Ice, no trees.

HARPER: Oh details! I'm sick of details! I'll plant them and grow them. I'll live off caribou fat, I'll melt it over the bonfires and drink it from long, curved goat-horn cups. It'll be great. I want to make a new world here. So that I never have to go home again.

MR. LIES: As long as it lasts. Ice has a way of melting . . .

HARPER: No. Forever. I can have anything I want here—maybe even companionship, someone who has . . . desire for me. You, maybe.

MR. LIES: It's against the by-laws of the International Order of Travel Agents to get involved with clients. Rules are rules. Anyway, I'm not the one you really want.

HARPER: There isn't anyone . . . maybe an Eskimo. Who could ice-fish for food. And help me build a nest for when the baby comes.

MR. LIES: There are no Eskimo in Antarctica. And you're not really pregnant. You made that up.

HARPER: Well all of this is made up. So if the snow feels cold I'm pregnant. Right? Here, I can be pregnant. And I can have any kind of a baby I want.

MR. LIES: This is a retreat, a vacuum, its virtue is that it lacks everything; deep-freeze for feelings. You can be numb and safe here, that's what you came for. Respect the delicate ecology of your delusions.

HARPER: You mean like no Eskimo in Antarctica.

MR. LIES: Correcto. Ice and snow, no Eskimo. Even hallucinations have laws.

HARPER: Well then who's that?

(*The Eskimo appears.*)

MR. LIES: An Eskimo.

HARPER: An antarctic Eskimo. A fisher of the polar deep.

MR. LIES: There's something wrong with this picture.

(*The Eskimo beckons.*)

HARPER: I'm going to like this place. It's my own National Geographic Special! Oh! Oh! (*She holds her stomach*) I think . . . I think I felt her kicking. Maybe I'll give birth to a baby covered with thick white fur, and that way she won't be cold. My breasts will be full of hot cocoa so she doesn't get chilly. And if it gets really cold, she'll have a pouch I can crawl into. Like a marsupial. We'll mend together. That's what we'll do; we'll mend.

Scene 4

Same day. An abandoned lot in the South Bronx. A homeless Woman is standing near an oil drum in which a fire is burning. Snowfall. Trash around. Hannah enters dragging two heavy suitcases.

HANNAH: Excuse me? I said excuse me? Can you tell me where I am? Is this Brooklyn? Do you know a Pineapple Street? Is there some sort of bus or train or . . . ?

I'm lost, I just arrived from Salt Lake. City. Utah? I took the bus that I was told to take and I got off—well it was the very last stop, so I had to get off, and I *asked* the driver was this Brooklyn, and he nodded yes but he was from one of those foreign countries where they think it's good manners to nod at everything even if you have no idea what it is you're nodding at, and in truth I think he spoke no English at all, which I think would make him ineligible for employment on public transportation. The public being English-speaking, mostly. Do you speak English?

(*The Woman nods.*)

HANNAH: I was supposed to be met at the airport by my son. He didn't show and I don't wait more than three and three-quarters hours for *anyone*. I should have been patient, I guess, I. . . . Is this . . .

WOMAN: Bronx.

HANNAH: Is that. . . . The *Bronx?* Well how in the name of Heaven did I get to the Bronx when the bus driver said . . .

WOMAN (*Talking to herself*): Slurp slurp slurp will you STOP that disgusting slurping! YOU DISGUSTING SLURPING FEEDING ANIMAL! Feeding yourself, just feeding yourself, what would it matter, to you or to ANYONE, if you just stopped. Feeding. And DIED?

(*Pause.*)

HANNAH: Can you just tell me where I . . .

WOMAN: Why was the Kosciusko Bridge named after a Polack?

HANNAH: I don't know what you're . . .

WOMAN: That was a joke.

HANNAH: Well what's the punchline?

WOMAN: I don't know.

HANNAH (*Looking around desperately*): Oh for pete's sake, is there anyone else who . . .

WOMAN (*Again, to herself*): Stand further off you fat loathsome whore, you can't have any more of this soup, slurp slurp slurp you animal, and the—I know you'll just go pee it all away and where will you do that? Behind what bush? It's FUCKING COLD out here and I . . .

Oh that's right, because it was supposed to have been a tunnel!

That's not very funny.

Have you read the prophecies of Nostradamus?

HANNAH: Who?

WOMAN: Some guy I went out with once somewhere, Nostradamus. Prophet, outcast, eyes like. . . . Scary shit, he . . .

HANNAH: Shut up. Please. Now I want you to stop jabbering for a minute and pull your wits together and tell me how to get to Brooklyn. Because you know! And you are going to tell me! Because there is no one else around to tell me and I am wet and cold and I am very angry! So I am sorry you're psychotic but just make the effort—take a deep breath—DO IT!

(*Hannah and the Woman breathe together.*)

HANNAH: That's good. Now exhale.

(*They do.*)

HANNAH: Good. Now how do I get to Brooklyn?

WOMAN: Don't know. Never been. Sorry. Want some soup?

HANNAH: Manhattan? Maybe you know . . . I don't suppose you know the location of the Mormon Visitor's . . .

WOMAN: 65th and Broadway.

HANNAH: How do you . . .

WOMAN: Go there all the time. Free movies. Boring, but you can stay all day.

HANNAH: Well. . . . So how do I . . .

WOMAN: Take the D Train. Next block make a right.

HANNAH: Thank you.

WOMAN: Oh yeah. In the new century I think we will all be insane.

Scene 5

Same day. Joe and Roy in the study of Roy's brownstone. Roy is wearing an elegant bathrobe. He has made a considerable effort to look well. He isn't well, and he hasn't succeeded much in looking it.

JOE: I can't. The answer's no. I'm sorry.

ROY: Oh, well, apologies . . .

I can't see that there's anyone asking for apologies.

(*Pause.*)

JOE: I'm sorry, Roy.

ROY: Oh, well, apologies.

JOE: My wife is missing, Roy. My mother's coming from Salt Lake to . . . to help look, I guess. I'm supposed to be at the airport now, picking her up but. . . . I just spent two days in a hospital, Roy, with a bleeding ulcer, I was spitting up blood.

ROY: Blood, huh? Look, I'm very busy here and . . .

JOE: It's just a job.

ROY: A job? A *job? Washington!* Dumb Utah Mormon hick shit!

JOE: Roy . . .

ROY: *WASHINGTON!* When Washington called me I was younger than you, you think I said "Aw fuck no I can't go I got two fingers up my asshole and a little moral nosebleed to boot!" When Washington calls you my pretty young punk friend you go or you can go fuck yourself sideways 'cause the train has pulled out of the station, and you are *out,* nowhere, out in the cold. Fuck you, Mary Jane, get outta here.

JOE: Just let me . . .

ROY: Explain? Ephemera. You broke my heart. Explain that. Explain that.

JOE: I love you. Roy.

There's so much that I want, to be . . . what you see in me, I want to be a participant in the world, in your world, Roy, I want to be capable of that, I've tried, really I have but . . . I can't do this. Not because I don't believe in you, but because I believe in you so much, in what you stand for, at heart, the order, the decency. I would give anything to protect you, but. . . . There are laws I can't break. It's too ingrained. It's not me. There's enough damage I've already done.

Maybe you were right, maybe I'm dead.

ROY: You're not dead, boy, you're a sissy.

You love me; that's moving, I'm moved. It's nice to be loved. I warned you about her, didn't I, Joe? But you don't listen to me, why, because you say Roy is smart and Roy's a friend but Roy . . . well, he isn't nice, and you wanna be nice. Right? A nice, nice man!

(*Little pause*)

You know what my greatest accomplishment was, Joe, in my life, what I am able to look back on and be proudest of? And I have helped make Presidents and unmake them and mayors and more goddam judges than anyone in NYC ever—AND several million dollars, tax-free—and what do you think means the most to me?

You ever hear of Ethel Rosenberg? Huh, Joe, huh?

JOE: Well, yeah, I guess I. . . . Yes.

ROY: Yes. Yes. You have heard of Ethel Rosenberg. Yes. Maybe you even read about her in the history books.

If it wasn't for me, Joe, Ethel Rosenberg would be alive today, writing some personal-advice column for *Ms.* magazine. She isn't. Because during the trial, Joe, I was on the phone every day, talking with the judge . . .

JOE: Roy . . .

ROY: Every day, doing what I do best, talking on the telephone, making sure that timid Yid nebbish on the bench did his duty to America, to history. That sweet unprepossessing woman, two kids, boo-hoo-hoo, reminded us all of our little Jewish mamas—she came this close to getting life; I pleaded till I wept to put her in the chair. Me. I did that. I would have fucking pulled the switch if they'd have let me. Why? Because I fucking hate traitors. Because I fucking hate communists. Was it legal? Fuck legal. Am I a nice man? Fuck nice. They say terrible things about me in the *Nation.* Fuck the *Nation.* You want to be Nice, or you want to be Effective? Make the law, or subject to it. Choose. Your wife chose. A week from today, she'll be back. SHE knows how to get what SHE wants. Maybe I ought to send *her* to Washington.

JOE: I don't believe you.

ROY: Gospel.

JOE: You can't possibly mean what you're saying.

Roy, you were the Assistant United States Attorney on the Rosenberg case, ex-parte communication with the judge during the trial would be . . . censurable, at least, probably conspiracy and . . . in a case that resulted in execution, it's . . .

ROY: What? Murder?

JOE: You're not well is all.

ROY: What do you mean, not well? Who's not well?

(*Pause.*)

JOE: You said . . .

ROY: No I didn't. I said what?

JOE: Roy, you have cancer.

ROY: No I don't.

(*Pause.*)

JOE: You told me you were dying.

ROY: What the fuck are you talking about, Joe? I never said that. I'm in perfect health. There's not a goddam thing wrong with me.

(*He smiles*)

Shake?

(*Joe hesitates. He holds out his hand to Roy. Roy pulls Joe into a close, strong clinch.*)

ROY (*More to himself than to Joe*): It's OK that you hurt me because I love you, baby Joe. That's why I'm so rough on you.

(*Roy releases Joe. Joe backs away a step or two.*)

ROY: Prodigal son. The world will wipe its dirty hands all over you.

JOE: It already has, Roy.

ROY: Now go.

(*Roy shoves Joe, hard. Joe turns to leave. Roy stops him, turns him around.*)

ROY (*Smoothing Joe's lapels, tenderly*): I'll always be here, waiting for you . . .

(*Then again, with sudden violence, he pulls Joe close, violently*)

What did you want from me, what was all this, what do you want, treacherous ungrateful little . . .

(*Joe, very close to belting Roy, grabs him by the front of his robe, and propels him across the length of the room. He holds Roy at arm's length, the other arm ready to hit.*)

ROY (*Laughing softly, almost pleading to be hit*): Transgress a little, Joseph.

(*Joe releases Roy.*)

ROY: There are so many laws; find one you can break.

(*Joe hesitates, then leaves, backing out. When Joe has gone, Roy doubles over in great pain, which he's been hiding throughout the scene with Joe.*)

ROY: Ah, Christ . . .
    Andy! Andy! Get in here! Andy!

(*The door opens, but it isn't Andy. A small Jewish Woman dressed modestly in a fifties hat and coat stands in the doorway. The room darkens.*)

ROY: Who the fuck are you? The new nurse?

(*The figure in the doorway says nothing. She stares at Roy. A pause. Roy looks at her carefully, gets up, crosses to her. He crosses back to the chair, sits heavily.*)

ROY: Aw, fuck. Ethel.

ETHEL ROSENBERG (*Her manner is friendly, her voice is ice-cold*): You don't look good, Roy.

ROY: Well, Ethel. I don't feel good.

ETHEL ROSENBERG: But you lost a lot of weight. That suits you. You were heavy back then. Zaftig, mit hips.

ROY: I haven't been that heavy since 1960. We were all heavier back then, before the body thing started. Now I look like a skeleton. They stare.

ETHEL ROSENBERG: The shit's really hit the fan, huh, Roy?

(*Little pause. Roy nods.*)

ETHEL ROSENBERG: Well the fun's just started.

ROY: What is this, Ethel, Halloween? You trying to scare me?

(*Ethel says nothing.*)

ROY: Well you're wasting your time! I'm scarier than you any day of the week! So beat it, Ethel! BOOO! BETTER DEAD THAN RED! Somebody trying to shake me up? HAH HAH! From the throne of God in heaven to the belly of hell, you can all fuck yourselves and then go jump in the lake because I'M NOT AFRAID OF YOU OR DEATH OR HELL OR ANYTHING!

ETHEL ROSENBERG: Be seeing you soon, Roy. Julius sends his regards.

ROY: Yeah, well send this to Julius!

(He flips the bird in her direction, stands and moves towards her. Halfway across the room he slumps to the floor, breathing laboriously, in pain.)

ETHEL ROSENBERG: You're a very sick man, Roy.

ROY: Oh God . . . ANDY!

ETHEL ROSENBERG: Hmmm. He doesn't hear you, I guess. We should call the ambulance.

(She goes to the phone)

Hah! Buttons! Such things they got now. What do I dial, Roy?

(Pause. Roy looks at her, then:)

ROY: 911.

ETHEL ROSENBERG *(Dials the phone)*: It sings! *(Imitating dial tones)* La la la . . .
Huh.
Yes, you should please send an ambulance to the home of Mister Roy Cohn, the famous lawyer.
What's the address, Roy?

ROY *(A beat, then)*: 244 East 87th.

ETHEL ROSENBERG: 244 East 87th Street. No apartment number, he's got the whole building.
My name? *(A beat)* Ethel Greenglass Rosenberg.
(Small smile) Me? No I'm not related to Mr. Cohn. An old friend.

(She hangs up)

They said a minute.

ROY: I have all the time in the world.

ETHEL ROSENBERG: You're immortal.

ROY: I'm immortal. Ethel. *(He forces himself to stand)*
I have *forced* my way into history. I ain't never gonna die.

ETHEL ROSENBERG *(A little laugh, then)*: History is about to crack wide open. Millennium approaches.

Scene 6

Late that night. Prior's bedroom. Prior 1 watching Prior in bed, who is staring back at him, terrified. Tonight Prior 1 is dressed in weird alchemical robes and hat over his historical clothing and he carries a long palm-leaf bundle.

PRIOR 1: Tonight's the night! Aren't you excited? Tonight she arrives! Right through the roof! Ha-adam, Ha-gadol . . .

PRIOR 2 *(Appearing, similarly attired)*: Lumen! Phosphor! Fluor! Candle! An unending billowing of scarlet and . . .

PRIOR: Look. Garlic. A mirror. Holy water. A crucifix. FUCK OFF! Get the fuck out of my room! GO!

PRIOR 1 *(To Prior 2)*: Hard as a hickory knob, I'll bet.

PRIOR 2: We all tumesce when they approach. We wax full, like moons.

PRIOR 1: Dance.

PRIOR: Dance?

PRIOR 1: Stand up, dammit, give us your hands, dance!

PRIOR 2: Listen . . .

(A lone oboe begins to play a little dance tune.)

PRIOR 2: Delightful sound. Care to dance?

PRIOR: Please leave me alone, please just let me sleep . . .

PRIOR 2: Ah, he wants someone familiar. A partner who knows his steps. *(To Prior)* Close your eyes. Imagine . . .

PRIOR: I don't . . .

PRIOR 2: Hush. Close your eyes.

(Prior does.)

PRIOR 2: Now open them.

(Prior does. Louis appears. He looks gorgeous. The music builds gradually into a full-blooded, romantic dance tune.)

PRIOR: Lou.

LOUIS: Dance with me.

PRIOR: I can't, my leg, it hurts at night . . .
Are you a ghost, Lou?

LOUIS: No. Just spectral. Lost to myself. Sitting all day on cold park benches. Wishing I could be with you. Dance with me, babe . . .

(Prior stands up. The leg stops hurting. They begin to dance. The music is beautiful.)

PRIOR 1 (*To Prior 2*): Hah. Now I see why he's got no children. He's a sodomite.

PRIOR 2: Oh be quiet, you medieval gnome, and let them dance.

PRIOR 1: I'm not interfering, I've done my bit. Hooray, hooray, the messenger's come, now I'm blowing off. I don't like it here.

(*Prior 1 vanishes.*)

PRIOR 2: The twentieth century. Oh dear, the world has gotten so terribly, terribly old.

(*Prior 2 vanishes. Louis and Prior waltz happily. Lights fade back to normal. Louis vanishes.*
Prior dances alone.
Then suddenly, the sound of wings fills the room.)

Scene 7

Split scene: Prior alone in his apartment; Louis alone in the park.
Again, a sound of beating wings.

PRIOR: Oh don't come in here don't come in . . . LOUIS!!

No. My name is Prior Walter, I am . . . the scion of an ancient line, I am . . . abandoned I . . . no, my name is . . . is . . . Prior and I live . . . *here and now,* and . . . in the dark, in the dark, the Recording Angel opens its hundred eyes and snaps the spine of the Book of Life and . . . hush! Hush!

I'm talking nonsense, I . . .

No more mad scene, hush, hush . . .

(*Louis in the park on a bench. Joe approaches, stands at a distance. They stare at each other, then Louis turns away.*)

LOUIS: Do you know the story of Lazarus?

JOE: Lazarus?

LOUIS: Lazarus. I can't remember what happens, exactly.

JOE: I don't. . . . Well, he was dead, Lazarus, and Jesus breathed life into him. He brought him back from death.

LOUIS: Come here often?

JOE: No. Yes. Yes.

LOUIS: Back from the dead. You believe that really happened?

JOE: I don't know anymore what I believe.

LOUIS: This is quite a coincidence. Us meeting.

JOE: I followed you.

From work. I . . . followed you here.

(*Pause.*)

LOUIS: You followed me.

You probably saw me that day in the washroom and thought: there's a sweet guy, sensitive, cries for friends in trouble.

JOE: Yes.

LOUIS: You thought maybe I'll cry for you.

JOE: Yes.

LOUIS: Well I fooled you. Crocodile tears. Nothing . . . (*He touches his heart, shrugs*)

(*Joe reaches tentatively to touch Louis's face.*)

LOUIS (*Pulling back*): What are you doing? Don't do that.

JOE (*Withdrawing his hand*): Sorry. I'm sorry.

LOUIS: I'm . . . just not . . . I think, if you touch me, your hand might fall off or something. Worse things have happened to people who have touched me.

JOE: Please.

Oh, boy . . .

Can I . . .

I . . . want . . . to touch you. Can I please just touch you . . . um, here?

(*He puts his hand on one side of Louis's face. He holds it there*)

I'm going to hell for doing this.

LOUIS: Big deal. You think it could be any worse than New York City?

(*He puts his hand on Joe's hand. He takes Joe's hand away from his face, holds it for a moment, then*) Come on.

JOE: Where?

LOUIS: Home. With me.

JOE: This makes no sense. I mean I don't know you.

LOUIS: Likewise.

JOE: And what you do know about me you don't like.

LOUIS: The Republican stuff.

JOE: Yeah, well for starters.

LOUIS: I don't not like that. I *hate* that.

JOE: So why on earth should we . . .

(*Louis goes to Joe and kisses him.*)

LOUIS: Strange bedfellows. I don't know. I never made it with one of the damned before.
I would really rather not have to spend tonight alone.

JOE: I'm a pretty terrible person, Louis.

LOUIS: Lou.

JOE: No, I really really am. I don't think I deserve being loved.

LOUIS: There? See? We already have a lot in common.

(*Louis stands, begins to walk away. He turns, looks back at Joe. Joe follows. They exit.*)

(*Prior listens. At first no sound, then once again, the sound of beating wings, frighteningly near.*)

PRIOR: That sound, that sound, it. . . . What is that, like birds or something, like a *really* big bird, I'm frightened, I . . . no, no fear, find the anger, find the . . . anger, my blood is clean, my brain is fine, I can handle pressure, I am a gay man and I am used to pressure, to trouble, I am tough and strong and. . . . Oh. Oh my goodness. I . . . (*He is washed over by an intense sexual feeling*) Ooohhhh. . . . I'm hot, I'm . . . so . . . aw Jeez what is going on here I . . . must have a fever I . . .

(*The bedside lamp flickers wildly as the bed begins to roll forward and back. There is a deep bass creaking and groaning from the bedroom ceiling, like the timbers of a ship under immense stress, and from above a fine rain of plaster dust.*)

PRIOR: OH!
PLEASE, OH PLEASE! Something's coming in here, I'm scared, I don't like this at all, something's approaching and I. . . . OH!

(*There is a great blaze of triumphal music, heralding. The light turns an extraordinary harsh, cold, pale blue, then a rich, brilliant warm golden color, then a hot, bilious green, and then finally a spectacular royal purple. Then silence.*)

PRIOR (*An awestruck whisper*): God almighty . . .
Very Steven Spielberg.

(*A sound, like a plummeting meteor, tears down from very, very far above the earth, hurtling at an incredible velocity towards the bedroom; the light seems to be sucked out of the room as the projectile approaches; as the room reaches darkness, we hear a terrifying CRASH as something immense strikes earth; the whole building shudders and a part of the bedroom ceiling, lots of plaster and lathe and wiring, crashes to the floor. And then in a shower of unearthly white light, spreading great opalescent gray-silver wings, the Angel descends into the room and floats above the bed.*)

ANGEL:
Greetings, Prophet;
The Great Work begins:
The Messenger has arrived.

(*Blackout.*)

PRODUCING *ANGELS IN AMERICA*

The productions we have studied so far—*And the Soul Shall Dance* at East West Players and at Northwest Asian American Theatre and *Joe Turner's Come and Gone* at the Oregon Shakespeare Festival—began with completed scripts. Each play had already had a number of successful productions and had achieved national recognition. For *Angels in America* we begin at a much earlier time in the life of the play. We examine the development of the play itself and the relationship between a new play and the performance process.

THE EUREKA THEATRE AND THE PLAYWRIGHT

More and more, American theatre companies are directly involved in the development of new plays. Sometimes playwrights work on their own and submit a new play to a theatre only after it has been completed. But there are also playwrights who are members of theatre companies or are invited or commissioned to write a play for a particular company. A commission involves payment that supports the actual writing of the play. In 1987, a small theatre company in San Francisco, the Eureka Theatre, used a grant from the National Endowment for the Arts to commission Tony Kushner to write a play. That play would become *Angels in America.*

The production history of *Angels in America* begins with Oskar Eustis, the Eureka's artistic director and ***dramaturg,*** and Tony Taccone, the theatre's producing director at that time. In this case, the development of the play itself was highly dependent on the production process. In the late 1980s, the Eureka Theatre was a small but active theatre committed to a "politically progressive aesthetic" and the production of plays that would be responsive to social issues.[3] Together, the artistic leaders of the theatre, Taccone and Eustis, sought out new plays or commissioned new work to create a vital and forward-looking repertory for their theatre and the politically conscious San Francisco audience that it attracted.

Oskar Eustis had just directed Kushner's first play, *A Bright Room Called Day,* and was inspired by the originality of Kushner's presentation of political ideas. In his capacity as dramaturg, Eustis began a dialogue with Kushner about what kind of play he might write for the Eureka Theatre. Kushner says of the origins of the new work, "I began *Angels* as a conversation, real and imaginary, between Oskar and myself."[4]

The Role of the Dramaturg

For years, European theatres have employed dramaturgs, whose role is to work with the playwrights in the shaping of their plays and to advise directors on questions of history, analysis, and interpretation. The position of dramaturg is a fairly recent addition to the production staffs of American theatres. Critic and producer Martin Esslin sees the role of the dramaturg as crucial to expanding the intellectual and cultural foundation of the American theatre: "The American dramaturg not only has to do the basic job of finding and nurturing scripts, but has also to work hard on helping to create that basic cultural atmosphere in which a healthy theatre can operate."[5] Robert Brustein, the founding director of the Yale Repertory Theatre and American Repertory Theatre, calls the dramaturg "the conscience of the theatre."[6] In this sense the dramaturg is concerned with developing a repertory of plays that challenges the audience as well as working with playwrights and directors to make sure that ideas are substantial and clearly articulated.

Oskar Eustis had been working in Germany and Switzerland as a director and dramaturg before he returned to the United States and joined the staff of the Eureka Theatre. He explains his original goals in assuming the role of dramaturg at the Eureka Theatre:

Oskar Eustis: *Being a dramaturg is an art form, not a science. What I felt needed to be done was to help work with playwrights to create a theatre that was more accessible, more political, more audience-friendly, and therefore more narratively based than the theatre I had done before.*[7]

Eustis describes the starting point in the development of two plays he commissioned for the Eureka that eventually went on to larger theatres, including some on Broadway—*Execution of Justice* by Emily Mann and *Angels in America* by Tony Kushner:

Oskar Eustis: *In both instances, I took a playwright who the Eureka had already produced and that we had had an exciting relationship with. With Emily Mann we had produced her play* Still Life *and had an amazing experience with it. Emily had loved the production. With Tony I had produced the professional premiere of* A Bright Room Called Day. *They were writers with whom I felt deep affinities, aesthetically, theatrically, and politically.*

Eustis looked to merge the interests of the Eureka Theatre with the concerns of the playwrights. He asked each playwright, "What play does it make sense for you to write for the Eureka Theatre?"

Oskar Eustis: *And both of them, for different reasons, ended up focusing on things that had to do with the gay community in San Francisco, with subjects that seemed to speak very directly to the audience that was there for us in San Francisco.*

Emily Mann turned to a true story about San Francisco itself. She wrote a courtroom drama based on the trial of Dan White, the city supervisor who shot and killed two city officials: another city supervisor, Harvey Milk, the first openly gay elected official in America, and George Moscone, the mayor of San Francisco. When Tony Kushner was invited to work with the Eureka Theatre, he knew that somehow he wanted to write a play that concerned Roy Cohn, AIDS in the gay community, and Mormons. How those subjects were to be connected, what form the play was to take, was still in the future.

One of the remarkable anecdotes about the evolution of *Angels in America* has to do with the company of the Eureka Theatre. The material that Kushner wanted to pursue had to do with gay men, but the core acting company of the Eureka Theatre was made up of three women and one man. The three women would need parts in whatever Kushner wrote.

In Context

PRODUCTION HISTORY OF *ANGELS IN AMERICA*

Date	Event
1987	Oskar Eustis commissions Tony Kushner to write a play for the Eureka Theatre.
1990	*Millennium Approaches* is staged in a workshop production at the Mark Taper Forum in Los Angeles, directed by Oskar Eustis.
1991	*Millennium Approaches* premieres at the Eureka Theatre in San Francisco, directed by David Esbjornson. *Perestroika* is given a staged reading but remains unfinished.
1992	*Millennium Approaches* opens at the Royal National Theatre's small black box theatre, the Cottesloe, in London, directed by Declan Donnellan. *Perestroika* would be added to the production in 1993.
1992	*Millennium Approaches* and *Perestroika* are produced together for the first time at the Mark Taper Forum in Los Angeles, codirected by Oskar Eustis and Tony Taccone.
1993	*Millennium Approaches* and *Perestroika* are produced together at the Walter Kerr Theatre on Broadway, directed by George C. Wolfe.

Oskar Eustis: *The play was modeled after the company members of the Eureka. The reason those parts exist in* Angels *is because that was the company of the Eureka Theatre. We spent a number of sleepless nights while Tony tried to figure out how to put three straight women into a show that is about the experience of gay men. But part of the reason why the show is so great is that Tony had to continually expand the range of the subject matter in order to get those actresses into the play. The play ended up taking on a scope that none of us suspected it was going to when we started.*

The Developmental Process

Angels in America went through a long and difficult developmental process that lasted six years until both plays were actually completed. Before the official premiere of *Millennium Approaches* at the Eureka Theatre in 1991, there were six workshop productions in San Francisco, Los Angeles, and at the Sundance Institute; about a dozen readings; endless informal discussions; and many revised drafts of the play. *Perestroika* was given an abbreviated staged reading when *Millennium Approaches* was being performed at the Eureka Theatre. Kushner did not finish the second play until just before its premiere in Los Angeles. *Perestroika* would be rewritten yet one more time before the entire piece opened on Broadway.

The developmental process was affected both by changes in personnel and by financial complications. After beginning the work on *Angels in America* at the Eureka Theatre, Tony Taccone became the associate artistic director of the Berkeley Repertory Theatre and Oskar Eustis became associate artistic director of the Mark Taper Forum in Los Angeles. David Esbjornson then became the director of the play at the Eureka Theatre. Following the production at the Mark Taper Forum, Eustis and Taccone concluded their formal relationship with the play, and George C. Wolfe, director of the Public Theatre in New York, guided the play on the final part of its journey. Until the play opened at the Mark Taper Forum in Los Angeles, the developmental process was guided by Oskar Eustis.

Oskar Eustis: *Many, many different formats were used, and I think all of them were certainly necessary to get us there. There were times when we were focusing on the arc of the characters. At other times we were focusing on the internal shape of the different scenes of different acts. There were times when we were trying to finish the story. And at times we were very much trying to figure out how to produce the thing as a whole, what our production method might be.*

Tony Kushner readily acknowledges the help of a variety of dramaturgs, theatre practitioners, and colleagues in the evolution of *Angels in America*. Some people were involved in the development of characters, scenes, and language; others gave crucial advice on cutting the script; and some were engaged with Kushner in dialogues and arguments about the ideas expressed by the play. Each reading or production made a major contribution to the writing process:

Tony Kushner: *It's deeply suspect that writers—especially male writers—feel that they have to produce everything completely on their own and that the act of writing becomes in part an act of denying that one is in any way reliant on other people. I've thought that maybe other writers simply don't need other people's help as much as I do, or maybe I'm just a bad writer. I suspect that some people are more solitary and really dredge it all out of their own souls. But even there, there may be ways in which people are feeding them about which they're not aware. . . . I haven't been diminished by admitting that other people have participated.*[8]

Although Kushner received input from many sources during the six-year gestation of *Angels in America*, the writing and rewriting were his work. Kushner is a playwright who makes continuous adjustments in his material, and *Angels* involved a legendary number of rewrites. Some of the actors who began the production in San Francisco were also part of the Los Angeles cast and eventually went on to New York, a rather unusual casting history. Ellen McLaughlin, the actor who played the Angel, memorized as many as twenty versions of a crucial scene in *Perestroika* before Kushner was satisfied. The rewrites continued on *Perestroika* throughout most of the rehearsal period in Los Angeles. The directors and actors who were staging two full plays that would run a total of seven hours had only a ten-week period of time to do their work and had to contend with changes in the script up until days before the production opened.

Tony Taccone: *There were lots of rewrites, and that was both thrilling and scary—thrilling because the writing was fantastic and scary because you have to constantly assess how many changes you can try to incorporate without driving everybody completely insane.*

Impact of the Theatre Space   Just as the writing of the play went through many stages, so the production of the play changed from theatre to theatre, which had an enormous impact on the final shape of the play. The home of the Eureka Theatre was a converted warehouse off Market Street in San Francisco. With a stage that measured twenty-five feet by twenty-five feet and an audience space of 200 seats, the theatre was only a little larger than East West Players or Northwest Asian American Theatre. Old wooden bleachers were used to form ten rows of seating accommodating twenty people per row. The existing pipes were exposed across the ceiling, lowering the height of the performance space and increasing the "rough" atmosphere of the interior of the building. The Brechtian idea of exposing the mechanics of the theatre meshed conveniently with the theatre space.

Tony Taccone: *It had a kind of raw but exciting feel. It was always a little too hot or too cold, but it had a lot of energy. Everything was exposed at the Eureka. You could never hide anything.*

The limitations of the stage space and the financial resources of the Eureka Theatre encouraged the development of a play that focused on the resources of the actors. For example, in writing the play for the Eureka Theatre, Kushner ended up creating a play with twenty-one characters for a total of eight actors—five men and three women. The range of

characters grew out of the needs of the original Eureka company with the addition of four men who were invited to join the group.

And yet as Kushner expanded the scope of the play in response to the company, he found he needed many more characters than there were actors. Kushner's intention was for the actors to play more than one part. The actors then had the responsibility of shifting between characters who existed in the present and characters who came out of the past or between realistic characters and fantasy characters.

Kathleen Chalfant, who played Hannah Pitt, Joe's Mormon mother from Salt Lake City, also played three other roles in *Millennium Approaches*—Ethel Rosenberg, the rabbi who conducts the funeral service for Louis's grandmother at the beginning of the play, and the doctor, Henry, who tells Roy Cohn that he has AIDS. The development of each character was helped by costume changes, varying hairstyles, and, for the rabbi, a long beard. But the emphasis was on Chalfant's creativity in drawing distinct characters and on her skill in quickly moving from character to character in performance. The double casting had stylistic and philosophical implications. Chalfant observed that "Not only did Tony want women to play men, but he wanted women to play male authority figures, which is rare."[9]

The double casting at the Eureka challenged the ingenuity of the actors and kept the audience from identifying each actor with only one role. The audience became more conscious of the actors as actors rather than only as certain characters. There was an awareness of an ensemble of actors working closely together to tell Kushner's complicated story. The actors also did most of the scene changes, which reinforced the audience's perception of the actors as arrangers of the event as well as inhabitants of the play. The necessities of the Eureka Theatre production—the double casting and having the actors change the sets—were subsequently written into the script to be used even at larger theatres with more substantial resources.

Refining the Balance Between Intimacy and Spectacle The Eureka production emphasized the intimate nature of the character relationships. Most of the scenes in *Angels in America* are between two characters and focus on personal details. In performance at the Eureka, the energy of the work went into the intensity and immediacy of the characters' needs and revelations.

Tony Taccone: *The simplicity of the show when it was done at the Eureka was brilliant. It was really straightforward and wonderfully clear. The play was in the lap of the audience, and that created an intimacy and urgency that made for a fantastic theatre experience.*

When the play moved to larger theatres, the spectacle became increasingly important, enlarging the background against which individual lives were seen.

Refining the balance between intimacy and spectacle—expanding Kushner's idea of a "fantasia"—became of primary importance in productions subsequent to the performances at the Eureka. For example, the presence of the Angel took on much larger dimensions at the Mark Taper Forum and then at the Walter Kerr Theatre in New York (Color Plate 37). The angel's entrance from eighteen inches at the Eureka Theatre became an entrance from thirty feet above the stage at the Mark Taper Forum.

Tony Taccone: *The Angel was flown in from high above with a halogen light behind her bright enough to light up the city of New York. There was a terrific amount of smoke and a very full sound track. It was spectacular.*

The much greater stage height at the Mark Taper and the more sophisticated flying apparatus allowed the producers to build the image of the Angel as a force of majestic power. This possibility contributed to Kushner's development of the emerging relationship between Prior and the Angel in *Perestroika*.

Act 2, scene 2 of *Perestroika*, a ferocious confrontation between Prior and the Angel, is

Ellen McLaughlin appears in her first incarnation as the Angel in the original production of Angels in America *at the Eureka Theatre. (See also Color Plate 37.)*

at the heart of Kushner's vision for the play. This is the scene that Ellen McLaughlin memorized in twenty different versions. It becomes a heroic and symbolic or allegorical battle for Prior's soul. The Angel turns out to be a conservative force who demands that human beings stop moving, that they stop trying to change.

ANGEL:
Forsake the Open Road:
Neither Mix nor Intermarry: Let Deep Roots
    Grow:
If you do not Mingle you will Cease to Progress:
Seek Not to Fathom the World and its Delicate
    Particle Logic:
You cannot Understand, You can only Destroy,
. . .
Turn back. Undo.[10]

Prior comes to understand that if he accepts the Angel's message of "stasis," it becomes his death sentence. He rejects the Angel's vision because he realizes that change is the only course of human action that can lead to "more life." Director Taccone describes the scene as a "wild landscape of evocative images that are all designed to create this huge conflict between a dying gay man, struggling to save his life, and an Angel who is not the miracle he is seeking."

In staging this confrontation in Los Angeles, the directors used the technology of the flying apparatus to create what Taccone calls a "fantastic, surreal wrestling match with an angel flying and leaping around the room and an actor who was both stunned and terrified." The scene became a theatricalized encounter between larger-than-life characters playing out a spiritual crisis. The choreographed battle—part dance, part high-wire gymnastics—merged with Kushner's poetic, dreamlike language to create a defining image for the play.

EXPANDING OPPORTUNITIES FOR THE DEVELOPMENT OF NEW PLAYS

Many of the most interesting plays come out of small theatres that do not have a commercial focus. Some of these plays may go on to larger regional theatres and to New York. The hallmark of an American play used to be its success on Broadway, but Broadway is no longer the final judge of a play's merit. At one time most major American plays originated in New York and then toured the country or moved on to regional theatres. Clearly, the course of many successful plays is now reversed. Like *Angels in America*, a play may originate in a regional theatre and work its way to Broadway. New York still has a remarkable concentration of talent and venues that can generate cutting-edge work and support long-running productions. But exciting theatre can emerge from any part of the country where theatres and audiences meet to consider questions about human existence from a new perspective.

In over twenty years of producing plays, the Eureka Theatre has supported the development of more than sixty new plays. Many other theatres also attempt to establish opportunities for new playwrights. In developing new work, theatres understand that they may provide only

the starting point for new plays that will become part of the larger American theatre.

Angels in America outgrew the boundaries of the Eureka Theatre. It became an event that took on a life of its own.

Tony Taccone: *It felt like an avalanche. It started out as a snowball and ended up coursing down the mountainside at a speed that none of us could possibly keep up with or predict.*

The original producers could have tried to contain the play, to keep it within the limits of the Eureka's production capabilities. No one had bargained for a six-year effort that would lead to a marathon extravaganza. But a good part of the energy that comes out of theatre work has to do with the unpredictable nature of whatever may evolve.

Oskar Eustis: *We came to a crisis point where we said, the Eureka cannot produce this play; it's not manageable. The play had taken on a scope that none of us had suspected when we started. It became apparent that it was going to be two evenings long, and that was catastrophic for my poor little theatre company, which had no way of believing that it could work or affording to pay for it.*

The work was telling us it had to be this thing that was larger than we could afford, and I really had two choices: to try to cut the ambition and scope of the piece to fit the Eureka or to say, let's go on this ride and see what happens. My decision was obvious. We went on the ride, and it led to extraordinary results. I think it's a perfect little model for what you have to do in this kind of process.

No previous paradigm is sufficient for creating important new work, because the whole point of it, the whole thing that makes it an art form, is that it is being invented and new. Otherwise, what you're doing is trying to fit new wine into old bottles. You might come up with something that sort of works. But you'll never come up with something that has the kind of galvanic effect that Angels *has, an artwork that is so uniquely, precisely itself. To produce* Angels in America *took years and years. You just have to be willing to get in the trenches and work for as long as it takes. I can't think of anything else that would be more worth doing with your time.*

SUMMARY

A play such as *Angels in America* that draws on many sources of theatrical expression reminds us to be wary of trying to define plays according to rigid categories. *Angels in America* tells a sweeping story of American life that functions on political and personal levels at the same time. Among the styles used by playwright Tony Kushner are realism, epic theatre, expressionism, and absurdism. The rapid shifts between kinds of characters and styles of language are in part influenced by the theatre of Bertolt Brecht. Kushner is also influenced by the plays of Caryl Churchill, who brings together characters from the past and characters from the present to create a historical perspective for contemporary issues. This device is seen in *Angels in America* in the character Ethel Rosenberg, the ancestor Priors, and most of all the character Roy Cohn. The flamboyant presentation of the Angel demonstrates how a theatrical image can be central to a play's expression.

The dramaturg is a relatively new position in the American theatre. In developing *Angels in America* at the Eureka Theatre, the playwright was assisted by Oskar Eustis, who originally commissioned the play and then worked closely on its development. The responsibilities of the dramaturg include new play development as well as research and analysis to help other theatre practitioners in the production of challenging plays.

TOPICS FOR DISCUSSION AND WRITING

If possible, read aloud in class the scenes from *Angels in America* that relate to the following questions:

1. Act 1, scene 9
   In Roy Cohn's confrontation with his doctor, what are the points he uses to construct his identity? What does his argument with his doctor convey about how he sees his place in the world? What does he need to defend against? Does his position express self-awareness?

2. Act 2, scene 9
   Study the shifts back and forth between the two pairs of characters in the scene. From the audience's viewpoint, how do the lines from one pair of characters comment on or contribute to the meaning of the lines from the other pair of characters? What is the cumulative effect of the split scene?

3. Act 3, scene 1
   How do you imagine the staging of the scene with the three Priors? What ideas are suggested by the discussion of the plagues of different centuries? Why would the two ancestor Priors be the ones to announce the coming of the Angel?

NOTES

1. Tony Kushner, *Thinking About the Longstanding Problems of Virtue and Happiness* (New York: Theatre Communications Group, 1995), x.

2. Tony Kushner, *Angels in America: Millennium Approaches* (New York: Theatre Communications Group, 1993), 74.

3. Tony Taccone, interviews with the author, 13 and 16 June 1996. All of Taccone's comments in this chapter come from these interviews.

4. Tony Kushner, acknowledgments to *Angels in America: Part Two: Perestroika* (New York: Theatre Communications Group, 1994), xi.

5. Martin Esslin, "Towards an American Dramaturg," in *Dramaturgy in American Theatre*, ed. Susan Jonas and Geoffrey S. Proehl (Orlando: Harcourt Brace, 1997), 27.

6. Robert Brustein, "From 'The Future of an Un-American Activity,'" in *Dramaturgy in American Theatre*, ed. Jonas and Proehl, 36.

7. Oskar Eustis, interview with the author, 2 June 1996. All of Eustis's remarks in this chapter come from this interview.

8. Susan Jonas, "Tony Kushner's Angels," in *Dramaturgy in American Theatre*, ed. Jonas and Proehl, 473.

9. Kathleen Chalfant, quoted in Eric Grode, "Two Men and a Mormon (And Ethel Rosenberg)," *TheaterWeek*, 20–26 September 1993, 15.

10. Kushner, *Angels: Perestroika*, 52–53.

SUGGESTIONS FOR FURTHER READING

Churchill, Caryl. *Top Girls*. New York: Samuel French, 1982.

One of the best known plays by Caryl Churchill; provides an excellent example of the historical framing techniques adapted by Tony Kushner.

Fisher, James. *The Theatre of Tony Kushner: Living Past Hope*. New York: Routledge, 2002.

An examination of the life and work of playwright Tony Kushner, including *Angels in America* and *Homebody/Kabul*. The author explores Kushner's dramatic innovations, thematic concerns, and the critical reception of the plays as well as their production histories.

Jonas, Susan, and Geoffrey S. Proehl, eds. *Dramaturgy in American Theatre*. Orlando: Harcourt Brace, 1997.

Essays on the nature of dramaturgy and the ways this new role is beginning to change the American theatre.

Kahn, David, and Donna Breed. *Scriptwork: A Director's Approach to New Play Development*. Carbondale: Southern Illinois University Press, 1995.

A book that explores and recommends a process for directors working with playwrights on the development of new scripts; includes interviews with directors and dramaturgs and commentary by Oskar Eustis. The authors were involved at the Eureka Theatre and at other theatres in the development of new plays.

Kushner, Tony. *Homebody/Kabul*. New York: Theatre Communications Group, 2002.

A play about the complex politics and historical circumstances that contribute to the social struggles in Afghanistan. The lives of three English characters are seen as they are disrupted by contact with the turmoil of Afghanistan. An English woman has disappeared in Kabul, leaving her husband and daughter to try to make sense of what may have happened to her. Like *Angels in America*, the play shapes personal experience as a representation of larger political and social concerns.

Kushner, Tony. *Plays by Tony Kushner*. New York: Broadway Play Publishing, 1992.

An anthology that includes Kushner's first play, *A Bright Room Called Day*—which moves back and forth between the present and pre-Hitler Germany—and his adaptation of Pierre Corneille's *The Illusion*.

Kushner, Tony. *Thinking About the Longstanding Problems of Virtue and Happiness*. New York: Theatre Communications Group, 1995.

A collection of writings that includes essays, the play *Slavs*, two poems, and a prayer about AIDS. The essays include insightful observations about the playwriting process and the history of *Angels in America*.

Osborn, M. Elizabeth, ed. *The Way We Live Now: American Plays and the AIDS Crisis*. New York: Theatre Communications Group, 1990.

A collection of excerpts from plays about AIDS, including work by Paul Vogel (*The Baltimore Waltz*), Terrence McNally (*Andre's Mother*), and Susan Sontag (*The Way We Live Now*); also contains an excerpt from *Angels in America* and an introduction by theatre critic Michael Feingold.

The Nature of Drama

Structure and Genre

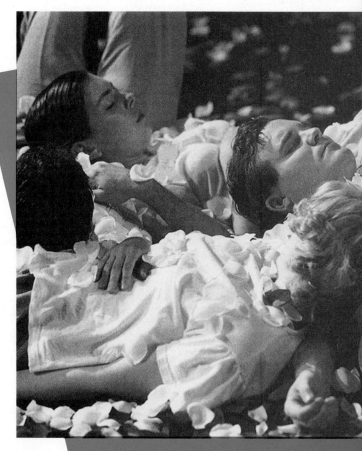

Drama is a unique art form with its own particular structural characteristics. We have distinguished theatre from film because theatre is performed live in front of an audience. We may also distinguish drama from other forms of written storytelling because of the way drama is built through character action and dialogue. A novelist writes descriptively, filling in details of the environment, atmosphere, character history, and psychology necessary to the reader's understanding of the work. The playwright works in a different medium, one in which the essence of the work is expressed through the nature of the characters and what they do and say.

The last section of the book presents two approaches to assessing dramatic form. Chapter 12 takes up the study of dramatic structure, the parts or elements of the drama and the relationship between those parts. Using the plays that we have read, the chapter looks at the building of the drama through character, plot, language, and spectacle. Chapter 13 then introduces another way of identifying dramatic characteristics through the study of genre. Genre divides the drama into categories—tragedy, comedy, melodrama, tragicomedy, and farce—and indicates the area of human experience addressed by the playwright. For example, tragedy confronts the significance of human mortality while comedy celebrates our ability to endure. Each genre considers human existense from a different perspective.

In Chapter 14 we focus on the genre of comedy through the study of another play and its production, *Dog Lady* by Milcha Sanchez-Scott. In *Dog Lady* we see the work of an American playwright who uses comedy to express the contradictions and struggles of her characters. Concerns about identity, male-female relationships, the importance of tradition, and realigning community values emerge from a lighthearted play about running a marathon. The production of the play at INTAR shows some of the techniques and creative approaches that theatre practitioners may use in staging a comedy.

Chapter 15 concludes Part Four with a final play, *Buried Child* by Sam Shepard. However, *Buried Child* is not accompanied by extensive background materials or a production analysis. Instead, the last chapter of the book offers students the opportunity to engage in the creative process and imagine their own production of this play.

CHAPTER 12

The Elements of Drama and Dramatic Structure

We have now studied three plays in some detail and surveyed a number of dramatic traditions. We therefore have the resources to make some observations about the structure of plays. A discussion of dramatic structure provides us with a way of summarizing the work of the playwright.

FUNDAMENTAL ELEMENTS OF STRUCTURE

At the center of the drama are its characters and the stories they tell through their actions. Character action may show events or human conflict or a movement of the human spirit. Drama is distinguished from fiction because its fundamental expression comes through character action. When the curtain goes up or the stage lights come on, one or more actors must enter the stage, impersonating characters who are involved in some kind of action. To this impersonation of characters all kinds of elaborations are added through plot, language, music, and spectacle.

This list of elements is similar to the one originally proposed by the Greek philosopher Aristotle. Writing in the fourth century B.C.E., Aristotle began a dialogue on the nature of the drama, particularly tragedy, that has continued through the ages to our own time. Aristotle's analysis, consisting of a series of lectures, is known as *The Poetics*. It should be noted, though, that in Aristotle's sequence of dramatic elements, plot comes before character.

Many drama teachers and critics have found Aristotle's list of structural elements to be a useful starting point in understanding the unique nature of the drama. To the five elements of the drama already mentioned, Aristotle added theme (or ideas), what he identified as "thought."

All of the first five elements (character, plot, language, music, and spectacle) are completely interrelated. We separate them in the following discussion only for the purpose of analysis rather than to suggest that character and plot or character and language exist independently of each other. Each element defines or shapes the others. We know who characters are by what they say or the actions they perform. But of all six structural elements, the ideas or thoughts in a play are the most difficult to separate from the other elements of dramatic expression. Form, that is the arrangement of character, plot, language, music, and spectacle, is what creates meaning. As we consider the structural components of the three plays we have read, we will see the emergence of further layers of "thought" created by the playwrights.

One of the most vivid characters of the Western theatre is Tartuffe, created by the great seventeenth-century French comic playwright Molière. Tartuffe is a supreme con artist who invades the life of a decent family with the goal of acquiring the family fortune. Hiding behind the mask of a devoutly religious man, he manages to indulge his obscene appetites. The photograph from the Hartford Stage Company (Connecticut) production of Tartuffe, directed by Mark Lamos, shows Tartuffe (David Patrick Kelly) attempting the seduction of Elmire (Maureen Anderson), his gullible benefactor's wife.

Character

The theatre celebrates what is extraordinary about life. The essential agents of the extraordinary in the drama are the characters. The characters who appear on the stage have remarkable qualities that may draw us to them, as we are drawn to Seth and Bertha in *Joe Turner's Come and Gone*, or that may repel us, as we are repelled by Roy Cohn in *Angels in America*. They may be ordinary characters, such as Hana in *And the Soul Shall Dance* or Prior in *Angels in America*, who behave in exceptional ways under difficult conditions. Or, like Emiko in *And the Soul Shall Dance*, they may be characters who are too large for the circumstances in which they are placed. The characters are our point of entry into the world of the play. They must take us with them. The characters must capture our attention and our imagination.

Part of what makes characters compelling is their will, their determination. Whatever the object of that determination, characters have overwhelming desires that propel them to action. Actors frequently begin their preparation for a role by seeking out the characters'

In a one-woman show, Tod Randolph creates a moving portrait of Virginia Woolf. Directed by Daniel Uaron for Shakespeare & Company, A Room of One's Own *dramatizes Woolf's painful internal struggles.*

motivations, that is, the characters' objectives or intentions. All characters who successfully hold the stage have some urgent goal that they strive to accomplish or some formidable obstacle to overcome. Herald Loomis is driven to find his wife. Seth is determined to make a decent life for himself and his wife, Bertha. Emiko is compelled to maintain her illusion that she will return to her old life in Japan. Roy Cohn is desperate to prevent his disbarment. Even in a play such as *Waiting for Godot,* in which the whole action is based on what could be a passive condition, waiting, the two main characters are driven to fill their time, compelled to converse, obsessed with puzzling out their situation.

Characters are defined by their actions, their motives, their histories, the selection of words that make up their vocabularies, and their reactions and responses to other characters. We learn more about them through what they say about themselves, what others say about them, and the physical descriptions provided by the playwright. For example, in *Angels in America,* the character of Roy Cohn is first defined through his relationship to the telephone. The playwright's description for act 1, scene 2 of the play, in which the character of Roy Cohn first appears, is as follows:

Roy and Joe in Roy's office. Roy at an impressive desk, bare except for a very elaborate phone system, rows and rows of flashing buttons which bleep and beep and whistle incessantly, making chaotic music underneath Roy's conversations. Joe is sitting, waiting. Roy conducts business with great energy, impatience and sensual abandon: gesticulating, shouting, cajoling, crooning, playing the phone, receiver and hold button with virtuosity and love. (Angels in America: Millennium Approaches, *act 1, scene 2*)

The intensity and sensuality of the character's interaction with the telephone provide a vivid physicalization of the character's nature. Here is one of the great manipulators in American history, the power player par excellence, lovingly plying the tool of his trade. The telephone is his link to the other power players, and the joy of modern technology allows Cohn to expand his influence according to the number of lines he can control. Cohn's opening line is vulgarly exuberant: "I wish I was an octopus, a fucking octopus. Eight loving arms and all those suckers. Know what I mean?" And while he plays the telephone as he would a musical instrument or a lover, he is acutely aware of being watched. Cohn is always "on." He is always dramatizing himself for effect.

Plot

Character action and plot are closely intertwined. The plot is the spine of the play and is made up of all the essential character actions or incidents. The significant events, the sequence

In Mark Medoff's play Children of a Lesser God, *the plot consists of the tightly woven interactions between a teacher and his deaf and hearing-impaired students. A love relationship between James and Sarah develops in spite of the difficulties of communication and Sarah's fierce struggle for independence. Gordon Davidson directed Phyllis Frelich and John Rubenstein in the production at the Mark Taper Forum.*

and pace of character entrances, the confrontations between characters, the changes in the situation, and the outcome of the various actions contribute to the development of the plot. In *Joe Turner's Come and Gone*, the plot revolves around the arrivals of the different characters at the boardinghouse and the interactions between them. Although the actions of all of the characters are important, the most important plot incidents have to do with the arrival of Herald Loomis, his search for his wife, his conflict with Seth, and his exchanges with Bynum.

A plot structure can be very simple, as is the plot of *And the Soul Shall Dance*, or it can be tremendously complicated, as is the plot of *Angels in America: Millennium Approaches*, with

its thirty-five scenes. It is through what happens in the drama that playwrights shape their ideas and their worldviews. To illustrate, let's compare the two plays by Yamauchi and Kushner.

In a realistic play, such as *And the Soul Shall Dance*, causality is extremely important to plot structure. The incidents are all closely linked in terms of both time and logic. One character action leads directly to another: the characters are brought together because the bathhouse has burned down; because Oka has stolen Emiko's money, Emiko is driven to sell her kimonos. In contrast, the plot structure of *Angels in America* is more arbitrary; Kushner organizes a sequence of events that lack the organic connections of a realistic drama. His jump-cut style juxtaposes snippets of different stories. It is only once the various plot threads begin to intertwine that we see an external logic at work.

A further example of causality in *And the Soul Shall Dance* is the inclusion of two contradictory characters, Emiko and Oka, who are married by proxy and come to live in hostile and isolated circumstances. Disaster thus becomes inevitable. The characters are set on a collision course from the outset. In contrast, there is no causal logic for the appearance of Prior 1 and Prior 2 in *Angels in America*, nor is there anything inevitable about the arrival of the Angel.

In her play, Yamauchi presents the closely interwoven detail of a small domestic drama as a way of illuminating what turns out to be a moment of great significance for all of the characters but particularly for the child, Masako. In contrast, Kushner presents a cosmic drama to comment on the relationship between individual conduct and national priorities.

Language

Although language is not present in all forms of drama and although many modern theatre practitioners have modified the centrality of words in the theatre, language is one of the great sources of vitality in the theatre. Language defines the characters and gives them au-

Under Milk Wood *was originally written by Welsh poet Dylan Thomas for radio. Frequently pro-*
duced on the stage, Under Milk Wood *evokes the inner life of a small Welsh town through the voices*
of its residents, who recount stories and memories and engage in brief, fragmentary dialogues. Thomas's
language is alive with richly textured sounds and eloquent imagery. The episodes are connected through
narration rather than plot. In the Hartford Stage Company production directed by Mark Lamos, ten
actors played the more than sixty characters.

thenticity and credibility. The speech rhythms and vocabulary of the characters in *And the Soul Shall Dance* and *Joe Turner's Come and Gone* are critical to the audience's perception of time, place, and character history. In *Angels in America*, Tony Kushner has a number of political arguments to make. What gives the play vitality is the gutsy language of the individual characters that makes them resonate as human beings, not as stick puppets of the playwright delivering prepared speeches. Dramatic language must somehow appeal to the audience's imagination and contribute to the sensory appeal of the play.

The vitality of Tony Kushner's language comes from the wit and biting sarcasm of his characters. The play is energized by its brashness and its humor. *Angels in America* uses a range of verbal approaches to match the odd and explosive mix of plot devices and characters. Much of the language is the intimate, domestic language of characters who share their lives, and this intimate language is at the heart of the play, the language with which the characters reveal themselves to each other. Frequently this language is sexually charged in an earthy and graphic way. At other times the language incorporates a sexual vocabulary that is

Playwright David Mamet interprets American life through harsh and repetitive language. Vocabulary is reduced to only essential phrases to give a concentrated sense of character and situation. In Glengarry Glen Ross, *real estate salesmen desperately compete for sales opportunities. The premiere production was directed by Gregory Mosher at the Goodman Theatre in Chicago.*

hostile and manipulative; in Roy Cohn's mouth, language becomes abuse. Some of the characters also use a kind of **camp** that is tied to the gay community—lines quoted from *The Wizard of Oz*, *A Streetcar Named Desire*, and *Come Back, Little Sheba*. The Angel speaks in heightened, mystic poetry; Hebrew words and phrases are used to imply the Angel's ancient biblical origins. Yiddish brings a sense of Jewish tradition and history to Ethel Rosenberg and Louis. And of great importance is the intellectual quality of the language as the characters struggle with ideas and arguments:

VOICE: I can't stay. I will return.
PRIOR: Are you one of those "Follow me to the other side" voices?

VOICE: No. I am no nightbird. I am a messenger . . .
PRIOR: You have a beautiful voice, it sounds . . . like a viola, like a perfectly tuned, tight string, balanced, the truth. . . . Stay with me.
VOICE: Not now. Soon I will return, I will reveal myself to you; I am glorious, glorious; my heart, my countenance and my message. You must prepare.
PRIOR: For what? I don't want to . . .
VOICE: No death, no:

A marvelous work and a wonder we undertake, an edifice awry we sink plumb and straighten, a great Lie we abolish, a great error correct, with the rule, sword and broom of Truth!

Color Plate 25 *The play* 36 Views *by Naomi Lizuka, shown here in production at the Public Theatre, presents many layers of meaning seen from different angles. The play takes its name and premise from the series of woodblock prints entitled "Thirty-six Views of Mount Fuji" by the Japanese artist Katsushika Hokusai. The play's concerns with the nature of art and East-West collisions are rendered through complex visual imagery as significant as the play's language. The lighting for the production by David Weiner has a major role in integrating the visual material and guiding the eye of the audience. The director is Mark Wing-Davey; set design is by Douglas Stein, and costumes are by Myung Hee Cho.*

Color Plate 26 *Sally Bowles, played here by Natasha Richardson in the 1997 revival of* Cabaret *directed by Sam Mendes, lives for her appearances at the Kit Kat Club.*

Color Plate 27   Into the Woods *has proven to be one of Sondheim's most popular creations with numerous productions in regional and community theatres all over the country in addition to Broadway success. Sondheim and his collaborator, James Lapine, have woven together a number of well-known fairy tales, including* Cinderella, Jack and the Beanstalk, *and* Little Red Riding Hood, *with characters entering each other's stories and complicating everyone's circumstances. The characters' greedy insistence on acquiring material possessions, new experiences, or new relationships leads to dissatisfaction at best and disaster at worst. Their quests all take place in the mysterious woods full of danger and surprises, designed here by Douglas W. Schmidt for the 2001 Broadway revival. The design of the woods must provide an environment for three hours of complex action where the characters lose and then find themselves.*

Color Plate 28   At the end of A Chorus Line, *the vulnerability and anxiety of the individual actors hoping to be cast is replaced by the confidence and unity of the chorus line. In the musical's finale, the actors have the chance to pull out all the stops as they sing and dance their triumph, wearing the production's signature gold tuxedoes and top hats.* A Chorus Line *is a tribute to the musical form itself.*

Color Plate 29 *The cast of* Rent *sings and dances "La Vie Bohème" on the tables of the Life Cafe with choreography by Marlies Yearby. In "La Vie Bohème" the characters sing of their social rebellion. Unlike the more structured choreography of* West Side Story *and* A Chorus Line, *the dancing in* Rent *has an informal, improvisational quality.*

Color Plate 30   *Deborah Yates, the girl in the yellow dress, confident and flirtatious, dances with two of her many admirers while Boyd Gaines looks on from the background, unable to join the dance.* Contact *was choreographed and directed by Susan Stroman with costumes by William Ivey Long.*

Color Plate 31 *The 1996 production of* A Doll's House *with Janet McTeer as Nora and Owen Beale as her husband, Torvald, brought a new intensity to their characters' relationship.*

Color Plate 32 *Liam Neeson plays John Proctor and Laura Linney plays Elizabeth Proctor in the 2002 Broadway revival of Arthur Miller's play* The Crucible *about the Salem witch trials, directed by Richard Eyre. In* The Crucible, *a rigid belief system is easily corrupted by lies when community members are falsely accused of witchcraft.*

Color Plate 33   In Wakako Yamauchi's play 12-1-A, the characters arrive at an internment camp with the one suitcase each they were allowed to bring and the identification tags they were required to wear. Becky Roscher, May Cha, Brian Kameoka, Chisao Hata, Phil Duong, S. H. Kim, and Tsune Tateoka play the characters who must learn to survive a new form of dislocation in a 1999 production directed by Stephanie Arnold.

Color Plate 34   In this 2002 production of Mother Courage at the Ma-Yi Theatre, Mother Courage (Ching Valdes Aran) bargains with a soldier who has stopped her wagon. While Mother Courage is preoccupied with matters of business, one of her sons slips away to join the army. This adaptation by Rodolfo Carlos Vera, directed by Tazewell Thompson, places the drama in the midst of conflict in the Philippines.

Color Plate 35 Bill Irwin is drawn to the philosophical concerns of playwright Samuel Beckett. He attempts to physicalize the suspension of Beckett's characters in a nightmare landscape. In 2001 Irwin did a solo performance of prose writing by Beckett entitled Texts for Nothing, photographed here at Seattle Repertory Theatre. The action of the piece consisted of Irwin trying to overcome the forces of nature that inevitably pull him down.

Color Plate 36 (following page) Mr. Lies emerges from Harper's hallucinations to help her escape when the reality of living with Joe Pitt becomes overwhelming, as seen in the New York production of Angels in America directed by George C. Wolfe.

Color Plate 37 (following page) By the time Angels in America was staged in New York, the Angel, still played by Ellen McGlaughlin, had become a stupendous creation that symbolized the entire work.

Color Plate 38 Lysistrata by Aristophanes is a comedy dating from the fifth century B.C.E. in
Athens, the same time period in which the great Greek tragedies were written. It is a play full of broad

Color Plate 39   When King Lear gives up his throne, he unleashes a bloody power struggle, as shown in this production of King Lear at Actors Theatre of Louisville. Lear sets in motion a sequence of events that eventually claim his life and the life of his only loyal daughter, Cordelia. The Louisville production, directed by Jon Jory, set the play in the deserts of the Middle East prior to the twentieth century.

Color Plate 40 *The tormented family reappears mysteriously at the end of* Six Characters in Search of an Author *at the Oregon Shakespeare Festival's second company in Portland, Oregon (now Portland Center Stage).*

Color Plate 41 *Stanley Ipkiss, played by Jim Carrey, re-creates himself as a bizarre, but romantic, hero dancing with Cameron Diaz in* The Mask. *The masked character fulfills the fantasies of the nice guy who always finishes last.*

Color Plate 42   *The visual art of Yolanda Lopez is connected in spirit to the plays of Milcha Sanchez-Scott. In the* Portrait of the Artist as the Virgin of Guadalupe, *Lopez creates an homage to working-class women. The young woman exuberantly jumps off the crescent moon that has served as a pedestal in the past, carrying with her the snake that symbolizes the tree of knowledge and sexuality as well as Aztec concepts of birth, death, and rebirth. The work is part of the artist's reconsideration of women taking control of their lives. The figure in this painting suggests Rosalinda running in* Dog Lady.

Color Plate 43   *The set for* Dog Lady, *designed by Ming Cho Lee, uses perspective painting to create an image of a Los Angeles barrio street with palm trees and the freeway in the distance. Through the designer's ingenuity, the narrow stage space at INTAR was transformed into a magical setting for Milcha Sanchez-Scott's characters.*

Color Plate 44 True West *continues Sam Shepard's exploration of familial conflict. Here two brothers, Austin (Todd Cerveris) and Lee (Ted Koch), fight for control of their relationship in the 2002 production at Arena Stage directed by Howard Shalwitz.*

British playwright Tom Stoppard pursues philosophical puzzles through a dazzling display of wit and verbal fireworks. In his play Arcadia, *the plot shifts back and forth between two sets of characters who live in different centuries but who inhabit the same setting and are engaged in a similar quest for knowledge. In the Portland Repertory Theatre (Oregon) production of* Arcadia, *Dennis Bigelow directed Winslow Corbett as the precocious Thomasina and William Harper as her tutor, Septimus Hodge.*

PRIOR: What are you talking about, I . . .

VOICE: I am on my way; when I am manifest,
  our Work begins:
  Prepare for the parting of the air,
  The breath, the ascent, . . .
  (act 2, scene 5)

The language of Wakako Yamauchi's play is marked by a poetic concentration and restraint. Within the framework of Japanese speech rhythms, the characters speak with economy and understatement. The language has none of the over-the-top verbal fireworks of *Angels in America*. It operates as if within a different musical scale. Because the characters function in a culture of public reserve, nuance and subtext become very important:

KIYOKO: She does! She hates me.

HANA: No. I don't think you have anything to do with it. It's this place. She hates it. This place is so lonely and alien.

KIYOKO: Then why didn't she go back? Why did they stay here?

HANA: You don't know. It's not so simple. Sometimes I think . . .

KIYOKO: Then why don't they make the best of it here? Like you?

HANA: That isn't easy either. Believe me. Sometimes . . . sometimes the longing for

Shakespeare frequently included songs in his plays. In this production of As You Like It, *set in the American West of the nineteenth century, Jacques (David Darlow) asks for a song. Directed by Michael Maggio at the Goodman Theatre.*

home . . . the longing fills me with despair. Will I never return again? Will I never see my mother, my father, my sisters again? But what can one do? There are responsibilities here . . . children . . . (*pause*) And another day passes . . . another month . . . another year. (act 2, scene 2)

August Wilson also brings to the theatre a unique character dialogue that reflects his many years of writing poetry before becoming a playwright. Individual characters are defined by their own speech patterns, and yet a strong contrapuntal structure that blends the many rhythms and patterns connects all of the speeches to make an almost-musical whole. Repetition is one of the devices that Wilson uses in creating these poetic rhythms. A character

may repeat himself, or a phrase may be passed from character to character:

BYNUM: You a farming man, Herald Loomis? You look like you done some farming.

LOOMIS: Same as everybody. I done farmed some, yeah.

BYNUM: I used to work at farming . . . picking cotton. I reckon everybody done picked some cotton.

SETH: I ain't! I ain't never picked no cotton. I was born up here in the North. My daddy was a freedman. I ain't never even seen no cotton!

BYNUM: Mr. Loomis done picked some cotton. Ain't you, Herald Loomis? You done picked a bunch of cotton.

LOOMIS: How you know so much about me?
How you know what I done? How much cotton I picked? (act 2, scene 2)

The short, exuberant exchanges that drive the play forward pause sometimes and open out into the storytelling of first one character and then another. Like a jazz solo improvisation, the storyteller lingers over his subject before the momentum of the play resumes.

Music

When Aristotle included music as one of the basic elements of the drama, he was referring to the musical accompaniment for the choruses and to the chorus members themselves who chanted parts of their text in the Greek tragedies. Almost all forms of theatre use music in one way or another. In opera all of the text is sung, as it is in most forms of Asian theatre. The modern musical alternates between spoken and sung text. In the Asian theatre, musicians almost always appear onstage and are visible throughout the entire performance. Inspired by the Chinese theatre, Bertolt Brecht saw songs as a fundamental way of commenting on character situations and choices. For Robert Wilson music is essential to his strange and elusive images (see Chapter 10). Even plays that don't incorporate music in the dramatic structure use music at various points throughout the production—before the play begins, between scenes, and often during the scenes as a kind of atmospheric background or underscoring of the action. This use of music as underscoring has an enormously important function in film.

For both Wakako Yamauchi and August Wilson, music makes a significant contribution to the rhythms of their plays and the feelings that the characters try to express. Yamauchi uses Japanese folk songs to highlight the texture of the characters' lives. The songs provide a certain nostalgia and connection to a distant homeland, but more important they provide the characters with a kind of special text that

Music is often a primary expressive element in plays that take a variety of forms and deal with serious subjects as well as more lighthearted ones. Cambodia Agonistes, *produced by the Pan Asian Repertory Theatre and directed by Tisa Chang, examined the forces that contributed to the genocide in Cambodia in the 1970s. With music by Louis Stewart and text and lyrics by Ernest Abuba, the production drew on classical Cambodian dance and the arts of Southeast Asia to create a surrealistic drama of good and evil. June Angela plays the Dancer (Mother Cambodia) who is beset by political figures from the East and the West, represented here by puppets.*

goes beyond the accepted language of polite social interaction. So the song "And the Soul Shall Dance" provides Emiko and Masako with a basis for communicating their mutual understanding of the life of the spirit. In *Joe Turner's Come and Gone*, folk songs and blues songs are interwoven into the text. Finding one's song is a major metaphor throughout the play. The

The Theatre de la Jeune Lune (Minneapolis) used a highly imaginative spectacle to capture the fantastic happenings in Carlo Gozzi's eighteenth-century play The Green Bird. In this scene, Renzo (John Bolding) and Barbarina (Felicity Jones) encounter Calmon, King of the Statues. Three designers, Henry Dunn, Steven Epp, and Vincent Gracieux, collaborated to create the set; Felicity Jones designed the costumes.

Juba is a song and dance that all of the characters share. The "Joe Turner Blues" has major thematic significance and is also sung by Bynum as a way of approaching Herald Loomis. And the child, Zonia, sings a children's song about tomorrow that develops her relationship to her father's journey.

Spectacle

Spectacle comes at the end of Aristotle's discussion of dramatic structure, and he all but dismisses it as the least important and least artistic element of the drama. Needless to say, there are many who would disagree. **Spectacle** encompasses everything from acting style and the blocking or movement of the actors to the most breathtaking scenic and special effects. As we have already observed, the playwright may include descriptions of the proposed spectacle, but the interpretation of a play through spectacle is in the hands of the director, the actors, the designers, and the technicians.

The playwright Henrik Ibsen (see Chapter 8) took great care in detailing the scenic elements of his plays. Particularly because individualized, realistic settings were not the norm at the time he wrote his plays, Ibsen's descriptions of the settings contributed greatly to the

developing style of realism as well as made clear the metaphoric significance of each play's environment. Following is his opening description of the scene for *A Doll House*, in which the environment is very inviting but ultimately stifling:

A comfortable room, tastefully, but not expensively furnished. A door to the right in the back wall leads to the entryway; another to the left leads to Helmer's study. Between these doors, a piano. Midway in the left-hand wall a door, and further back a window. Near the window a round table with an armchair and a small sofa. In the right-hand wall, toward the rear, a door, and nearer the foreground a porcelain stove with two armchairs and a rocking chair beside it. Between the stove and the side door, a small table. Engravings on the walls. An etagere with china figures and other small art objects; a small bookcase with richly bound books; the floor carpeted; a fire burning in the stove. It is a winter day.[1]

In *And the Soul Shall Dance*, the playwright suggests simple settings in keeping with a realistic presentation of the material. The East West Players' production of the play with the kabuki-inspired unfolding houses and the rolling tumbleweed added a layer to the cultural context of the play by referencing the Japanese theatre as a backdrop to the Japanese American experience.

For a theatre artist such as Robert Wilson, spectacle is the soul of the drama. Wilson conceptualizes with images rather than with words. His initial plan for a theatre piece consists of sequences of sketches that outline a progression of evolving images. Verbal text plays a part in his dramas, but it is a subsidiary part rather than the foundation.

The twentieth-century theatre philosopher Antonin Artaud wrote in his visionary book *The Theatre and Its Double* that the theatre is a three-dimensional space that must be filled with a concrete poetry of its own.

> I say that the stage is a concrete physical place which asks to be filled, and to be given its own concrete language to speak.
>
> I say that this concrete language, intended for the senses and independent of speech, has first to satisfy the senses, that there is a poetry of the senses as there is a poetry of language, and that this concrete physical language to which I refer is truly theatrical only to the degree that the thoughts it expresses are beyond the reach of the spoken language.[2]

> The problem is to make space speak, to feed and furnish it; like mines laid in a wall of rock which all of a sudden turns into geysers and bouquets of stone.[3]

When Aristotle suggested a diminished place for spectacle in the drama, he may have been deferring to his teacher, the philosopher Plato, who would have eliminated the theatre altogether because of its illusionary nature. But whatever the reason for Aristotle's dismissal of spectacle, the Greek theatre set on a hillside overlooking the sea, with its masked choruses dancing and gods descending from above, had much more in common with the primacy of spatial poetry of which Artaud writes than Aristotle's evaluation admits.

THE ORGANIZATION OF THE DRAMA IN SPACE AND TIME

Some playwrights believe that a credible theatre event depends on not stretching events across too much time or too much space. In certain historical periods of the drama, place was restricted to a single setting and time to a single day. Nevertheless, most playwrights have great faith in the ability of the audience's imagination to keep up with their leaps through the calendar and around the globe. For these dramatists, space and time are organized according to the needs of their material. The plays of Shakespeare are prime examples, with their scenes that shift quickly between castle and battleground or even from nation to nation and with their events that chronicle a span of months or even years.

In *Joe Turner's Come and Gone*, August Wilson creates an action that takes place in Seth and Bertha's boardinghouse over a period of two weeks. The action of *And the Soul Shall Dance* shifts back and forth between two small houses in the Imperial Valley during a time span of about nine months. The time covered by the action of *Angels in America: Millennium Approaches* extends from October 1985 to January 1986 (although *Perestroika* takes the play all the way to 1990). And the thirty-five scenes of the play move between a multiplicity of locations within New York and even to Salt Lake City, as well as into the nightmares and hallucinations of the characters. The time is close to the present, but characters emerge from the past to create a distorted sense of time just as we move in and out of realistic and expressionistic spaces. And although there seems to be a much more concentrated and realistic approach to time in *And the Soul Shall Dance* and *Joe Turner's Come and Gone* than in *Angels in America*, both of these largely realistic plays offer variations on the sequential progression of time. Because *And the Soul Shall Dance* represents Masako's memory, the play may be said to move backward in time as well as forward. And in *Joe Turner's Come and Gone*, the telling of stories interrupts a sequential, realistic sense of time and opens out moments of consciousness into an almost mythical time frame in which large, symbolic actions and legendary figures replace the everyday goings-on of the boardinghouse kitchen.

As the title suggests, Six by Ives *is made up of six one-act plays that together form an evening of the-atre, although each play may be performed separately. Playwright David Ives uses the one-act form to explore the different dynamics of relationships, inventing clever and lively variations on male–female encounters to keep the material fresh and amusing. Photographed here are Karen Trumbo, Sharonlee McLean, William Harper, and Michael Mendelson in "All in the Timing." The production at Portland Repertory Theatre was directed by Dennis Bigelow.*

The Duration of the Performance

In addition to the fictional time created by the stage action, another factor of great importance to the shaping of the drama is the actual time or duration of the theatre event. In Western society, going to the theatre is usually considered an afternoon or evening event. We think of the theatre as providing a concentrated experience that will last from two to three hours; *And the Soul Shall Dance* and *Joe Turner's Come and Gone* fulfill this expectation. But there are also many one-act plays that may range in time from a few minutes to one hour. One-acts are frequently grouped together to form one program or one evening of theatre. Festivals of one-act plays by different playwrights have been popularized by such theatres as Actors Theatre of Louisville, which sponsors the annual Humana Festival. And in recent years various theatres have experimented with very long performances such as the combined parts of *Angels in America*, which lasts about seven hours. Other marathon presentations have featured the work of Robert Wilson and dramatizations of novels such as *Nicholas Nickleby*, by Charles Dickens. Lengthy productions allow the audience to experience a shift in consciousness. Time seems to become suspended as the audience members become immersed in the world of the performance. In the words of Robert Wilson:

> Most theatre deals with speeded-up time, but I use the kind of natural time in which it takes

the sun to set, a cloud to change, a day to dawn. I give you time to reflect, to meditate about other things than those happening on stage. I give time and space in which to think.[4]

It is not uncommon in Asian theatre for the audience to spend all day or all night at the theatre or even several days at a time. For such productions, unwavering concentration is not expected of the audience: in addition to watching the performance, theatregoers socialize, eat, drink, and even nap during the course of the event.

Building the Drama: The Internal Rhythm

Within the plot structures of all dramas, no matter what form they may take, there is an internal rhythm, a relationship between the parts that involves the audience progressively in the theatre experience. As the play or performance changes and develops, the audience's understanding of and commitment to the theatre work increases. Usually this internal rhythm has to do with conflict and rising tension or suspense. What is at stake becomes increasingly important and at the same time more difficult to obtain. Expectations on the verge of fulfillment collapse, and characters must begin again with greater obstacles or change course altogether. Mistaken assumptions lead to disastrous choices that cannot be reversed or require a more heroic effort yet. Character needs are set against each other in such a way that physical or psychological battle is inevitable. Sometimes the internal rhythm of the drama has to do with the building or layering of image upon image or the accumulation of sensory experiences. The interplay between the areas of information or the incidents in the presentation of an epic story create a tension of their own. In this last section of the chapter we examine the more traditional conflict structure that is responsible for building the drama in most of the plays we have studied thus far.

In Topdog/Underdog *by Suzan-Lori Parks, the Pulitzer Prize-winning play for 2002, two brothers search for their place in America and in their own family. Challenging each other through the street con game three-card monte, the brothers engage in a deadly battle of rising tensions. Here Don Cheadle and Jeffrey Wright appear in the 2001 production at the Public Theatre directed by George C. Wolfe.*

Conflict, Rising Tension, and Resolution

Conflict can occur between individual characters, between groups of characters, or between characters and institutions such as governments or religion. Conflict may be internal—that is, within an individual character. Most plays have at least several layers of conflicts, and they have some form of rising tension—a series of escalating confrontations that heighten the conflict and raise the stakes. Frequently, through these confrontations, characters discover new information that changes or reverses their expectations and therefore also intensifies the urgency of their needs or motivations.

In *And the Soul Shall Dance*, the conflict between the Okas generates rising tension that

In this scene from And the Soul Shall Dance, *Emiko finally must face the reality of her situation when she realizes that she will not be able to sell her kimonos. Hana, Masako, and Emiko all experience this devastating moment of recognition in the production at East West Players.*

draws in all of the other characters. Some of the hostility we witness directly in their two violent scenes; some we learn of through Kiyoko's distraught response when she escapes in the middle of the night to seek the Muratas' assistance. In the final confrontation between Oka and Emiko, Oka reveals that he has spent Emiko's savings on Kiyoko. With this terrible reversal of her situation, the urgency of Emiko's motivation increases dramatically. She must now part with her only real treasures if she is to retain any hope of returning to Japan. Thus we have the climactic scene in which Emiko tries to sell her kimonos to Hana and Masako.

Frequently, final climactic scenes are explosive, as in *Joe Turner's Come and Gone* when Loomis pulls out his knife; such scenes may build to almost unbearable suspense that catches audiences with its intensity and then allows them to collect themselves in the final moment of resolution that follows. In *And the Soul Shall Dance,* however, the climactic scene, the kimono scene, has a certain stillness. Despite her desperation, Emiko gathers herself and ventures out beyond her own house for the first time in the play to make one last attempt to

function in the real world. She is motivated by financial need and the illusion of financial possibilities. We do not know whether Emiko has anything to return to in Japan or whether she has any inner resources left to make a new life for herself. She appears to sustain herself with illusions. Her motive grows more complex as her options shrink. As much as she is concerned about the money for herself, it is Masako to whom she wants the kimonos to go. She wants to pass something of what she has known to someone for whom it will make a difference.

Yamauchi takes her time with the resolution and ending of her play. The resolution has three parts. First is the defeat or loss for Emiko, her recognition that there is no way out of her situation. Second is the drawing together of the Murata family in response to the disturbance and suffering that they have witnessed in their neighbors' unhappy lives. The play could have conceivably ended with either of these moments, but the playwright chose to finish with the brief scene on the desert between Emiko and Masako. Emiko, dressed in one of her beautiful kimonos, with her hair down, dances and sings. She has now withdrawn completely into her own world. Masako watches her, hidden behind a shrub. When Emiko senses her presence, she makes one further gesture before she exits. She "empties out her sleeve of imaginary flowers at Masako."

This seems to be the passing of her spirit that Emiko could not achieve through the sale of her kimonos. The domestic drama concludes with the previous scene of the kimonos and the wind chimes. The spiritual drama finishes with this silent little epilogue. We do not know if this scene is real or a function of Masako's memory or imagination. What is important is that Masako has received a gift from Emiko that her own mother could not give her. As Masako picks up the branch that Emiko has dropped, we know that her life is forever changed.

SUMMARY

The playwright constructs a drama through character, plot, language, ideas, music, and spectacle. Different playwrights shape the elements according to the needs of the ideas they wish to express. The placement of the play in one or more locations and the movement of the play through time are also important factors in the construction of the drama. Many plays have an internal rhythm that evolves out of conflict. Rising tension that results in some kind of climactic action is frequently the basis of dramatic plotting. However, a number of dramas move away from this model. The climax may be diffused or the pattern of character interaction or plot incidents may not move in a linear progression of increasing tension but may use repetition or a layering of images to create a cumulative awareness of the dramatic situation.

TOPICS FOR DISCUSSION AND WRITING

1. How many levels of conflict are part of the structure of *Joe Turner's Come and Gone?* Cite examples of internal conflict, conflict between characters, and conflict between groups of characters or between characters and institutions.

2. Create an idea for a brief two- or three-character play. Make a cast list in which you briefly describe each character. Create a plot outline in which you list the major events of the play. Focus on the important character actions and the conflicts between the characters.

3. Choose one of the three plays that we have read thus far. How does the language of the play affect your responses to the material? Does the language provoke images or associations in your own mind? Does the language prompt emotional or physical responses? What mood or feeling does the language create? How would you describe the playwright's use of language to someone who has not read the play?

NOTES

1. Henrik Ibsen, *A Doll House*, in *Henrik Ibsen: The Complete Major Prose Plays*, trans. Rolfe Fjelde (New York: New American Library, 1978), 125. Fjelde translates the title as *A Doll House*, though most American productions use the title *A Doll's House*.

2. Antonin Artaud, *The Theatre and Its Double* (New York: Grove Press, 1958), 37.

3. Artaud, 98.

4. Robert Wilson, quoted in a brochure from the UCLA Extension, "Robert Wilson: Artist in Residence," May 1985.

SUGGESTIONS FOR FURTHER READING

Bermel, Albert. *Contradictory Characters: An Interpretation of Modern Theatre.* Evanston, IL: Northwestern University Press, 1996.

A study of character conflict in drama between characters, between character and the environment and most particularly within individual characters. The text analyzes plays by Ibsen, Strindberg, Chekhov, O'Neill, Beckett, and Brecht.

Betsko, Kathleen, and Rachel Koenig. *Interviews with Contemporary Women Playwrights.* New York: Beech Tree Books, 1987.

> A wealth of ideas about writing for the theatre and the changes being brought about by the greater participation of women playwrights, including Caryl Churchill, Maria Irene Fornes, Beth Henley, Emily Mann, Marsha Norman, and Ntozake Shange.

Cole, Toby, ed. *Playwrights on Playwriting.* New York: Hill and Wang, 1961.

> A collection of essays by major European and American playwrights on the craft of playwriting, including notes on the creation of specific plays; begins with Ibsen and concludes with Ionesco.

Corrigan, Robert, and James L. Rosenberg. *The Context and Craft of Drama.* San Francisco: Chandler, 1964.

> A collection of essays by distinguished critics on the essence of the drama; addresses questions such as what is a play? How does it work? What is plot? What is the function of language in the drama? What is the role of the audience?

Esslin, Martin. *Anatomy of Drama.* New York: Hill and Wang, 1977.

> A simple but eloquent discussion about the nature of the drama and the place of the audience in determining its meaning.

George, Kathleen. *Rhythm in Drama.* Pittsburgh: University of Pittsburgh Press, 1980.

> A careful analysis of the many factors that in combination make up the rhythm of a play.

McLaughlin, Buzz. *The Playwright's Process: Learning the Craft from Today's Leading Dramatists.* New York: Back Stage Books, 1997.

> A hands-on breakdown of the playwriting process, with commentary on all of its stages by leading American playwrights such as Edward Albee, John Guare, Tina Howe, Arthur Miller, and Emily Mann.

Sona, Kathy, Gretchen Van Lente, and Todd Miller. *Dramatists Sourcebook: 2002–2003 Edition.* New York: Theatre Communications Group, 2002.

> A discussion of opportunities for playwrights, translators, composers, lyricists, and librettists. This book includes advice on submitting work for production and publication as well as listings of producing theatres, publishers, prizes, grants, and other resources.

CHAPTER 13

Genre

In the preceding chapters we looked at the playwright's artistic vision and the development of that vision through style and dramatic construction. In this chapter we consider another dimension of the drama: the way the drama views human existence or divides human experience. In simple terms, we divide drama into the serious and the comic, into tragedy and comedy. To these divisions we can add tragicomedy, a form of drama that moves between serious and comic views. The term **genre** refers to a specific division, or classification, of drama. The most frequently used classifications, or genres, of drama are tragedy, comedy, melodrama, tragicomedy, and farce.

INTRODUCTION TO GENRE

In thinking about genres, we must remember that categorization is a tool for exploration, not an end itself. Furthermore, genres frequently merge or overlap rather than adhere to neat and tidy boundaries. The organization of the drama into genres offers a way to examine the shifting viewpoint on human experience and a comparable shift in the audience's response to the drama.

What makes the study of genre worthwhile is the insight that each particular form of drama contributes to our understanding of the relationship between human beings and the world or the universe. Studying genre leads us to consider some of the most troublesome questions about human existence. How much control do we have over our own lives? Are human beings responsible for their own actions? Are we merely victims of circumstance? Are human beings capable of heroic action, or do we often blunder at the critical moment or fail to recognize the significant issues? How high or low is our aim? Are we free, or is there an external force, either divine or random, that ultimately controls, contradicts, or renders meaningless all of our actions?

TRAGEDY AND COMEDY

Genre begins with tragedy and comedy, the most basic—though not necessarily opposite—parts of the dramatic experience. Tragedy and comedy are two different ways of understanding the fundamental rhythms of the human life cycle. Tragedy frequently ends in disaster. Although violence and death are central to most tragedies, it is the awareness of our mortality that seems most relevant to the tragic understanding of life. Tragedy explores the notion that no matter how great our human achievement, life is finite. We cannot overcome our mortality, nor can we overcome the hostilities or inconsistencies in the universe. The limitations of human mortality are addressed in the following passage from the Greek poet Pindar:

> One is the race of gods and of men; from one mother we both draw our breath. Yet are our powers poles apart; for we are nothing, but for them the brazen Heaven endures forever, their secure abode.[1]

Pindar suggests that human beings are godlike in their aspirations. But the gods, however we interpret them or whatever forces they

---

CHARACTERISTICS OF COMEDY

- Comedy celebrates the continuation of life, the success of generations through love and rebirth.
- The plot of comedy usually involves an outrageous idea or fantastic scheme that disrupts the normal workings of the community and leads to chaos.
- Comedy usually looks at characters as part of a social group.
- Comic characters tend to reflect human weakness.
- Comedy often takes place in the realm of the ludicrous.
- The world of comedy is a protected world where there is no pain.
- Comedy ends with a reconciliation or happy resolution, frequently including an engagement or marriage.
- Comedy exists to make us laugh, but its underlying subject matter is often serious and involves some kind of social critique.
- The performance of comedy depends on broad physicality, timing, and rapport between actor and audience.

---

represent, are constant. They do not die. Human beings, for all their intelligence, courage, and will, can never achieve the immortality of the gods or the constant forces of the universe.

In contrast to tragedy, comedy looks to the continuation of life rather than to its finality. In spite of all the pitfalls and the setbacks, in spite of the pettiness of human behavior and our foolish self-importance, life goes on. Comedy focuses on the success of generations rather than on the mortality of the individual. Through love and rebirth, there is continuance.

The plot of comedy usually begins with an outrageous idea or a fantastic scheme that disrupts the normal workings of the community. Incongruous events are frequently complicated by mistaken identity and misunderstandings.

A Midsummer Night's Dream *by William Shakespeare is a comedy based on mistaken identity and the separation of lovers who are all reconciled at the end. Here, asleep in the bewitched woods, are Hermia, Helena, Demetrius, and Lysander played by Jennifer Mudge Tucker, Vanessa Hidary, Eric Tucker, and Mauro Hantman in the Trinity Repertory Company production.*

Gullibility, greed, egotism, and hypocrisy appear to rule the day. Lovers are separated, fortunes are lost, and chaos seems to reign supreme. But common sense prevails, the misunderstandings are resolved, and the reconciliation of all the separated factions leads to the affirmation of true love. Comedies frequently end in marriage or engagements.

Comedy exists to make us laugh. But the brilliance of comedy lies in its ability to take on the most serious subjects while evoking the deepest laughter. Perhaps we laugh hardest at the exposure of things that concern us the most or, as Bill Irwin has observed, that frighten us the most. War, religion, politics, generational conflict, and sexual relationships are common subjects of comedy.

Origins in Greek Drama

The original designations of tragedy and comedy in the theatre were arrived at simply. In the early Greek theatre, all plays that dealt with lofty and serious subjects were called tragedies. The word *tragedy* is derived from the Greek word that means "goat song"—a song that was sung in honor of Dionysus. Plays that dealt

with human weakness and folly were called comedies.

The Greeks were certainly aware of the proximity of tragedy and comedy in describing human experience. Originally, comedies were performed as companion pieces to tragedies to complete the picture of human endeavor. The tragic side looked to the human actor engaged in noble causes. The comic side revealed that underneath the heroic guise, humans are terrified and capable of the most ridiculous posturing and mistakes (Color Plate 38). In the Greek theatre the genres were maintained as separate but complementary entities. In contrast, contemporary playwrights frequently mix comic and tragic elements in the same play because that approach seems to most effectively reflect their understanding of life's rhythms in today's world.

Aristotle on Tragedy and Comedy

In his series of lectures that were collected under the title *The Poetics* (see Chapter 12), Aristotle described the nature of tragedy. In defining tragedy, he included a few asides on the nature of comedy. Aristotle summarized the distinction between tragedy and comedy in two statements. In the first he wrote:

> Comedy aims at representing men as worse,
> Tragedy as better than in actual life.[2]

We may interpret "better than in actual life" to mean that the characters in tragedy come from noble houses. And Aristotle in fact writes later in *The Poetics* that a tragic character must be "highly renowned and prosperous."[3] Tragic characters by their royal birth, are distinguished from ordinary citizens. But Aristotle's "better" refers more significantly to character, behavior, and choices. In tragic characters, nobility of conduct corresponds to nobility of position.

In Aristotle's second statement on comedy he wrote:

> Comedy is, as we have said, an imitation of characters of a lower type—not, however, in the full sense of the word bad, the Ludicrous being merely a subdivision of the ugly. It consists in some defect or ugliness which is not painful or destructive. To take an obvious example, the comic mask is ugly and distorted, but does not imply pain.[4]

Comedy's "imitation of characters of a lower type" suggests conduct that may make audience members feel superior—or that may make them recognize themselves at their worst. Aristotle uses the word *ludicrous* to further delineate the particular area of behavior comedy addresses. *Ludicrous* implies the contradictions in life that make our efforts ridiculous. When Harpo Marx uses huge scissors to cut off pieces of a formal dinner jacket worn by a pompous diplomat while he is conducting serious business, we are in the realm of the ludicrous. Ludicrous has to do with the loss of control, with the incongruous, with the undercutting of whatever we take too seriously.

Comedy: A World Without Pain

In his second statement, Aristotle made another simple observation about comedy that has far greater significance than the words communicate at first reading: "It consists in some defect or ugliness which is not painful or destructive. To take an obvious example, the comic mask is ugly and distorted, but does not imply pain." The implication here is that comic characters may do all kinds of ridiculous things and may suffer temporary losses, but they are not in pain. And most particularly, the audience does not respond to them as if they were suffering. When we laugh in the theatre, we laugh at the incongruous, we laugh at the foolish, we laugh at ourselves, but we do not laugh if we believe that people are genuinely in pain.

A Look at Tartuffe

As a model of comedy, we turn to the work of the great French playwright Jean-Baptiste Molière (1622–1673), who wrote shortly after the time of Shakespeare. In one of his best-loved and most frequently performed plays, *Tartuffe* (1664), Molière took on a serious subject, religious hypocrisy, which he used as the basis for his comedy. Molière subtitled his play *The Imposter*, which helps us to see immediately that we, the audience, are not expected to be taken in by the charade played out by the hypocrite Tartuffe. Rather than simply exposing or critiquing those who make a great show of religious faith while indulging in scandalous behavior, Molière explored the damage done when supposedly reasonable and responsible people allow themselves to be fooled by false piety.

In *Tartuffe*, the central character, Orgon, is a prosperous businessman married to a very attractive and intelligent woman, Elmire, who is the stepmother of his two young-adult children, Mariane and Damis. Their stable family life is completely disrupted when Orgon becomes infatuated with a man, *Tartuffe*, who makes public declarations of religious faith, poverty, and modest behavior but who in reality is a glutton, a scoundrel, and a thief. The playwright Molière was most concerned about the way Orgon abandons the sensible and prudent conduct of his business affairs and family relationships in his rush to become Tartuffe's

In this photo Mariane looks on in horror and her father, Orgon, reacts with increasing anger as the maid, Dorine, describes what Mariane's life will be like if she is forced by her father to marry the religious hypocrite, Tartuffe. The 1999 American Conservatory Theatre production, directed by Charles Randolph-Wright, moved the period of the play forward to the twentieth century, underscoring the relevance of the play's themes for our own times. Anika Noni Rose plays Mariane, Steven Anthony Jones plays Orgon, and Roxanne Raja plays Dorine.

benefactor. Orgon brings Tartuffe to live in his house, and then determines to marry his young daughter Mariane to the much older and physically repulsive Tartuffe. Orgon finally disinherits his family and turns all of his worldly goods over to Tartuffe. Orgon recognizes his catastrophic folly only when Tartuffe tries to seduce Orgon's wife, Elmire.

Although Tartuffe's power over Orgon is essential to the unfolding of the play, much of the play's action consists of Orgon's family trying with increasing urgency to make Orgon see Tartuffe as he really is. In the following scene

(from act 2, scene 2), the maid, Dorine, tries to save Mariane from her father's ruinous plan to marry her to Tartuffe. Molière frequently endowed the servants in his plays with the common sense and moderation of behavior that he clearly admired and that many of his upper-class characters lack.

ORGON (*to* DORINE): What are you doing there?
   I gather that you find a fascination
   In trying to overhear our conversation?
DORINE: There is a rumor going around here,
   Chance or conjecture, I have no idea;

But when I heard these two were to wed,
I just assumed someone was off his head.

ORGON: What? Do you doubt it then?

DORINE: Indeed I do;
Yes, even though I've heard it now from you.

ORGON: You will believe it soon, before I'm
done.

DORINE: Yes, yes, I know; you like to have your
fun.

ORGON: I'm telling you what soon you will
attest.
(*To* MARIANE): I tell you, daughter, it's no jest.

DORINE: Nonsense!
(*To* MARIANE): Don't mind the games your
father plays with you:
Just jokes.

ORGON: I say. . .

DORINE: No matter what you do,
They won't believe you.

ORGON: I am getting mad . . .

DORINE: All right, they will, then; and that *is*
too bad.
What, sir? Can you, who always have
appeared
So wise, with your mustache and solemn
beard,
Be fool enough to try . . .

ORGON: Listen to me:
You give yourself a lot of liberty,
My girl. I won't put up with it, I swear.

DORINE: Now, let's not get excited, sir; there,
there.
How could you dream up such a silly plot?
Your daughter for a bigot? I hope not.
He has to have his mind on other things.
Besides, what do you think this union brings?
And when you are so wealthy, why select
A beggar son-in-law . . .?

ORGON: What disrespect!
If he is poor, that is no cause to sneer.
His is a misery we must revere.
He stands above our pomp by his austerity.
Since he has sacrificed his own prosperity
By his disdain for all things transitory
And his concern for true, eternal glory.
But my assistance may facilitate
His restoration to his old estate.

In his district he holds important lands,
And he's a gentleman just as he stands.

DORINE: Oh yes, he says so, and that vanity
Does not sit well, sir, with his piety.
If holy living really is his aim,
He should prate less about his birth and
name;
And true devoutness seeks a low condition
Which will not suffer outbursts of ambition.
So why this pride? . . . But you are looking
grim.
Enough about his rank; how about him?
Is he the sort of man you could prefer
To have possession of a girl like her?
And shouldn't you consider what is seemly,
And fear the consequences most extremely?
The danger to a girl's virtue is great
When she is wed to an unwelcome mate;
Her aim to live in modesty and honor
Rests on the type of man you wish upon her,
And many a man with horns upon his brow
Has made his wife the person she is now.
Fidelity is difficult, in short,
Toward certain husbands of a certain sort.
Marry your daughter where she cannot love,
You'll answer for her sins to Heaven above.
The dangers of your enterprise are grave.

ORGON (*to* MARIANE): Now *I* must learn from
her how to behave!

DORINE: Take my advice, and you'd do well
enough.

ORGON: Daughter, let's not waste time upon
this stuff.
I am your father; I know what's best for you.
I *had* promised you to Valère, that's true;
But I am told he gambles more than he
ought,
And, worse yet, I suspect him of free thought.
I don't often see him at church, I know.

DORINE: Should he go running there just when
you go,
Like some who go there only to be seen?

ORGON: I did not ask for your advice, Dorine.
At all events, Heaven views Tartuffe with
pleasure;
And that is, after all, our greatest treasure.
This marriage will be all you could desire,

Full of sweet joys of which you'll never tire.
You'll live together, in your faithful loves,
Just like two children, like two turtledoves;
No quarrel will take place between you two;
You'll do with him just as you want to do.
DORINE: She'll make a fool of him; just wait
and see.
ORGON: What talk!
DORINE: He's built for it, believe you me.
Against the power of his horoscope
Your daughter's virtue, sir, has little hope.
ORGON: Stop interrupting me, and just be quiet.
We're minding our affairs; why don't you
try it?
DORINE: I speak of this, sir, only for your sake.

(*She interrupts* ORGON *every time he turns to speak to his daughter.*)

ORGON: Just hush; spare me the interest you
take.
DORINE: If I didn't love you . . .
ORGON: Just don't love me, pray.
DORINE: I *will* love you, no matter what you say.
ORGON: Oh!
DORINE: Your good name fills me with too
much pride
To see you ridiculed on every side.
ORGON: Quiet!
DORINE: My conscience will not let me rest
If I allow this match and don't protest.
ORGON: Quiet, you serpent! Wipe that
impudent smile . . .
DORINE: Oh! So much piety, and so much bile!
ORGON: Yes, all this nonsense heats my bile,
that's true;
And I don't want another word from you.
DORINE: All right, but just the same, my
thoughts are there.
ORGON: Think, if you like; but better have a care.
Not a word, or . . . enough.

(*To Mariane*)

Now, I have weighed
Everything wisely.
DORINE: Silence, I'm afraid,
Will drive me mad.

(ORGON *turns his head toward her; she is silent.*)

ORGON: True, he's no pretty boy.
And yet Tartuffe . . .
DORINE: That snout! Oh, what a joy!
ORGON: . . . Without his other gifts, would be a
catch
Well worth considering . . .

(*Turns to* DORINE, *crosses his arms, and watches her.*)

DORINE: A splendid match!
If I were she, no man would marry me
Against my will and with impunity.
Soon after, I would make him understand
That women have their vengeance close at
hand.
ORGON (*to* DORINE): You disregard my orders,
is that true?
DORINE: What's your complaint? I'm not
speaking to you.
ORGON: Who *are* you talking to?
DORINE: To me; that's all.
ORGON: All right. To punish her colossal gall,
I'll have to let her have the back of my hand.

(DORINE *is behind* ORGON, *encouraging* MARIANE *to speak up and resist. At this and each of the following pauses,* ORGON *turns and sets to slap* DORINE, *who each time either freezes, silent and motionless, or changes her signal to* MARIANE *into an innocent gesture.*)

Daughter, you should approve of what I've
planned . . .
The man I've chosen . . . for your fiancé . . .
(*To* DORINE) Not talking to yourself?
DORINE: Nothing to say.
ORGON: Just one more little word.
DORINE: The word is mum.
ORGON: I'm waiting for you.
DORINE: I should be so dumb!
ORGON: In short, you must obey the master's
voice,
And show yourself compliant to my choice.
DORINE (*fleeing*): I wouldn't marry that man on
a bet.

(ORGON *tries to slap her, but misses.*)

ORGON: That pest will make me lose my temper
yet;

I'd best dismiss her, to avoid that sin.
I can't go further in the state I'm in.
Her insolence has vexed me so, I swear,
I'd better go and get a breath of air.[5]

In *Tartuffe*, Molière included many of the traditional elements of comedy. Orgon's ill-conceived scheme brings misunderstanding and then chaos to his family, resulting in broken engagements and lost fortunes. Molière in fact took his characters to the brink of disaster when Tartuffe is ready to throw the dispossessed family into the street. But in a celebrated reversal, the king's messenger arrives to restore both common sense and the characters to their rightful places. The suffering that is threatened by Tartuffe does not come to pass, and the characters remain in a protected world in which they are buffered from the consequences of their actions.

Zoe Wanamaker, in a recent production of Electra, *demonstrates the emotional intensity of the situations facing characters in Greek tragedy that lead to intense audience involvement and catharsis.*

Tragedy: Catharsis and Awareness

The audience experience in tragedy is quite different from that in comedy. In tragedy we feel the pain and suffering of the characters intensely. The audience empathizes with the tragic characters and shares in their inner journeys. The identification with the suffering in tragedy brings about an emotional release or cleansing of the spirit that is referred to as catharsis. Catharsis is one of the most discussed and debated concepts in the study of drama. To understand catharsis, imagine that you have witnessed an ordeal and have been caught up in the terrible tensions of the situation. When those conflicts and tensions are finally resolved, you feel both a relief and a heightened awareness. The same emotional experience occurs in tragedy: the tragic character comes to a new understanding or a greater wisdom through his or her suffering, and we in the audience come to a new awareness of life's meaning. This experience that combines emotional sensitivity with insight into life's most difficult questions brings us a degree of exhilaration at the same time that we are deeply moved by the struggle we have witnessed.

Plot Summaries of Selected Tragedies

Today we are surrounded by comedies—on the stage, on television, and in the movies. We have abundant material to draw on in our attempt to identify the distinguishing qualities of comedy. But we have only a generalized sense of the "tragic," which we tend to think of in terms of painful incidents that end in loss, disaster, or death. We do not have a large, well-known body of contemporary theatre works to create a frame of reference for identifying that part of human experience explored by tragedy.

To provide a partial foundation for our discussion of tragedy, we include here brief plot summaries of the plays most frequently cited in discussions of tragedy. To the tragedies listed, written in either the fifth century B.C.E. or Elizabethan England, could be added more plays from either of these periods as well as the tragedies of Racine, written in seventeenth-century France. But even with these additions, we quickly see that a huge area of literary and

Medea *by Euripides centers on the betrayal of Medea by her husband, Jason. Medea has dedicated her life to Jason, giving up her country and using all of her powers to secure his fortune. But Jason is a character always seeking his own advantage. The play begins as Jason has taken a new, younger wife, the daughter of the king. In this photo we see the terrible revenge that Medea undertakes, the murder of her children with Jason. Barbara Berlovitz as Medea drags the bodies of her dead children behind her as Jason grieves in the 2002 production by the Theatre de la Jeune Lune directed by Steven Epp.*

dramatic study is based on a very small sample of plays.

Oedipus Rex *(Sophocles)*   When Oedipus is a young man, he is told by an oracle that he is fated to kill his father and marry his mother and have children with her. Horrified at such a future, he leaves the home and kingdom of his parents, not knowing that he is, in fact, an adopted child. Unwittingly, he travels to the city of his actual parents where the prophecy comes true. Oedipus murders his father King Laius and marries his mother Queen Jocasta. Because Laius is dead, the people of Thebes choose Oedipus to be their new king. The play focuses on the day, many years after Oedipus's arrival in Thebes, the true city of his birth, that Oedipus comes to know who he really is.

Antigone *(Sophocles)*   The sons of Oedipus, Eteocles and Polyneices, have both been killed battling each other for the throne. Their uncle, Creon, declares that one is a hero and will be buried appropriately and that the other is a traitor and will be left unburied with his remains to be destroyed by the elements. Creon, who has become the king on the death of Oedipus's sons, further decrees that anyone attempting to bury the abandoned body will be stoned to death. The young men's sister, Antigone, refuses to obey her uncle's decree and performs burial rites for her brother. Creon has Antigone imprisoned in a cave, where she commits suicide.

The Oresteia *(Aeschylus)*   Agamemnon, the Greek king and general who leads the Greek army against Troy in the ten-year Trojan War, is killed by his wife, Clytaemnestra, on his return from the war. Clytaemnestra is then killed by her son, Orestes, as revenge for his father's death. Orestes is tried for murder in a trial by jury and acquitted.

Hamlet (*Shakespeare*)   Hamlet's father, King Hamlet, is murdered by his uncle Claudius, who is the dead king's brother. Claudius then marries Hamlet's mother, Gertrude, and takes the throne of Denmark. Young Prince Hamlet fears that his uncle has murdered his father but lacks conclusive proof. In the course of Hamlet's attempt to prove his uncle a murderer and avenge his father's death, violence claims eight lives, including those of Hamlet, Claudius, and Gertrude.

Macbeth (*Shakespeare*)   Macbeth is presented with visions of future power by three witches whom he meets on the heath. The witches' mysterious prophecies fire his own ambitions. He and his wife Lady Macbeth embark on a course of murder, beginning with the reigning king, that ultimately leads to their downfall (Color Plate 17).

King Lear (*Shakespeare*)   Seeking to bind his three daughters more closely to him, King Lear divides up his kingdom and bestows what would be his children's inheritance in advance of his death. He makes the division of his kingdom in a public ceremony, in which he expects his daughters to declare their love for him above all else. His treacherous older daughters easily proclaim the adulation they know he awaits. Cordelia, however, his youngest daughter (for whom the ceremony is probably staged), refuses to compromise herself with false flattery to surpass her sisters. Lear banishes Cordelia, opening the way for a vicious power struggle that results in the deaths of both Lear and Cordelia (Color Plate 39).

Common Themes of Tragedy

A Struggle over Succession   As these six plot summaries show, the major tragedies all deal with power struggles over succession. Oedipus unknowingly kills the legitimate king, his father, and then taints his own children and heirs through incest. Creon imprisons his rebellious niece, Antigone, to consolidate his own power as king following the deaths of the two legitimate heirs to the throne. Clytemnaestra kills her husband to avenge the death of their daughter and then assumes the leadership of the state; Orestes, Clytemnaestra's son, kills his mother to reclaim the throne he believes by right should be his. Claudius and Macbeth both scheme for power and murder the legitimate king. And by giving up his power prematurely, King Lear unleashes a bloody struggle for control of the kingdom.

Although succession is not necessarily the primary focus of tragedy, it is integral to many of the works of the past that we categorize as tragedy. Crisis over succession exposes a society at its most vulnerable. Tragedy explores a breakdown or challenge to a society's system of values. And it is during these times of vulnerability that the choices of the characters in terms of moral issues are the most difficult and significant.

A Rupturing of Family and Societal Bonds   Classical tragedies test the moral foundations of human civilization. Tragedies take place when the bonds that tie human society together are ruptured. The family is almost always at the center of tragedy, and it is a royal family that represents both the larger society and the essential relationships between family members. Tragic characters become engaged in conflict leading to or in response to the transgression of principles deemed sacred by the community. All the major tragedies involve royal or aristocratic characters who kill members of their own families. The health or disruption in that royal family is intricately tied to the social and political health of the community.

The relationship of the tragic characters to this wrenching of fundamental values changes from play to play and playwright to playwright. Some characters—such as Oedipus, unknowingly, and King Lear, knowingly—initiate all of the events that lead to catastrophe. Others, such as Hamlet and Antigone, must respond to

CHARACTERISTICS OF TRAGEDY

- Tragedy deals with serious subjects and characters who are confronted with their own mortality.
- Many tragic plots revolve around a crisis over succession to a throne, representing a rupture in the bonds that tie families and society together.
- Murder and death occur frequently in tragedy and usually as a result of the transgression of sacred principles.
- Tragic characters come from aristocratic or royal families and usually exhibit admirable behavior.
- Tragic characters act alone and take responsibility for their choices and actions.
- The audience empathizes with tragic characters, identifies with their suffering, and often experiences catharsis.

The tragedies of Euripides frequently explore characters overcome by their passions. The Bacchai *examines an entire society whose people have lost touch with fundamental elements of their own human nature. The character Dionysus, part man and part god, arrives in their community to force them to recognize themselves first through madness and then through murder. Here Dionysus (Greg Hicks) seduces Pentheus (William Houston), the youthful leader of Thebes with a vision of a freer life outside the restrictions of a repressive, militaristic society. Peter Hall directed the 2002 production at the Royal National Theatre of Great Britain.*

situations initiated by others. What the characters share is an unwillingness to let other characters or circumstances shape their individual destinies. They are determined, even at the cost of their own lives and sometimes the lives of others, to find a course of action that is true to their own natures and true to a value system as they understand it. Some of them, such as King Lear, Creon, and Macbeth, make enormous errors of judgment or miscalculations. Some, such as Oedipus, are caught in such a tangled web that extrication is impossible. Some, such as Hamlet and Antigone, give their lives to restore justice. For all of these tragic characters, there is great suffering in the actions that they choose, and through that suffering comes not only wisdom but also self-determination. They have defined themselves.

Isolation of the Tragic Character Whereas comedies look at characters as part of a social unit, tragedies examine characters who stand alone. Hamlet was part of the court of Denmark

before the play opens; he had family, friends, a woman who loved him, and the highest regard of the people of Denmark. Part of his tragedy is that he becomes increasingly isolated as he pursues his course of action. His father is dead. He is betrayed by his friends Rosencrantz and Guildenstern, attacked by his uncle Claudius, rejected by Ophelia, and abandoned by his mother.

Isolated, the tragic hero or character struggles with a hideous situation: Hamlet's father has been murdered, and the apparent murderer now wears the crown and has married Hamlet's mother; the body of Antigone's brother lies unburied, to be torn apart by wild dogs and vultures, and the king has decreed that anyone burying the body will be stoned to death; Oedipus's people are dying of plague because an old murder goes unpunished. The tragic character determines to follow his or her own conscience in addressing these situations rather than accept the solutions of others or the supposed decrees of fate.

The Acceptance of Responsibility   Although the circumstances with which they are presented are not always of their own making, tragic characters take full responsibility for their actions. Tragedy is about human potential and our ability to choose for ourselves and take responsibility for the consequences of those choices. It is no coincidence that the great tragedies were written in periods of optimism about the ability of human beings to control their own destiny. The fifth century B.C.E. saw the rise of both Athenian democracy and the Athenian empire. In Shakespeare's time, the English navy defeated the Spanish Armada and then pursued Queen Elizabeth's goals of building an empire.

Can Tragedy Exist Today?

Because the drama has changed and our philosophical perspective has changed, we might question whether tragedy can exist today. Certainly, the tragedies that we use as our reference points were written during times when the drama saw royal characters rather than common characters as the best personages to convey their meaning. These characters were seen as larger than life as they undertook epic struggles with the universe. They spoke a poetic, highly charged language that also lifted them out of the realm of ordinary existence. And they were further enlarged by their relationship to myths or legends. They were characters ready to fight the gods or fate.

Today, much of our drama frames human action in realistic terms and examines the struggles of average people to overcome economic and social problems. Our sense of the universe and our place in it has changed. The vastness of the universe defies comprehension; human beings have become no more than flecks barely registering on the surface of endless space and time. Because so much of our lives seems out of our control, much of today's nonrealistic drama has focused on the absurd, on our inability to give meaning to our brief passage on the planet. The idea of taking responsibility for our actions, which is at the heart of tragedy, may seem impossible or irrelevant.

If indeed tragedy is possible today, it cannot be produced from the models of Greek or Elizabethan tragedy. It will have to take a different course. The very nature of democracy, for example, precludes a tragedy of the aristocracy; nonetheless, several playwrights, including Arthur Miller and Eugene O'Neill, have contributed to an American idea of tragedy. And playwright August Wilson provides tantalizing possibilities of a tragic view in *Joe Turner's Come and Gone*. The central character, Herald Loomis, has a larger-than-life quality that comes from both the intensity of his feelings and the symbolic nature of his character. And he speaks a language that is poetic and charged. His name, Herald Loomis, suggests that he brings redemption; he is the "herald" of the light. He emerges from a background of slavery and the chain gang, a background comparable to the harrowing circumstances of classical tragedy.

Just as the tragic figures of ancient Greece or Elizabethan England represented their communities, so Herald Loomis represents his community—all of the enslaved. He endures terrible suffering, and through that suffering he comes to wisdom. Like Oedipus, he is searching for himself, and he reviews his past and those closest to him as he comes to recognize and take his place in the world. Although, like Hamlet, much of his suffering is not of his own making, the play focuses on his spiritual crisis, for which he *is* responsible. And ultimately he chooses the path of self-determination, acting symbolically when he cuts himself. Freedom is central to classical tragedy, and it is central to Herald Loomis. He is not waiting for someone else to bleed or suffer for him. He will suffer for himself. And in that moment of accepting himself, he discharges the spectral chains of Joe Turner.

In its own way, *Joe Turner's Come and Gone* may also deal with the struggle over succession. Herald Loomis may not be a king, but he is a representative of a people enslaved by another people. By throwing off the oppressor and reclaiming himself, Herald Loomis asserts the rights of black people to participate fully in society. His actions help bring change in succession to the rights of the nation. August Wilson places his characters in a world that has meaning and a moral framework.

MELODRAMA

We may see very little tragedy in the theatre and films of today, yet we do see a great deal of another genre, **melodrama.** Melodrama has its origins in very simple conflicts of good and evil. Melodrama externalizes the cause of our problems; there is little internal conflict or probing of moral issues. The nature of good and evil is clear at the outset. The hero may have terrifying obstacles to overcome, but one of them is not himself; nor does he set in motion the forces that threaten him. The hero is identified as male in this case because in contemporary melodrama, women usually still play supporting roles.

In early melodrama, a helpless young woman would be held hostage in some gruesome way by an obvious villain—only to be rescued at the last possible moment by a courageous and virtuous young man. This was a celebrated formula on the early American stage that has made a transition very easily and

Early film made the most of melodramatic plots in which young women were threatened by villains. The scene depicted here comes from a 1919 film, Chelsea 7750. *Although such damsel-in-distress scenes are the most vivid representations of melodramatic form, melodrama encompasses a range of plots in which good and evil are clearly opposed.*

happily and largely unchanged into Hollywood movies. Steven Spielberg and George Lucas have based much of their film careers on this formula. A lively version of the damsel in distress takes place in the third film of George Lucas's *Star Wars* trilogy, *Return of the Jedi.* Princess Leia and Han Solo have been taken captive by the evil and disgusting Jabba the Hutt. Solo, weak and blinded from having been imprisoned in ice, is temporarily unable to defend Leia from the vile Jabba, "the slimy piece of worm-ridden filth." Leia, for all her 1980s courage and independence, is dressed seductively in a bikini with a metal collar and chain about her neck. Jabba holds the chain and uses it to pull Leia closer to his voluminous flesh. It is a particularly gross version of the villain taking advantage of the heroine, a new way of tying her to the railroad tracks. At this point Luke Skywalker, now a Jedi knight, arrives. But

In a modern sci-fi version of the damsel in distress, Princess Leia (Carrie Fisher) bides her time as Jabba the Hutt flaunts his power in Return of the Jedi. *Luke Skywalker, like the heroes in early melodrama, must overcome the evil forces of Jabba the Hutt and Rancor to save Leia and Han Solo.*

he must face more evil before he can win the release of his friends. First he must outwit the horrible Rancor, and then they must all take on the dreaded Sarlac, the vast, pulsing mouth on the desert floor, filled with hundreds of tusklike teeth. As the battle builds, the well-known *Star Wars* theme music supports the action. Like the early stage melodramas from which the name of this genre is taken, music is an extraordinarily important part of the action film experience, building a sense of fear or triumph as needed.

The melodramatic theme and variations on the good guy who takes on the many incarnations of the forces of evil, all with state-of-the-art special effects, are at the heart of a long list of Hollywood movies, from the Indiana Jones and James Bond movies to the more recent *Die Hard*, *Speed*, and *Independence Day*. Sometimes there are whole cities of innocent people to be rescued instead of an individual woman, but the basic premise is the same.

The popularity of such movies is due to more than simply the rush of the special effects. The world is a difficult place. Contemporary life is stressful. We worry about everything from financial difficulties to crime to international tensions to overpopulation and its effect on the environment. There is great and simple satisfaction in being clear on the distinction between good and evil and in seeing the triumph of the good and the crushing of the bad. Although we may celebrate such triumph in the moment, we know that life is much more complicated than in the movies and that celluloid villains and heroes are as thin as the film on which their exploits are recorded.

Pure melodrama is most easily identified in action movies and popular drama from the nineteenth century. More serious drama that clearly opposes the forces of good and evil can also be described in part by the term *melodrama*. With Roy Cohn as the obvious villain, *Angels in America* can be seen to have some melodramatic tendencies. And the work of playwright Lillian Hellman (discussed in Chapter 8) is also sometimes categorized as melodrama because it examines the way evil spreads when good people do not fight it.

TRAGICOMEDY

Tragicomedy is a form of drama that has particular resonance today. The plays that fall into this classification are not merely plays that combine serious and comic elements. *Hamlet,* for example, has a generous amount of comedy and humor, yet we are clear that it is a tragedy. Similarly, there are some tragicomic—as well as melodramatic—tendencies in *Angels in America*, yet because the play focuses on the possibility of social and personal change, it does not fall under the category of tragicomedy.

Tragicomic plays are concerned with human awareness rather than a program of social change. In particular, they tend to explore an existential philosophical position. In simple terms, existentialism has to do with relativity—a belief that no fixed meaning underlies human existence and that the best we can do is to invent a framework for meaning that will be highly personal and individual and will inevitably have to change. What distinguishes tragicomedy is the way one perspective undercuts or changes the other. There is an interplay between the serious and comic sides of a situation that results in an unstable landscape, a kind of shifting geography where the footing is hard to maintain. The truth of the situation becomes elusive or impossible to ascertain, as is the case in Luigi Pirandello's *Six Characters in Search of an Author*.

Six Characters in Search of an Author presents the bizarre situation in which a group of characters arrives at a theatre where actors are rehearsing a play (Color Plate 40). The characters request and then insist that the actors put on the story of the characters' lives instead of the play that they are rehearsing. The characters claim that their playwright abandoned them partway through the process of making them into a play, and now they are desperate to have the opportunity to play out their drama. Built into this confusing structure of actors playing actors who are then impersonating characters who are actually present are all kinds of questions about the nature of reality. The Father, who is one of the six characters, articulates the isolation that results from the inability to communicate:

We all have a world of things inside ourselves
  and each one of us has his own private
world. How can we understand each other if the words I use have the sense and the value that I expect them to have, but whoever is listening to me inevitably thinks that those same words have a different sense and value, because of the private world he has inside himself too. We think that we understand each other, but we never do.[6]

Later he comments to the director on the changing nature of reality for everyone:

I'm only asking to try to find out if you really see yourself now in the same way that you saw yourself, for instance, once upon a time in the past, with all the illusions you had then, with everything inside and outside yourself as it seemed then—and not only seemed, but really was! Well then, look back on those illusions, those ideas that you don't have anymore, on all those things that no longer seem the same to you. Don't you feel that not only this stage is falling away from your feet but so is the earth itself, and that all these realities of today are going to seem tomorrow as if they had been an illusion.[7]

Pirandello's play challenges the audience not to be relentless in pursuing the truth about one another because the truth is impossible to ascertain. In the difficult areas of human relationships, Pirandello suggests that compassion may be the best that we can offer.

Plays that communicate the existential, tragicomic perspective embodied by *Six Characters* range from the realistic plays of Anton Chekhov to the absurd plays of Samuel Beckett. Tragicomedy probably offers the least affirmation of any of the theatrical genres. These plays are usually disturbing and present more questions than answers. The mixture of forms as well as the frequently provoking stage images are deliberate challenges to complacency or certainty. Tragicomedy offers neither the catharsis of tragedy, the moral satisfaction of melodrama, nor the emotional release through laughter of comedy or farce. The laughter of tragicomedy is laughter that is interrupted when we are reminded once again of how genuinely painful the situation actually is.

The characters are cut off from a fixed value system and at the same time are cut off from one another. The condition of loneliness or alienation is at the heart of tragicomedy. We have observed that tragic characters are also alone, but their isolation heightens the grandeur and courage of their actions. The scale of the characters in tragicomedy is greatly reduced. These are small characters beset by anxiety, failure, and emptiness.

American playwrights who write tragicomedy include both Edward Albee and Sam Shepard, whose *Buried Child* appears in full in Chapter 15 of this book. Both Albee and Shepard focus on breakdowns in the American family—breakdowns that result from the spiritual isolation of the characters. Shepard's distinctly American characters are rough around the edges, restless, and in search of something that can be called home. Humor in Shepard's plays is interrupted by the very real threat of violence that always simmers underneath the surface. By contrast, Albee's characters, in such plays as *Who's Afraid of Virginia Woolf?* and *A Delicate Balance*, are more educated and upperclass than are Shepard's, but their education becomes part of the source of their spiritual crisis.

Like the American tragicomic playwrights, Chekhov focuses on a realistic social group of family, friends, and associates. Of all the tragicomic playwrights, Chekhov seems to be the most gentle with his characters and yet the most unforgiving. As a group, his plays present situations in which the gulf between people cannot be bridged. The isolation and self-focus are complete. In the poignant final moments of Chekhov's *Cherry Orchard*, the characters all quickly make plans to depart. But they are so self-absorbed with their personal needs that they fail to provide for the care of their aged servant, Firs. Each exits thinking someone else has arranged to take Firs to a nursing home.

As they go off, cheerfully or tearfully calling out their good-byes, with the house bolted and secured from the outside, it becomes apparent to the audience that Firs has been forgotten. The last image of the play is of Firs, locked alone in the house to die, with the sound first of a breaking string and then of an axe chopping down the cherry trees.

The ending of Beckett's *Waiting for Godot* is widely considered a definitional moment in tragicomedy, when the two tramps repeat for the last time, "Let's go." But once again, they cannot leave the stage and remain sitting, waiting into eternity as the light fades. What sustains these two characters in the end is their companionship, however difficult and contentious. There is genuine affection between the two characters, and they choose to stay together rather than part.

Tragicomic plays involve human desperation, yet they are some of the most eloquent theatrical works of our times. In their arresting and imaginative creation lies the challenge of the playwright to confront our own illusions—about ourselves and the world we inhabit—without any of the protective devices that we usually employ to hold back the truth.

FARCE

Whereas comedy generally takes as its subject some kind of social critique, **farce** is concerned with the humorous possibilities of the moment. Farce attacks pretentiousness of all kinds and uses the social situation as a launching pad for the ridiculous. Farce is about anarchy, about breaking all the rules. Taking on authority is one of the trademarks of farce, and frequently the characters are only one step ahead of the law. In the film *Animal House*, the Deltas, a group of low-life fraternity brothers, scheme to destroy the obnoxious dean and his pal the mayor as well as the rich and condescending members of the student elite. This film is a classic example of a farce involving a rowdy assault on authority.

The Marx Brothers honed their acting skills in vaudeville before turning their special brand of lunacy into films. Animals were frequently featured as part of their performance onstage and in the movies. French theatre practitioners Antonin Artaud and Samuel Beckett acknowledged the Marx Brothers' influence on their own work well before the comedy team was taken seriously in the United States. Major Marx Brothers films include Duck Soup *and* A Night at the Opera.

Similarly, in the Marx Brothers' films, Groucho, Harpo, and Chico invade various forms of high society and bring them crashing down.

Farce almost always highlights actors rather than playwrights. Performances are memorable not because of the playwright's words but because of the comic genius of the actor. Farce has a brilliant history in the United States if we consider as a whole the work of actors on the stage, in film, and on television. It is not surprising that farce would flourish in a nation whose origins are revolutionary and whose goals are democratic. The actors of farce rebel against notions of aristocracy, against the imposition of high

culture, against institutions that have lost touch with the people, against all forms of arbitrary rules and hierarchical power structures.

Jim Carrey is an actor known for creating characters who have a wild, anarchic streak. He performs with a highly energized physical abandon that seems to defy the bodily limitations of most humans. In films such as *The Mask* and *Liar Liar*, he challenges authority with an attitude of defiance well-suited to contemporary farce. His film *The Mask* offers another model of a typical plot in farce. Carrey's character, Stanley Ipkiss, is the little man at the bottom of the ladder at the bank where he works. He is taken advantage of by everyone, abused by his landlady, swindled by his auto mechanics. He wears the ultimate in "geek" ties and pajamas. But by placing a mysterious mask on his face, Carrey breaks through all the social restraint of his "Mr. Nice Guy" role, throws caution to the wind, and becomes the embodiment of physical and spiritual anarchy. With a ludicrous green face and an outrageously suave wardrobe, he robs the bank where he works, defeats the town gangsters, and has the police dancing in the streets while he plays the maracas in his persona as "Cuban Pete." With the broadest possible physical humor, sometimes even rendered through cartoon images, he revenges himself on everyone who previously pushed him around. Carrey's character says of the power of the mask, "It brings your innermost desires to life." The same could be said of farce (Color Plate 41).

SUMMARY

The division of drama into genres is a way of identifying different perspectives on human existence. Tragedy focuses on human mortality and often ends in death or disaster. But tragedy is not a pessimistic form of drama. Tragic characters assume heroic stature as they struggle to control their own destinies and take responsibility for the consequences of their actions. Tragedy flourished as a form of drama in the Greek and Elizabethan theatres, which produced such masterpieces as *Oedipus Rex* and *Hamlet*.

Comedy is concerned with the human ability to endure. Comedy looks at the way human weakness leads to the ridiculous and the ludicrous. But in spite of all their failures, comic characters find a way to go on. Comedy frequently involves a group of characters separated by misunderstanding who are reconciled in the end, as in Molière's *Tartuffe*.

Tragicomedy reflects the anxiety of life. Plays of this genre shift between serious and comic perspectives, and each view undermines the other. In plays such as *Six Characters in Search of an Author* and *Waiting for Godot*, the nature of reality is uncertain, and no fixed meaning underlies the characters' existence. The plays emphasize the characters' frailty and isolation. Tragicomedy also challenges traditional ideas of dramatic structure by questioning the ability of language to communicate or the ability of characters to act in any purposeful way.

Two other genres, melodrama and farce, have become very popular on television and in film as well as in the theatre. Melodrama builds on clear-cut conflicts between good and evil. Farce is a comic form that attacks pretentiousness and all forms of authority.

TOPICS FOR DISCUSSION AND WRITING

1. What are the fundamental differences between tragedy and comedy? How can they be considered as complementary genres rather than as opposites?

2. How does comedy offer social criticism? What kind of social commentary does *Tartuffe* make? Where do you see social criticism in other comedies in the theatre or in films? Because we laugh, do we take social criticism less seriously in comedy than in other genres?

3. What is the philosophical perspective expressed by tragicomedy? What view of life is expressed by the situation of the characters in *Waiting for Godot*?

NOTES

1. Pindar, quoted in H. D. F. Kitto, *The Greeks* (Baltimore: Penguin, 1962), 10.

2. Aristotle, *The Poetics*, trans. S. H. Butcher (New York: Hill and Wang, 1968), 52.

3. Aristotle, 76.

4. Aristotle, 59.

5. Jean-Baptiste Molière, *"Tartuffe" and Other Plays*, ed. and trans. Donald Frame (New York: New American Library, 1967), act 2, scene 2, pp. 257–62.

6. Luigi Pirandello, *Six Characters in Search of an Author*, trans. John Linstrum (London: Methuen, 1986), act 1.

7. Pirandello, act 3.

SUGGESTIONS FOR FURTHER READING

Aristotle. *Aristotle's Poetics*. Translated by S. H. Butcher, with an introduction by Francis Fergusson. New York: Hill and Wang, 1968.

Aristotle's classic treatise on the nature of the tragic drama; written in the fifth century B.C.E. in Athens. Sophocles and his play *Oedipus Rex* set the standard by which other works are judged. Aristotle takes a particularly secular view of tragedy and interprets the significance of the works as they are reflected in the behavior of the central characters.

Bermel, Albert. *Farce*. New York: Simon and Schuster, 1982.

A book that "celebrates the danger, destruction and torment" of farce through the examination of scripts, live performances, and movies; looks at farce in all eras of the theatre and pays particular attention to the genre in contemporary American theatre and film.

Corrigan, Robert, ed. *Tragedy: Vision and Form*. San Francisco: Chandler, 1965.

A collection of essays that explores essential issues in tragedy, such as the tragic character, or hero, the human perception that defines tragedy, the possibilities of modern tragedy, and the experience of tragedy for the audience; also includes a section that examines melodrama in relation to tragedy.

Fergusson, Francis. *The Idea of a Theater*. Princeton: Princeton University Press, 1968.

A book that views Sophocles' *Oedipus* and Shakespeare's *Hamlet* as plays at the center of their communities. Fergusson examines these plays and others in relation to Aristotle's theory of tragedy, among others, and develops his own idea of the "tragic rhythm," which takes into account the mythic and ritualistic backgrounds of tragedy.

Jenkins, Ron. *Acrobats of the Soul: Comedy and Virtuosity in Contemporary American Theatre*. New York: Theatre Communications Group, 1988.

A look at the performance elements of comedy through the stage work of Bill Irwin, the Pickle Family Circus, the Flying Karamazov Brothers, and Cirque du Soleil, among others; examines circuses, magic acts, vaudeville, and street performances to give a sense of the vitality and skills of the comic actor; written by a trained clown who is equally aware of the social critique and the performance sophistication combined by the comic actor.

Kerr, Walter. *Tragedy and Comedy*. New York: Da Capo Press, 1985.

A study of drama and human experience that explores the idea that tragedy and comedy come from the same sources and that they are inextricably intertwined. Kerr begins with the classics of comedy and tragedy from ancient Greece as well as Shakespeare and Molière and then moves into the realm of tragicomedy to expand his notions through the works of Beckett and Chekhov.

Kitto, H. D. F. *Form and Meaning in Drama*. London: Methuen, 1956.

A study of six Greek tragedies and *Hamlet* that explores the nature of the tragic form and makes a strong case for a religious interpretation of tragedy that contrasts with Aristotle's focus on the centrality of the tragic hero.

Storm, William. *After Dionysus: A Theory of the Tragic*. Ithaca: Cornell University Press, 1998.

An analysis of tragedy that begins with Euripides' play *The Bacchae*, in which Pentheus is torn apart physically and his mother, Agave, is destroyed psychologically. Storm uses the disasters of these two characters to build a Dionysian foundation for tragedy that he further develops through the examination of *Agamemnon*, *King Lear*, and *The Seagull*.

CHAPTER 14

Choosing a Genre: Comedy

Looking at Dog Lady *by* Milcha Sanchez-Scott

To further our study of genre, we examine one more American play through its text and in performance, *Dog Lady* by Milcha Sanchez-Scott. In *Dog Lady* the playwright uses the genre of comedy to reflect on changing family and social relationships. The choice of comedy as the vehicle for her ideas affects the structure of the play itself and the way the play is performed on the stage. Sanchez-Scott's comedy offers a view of life that is resilient and durable even as we see the confusion and foolishness that accompany much of human activity.

EXPLORING THE TEXT OF *DOG LADY*

Dog Lady contains many of the characteristics of comedy discussed in Chapter 13. The action is driven by a fantastic idea. A proper, young Catholic woman is possessed by the spirit of a dog so that she may run fast enough to win a marathon. The marathon is sponsored by the local church, which is offering a trip to Rome as first prize. In the imaginary world of the play, the Catholic Church is both the source of tradition and, surprisingly, the source of change. The winner's athletic achievement, her quest, will be validated and blessed by the center of world Catholicism.

PLOT AND CHARACTERS

Because *Dog Lady* is a one-act, the storytelling is compressed. The characters cannot be developed gradually but must be quickly established, and the details with which they are drawn must be concentrated and revealing. Sanchez-Scott uses a fairly large cast for a one-act because she is giving us the whole social group, which also means each character must be sharply defined in a very brief period of time. Sanchez-Scott says that a simple plot structure based on a physical idea allows her to develop her comedy within the one-act framework.

> I just hang everything on the simplest plot/ story that I can find. What inspires me are visual images. I think almost every play of mine has been about movement: running, swimming, fighting, dancing, rhythm.[1]

For this play, Sanchez-Scott says she began with the idea of a long-distance runner. One of the two main characters, Rosalinda Luna, is such a runner who lives in the "barrio" in Los Angeles. She is in training for "Our Lady of a Thousand Sorrows Marathon," sponsored by the local Catholic church. Because of their poverty, Rosalinda's mother, María Pilar Luna, cannot afford Rosalinda's entry fee. But the local priest, Father Estefan, has gone door to door to collect donations from the Lunas' friends and neighbors to pay Rosalinda's fees. Only one neighbor has been ignored, Luisa Ruiz, the *curandera* (healer) who lives next door. Determined to contribute something to help Rosalinda, who has always been very kind to her, Luisa Ruiz creates a magic potion that gives Rosalinda the speed and spirit of a dog. Rosalinda's transformation leads to startling and chaotic consequences. Through the playing out of this ludicrous action, the identities of Rosalinda and her sister Jesse undergo major changes.

Rosalinda's transformation into a free-spirited, caninelike person creates chaos in the neighborhood. She leaps and soars over parked cars, eats raw meat, catches frisbees in her teeth,

In a midnight ceremony, the curandera *gives Rosalinda an amulet that has the power of the dog spirit. Production at INTAR directed by Max Ferra in 1984.*

and runs with a pack of her fellow creatures—attacking mailmen and trampling gardens. Incongruous events disrupt the harmony of the social group. Rosalinda's admirer, Raphael, feels abandoned and in his desperation pulls out his knife. The mailman collapses. Rosalinda's mother is terrified. Accusations fly of drug use and madness. The *curandera* who supplied the potion is condemned by all. Misunderstanding runs rampant. Within the plot are the seeds of Sanchez-Scott's social concerns about the restrictions placed on young Latina women in particular and young American women in general by traditional social expectations: the expectations of family, of religion, of the Latino community, and of the larger American society.

> I saw this woman, Chicana, a huge woman wearing a white dress, pushing this little boy in a stroller, crossing the street to go to the park. She looked just like a ship. The wind was blowing and with her dark olive complexion, she looked like an angel sailing ship carrying this little boy. These are the things that I find. It's important to me to see these things every day.[2]
>
> —MILCHA SANCHEZ-SCOTT

THE PLAYWRIGHT'S SOURCES: AN INTERSECTION OF CULTURES

Milcha Sanchez-Scott was born in 1955 on the island of Bali to a rich international heritage. From her mother came a Chinese, Indonesian, and Dutch background, from her father a Mexican and Colombian ancestry. But her early years were also marked by international tensions. At the same time that Wakako Yamauchi and her parents were held in an internment camp by the U.S. government during World War II in Poston, Arizona, Milcha Sanchez-Scott's father was imprisoned by the Japanese in Indonesia. Incarcerated again for political reasons in the 1950s, he spent the earliest part of Sanchez-Scott's childhood as a political prisoner. Following her father's release from prison, he resumed his career in international agriculture working for the United Nations.

At the age of five, Milcha Sanchez-Scott was sent to England to St. Agnes, a Catholic girls' boarding school, while her parents traveled in Europe as part of her father's work. Sanchez-Scott remembers going out onto the balcony of the school dormitory at night and howling out her grief at this separation and dislocation. Summers were spent with her family in Colombia. From her Colombian relatives, Sanchez-Scott learned a vivid, poetic language that encourages thoughts to be expressed as images. Spanish, she says, is "a lyrical language, a language of poetry that (allows) people's souls to sing. That's where the magic is. It's the way Spanish is spoken. It's like you swallowed candles and you're lit from within."

Her storytelling began in Colombia, where family members told one another their dreams over breakfast each morning. Because she was frequently alone at school, she spent much of her childhood making little stages for her dolls and puppets, all the while creating scenarios in her head. One of Sanchez-Scott's plays, *Roosters*, has a scene of a young teenage girl using her dolls to play the Catholic saints who, she hopes, will intervene on her behalf; in another scene, the girl writes scathing epitaphs on small cardboard gravestones with colored markers to comment on her relatives' latest betrayals. These episodes are, in fact, based on the way Sanchez-Scott played as a child.

Sanchez-Scott's identity as a writer took another turn when her family moved again when she was fourteen, this time to southern California. Her international upbringing and background had not prepared her for the racial discrimination that she would face even before she climbed on the school bus for the first time; she was not prepared to be the object of white teenage prejudice against Mexican Americans and Mexican immigrants. Her identification with the predominately Mexican Latino community increased when her father made her do field work one summer to pay for a costly prank she had participated in at school.[3] Later, while she was auditioning for roles as a television actress, she supported herself working at an employment agency that placed Latina women as domestics. The experience with field work and domestic employment became very important as she began to write about the lives of Latino people living in the southwestern United States. While she was observing people in difficult situations, what struck her most was the positive attitude, the celebration of life. This would become a source for the laughter and exuberance in her own plays:

> But what really mattered was seeing how people manage . . . to feed their children, to be in good humor, to be balanced. These immigrant women who had their feet on the ground, and their eyes on the stars, and their hearts full of love, strengthened me. It was like meeting at the river.[4]

Milcha Sanchez-Scott has written a group of four coming-of-age plays: *Latina, Dog Lady, The Cuban Swimmer*, and *Roosters*. These plays are placed firmly in the American Latino community with which Sanchez-Scott has been identified since coming to the United States. All four plays use comedy to address serious social issues. Three of the plays have varying degrees of darker undertones. The play that we are studying, *Dog Lady*, is pure comedy.

CHARACTERISTICS OF THE PLAY

The sources of this play, the cultural context, bring together Sanchez-Scott's association with the Mexican American community in Los Angeles and her own South American background. She draws on the bilingualism of the Latinos in the United States and the magical realist literary movement of Latin America. *Dog Lady* is also part of a movement shaped by Latina writers, playwrights, and visual artists that is concerned with gender issues in the Latino community. We will explore the elements of the play that respond to these influences.

Blended Language

Dog Lady is written in a language that combines English and Spanish. Such a blending of English and Spanish is frequently used in Chicano or Hispanic American fiction, poetry, and drama because it reflects the use of language in Latino communities. While the term *bilingual* is frequently used to describe such literature or speech practices, another term, *interlingual*, may be more accurate. Bilingual implies two separate languages. That is, bilingualism suggests that the speaker is switching back and forth between two completely different languages like a translator at an international conference. Interlingualism indicates the development of a new language that presents a fusion of English and Spanish languages and a fusion of the cultural experiences of the two language communities.

Cultural critic Juan Bruce-Novoa emphasizes that neither English nor Spanish alone communicates the same meaning that the blended language achieves.[5] The interlingual text is discussed in a more personal, political context by Gloria Anzaldúa in *Borderlands: La Frontera:*

> For a people who are neither Spanish nor live in a country in which Spanish is the first language: for a people who live in a country in which English is the reigning tongue but who are not Anglo; for a people who cannot entirely identify with either standard (formal, Castillian) Spanish nor standard English, what recourse is left to them but to create their own language . . . neither *español ni ingles*, but both.[6]

The use of blended English and Spanish gives Sanchez-Scott's text a distinct flavor and rhythm as well as giving the characters authenticity. The blending of languages also contributes to the play's humor. When Rosalinda is transformed into a dog, the younger sister, Jesse, is awestruck when she sees her sister leap over a black Chevy Impala like "la Wonder Woman":

JESSE: OK, OK. That's when I see Rosalinda, with Pepe and Bobo. I yell at her, I say, "Rosalinda, Mom says to come home," that's when she barked at me. Then she turns around and runs up to this car . . . It was a black Impala . . . So she runs up to this car, and Mom . . . you won't believe this . . . she jumps over the car! . . . The black Impala, she jumps over it! . . . Just like la Wonder Woman . . .

By the simple addition of the Spanish article "la," which means "the," the cultural identity of Wonder Woman is changed. She becomes Rosalinda from the barrio who now has the power to challenge a traditional source of Latino machismo, the black Chevrolet. It is an exuberantly humorous image. Rosalinda is both a dog and "la Wonder Woman," sailing over parked cars.

In another scene, the mailman, Orlando, staggers in, having been attacked by a pack of dogs that now includes Rosalinda, and says, "La Rosalinda se freakió." The English slang "to freak or freak out" is changed into a slang version of a reflexive Spanish verb with all the emphasis of the additional vowel sounds. Sanchez-Scott frequently follows the Spanish words with an English equivalent so that the non-Spanish-speaking reader will have very little trouble following the text. Sanchez-Scott actually uses a far more restrained version of blended language than do many other Latino writers.

Magical Realism

The blending of English and Spanish and the placement of the play in a Los Angeles barrio are two of the sources of the cultural context that shape Milcha Sanchez-Scott's work *Dog Lady*. In addition, Sanchez-Scott brings to her writing the lyricism and philosophical perspective of her South American background, which associates her with the artistic movement of *magical realism*. The language of magical realism is characterized by an extravagant lyricism in which imagery and metaphor are primary tools of the storytelling. Exaggeration of an astounding degree is central to the works gathered together as magical realism. Elements of fantasy or surrealism exist in otherwise realistic situations or settings and infuse everything

with their presence. The reader or audience member may be surprised by the extraordinary occurrences, but the characters in the play or story are not. Much magical realist work also tends to portray a world in which more traditional beliefs in spirits persist alongside modern, technological society. For Sanchez-Scott, healers (*curanderas*), herbal medicines, animals with magical powers, and spirit worship merged with Catholic worship are all part of the perspective of the characters who live in the urban, technological world of Los Angeles.

The language used by Milcha Sanchez-Scott places her in the tradition of magical realism as does the occurrence in her plays of miracles or magical transformations. Tropical islands emerge from pieces of fruit, human characters become animals, roosters dance, characters walk on water and ascend to the heavens. Characters pray to the spirits, the stars, and the moon as well as to the Catholic hierarchy. And the figure of the *curandera*, whom Sanchez-Scott remembers vividly from *bellarios* (healing ceremonies) from her childhood in Colombia, appears in one form or another in all four of the early related plays. The *curandera* becomes the connection to the spirit world. The shared action of the older woman, the *curandera*, and the central character, in each play a girl or young woman, makes possible the miraculous transcendence.

Reinterpreting Catholic Imagery: The Virgin of Guadalupe

This alliance with magical realism is given further definition by Sanchez-Scott's focus on Latina women in the United States struggling with their place at the center of a complex intersection of cultures—struggling with their identity. As Sanchez-Scott approaches issues of changing identity and gender, she joins another vibrant contemporary movement of Hispanic artists seeking social change by examining interrelated historical and cultural forces. In

Chapter 11 we discussed Caryl Churchill's strategies for questioning or breaking down gender assumptions. Churchill uses devices such as cross-gender casting as well as bringing together characters from different time periods to relate contemporary situations to historical backgrounds.

One of the major strategies of Latina artists of Mexican and Central American heritage in addressing gender issues is the manipulation of religious imagery important to their communities, particularly the image of the Virgin of Guadalupe, who holds a place of central significance. The Virgin of Guadalupe is the meeting point of European and indigenous cultures, the cross-cultural incarnation of the European Virgin Mary brought by the Spanish to the Americas. The dark Virgin of Guadalupe supposedly first appeared in 1531 to the Indian Juan Diego in Mexico, very close to the shrine of Tonantzin, who was the foremost Aztec goddess, the goddess of corn and regeneration. The connection of Guadalupe to Tonantzin is inescapable and follows the pattern of invaders who build their churches on indigenous religious sites. The Virgin of Guadalupe has become a complex figure who has been seen for centuries as a representation of both faith and liberation. Her image was carried in revolutions in Mexico and on marches led by Cesar Chavez to organize migrant farmworkers in the 1960s and 1970s in California.

Although Guadalupe historically has an activist component, she became the "traditional role model" promoted by Mexican Catholicism as the ideal for women: "woman as nurturer, protector, and comforter."[7] In a tradition referred to as "marianismo," Guadalupe has also been seen as reinforcing the passivity of Hispanic women. The traditional representation of the Virgin of Guadalupe shows a saintly woman with head bowed and covered by a demure blue cloak. She is a model of submission. By laying claim to this most central image of Hispanic womanhood and recasting the image with ancient and contemporary significance, Latina writers and artists have transformed this religious icon into a repository of lost history and a symbol of power, activism, and liberation.

The artwork of Yolanda Lopez shares the buoyancy and humor of Milcha Sanchez-Scott's approach to gender questions. Yolanda Lopez has created a *triptych*, a work in three parts, that presents images of the Virgin of Guadalupe corresponding to three generations of women. The women that Lopez uses as models for the paintings are her grandmother, her mother, and herself. In a compelling coincidence, Rosalinda, running through the barrio, recalls Lopez's painting of herself, "Portrait of the Artist as the Virgin of Guadalupe." In the painting, Lopez/Guadalupe is the runner with pink dress flying up over muscular brown legs in white running shoes and with her short, black hair on her now bare head blowing free in the wind (see Color Plate 42).

While there is no mention of the Virgin of Guadalupe in *Dog Lady*, the race in which Rosalinda is running is, of course, "Our Lady of a Thousand Sorrows Marathon." The Virgin Mary takes many forms, reflective of different moments of spiritual insight in the many communities worldwide that are part of the Catholic Church. The Virgin of Guadalupe is one of those forms, as is *La Dolorosa*, or Our Lady of Sorrow. Our Lady of a *Thousand* Sorrows is the playwright's magical realist exaggeration of the Catholic representation of and the stereotypical internalization of that representation by women such as Rosalinda's mother, María Pilar, with all of her suffering.

As the starting point for her comedy, Sanchez-Scott has created a most incongruous situation: Catholic girls running through the streets in honor of the suffering of Catholic women. Just as Yolanda Lopez has liberated the Virgin of Guadalupe from her passivity and sorrow, Milcha Sanchez-Scott does the same. Rosalinda's very existence turns the old imagery upside down. Far from patiently waiting at home to fulfill some kind of biological destiny, Rosalinda intends to seize the world.

For both Lopez and Sanchez-Scott, a critical issue in the challenge to the traditional image of women is the liberation and physicality of the runner. There is an earth-shaking difference between young women running free through the streets in honor of the Virgin Mary and women on their knees crossing the huge cobblestone courtyard in front of the Basilica of the Virgin of Guadalupe in Mexico City; the latter has been considered one of the ultimate forms of reverence. In both Lopez's painting and Sanchez-Scott's play, the body is active and uncovered, not in an objectified way, but as an expression of female strength. The two characters are doing nothing less than reclaiming the female body. Binding, inhibiting clothing is cast aside, and the strength of the natural world is symbolically associated with women as it has often been associated with men. Yolanda Lopez's runner holds a snake in her hand, the snake that once adorned women's heads until it was incorporated into women's fall from grace and placed under Mary's foot. And Rosalinda is given the strength of the dog.

A Latina Identity

While Rosalinda is reshaping the identity of American Catholic girls from the barrio, Sanchez-Scott is clear about the creation of a Latina identity rather than an "Anglo" one. After Rosalinda has turned into a dog, another neighbor, Mrs. Amador, comes onstage outraged, carrying a broken rosebush. Again, in typical dog fashion, Rosalinda has trampled Mrs. Amador's garden. Growing in that garden are a collection of roses named for famous wives of American presidents, icons of white American culture:

MRS. AMADOR: Rosalinda *y los perros* [dogs] destroyed my rose garden.
MARÍA PILAR: No . . . No . . .

MRS. AMADOR: *Sí, sí,* all my roses. La Yellow Rose de Texas . . . las tea roses, La Eleanor Roosevelt . . . La Jacqueline Kennedy . . . *y esta* (*Holding up broken rosebush.*) La Mamie Eisenhower.

Rosalinda will be neither her mother's passive daughter nor a submissive Catholic woman, nor in their place will she aspire to traditional role models from the dominant "Anglo" culture.

In broadening the issues of Latina identity, Sanchez-Scott explores the idea of borders, geography, and patterns of migration. When Rosalinda Luna runs, she calls out a series of cities and locations as she goes from Mexico City to Tijuana, then up the West Coast of the United States, across Canada to Alaska and then finally across the Bering Strait to Russia: "Mexico City, Acapulco, Puerto Vallarta, La Paz, Santa Rosalia, Encinada, Tijuana, San Diego, La Orange County, Los Angeles, Santa Barbara, San Jose, San Francisco, Seattle, Portland, Vancouver, Alaska, the Bering Strait, Russia. . . ." What she is mapping is a reversal of the pattern of migration that archaeological research tells us first brought people to the Americas. Rosalinda Luna is a young American woman determined to explore the world:

ROSALINDA: I'm going to run around the world, over oceans and islands and continents. I'm going to jump over the Himalayas, skip the Spanish steps and dip my toes in the Blue Nile.

But in the specific, reversed mapping of the migration route of early American peoples, there is also a suggestion that Rosalinda is reclaiming land that was taken from indigenous people. As a woman and as a person of Latino ancestry living in the United States, Rosalinda is laying claim to her full identity as a citizen of the world.

Dog Lady

Milcha Sanchez-Scott

CHARACTERS

RAPHAEL
ORLANDO, *the mailman*
ROSALINDA LUNA, *the runner*
MARÍA PILAR LUNA, *Rosalinda's mother*
JESSE LUNA, *Rosalinda's younger sister*
LUISA RUIZ, *the Dog Lady*
MRS. AMADOR, *a neighbor*

TIME, *Summer.*
PLACE, *Los Angeles: a small barrio off the Hollywood freeway.*

FIRST DAY

Early summer morning. The residential section of Castro Street. There is a large sun, and the sunlight has the particular orange hue that indicates the Santa Ana weather condition.

We see two front yards, enclosed by a low stone or cement fence. One yard is very neat, tidy, almost manicured, with a rotating sprinkler watering the green lawn. The other yard is jungle-like, with strange plants in odd places, rubber tires, all kinds of other rubbish, and a sign in front that reads: "CURANDERA— HEALER". Each yard has a mailbox and on the far side of the neat house, there is a jacaranda tree.

Leaning against the fence is RAPHAEL, a dark, brutal-looking young man of eighteen or nineteen. He has smoldering dark eyes. His is wearing a Cuban T-shirt, khaki pants, a dark felt hat. He is staring at the neat house.

RAPHAEL: (*Like music.*) Rosalinda! (*Enter OR-LANDO, the mailman, carrying his bag. RAPHAEL runs away before ORLANDO can see him.*)

ORLANDO: (*Walking*) Neither rain, nor sleet, nor snow. . . . Says nothing about the heat . . . not one word about the heat. (*He opens the mailbox of the messy yard and rummages through his bags.*) Nada, ni modo, nothing for you, Doña Luisa. (*Reading sign.*) "Curandera . . . healer." (*Shakes his head.*) It takes all kinds. (*ROSALINDA comes out of the neat house. She is 18 years old, wearing a jogging shorts outfit. She is quite pretty and feminine. She does some warm-up stretches.*) Hola Rosalinda, ay qué hot! . . . It's a scorcher . . . it's a sauna . . . you could fry eggs on the sidewalk . . . it's so hot that . . . You gonna run? Today?

ROSALINDA: I'm gonna win, Orlando.

ORLANDO: You're gonna die! This heat could affect your brain.

ROSALINDA: (*Getting into starting position.*) I'm going to run around the world. Today Africa, tomorrow India and Saturday . . .

ORLANDO: The Big One.

ROSALINDA: Rome!

ORLANDO: On your mark. Get set. The whole barrio's behind you. . . . Go! (*ROSALINDA runs off. Yelling to ROSALINDA.*) May all the Angels come down and blow you over the finish line. (*Walking off.*) Wish we had some rain, some sleet, some snow. (*Exit ORLANDO. The sun moves up a fraction in the sky to indicate passage of time. In front of the neat yard of the Luna family we see MARÍA PILAR LUNA, ROSALINDA's mother, wearing a fresh housedress and apron. She is standing on the newly swept cement path that leads to her front porch. She has a very determined look as her eyes scan the street. The Lunas' neighbor, LUISA RUIZ, is slowly making her way through the rubble and rubbish in her front yard. She is dressed in a torn, stained, dingy white bathrobe. Although her lips are painted a bright red, her hair has not been combed. The overall effect is that she looks not unlike her front yard.*)

MARÍA PILAR: Rosalinda! Rosalinda!

LUISA RUIZ: *Buenos días,* María Pilar. It's a beautiful Santa Ana Day, *que no?*

MARÍA PILAR: *Buenos días,* Doña Luisa. *Sí, sí* it's a beautiful day. Rosalinda! *Ay, dónde está, esa muchacha?* Rosalinda!

LUISA RUIZ: Are you looking for Rosalinda?

MARÍA PILAR: No, I'm doing this for the good of my health.

LUISA RUIZ: Oh. Maybe a tea of wild pepper grass.

MARÍA PILAR: I'm only joking, Doña Luisa, I'm already under the doctor's care, thank you.

LUISA RUIZ: Oh. You're welcome.

MARÍA PILAR: Rosalinda! Rosalinda!

LUISA RUIZ: Where is she?

MARÍA PILAR: Ay, Doña Luisa, believe me, if I knew where Rosalinda was, I wouldn't be calling for her. Rosalinda!

LUISA RUIZ: Sometimes if you whistle, they come. El Bobo only comes when I whistle.

MARÍA PILAR: El Bobo?

LUISA RUIZ: The big one. He's a . . . a . . . Labrador retriever. He only comes when I whistle. Once the people complained so I got one of them ultrasonic dog whistles, but when I blow it, Mr. Mura says it opens up his garage door.

MARÍA PILAR: Doña Luisa, my daughter is not a dog to be whistled for.

LUISA RUIZ: Oh. Now El Pepe, he's the cockapoo, they're not so independent, you know. He comes whenever you just call him.

MARÍA PILAR: Rosalinda! (*Holding her stomach.*) Ay, this screaming is making me acid. (*She yells toward the house.*) Jesse! Jesse! Andale, baby, get me the Rolaids. They're on top of *la llelera.* You hear me, Jesse?

LUISA RUIZ: You just say "Pepe, Pepe" and he just comes running, wagging his tail, happy to see you. Not like Esmerelda, she's the collie that stays in the window all the time.

MARÍA PILAR: Jesse! The Rolaids!

JESSE: (*Offstage*) I can't find them, Mom.

MARÍA PILAR: On top of la refrigerator, I said.

JESSE: (*Offstage*) There's only bananas on top of the refrigerator.

MARÍA PILAR: *Ay San Fernando de los Flojos,* when will you cure that lazy child? *Con permiso,* Doña Luisa. (*She starts to leave. Grabbing María Pilar by the sleeve, LUISA RUIZ points to the window of her own house.*)

LUISA RUIZ: There she is. There's Esmerelda. You see her? Eh, you see her?

MARÍA PILAR: Yes, yes Doña Luisa, I can see her.

LUISA RUIZ: I call her "La Princesa," she's a real snob, that one, just like royalty. Sits there all day.

MARÍA PILAR: That's because the dog is blind, Doña Luisa. And you should . . .

LUISA RUIZ: (*Interrupting.*) They gave her to me that time I was an extra in the movies . . . the man said that she was the daughter of Lassie and she had belonged to La Liz Taylor.

MARÍA PILAR: You should take that animal to the veterinarian and . . .

LUISA RUIZ: (*Interrupting.*) It's the cataracts in her eyes. I can cure that. I know there is something I can use to cure that.

MARÍA PILAR: (*Walking briskly to house.*) Jesse! Jesse! María de Jesús. (*JESSE comes out the back door. She looks disheveled.*)

JESSE: Mom! Don't call me that.

MARÍA PILAR: Ay, if your Sainted Father *que Dios lo tenga en la Gloria* . . . (*Crosses herself.*) could see you now. Jesse, *por favor,* stand up straight and comb your hair. (*She exits into house.*)

JESSE: What for? I'm not going anyplace. I never go anyplace. Nobody even knows that I'm alive. (*JESSE slumps her way to LUISA RUIZ, who is busy studying the sky.*) I'm just drifting.

LUISA RUIZ: (*Looking at sky.*) Like a cloud.

JESSE: (*Looking at sky.*) Yeah.

LUISA RUIZ: (*No longer looking up.*) It was such a little cloud.

JESSE: (*Still looking at sky.*) A baby cloud, all fat and happy. . . .

LUISA RUIZ: But it got bigger and bigger . . .

JESSE: (*Looking up.*) It didn't know what to do, what to say. It wasn't ready. . . .

LUISA RUIZ: . . . and bigger until it blinded her.

JESSE: (*Looking at LUISA RUIZ.*) Huh?

LUISA RUIZ: The clouds in Esmerelda's eyes.

JESSE: The cataracts.

LUISA RUIZ: I put the pollen of the yellow passion flower on them, which is very strong, Jesse, they say within the flower are the symbols of the crucified Christ.

JESSE: I knew you were talking about the cataracts.

LUISA RUIZ: But it had no effect. I made a tea of that weed they call Juan Simón. . . . (*RAPHAEL appears, lurking around the edge of the yard.*) It had no effect, but I still have the ginseng root in the shape of a cross. . . . (*She starts walking back to her house, mumbling to herself.*) The ginseng root with the leaf of the aloe plant. . . . (*She exits.*)

JESSE: (*Yelling to RAPHAEL.*) My sister's not home! She's not interested in you. She's going to see the world. So you can stop hanging around the house. (*JESSE and RAPHAEL stand, stare at each other for a beat. JESSE picks up a rock. Exit RAPHAEL. JESSE shouts after him.*) And you can stop calling on the phone and hanging up. I know it's you . . . (*Softly.*) I recognize your breathing.

FIRST NIGHT

Lights change to night. The stage is dark, except for a large three-quarter moon and the small light in the bedroom window of the Luna house. We hear crickets and the howling of a dog. Enter ROSALINDA from the house, in sweatshirt and pants.

ROSALINDA: (*Running in place.*) I'm going to run around the world, over oceans and islands and continents. I'm going to jump over the Himalayas, skip the Spanish Steps and dip my toes in the Blue Nile. I'm going to see places I've never seen and meet people I've never known, Laplanders, Indonesians, Ethiopians. . . . (*Pointing and waving to imaginary people.*) Ay, mira los Japoneses, y los Chinitos and who are those giants? *Ay Dios, los Samoans!* And I will speak many tongues like the Bible. . . . (*Shaking hands with imaginary people.*) *Mucho gusto, yo soy* Rosalinda. *Je suis* Rosalinda, *comment allez-vous? Io sono* Rosalinda. *Jumbo!* Me Rosalinda from America. (*JESSE appears in window. The alarm clock in JESSE's hand goes off.*) Shhhh! Somebody might hear me.

JESSE: Somebody might mug you.

ROSALINDA: I'm too fast. (*She gets into starting position.*)

JESSE: Jeez, I wish we had a stopwatch. It's hard with this alarm clock. . . . Which way are you going tonight?

ROSALINDA: The northern route. Over the Pole.

JESSE: Say hello to the Eskimos.

ROSALINDA: Oh please, Jesse, hurry up.

JESSE: OK, OK. When the little hand hits twelve . . . on your mark . . . get set . . . go!

ROSALINDA: (*Running.*) There's Fresno . . . San Francisco . . . Portland. . . . (*She exits.*)

JESSE: Weird. (*Enter RAPHAEL. Seeing him, JESSE hides behind window curtain. RAPHAEL paces up and down in front of the house, looking at the window. He picks up a small stone and throws it through window. Loudly, from behind curtain.*) Hey!

RAPHAEL: Psst . . . Rosalinda . . . Rosalinda . . .

JESSE: (*In a breathy, sexy voice.*) Yeeesss?

RAPHAEL: Rosalinda, I know you got things on your mind with your big race on Saturday *pero* a man can only be ignored so much. (*Pause*) Listen, Rosalinda, *me voy a declarar. Sí,* I'm going to declare myself. (*Pause.*) "Rosalinda": a poem by Raphael Antonio Piña.
You are once
You are twice
You are three times a lady
And that is why you'll always
Be my one and only baby.
When I see you running

Running through the barrio
With your legs so brown and fine
Oh Rosalinda, Rosalinda,
Won't you be mine?

JESSE: (*Throwing a shoe out the window.*) Oh Christ.

RAPHAEL: Ay, Rosy, don't be mean.

JESSE: Her name isn't Rosy. So stop calling her Rosy. She's not gonna answer to Rosy.

RAPHAEL: Oh, you again.

JESSE: Ay Rosalinda! Quick somebody hold me back, I'm about to declare myself.

RAPHAEL: Listen you . . . you . . .

JESSE: My name is Jesse. I live here too ya know.

RAPHAEL: Where is Rosalinda?

JESSE: She's not home. She's running. She's in training and she doesn't see boys when she's training.

RAPHAEL: I'm not a boy, I'm a man.

JESSE: Oh yeah! . . . Well . . . eh . . . er . . . you're not her type. (*RAPHAEL starts to exit.*) Hey Raphael!

RAPHAEL: Yeah.

JESSE: You know your poem?

RAPHAEL: Yeah.

JESSE: It wasn't bad.

RAPHAEL: Thanks. . . . Good night Jesse. (*He exits.*)

JESSE: Good night Raphael Antonio Piña.

ROSALINDA: (*Offstage.*) Mexico City, Acapulco, Puerto Vallarta, La Paz, Santa Rosalia, Encinada . . . (*She enters.*) Tijuana, San Diego, La Orange County, Los Angeles . . . Castro Street. (*Looking up at JESSE.*) How did I do?

JESSE: Huh . . . ? I . . . I lost track. (*ROSALINDA sighs and gets into starting position again.*)

ROSALINDA: OK, one more time.

JESSE: Go!

ROSALINDA: (*Running.*) Santa Barbara, San Jose, San Francisco . . . (*She exits running. ROSALINDA's voice is heard sounding further and further away, as lights slowly change to day. Continued; offstage.*) Seattle, Portland, Vancouver, Alaska, the Bering Strait, Russia . . .

SECOND DAY

Early morning. Same large sun as First Day. MARÍA PILAR, wearing a fresh housedress and apron, is standing in front of her house, scanning the street. LUISA RUIZ, wearing the same outfit as on 1st Day, is coming out of her house.

MARÍA PILAR: Rosalinda! Rosalinda!

LUISA RUIZ: *Buenos días,* María Pilar.

MARÍA PILAR: *Buenos días,* Doña Luisa.

LUISA RUIZ: It's a beautiful day *con mucho viento.* Some people call it the Santa Ana wind. Some people call it the Devil Wind. Some people call it *El Siroco.* And some people—

MARÍA PILAR: *Sí sí,* it's a very windy day. Rosalinda! Running, running, that's all that girl thinks about. Ay and my stomach secreting the acid all morning.

LUISA RUIZ: Running, running that's all El Bobo and Pepe think about too. They wake up, sniff the air and off they go. I think it's something they smell in Mrs. Amador's rose garden. Maybe it's a dead bird. (*She sniffs the air.*) No. Maybe Mrs. Amador is making *chicharrones* . . . (*She sniffs the air.*) No . . . (*She sniffs more thoughtfully.*) It must be that patch of wild peppermint. They say the scent is very invigorating. Maybe that's where La Rosalinda is.

MARÍA PILAR: Doña Luisa, my daughter does not have the custom to go smelling things in other people's garden.

LUISA RUIZ: Oh.

MARÍA PILAR: She runs to practice.

LUISA RUIZ: Oh.

MARÍA PILAR: She runs because this Saturday she is entered in Our Lady of a Thousand Sorrows Marathon.

LUISA RUIZ: No! . . . *Sí?*

MARÍA PILAR: *Sí,* Father Estefan himself went from door to door to collect money for her entrance fee.

LUISA RUIZ: Oh, *pero* he didn't ask me for money. He never came to my door.

MARÍA PILAR: *Válgame Dios,* three hundred young girls from all the Catholic Diocese in

California. Ay, I don't know what those priests can be thinking. All that running shakes up a woman's insides.

LUISA RUIZ: He never came to my door. . . . I didn't give anything. . . . This Saturday? . . . That's tomorrow.

MARÍA PILAR: They are making them run from Elysian Park to the Mission downtown.

LUISA RUIZ: Oh. That's far . . . El Bobo could run that far.

MARÍA PILAR: It's not for dogs. It's for Catholic girls.

LUISA RUIZ: Maybe it's not too late for me to give . . .

MARÍA PILAR: I cannot give to her the things she wants. I am a woman alone. Now if her Sainted Father, *que Dios lo tenga en la Gloria* . . . (*Crosses herself.*) were down here with us today . . .

LUISA RUIZ: But it is important to give.

MARÍA PILAR: To give, ah *sí*, to give, *mira no más,* it's easy for you to say give . . . and for him, my husband . . . (*Raising her hand to heaven.*) *charlando* up there, playing the big macho with all the angels and the saints . . . does he listen when Rosalinda says she wants to be educated . . . she wants to see the world? Does he lift a finger? Does he put in a good word for us? No, *se hace sordo,* he pretends not to hear me. *Gracias a Dios,* Rosalinda knows how to work. She gets that from me.

LUISA RUIZ: She looks so pretty working at La Dairy Queen in her white uniform, just like a nurse. She always gives me free cones, soft-serve she calls it. She goes up to that big steel machine, she presses the red button, and zas! Out comes the ice cream, like a clean white snake it comes round and round and round. Rosalinda twirls the cone. She never spills a drop. When it just gets so high she stops, just like that. She never spills a drop. Then she leans over the counter, with a big smile, and says, "This is for you, Doña Luisa." That girl knows how to give.

MARÍA PILAR: I cry, I beg him, "Juanito, *mi amor,*" I say, "help us. It's our duty as parents to provide for our children. *Por favor, Papacito lindo,* I'm already sewing ten hours a day just to put food in our mouths." Did I hear from him? Nothing. *Ni una palabra. Condenado viejo.* . . . It took Father Estefan to put her in this race. Just think if she wins *el gran premio* it is a trip to Rome and all the expenses paid . . . but he . . . (*Indicating husband in heaven.*) didn't even help me with the entrance fee or the Nike running shoes. Father Estefan himself had to go door-to-door.

LUISA RUIZ: (*To MARÍA PILAR's husband in heaven.*) I swear he never came to my door.

MARÍA PILAR: She has to run like a dog to get somewhere in life. Ay, this acid is killing me. Jesse!

LUISA RUIZ: Run like a dog . . . ?

MARÍA PILAR: Jesse, the Rolaids. (*JESSE is coming out the back door, looking more disheveled than usual.*)

JESSE: I can't find them Mom.

MARÍA PILAR: María de Jesús! Look at you! *Por favor,* do something. Comb your hair. Stand up straight. Be a señorita. (*Exit MARÍA PILAR into house. JESSE walks up to the fence and LUISA RUIZ*).

JESSE: Please stop calling me that! It's weird. . . . I was real cute until I was twelve . . . people always pinching my cheeks. (*Pinching her own cheeks.*) "Ay qué preciosa!" "Ay qué belleza." But now it's all this pressure.

LUISA RUIZ: Run like a dog. . . .

JESSE: Yeah, far away. . . . No, wouldn't do any good, I think it's some kinda contagious disease, no matter where you go people expect you to comb your hair and stand up straight. I try, but my hair keeps falling into my face and my body just has this . . . terminal slouch . . . it's like I got a hunchback's blood . . . or—

MARÍA PILAR: (*Offstage.*) Jesse! Jesse! What is this *porquería* under your bed?

JESSE: Maybe I wasn't meant to be a señorita.

MARÍA PILAR: (*Offstage.*) Dr. Pepper, Twinkies, Cheetos . . . (*JESSE sighs and slumps her way into the house.*)

LUISA RUIZ: She has to run like a dog. . . . (*She exits slowly toward her house.*)

MARÍA PILAR: (*Offstage.*) Snickers, Ding-Dongs, Ho-Ho's, Susie-Qs, a pizza! (*MARÍA PILAR's voice fades. Light changes to night.*)

SECOND NIGHT

Moon is fuller than First Night, but not yet full. There is a soft, low-energy sound under this scene, like something vibrating.

LUISA RUIZ, wearing a dark kimono, is standing in front of her doorway. She is holding her hands in front of her body, with a red flannel cloth over them. RAPHAEL appears, lurking around the edges of the yard. Seeing LUISA RUIZ, he hides behind the jacaranda tree. As ROSALINDA comes out of her house in her running outfit, LUISA RUIZ beckons to her with both hands and the red flannel cloth. This gesture is slow, as though she is hypnotizing ROSALINDA.

LUISA RUIZ: *Ancho y profundo en pasos en el corazón en el Espíritu Santo. Espíritu Bendito.* (*ROSALINDA slowly waves to LUISA RUIZ and stands before her. LUISA RUIZ makes the sign of the cross on ROSALINDA. ROSALINDA kneels in front of LUISA RUIZ, who then opens her hands and carefully holds out a special Yu-Yu amulet—a small red flannel bag, the size of a large book of matches, which is filled with special herbs and potions and hung around the neck by a drawstring. LUISA RUIZ holds the Yu-Yu high above her own head.*) *Niño Santo Lobo.* (*She brings the Yu-Yu down and hangs it around ROSALINDA's neck as she starts her chant over and around ROSALINDA.*)
Cristo Santo de los Lagos y las Montañas dice—
(*She claps.*)
Madre Santa de las Valles dice—
(*Clap.*)
Padre Santo de la Sombra y el Sol dice—
(*Clap.*)
Virgencita de la Niebla dice—
(*Clap.*)
Niño Santo de las Criaturas dice—
(*Clap.*)
Santa Ana de los Vientos Secos dice—
(*Clap.*)

Espíritu Santo de la Chupa Rosa dice—
(*Clap.*)
Espíritu Santo de la Mariposa dice—
(*Clap.*)
San Bernardo de los Perros dice—
(*Clap.*)
Dios te bendiga
Cristo Santo te bendiga.

(*We hear a dog howl. RAPHAEL exits. Low-energy sound fades into sound of TV cartoons as lights change to day.*)

THIRD DAY

Early morning. Same large sun as First and Second Days. Sound of TV cartoons continues. MARÍA PILAR comes out from her house.

MARÍA PILAR: Rosalinda! (*Yells toward house.*) Jesse! Jesse! Turn off those cartoons, you hear me? I want you to go after your sister.

JESSE: (*In the window.*) Mom . . . it's seven o'clock. It's Saturday.

MARÍA PILAR: Now, Jesse. Do you hear me?

JESSE: Jeez, what's the big deal? (*JESSE disappears from window. Sound of cartoons goes off.*)

MARÍA PILAR: Your sister has to come back here and have a good breakfast. Then we have to go to la special mass for the runners where Father Estefan is going to bless her feet before the race. *Andale,* Jesse. Hurry up. (*JESSE comes out, looking very sleepy, wearing her pajamas with a skirt on top.*)

JESSE: I don't believe this.

MARÍA PILAR: You don't believe anything *y mira no más,* how you look. At your age I was up at five. I was already washed, dressed and making tortillas for all the men in the house.

JESSE: (*Rolling up pj legs.*) Take it easy, Mom, I'm going. (*She exits.*)

MARÍA PILAR: (*Calling after JESSE.*) And stop at the market and get some orange juice for your sister. Tell them to charge it to my account . . . and tell them I'll pay them next week. (*To husband in heaven.*) Ay, Juanito, you better keep your eye on that child.

ORLANDO: (*Enters.*) *Reader's Digest* . . . bill from Dr. Mirabel. . . . *Buenos días,* María Pilar. (*Handing her mail.*) Well today's the big day . . . eh. And the whole barrio's gonna be there. How's Rosalinda?

MARÍA PILAR: Ay Orlando, how do I know? I am only her mother, I am the last person to know where she is or how she is. Have you seen Rosalinda?

ORLANDO: Now don't start worrying, she's just warming up for the big race . . . whew! *Qué* hot . . . looks like it's going to be another scorcher.

MARÍA PILAR: Running, running. The whole thing is affecting my nerves.

ORLANDO: It's the Santa Ana winds, they affect people.

MARÍA PILAR: *Por favor* Orlando, if you see her tell her to come home.

ORLANDO: Of course María Pilar, "Go home at once," that's what I'll tell her. (*Turning to go.*) See you at the race. (*He exits.*)

MARÍA PILAR: (*Walking to house.*) Big race or no big race a person should tell their mother, a person should eat their breakfast. (*Exit MARÍA PILAR. Sun moves up a fraction in the sky to indicate passage of time. ROSALINDA zooms past the house. Enter JESSE, running, carrying a paper bag; one of her pj legs has fallen down.*)

JESSE: Amaa! Amaa!

MARÍA PILAR: (*Comes out of house.*) Ay por Dios, Jesse, walk *como una dama* . . . *un* lady.

JESSE: Ma, wait'll I tell you what Rosalinda did.

MARÍA PILAR: And where's your sister? Did you tell her about la special mass?

JESSE: I tried, Mom, but she just barked at me. OK. I'm walking down Castro Street. I'm right in front of Arganda's Garage. When Manny Arganda slides out from under a '68 Chevy, stands up and says, "Hey Essé, what's with jur seester?" I tell him to drop dead. He says, "OK. Essé, hab a nice dey." He thinks he's so cool.

MARÍA PILAR: Jesse.

JESSE: OK, OK. That's when I see Rosalinda, with Pepe and Bobo. I yell at her, I say, "Rosalinda, Mom says to come home,"

that's when she barked at me. Then she turns around and runs up to this car. . . . It was a black Impala with a little red racing stripe all along the side and real pretty red letters on the door that said "Danny Little Red Lopez."

MARÍA PILAR: *Por favor* Jesse.

JESSE: OK, OK. So she runs up to the car, and Mom . . . you won't believe this . . . she jumps over the car! . . . The black Impala, she jumps over it! . . . Just like la Wonder Woman . . . and she wasn't even breathing hard.

MARÍA PILAR: Jesse, why do you lie?

JESSE: Mom, it's exactly what happened. And when I went to the market they said Rosalinda charged a pound of chopped meat and bones.

MARÍA PILAR: That's ridiculous. Your sister never eats meat. Didn't you tell her to get home and about the mass?

JESSE: I couldn't catch her. She's so fast. The last time I saw her she's standing by the stoplight going like this. . . . (*Does an imitation of a dog running in place. Paws out, tongue out like a dog, panting.*)

MARÍA PILAR: Ave María Santísima, I told her never to bounce like that. She's gonna break her eggs.

JESSE: Not eggs, chopped beef.

MARÍA PILAR: I'm talking about her ovaries.

JESSE: Ovaries?

MARÍA PILAR: She's going to ruin her ovaries running like that.

JESSE: Ah Mom, I'm sure . . .

MARÍA PILAR: *La verdad!* Any doctor will tell you bouncing and riding a motorcycle is going to break your eggs.

JESSE: Uuggh. Disgusting. I'm going in for a soda.

MARÍA PILAR: No señorita, not before your breakfast.

JESSE: Eeewww Mom, please, I don't want breakfast. I just want a soda.

MARÍA PILAR: All right baby, all right. You stay here in case your sister runs by and I'll get you the soda . . . but don't drink it too fast. If you drink ice-cold soda too fast it gives you bad gas.

JESSE: Mom!

MARÍA PILAR: Ah *sí*, you laugh *pero* I've known people who have died of these things. (*Exits to house.*)

JESSE: Oh yeah? When I'm eighteen I'm going to ride a big black Harley Davidson motorcycle that has "La Jesse" painted on the side of the gas tank. I'll be jumping over cars, zooming along dusty, bumpy desert trails, and doing loop-dee-loos on the Ventura Freeway. All this, while drinking an ice . . . cold . . . soda real fast before breakfast! (*We hear the sound of a pack of dogs barking and see ROSALINDA running from U.L. to U.R.—a flash of her flying, wild black hair as she runs by. Jesse runs after ROSALINDA.*) Rosalinda! Rosalinda! (*As she exits.*) Rosalinda Mom says for you—(*More barking. Offstage.*) Rosalinda wait . . . ! (*MARÍA PILAR runs out the back door with a bottle of soda and a glass in her hands.*)

MARÍA PILAR: Jesse . . . ! Rosalinda . . . ! Come back here. This is no time to be playing. (*MARÍA PILAR runs around the back of the house and comes out in front. Enter MRS. AMADOR. She is out of breath, her hair is askew. She is splattered with mud and rose petals. She carries a broken rose-bush. She leans against the fence, trying to catch her breath.*) Señora! *Qué le pasa?* (*Out of breath, MRS. AMADOR struggles to speak.*) *Andale* Mrs. Amador, make an effort. Speak to me.

MRS. AMADOR: Rosalinda . . . ! The dogs . . . !

MARÍA PILAR: *Qué? Qué? Qué dices de* Rosalinda?

MRS. AMADOR: Rosalinda *y los perros* destroyed my rose garden.

MARÍA PILAR: No . . . No . . .

MRS. AMADOR: *Sí, sí,* all my roses. La Yellow Rose de Texas . . . las tea roses, La Eleanor Roosevelt . . . La Jacqueline Kennedy . . . *y esta* . . . (*Holding up broken rosebush.*) La Mamie Eisenhower. (*The sound of dogs barking is heard.*) Here they come . . . here they come . . . (*ROSALINDA runs through, U.R. to U.L., followed by a worn-out JESSE.*)

JESSE: (*Running to her mother.*) Mom, Mom you should see Rosalinda! She's chasing cars down Castro Street! She's . . . !

MRS. AMADOR: (*Interrupting.*) You should see what she did to my rose garden!!

MARÍA PILAR: I'm telling you it was those dogs next door.

MRS. AMADOR: *Pero* Rosalinda was with them! She was one of them. All wild-looking she was *así, mira* . . . (*Baring her teeth, imitating ROSALINDA's wild look.*) Ay! And blood all around her mouth. (*Crossing herself.*) It makes me tremble to think of it.

MARÍA PILAR: Blood around her mouth.

JESSE: Aw Mom, that was just from the raw meat she was eating. (*Enter ORLANDO, in a state of disarray, strap on mailbag broken, pants leg torn.*)

ORLANDO: La Rosalinda *se freakió.*

MARÍA PILAR: Where is she!? Where did she go?

JESSE: She's OK, Mom, she's over at the park catching frisbees between her teeth. She's really good. You should see her.

MRS. AMADOR: She's on drugs. I've seen it. They go crazy.

JESSE: She's not crazy.

MARÍA PILAR: (*Crying.*) She can't even take Contac.

MRS. AMADOR: That's how they start. First the Contac and then the—(*LUISA RUIZ enters to her front yard.*)

LUISA RUIZ: Pepe! Pepe! Bobo! (*Enter RAPHAEL running.*)

RAPHAEL: Jesse! Jesse! Rosalinda's in . . . (*Seeing LUISA RUIZ and pointing at her.*) She's the one! La Dog Lady! She gave her something. She put a curse on her. She turned her into a dog! I seen her do it.

MARÍA PILAR: (*To LUISA RUIZ.*) What have you done to my daughter?

MRS. AMADOR: Drugs! She gave her drugs. She's a pusher.

RAPHAEL: I seen her. She put something around her neck. And said spooky words over her.

MARÍA PILAR: (*Taking LUISA RUIZ by the shoulders, shaking her.*) What did you do to Rosalinda? What did you give her?

MRS. AMADOR: Speed! I bet that's what she gave her.

ORLANDO: (*Pulling MARÍA PILAR away from LUISA RUIZ.*) Give her a chance to talk. *Orale,* Doña Luisa. Did you give Rosalinda something?

LUISA RUIZ: She had to run like a dog . . . I gave her the Spirit . . . the Dog Spirit. It won't hurt her.

MRS. AMADOR: (*Crossing herself.*) Devil's work. *Ave, Dios,* she's a *bruja,* a witch. Where's my cross? (*Searching for cross at her neck.*) Jesse! Don't look at her. (*Pulling JESSE's face away.*) Nobody look at her eyes. (*All shield their eyes, except ORLANDO.*)

ORLANDO: *Cálmanse! Y* stop talking nonsense.

MRS. AMADOR: *Qué* nonsense and *qué nada!* Didn't Father Estefan himself say that she made the dog in the window blind with all them herbs she put in the dog's eyes? Didn't he? Didn't he?

MARÍA PILAR: *Sí, sí,* he said to keep away from her. (*Crying.*) She's turned my daughter into a dog.

JESSE: Mom! (*RAPHAEL, shielding his eyes, pulls a switchblade and points it at LUISA RUIZ's throat.*)

RAPHAEL: Turn her back, Dog Lady.

ORLANDO: Raphael . . . put it away. Now everybody calm down. It's just these damn Santa winds. It drives people crazy.

JESSE: She's not crazy.

MARÍA PILAR: *Por favor* Doña Luisa, you're a powerful woman. . . . I beg you, bring me back my daughter. (*LUISA RUIZ rummages in her pockets and pulls out an ultrasonic dog whistle. As she pulls it out, everybody stands back. She blows it. MRS. AMADOR crosses herself, gasps, and points across the street.*)

MRS. AMADOR: Ay! *Mira* Mr. Mura's garage door opened all by itself. (*They all turn around and look in shocked silence. RAPHAEL drops his knife. One by one all cross themselves, except for LUISA RUIZ and JESSE. JESSE stands up on the fence and looks up and down the street.*)

JESSE: Here she comes. Wow! Rosalinda that was great. (*ROSALINDA enters running. She continues running in place. Her hair is messy and wild. She is splattered with mud and rose petals. She has a keenly determined look in her eyes and holds a frisbee between her teeth.*)

MARÍA PILAR: Rosalinda, where were you? And why didn't you come when I called? (*ROSALINDA drops frisbee at MARÍA PILAR's feet.*) No señorita, I'm not playing games with you.

MRS. AMADOR: (*Passing her hands before ROSALINDA's face.*) Rosalinda . . . how do you feel?

JESSE: Fine! She feels fine!

ORLANDO: You're all right, eh Rosalinda?

JESSE: Of course she's all right.

MARÍA PILAR: Rosalinda, I want you to go to bed.

JESSE: Not now, she'll be late for the race, Ready? Rome, here comes Rosalinda. (*Exit ROSALINDA, running. The others look at one another. Then all run offstage after ROSALINDA, except for LUISA RUIZ, and RAPHAEL, who lags slowly behind.*)

RAPHAEL: (*Exiting slowly.*) A man can only take so much. She's never home, she's a lot of trouble, running, jumping, barking. Women! (*LUISA RUIZ stands onstage alone for a beat. We hear the sound of dogs barking. She goes to the alleyway.*)

LUISA RUIZ: Pepe! Bobo! No, you can't go . . . it's only for Catholic girls. We're not invited. (*She runs offstage after the dogs.*)

THIRD NIGHT

There is a full moon. The sound of a mariachi band playing "Guadalahara," and other party sounds. MARÍA PILAR in front of her house, in a party dress, hanging a banner proclaiming "Rosalinda Number One." Enter MRS. AMADOR carrying a big plate.

MRS. AMADOR: *Tamales estilo Jalisco.*

MARÍA PILAR: Just think, she's going to Rome and all the expenses paid.

MRS. AMADOR: What about the woof! woof! (*ROSALINDA comes out of the house. MRS. AMADOR jumps back and looks at ROSALINDA very cautiously.*)

ROSALINDA: She hasn't come yet? She said she would come.

MARÍA PILAR: Now don't get excited, if Doña Luisa said she would come, then she will come.

MRS. AMADOR: *Sí,* don't get excited. Nothing to get excited about.

ROSALINDA: Oh Mom, isn't it wonderful! I'm going to see the world. (*Looking up at the sky.*) I'm going to see the universe. . . . I am going to dance on Venus, skate on Saturn's rings, dive into the Milky Way and wash my hair with stars.

MRS. AMADOR: Is she getting excited? (*ROSALINDA and MARÍA PILAR are looking up to the sky. Seeing them, MRS. AMADOR very cautiously starts to look up.*)

MARÍA PILAR: Ay, Juanito . . . I feel your soft brown eyes on me . . . on Rosalinda . . . on Jesse . . . Jesse? Rosalinda, where's Jesse?

ROSALINDA: (*Still gazing at the sky.*) I don't know Mom.

MRS. AMADOR: (*Eyeing the sky with great suspicion.*) Is somebody there? (*MRS. AMADOR continues to stare straight up to the sky throughout the rest of this scene. Enter ORLANDO and RAPHAEL, both very dressed up. RAPHAEL carries a big bouquet of flowers.*)

ORLANDO: *Orale,* Rafa, give her the flowers.

RAPHAEL: Now?

MARÍA PILAR: Ay look Rosalinda, it's Orlando and Raphael. . . . *Pasen, pasen* . . . ay, where is Jesse? Rosalinda. I'll get her. (*ROSALINDA goes toward house as LUISA RUIZ comes out of her house in a faded cocktail dress, a large flower in her hair.*)

MARÍA PILAR: *Ay qué bonita se ve, me da tanto gusto a ver* La Doña Luisa.

LUISA RUIZ: Oh! Thank you, María Pilar. (*She looks up to the sky.*) It's a beautiful night.

MARÍA PILAR: *Sí.* God works in mysterious ways, Doña Luisa. (*Enter JESSE. She has been transformed into a beautiful young princess. She stands next to ROSALINDA. RAPHAEL stands before them, holding the bouquet of flowers, awestruck at JESSE. All stare at JESSE in silence except for MRS. AMADOR, who is still staring at the sky.*)

ORLANDO: Look at La Jesse!

MARÍA PILAR: Ay Juanito. (*She crosses herself.*) She combed her hair.

LUISA RUIZ: She looks just like a princess.

ORLANDO: (*Nudging RAPHAEL.*) Now Rafa! Now. (*RAPHAEL, staring at JESSE, tears the bouquet of flowers in half, giving half to ROSALINDA and half to JESSE.*) *Y la fiesta pues?* . . . I am gonna dance with you, Doña Luisa. (*ORLANDO takes LUISA RUIZ arm-in-arm and exits into the house as MARÍA PILAR moves to MRS. AMADOR, who is still staring into the sky, holding plate of tamales.*)

MARÍA PILAR: *Andale,* Mrs. Amador, it's time for the tamales.

MRS. AMADOR: (*Still looking at the sky.*) Is somebody watching us? (*MARÍA PILAR takes MRS. AMADOR into the house, followed by RAPHAEL.*)

ROSALINDA: I'm proud of you Jesse.

JESSE: (*To ROSALINDA.*) You're going to see the world . . . all those places . . . all the things that will happen to you . . .

ROSALINDA: I'll be back.

JESSE: You'll be different.

ROSALINDA: We're sisters forever.

JESSE: Rosalinda? . . . Can I see it? (*ROSALINDA brings out the Yu-Yu from under her blouse.*) Can I touch it? . . . Did . . . did you really turn into a dog?

ROSALINDA: (*Taking Yu-Yu off her neck, holding it in her hands.*) You have to work very hard.

JESSE: I know. (*ROSALINDA puts Yu-Yu around JESSE's neck. She exits into the house. JESSE turns around and stares at the moon. She slowly walks up Castro Street toward the moon as lights slowly fade and we hear MARÍA PILAR's voice.*)

MARÍA PILAR: (*Offstage.*) Jesse! Jesse!

END OF PLAY

PROPERTY LIST

First Day

Onstage
Rotating sprinkler
Strange plants
Rubber tires
Rubbish
Sign: "CURANDERA—HEALER"

2 mailboxes
Jacaranda tree
Rock

Offstage
Mailbag (Orlando)
Alarm clock (Jesse)
Shoe (Jesse)

First Night

Onstage
Small stone

Second Night

Onstage
Red flannel cloth
Yu-Yu amulet

Third Day

Offstage
Paper bag (Jesse)
Bottle of soda and glass (María Pilar)
Broken rosebush (Mrs. Amador)
Switchblade (Raphael)
Ultrasonic dog whistle (Luisa Ruiz)
Frisbee (Rosalinda)

Third Night

Onstage
Banner: "Rosalinda Number One"

Offstage
Big plate of tamales (Mrs. Amador)
Big bouquet of flowers (Raphael)

PRODUCING *DOG LADY*

The production of *Dog Lady* that we consider here was done by an organization called International Arts Relations, or INTAR. INTAR has functioned much like East West Players as an umbrella organization for the production of new plays and musicals by Hispanic Americans as well as the most prominent work from the Latin American theatre. In addition to the production of her plays at INTAR, Milcha Sanchez-Scott's participation in the INTAR playwrights' laboratory led to the development of her next major play, *Roosters*.

INTAR

INTAR was founded in 1966 by artistic director Max Ferra to promote Spanish-language theatre for the Spanish-speaking peoples of New York City. INTAR began in a condemned tenement building as an organization committed to providing low-income access to the theatre. It joined a growing movement of Spanish-speaking or interlingual theatres developing on both the East and West coasts such as El Teatro Campesino in northern California or the Puerto Rican Traveling Company in New York. Today playwrights of Cuban, Mexican, Puerto Rican, and Central and South American heritages are contributing vibrant plays to American theatre organizations across the country. As one of the oldest Latino theatres of the period from the 1960s to the present, INTAR has had a significant impact on the careers of many Latino playwrights. INTAR is still located in a small, off-Broadway theatre where creativity is the most important resource as it was when Max Ferra directed *Dog Lady* in 1984.

SET DESIGN AND MING CHO LEE

For the production of Milcha Sanchez-Scott's companion one-acts, *Dog Lady* and *The Cuban Swimmer*, Max Ferra invites Ming Cho Lee to

do the set design. One of the foremost designers in the United States, Lee is known for his
work with the New York Shakespeare Festival,
the New York City Opera, the Metropolitan
Opera, and the Martha Graham Dance Company, as well as on Broadway and in many of the
resident theatre companies in North America.
Lee usually works with far larger budgets than
the resources of a small not-for-profit off-
Broadway theatre will allow.

Max Ferra sees in Sanchez-Scott's one-acts
a special quality of lightness and simplicity that
he compares to a kite caught up in the air currents. He believes that the artistic perspectives
of Milcha Sanchez-Scott and Ming Cho Lee
are complementary and will make for a productive creative partnership. Ming Cho Lee agrees.
He is particularly fascinated by *Dog Lady* and
the vivid way it captures the Hispanic world.
The INTAR production of *Dog Lady* is shaped
by the way Ming Cho Lee physicalizes his
imaginative response to the world of the play.

Lee will be working in the INTAR theatre
that he describes as a "brownstone, railroad flat
of a theatre" because of its long, narrow space,
brick interior, and spartan arrangements. The
entire space, audience and stage, is 21 feet wide
and 59 feet deep. That is divided into a stage
space of 21 feet wide and 24 feet deep and a
seating area of 21 feet wide and 35 feet deep for
the 99 seats of this equity waiver theatre. In designing the set for *Dog Lady*, Ming Cho Lee is
guided by the nature of the INTAR theatre
space as well as the structure, tone, and images
of the play.

Pop Art and Forced Perspective

Because Lee sees the play as having a "parable
or fairy-tale quality," he has decided to do a
"pop art realistic" version of a Los Angeles
street scene but with "a very forced perspective."[8] Through painting technique, the street
scene appears to continue off into the distance
because the houses grow smaller upstage. For
perspective to work in the theatre, everyone

must share the same view of the vanishing
point. In theatres with wide audience spaces or
audience spaces that wrap around part or all of
the stage, creating a forced perspective is not
possible. When perspective painting was first
introduced into the theatre during the Italian
Renaissance in the early sixteenth century, the
perspective was drawn essentially from the
Duke's seat in the center of the palace room
that functioned as a theatre. One's importance
at court would dictate how close one sat to the
royal seat and therefore how much of the perspective effect one was able to enjoy. But because the audience space at INTAR is quite
narrow, everyone can, in fact, share the same
visual point of view that allows the perspective
to work. "The idea was that when people walk
in, they think that they are looking at a magical
realism recreation of the Los Angeles barrio."
Small stucco houses line the street painted
brightly in blues, pinks, and yellows, more
color than Ming Cho Lee usually uses in his
sets. "Seedy looking" palm trees rise above the
houses and off in the distance the freeway can
be seen. The sky is a glaring white color that
suggests a smoggy heat (see Color Plate 43).

The street scene was first suggested by an
impressionist painting brought to the planning
process by director Max Ferra. Ming Cho Lee
interpreted the street by drawing on his own
memories of Los Angeles in the 1950s when he
was a student at Occidental College and on
photographs sent to him by playwright Milcha
Sanchez-Scott. The set captures a sense of both
an actual, recognizable place and a magical
place given to the unexpected. The use of the
perspective is a crucial factor in first establishing the sense of place and then in contributing
to the humor in the production.

Breaking the Illusion

When plays were originally done with perspective scenery, the actors performed at the front
edge of the stage. Because the painted objects
must be made smaller as they are placed farther

upstage to create the sense of distance or the vanishing point, if actors move upstage and stand next to the smaller objects, the illusion is destroyed. Stories are told of some stage directors even arranging crowd scenes using children or midgets upstage to create the effect that, like the painted buildings, the people, too, were getting smaller in the distance.

However, the illusion of the perspective painting in the *Dog Lady* set—with the smaller houses upstage—is created for a purpose other than giving a sense of distance. The actors move upstage deliberately to challenge or break the illusion of the perspective. They appear to become huge because they tower over the tiny houses and the ribbonlike rendering of the freeway. The actors become taller yet because the stage is steeply "raked." That is, the stage floor itself rises on an angle as you move upstage. For example, when Rosalinda does her training runs that seem to take her round the world she moves upstage and runs in an exaggerated slow motion. She becomes a giant, circumnavigating what has become an almost toy planet. The relationship of the characters to the physical world keeps changing, and this technique works as a visual surprise to keep the audience off balance as the incidents in the play also continue to startle. Lee gives us a playful, lighthearted image of a Los Angeles barrio and builds into it a shifting perspective that allows the characters to occupy differing levels of reality. When the actors are **downstage,** the houses appear to be normal size. As soon as the actors move upstage, the neighborhood seems to shrink.

STAGING AND ACTING

The staging of *Dog Lady* and the acting style in conjunction with the set make clear to the audience that the characters live in the protected world of comedy. The acting has an exaggerated, cartoonish quality that is both a little flatter than life and at the same time larger than life. There is less internal focus to the acting

than in the productions of *And the Soul Shall Dance* and *Joe Turner's Come and Gone*. In those performances each character brings the weight of a difficult and important personal history with him or her. The past with its memories is always present. In contrast, in *Dog Lady*, the characters seem to exist only in the present. There is subtext, but not the reference to memory.

Most of the action takes place downstage and has a presentational rather than a representational or realistic quality. The set is less of an environment than a background for the action. Rather than the actors inhabiting the set as they do Bertha's kitchen, the set becomes part of a game the actors are playing for us, particularly with the visual tricks of the shrinking houses. The actors in *Dog Lady* face out and play to the audience as much as they play to each other. The audience is less the invisible witness of realism; it is more a partner overtly acknowledged by the actors.

The movement of the actors is obviously stylized rather than staged to create the appearance of reality. When Rosalinda runs, she always shifts into slow motion to indicate that she is covering great distances. Her transformation into a dog is indicated suggestively with her hands simply raised and cupped as paws, the infamous Frisbee in her mouth. Before Rosalinda's entrance as a dog, the other characters enter, each with their astonished response to her offstage canine exploits. The characters all stand in a line as if they are too amazed to stand alone, their heads moving precisely together, all the bodies leaning in the same direction.

Sight Gags

Sight gags become important. When María Pilar sends Jesse to find Rosalinda, Jesse is in her pajamas. Jesse pulls a skirt over the pajamas and pulls up the pajama bottoms so that they are out of sight under the skirt. When she returns to tell her story about Manny Argando, the black Impala, and the chopped meat and

Rosalinda (Jeannette Mirabel) appears as a dog to terrorize Mrs. Amador, who is already furious about her rose garden. The dog character is created through gesture and attitude, not through any change in costume or makeup.

bones, one pajama leg has slipped down. So the humor of her story is punctuated by her utter disregard for her own appearance. A moment later Orlando, the mailman, enters. It is clear from his appearance that, in the tradition of dogs and mailmen, he has been attacked by Rosalinda and her pack, her newly found comrades in crime. His trousers are badly torn and dangling as if they have been torn by large canine teeth, his hat is askew, and he carries one shoe in his hand. He staggers in and falls onto the step as he says, "*La Rosalinda se freakió.*" The costume designer, Connie Singer, is responsible for creating ideas of character and sociological background. But like the work of scene designer Ming Cho Lee, her work makes a major contribution to the humor in the performance.

Vocal Style

The vocal delivery of the actors is also exaggerated. These are not seemingly overheard conversations, but lines delivered for the audience's benefit. The actor playing the mother, María Pilar, has an almost operatic style as she details her various woes with obvious relish and gusto. In her early scene with Luisa Ruiz, the *curandera*, she begins with great pride in her daughter's running and the assistance of Father Estefan. She then becomes very melodramatic over being a "woman alone" who must struggle to provide for her daughters. The self-pity is followed by a scathing commentary on her dead husband's failure to help. Sarcastically, she calls to him in heaven. She is reduced to tears at his lack of response and then finally unleashes a

Rosalinda and Jesse (Elizabeth Peña) enjoy Rosalinda's transformation, while the rest of the cast reacts with varying degrees of dismay. The acting style is far more presentational than the more realistic acting in Joe Turner's Come and Gone *and* And the Soul Shall Dance.

blast of anger at the *"condenado viejo"* (old sinner). It is almost as if an aria has been made of her shifting moods, and the actor enjoys it as much as the audience.

USING COMEDY TO SHIFT THE WORLDVIEW

In *Dog Lady*, Milcha Sanchez-Scott incorporates many of the traditional expectations of comedy and realigns them. A small community is disrupted by misunderstanding and tangled events. Luisa Ruiz tries to help Rosalinda and seems to create chaos. Love is confused and unrequited. Raphael loves Rosalinda, who thinks only about running. Jesse loves Raphael, who thinks only about Rosalinda. Like most comedies the play ends with triumph and reconciliation. Rosalinda has won the race and will go to Rome, the first step in her journey out into the world. There is a party of celebration and the outcast, Luisa Ruiz, becomes the honored guest. Jesse is transformed from an awkward adolescent into a radiant young woman. Raphael, who has had eyes only for Rosalinda, is suddenly captivated by Jesse.

The INTAR production deftly underscores the shift in worldview that Sanchez-Scott establishes through her material. In another time Rosalinda (beautiful rose) would be a fairy princess waiting to be rescued by a prince. Now the fair one has become an athlete with her own quest who is helped by a Latina

In the final scene of Dog Lady *the mood of the play shifts from exaggeration to intimacy. The set becomes more an environment for dreams than the toy planet of earlier scenes. Through acting style, placement of the characters, and lighting, the performance leads to revelation, changing the focus from the physical and verbal humor of the first part of the play.*

version of the fairy godmother, the *curandera*. Rather than kissing a frog who turns into a prince, Rosalinda moves farther away from the passive, fairy-tale image by becoming an animal herself, unpredictable and even ferocious. The sister living in her shadow does not dream of a beautiful transformation (although she does dream of Rafael) but of roaring away on her own Harley Davidson. The final moment of the play is not a love scene or betrothal involving

Raphael and Rosalinda or Raphael and Jesse. The final scene is between the two sisters, both lovely in their fiesta dresses. Rosalinda is now in a black dress with her hair unbound from the sweatband she has worn throughout the play, and Jesse is in a soft white dress instead of the pajamas under a skirt with one leg rolled up and the other falling down.

In this final scene the pace of the performance slows down and the actors lose the cartoonish, exaggerated quality of the earlier scenes. The sisters sit together on the front step of the Luna house and share the most personal moments of the production. They lean against each other, their faces very close together. When Jesse says, "all the things that will happen to you," she is wistful and sad. There is a clear sense of the unspoken, her sense of loss in feeling that magical things will not happen to her. And Jesse's subsequent "you'll be different" carries a tinge of resentment.

Jesse's subtext, her longing for the world that is opening up to Rosalinda, sets the stage for their focus on the amulet given to Rosalinda by the *curandera*, the apparent source of Rosalinda's power. Rosalinda shows Jesse the *yu-yu*, holding it reverently as a great treasure, and the amulet seems to emit a magical aura perceived by both young women. The scene is played very deliberately. Jesse reaches to touch the amulet. And then there is a long pause while Rosalinda makes up her mind. She takes the amulet from around her neck and gives it to Jesse. They touch cheeks in the Latina manner. The play and the production suggest that the power to reach, to become, to transcend, is a gift that comes out of the relationships of these women, the *curandera* with her ties to the earth and traditional ways and the sisters with their courage to take on the world.

Jesse stands and Rosalinda exits into the house. Jesse puts on the amulet, and her facial expression changes. The haunted look of vulnerability and longing disappears, replaced by a more knowing expression, an awareness. She gives the audience one last, mysterious look and slowly walks upstage bathed in the moonlight, "*la luna*," leaving her mother's cries of "Jesse, Jesse" behind.

SUMMARY

In *Dog Lady*, Milcha Sanchez-Scott uses comedy to explore questions of gender, religion, and social organization. She takes an outrageous situation in which a young woman becomes a dog to win a race and disrupts the entire community. Tales of Rosalinda's amazing exploits reverse all of the community expectations of female behavior. The play follows the usual pattern in comedy of reconciliation, but in the end Rosalinda and Jesse both go their own ways instead of returning to the traditional social structure.

The work of Milcha Sanchez-Scott is influenced by the playwright's childhood in Colombia and her formative years living as part of the Mexican American community in southern California. Other sources include the literary movement of magical realism as well as the feminist movement involving visual artists and writers. The blending of English and Spanish reflects the use of language in the Latino community and contributes to the rhythms of the characters' speeches and the vividness of the play's vocabulary.

The style of the production at INTAR, in terms of both design and acting, was very important to the audience's experience of the comedy. For *Dog Lady*, set designer Ming Cho Lee created a magical world through perspective painting. The set seemed to grow or shrink, depending on the placement of the actors, and served as a presentational background rather than a realistic environment for the actors. The acting style involved exaggeration and suggestion, with the actors acknowledging the presence of the audience.

TOPICS FOR DISCUSSION AND WRITING

1. Chapter 13 on genre makes the point that ultimately the world of comedy is a protected one, a world without suffering. *Dog Lady* offers an example of such a protected world. How does the absence of pain contribute to the comedy? Is comedy always without suffering or pain?

2. Usually, associating a girl or woman with a dog would have a negative connotation. What different meanings are suggested by the symbol of the dog in this play?

3. What kinds of changes occur in the characters in *Dog Lady?* What changes do you think the playwright would like to see in our own society?

NOTES

1. Milcha Sanchez-Scott, interview with the author, 1 June 1994.

2. Milcha Sanchez-Scott, interview with the author, 1 June 1994.

3. There continues to be evolution within the communities of Latin American heritage about the words of identification used to designate national ancestry. "Chicano" emerged as a radical term in the 1960s identifying Americans of Mexican heritage who were associated with political activity. At that time, "Hispanic" began to be considered an outdated term originated by "Anglos." But for some the word "Chicano" had other pejorative connotations or limitations because of its reference to Mexican heritage rather than a wider grouping of Latin American nations. The more recent "Latino" and "Latina" (in reference to women) were adopted to refer to any Americans of Latin American descent. "Hispanic" has become a more widely used term again and refers to people of Spanish-speaking origins so that it could also refer to Europeans. Some people use the terms interchangeably; others have strong preferences. The debate is not unlike that within the African American community over the words "black," "African American," "Afro-American," and the rarely used "Negro."

4. M. Elizabeth Osborn, *On New Ground: Contemporary Hispanic-American Plays* (New York: Theatre Communications Group, 1987), 245.

5. Juan Bruce-Novoa, *Retrospace: Collected Essays on Chicano Literature, Theory, and History* (Houston: Arte Publico Press, 1990), 49–50.

6. Gloria Anzaldúa, *Borderlands: La Frontera* (San Francisco: Aunt Lute Book Company, 1987), 20.

7. Erasmo Gamboa and Carolyn M. Buan, *Nosotros: The Hispanic People of Oregon* (Portland: The Oregon Council for the Humanities, 1995), 108.

8. All of Lee's comments are from an interview with the author, May 1996.

SUGGESTIONS FOR FURTHER READING

Brading, D. A. *Mexican Phoenix: Our Lady of Guadalupe: Image and Tradition Across Five Centuries.* Cambridge: Cambridge University Press, 2001.

> An authoritative history of the position of the Virgin of Guadalupe in the Mexican Catholic Church and in relation to international Catholicism.

Cisneros, Sandra. *Woman Hollering Creek and Other Stories.* Madison, WI: Turtleback Books, 1992.

> A book of short stories from a leading Latina author who focuses on the experiences of Mexican Americans. The story "Little Miracles, Kept Promises" offers a contemporary exploration of ways in which the figure of the Virgin of Guadalupe can be reinterpreted to offer strength to those who do not follow a traditional path. Other writings of Cisneros include *The House on Mango Street* and *Caramelo.*

Gonzalez, Jose Cruz, and Juliette Carrillo, eds. *Latino Plays from South Coast Repertory.* New York: Broadway Play Publishing, 2000.

> This book features plays developed through the South Coast Repertory Theatre's Hispanic Playwrights Project, which has functioned since 1986 to provide opportunities for Latino playwrights, actors, and directors. South Coast Repertory Theatre, in Costa Mesa, California, is a major regional theatre that has chosen to integrate Latino theatre as a fundamental part of its programming. Plays by Jose Rivera, Cherrie Moraga, and Octavio Solis are included.

Huerta, Jorge, ed. *Necessary Theater: Six Plays About the Chicano Experience.* Houston: Arte Publico Press, 1989.

> An anthology of Chicano plays focusing largely on the West Coast experience of Mexican Americans. The introductory material provides a helpful overview of the development of Latino theatre in the United States during the 1960s through the work of El Teatro Campesino and El Teatro de la Esperanza. The plays include *Latina* by Milcha Sanchez-Scott and Jeremy Blahnik and *The Shrunken Head of Pancho Villa* by Luis Valdez.

Kanellos, Nicolas. *A History of Hispanic Theatre in the United States: Origins to 1940.* Austin: University of Texas Press, 1990.

> A fascinating history of nineteenth- and early twentieth-century Hispanic theatre productions from southern California to Texas to New York and Florida. Kanellos documents the work of

touring companies from Mexico as well as new plays written in the United States by immigrants from Mexico, South America, Spain, Puerto Rico, and Cuba.

Lippard, Lucy R. *Mixed Blessings: New Art in a Multicultural America*. New York: Pantheon Books, 1990.

A study of the way visual art reflects culture. This book includes a number of Latino artists whose work is highly theatrical and is also connected to many of the same impulses that inspire the work of Latino playwrights.

Osborn, M. Elizabeth, ed. *On New Ground: Contemporary Hispanic-American Plays*. New York: Theatre Communications Group, 1987.

An anthology of Latino plays that includes *Roosters* by Milcha Sanchez-Scott, this book expands the coverage of Latino theatre. It includes playwrights of Cuban, Puerto Rican, and South American heritage such as Maria Irene Fornes, Eduardo Machado, and Jose Rivera.

Sandoval-Sanchez, Alberto, and Nancy Saporta Sternbach, eds. *Puro Teatro: A Latina Anthology*. Tucson: University of Arizona Press, 2000.

An anthology of plays by Latina playwrights that includes full-length plays, one-acts, performance pieces, and writings called *testimonios*, which are statements in creative, personal form about how individuals became playwrights. The book focuses on the rapidly increasing participation of women in Latino theatre.

Svich, Caridad, and Maria Teresa Marrero, eds. *Out of the Fringe: Contemporary Latina/Latino Theatre and Performance*. New York: Theatre Communications Group, 2000.

This is an anthology of recent Latino plays with several essays that explore what the editors identify as the "first, second, and third waves" of Latino playwriting. The book identifies the new subjects and new forms explored during the last three decades of Latino theatre. The playwrights include Luis Alfaro, Migdalia Cruz, Nilo Cruz, Naomi Lizuka, and Oliver Mayer.

CHAPTER 15

The Project

Looking at Buried Child *by* Sam Shepard

In our study of theatre, we have moved from the most basic element of theatre—the impulse in human nature to perform—to the complex development of that performance impulse in the production of plays. In coming to understand the theatre, we have examined the structure of plays, the work of theatre artists, and the relationship between the expression of ideas in performance and the audience. The purpose of this final chapter is to give you the opportunity to integrate the materials presented in the book by participating in the production process. The goal of this culminating project is for groups of students to collaborate on the hypothetical production of a play. You will need to study the play to be produced, consider the ideas of the playwright, and contribute to an interpretation of those ideas in a theatre of your choosing for an audience of your peers.

Several approaches to the production project are possible, depending on the size and organization of your class. The project may be collaborative or individual. The project may culminate in the presentation of scenes to your class and/or in the presentation of a production plan. If the project is done individually, your results may be turned in to the instructor rather than presented to the class. The collaborative

project is designed for small classes or large classes that also have discussion sections. Large classes without discussion sections will need to modify the collaborative process or use the individual approach.

PREPARING A PRODUCTION

The collaborative project should be done in groups of approximately five to seven. If possible, groups should include students who are interested in design and students who are interested in performance. After the groups have been organized, each group will meet and decide who will take on the different individual responsibilities as they are described in the "Project Assignments" section of this chapter. One person needs to assume the role of the director. Each group does not need to do all of the possible assignments. Students should choose the area that interests them most and with which they are most comfortable.

After reading the play, each group will hold their first meeting to decide on the distribution of responsibilities. Then each student will begin work on his or her particular assignment. The group should meet for the second time when the members have completed enough preliminary thinking to allow the group to brainstorm and make the group decisions listed on pages 438–439.

Group members will present their production plan to the class, showing the poster design, scene design, and costume designs and outlining the stylistic choices they have made and explaining how those choices interpret the ideas in the play. The production presentation may also include the presentation of a scene from the play. If time restrictions do not allow a class presentation, the director will write an overview of the stylistic choices. As an alternative presentation plan, each group may display the visual materials they have developed, and the class time may be used for the presentation of scenes.

If the project is to be completed individually, each student should choose one of the assignments and develop his or her project as described in the "Project Assignments" section. Each student will need to make the decisions listed under "Group Decisions" on an individual basis.

BURIED CHILD AND ALTERNATIVE PLAY CHOICES

The play included in this chapter and meant to be used as the subject of the production project is *Buried Child*, by Sam Shepard. Although the assignments have been created with *Buried Child* in mind, they may be adapted to other plays, including the four plays that we have already read. Additional contemporary plays recommended as alternatives for the production project are *The Art of Dining*, by Tina Howe; *Proof*, by David Auburn; and *The Guys*, by Anne Nelson. As one further alternative, some classes may wish to explore a play from an earlier period chosen by the instructor.

Introduction to Sam Shepard

Sam Shepard is a contemporary playwright whose plays test the American experience against popular American mythology. In his work, cowboys, musicians, and screenwriters inhabit an American landscape whose promise of space, freedom, and renewal has become a lie. Characters seek out their roots or connections to the past and find homes where the family members don't recognize one another or else engage in bitter hostilities.

Born on November 5, 1943, in Fort Sheridan, Illinois, Sam Shepard (originally named Samuel Shepard Rogers III) spent the first years of his life moving between military bases while his father served in the Army Air Corps. Upon his father's retirement from the army, the family settled in southern California, first South Pasadena and then Duarte, where his mother worked as a school teacher and his father went to college on the G.I. Bill. Although he would become legendary for his rebellious behavior and attitude, as a child Shepard was involved in traditional school activities as well as raising animals and doing farmwork. But he had a very contentious relationship with his father, who was strict and unpredictable. Shepard escaped family pressures and the boredom of small town life by identifying with the adventures of characters in Hollywood westerns and later by participating in plays when he attended Mount San Antonio Community College. When he was nineteen years old, he dropped out of college to join a small, traveling religious theatre company that eventually took him to New York City.

In 1963 Shepard shared a room with Charles Mingus Jr., the son of the great jazz musician. He became immersed in the bohemian East Village world of jazz, rock and roll, and theatre, as well as the drug culture. Shepard had begun playing drums when he was thirteen, and in New York he joined a band and started to write plays. He has been quoted as saying that what he really wanted to be was a rock-and-roll star not a playwright.

> The people that were most admirable to me were, first, musicians. They had an instrument, they could play alone, by themselves; that was their craft. . . . Next, I admired painters. I wanted something like that, something tangible that I could work on, something that I did by myself.[1]

That "something" became strange plays inhabited by wild characters speaking a hallucinatory kind of language. Far from the traditional form of American realism with well-made family dramas, Shepard's first plays featured bizarre actions and characters who changed their identities from moment to moment with no explanation or motivation. He acknowledges the deep impression that Samuel Beckett's *Waiting for Godot* made on him when he was still a teenager, but the dramas he wrote were the product of an original imagination that had been shaped by the explosiveness of the sixties and the icons of pop culture.

As a playwright Shepard draws heavily on his family history and his own experiences. Many of his early plays were based on his latest relationship. His father, who became a reclusive alcoholic living in Santa Fe, New Mexico, recurs in a number of the plays, and his father's family, whom he visited when he was sixteen, became the models for *Buried Child*. But he uses his relationships and his family history as a way of exploring basic truths about life in the United States rather than as a way of constructing a theatrical autobiography, as did Eugene O'Neill in *Long Day's Journey into Night*.

Shepard was deeply involved in the experimental off-off-Broadway theatre of Theatre Genesis, Caffe Cino, and Cafe La Mama during the sixties, where his plays were central to new movements in the American theatre. But after a period of almost manic productivity and searing relationships, Shepard consciously removed himself from the debilitating subculture of substance abuse by moving with his wife, O-lan, and baby son to London for several years. At a distance from the United States, he began to mature as a playwright with his first major work, *The Tooth of Crime*.

Deciding to return to his Western roots, Shepard moved to San Francisco, where he began a decade-long association with the Magic Theatre. With plays such as *True West, Fool for Love*, and *Buried Child*, Shepard earned a reputation as one of America's most prominent playwrights. Shepard's later plays are a mixture of realism and theatre of the absurd. They are characterized by a surprising use of symbols and bizarre character behavior. The plays can be very funny and at the same time highly disturbing because violence continuously threatens to surface.

> If the experience of being confronted by a theater event brings some shock to your reality, brings you in some kind of new touch with yourself—then it's important. But if you leave the theater with a lot of theories about how to approach the world . . . well, that just lasts for a while.[2]

The premiere production of the revised version of Buried Child *by Sam Shepard was produced by Steppenwolf Theatre Company of Chicago under the direction of Gary Sinise. In a view of the generations, Dodge (James Gammon), Tilden (Ted Levine), and Vince (Ethan Hawke) offer an unsettling representation of the past and the future.*

During this very productive period in northern California, Shepard was invited to take a role in the film *Days of Heaven*, which was the beginning of the refocusing of his energies. He began a second career acting in the movies, with appearances in such films as *The Right Stuff, Crimes of the Heart,* and *Country.*

Buried Child received the 1979 Pulitzer Prize for drama when it was first produced. The premiere production was at the Magic Theatre in San Francisco and opened on June 27, 1978, followed by a New York production that opened on October 19, 1978. The play then had numerous professional productions in regional theatres. It was revived by the Steppenwolf Theatre Company of Chicago in 1995 in a production that was directed by Gary Sinise, who has been closely associated with Shepard's work over a period of years. The new production of *Buried Child* moved to New York following its success in Chicago. For the 1995 production, Shepard revised the play—an unusual move for a play so highly regarded in its original version. The revised version of *Buried Child* is included in this text.

The year 1996 marked a major return to the theatre for Sam Shepard, following a period in which he had been absorbed by film work. In addition to the new production of *Buried Child*, Shepard's work was featured by the Signature Theatre in New York City, a theatre company that devotes its entire season to the work of a major American playwright (Color Plate 44).

Alternative Play Choices

The Art of Dining, by Tina Howe

Realism: comedy

Four women, five men

Interior of a restaurant and the restaurant kitchen

A couple try to fulfill their dreams of owning and running their own restaurant. Food becomes a metaphor for all of the characters' inner struggles, conflicts, and dreams.

Strong two-person scenes with male-female casting

Proof, by David Auburn

Realism

Two women, two men

The back porch of a house in Chicago

A young woman faces an unknown future after the death of her father. In confrontations with her sister and one of her father's former students, she tries to assess how much she may have inherited of her father's genius and his mental illness.

Strong two- and three-person scenes with male-female and female-female casting

The Guys, by Anne Nelson

Realism

One woman, one man

A writer helps a fire captain write the eulogies for firefighters lost in the collapse of the World Trade Center.

A modest living room

Strong male-female scenes

WORKING ON THE PROJECT

Sequence of Work

1. Read the play.
2. *Group Meeting #1.* Begin group discussion topics. Choose individual assignments. Choose a director. Decide *if* you are going to present a scene, and, if so, cast actors.
3. Begin individual research. Begin scene rehearsals.
4. *Group Meeting #2.* Work through group decisions. Establish a calendar for completion of the work. Share initial findings.
5. Complete research and continue rehearsals.
6. Complete design for each area, including set, costumes, music, poster, program note.
7. *Group Meeting #3.* Present designs to other members of the group. Hold a final dress rehearsal with everyone present if you are presenting a scene.
8. Present project to class.

Topics for Group Discussion (Group Meeting #1)

1. What are your initial reactions to the play? What surprises or intrigues you about the character relationships? What in the relationships seems familiar to you? What seems strange?
2. What does the title of the play *Buried Child* mean? What is actually said about the buried child during the course of the play? Who seem to be the parents of the buried child? What is Dodge's reaction to the child? Tilden appears at the end of the play carrying a baby up the stairs. Is the buried child his? Does Vince have any connection to the buried child? Is the family's inability to recognize Vince related to their denial of the child? Is the buried child actual or symbolic or both? What possible images and meanings are suggested to you by the idea of the buried child? What does the buried child reflect about the nature of this family?
3. What are other significant symbols in the play? What is the interplay or balance between symbols or images of decay and symbols or images of regeneration?

Group Decisions (Group Meeting #2)

1. What theatre is to be used for your hypothetical production? What would be the most appropriate spatial arrangement (proscenium? thrust? arena?) and actor-audience relationship? How large should the theatre be? How close should the audience be to the action? If possible, choose a theatre on your campus or in your community that you think would be a good space in which to produce the play. Find out the dimensions of the theatre and the number of seats in the auditorium.
2. What style do you think will be appropriate for your production? How realistic should the sets and costumes be? How much detail

should they have? Is the setting to be complete with walls and windows, or is the set to be suggestive or expressionistic? Does the environment give the appearance of reality, or is it distorted in some way? What pieces of furniture and architectural features (such as staircase, porch) seem essential? Do the costumes seem real, or are they exaggerated?

3. What metaphors or images seem helpful in thinking about the play?

4. What colors best communicate the feelings of the play?

PROJECT ASSIGNMENTS

The Director

The director will lead the discussion on the group topics and questions. The director will develop a written response to questions 8 and 9 in the "Scene Design" section (pages 440–441) and question 6 in the "Costume Design" section (page 442). These issues should be discussed at Group Meeting #2.

The director will write a summary of the ideas for the production based on his or her understanding of the play and the group responses. If scenes from the same play are to be presented to the class, the directors from the different groups will meet to make sure each group produces a different scene. As part of the director's written project, the director will analyze the content of the scene and its relationship to the play; that is, he or she will identify the important actions or issues in the scene and determine how they contribute to the play's meaning.

Character Analysis

Choose one character. Anyone performing a scene from *Buried Child* or another play should do the analysis for the character that he or she is playing. If scenes are not to be presented,

the character analysis may be done for any character.

1. What does your character say about himself or herself? Make a list quoting all the lines by act and scene.

2. What do the other characters say about your character? Make a list quoting all of the lines by act and scene.

3. What are the motives that drive your character? List the things that he or she wants from the other characters in the play. What seems to be the dominant motive for your character?

4. How does your character change during the course of the play? What are the important realizations that your character comes to during the play? What provokes the realizations? Where does the character begin? Where does the character end?

5. What is the history of your character? Put together all of the information given by the playwright, your character, and the other characters.

6. What is your character's relationship to the family? How does it change?

7. What does your character look like? Find several pictures that show clothes, physicality, or outlook.

Scene Design

This assignment may be shared by two students.

Assessing the Environment: "The House"

1. How does the playwright describe the house?

2. Make a list of all the things the characters say about the house.

3. Determine what the play establishes about the time in which the house would have been built and the location of the house. Find pictures of houses built in that

Buried Child, *by Sam Shepard, offers an absurdist view of life in America. The play is filled with dark humor as the characters attack each other in grotesque attempts at self-justification. James Gammon plays Dodge, Kellie Overbey plays Shelly, and Leo Burmester plays Bradley.*

approximate time and general area of the country.

4. What seems to be the impact of the house on the different characters? How much warmth or comfort does the house provide? Is the house a refuge for the characters or a trap? What kind of memories does the house hold for the family members? What aspects of the family history does the house represent?

5. Collect exterior and interior pictures of houses that give the feeling of the house suggested by the script.

6. What parts of the house are most important to the play? What parts of the house have to be seen onstage by the audience?

What other parts of the house or yard must be indicated in some way during the play's action?

7. What pieces of furniture and appliances are referred to by the characters or in the stage directions? Make a list of everything that is necessary to the action of the play. What other furniture pieces seem useful to the character action or to communicating either the period or the atmosphere of the house? How old and in what condition are the furnishings?

8. What artifacts of the characters' lives might be part of the physical environment? For example, are memories of the family history represented in some way through

With set by Robert Brill and lighting by Kevin Rigdon, the Steppenwolf production of Buried Child *presented an ominous view of the characters' world. Tilden wears Shelly's rabbit coat as he introduces her to the family's disturbing secret.*

photographs or sports trophies? Is one character's point of view more important than another's in determining the details of the physical environment? Does someone seem to own or dominate the space?

9. What are the basic character actions in the play? What are the necessary entrances and exits and the physical character actions that the stage space must accommodate and support?

Designing the Set

1. *Ground plan.* In collaboration with the director, work out a ground plan that will allow for the kind of interactions indicated in the script. What are the necessary pieces of furniture? What would be the most effective placement of entrances, doors, walls, and pieces of furniture? If possible, consult with the scene designer in your theatre department or with a scene design student on the development of your ground plan. The ground plan may be drawn very simply on a diagram of the stage that you are using, with geometric shapes used to indicate furniture drawn to scale.

   If you do not do a rendering or a model of your set, then use pictures from your research to accompany the ground plan to demonstrate the mood of the house and the style of architecture and furnishings.

2. *Optional.* Draw or paint a rendering of your set, *or* build a scale model of the set.

Costume Design

1. Make a list of all the references in the stage directions to costuming.

2. Make a list of the references in the dialogue to articles of clothing.

3. What symbols are associated with the costumes?

4. What period(s) do the costumes come from? Are the style and time period of Vince's and Shelly's costumes different from the costumes worn by the rest of the family? Do the costumes date the characters?

5. What is the range of colors that express the lives of the characters? Are specific colors called for in the script? How would contrasting use of colors appropriately identify the differences between characters?

6. What character qualities help to identify the kind of clothing each might wear? What clothing pieces seem appropriate, given circumstances such as jobs or activities performed, social status, and character outlook? How do you think the characters feel about what they wear? Do they hide or cover themselves in some way with their clothes? Do any of the characters try to call attention to themselves with their clothing? Are there major costume changes during the play? What do the costume changes signify?

7. Draw or find pictures of costumes that you think would be appropriate for each character. Go to a fabric store and buy small pieces of fabric that you would use to make the costumes for each character. Attach the appropriate fabric swatches to the drawing of each costume.

Music

Music is often a critical factor in setting the mood for a play and in providing transitions between scenes and at the beginning and end of acts. Sometimes the music is chosen by the director and sometimes jointly by the director and the sound designer. Music in the theatre is usually used more sparingly than in films, which often have elaborate scores.

Study the script of *Buried Child* for mood as well as references to music. We know that Sam Shepard has a particular interest in rock and roll. Do you find any sense of that interest in this particular play? Which characters might you associate music with? Does Vince bring music with him, or does music seem attached to Dodge and Halie's house? Is the music contemporary, or does it reflect an earlier period? Does the music undergo a change or a progression during the course of the play as the characters change?

Decide on all of the places in the script where you think music would be appropriate. Select the music that you think should be played at each cue. Make a tape of the music you would recommend for your production. Make a cue sheet that lists each place in the script that music is to be played and the title of the selection that you have chosen.

Write a short paper to accompany your tape and cue sheet; explain the thinking behind your musical selections. Explain the relationship between the music and your understanding of the play.

Program Note

Write a program note for a production of the play. In writing the program note, decide what kind of information would be most helpful and also most interesting to an audience of your peers. The program note may include biographical material on the playwright, historical background on issues in the play, thematic exploration of the play itself (which could also include references to other plays of the playwright), and previous, noteworthy productions of the same play. The program note may also refer to the changes that the playwright has recently made in the play.

Poster

Design a poster to advertise your group's production. Look at posters from your college or university's theatre department or another theatre in your community to determine the kind of information that should go on the poster. Decide on fictional dates and times for your production for the purposes of your poster. Consult with the director and the costume and set designers for possible images and colors for the poster.

In designing the poster you should focus on clarity. The lettering of the play's title and the playwright's name is very important in communicating effectively to potential ticket buyers; the lettering needs to be strong and clear. Further, any image you decide to use must be compelling and give some sense of the mood of the production. Poster imagery must be fairly simple given the amount of space available and the need to quickly attract the viewers' attention.

CONCLUSION

You are preparing a hypothetical production. You are working with unfamiliar materials and new approaches and methods. You may come up with ideas that might not work in an actual production, although you might just as likely arrive at some remarkable ideas. What is important is starting from a point of exploration, of asking questions rather than beginning with answers. The production project is meant to allow you to participate in a process of discovery. To do that you must be willing to take risks, to try out possibilities and see where they may lead. If such a process is to be successful, it requires commitment on your part—commitment to be prepared, to be open with the other members of your group, to follow through on your part of the production.

This kind of commitment is the starting point for all theatre practitioners. The theatre continues in every age because of the passionate commitment of theatre artists to work collectively to bring stories, images, and ideas to life on the stage. Every group of theatre artists shares something with the actors in Sarajevo (see Chapter 2), for whom working in the theatre was an affirmation of life itself. The live performance produced by theatre artists in the presence of the audience is a celebration of the human spirit.

Buried Child

Sam Shepard

CHARACTERS

DODGE, *in his seventies*
HALIE, *Dodge's wife; mid sixties*
TILDEN, *their oldest son*
BRADLEY, *their next oldest son, an amputee*
VINCE, *Tilden's son*
SHELLY, *Vince's girlfriend*
FATHER DEWIS, *a Protestant minister*

ACT ONE

Scene: day. Old wooden staircase down left with pale, frayed carpet laid down on the steps. The stairs lead offstage left up into the wings with no landing. Up right is an old, dark green sofa with the stuffing coming out in spots. Stage right of the sofa is an upright lamp with a faded yellow shade and a small night table with several small bottles of pills on it. Down right of the sofa, with the screen facing the sofa, is a large old-fashioned brown TV. A flickering blue light comes from the screen, but no image, no sound. In the dark, the light of the lamp and the TV slowly brighten in the black space. The space behind the sofa, upstage, is a large, screened-in porch with a board floor. A solid interior door to stage right of the sofa leads from the porch to the outside. Beyond that are the shapes of dark elm trees.

Gradually the form of Dodge is made out, sitting on the couch, facing the TV, the blue light flickering on his face. He wears a well-worn T-shirt, suspenders, khaki work pants, and brown slippers. He's covered himself in an old brown blanket. He's very thin and sickly looking, in his late seventies. He just stares at the TV. More light fills the stage softly. The sound of light rain. Dodge slowly tilts his head back and stares at the ceiling for a while, listening to the rain. He lowers his head again and stares at the TV. He starts to cough slowly and softly. The coughing gradually builds. He holds one hand to his mouth and tries to stifle it. The coughing gets louder, then suddenly stops when he hears the sound of his wife's voice coming from the top of the staircase.

HALIE'S VOICE: Dodge? (*DODGE just stares at the TV. Long pause. He stifles two short coughs.*) Dodge! You want a pill, Dodge? (*He doesn't answer. Takes a bottle out from under cushion of sofa and takes a long swig. Puts the bottle back, stares at TV, pulls blanket up around his neck.*) You know what it is, don't you? It's the rain! Weather. That's it. Every time. Every time you get like this, it's the rain. No sooner does the rain start than you start. (*Pause.*) Dodge? (*He makes no reply. Pulls a pack of cigarettes out from his sweater and lights one. Stares at TV. Pause.*) You should see it coming down up here. Just coming down in sheets. Blue sheets. The bridge is pretty near flooded. What's it like down there? Dodge? (*DODGE turns his head back over his left shoulder and takes a look out through the porch. He turns back to the TV.*)

DODGE: (*To himself.*) Catastrophic.

HALIE'S VOICE: What? What'd you say, Dodge?

DODGE: (*Louder.*) It looks like rain to me! Plain old rain!

HALIE'S VOICE: Rain? Of course it's rain! Are you having a seizure or something! Dodge? (*Pause.*) I'm coming down there in about five minutes if you don't answer me!

DODGE: Don't come down.

HALIE'S VOICE: What!

DODGE: (*Louder.*) Don't come down! (*He has another coughing attack. Stops.*)

HALIE'S VOICE: You should take a pill for that! I don't see why you just don't take a pill. Be done with it once and for all. Put a stop to it. (*He takes bottle out again. Another swig. Returns bottle.*) It's not Christian, but it works. It's not necessarily Christian, that is. A pill. We don't know. We're not in a position to answer something like that. There's some things the ministers can't even answer. I, personally, can't see anything wrong with it. A pill. Pain is pain. Pure and simple. Suffering is a different matter. That's entirely different. A pill seems as good an answer as any. Dodge? (*Pause.*) Dodge, are you watching baseball?

DODGE: No.

HALIE'S VOICE: What?

DODGE: (*Louder.*) No! I'm *not* watching baseball.

HALIE'S VOICE: What're you watching? You shouldn't be watching anything that'll get you excited!

DODGE: Nothing gets me excited.

HALIE'S VOICE: No horse racing!

DODGE: They don't race here on Sundays.

HALIE'S VOICE: What?

DODGE: (*Louder.*) They don't race on Sundays!

HALIE'S VOICE: Well they shouldn't race on Sundays. The Sabbath.

DODGE: Well they don't! Not here anyway. The boondocks.

HALIE'S VOICE: Good. I'm amazed they still have that kind of legislation. Some semblance of morality. That's amazing.

DODGE: Yeah, it's amazing.

HALIE'S VOICE: What?

DODGE: (*Louder.*) It *is* amazing!

HALIE'S VOICE: It is. It truly is. I would've thought these days they'd be racing on Christmas even. A big flashing Christmas tree right down at the finish line.

DODGE: (*Shakes his head.*) No. Not yet.

HALIE'S VOICE: They used to race on New Year's! I remember that.

DODGE: They never raced on New Year's!

HALIE'S VOICE: Sometimes they did.

DODGE: They never did!

HALIE'S VOICE: Before we were married they did!

DODGE: "Before we were married." (*DODGE waves his hand in disgust at the staircase. Leans back in sofa. Stares at TV.*)

HALIE'S VOICE: I went once. With a man. On New Year's.

DODGE: (*Mimicking her.*) Oh, a "man."

HALIE'S VOICE: What?

DODGE: Nothing!

HALIE'S VOICE: A wonderful man. A breeder.

DODGE: A what?

HALIE'S VOICE: A breeder! A horse breeder! Thoroughbreds.

DODGE: Oh, thoroughbreds. Wonderful. You betcha. A breeder-man.

HALIE'S VOICE: That's right. He knew everything there was to know.

DODGE: I bet he taught you a thing or two huh? Gave you a good turn around the old stable!

HALIE'S VOICE: Knew everything there was to know about horses. We won bookoos of money that day.

DODGE: What?

HALIE'S VOICE: Money! We won every race I think.

DODGE: Bookoos?

HALIE'S VOICE: Every single race.

DODGE: Bookoos of money?

HALIE'S VOICE: It was one of those kind of days.

DODGE: New Year's!

HALIE'S VOICE: Yes! It might've been Florida. Or California! One of those two.

DODGE: Can I take my pick?

HALIE'S VOICE: It was Florida!

DODGE: Aha!

HALIE'S VOICE: Wonderful! Absolutely wonderful! The sun was just gleaming. Flamingos. Bougainvilleas. Palm trees.

DODGE: (*To himself, mimicking her.*) Flamingos. Bougainvilleas.

HALIE'S VOICE: Everything was dancing with life! Colors. There were all kinds of people from everywhere. Everyone was dressed to the nines. Not like today. Not like they dress to-day. People had a sense of style.

DODGE: When was this anyway?

HALIE'S VOICE: This was long before I knew you.

DODGE: Must've been.

HALIE'S VOICE: Long before. I was escorted.

DODGE: To Florida?

HALIE'S VOICE: Yes. Or it might've been California. I'm not sure which.

DODGE: All that way you were escorted?

HALIE'S VOICE: Yes.

DODGE: And he never laid a finger on you I suppose? This gentleman breeder-man. (*Long silence.*) Halie? Are we still in the land of the living? (*No answer. Long pause.*)

HALIE'S VOICE: Are you going out today?

DODGE: (*Gesturing toward rain.*) In this?

HALIE'S VOICE: I'm just asking a simple question.

DODGE: I rarely go out in the bright sunshine, why would I go out in this?

HALIE'S VOICE: I'm just asking because I'm not doing any shopping today. And if you need anything you should ask Tilden.

DODGE: Tilden's not here!

HALIE'S VOICE: He's in the kitchen. (*DODGE looks toward L., then back toward TV.*)

DODGE: All right.

HALIE'S VOICE: What?

DODGE: (*Louder.*) All right! I'll ask Tilden!

HALIE'S VOICE: Don't scream. It'll only get your coughing started.

DODGE: Scream? Men don't scream.

HALIE'S VOICE: Just tell Tilden what you want and he'll get it. (*Pause.*) Bradley should be over later.

DODGE: Bradley?

HALIE'S VOICE: Yes. To cut your hair.

DODGE: My hair? I don't need my hair cut! I haven't hardly got any hair left!

HALIE'S VOICE: It won't hurt!

DODGE: I don't need it!

HALIE'S VOICE: It's been more than two weeks Dodge.

DODGE: I don't need it! And I never did need it!

HALIE'S VOICE: I have to meet Father Dewis for lunch.

DODGE: You tell Bradley that if he shows up here with those clippers, I'll separate him from his manhood!

HALIE'S VOICE: I won't be very late. No later than four at the very latest.

DODGE: You tell him! Last time he left me near bald! And I wasn't even awake!

HALIE'S VOICE: That's not my fault!

DODGE: You put him up to it!

HALIE'S VOICE: I never did!

DODGE: You did too! You had some fancy, idiot house social planned! Time to dress up the corpse for company! Lower the ears a little! Put up a little front! Surprised you didn't tape a pipe to my mouth while you were at it! That woulda looked nice! Huh? A pipe? Maybe a bowler hat! Maybe a copy of the *Wall Street Journal* casually placed on my lap! A fat labrador retriever at my feet.

HALIE'S VOICE: You always imagine the worst things of people!

DODGE: That's the least of the worst!

HALIE'S VOICE: I don't need to hear it! All day long I hear things like that and I don't need to hear more.

DODGE: You better tell him!

HALIE'S VOICE: You tell him yourself! He's your own son. You should be able to talk to your own son.

DODGE: Not while I'm sleeping! He cut my hair while I was sleeping!

HALIE'S VOICE: Well he won't do it again.

DODGE: There's no guarantee. He's a snake, that one.

HALIE'S VOICE: I promise he won't do it without your consent.

DODGE: (*After pause.*) There's no reason for him to even come over here.

HALIE'S VOICE: He feels responsible.

DODGE: For my hair?

HALIE'S VOICE: For your appearance.

DODGE: My appearance is out of his domain! It's even out of mine! In fact, it's disappeared! I'm an invisible man!

HALIE'S VOICE: Don't be ridiculous.

DODGE: He better not try it. That's all I've got to say.

HALIE'S VOICE: Tilden will watch out for you.

DODGE: Tilden won't protect me from Bradley!

HALIE'S VOICE: Tilden's the oldest. He'll protect you.

DODGE: Tilden can't even protect himself!

HALIE'S VOICE: Not so loud! He'll hear you. He's right in the kitchen.

DODGE: (*Yelling off L.*) Tilden!

HALIE'S VOICE: Dodge, what are you trying to do?

DODGE: (*Yelling off L.*) Tilden, get your ass in here!

HALIE'S VOICE: Why do you enjoy stirring things up?

DODGE: I don't enjoy anything!

HALIE'S VOICE: That's a terrible thing to say.

DODGE: Tilden!

HALIE'S VOICE: That's the kind of statement that leads people right to an early grave.

DODGE: Tilden!

HALIE'S VOICE: It's no wonder people have turned their backs on Jesus!

DODGE: TILDEN!!

HALIE'S VOICE: It's no wonder the messengers of God's word are shouting louder now than ever before. Screaming to the four winds.

DODGE: TILDEN!!!! (*DODGE goes into a violent, spasmodic coughing attack as TILDEN enters from L., his arms loaded with fresh ears of corn. TILDEN is DODGE's oldest son, late forties, wears heavy construction boots covered with mud, dark green work pants, a plaid shirt and a faded brown windbreaker. He has a butch haircut, wet from the rain. Something about him is profoundly burned-out and displaced. He stops C. with the ears of corn in his arms and just stares at DODGE until he slowly finishes his coughing attack. DODGE looks up at him slowly. DODGE stares at the corn. Long pause as they watch each other.*)

HALIE'S VOICE: Dodge, if you don't take that pill nobody's going to force you. Least of all me. There's no honor in self-destruction. No honor at all. (*The two men ignore the voice.*)

DODGE: (*To TILDEN.*) Where'd you get that?

TILDEN: Picked it.

DODGE: You picked all that? (*TILDEN nods.*) You expecting company?

TILDEN: No.

DODGE: Where'd you pick it from?

TILDEN: Right out back.

DODGE: Out back where!

TILDEN: Right out in back.

DODGE: There's nothing out there—in back.

TILDEN: There's corn.

DODGE: There hasn't been corn out there since about nineteen thirty-five! That's the last time I planted corn out there!

TILDEN: It's out there now.

DODGE: (*Yelling at stairs.*) Halie!

HALIE'S VOICE: Yes dear! Have you come to your senses?

DODGE: Tilden's brought a whole bunch of sweet corn in here! There's no corn out back is there?

TILDEN: (*To himself.*) There's tons of corn.

HALIE'S VOICE: Not that I know of!

DODGE: That's what I thought.

HALIE'S VOICE: Not since about nineteen thirty-five!

DODGE: (*To TILDEN.*) That's right. Nineteen thirty-five. That was the last of it.

TILDEN: It's out there now.

DODGE: You go and take that corn back to wherever you got it from!

TILDEN: (*After pause, staring at DODGE.*) It's picked. I picked it all in the rain. Once it's picked you can't put it back.

DODGE: I haven't had trouble with the neighbors here for fifty-seven years. I don't even know who the neighbors are! And I don't wanna know! Now go put that corn back where it came from! (*TILDEN stares at DODGE then walks slowly over to him and dumps all the corn on DODGE's lap and steps back. DODGE stares at the corn then back to TILDEN. Long pause.*) Are you having trouble here, Tilden? Are you in some kind of trouble again?

TILDEN: I'm not in any trouble.

DODGE: You can tell me if you are. I'm still your father.

TILDEN: I know that.

DODGE: I know you had a little trouble back there in New Mexico. That's why you came out here. Isn't that the reason you came back?

TILDEN: I never had any trouble.

DODGE: Tilden, your mother told me all about it.

TILDEN: What'd she tell you? (*TILDEN pulls some chewing tobacco out of his jacket and bites off a plug.*)

DODGE: I don't have to repeat what she told me! She told me all about it!

TILDEN: Can I bring my chair in from the kitchen?

DODGE: What?

TILDEN: Can I bring in my chair from the kitchen?

DODGE: That's not a chair it's a stool. Milking stool.

TILDEN: Can I bring it in here?

DODGE: Sure. Bring it in here. Bring it on in here. Just don't call it a chair when it's a stool. (*TILDEN exits L. DODGE pushes all the corn off of his lap onto the floor. He pulls the blanket off angrily and tosses it at one end of the sofa, pulls out the bottle and takes another swig. TILDEN enters again from L. with a milking stool and a pail. DODGE hides the bottle quickly under the cushion before TILDEN sees it. TILDEN sets the stool down by the sofa, sits on it, puts the pail in front of him on the floor. TILDEN starts picking up the ears of corn one at a time and husking them. He throws the husks and silk in the center of the stage and drops the ears into the pail each time he cleans one. He repeats this process as they talk. After pause.*) Pretty good-lookin' corn.

TILDEN: Golden.

DODGE: Hybrid?

TILDEN: What?

DODGE: Some kinda fancy hybrid?

TILDEN: You planted it. I don't know what it is. (*Pause.*)

DODGE: I never planted it. (*Pause.*) Tilden, look, you can't stay here forever. You know that, don't you? (*TILDEN spits in spittoon.*)

TILDEN: I'm not.

DODGE: I know you're not. I'm not worried about that. That's not the reason I brought it up.

TILDEN: What's the reason?

DODGE: The reason is I'm wondering what you're gonna do with yourself.

TILDEN: You're not worried about me, are you?

DODGE: I'm not worried about you. No. I'm just wondering.

TILDEN: You weren't worried about me when I wasn't here. When I was in New Mexico.

DODGE: No, I wasn't worried about you then either.

TILDEN: You shoulda worried about me then.

DODGE: Why's that? You didn't do anything down there, did you? Nothin' serious.

TILDEN: I didn't do anything. No.

DODGE: Then why should I have worried about you?

TILDEN: Because I was by myself.

DODGE: By yourself?

TILDEN: Yeah. I was by myself more than I've ever been before.

DODGE: Why was that? (*Pause.*)

TILDEN: Could I have some of that whiskey you've got?

DODGE: What whiskey? I haven't got any whiskey.

TILDEN: You've got some under the sofa.

DODGE: I haven't got anything under the sofa! Now mind your own damn business! Judas Priest, you come into the house outa the middle of nowhere, haven't heard or seen you in twenty-some years and suddenly you're making accusations.

TILDEN: I'm not making accusations.

DODGE: You're accusing me of hoarding whiskey under the sofa!

TILDEN: I'm not accusing you.

DODGE: You just got through telling me that I had whiskey under the sofa!

HALIE'S VOICE: Dodge?

DODGE: (*To TILDEN.*) Now she knows about it!

TILDEN: She doesn't know about it.

DODGE: She knows!

HALIE'S VOICE: Dodge, are you talking to your-self down there?

DODGE: I'm talking to Tilden!

HALIE'S VOICE: Tilden's down there?

DODGE: He's right here!

HALIE'S VOICE: What?

DODGE: (*Louder.*) He's right here!

HALIE'S VOICE: What's he doing?

DODGE: (*To TILDEN.*) Don't answer her.

TILDEN: (*To DODGE.*) I'm not doing anything wrong.

DODGE: (*To TILDEN.*) I know you're not.

HALIE'S VOICE: What's he doing down there!

DODGE: (*To TILDEN.*) Don't answer. Whatever you do, don't answer her.

TILDEN: I'm not.

HALIE'S VOICE: Dodge! (*The men sit in silence. DODGE lights a cigarette. TILDEN keeps husking corn, spits tobacco now and then in spittoon.*) Dodge! He's not drinking anything, is he? You see to it that he doesn't drink anything! You've gotta watch out for him. It's our re-sponsibility. He can't look after himself any-more, so we have to do it. Nobody else will do it. We can't just send him away some-where. If we had lots of money we could send him away. But we don't. We never will. That's why we have to stay healthy. You and me. Nobody's going to look after us. Bradley can't look after us. Bradley can hardly look after himself. I was always hoping that Tilden would look out for Bradley when they got older. After Bradley lost his leg. Tilden's the oldest. I always thought he'd be the one to take responsibility. I had no idea in the world that Tilden would be so much trouble. Who would've dreamed. Tilden was an All-American, don't forget. Don't forget that. Fullback. Or quarterback. I forget which.

TILDEN: (*To himself.*) Halfback.

DODGE: Don't make a peep. Just let her babble. (*TILDEN goes on husking.*)

HALIE'S VOICE: Then when Tilden turned out to be so much trouble, I put all my hopes on Ansel. Of course Ansel wasn't as handsome, but he was smart. He was the smartest probably. I think he probably was. Smarter than Bradley, that's for sure. Didn't go and chop his leg off with a chain saw. Smart enough not to go and do that. I think he was smarter than Tilden too. Especially after Tilden got in all that trouble. Doesn't take brains to go to jail. Anybody knows that. Course then when Ansel passed that left us all alone. Same as being alone. No different. Same as if they'd all died. He was the smartest. He could've earned lots of money. Lots and lots of money.

DODGE: Bookoos. (*HALIE enters slowly from the top of the staircase as she continues talking. Just her feet are seen at first as she makes her way down the stairs a step at a time. She appears dressed completely in black, as though in mourning. Black handbag, hat with a veil, and pulling on elbow-length black gloves. She is about sixty-five with pure white hair. She remains absorbed in what she's say-ing as she descends the stairs and doesn't really no-tice the two men who continue sitting there as they were before she came down, smoking and husking.*)

HALIE: He would've took care of us, too. He would've seen to it that we were repaid. He was like that. He was a hero. Don't forget that. A genuine hero. Brave. Strong. And very intelligent.

TILDEN: Ansel was a hero?

HALIE: Ansel could've been a great man. One of the greatest. I only regret that he didn't die in action. It's not fitting for a man like that to die in a motel room. A soldier. He could've won a medal. He could've been decorated for valor. I've talked to Father Dewis about putting up a plaque for Ansel. He thinks it's a good idea. He agrees. He knew Ansel when he used to play basketball. Went to every game. Ansel was his favorite player. He even recommended to the City Council that they put up a statue of Ansel. A big, tall statue with a basketball in one hand and a rifle in the other. That's how much he thinks of Ansel.

TILDEN: Ansel was a hero? (*DODGE kicks him. HALIE reaches the stage and begins to wander around, still absorbed in pulling on her gloves, brushing lint off her dress and continuously talking to herself as the men just sit.*)

HALIE: Of course, he'd still be alive today if he hadn't married into the Catholics. The Mob. How in the world he never opened his eyes to that is beyond me. Just beyond me. Everyone around him could see the truth. Even Tilden. Tilden told him time and again. Catholic women are the Devil incarnate. He wouldn't listen.

TILDEN: I don't remember that. I must've been gone somewhere.

HALIE: He was blind with love. Blind. I knew. Everyone knew. The wedding was more like a funeral. You remember? All those Italians. All that horrible black, greasy hair. The rancid smell of cheap cologne. I think even the priest was wearing a pistol. When he gave her the ring I knew he was a dead man. I knew it. As soon as he gave her the ring. But then it was the honeymoon that killed him. The honeymoon. I knew he'd never come back from the honeymoon. (*She stops abruptly and stares at the corn husks. She looks around the space as though just waking up. She turns hard and looks hard at TILDEN and DODGE who continue sitting calmly. She looks again at the corn husks. Pointing to the husks.*) What's this in my house! (*Kicks husks.*) What's all this mess? (*TILDEN stops husking and stares at her. To DODGE.*) And you encourage him! (*DODGE pulls blanket over himself again.*)

DODGE: You're going out in the rain for a little soiree.

HALIE: It's not raining now, is it. (*TILDEN starts husking again.*)

DODGE: Not in Florida it's not.

HALIE: We're not in Florida!

DODGE: It's not raining at the racetrack.

HALIE: Have you been taking those pills? Those pills always make you talk crazy. Tilden, has he been taking those pills? Those teeny little blue pills.

TILDEN: He hasn't took anything.

HALIE: (*To DODGE.*) What've you been taking?

DODGE: It's not raining in California or Florida or at the racetrack. Only in Illinois. This is the only place it's raining. All over the rest of the world it's bright golden sunshine. (*HALIE goes to the night table next to the sofa and checks the bottle of pills.*)

HALIE: Which ones did you take? Tilden, you must've seen him take something.

TILDEN: He never took a thing.

HALIE: Then why's he talking crazy?

DODGE: Crazy. Crazy, crazy, crazy.

TILDEN: I've been here the whole time.

HALIE: Then you've both been taking something!

TILDEN: I've just been husking the corn.

HALIE: Where'd you get that corn anyway? Why is the house suddenly full of corn?

DODGE: Bumper crop! Unexplainable.

HALIE: (*Moving C.*) We haven't had corn here for over thirty years.

TILDEN: The whole back lot's full of corn. Far as the eye can see. Like an ocean.

DODGE: (*To HALIE.*) Things keep happening while you're upstairs, ya know. The world doesn't stop just because you're upstairs. Corn keeps growing. Rain keeps raining.

HALIE: I'm not unaware of the world around me! Thank you very much. It so happens that I have an overall view from the upstairs. A panorama. The backyard's in plain view of my window. And there's no corn to speak of. Absolutely none.

DODGE: Tilden wouldn't lie. If he says there's corn, there's corn.

HALIE: What's the meaning of this corn Tilden!

TILDEN: It's a mystery to me. I was out in back there. And the rain was coming down. And I didn't feel like coming back inside. I didn't feel the cold so much. I didn't mind the wet. So I was just walking. I was muddy but I didn't mind the mud so much. And I looked up. And I saw this stand of corn. In fact I was standing in it. Surrounded. It was over my head.

HALIE: There isn't any corn outside Tilden! There's no corn! It's not the season for corn.

Now, you must've either stolen this corn or you bought it.

DODGE: He doesn't have a red cent to his name. He's totally dependent.

HALIE: (*To TILDEN.*) So you stole it!

TILDEN: I didn't steal it. I don't want to get kicked out of Illinois. I was kicked out of New Mexico and I don't want to get kicked out of Illinois.

HALIE: You're going to get kicked out of this house, Tilden, if you don't tell me where you got that corn! (*TILDEN starts crying softly to himself but keeps husking corn. Pause.*)

DODGE: (*To HALIE.*) Why'd you have to tell him that? Who cares where he got the corn? Why'd you have to go and threaten him with expulsion?

HALIE: (*To DODGE.*) It's your fault you know! You're the one that's behind all of this! I suppose you thought it'd be funny! Some joke! Cover the house with corn husks. You better get this cleaned up before Bradley sees it.

DODGE: Bradley's not getting in the front door!

HALIE: (*Kicking husks, striding back and forth.*) Bradley's going to be very upset when he sees this. He doesn't like to see the house in disarray. He can't stand it when one thing is out of place. The slightest thing. You know how he gets.

DODGE: Bradley doesn't even live here!

HALIE: It's his home as much as ours. He was born in this house!

DODGE: He was born in a hog wallow.

HALIE: Don't you say that! Don't you ever say that!

DODGE: He was born in a goddamn hog wallow! That's where he was born and that's where he belongs! He doesn't belong in this house! (*HALIE stops.*)

HALIE: I don't know what's come over you, Dodge. I don't know what in the world's come over you. You've become an evil, spiteful, vengeful man. You used to be a good man.

DODGE: Six of one, a half-dozen of another.

HALIE: You sit here day and night, festering away! Decomposing! Smelling up the house with your putrid body! Hacking your head off 'til all hours of the morning! Thinking up mean, evil, stupid things to say about your own flesh and blood!

DODGE: He's not my flesh and blood! My flesh and blood's out there in the backyard! (*They freeze. Long pause. The men stare at her.*)

HALIE: (*Quietly.*) That's enough, Dodge. That's quite enough. You've become confused. I'm going out now. I'm going to have lunch with Father Dewis. I'm going to ask him about a monument for Ansel. A statue. At least a plaque.

DODGE: That oughta heal things up. A statue. (*She crosses to the door up R. She stops.*)

HALIE: If you need anything, ask Tilden. He's the oldest. I've left some money on the kitchen table.

DODGE: I don't need a thing.

HALIE: No, I suppose not. (*She opens the door and looks out through porch.*) Still raining. I love the smell just after it stops. The ground. It's like the ground is breathing. I won't be too late. (*She goes out door and closes it. She's still visible on the porch as she crosses toward L. screen door. She stops in the middle of the porch, speaks to DODGE but doesn't turn to him.*) Dodge, tell Tilden not to go out in the back lot anymore. I don't want him back there in the rain. He's got no business out there.

DODGE: You tell him yourself. He's sitting right here.

HALIE: He never listens to me Dodge. He's never listened to me in the past.

DODGE: I'll tell him.

HALIE: We have to watch him just like we used to now. Just like we always have. He's still a child.

DODGE: I'll watch him.

HALIE: Good. We don't want to lose him. I couldn't take another loss. Not at this late date. (*She crosses to screen door, L., takes an umbrella off a hook and goes out the door. The door slams behind her. Long pause. TILDEN husks corn, stares at pail. DODGE lights a cigarette, stares at TV.*)

TILDEN: (*Still husking.*) You shouldn't a told her that.

DODGE: (*Staring at TV.*) What?

TILDEN: What you told her. You know.

DODGE: What do you know about it?

TILDEN: I know. I know all about it. We all know.

DODGE: So what difference does it make? Everybody knows, everybody's forgot.

TILDEN: She hasn't forgot.

DODGE: She should've forgot.

TILDEN: It's different for her. She couldn't forget that. How could she forget a thing like that?

DODGE: I don't want to talk about it!

TILDEN: Why'd you tell her it was *your* flesh and blood?

DODGE: I don't want to talk about it.

TILDEN: What do you want to talk about?

DODGE: I don't want to talk about anything! I don't want to talk about troubles or what happened fifty years ago or thirty years ago or the racetrack or Florida or the last time I seeded the corn! I don't want to talk period. Talking just wears me thin.

TILDEN: You don't wanna die do you?

DODGE: No, I don't particularly wanna die either.

TILDEN: Well, you gotta talk or you'll die.

DODGE: Who told you that crap?

TILDEN: That's what I know. I found that out in New Mexico. I thought I was dying but I just lost my voice.

DODGE: Were you with somebody? A woman? A woman'll make you think you're dying, sure as shooting.

TILDEN: I was alone. I thought I was dead.

DODGE: Might as well have been. What'd you come back here for?

TILDEN: I didn't know where else to go.

DODGE: You're a grown man. You shouldn't be needing your parents at your age. It's unnatural. There's nothing we can do for you now anyway. Couldn't you make a living down there? Couldn't you find some way to make a living? Support yourself? What'dya come back here for? You expect us to feed you forever?

TILDEN: I didn't know where else to go.

DODGE: I never went back to my parents. Never. Never even had the urge. I was independent. Always independent. Always found a way. Self-sufficient.

TILDEN: I didn't know what to do. I couldn't figure anything out.

DODGE: There's nothing to figure out. You just forge ahead. What's there to figure out? (*TILDEN stands.*)

TILDEN: I was standing. It was night. I was full of the smell of New Mexico. It's different than Illinois. Totally different. Foreign, almost. My lungs were full of it. Like pine smoke and mesquite. That was it. It was foreign. So I left there and I came back here. (*He starts to leave.*)

DODGE: Where are you going?

TILDEN: Out back.

DODGE: You're not suppose to go out there. You heard what she said. Don't play deaf with me!

TILDEN: I like it out there.

DODGE: In the rain?

TILDEN: Especially in the rain. I like the feeling of it. Feels like it always did.

DODGE: You're supposed to watch out for me. Get me things when I need them.

TILDEN: What do you need?

DODGE: I don't need anything yet! But I might. I might need something any second. Any second now. I can't be left alone for a minute! (*DODGE starts to cough.*)

TILDEN: I'll be right outside. You can just yell.

DODGE: (*Between coughs.*) No! It's too far! You can't go out there! It's too far! You might not even hear me! I could die here and you'd never hear me!

TILDEN: (*Moving to pills.*) Why don't you take a pill? You want a pill? (*DODGE coughs more violently, throws himself back against the sofa, clutches his throat. TILDEN stands by helplessly.*)

DODGE: Water! Get me some water! (*TILDEN rushes off L. DODGE reaches out for the pills, knocking some bottles to the floor, coughing in spasms. He grabs a small bottle, takes out pills and swallows them. TILDEN rushes back in with a glass of water. DODGE takes it and drinks, his coughing subsides.*)

TILDEN: You all right now? (*DODGE nods. Drinks more water. TILDEN moves in closer to him. DODGE sets glass of water on the night table. His coughing is almost gone.*) Why don't you lay down for a while? Just rest a little. (*TILDEN helps DODGE lie down on the sofa. Covers him with blanket.*)

DODGE: You're not going outside are you?

TILDEN: No.

DODGE: I don't want to wake up and find you not here.

TILDEN: I'll be here. (*TILDEN tucks blanket around DODGE.*)

DODGE: You'll stay right here?

TILDEN: I'll stay in my chair.

DODGE: That's not a chair. That's my old milking stool.

TILDEN: I know.

DODGE: Don't call it a chair.

TILDEN: I won't. (*TILDEN tries to take DODGE's baseball cap off.*)

DODGE: What're you doing! Leave that on me! Don't take that offa me! That's my cap! (*TILDEN leaves the cap on DODGE.*)

TILDEN: I know.

DODGE: Bradley'll shave my head if I don't have that on. That's my cap.

TILDEN: I know it is.

DODGE: Don't take my cap off.

TILDEN: I won't.

DODGE: You stay right here now.

TILDEN: (*Sits on stool.*) I will.

DODGE: Don't go outside. There's nothing out there. Never has been. It's empty.

TILDEN: I won't.

DODGE: Everything's in here. Everything you need. Money's on the table. TV. Is the TV on?

TILDEN: Yeah.

DODGE: Turn it off! Turn the damn thing off! What's it doing on?

TILDEN: (*Turns off TV, light goes out.*) You left it on.

DODGE: Well turn it off.

TILDEN: (*Sits on stool again.*) It's off.

DODGE: Leave it off.

TILDEN: I will.

DODGE: When I fall asleep you can turn it back on.

TILDEN: Okay.

DODGE: You can watch the ball game. White Sox. You like the White Sox don't you?

TILDEN: Yeah.

DODGE: You can watch the White Sox. Pee Wee Reese. Pee Wee Reese. You remember Pee Wee Reese?

TILDEN: No.

DODGE: Was he with the White Sox?

TILDEN: I don't know.

DODGE: Pee Wee Reese. (*Falling into sleep.*) Bases loaded. Top a the sixth. Bases loaded. Runner on first and third. Big fat knuckle ball. Floater. Big as a blimp. Cracko! Ball just took off like a rocket. Just pulverized. I marked it. Marked it with my eyes. Straight between the clock and the Burma Shave ad. I was the first kid out there. First kid. I had to fight hard for that ball. I wouldn't give it up. They almost tore the ears right off of me. But I wouldn't give it up. (*DODGE falls into deep sleep. TILDEN just sits staring at him for a while. Slowly he leans toward the sofa, checking to see if DODGE is well asleep. He reaches slowly under the cushion and pulls out the bottle of booze. DODGE sleeps soundly. TILDEN stands quietly, staring at DODGE as he uncaps the bottle and takes a long drink. He caps the bottle and sticks it in his hip pocket. He looks around at the husks on the floor and then back to DODGE. He moves C. and gathers an armload of corn husks then crosses back to the sofa. He stands holding the husks over DODGE and looks down at him as he gently spreads the corn husks over the whole length of DODGE's body. He stands back and looks at DODGE. Pulls out bottle, takes another drink,*) *returns bottle to his hip pocket. He gathers more husks and repeats the procedure until the floor is clean of corn husks and DODGE is completely covered in them except for his head. TILDEN takes another long drink, stares at DODGE sleeping then quietly exits L. Long pause as the sound of rain continues. DODGE sleeps on.*

The figure of BRADLEY appears U.L., outside the screen porch door. He holds a wet newspaper over his head as a protection from the rain. He seems to be struggling with the door then slips and almost falls to the ground. DODGE sleeps on, undisturbed.)

BRADLEY: Sonuvabitch! Sonuvagoddamnbitch! Always some obstacle. (*BRADLEY recovers his footing and makes it through the screen door onto the porch. He throws the newspaper down, shakes the water out of his hair, and brushes the rain off his shoulders. He is a big man dressed in a gray sweatshirt, black suspenders, baggy dark blue pants, and black janitor's shoes. His left leg is wooden, having been amputated above the knee. He moves with an exaggerated, almost mechanical limp. The squeaking sounds of leather accompany his walk coming from the harness and hinges of the false leg. His arms and shoulders are extremely powerful and muscular due to a lifetime of dependency on the upper torso doing all the work for the legs. He is about five years younger than TILDEN. He moves laboriously to the R. door and enters, closing the door behind him. He doesn't notice DODGE at first. He moves toward the staircase. Calling upstairs.)* Mom! (*He stops and listens. Turns U. and sees DODGE sleeping. Notices corn husks. He moves slowly toward sofa. Stops next to pail and looks into it. Looks at husks. DODGE stays asleep. BRADLEY talks to himself.)* Corn. (*Pause.*) Harvest's over, Pops. (*He looks at DODGE's sleeping face and shakes his head in disgust. He pulls out a pair of black electric hair clippers from his pocket. Unwinds the cord and crosses to the lamp. He jabs his wooden leg behind the knee, causing it to bend at the joint and awkwardly kneels to plug the cord into a floor outlet. He pulls himself to his feet again by using the sofa as leverage. He moves to DODGE's head and again jabs his false leg. Goes down on one knee. He violently knocks away some of the corn husks then jerks off DODGE's baseball cap and throws it down C. DODGE stays asleep. BRADLEY switches on the clippers. Lights start dimming. BRADLEY cuts DODGE's hair while he sleeps. Lights dim slowly to black with the sound of clippers and rain.)*

ACT TWO

Scene: same set as Act One. Night. Sound of rain. DODGE still asleep on sofa. His hair is cut extremely short and in places the scalp is cut and bleeding. His cap is still center stage. All the corn and husks, pail and milking stool have been cleared away. The lights come up to the sound of a young girl laughing offstage left. DODGE remains asleep. SHELLY and VINCE appear up left outside the screen porch door sharing the shelter of VINCE's overcoat above their heads. SHELLY is about nineteen, black hair, very beautiful. She wears tight jeans, high heels, purple T-shirt and a short rabbit fur coat. Her makeup is exaggerated and her hair has been curled. VINCE is TILDEN's son, about twenty-two, wears a plaid shirt, jeans, dark glasses, cowboy boots and carries a black saxophone case. They shake the rain off themselves as they enter the porch through the screen door.

SHELLY: (*Laughing, gesturing to house.*) This is it? I don't believe this is it!

VINCE: This is it.

SHELLY: This is the house?

VINCE: This is the house.

SHELLY: I don't believe it!

VINCE: How come? It's just a house.

SHELLY: It's like a Norman Rockwell cover or something.

VINCE: What's a matter with that? It's American.

SHELLY: American? Where's the milkman and the little dog? What's the little dog's name? Spot. Spot and Jane. Dick and Jane and Spot. See Spot run.

VINCE: Come on! Knock it off. It's my heritage. (*She laughs more hysterically, out of control.*) Have some respect would ya!

SHELLY: (*Trying to control herself.*) I'm sorry.

VINCE: I don't want to go in there with you acting like an idiot.

SHELLY: Yes sir!

VINCE: Well I don't. I haven't had any contact with them for years. I just don't want them to think I've suddenly arrived out of the middle of nowhere completely deranged.

SHELLY: What do you want them to think then? (*Pause.*)

VINCE: Nothing. Let's just go in. (*He crosses porch toward R. interior door. SHELLY follows him. He opens the R. door slowly. VINCE sticks his head in, doesn't notice DODGE sleeping. Calls out toward staircase.*) Grandma! (*SHELLY breaks into laughter, unseen behind VINCE. VINCE pulls his head back outside and pulls door shut. We hear their voices again without seeing them.*)

SHELLY: (*Stops laughing.*) I'm sorry. I'm sorry Vince. I really am. I really am sorry. I won't do it again. I couldn't help it.

VINCE: It's not all that humorous.

SHELLY: I know it's not. I'm sorry.

VINCE: I mean this is a tense situation for me! I haven't seen them for over six years. I don't know what to expect.

SHELLY: I know. I won't do it again. Scout's honor. Just don't say "Grandma," okay? (*She giggles, stops.*) I mean if you say "Grandma," I don't know if I can control myself.

VINCE: Well try!

SHELLY: Okay. Sorry. (*He opens the door again. VINCE sticks his head in then enters. SHELLY follows behind him. VINCE crosses to staircase, sets down saxophone case and overcoat, looks up staircase. SHELLY notices DODGE's baseball cap. Crosses to it. Picks it up and puts it on her head. VINCE goes up the stairs and disappears at the top. SHELLY watches him then turns and sees DODGE on the sofa. She takes off the baseball cap.*)

VINCE: (*From upstairs.*) Grandma! (*From upstairs.*) Grandma! (*SHELLY crosses over to DODGE slowly and stands next to him. She stands at his head, reaches out slowly and touches one of the cuts. The second she touches his head, DODGE jerks up to a sitting position on the sofa, eyes open.*

SHELLY gasps. DODGE looks at her, sees his cap in her hands, quickly puts his hand to his bare head. He glares at SHELLY then whips the cap out of her hands and puts it on. SHELLY backs away from him. DODGE stares at her.)

SHELLY: I'm uh—with Vince. (*DODGE just glares at her.*) He's upstairs. (*DODGE looks at the staircase then back at SHELLY. Calling upstairs.*) Vince!

VINCE: Just a second!

SHELLY: You better get down here!

VINCE: Just a minute! I'm looking at the pictures. (*DODGE keeps staring at her.*)

SHELLY: (*To DODGE.*) We just got here. We drove out from New York. Pouring rain on the freeway so we thought we'd stop by. I mean Vince was planning on stopping anyway. He wanted to see you. He said he hadn't seen you in a long time. Pay you a little visit. (*Pause. DODGE just keeps staring at her.*) We were going all the way through to New Mexico. To see his father. I guess his father lives out there. In a trailer or something. (*Louder.*) We thought we'd stop by and see you on the way. Kill two birds with one stone, you know? (*She laughs, DODGE stares; she stops laughing.*) I mean Vince has this thing about his family now. I guess it's a new thing with him. I kind of find it hard to relate to. But he feels it's important. You know. I mean he wants to get to know you again. After all this time. Reunite. I don't have much faith in it myself. Reuniting. (*Pause. DODGE just stares at her. She moves nervously to staircase and yells up to VINCE.*) Vince will you come down here please! (*VINCE comes halfway down the stairs.*)

VINCE: I guess they went out for a while. (*SHELLY points to sofa and DODGE. VINCE turns and sees DODGE. He comes all the way down staircase and crosses to DODGE. SHELLY stays behind, near the staircase, keeping her distance.*) Grandpa? (*DODGE looks up at him, not recognizing him.*)

DODGE: Did you bring the whiskey? (*VINCE looks back at SHELLY then back to DODGE.*)

VINCE: Grandpa, it's me. Vince. I'm Vince. Tilden's son. You remember? (*DODGE stares at him.*)

DODGE: You didn't do what you told me. You didn't stay here with me.

VINCE: Grandpa, I haven't been here until just now. I just got here.

DODGE: You left. Abandoned me. You went outside like we told you not to do. You went out there in back. In the rain. (*VINCE looks back at SHELLY. She moves slowly toward the sofa.*)

SHELLY: Is he okay?

VINCE: I don't know. (*Takes off his shades.*) Look, Grandpa, don't you remember me? Vince. Your grandson. I know it's been a while. My hair's longer, maybe. (*DODGE stares at him then takes off his baseball cap.*)

DODGE: (*Points to his head.*) See what happens when you leave me alone? See that? That's what happens. (*VINCE looks at DODGE's head, then reaches out to touch it. DODGE slaps VINCE's hand away with the cap and puts it back on his head.*)

VINCE: What's going on Grandpa? Where's Halie?

DODGE: Don't worry about her. She won't be back for days. She's absconded. She says she'll be back but she won't be. (*He starts laughing.*) There's life in the old girl yet! (*Stops laughing.*)

VINCE: How did you do that to your head?

DODGE: I didn't do it! Don't be ridiculous! Whadya think I am, an animal?

VINCE: Well who did then? (*Pause. DODGE stares at VINCE.*)

DODGE: Who do you think did it? Who do you think? (*SHELLY moves toward VINCE.*)

SHELLY: Vince, maybe we oughta go. I don't like this. I mean this isn't my idea of a good time.

VINCE: (*To SHELLY.*) Just a second. (*To DODGE.*) Grandpa, look, I just got here. I just now got here. I haven't been here for six years. I don't know anything that's happened. (*Pause. DODGE stares at him.*)

DODGE: You don't know anything?

VINCE: No.

DODGE: Well that's good. That's good. It's much better not to know anything. Much, much better.

VINCE: Isn't there anybody here with you? (*DODGE turns slowly and looks off to L.*)

DODGE: Tilden's here.

VINCE: No, Grandpa, Tilden's in New Mexico. That's where I was going. I'm going out there to see him. We just stopped off here because it was on the way. (*DODGE turns slowly back to VINCE.*)

DODGE: Well, you're gonna be disappointed. (*VINCE backs away and joins SHELLY. DODGE stares at them.*)

SHELLY: Vince, why don't we spend the night in a motel and come back in the morning? We could have breakfast. A shower. Maybe everything would be different.

VINCE: Don't be scared. There's nothing to be scared of. He's just old.

SHELLY: I'm not scared!

DODGE: You two are not my idea of the perfect couple!

SHELLY: (*After pause.*) Oh really? Why's that?

VINCE: Shh! Don't aggravate him.

DODGE: There's something wrong between the two of you. Something not compatible. Like chalk and cheese.

VINCE: Grandpa, where did Halie go? Maybe we should call her. I don't understand why you're here all by yourself. Isn't anybody looking after you?

DODGE: What are you talking about? Do you know what you're talking about? Are you just talking for the sake of talking? Lubricating the gums?

VINCE: I'm just trying to—

DODGE: Halie is out with her boyfriend. The Right Reverend Dewis. He's not a breeder-man but a man of God. Next best thing I suppose.

VINCE: I'm trying to figure out what's going on here!

DODGE: Good luck.

VINCE: I expected everything to be different. I mean the same. Like it used to be.

DODGE: Who are you to expect anything? Who are you supposed to be?

VINCE: I'm Vince! Your grandson! You've gotta remember me.

DODGE: Vince. My grandson. That's rich!

VINCE: Tilden's son.

DODGE: Tilden's son, Vince. He had *two,* I guess.

VINCE: Two? No look, you haven't seen me for a long time.

DODGE: When was the last time?

VINCE: I don't remember exactly. We had a big dinner. A reunion, kind of. Turkey. You made some comment about Dad's fastball. I was a kid, I guess. It was quite a while ago.

DODGE: You don't remember.

VINCE: No. Not really. I mean—we were all sitting at the table. All of us—and you and Bradley were making fun of Dad's fastball. And—

DODGE: You don't remember. How am I supposed to remember if you don't.

VINCE: I remember being there. I just don't remember the details.

SHELLY: Vince, come on. This isn't going to work out. I've got a strong feeling.

VINCE: (*To SHELLY.*) Just take it easy.

SHELLY: I'm taking it easy! He doesn't even know who you are!

VINCE: (*Crossing to DODGE.*) Of course he knows who I am. He's just tired or something. Grandpa, look—I don't know what's happened here, but—

DODGE: Stay where you are! Keep your distance! (*VINCE stops. Looks back at SHELLY then to DODGE.*)

SHELLY: Vince, this is really making me nervous. I mean he doesn't even want us here. He doesn't even like us.

DODGE: She's a beautiful girl.

VINCE: Thanks.

DODGE: Very "fetching," as they used to say.

SHELLY: Oh my God.

DODGE: (*To SHELLY.*) What's your name, girlie girl?

SHELLY: Shelly.

DODGE: Shelly. That's a man's name isn't it?

SHELLY: Not in this case.

DODGE: (*To VINCE.*) She's a smart-ass too.

SHELLY: Vince! Can we go?

VINCE: Grandpa look—look at me for a second. Try to remember my face.

DODGE: She wants to go. She just got here and she wants to go. Itchy.

VINCE: This is kind of strange for her. I mean, it's strange enough for me—

DODGE: She'll get used to it. (*To SHELLY.*) What part of the country do you hail from, girlie?

SHELLY: Originally?

DODGE: That's right. Originally. At the very start.

SHELLY: LA.

DODGE: LA. Stupid country.

SHELLY: I can't stand this Vince! This is really unbelievable!

DODGE: It's stupid! LA is stupid! So is Florida. All those Sunshine States. They're all stupid! Do you know why they're stupid?

SHELLY: Illuminate me.

VINCE: Shelly. Don't!

DODGE: I'll tell you why. Because they're full of smart-asses! That's why. (*SHELLY turns her back to DODGE, crosses to staircase and sits on bottom step. To VINCE.*) Now she's insulted.

SHELLY: Vince?

DODGE: She's insulted! Look at her! In my house she's insulted! She's over there sulking because I insulted her!

VINCE: Grandpa—

SHELLY: (*To VINCE.*) This is really terrific. This is wonderful. And you were worried about me making the right first impression!

DODGE: (*To VINCE.*) She's a fireball isn't she? Regular fireball. I had some a them in my day. Temporary stuff. Never lasted more than a week.

VINCE: Grandpa—look—

DODGE: Stop calling me Grandpa will ya! It's sickening. "Grandpa." I'm nobody's grandpa! Least of all yours.

VINCE: I can't believe you don't recognize me. I just can't believe it. It wasn't that long ago.

(*DODGE starts feeling around under the cushion for the bottle of whiskey. SHELLY gets up from the staircase.*)

SHELLY: (*To VINCE.*) Maybe you've got the wrong house. Did you ever think of that? Maybe this is the wrong address!

VINCE: It's not the wrong address! I recognize the yard. The porch. The elm tree. The house. I was standing right here in this house. Right in this very spot.

SHELLY: Yeah but do you recognize the people? He says he's not your grandfather.

VINCE: He *is* my grandpa! I know he's my grandpa! He's *always* been my grandpa. He always *will be* my grandpa!

DODGE: (*Digging for bottle.*) Where's that bottle!

VINCE: He's just sick or something. I don't know what's happened to him. Delirious.

DODGE: Where's my goddamn bottle! (*DODGE gets up from sofa and starts tearing the cushions off it and throwing them D., looking for the whiskey.*) They've stole my bottle!

SHELLY: Can't we drive on to New Mexico? This is terrible, Vince! I don't want to stay here. In this house. I thought it was going to be turkey dinners and apple pie and all that kinda stuff.

VINCE: Well I hate to disappoint you!

SHELLY: I'm not disappointed! I'm fuckin' terrified! I wanna go! (*DODGE yells toward L.*)

DODGE: Tilden! Tilden! They stole my bottle! (*DODGE keeps ripping away at the sofa looking for his bottle, he knocks over the nightstand with the bottles. VINCE and SHELLY watch as he starts ripping the stuffing out of the sofa.*)

VINCE: (*To SHELLY.*) He's lost his mind or something. I've got to try to help him.

SHELLY: You help him! I'm leaving! (*SHELLY starts to leave. VINCE grabs her. They struggle as DODGE keeps ripping away at the sofa and yelling.*)

DODGE: Tilden! Tilden get your ass in here! Tilden!

SHELLY: Let go of me!

VINCE: You're not going anywhere! I need you to stay right here!

SHELLY: Let go of me you sonuvabitch! I'm not your property! (*Suddenly TILDEN walks on from L. just as he did before. This time his arms are full of carrots. DODGE, VINCE and SHELLY stop suddenly when they see him. They all stare at TILDEN as he crosses slowly C. with the carrots and stops. DODGE sits on sofa, exhausted.*)

DODGE: (*Panting, to TILDEN.*) Where in the hell have you been?

TILDEN: Out back.

DODGE: Where's my bottle?

TILDEN: Gone. (*TILDEN and VINCE stare at each other. SHELLY backs away.*)

DODGE: (*To TILDEN.*) You stole my bottle!

VINCE: (*To TILDEN.*) Dad? What're you doing here?

SHELLY: Oh brother. (*TILDEN just stares at VINCE.*)

DODGE: You had no right to steal my bottle! No right at all! Who do you think you are?

VINCE: (*To TILDEN.*) It's Vince. I'm Vince. (*TILDEN stares at VINCE then looks at DODGE then turns to SHELLY.*)

TILDEN: (*After pause.*) I picked these carrots. If anybody wants any carrots, I picked 'em.

SHELLY: (*To VINCE.*) Now, wait a minute. This is your father? The one we were going to visit?

VINCE: (*To TILDEN.*) Dad, what're you doing here? What's going on? (*TILDEN just stares at VINCE, holding carrots, DODGE pulls the blanket back over himself.*)

SHELLY: This is actually your father? The one in New Mexico?

DODGE: (*To TILDEN.*) You're going to have to get me another bottle! You gotta get me a bottle before Halie comes back! There's money on the table. (*Points to L. kitchen.*)

TILDEN: (*Shaking his head.*) I'm not going down there. Into town. I never do well in town. (*SHELLY crosses to TILDEN. TILDEN stares at her.*)

SHELLY: (*To TILDEN.*) Are you Vince's father?

TILDEN: (*To SHELLY.*) Vince?

SHELLY: (*Pointing to VINCE.*) This is supposed to be your son! Is he your son? Do you recognize him? I'm just along for the ride here.

I thought everybody knew each other! (*TILDEN stares at VINCE. DODGE wraps himself up in the blanket and sits on sofa staring at the floor.*)

TILDEN: I had a son once but we buried him. (*DODGE quickly looks at TILDEN. SHELLY looks to VINCE.*)

DODGE: You shut up about that! You don't know anything about that!

VINCE: Dad, I thought you were in Bernalillo. We were going to drive down there and see you.

TILDEN: Long way to drive. Terrible distance.

VINCE: What's happened, Dad? Has something happened? I thought everything was all right. What's happened to Halie? What're you doing back here?

TILDEN: She left. Church or something. It's always church. God or Jesus. Or both.

SHELLY: (*To TILDEN.*) Do you want me to take those carrots for you?

VINCE: Shelly—(*TILDEN stares at her. She moves in close to him. Holds out her arms. TILDEN stares at her arms then slowly dumps the carrots into her arms. SHELLY stands there holding the carrots.*)

TILDEN: (*To SHELLY.*) You like carrots?

SHELLY: Sure. I like all kinds of vegetables. I'm a vegetarian.

DODGE: (*To TILDEN.*) Hitler was a vegetarian. You gotta get me a bottle before Halie comes back! (*DODGE hits sofa with his fist. VINCE crosses up to DODGE and tries to console him. SHELLY and TILDEN stay facing each other.*)

TILDEN: (*To SHELLY.*) Backyard's full of carrots. Corn. Potatoes.

SHELLY: You're Vince's father, right? His real father. I'm just asking.

TILDEN: All kinds of vegetables. You like vegetables?

SHELLY: (*Laughs.*) Yeah. I love vegetables.

TILDEN: We could cook these carrots ya know. You could cut 'em up and we could cook 'em. You and me.

SHELLY: All right. Sure. Whatever works.

VINCE: Shelly, what're you doing?

TILDEN: I'll get you a pail and a knife.

SHELLY: Okay.

VINCE: Shelly!

TILDEN: I'll be right back. Don't go.

VINCE: Dad, wait a second. (*TILDEN exits off L.*) What the hell is going on here? What's happened to everybody. (*SHELLY stands C., arms full of carrots. VINCE stands next to DODGE. SHELLY looks toward VINCE then down at the carrots.*)

DODGE: (*To VINCE.*) You could get me a bottle. (*Pointing off L.*) There's money on the table.

VINCE: Grandpa why don't you lay down for a while?

DODGE: I don't wanna lay down for a while! Every time I lay down something happens! (*Whips off his cap, points at his head.*) Look what happens! That's what happens! (*Pulls his cap back on.*) You go lay down and see what happens to you! See how you like it! They'll steal your bottle! They'll cut your hair! They'll murder your children! That's what'll happen. They'll eat you alive.

VINCE: Just relax for a while. Maybe things will come back to you. (*Pause.*)

DODGE: You could get me a bottle ya know. There's nothing stopping you from getting me a bottle.

SHELLY: Why don't you get him a bottle Vince? Maybe it would help everybody identify each other.

DODGE: (*Pointing to SHELLY.*) There, see? She thinks you should get me a bottle. She's a smart cookie. Suddenly, she got smart. (*VINCE crosses to SHELLY.*)

VINCE: Shelly, what're you doing with those carrots.

SHELLY: I'm waiting for your father.

DODGE: She thinks you should get me a bottle!

VINCE: Shelly put the carrots down will ya! We gotta deal with the situation here! I'm gonna need your help. I don't know what's going on here but I need some help to try to figure this out.

SHELLY: I'm helping.

VINCE: You're only adding to the problem! You're making things worse! Put the carrots down! (*VINCE tries to knock the carrots out of her arms. She turns away from him, protecting the carrots.*)

SHELLY: Get away from me! Stop it! (*VINCE stands back from her. She turns to him still holding the carrots.*)

VINCE: (*To SHELLY.*) Why are you doing this? Are you trying to make fun of me? This is my family you know!

SHELLY: You coulda fooled me! I'd just as soon not be here myself. I'd just as soon be a thousand miles from here. I'd rather be any-where but here. You're the one who wants to stay. So I'll stay. I'll stay and I'll cut the car-rots. And I'll cook the carrots. And I'll do whatever I have to do to survive. Just to make it through this thing.

VINCE: Put the carrots down Shelly. The carrots aren't going to help. The carrots have noth-ing to do with the situation here. (*TILDEN en-ters from L. with pail, milking stool, and a knife. He sets the stool and pail C. for SHELLY. SHELLY looks at VINCE then sits down on stool, sets the car-rots on the floor and takes the knife from TILDEN. She looks at VINCE again then picks up a carrot, cuts the ends off, scrapes it and drops it in the pail. She repeats this, VINCE glares at her. She smiles.*)

DODGE: She could get me a bottle. She's the type a girl that could get me a bottle. Easy. She'd go down there. Slink up to the counter. They'd probably give her two bottles for the price of one. She could do that. She has that air about her. (*SHELLY laughs. Keeps cutting carrots. VINCE crosses up to DODGE, looks at him. TILDEN watches SHELLY's hands. Long pause.*)

VINCE: (*To DODGE.*) I haven't changed that much. I mean physically. Physically I'm just about the same. Same size. Same weight. Everything's the same. (*DODGE keeps staring at SHELLY while VINCE talks to him.*)

DODGE: She's a beautiful girl. Exceptional. (*VINCE moves in front of DODGE to block his view of SHELLY. DODGE keeps craning his head around to see her as VINCE demonstrates tricks from his past.*)

VINCE: Look. Look at this. Do you remember this? I used to bend my thumb behind my knuckles. You remember? I used to do it at the dinner table. Way back when. You told me, one day it would get stuck like this and I'd never be able to throw a baseball. (*VINCE bends a thumb behind his knuckles for DODGE and holds it out to him. DODGE takes a short glance then looks back at SHELLY. VINCE shifts position and shows him something else.*) What about this? (*VINCE curls his lips back and starts drumming on his teeth with his fingernails making little tapping sounds. DODGE watches a while. TILDEN turns toward the sound. VINCE keeps it up. He sees TILDEN taking notice and crosses to TILDEN as he drums on his teeth. DODGE turns TV on and watches it.*) You remember this Dad? Rooty-tooty? "St. James Infirmary"? "When the Saints Go Marching In"? (*VINCE keeps on drumming for TILDEN. TILDEN watches a while, fascinated, then turns back to SHELLY. VINCE keeps up the drumming on his teeth, crosses back to DODGE doing it. SHELLY keeps working on the carrots, talking to TILDEN.*)

SHELLY: (*To TILDEN.*) He drives me crazy with that sometimes.

VINCE: (*To DODGE.*) I know! Here's one you'll remember. You used to kick me out of the house for this one. (*VINCE pulls his shirt out of his belt and holds it tucked under his chin with his stomach exposed. He grabs the flesh on either side of his belly button and pushes it in and out to make it look like a mouth talking. He watches his belly button and makes a deep-sounding cartoon voice to synchronize with the movement. He demonstrates it to DODGE then crosses down to TILDEN doing it. Both DODGE and TILDEN take short, uninter-ested glances then ignore him. Deep cartoon voice.*) "Hello. How are you? I'm fine. Thank you very much. It's so good to see you looking well this fine Sunday morning." It's the same old me. Same old dependable me. Never change. Never alter one iota. (*VINCE stops. Tucks his shirt back in.*)

SHELLY: Vince, don't be pathetic will ya! They're not gonna play. Can't you see that? (*SHELLY keeps cutting carrots. VINCE slowly moves toward TILDEN. TILDEN keeps watching SHELLY.*)

VINCE: (*To SHELLY.*) I don't get it. I really don't get it. Maybe it's me. Maybe I forgot something.

DODGE: (*From sofa.*) You forgot to get me a bottle! That's what you forgot. Anybody in this house could get me a bottle. Anybody! But nobody will. Nobody understands the urgency! Peelin' carrots is more important. Playin' piano on your teeth! Well I hope you all remember this when you get up in years. When you find yourself immobilized. Dependent on the whims of others. (*VINCE moves up toward DODGE. Pause as VINCE looks at him. SHELLY continues cutting carrots. Pause. VINCE moves around, stroking his hair, staring at DODGE and TILDEN. VINCE and SHELLY exchange glances. DODGE watches TV.*)

VINCE: Boy! This is amazing. This is truly amazing. (*Keeps moving around.*) What is this anyway? Am I being punished here or what? Is that it? Some kind of banishment? Some kind of wicked warped exile? Just tell me. I can take it. Lay it on me. What was it? Did I betray some secret ancient family taboo, way back when? Did I cross the line somehow when I wasn't looking? What exactly was it?

SHELLY: Vince, what are you doing that for? They don't care about any of that. They just don't recognize you, that's all. They don't have a clue.

VINCE: How could they not recognize me! How in the hell could they not recognize me! I'm their son! I'm their flesh and blood. Anybody can see we're related.

DODGE: (*Watching TV.*) You're no son of mine. I've had sons in my time—plenty of sons but you're not one of 'em. I know them by their scent. (*Long pause. VINCE stares at DODGE.*)

VINCE: All right. All right look—I'll get you a bottle. I'll get you a goddamn bottle.

DODGE: You will?

VINCE: Yeah, sure, you bet. If that's what it takes, I'll get you a bottle. Then maybe you can tell me what's going on here.

SHELLY: You're not going to leave me here alone are you?

VINCE: (*Moving to her.*) You suggested it! You said, "Why don't I go get him a bottle." So I'll go get him a bottle! That's what I'll do. Maybe it'll help jar things loose.

SHELLY: But I can't stay here by myself.

DODGE: Don't let her talk you out of it! She's a bad influence. I could see it the minute she stepped in here.

VINCE: Shelly, I gotta go out for a while. I just gotta get outta here. Think things through by myself. I'll get a bottle and I'll come right back.

SHELLY: I don't know if I can handle this Vince.

VINCE: You'll be okay. Nothing's going to happen. They're not dangerous or anything.

SHELLY: Can't we just go?

VINCE: No! I gotta find out what's going on here. Something has fallen apart. This isn't how it used to be. Believe me. This is nothing like how it used to be . . .

SHELLY: Look, you think you're bad off, what about me? Not only don't they recognize me but I've never seen them before in my life. I don't know who these guys are. They could be anybody!

VINCE: They're not anybody!

SHELLY: That's what you say.

VINCE: They're my family for Christ's sake! I should know who my own family is! Now give me a break. It won't take that long. I'll just go out and I'll come right back. Nothing'll happen. I promise. (*SHELLY stares at him. Pause.*)

SHELLY: Unbelievable.

VINCE: Nothing'll happen. (*He crosses up to DODGE.*) I'm gonna go out now, Grandpa, and I'll pick you up a bottle. Okay?

DODGE: Persistence see? That's what it takes. Persistence. Persistence, fortitude and determination. Those are the three virtues. That's how the country was *founded*. You stick with those three and you can't go wrong. (*Pointing off L.*) Money's on the table. In the kitchen. (*VINCE moves toward SHELLY.*)

VINCE: (*To SHELLY.*) You'll be all right, Shelly. I won't be too long.

SHELLY: (*Cutting carrots.*) I'll just keep real busy while you're gone. I love vegetables. (*VINCE exits. TILDEN keeps staring down at SHELLY's hands.*)

VINCE: (*Re-entering, to TILDEN.*) You want anything, Dad?

TILDEN: (*Looks up at VINCE.*) Me?

VINCE: Yeah, you. "Dad." That's you. From the store? I'm gonna get Grandpa a bottle. Do you want anything from the store?

TILDEN: He's not supposed to drink. Halie wouldn't like it. She'd be disappointed.

VINCE: He wants a bottle.

TILDEN: He's not supposed to drink.

DODGE: (*To VINCE.*) Don't negotiate with him! He's the one who stole my bottle! Don't make any transactions until you've spoken to me first! He'll steal you blind!

VINCE: (*To DODGE.*) Tilden says you're not supposed to drink.

DODGE: Tilden's lost his marbles! Look at him! He's around the twist. Take a look at him. He's come unwound. (*VINCE stares at TILDEN. TILDEN watches SHELLY's hands as she keeps cutting carrots.*) Now look at me. Look here at me! (*VINCE looks back to DODGE.*) Now, between the two of us, who do you think is more trustworthy? Him or me? Can you trust a man who keeps bringing in vegetables from out of nowhere? Take a look at him. (*VINCE looks back at TILDEN.*)

SHELLY: Go get the bottle Vince. Just go get the bottle.

VINCE: I'll be right back. (*VINCE crosses L.*)

DODGE: Where are you going?

VINCE: I'm going to get the money.

DODGE: Then where are you goin'?

VINCE: Liquor store.

DODGE: Don't go off anyplace else. Don't go off some place and drink by yourself. Come right back here.

VINCE: I will. (*VINCE exits L.*)

DODGE: (*Calling after VINCE.*) You've got responsibility now! And don't go out the back way

either! Come out through this way! I wanna see you when you leave! Don't go out the back.

VINCE: (*Off L.*) I won't! (*DODGE turns and looks at TILDEN and SHELLY.*)

DODGE: Untrustworthy. Probably drown himself if he went out the back. Fall right in a hole. I'd never get my bottle.

SHELLY: I wouldn't worry about Vince. He can take care of himself.

DODGE: Oh he can, huh? Independent. (*VINCE comes on again from L. with two dollars in his hand. He crosses R. past DODGE. To VINCE.*) You got the money?

VINCE: Yeah. Two bucks.

DODGE: Two bucks. Two bucks is two bucks. Don't sneer.

VINCE: What kind do you want for two bucks?

DODGE: Whiskey! Gold Star Sour Mash. Use your own discretion.

VINCE: Okay.

DODGE: Nothin' fancy! (*VINCE crosses to R. door. Opens it. Stops when he hears TILDEN.*)

TILDEN: (*To VINCE.*) You drove all the way from New Mexico?

VINCE: (*From porch.*) No, I—look—while I'm gone, try to remember who I am. Try real hard to remember. Use your imagination. It might suddenly come back to you. In a flash. (*VINCE turns and looks at TILDEN. They stare at each other. VINCE shakes his head, goes out the door, crosses porch and exits out screen door. TILDEN watches him go. Pause.*)

TILDEN: That's a long, lonely stretch of road. I've driven that stretch before and there's no end to it. You feel like you're going to fall right off into blackness.

SHELLY: You really don't recognize him? Either one of you? (*TILDEN turns again and stares at SHELLY's hands as she cuts carrots.*)

DODGE: (*Watching TV.*) Recognize who?

SHELLY: Vince.

DODGE: What's to recognize? (*DODGE lights a cigarette, coughs slightly and stares at TV.*)

SHELLY: It'd be cruel if you recognized him and didn't tell him. Wouldn't be fair.

DODGE: Cruel.

SHELLY: Well it would be. I mean it's not really possible, is it, that he's not related to you at all? Just a stranger? He seems so sure about it. (*DODGE just stares at TV, smoking.*)

TILDEN: I thought I recognized him. I thought I recognized something about him.

SHELLY: You did?

TILDEN: I thought I saw a face inside his face.

SHELLY: Well it was probably that you saw what he used to look like. You haven't seen him for six years.

TILDEN: I haven't?

SHELLY: That's what he says. (*TILDEN moves around in front of her as she continues with carrots.*)

TILDEN: Where was it I saw him last?

SHELLY: I have no idea. I've only known him for a few months, myself. He doesn't tell me everything.

TILDEN: He doesn't?

SHELLY: Not stuff like that.

TILDEN: What does he tell you?

SHELLY: You mean in general?

TILDEN: Yeah. (*TILDEN moves around behind her.*)

SHELLY: Well he tells me all kinds of things.

TILDEN: Like what?

SHELLY: I don't know! I mean I can't just come out and tell you how he feels.

TILDEN: How come? (*TILDEN keeps moving around her slowly in a circle.*)

SHELLY: Because it's stuff he told me privately!

TILDEN: And you can't tell me?

SHELLY: I don't even know you! I'm not even sure *he* knows you.

DODGE: Tilden, go out in the kitchen and make me some coffee! Leave the girl alone. She's nervous. She's ready to jump ship any second.

SHELLY: (*To DODGE.*) He's all right. (*TILDEN ignores DODGE, keeps moving around SHELLY. He stares at her hair and coat. DODGE stares at TV.*)

TILDEN: You mean you can't tell me anything?

SHELLY: I can tell you some things. I mean we can have a conversation.

TILDEN: We can?

SHELLY: Sure. We're having a conversation right now.

TILDEN: We are?

SHELLY: Yes. That's what we're doing. It's easy.

TILDEN: But there's certain things you can't tell me, right?

SHELLY: Right.

TILDEN: There's certain things I can't tell you either.

SHELLY: How come?

TILDEN: I don't know. Nobody's supposed to hear it.

SHELLY: Well, you can tell me anything you want to.

TILDEN: I can?

SHELLY: Sure.

TILDEN: It might not be very nice.

SHELLY: That's all right. I've been around.

TILDEN: It might be awful.

SHELLY: Well, can't you tell me anything nice? (*TILDEN stops in front of her and stares at her coat. SHELLY looks back at him. Long pause.*)

TILDEN: (*After pause.*) Can I touch your coat?

SHELLY: My coat? (*She looks at her coat then back to TILDEN.*) Sure.

TILDEN: You don't mind?

SHELLY: No. Go ahead. (*SHELLY holds her arm out for TILDEN to touch. DODGE stays fixed on TV. TILDEN moves in slowly toward SHELLY, staring at her arm. He reaches out very slowly and touches her arm, feels the fur gently then draws his hand back. SHELLY keeps her arm out.*) It's rabbit.

TILDEN: Rabbit. (*He reaches out again very slowly and touches the fur on her arm then pulls back his hand again. SHELLY drops her arm.*)

SHELLY: My arm was getting tired.

TILDEN: Can I hold it? (*Pause.*)

SHELLY: The coat? Sure. I guess. (*SHELLY takes off her coat and hands it to TILDEN. TILDEN takes it slowly, feels the fur then puts it on. SHELLY watches as TILDEN strokes the fur slowly. He smiles at her. She goes back to cutting carrots.*) You can have it if you want.

TILDEN: I can?

SHELLY: Yeah. I've got a raincoat in the car. That's all I need.

TILDEN: You've got a car?

SHELLY: Vince does. (*TILDEN walks around stroking the fur and smiling at the coat. SHELLY watches him when he's not looking. DODGE sticks with TV, stretches out on sofa wrapped in blanket.*)

TILDEN: (*As he walks around.*) I had a car once! I had a white car! I drove. I went everywhere. I went to the mountains. I drove in the snow.

SHELLY: That must've been fun.

TILDEN: (*Still moving, feeling coat.*) I drove all day long sometimes. Across the desert. Way out across the desert. I drove past tiny towns. Anywhere. Past palm trees. Lightning. Anything. I would drive through it. I would drive through it and I would stop and I would look around and I would see things sometimes. I would see things I wasn't supposed to see. Like deer. Hawks. Owls. I would look them in the eye and they would look back and I could tell I wasn't supposed to be there by the way they looked at me. So I'd drive on. I would get back in and drive! I loved to drive. There was nothing I loved more. Nothing I dreamed of was better than driving. I was independent.

DODGE: (*Eyes on TV.*) Pipe down would ya! Stop running off at the mouth. (*TILDEN stops. Stares at SHELLY.*)

SHELLY: Do you do much driving now?

TILDEN: Now? Now? I don't drive now.

SHELLY: How come?

TILDEN: I'm older.

SHELLY: You're not that old.

TILDEN: I'm not a kid.

SHELLY: You don't have to be a kid to drive.

TILDEN: It wasn't driving then.

SHELLY: What was it?

TILDEN: Adventure. I went everywhere. I had a sensation of myself.

SHELLY: Well you can still do that.

TILDEN: Not now.

SHELLY: Why not?

TILDEN: I just told you. You don't understand. If I told you something you wouldn't understand it.

SHELLY: Told me what?

TILDEN: Told you something that's true.

SHELLY: Like what?

TILDEN: Like a baby. Like a little tiny baby.

SHELLY: Like when you were little?

TILDEN: If I told you you'd make me give your coat back.

SHELLY: I won't. I promise. Tell me. Please.

TILDEN: I can't. Dodge won't let me.

SHELLY: He won't hear you. It's okay. He's watching TV. (*Pause. TILDEN stares at her. Moves slightly toward her.*)

TILDEN: We had a baby. Little baby. Could pick it up with one hand. Put it in the other. (*TILDEN moves closer to her. DODGE takes more interest.*) So small that nobody could find it. Just disappeared. We had no service. No hymn. Nobody came.

DODGE: Tilden!

TILDEN: Cops looked for it. Neighbors. Nobody could find it. (*DODGE struggles to get up from sofa.*)

DODGE: Tilden? You leave that girl alone! She's completely innocent. (*DODGE keeps struggling until he's standing.*)

TILDEN: Finally everybody just gave up. Just stopped looking. Everybody had a different answer. (*DODGE struggles to walk toward TILDEN and falls. TILDEN ignores him.*)

DODGE: Tilden! What are you telling her? (*DODGE starts coughing on the floor. SHELLY watches him from the stool.*)

TILDEN: Little tiny baby just disappeared. It's not hard. It's so small. Almost invisible. Hold it in one hand. (*SHELLY makes a move to help DODGE. TILDEN firmly pushes her back down on the stool. DODGE keeps coughing.*)

DODGE: Tilden! Don't tell her anything! She's an outsider!

TILDEN: He's the only one who knows where it is. The only one. Like a secret buried treasure. Won't tell any of us. (*DODGE's coughing subsides. SHELLY stays on stool staring at DODGE. TILDEN slowly takes SHELLY's coat off and holds it out to her. Long pause. SHELLY sits there trembling.*) You probably want your coat back now. I would if I was you. (*SHELLY stares at coat but doesn't move to take it. The sound of BRADLEY's leg squeaking is heard off L. The others onstage remain still. BRADLEY appears U.L. outside the screen door wearing a yellow rain slicker. He enters through screen door, crosses porch to R. door and enters stage. Closes door. Takes off rain slicker and shakes it out. He sees all the others and stops. TILDEN turns to him. BRADLEY stares at SHELLY. DODGE remains on floor.)*

BRADLEY: What's going on here? *(Motioning to SHELLY.)* Who's that? *(SHELLY stands, moves back away from BRADLEY as he crosses toward her. He stops next to TILDEN. He sees coat in TILDEN's hand and grabs it away from him.)* Who's she supposed to be?

TILDEN: She's driving to New Mexico. She has a car. *(BRADLEY stares at her. SHELLY is frozen. BRADLEY limps over to her with the coat in his fist. He stops in front of her.)*

BRADLEY: *(To SHELLY, after pause.)* Vacation? *(SHELLY shakes her head "no," trembling. To SHELLY, motioning to TILDEN.)* You taking him with you? *(SHELLY shakes her head "no." BRADLEY crosses back to TILDEN.)* You oughta. No use leaving him here. Doesn't do a lick of work. Doesn't raise a finger. *(Stopping, to TILDEN.)* Do ya? *(To SHELLY.)* Course he used to be a All-American. Quarterback or fullback or somethin'.

TILDEN: Halfback.

BRADLEY: He tell you about that? Brag on himself? *(SHELLY shakes her head "no.")* Yeah, he used to be a big deal. Wore letterman's sweaters. Had medals hanging all around his neck. Real purty. Big damn deal. *(He laughs to himself, notices DODGE on floor, crosses to him, stops.)* This one too. *(To SHELLY.)* You'd never think it to look at him, would ya? All paunchy and bloated. *(SHELLY shakes her head again. BRADLEY stares at her, crosses back to her, clenching the coat in his fist. He stops in front of SHELLY.)* Women like that kinda thing don't they?

SHELLY: What?

BRADLEY: Importance. Importance in a man.

SHELLY: I don't know.

BRADLEY: Yeah. Ya know, ya know. Don't give me that. *(Moves closer to SHELLY.)* You're with Tilden?

SHELLY: No.

BRADLEY: *(Turning to TILDEN.)* Tilden! She with you? *(TILDEN doesn't answer. Stares at floor.)* Tilden! You're gonna run now. Run like a scalded dog! *(TILDEN suddenly bolts and runs off U.L. BRADLEY laughs. Talks to SHELLY. DODGE starts moving his lips silently as though talking to someone invisible on the floor. Laughing.)* Scared to death! He was always scared. Scared of his own shadow. *(BRADLEY stops laughing. Stares at SHELLY.)* Some things are like that. They just tremble for no reason. Ever noticed that? They just shake? *(SHELLY looks at DODGE on the floor.)*

SHELLY: Can't we do something for him?

BRADLEY: *(Looking at DODGE.)* We could shoot him. *(Laughs.)* Put him out of his misery.

SHELLY: Shut up! *(BRADLEY stops laughing. Moves in closer to SHELLY. She freezes. BRADLEY speaks slowly and deliberately.)*

BRADLEY: Hey! Missus. Don't talk to me like that. Don't talk to me in that tone of voice. There was a time when I had to take that tone a voice from pretty near everyone. *(Motioning to DODGE.)* Him, for one! When he was a whole man. Full of himself. Him and that half-brain that just ran outa here. They don't talk to me like that now. Not anymore. Everything's turned around now. Full circle. Isn't that funny?

SHELLY: I'm sorry.

BRADLEY: Open your mouth.

SHELLY: What?

BRADLEY: *(Motioning for her to open her mouth.)* Open up. *(She opens her mouth slightly.)* Wider. *(She opens her mouth wider.)* Keep it like that. *(She does. Stares at BRADLEY. With his free hand he puts his fingers into her mouth. She tries to pull away.)* Just stay put! *(She freezes. He keeps his fingers in her mouth. Stares at her. Pause. He pulls his hand out. She closes her mouth, keeps her eyes on him. BRADLEY smiles. He looks at DODGE on* the floor and crosses over to him. SHELLY watches him closely. BRADLEY stands over DODGE and smiles at SHELLY. He holds her coat up in both hands over DODGE, keeps smiling at SHELLY. He looks down at DODGE then drops the coat so that it lands on DODGE and covers his head. BRADLEY keeps his hands up in the position of holding the coat, looks over at SHELLY and smiles. The lights black out.)

ACT THREE

Scene: same set. Morning. Bright sun. No sound of rain. Everything has been cleared up again. No sign of carrots. No pail. No stool. VINCE's saxophone case and overcoat are still at the foot of the staircase. BRADLEY is asleep on the sofa under DODGE's blanket, his head toward stage left. BRADLEY's wooden leg is leaning against the sofa right by his head. The shoe is left on. The harness hangs down. DODGE is sitting on the floor, propped up against the TV set facing stage left, wearing his baseball cap. SHELLY's rabbit fur coat covers his chest and shoulders. He stares toward stage left. He seems weaker and more disoriented. The lights rise slowly to the sound of birds. The two men remain for a while in silence. BRADLEY sleeps very soundly. DODGE hardly moves. SHELLY appears from stage left with a big smile, slowly crossing toward DODGE balancing a steaming cup of broth in a saucer. DODGE just stares at her as she gets close to him.

SHELLY: (*As she crosses.*) This is going to make all the difference in the world, Grandpa. You don't mind me calling you Grandpa do you? I mean I know you minded when Vince called you that but you don't even know him.

DODGE: I'm nobody's Grandpa. He skipped town with my money you know. I'm gonna hold you as collateral.

SHELLY: He'll be back. Don't you worry. He always comes back.

DODGE: The faithful type.

SHELLY: No. Determined. (*She kneels down next to DODGE and puts the cup and saucer in his lap.*)

DODGE: It's morning already! When did it get to be morning? Not only didn't I get my bottle but he's got my two bucks! I'm surrounded by thieves.

SHELLY: Try to drink this, okay? Don't spill it.

DODGE: What is it?

SHELLY: Beef bouillon. It'll warm you up.

DODGE: Bouillon! I don't want any goddamn bouillon! Get that stuff away from me!

SHELLY: I just got through making it.

DODGE: I don't care if you just spent all week making it! I ain't drinking it!

SHELLY: Well, what am I supposed to do with it? I'm trying to help you out. Besides, it's good for you.

DODGE: Get it away from me! (*SHELLY stands up with cup and saucer.*) What do you know what's good for me anyway? (*She looks at DODGE then turns away from him, crosses to staircase, sits on bottom step and drinks the bouillon. DODGE stares at her.*) You know what'd be good for me?

SHELLY: What?

DODGE: A little backrub. A little contact.

SHELLY: Oh no. I've had enough contact for a while. Thanks anyway. (*She keeps sipping the bouillon, stays sitting. Pause as DODGE stares at her.*)

DODGE: Why not? You got nothing better to do. That fella's not gonna be back here. You're not expecting him to show up again are you?

SHELLY: Sure. He'll show up. He left his horn here.

DODGE: His horn? (*Laughs.*) You're his horn?

SHELLY: Very funny.

DODGE: He's run off with my money! That's what he did. He's not coming back here.

SHELLY: He'll be back. This is where he's from. He knows that. He's convinced. And so am I.

DODGE: You're a funny chicken, you know that?

SHELLY: Funny?

DODGE: Full of hope. Faith. Faith and hope. You're all alike you hopers. If it's not God then it's a man. If it's not a man then it's a woman. If it's not a woman then it's politics or bee pollen or the future of some kind. Some kind of future.

SHELLY: Bee pollen?

DODGE: Yeah, bee pollen. (*Pause.*)

SHELLY: (*Looking toward porch.*) I'm glad it stopped raining. (*DODGE looks toward porch then back at SHELLY.*)

DODGE: That's what I mean. See, you're glad it stopped raining. Now you think everything's gonna be different. Just 'cause the sun comes out.

SHELLY: It's already different. Last night I was scared.

DODGE: Scared a what?

SHELLY: Just scared.

DODGE: Yeah, well we've all got an instinct for disaster. We can smell it coming.

SHELLY: It was your son. Bradley. He scared me.

DODGE: Bradley? (*Looks at BRADLEY.*) He's a push-over. 'Specially now. All ya gotta do is take his leg and throw it out the back door. Helpless. Totally helpless. (*SHELLY turns and stares at BRADLEY's wooden leg then looks at DODGE. She sips bouillon.*)

SHELLY: You'd do that?

DODGE: Me? I've hardly got the strength to breathe.

SHELLY: But you'd actually do it if you could?

DODGE: Don't be so easily shocked, girlie. There's nothing a man can't do. You dream it up and he can do it. Anything. It boggles the imagination.

SHELLY: You've tried I guess.

DODGE: Don't sit there sippin' your bouillon and judging me! This is my house!

SHELLY: I forgot.

DODGE: You forgot? Whose house did you think it was?

SHELLY: Mine. (*DODGE just stares at her. Long pause. She sips from cup.*) I know it's not mine but I had that feeling.

DODGE: What feeling?

SHELLY: The feeling that nobody lives here but me. I mean everybody's gone. You're here, but it doesn't seem like you're supposed to be. (*Pointing to BRADLEY.*) Doesn't seem like he's supposed to be here either. I don't know what it is. It's the house or something. Something familiar. Like I know my way around here. Did you ever get that feeling? (*DODGE stares at her in silence. Pause.*)

DODGE: No. No, I never did. I get lost in the hallway sometimes. (*SHELLY gets up. Moves around space holding cup.*)

SHELLY: Last night I went to sleep up there in that room.

DODGE: What room?

SHELLY: That room up there with all the pictures. All the crosses on the wall.

DODGE: Halie's room?

SHELLY: Yeah. Whoever "Halie" is.

DODGE: She's my wife.

SHELLY: So you remember her?

DODGE: Whadya mean! 'Course I remember her. She's only been gone a day—half a day. However long it's been.

SHELLY: Do you remember her when her hair was bright red? Standing in front of an apple tree?

DODGE: What is this, the third degree or something! Who're you to be askin' me personal questions about my wife!

SHELLY: You never look at those pictures up there?

DODGE: What pictures!

SHELLY: Your whole life's up there hanging on the wall. Somebody who looks just like you. Somebody who looks just like you used to look.

DODGE: That isn't me! That never was me! This is me. Right here. This is it. The whole shootin' match, sittin' right here in front of you. That other stuff was a sham.

SHELLY: So the past never happened as far as you're concerned?

DODGE: The past? Jesus Christ. The past is passed. What do you know about the past?

SHELLY: Not much. I know there was a farm. (*Pause.*)

DODGE: A farm?

SHELLY: There's a picture of a farm. A big farm. A bull. Wheat. Corn.

DODGE: Corn?

SHELLY: All the kids are standing out in the corn. They're all waving these big straw hats. One of them doesn't have a hat.

DODGE: Which one was that?

SHELLY: There's a baby. A baby in a woman's arms. The same woman with the red hair. She looks lost standing out there. Like she doesn't know how she got there.

DODGE: She knows! I told her a hundred times it wasn't gonna be the city! I gave her plenty of warning.

SHELLY: She's looking down at the baby like it was somebody else's. Like it didn't even belong to her.

DODGE: That's about enough outta you! You got some funny ideas, sister. Some damn funny ideas. You think just because people propagate they have to love their offspring? You never seen a bitch eat her puppies? Where are you from anyway?

SHELLY: LA. We already went through that.

DODGE: That's right, LA I remember.

SHELLY: Stupid country.

DODGE: That's right! No wonder. Dumber than dirt. (*Pause.*)

SHELLY: What's happened to this family anyway?

DODGE: You're in no position to ask! What do you care? You some kinda social worker?

SHELLY: I'm Vince's friend.

DODGE: Vince's friend! That's rich. That's real rich. "Vince"! "Mr. Vince"! "Mr. Thief" is more like it! His name doesn't mean a hoot in hell to me. Not a tinkle in the well. You know how many kids I've spawned? Not to mention grandkids and great-grandkids and great-great-grandkids after them?

SHELLY: And you don't remember any of them?

DODGE: What's to remember? Halie's the one with the family album. She's the one you should talk to. She'll set you straight on the heritage if that's what you're interested in. She's traced it all the way back to the grave.

SHELLY: What do you mean?

DODGE: What do you think I mean? How far back can you go? A long line of corpses! There's not a living soul behind me. Not a one. Who gives a damn about bones in the ground?

SHELLY: What was Tilden trying to tell me last night? (*DODGE stops short. Stares at SHELLY. Shakes his head. He looks off L. DODGE's tone changes drastically.*)

DODGE: Tilden? (*Turns to SHELLY, calmly.*) Where is Tilden?

SHELLY: What was he trying to say about the baby? (*Pause. DODGE turns toward L.*)

DODGE: What's happened to Tilden? Why isn't Tilden here?

SHELLY: Bradley chased him out.

DODGE: (*Looking at BRADLEY asleep.*) Bradley? Why is he on my sofa? (*Turns back to SHELLY.*) Have I been here all night? On the floor?

SHELLY: He wouldn't leave. I hid outside until he fell asleep.

DODGE: Outside? Is Tilden outside? He shouldn't be out there in the rain. He'll get himself into trouble. He doesn't know his way around here anymore. Not like he used to. He went out West and got himself into trouble. Deep trouble. We don't want any of that around here.

SHELLY: What did he do? (*Pause.*)

DODGE: (*Quietly stares at SHELLY.*) Tilden? He got mixed up. That's what he did. We can't afford to leave him alone. Not now. (*Sound of HALIE laughing comes from off L. SHELLY stands, looking in direction of voice, holding cup and saucer, doesn't know whether to stay or run. Motioning to SHELLY.*) Sit down! Sit back down! (*SHELLY sits. Sound of HALIE's laughter again. To SHELLY in a heavy whisper, pulling coat up around him.*) Don't leave me alone now! Promise me? Don't go off and leave me alone. I need somebody here with me. Tilden's gone now and I need someone. Don't leave me! Promise!

SHELLY: (*Sitting.*) I won't. (*HALIE appears outside the screen porch door, U.L. with FATHER DEWIS. She is wearing a bright yellow dress, no hat, white gloves and her arms are full of yellow roses. FATHER DEWIS is dressed in traditional black suit, white clerical collar and shirt. He is a very distinguished gray-haired man in his sixties. They are both slightly drunk and feeling giddy. As they enter the porch through the screen door, DODGE pulls the rabbit fur coat over his head and hides. SHELLY stands again. DODGE drops the coat and whispers intently to SHELLY. Neither HALIE nor FATHER DEWIS are aware of the people inside the house.)*

DODGE: *(To SHELLY in a strong whisper.)* You promised! *(SHELLY sits on stairs again. DODGE pulls coat back over head. HALIE and FATHER DEWIS talk on the porch as they cross toward R. interior door.)*

HALIE: Oh Father! That's terrible! That's absolutely terrible! Aren't you afraid of being punished? *(She giggles.)*

DEWIS: Not by the Italians. They're too busy punishing each other. *(They both break out in giggles.)*

HALIE: What about God?

DEWIS: Well, prayerfully, God only hears what he wants to. That's just between you and me of course. In our heart of hearts we know we're every bit as wicked as the Catholics. *(They giggle again and reach the R. door.)*

HALIE: Father, I never heard you talk like this in Sunday sermon.

DEWIS: Well, I save all my best jokes for private company. Pearls before swine you know. *(They enter the room laughing and stop when they see SHELLY. SHELLY stands. HALIE closes the door behind FATHER DEWIS. DODGE's voice is heard under the coat talking to SHELLY.)*

DODGE: *(Under coat, to SHELLY.)* Sit down, sit down! Don't let 'em buffalo you. *(SHELLY sits on stair again. HALIE looks at DODGE on the floor, then looks at BRADLEY asleep on the sofa and sees his wooden leg. She lets out a shriek of embarrassment for FATHER DEWIS.)*

HALIE: Oh my gracious! What in the name of Judas Priest is going on in this house! *(She hands over the roses to FATHER DEWIS.)* Excuse me Father. *(HALIE crosses to DODGE, whips the coat off him and covers the wooden leg with it. BRADLEY stays asleep.)* You can't leave this house for a second without the devil blowing in the front door!

DODGE: Gimme back that coat! Gimme back that goddamn coat before I freeze to death!

HALIE: You're not going to freeze! The sun's out in case you hadn't noticed!

DODGE: Gimme back that coat! That coat's for live flesh not dead wood. *(HALIE whips the blanket off BRADLEY and throws it on DODGE. DODGE covers his head again with blanket. BRADLEY's amputated leg can be faked by having it under a cushion on the sofa. BRADLEY's fully clothed. He sits up with a jerk when the blanket comes off him.)*

HALIE: *(As she tosses blanket.)* Here! Use this! It's yours anyway! Can't you take care of yourself for once!

BRADLEY: *(Yelling at HALIE.)* Gimme that blanket! Gimme back that blanket! That's my blanket! *(HALIE crosses back toward FATHER DEWIS who just stands there with the roses. BRADLEY thrashes helplessly on the sofa trying to reach the blanket. DODGE hides himself deeper in the blanket. SHELLY looks on from staircase, still holding cup and saucer.)*

HALIE: Believe me, Father, this is not what I had in mind when I invited you in. I keep forgetting how easily things fall to pieces when I'm not here to hold them together.

DEWIS: Oh, no apologies please. I wouldn't be in the ministry if I couldn't face real life. *(FATHER DEWIS laughs self-consciously. HALIE notices SHELLY and crosses over to her. SHELLY stays sitting. HALIE stops and stares at her.)*

BRADLEY: I want my blanket back! Gimme my blanket! *(HALIE turns toward BRADLEY and silences him.)*

HALIE: Shut up Bradley! Right this minute. I've had enough! It's shameful the way you carry on. *(BRADLEY slowly recoils, lies back down on the sofa, turns his back toward HALIE and whimpers softly. HALIE directs her attention to SHELLY again. Pause.)*

BRADLEY: You gave me that blanket.

HALIE: Enough. *(To SHELLY.)* What are you doing with my cup and saucer?

SHELLY: *(Looking at cup, back to HALIE.)* I made some bouillon for Dodge.

HALIE: For Dodge?

SHELLY: Yeah.

HALIE: My husband, Dodge.

SHELLY: Yes.

HALIE: You're here in my house making bouillon for my husband.

SHELLY: Yes.

HALIE: Well, did he drink it?

SHELLY: No.

HALIE: Did you drink it?

SHELLY: Yes. (*HALIE stares at her. Long pause. She turns abruptly away from SHELLY and crosses back to FATHER DEWIS.*)

HALIE: Father, there's a stranger in my house. What would you advise? What would be the Christian thing?

DEWIS: (*Squirming.*) Oh, well . . . I . . . I really—is she a trespasser?

HALIE: We still have some whiskey, don't we? A drop or two? (*DODGE slowly pulls the blanket down and looks toward FATHER DEWIS. SHELLY stands.*)

SHELLY: Listen, I don't drink or anything. I just— (*HALIE turns toward SHELLY viciously.*)

HALIE: You sit back down! (*SHELLY sits again on stair. HALIE turns again to DEWIS.*) I think we still have plenty of whiskey left! Don't we Father?

DEWIS: Well, yes. I think so. You'll have to get it. My hands are full. (*HALIE giggles. Reaches into DEWIS's pockets, searching for bottle. She smells the roses as she searches. DEWIS stands stiffly. DODGE watches HALIE closely as she looks for bottle.*)

HALIE: Roses. The most incredible things, roses! Aren't they incredible, Father?

DEWIS: Yes. Yes they are.

HALIE: They almost cover the stench of sin in this house. Hanky-panky. Just magnificent! The smell. We'll have to put some at the foot of Ansel's statue. On the day of the unveiling. (*HALIE finds a silver flask of whiskey in DEWIS's vest pocket. She pulls it out. DODGE looks on eagerly. HALIE crosses to DODGE, opens the flask and takes a sip. To DODGE.*) Ansel's getting a statue, Dodge. Did you know that?

Not a plaque but a real live statue. A full bronze. Tip to toe. A basketball in one hand and a rifle in the other.

BRADLEY: (*His back to HALIE.*) He never played basketball!

HALIE: You better shut up, Bradley! You shut up about Ansel! Ansel played basketball better than anyone! And you know it! He was an All-American! There's no reason to take the glory away from others. Especially when one's own shortcomings are so apparent. (*HALIE turns away from BRADLEY, crosses back toward DEWIS sipping on the flask and smiling. To DEWIS.*) Ansel was a great basketball player. Make no mistake. One of the greatest.

DEWIS: I remember Ansel. Handsome lad. Tall and strapping.

HALIE: Of course! You remember. You remember how he could play. (*She turns toward SHELLY.*) Of course, nowadays they play a different brand of basketball. More vicious. Isn't that right, dear?

SHELLY: I don't know. (*HALIE crosses to SHELLY, sipping on flask. She stops in front of SHELLY.*)

HALIE: Much, much more vicious. They smash into each other. They knock each other's teeth out. There's blood all over the court. Savages. Barbaric, don't you think? (*HALIE takes the cup from SHELLY and pours whiskey into it.*) They don't train like they used to. Not at all. They allow themselves to run amuck. Drugs and women. Women mostly. (*HALIE hands the cup of whiskey back to SHELLY slowly. SHELLY takes it.*) Mostly women. Girls. Sad, pathetic little skinny girls. (*She crosses back to FATHER DEWIS.*) It's just a reflection of the times, don't you think Father? An indication of where we stand?

DEWIS: I suppose so, yes. I've been so busy with the choir—

HALIE: Yes. A sort of bad omen. Our youth becoming monsters.

DEWIS: Well, I uh—wouldn't go quite that far.

HALIE: Oh you can disagree with me if you want to, Father. I'm open to debate. (*She moves toward DODGE.*) I suppose, in the long run, it doesn't matter. When you see the way things deteriorate before your very eyes. Everything running down hill. It's kind of silly to even think about youth.

DEWIS: No, I don't think so. I think it's important to believe in certain things. Certain basic truths. I mean—

HALIE: Yes. Yes, I know what you mean. I think that's right. I think that's true. (*She looks at DODGE.*) Certain basic things. We can't shake the fundamentals. We might end up crazy. Like my husband. You can see it in his eyes. You can see the madness almost oozing out. (*DODGE covers his head with the blanket again. HALIE takes a single rose from DEWIS and moves slowly over to DODGE.*) We can't not believe in something. We can't stop believing. We just end up dying if we stop. Just end up dead. (*HALIE throws the rose gently onto DODGE's blanket. It lands between his knees and stays there. Long pause as HALIE stares at the rose.*)

BRADLEY: Ansel never played basketball.

HALIE: Bradley, I'm warning you. (*SHELLY stands suddenly. HALIE doesn't turn to her but keeps staring at the rose.*)

SHELLY: (*To HALIE.*) Don't you wanna know who I am? Don't you wanna know what I'm doing here! Standing in the middle of your house. I'm not dead! (*SHELLY crosses toward HALIE. HALIE turns slowly to her.*)

HALIE: Did you drink your whiskey?

SHELLY: No! And I'm not going to either!

HALIE: Well that's a firm stand. It's good to have a firm stand.

SHELLY: I don't have any stand at all. I'm just trying to put all this together. (*HALIE laughs and crosses back to DEWIS.*)

HALIE: (*To DEWIS.*) Surprises, surprises! Did you have any idea we'd be returning to this?

DEWIS: Well, actually—

SHELLY: I came here with your grandson for a little visit! A little innocent friendly visit.

HALIE: My grandson?

SHELLY: Yes! That's right. The one no one seems to remember.

HALIE: (*To DEWIS.*) This is getting a little far-fetched.

SHELLY: I told him it was stupid to come back here. To try to pick up from where he left off.

HALIE: Where was that?

SHELLY: Wherever he was when he left here! Six years ago! Ten years ago! Whenever it was! I told him nobody cares. I told him nobody cares anymore. Nobody's going to care.

HALIE: Didn't he listen?

SHELLY: No! No he didn't. We had to stop off at every tiny little meatball town that he remembered from his boyhood!

HALIE: My grandson?

SHELLY: Every dumb little donut shop he ever kissed a girl in. Every drive-in. Every drag strip. Every football field he ever broke a bone on.

HALIE: (*Suddenly alarmed, to DODGE.*) Where's Tilden?

SHELLY: Don't ignore me! I'm telling you something!

HALIE: Dodge! Where's Tilden gone? (*SHELLY moves violently toward HALIE.*)

SHELLY: (*To HALIE.*) I'm talking to you! I'm standing here talking to you. (*BRADLEY sits up fast on the sofa, SHELLY backs away.*)

BRADLEY: (*To SHELLY.*) Don't you yell at my mother!

HALIE: Dodge! (*She kicks DODGE.*) I told you not to let Tilden out of your sight! Where's he gone to?

DODGE: Gimme a drink and I'll tell ya.

DEWIS: Halie, maybe this isn't the right time for a visit. (*HALIE crosses back to DEWIS.*)

HALIE: (*To DEWIS.*) I never should've left! I never, never should've left! Tilden could be anywhere now! Anywhere! He's not in control of his faculties. He wanders. You know how he wanders. Dodge knew that. I told him when I left here. I told him specifically to watch out for Tilden. (*BRADLEY reaches down, grabs DODGE's blanket and yanks it off him. He lays down on the sofa and pulls the blanket over his head.*)

DODGE: He's got my blanket again! He's got my blanket!

HALIE: (*Turning to BRADLEY.*) Bradley! Bradley, put that blanket back! (*HALIE moves toward BRADLEY. SHELLY suddenly throws the cup and saucer against the R. door. DEWIS ducks. The cup and saucer smash into pieces. HALIE stops, turns toward SHELLY. Everyone freezes. BRADLEY slowly pulls his head out from under blanket, looks toward R. door, then to SHELLY. SHELLY stares at HALIE. DEWIS cowers with roses. SHELLY moves slowly toward HALIE. Long pause. SHELLY speaks softly.*)

SHELLY: (*To HALIE.*) I am here! I am standing right here in front of you. I am breathing. I am speaking. I am alive! I exist. *DO YOU SEE ME?*

BRADLEY: (*Sitting up on sofa.*) We don't have to tell you anything, girl. Not a thing. You're not the police are you? You're not the government. You're just some prostitute that Tilden brought in here.

HALIE: Language! I won't have that language in my house! Father I'm—

SHELLY: (*To BRADLEY.*) You stuck your hand in my mouth and you call me a prostitute! What kind of a weird fucked-up yo-yo are you?

HALIE: Bradley! Did you put your hand in this girl's mouth? You have no idea what kind of diseases she might be carrying.

BRADLEY: I never did. She's lying. She's lying through her teeth.

DEWIS: Halie, I think I'll be running along now. I'll just put the roses in the kitchen. Keep them fresh. A little sugar sometimes helps. (*DEWIS moves toward L. HALIE stops him.*)

HALIE: Don't go now, Father! Not now. Please— I'm not sure I can stay afloat.

BRADLEY: I never did anything, Mom! I never touched her! She propositioned me! And I turned her down. I turned her down flat! She's not my type. You know that Mom. (*SHELLY suddenly grabs her coat off the wooden leg and takes both the leg and coat D., away from BRADLEY.*) Mom! Mom! She's got my leg!

She's taken my leg! I never did anything to her! She's stolen my leg! She's a devil Mom. How did she get in our house? (*BRADLEY reaches pathetically in the air for his leg. SHELLY sets it down for a second, puts on her coat fast and picks up the leg again. DODGE starts coughing again softly.*)

HALIE: (*To SHELLY.*) I think we've had about enough of you young lady. Just about enough. I don't know where you came from or what you're doing here but you're no longer welcome in this house.

SHELLY: (*Laughs, holds leg.*) No longer welcome!

BRADLEY: Mom! That's my leg! Get my leg back! I can't do anything without my leg! She's trying to torture me. (*BRADLEY keeps on making whimpering sounds and reaching for his leg.*)

HALIE: Give my son back his leg. Right this very minute! Dodge, where did this girl come from? (*DODGE starts laughing softly to himself in between coughs.*)

DODGE: She's a pistol, isn't she?

HALIE: (*To DEWIS.*) Father, do something about this would you! I'm not about to be terrorized in my own house!

DEWIS: This is out of my domain.

BRADLEY: Gimme back my leg!

HALIE: Oh, shut up Bradley! Just shut up! You don't need your leg now! Just lay down and shut up! I've never heard such whining. (*BRADLEY whimpers, lies down and pulls blanket around him. He keeps one arm outside blanket, reaching out toward his wooden leg. DEWIS cautiously approaches SHELLY with the roses in his arms. SHELLY clutches the wooden leg to her chest as though she's kidnapped it.*)

DEWIS: (*To SHELLY.*) Now, honestly, dear, wouldn't it be better to talk things out? To try to use some reason? No point in going off the deep end. Nothing to be gained in that.

SHELLY: There isn't any reason here! I can't find a reason for anything.

DEWIS: There's nothing to be afraid of. These are all good people. All righteous souls.

SHELLY: I'm not afraid!

DEWIS: But this is not your house. You have to have some respect.

SHELLY: You're the strangers here, not me.

HALIE: This has gone on far enough!

DEWIS: Halie, please. Let me handle this. I've had some experience.

SHELLY: Don't come near me! Don't anyone come near me. I don't need any words from you. I'm not threatening anybody. I don't even know what I'm doing here. You all say you don't remember Vince, okay, maybe you don't. Maybe it's Vince that's crazy. Maybe he's made this whole family thing up. I don't even care anymore. I was just coming along for the ride. I thought it'd be a nice gesture. Besides, I was curious. He made all of you sound familiar to me. Every one of you. For every name, I had an image. Every time he'd tell me a name, I'd see the person. In fact, each of you was so clear in my mind that I actually believed it was you. I really believed that when I walked through that door that the people who lived here would turn out to be the same people in my imagination. Real people. People with faces. But I don't recognize any of you. Not one. Not even the slightest resemblance.

DEWIS: Well you can hardly blame others for not fulfilling your hallucination.

SHELLY: It was no hallucination! It was more like a prophecy. You believe in prophecy, don't you, Father?

HALIE: Father, there's no point in talking to her any further. We're just going to have to call the police.

BRADLEY: No! Don't get the police in here. We don't want the police in here. This is our home.

SHELLY: That's right. Bradley's right. Don't you usually settle your affairs in private? Don't you usually take them out in the dark? Out in the back?

BRADLEY: You stay out of our lives! You have no business interfering!

SHELLY: I don't have any business period. I got nothing to lose. I'm a free agent. (*She moves around, staring at each of them.*)

BRADLEY: You don't know what we've been through. You don't know anything about us!

SHELLY: I know you've got a secret. You've all got a secret. It's so secret, in fact, you're all convinced it never happened. (*HALIE moves to DEWIS.*)

HALIE: Oh, my God, Father! Who is this person?

DODGE: (*Laughing to himself.*) She thinks she's going to get it out of us. She thinks she's going to uncover the truth of the matter. Like a detective or something.

BRADLEY: I'm not telling her anything! Nothing's wrong here! Nothing's ever been wrong! Everything's the way it's supposed to be! Nothing ever happened that's bad. Everything is all right here! We're all good people! We've always been good people. Right from the very start.

DODGE: She thinks she's gonna suddenly bring everything out into the open after all these years.

DEWIS: (*To SHELLY.*) Can't you see that these people want to be left in peace? Don't you have any mercy? They haven't done anything to you.

DODGE: She wants to get to the bottom of it. (*To SHELLY.*) That's it, isn't it? You'd like to get right down to bedrock? Look the beast right dead in the eye. You want me to tell ya? You want me to tell ya what happened? I'll tell ya. I might as well. I wouldn't mind hearing it hit the air after all these years of silence.

BRADLEY: No! Don't listen to him. He doesn't remember anything!

DODGE: I remember the whole thing from start to finish. I remember the day he was born. (*Pause.*)

HALIE: Dodge, if you tell this thing—if you tell this, you'll be dead to me. You'll be just as good as dead.

DODGE: That won't be such a big change, Halie. See this girl, this little girl here, she wants to know. She wants to know something more. And I got this feeling that it doesn't make a bit a difference. I'd sooner tell it to a stranger than anybody else. I'd sooner tell it to the four winds.

BRADLEY: (*To DODGE.*) We made a pact! We made a pact between us! You can't break that now!

DODGE: I don't remember any pact. (*Silence.*) See, we were a well-established family once. Well-established. All the boys were grown. The farm was producing enough milk to fill Lake Michigan twice over. Me and Halie here were pointed toward what looked like the middle part of our life. Everything was settled with us. All we had to do was ride it out. Then Halie got pregnant again. Out the middle a nowhere, she got pregnant. We weren't planning on havin' any more boys. We had enough boys already. In fact, we hadn't been sleepin' in the same bed for about six years.

HALIE: (*Moving toward stairs.*) I'm not listening to this! I don't have to listen to this!

DODGE: (*Stops HALIE.*) Where are you going! Upstairs! You'll just be listenin' to it upstairs! You go outside, you'll be listenin' to it outside. Might as well stay here and listen to it. (*HALIE stays by stairs. Pause.*) Halie had this kid see. This baby boy. She had it. I let her have it on her own. All the other boys I had had the best doctors, the best nurses, everything. This one I let her have by herself. This one hurt real bad. Almost killed her, but she had it anyway. It lived, see. It lived. It wanted to grow up in this family. It wanted to be just like us. It wanted to be part of us. It wanted to pretend that I was its father. She wanted me to believe in it. Even when everyone around us knew. Everyone. All our boys knew. Tilden knew.

HALIE: You shut up! Bradley, make him stop!

BRADLEY: I can't.

DODGE: Tilden was the one who knew. Better than any of us. He'd walk for miles with that kid in his arms. Halie let him take it. All

night sometimes. He'd walk all night out there in the pasture with it. Talkin' to it. Singin' to it. Used to hear him singing to it. He'd make up stories. He'd tell that kid all kinds of stories. Even when he knew it couldn't understand him. We couldn't let a thing like that continue. We couldn't allow that to grow up right in the middle of our lives. It made everything we'd accomplished look like it was nothin'. Everything was canceled out by this one mistake. This one weakness.

SHELLY: So you . . .

DODGE: I killed it. I drowned it. Just like the runt of a litter. Just drowned it. There was no struggle. No noise. Life just left it. (*HALIE moves toward BRADLEY.*)

HALIE: (*To BRADLEY.*) Ansel would've stopped him! Ansel would've stopped him from telling these lies! He was a hero! A man! A whole man! What's happened to the men in this family! Where are the men! (*Suddenly VINCE comes crashing through the screen porch door U.L., tearing it off its hinges. Everyone but DODGE and BRADLEY back away from the porch and stare at VINCE, who has landed on his stomach on the porch in a drunken stupor. He is singing loudly to himself and hauls himself slowly to his feet. He has a paper shopping bag full of empty booze bottles. He takes them out one at a time as he sings and smashes them at the opposite end of the porch, behind the solid interior door, R. SHELLY moves slowly toward R., holding wooden leg and watching VINCE.*)

VINCE: (*Singing loudly as he hurls bottles.*) "From the halls of Montezuma to the shores of Tripoli. We will fight our country's battles in the air on land and sea." (*He punctuates the words "Montezuma," "Tripoli," "battles," and "sea" with a smashed bottle each. He stops throwing for a second, stares toward R. of the porch, shades his eyes with his hand as though looking across to a battlefield, then cups his hands around his mouth and yells across the space of the porch to an imaginary army. The others watch in terror and expectation. To imagined army.*) Have you had enough over there! 'Cause there's a lot more here where that came from! (*Pointing to paper bag full of bottles.*) A helluva lot more! We got enough over here to blow ya from here to Kingdom come! (*He takes another bottle, makes high whistling sound of a bomb and throws it toward R. porch. Sound of bottle smashing against wall. This should be the actual smashing of bottle and not tape sound. He keeps yelling and heaving bottles one after another. VINCE stops for a while, breathing heavily from exhaustion. Long silence as the others watch him. SHELLY approaches tentatively in VINCE's direction, still holding BRADLEY's wooden leg.*)

SHELLY: (*After silence.*) Vince? (*VINCE turns toward her. Peers through screen.*)

VINCE: Who? What? Vince who? Who's that in there? Is someone in there? (*VINCE pushes his face against the screen from the porch and stares in at everyone.*)

DODGE: Where's my goddamn bottle!

VINCE: (*Looking in at DODGE.*) What? Who is that? Who's speaking. Who's voice is that?

DODGE: It's me! Your grandfather! Don't play stupid with me! Where's my two bucks!

VINCE: Grandfather? Grandfather? You mean the father of my father? The son of my great-grandfather? That one? When did this start?

DODGE: Where's my bottle! (*HALIE moves away from DEWIS, U., peers out at VINCE, trying to recognize him.*)

HALIE: Vincent? Is that you, Vincent? (*SHELLY stares at HALIE then looks out at VINCE.*)

VINCE: (*From porch.*) Vincent who? What is this! Who are you people?

SHELLY: (*To HALIE.*) Hey, wait a minute. Wait a minute!

HALIE: (*Moving closer to porch screen.*) We thought you were a murderer or something. Barging in through the door like that.

VINCE: A murderer? No, no, no! How could I be a murderer when I don't exist? A murderer is a living breathing person who

takes the life and breath away from another living breathing person. That's a murderer. You've got me mixed up with someone else.

BRADLEY: (*Sitting up on sofa.*) You get off our front porch you creep! What're you doing out there breaking bottles? Who are these foreigners anyway! Where did they all come from?

HALIE: (*Moving toward porch.*) Vincent, what's got into you! Why are you acting like this?

VINCE: Who's that? Who's that speaking?

SHELLY: (*Approaching HALIE.*) You mean you know who he is?

HALIE: Of course I know who he is! That's more than I can say for you missie.

DODGE: Where's my goddamn bottle? (*HALIE turns back toward DEWIS and crosses to him. VINCE sings.*)

VINCE: "From the halls of Montezuma to the shores of Tripoli. We will fight our country's battles in the air on land and sea . . ."

HALIE: (*To DEWIS.*) Father, why are you just standing around here when everything's falling apart? Can't you rectify this situation? (*DODGE laughs, coughs.*)

DEWIS: I'm just a guest here, Halie. I don't know what my position is exactly. This is outside my parish anyway. I'm in the quiet part of town.

SHELLY: Vince! Knock it off will ya! I want to get out of here! This is enough.

VINCE: (*To SHELLY.*) Have they got you prisoner in there, dear? (*VINCE starts to sing again, throwing more bottles as things continue.*)

SHELLY: I'm coming out there, Vince! I'm coming out there and I want us to get in the car and drive away from here. Anywhere. Just away from here. Far, far away. (*SHELLY moves toward VINCE's saxophone case and overcoat. She sets down the wooden leg D.L. and picks up the saxophone case and overcoat. VINCE watches her through the screen. SHELLY moves to R. door and opens it.*)

VINCE: We'd never make it. We'd drive and we'd drive and we'd drive and we'd never make it. We'd think we were getting farther and farther away. That's what we'd think.

SHELLY: I'm coming out there now, Vince.

VINCE: Don't come out. Don't you dare come out here. It's off limits. Taboo territory. (*VINCE pulls out a big folding hunting knife and pulls open the blade. He jabs the blade into the screen and starts cutting a hole big enough to climb through. BRADLEY cowers in a corner of the sofa as VINCE rips open the screen. DEWIS takes HALIE by the arm and pulls her toward staircase.*)

DEWIS: Halie, maybe we should go upstairs until this blows over. I'm completely at a loss.

HALIE: I don't understand it. I just don't understand it. He was the sweetest little boy! There was no indication. (*DEWIS drops the roses beside the wooden leg at the foot of the stair-case then escorts HALIE quickly up the stairs. HALIE keeps looking back at VINCE as they climb the stairs.*) There wasn't a mean bone in his body. Everybody loved Vincent. Everyone. He was the perfect baby. So pink and perfect.

DEWIS: He'll be all right after a while. He's just had a few too many that's all.

HALIE: He used to sing in his sleep. He'd sing. In the middle of the night. The sweetest voice. Like an angel. (*She stops for a moment.*) I used to lie awake listening to it. I used to lie awake thinking it was all right if I died. Because Vincent was an angel. A guardian angel. He'd watch over us. He'd watch over all of us. He would see to it that no harm would come. (*DEWIS takes her all the way up the stairs. They disappear above. VINCE is now climbing through the porch screen onto the sofa. BRADLEY crashes off the sofa, holding tight to his blanket, keeping it wrapped around him. SHELLY is outside on the porch. VINCE holds the knife in his teeth once he gets the hole wide enough to climb through. BRADLEY starts crawling slowly toward his wooden leg, reaching out for it.*)

DODGE: (*To VINCE.*) Go ahead! Take over the house! Take over the whole goddamn house! You can have it! It's yours! It's been a pain in the neck ever since the very first

mortgage. I'm gonna die any second now. Any second. You won't even notice. So I'll settle my affairs once and for all. (*As DODGE proclaims his last will and testament, VINCE climbs into the room, knife in mouth and strides slowly around the space, inspecting his inheritance. He casually notices BRADLEY as he crawls toward his leg. VINCE moves to the leg and keeps pushing it with his foot so that it's out of BRADLEY's reach then goes on with his inspection. He picks up the roses and carries them around smelling them. SHELLY can be seen outside on the porch, moving slowly C. and staring in at VINCE. VINCE ignores her.*) The house goes to my grandson, Vincent. That's fair and square. All the furnishings, accoutrements and paraphernalia therein. Everything tacked to the walls or otherwise resting under this roof. My tools—namely my band saw, my skill saw, my drill press, my chain saw, my lathe, my electric sander all go to my eldest son, Tilden. That is, if he ever shows up again. My Benny Goodman records, my harnesses, my bits, my halters, my brace, my rough rasp, my forge, my welding equipment, my shoeing nails, my levels and bevels, my milking stool—no, not my milking stool—my hammers and chisels and all related materials are to be pushed into a gigantic heap and set ablaze in the very center of my fields. When the blaze is at its highest, preferably on a cold, windless night, my body is to be pitched into the middle of it and burned 'til nothing remains but ash. (*Pause. VINCE takes the knife out of his mouth and smells the roses. He's facing toward audience and doesn't turn around to SHELLY. He folds up knife and pockets it.*)

SHELLY: (*From porch.*) I'm leaving, Vince. Whether you come or not, I'm leaving. I can't stay here.

VINCE: (*Smelling roses.*) You'll never make it. You'll see.

SHELLY: (*Moving toward hole in screen.*) You're not coming? (*VINCE stays D., turns and looks at her.*)

VINCE: I just inherited a house. I've finally been recognized. Didn't you hear?

SHELLY: (*Through hole, from porch.*) You want to stay here?

VINCE: (*As he pushes BRADLEY's leg out of reach.*) I've gotta carry on the line. It's in the blood. I've gotta see to it that things keep rolling. (*BRADLEY looks up at him from floor, keeps pulling himself toward his leg. VINCE keeps moving it.*)

SHELLY: What happened to you, Vince? You just disappeared. (*Pause. VINCE delivers the following speech front.*)

VINCE: I was gonna run last night. I was gonna run and keep right on running. Clear to the Iowa border. I drove all night with the windows open. The old man's two bucks flapping right on the seat beside me. It never stopped raining the whole time. Never stopped once. I could see myself in the windshield. My face. My eyes. I studied my face. Studied everything about it as though I was looking at another man. As though I could see his whole race behind him. Like a mummy's face. I saw him dead and alive at the same time. In the same breath. In the windshield I watched him breathe as though he was frozen in time and every breath marked him. Marked him forever without him knowing. And then his face changed. His face became his father's face. Same bones. Same eyes. Same nose. Same breath. And his father's face changed to his grandfather's face. And it went on like that. Changing. Clear on back to faces I'd never seen before but still recognized. Still recognized the bones underneath. Same eyes. Same mouth. Same breath. I followed my family clear into Iowa. Every last one. Straight into the corn belt and further. Straight back as far as they'd take me. Then it all dissolved. Everything dissolved. Just like that. And that two bucks kept right on flapping on the seat beside me. (*SHELLY stares at him for a while then reaches through the hole in the screen and sets the saxophone case and VINCE's overcoat on the sofa. She looks at VINCE again.*)

SHELLY: Bye Vince. I can't hang around for this. I'm not even related. (*She exits L. off the porch. VINCE watches her go. BRADLEY tries to make a lunge for his wooden leg. VINCE quickly picks it up and dangles it over BRADLEY's head like a carrot. BRADLEY keeps making desperate grabs at the leg. DEWIS comes down the staircase and stops halfway, staring at VINCE and BRADLEY. VINCE looks up at DEWIS and smiles. He keeps moving backwards with the leg toward U.L. as BRADLEY crawls after him.*)

VINCE: (*To DEWIS as he continues torturing BRADLEY.*) Oh, excuse me, Father. Just getting rid of some of the vermin in the house. This is my house now, ya know? All mine. Everything. Except for the power tools and stuff. I'm gonna get all new equipment anyway. New plows, new tractor, everything. All brand-new. (*VINCE teases BRADLEY closer to the U.L. corner of the stage.*) Start right off on the ground floor. (*VINCE throws BRADLEY's wooden leg far offstage L. BRADLEY follows his leg offstage, pulling himself along on the ground, whimpering. As BRADLEY exits, VINCE pulls the blanket off him and throws it over his own shoulder. He crosses toward DEWIS with the blanket and smells the roses. DEWIS comes to the bottom of the stairs.*)

DEWIS: You'd better go up and see your grandmother. I think you should. It would be the Christian thing.

VINCE: (*Looking upstairs, back to DEWIS.*) My grandmother? There's nobody else in this house. Except for you. And you're leaving aren't you? (*DEWIS crosses toward R. door. He turns back to VINCE.*)

DEWIS: She's going to need someone. I can't help her. I don't know what to do. I don't know what my position is here. I'm quite out of my depths. I'll be the first to admit it. I thought, by now, the Lord would have given me some sign, some guidepost, but I haven't seen it. No sign at all. Just—(*VINCE just stares at him. DEWIS goes out the door, crosses porch and exits L. VINCE listens to him leaving. He smells roses, looks up the staircase then smells roses again. He turns and looks U. at DODGE. He crosses up to him and bends over, looking at DODGE's open eyes. DODGE is dead. His death should have come completely unnoticed. VINCE lifts the blanket, then covers DODGE's head. He puts DODGE's cap on his own head and smells the roses while staring at DODGE's body. Long pause. VINCE places the roses on DODGE's chest then lays down on the sofa, arms folded behind his head, staring at the ceiling, his body in the same position as DODGE's. After a while, HALIE is heard coming from above the staircase. The lights start to dim imperceptively as HALIE speaks. VINCE keeps staring at the ceiling.)*

HALIE'S VOICE: Dodge? Is that you Dodge? Tilden was right about the corn you know. I've never seen such corn. Have you taken a look at it lately? Dazzling. Tall as a man already. This early in the year. Carrots too. Potatoes. Peas. It's like a paradise out there, Dodge. You oughta take a look. A miracle. I've never seen it like this. Maybe the rain did something. Maybe it was the rain. (*As HALIE keeps talking offstage, TILDEN appears from L., dripping with mud from the knees down. His arms and hands are covered with mud. In his hands he carries the corpse of a small child at chest level, staring down at it. The corpse mainly consists of bones wrapped in muddy, rotten cloth. He moves slowly D. toward the staircase ignoring VINCE on the sofa. VINCE keeps staring at the ceiling as though TILDEN wasn't there. As HALIE continues, TILDEN slowly makes his way up the stairs. His eyes never leave the corpse of the child. The lights keep fading.*) Good hard rain. Takes everything straight down deep to the roots. The rest takes care of itself. You can't force a thing to grow. You can't interfere with it. It's all hidden. Unseen. You just gotta wait 'til it pops up out of the ground. Tiny little shoot. Tiny little white shoot. All hairy and fragile. Strong though. Strong enough to crack the earth even. It's a miracle, Dodge. I've never

seen a crop like this in my whole life. Maybe it's the sun. Maybe that's it. Maybe it's the sun. (*TILDEN disappears above. Silence. Lights go to black.*)

End of Play

PROPERTY LIST

Umbrella (HALIE)
Bottle of whiskey (DODGE)
Old, brown blanket (DODGE)
Pack of cigarettes (DODGE)
Lighter or matches (DODGE)
Bunch of fresh corn (TILDEN)
Chewing tobacco (TILDEN)
Milking stool (TILDEN)
Pail (TILDEN)
Spittoon (TILDEN)
Elbow-length gloves (HALIE)
Bottles of pills (HALIE, DODGE)
Glass of water (TILDEN)
Baseball cap (DODGE)
Wet newspaper (BRADLEY)
Black, electric hair clippers, with cord (BRADLEY)
Overcoat (VINCE)
Black saxophone case (VINCE)
Sunglasses (VINCE)
Bunch of carrots (TILDEN)
Knife (TILDEN)
2 one-dollar bills (VINCE)
Rabbit fur coat (SHELLY)
Wooden leg (BRADLEY)
Cup and saucer with broth (SHELLY)
Bouquet of yellow roses (HALIE)
Silver flask of whiskey (FATHER DEWIS)
Paper bag of empty booze bottles (VINCE)
Corpse of child, wrapped in muddy, rotten cloth (TILDEN)

SOUND EFFECTS

Light rain
Birds

The two reviews that follow are both from the *New York Times*. The first is a review of the original New York production and was published on November 7, 1978. The second, printed May 1, 1996, reviews the 1995 revival, produced on Broadway in 1996.

Stage: Sam Shepard Offers "Buried Child"
By Richard Eder

Sam Shepard does not merely denounce chaos and anomie in American life, he mourns over them. His corrosive images and scenes of absurdity never soften to concede the presence of a lament, but it is there all the same.

Denunciation that has no pity in it is pamphleteering at best and a striking of fashionable attitudes at worst, and it is fairly common on the contemporary stage. Mr. Shepard is an uncommon playwright and uncommonly gifted and he does not take denouncing for granted. He wrestles with it at the risk of being thrown.

Recently he has been writing about families. "Curse of the Starving Class" used the image of physical hunger as a symbol of moral starvation. It was a fierce, funny, unmanageable play whose imagery never quite worked.

"Buried Child", now at the Theater for the New City, takes the same theme. As a piece of writing, it may be less interesting but it seems to work far better on the stage. In the very gifted production directed by Robert Woodruff, it manages to be vividly alive even as it is putting together a surreal presentation of American intimacy withered by rootlessness.

It takes the form of a homecoming. Vince, who has been away for six years, comes home bringing his saxophone and his Los Angeles girlfriend. Home is an Illinois farm where his grandparents live. It was flourishing once and he comes with the most bucolic memories and a determination to get to know his family and his roots.

What he finds is a house of the dying, full of grotesques clinging to guilty secrets. His grandmother preaches morality and goes out on all-night bashes with the local clergyman. His grandfather is a bitter, self-absorbed drunk who, as it turns out, has murdered an unwanted child. Vince's father, Tilden, is half-crazed; he keeps bringing in armloads of corn and carrots that grow even though nobody has planted them. Finally, there is a brutal uncle who has lost a leg to a chain saw.

It is a far cry from the apple pie, turkey, and kindly old relatives that Shelly, the girl, has been told to expect. By the time the visit is over, she has been insulted, assaulted, set to peel Tilden's supernatural carrots, and generally abused. Vince, who had thought of the visit as a voyage through memory, fares even worse. His memories don't remember him. His relatives ignore him or send him out to buy whisky.

Dodge, the fierce, dying grandfather who is the shattered heart of this American household, has no use for progeny or for any future. "You're all alike, you hopers," he tells Shelly, and clings to his whisky, his television and a battered baseball cap. The future is meaningless to him and the past is even more meaningless. "I'm descended from a long line of corpses," he says, "and there's not a living soul behind me." Shepard's America has poisoned its roots and destroyed its life.

But onstage each of these grotesques has as much individuality and vitality as the worst of William Faulkner's Snopeses. The director, Robert Woodruff, has seen to it that the play's judgments never eclipse their humanity. Each character is played in such a way that the symbolic function grows out of a very concrete humanity. We do not always understand these figures but we are almost always affected by them.

Richard Hamilton plays Dodge as if he were a scrawny old fighting cock. He sits feebly under his blanket, but one fierce hand whips out a whisky flask with the speed of a cobra's strike the moment the coast is clear. His eye glitters; it is mostly fixed in a senile introspection, but when it flashes upon another character it is like a spotlight.

Tom Noonan makes the hulking, inchoate Tilden a moving and powerful figure. He, more than any of the others, is the victim of the family's rootlessness; he dumbly reflects the play's mute compassion. So does Shelly, the girl. Mary McDonnell gives a splendid performance, making her grow from shallowness to experience with a tough and winning vitality. Jay Sanders, Jacqueline Brookes, Christopher McCann and Bill Wiley are all good in the somewhat less interesting roles of the cripple, the grandmother, Vince, and the clergyman.

A Sam Shepard Revival Gets Him to Broadway

By Ben Brantley

Children do grow up in the most unexpected ways, even, it would seem, a certain dead baby beneath an Illinois farm yard. Seeing the Steppenwolf Theater Company's inspired revival of Sam Shepard's "Buried Child," which opened last night at the Brooks Atkinson Theater, you may find yourself thinking, "My, how big you've gotten."

That isn't just because this new, dazzlingly acted production, which once seemed to represent the very essence of Off Broadway cool, comfortably fills a big Broadway stage. This fierce testimony to the theory that you really can't go home again (and if you try, be prepared for the consequences) actually appears to have grown more resonant, funnier and far more accessible in the 17 years since it won the Pulitzer Prize.

In the late 1970's, Mr. Shepard was deeply fashionable, everyone's favorite crossover from the avant-garde. But like all golden boys, he eventually began to tarnish in his public's mind. There was a backlash of feeling that identified him as a relic of a chapter in experimental theater, saturated in symbolism, willfully obscure and given to bashing the American Dream with two heavy hands.

Stuff and nonsense. In this exuberant staging by Gary Sinise, "Buried Child" emerges as a play for the ages, no more confined to the moment in which it was conceived than such works with similar themes as Harold Pinter's "Homecoming" or Edward Albee's "Delicate Balance."

The presence of Mr. Albee's play on Broadway in the acclaimed Lincoln Center revival makes this a happy season for unhappy families. Mr. Albee's bitingly elegant sophisticates in "Balance" may seem to have little in common with Mr. Shepard's down-and-dirty rural folk.

But it's worth noting that both plays are haunted by the specter of a dead infant and portray grown-up children limping back to the nest. More important, the two playwrights share a gift that guarantees the survival of their work: a rhythmic sense of speech and imagery that finds the dark, scary poetry behind every domestic arrangement.

In many ways, the experience of Vince (Jim True), the young man in "Buried Child," is that of everyone who goes back to the family fold after a long absence. To some degree the play shares the sensibility of the stories that college students, who are just beginning to see the world they grew up in with some distance, often tell each other: the "my family is weirder than yours" anecdotes that occupy long nights in dormitories.

Mr. Shepard takes that perspective further to locate a chilling paradox: even as the characters in "Buried Child" are inextricably bound to each other by shared histories and dark secrets, they are also irretrievably alone. The long-married Halie and Dodge (Lois Smith and James Gammon), the decrepit matriarch and patriarch, begin the play with a hilariously weary quarrel they seem to have been having forever. But while they speak the same language, they don't really hear each other.

And when Vince first appears, Dodge, his grandfather, and Tilden (Terry Kinney), Vince's dim-witted hulk of a father, don't recognize him. Dodge further insists that his other son, the one-legged, cretinous Bradley (Leo Burmester), doesn't belong with them, but then Dodge himself tends to get lost in the house's halls. Actually, the only person who says she feels at home in the place is Vince's girlfriend, Shelly (Kellie Overbey), and she's never been there before. The idea of the sanctuary of home is clearly, to borrow another title of Mr. Shepard's, a lie of the mind.

It all sounds kind of metaphysical, doesn't it? But watching this production is a startlingly visceral experience. Mr. Sinise and his excellent cast and design team have deliciously scaled up the play's Gothic side. Mr. Shepard's revisions of his original script illuminate both the thematic content and the flatout funny absurdity. (The new quibbles over semantics—like Dodge's "Scream? Men don't scream"—are priceless.)

Robert Brill's decaying, screened-in living room, with walls that seem to climb to the heavens and a long, sinister staircase, really is a place to get lost in. This is a house that devours its inhabitants, like the spooky mansions in horror movies. The feeling is underscored by the punctuation of lightning and thunder. (The lighting and sound are by Kevin Rigdon and Rob Milburn.)

The cast, all but two of whom appeared in the production earlier this season in Chicago, is close to perfection, at once grotesquely surreal and as prosaic as a Walker Evans photograph. Ms. Smith and Mr. Gammon are magnificent, giving comic gargoyles the stature of figures in Greek tragedy. They are obscenely funny, yet when their characters touch on the black secret of their family's past, they exude a real, fathomless anguish.

Mr. Gammon's Dodge is the play's rotting center, a rasping, barking old man whose voice seems to come from a terminal, decades-old cough. Even though he mostly remains stationary beneath a stiff, filthy blanket, he seems to be everywhere on the stage. Ms. Smith, a bizarre counterpoint of ladylike hand gestures and a lewd, wide-legged, pelvis-forward walk, is equally stunning. She shifts unflinchingly from pious homilies about the decline of manners to raucous physical slapstick.

In Chicago, Ted Levine's pathetic Tilden, the guy who keeps bringing in armfuls of vegetables from the supposedly barren backyard, was so good as to seem irreplaceable. But Mr. Kinney makes the part his own with an eerie, centered quietness and a heartbreaking vulnerability. (His high, gleaming forehead comes to seem like a target.) And Mr. Burmester is as good as ever as the satanic bully who can turn instantly into a sobbing brat.

Ms. Overbey has definitely improved on her Chicago performance, and she now holds her own, using a comically shrill shrewdness. And Jim Mohr brings wonderful deadpan timing to his small but telling role as a visiting minister.

The replacement of Ethan Hawke by Mr. True is a mixed blessing. Mr. True is fine in the play's second act, as the outraged young man in search of reassurance. But he's not comfortable yet with Vince's savage metamorphosis in the third act, and his concluding monologue—in which he speaks of seeing his face dissolve into those of his ancestors—has the stiffness of an audition piece.

This is unfortunate, since the uncertainty of identity is the key to "Buried Child." But otherwise the theme is beautifully realized: in the ways in which the characters keep trying to find their images in a fragment of a broken mirror; in Ms. Smith's astonishing, unexplained change of appearance between the first and third acts.

"Buried Child" operates successfully on so many levels that you get dizzy watching it. It has the intangible spookiness of nightmares about home and dispossession, yet it involves you in its tawdry, mystery-driven plot with the old-fashioned verve of an Erskine Caldwell novel.

Great plays always exist on more than one level, of course, something of which the American dramas on Broadway have too rarely reminded us in recent years. It is remarkable to realize that this production is Mr. Shepard's Broadway debut. His presence there, along with that of Mr. Albee after a long exile, hearteningly suggests that the Great White Way, after an extended second childhood of musical revivals and frothy comedies, may be ready to grow up again.

NOTES

1. Don Shewey, *Sam Shepard* (New York: Da Capo Press, 1997), 32.

2. Shewey, p. 67.

SUGGESTION FOR FURTHER READING

Shewey, Don. *Sam Shepard.* New York: Da Capo Press, 1997.

In this study of the relationship between Shepard's personal life and his work as a playwright and film actor, Shewey explores the sources and impact of Shepard subjects: rock and roll, Hollywood movies, drug culture, and family relationships. Also included is worthwhile material on the development of the off-off-Broadway theatre in New York in the 1960s and 1970s and the evolution of the Magic Theatre in San Francisco.

Glossary

act 1. To play a role on the stage in front of an audience. 2. The basic division of a play. *Joe Turner's Come and Gone* is divided into two acts.

acting in quotes The Brechtian concept of acting in which actors comment on the actions of the characters they are playing rather than maintain continuous identification with the character.

action The movement of the actors and the unfolding of a play's events. Action may be physical or psychological.

actor The central artist of the theatre who creates a dramatic story on the stage through words and gestures. Frequently the actor expresses the language of a playwright; theatre, however, can exist without playwrights, but it cannot exist without actors.

alienation effect The Brechtian idea of distancing the audience from a performance through breaks in the narrative and the suspense to promote critical awareness.

amplification The augmentation of sound through electronic means.

arena stage A round or square stage completely surrounded by the audience.

audition The process through which actors seeking roles in a play or positions with a theatre company present monologues or scene readings for a director.

avant-garde New ideas of drama and performance that push back boundaries and challenge the assumptions of accepted theatre traditions.

beat The basic units of an actor's role defined by changes in character motivation.

Beijing Opera A form of Chinese theatre first introduced in 1790 that relies on music, singing, and acrobatics to express dramas based on the traditional Chinese way of life. Domestic relationships and military conquests are frequently the subjects of Beijing Opera, which also uses mythical subjects to reinforce accepted values.

black box A flexible theatre space in which the stage space and the configuration of the audience space can be changed from production to production.

blocking All of the movement of the actors on the stage during a play.

blues Songs that are part of the African American oral tradition. Descended from slave songs, the blues became a major outlet for community concerns and stories.

book The scripted action and dialogue of a musical—as distinguished from the music and lyrics of the songs.

book musical A musical with an integrated plot such as *Oklahoma!* and *My Fair Lady*.

Broadway The long street that runs through the heart of Manhattan, home to the largest concentration of professional theatres in New York City.

camp A linguistic form of parody.

catharsis The release of emotion experienced by audience members watching a play. Aristotle understood this emotional release to be one of the essential elements of the experience of watching a tragedy.

character The people in a play. The theatre is distinguished from other forms of storytelling because of the presence of characters onstage who are engaged in action.

chorus In classical Greek theatre, a group of fifteen or more actors who chanted their lines in unison and sometimes functioned as a character in the play and sometimes provided commentary on the dramatic situation. The chorus added to the rhythmic structure of the performances through singing and dancing.

City Dionysia A festival in ancient Athens that became a major event for the presentation of drama. The festival was held in honor of the god Dionysus, who is closely associated with the Greek theatre.

collaborative art The group effort required to produce theatre, as opposed to the separate work of individuals.

comedy   The dramatic genre that focuses on human weakness through humor. Comedy celebrates the regeneration of life through love and reconciliation.

community aesthetics   The artistic expression formulated over many years that has precise meaning for a particular community; includes accepted traditions and conventions.

concept musical   A musical organized around a theme, with the songs or musical numbers functioning as connected episodes; examples include *A Chorus Line* and *Bring in da Noise Bring in da Funk*.

costume designer   The theatre artist responsible for interpreting plays through the costumes created for the actors.

cross-gender casting   The casting of actors of the opposite sex in roles written for either men or women. In many early theatres, men played the roles of women characters. In recent productions, cross-gender casting has been used as a strategy to explore issues of gender identity.

cue   The line of dialogue, musical moment, or piece of stage action that is the signal for a character entrance or any change in lights or scenery. For a play to run smoothly, every participant must pay scrupulous attention to the cues.

Cultural Revolution   The cultural upheaval initiated by Mao Zedong and his wife Jiang Qing in 1966 with the goal of reforming Chinese society. During the Cultural Revolution, traditional forms of theatre were repressed and replaced with model performances that presented an obvious political point of view.

cyclorama   A very large piece of light-colored fabric stretched across the back of the stage that serves to create expansive lighting effects and to silhouette actors.

dialogue   The language spoken by two or more characters in the play.

Dionysus   The Greek god of fertility in whose honor plays were performed in ancient Greece.

director   The theatre practitioner who has primary responsibility for the interpretation of a play. The director creates the stage action and unifies all the elements of the production.

downstage   The front of the stage or area of the stage closest to the audience.

drama   The written text of a play as it is constructed by the playwright.

dramatic ritual   A ceremony, frequently religious, that expresses community values or beliefs through performance. Participants enact community stories that have been passed down through generations. Dramatic rituals are performed for the welfare of the community and usually involve repetition of the drama in a set form.

dramaturg   A theatre practitioner concerned with selecting plays for a theatre company, working with playwrights on the development of new scripts, and working with directors on research issues.

ekkyklema   The wheeling cart on which the bodies of dead characters were displayed in Greek tragedy. The ekkyklema showed the results of violence that had taken place offstage.

ensemble   A group of actors who work closely together and share the responsibility for the performance of a play.

environmental sound   Sound effects that may be live or recorded that contribute to the interpretation of the play or are an expressive part of the performance.

epic theatre   A theatrical style that emphasizes a historical approach to the subject and uses an episodic structure. Epic theatre also uses devices such as songs and signs to interrupt the action of the play so that emotional distance is created.

episodic art   Visual art and theatre that tell a story through a sequence of connected images or episodes. The church-related art of the Middle Ages was particularly known for employing an episodic form.

equity theatre   A theatre company or producing organization that performs in a theatre space that seats an audience of one hundred or more patrons and that pays its actors according to a union contract.

equity waiver theatre   A professional theatre with ninety-nine or fewer seats that is thereby exempt from certain regulations of the Actors Equity union.

expressionism   A theatrical style that uses exaggeration and distortion in both design and acting to reflect the interior world of the characters.

external acting approach   An acting approach that begins with text and movement rather than the psychological analysis of character.

farce   An extreme form of comedy involving challenges to authority that frequently result in anarchy.

genre   The division of dramas into categories such as tragedy and comedy as they represent different kinds of human experience.

German expressionism   An artistic movement in the visual and performing arts that prevailed in Germany from 1905 to 1922; it merged aesthetic and political views.

gestural acting   An approach to acting influenced by Bertolt Brecht and Asian performance techniques that relies on distilling the essence of character through concentrated physical gestures.

glory   A scenic device used in the Italian court theatre to fly large groups of characters such as angels.

gobo   A stencil placed inside a lighting instrument to create a pattern of reflected light on the floor or on a cyclorama or scenic unit.

ground plan   The basic diagram for the placement of furniture, walls, doors, and levels such as stairs; evolves through collaboration by the scene designer and the director.

HUAC   The Congressional committee organized to monitor "un-American activities." From the late 1930s to the 1950s the committee functioned to censor the content of American theatre and film.

improvisation   The spontaneous invention of actors used to explore text, character, or situation; a tool used by actors to freely create actions and language. Improvisation can be used in either rehearsal or performance.

inner monologue   The unspoken thoughts that accompany an actor's lines in method acting. The actor responds to the character's situation with a stream of spontaneous thoughts as if the actor were in the character's place.

internal acting approach   An acting approach that is based on a psychological investigation of character and actor identification with character; involves imagining character history and placing oneself in the character's position.

interpretive art   Theatre performance that evolves out of the interpretation of the playwright's script. Directors, actors, and designers are interpretive artists.

kabuki   A popular Japanese theatre form that began in the sixteenth century; highly stylized with elaborate action, exaggerated gestures and speech patterns, and magnificent costumes, makeup, and wigs.

kachina cycle   A sequence of ritual ceremonies performed by the Hopi people of the American Southwest that promotes the welfare of their community. The kachinas are the guardian spirits of the Hopi, who believe that the kachinas participate with them in dramatic ceremonies performed to ensure the success of the harvest and to preserve the Hopi way of life.

kathakali   A form of dance drama from southern India in which the actors express a story through movement and complex hand gestures accompanied by musicians and singers who communicate the text. The actors play character types as in the Beijing Opera and spend years in intense training to perfect the strenuous and complicated movement skills. The dramas themselves are based on the *Ramayana* and the *Mahabharata*, two epic Sanskrit poems.

kuroko   A performer dressed in black (with a hood) in the tradition of the kabuki theatre; changes scenery and props and helps actors with onstage costume changes.

language   The dialogue of a play written from the multiple points of view of the characters. Dramatic language may be realistic or poetic.

light plot   A diagram that shows the position and type of each lighting instrument to be used for a given production. This diagram is used as a tool in discussions between the lighting designer and the director and is also used by the technicians who hang the lights in the theatre.

lighting designer   The theatre artist responsible for interpreting plays through the use of light to create atmosphere and imagery and to make the action visible.

mask   A fundamental device for establishing character that covers the human face and has been used in dramatic presentations throughout the world since the beginning of theatre.

melodrama   A dramatic genre that presents the conflict between good and evil.

method acting   An internal approach to acting used in the United States that was influenced by the work of Constantin Stanislavsky. Method acting uses a close study of character psychology to determine the character's sequence of intentions or objectives. Method acting also relies on the actor's own life experiences as a major source of material for character creation.

musical theatre A form of theatre in which dialogue, singing, and dance are integrated to communicate character and plot.

mystery cycle A medieval theatre form based on biblical teachings. Episodic in structure, the mystery cycles were composed of many individual playlets.

nonrealism A theatrical style that offers a way of interpreting human experience different from the illusion of daily life created by realism. Some nonrealistic theatrical styles are expressionism, symbolism, and surrealism. Nonrealistic styles emphasize bold theatrical imagery and gestural acting.

nontraditional casting The casting of actors of different racial backgrounds in plays that were written for a nonpluralistic society, such as the plays of Shakespeare.

pageant wagons Traveling stages drawn by horses or people on which the playlets of the medieval mystery cycles were performed in England.

parody The imitation of a style of writing (for example, songs or plays) for comic effect or ridicule.

perform To engage in the presentation of theatre, dance, or music. In the theatre, performance involves the manipulation of the persona presented by the actor.

performance The live presentation of a play.

period style Presentational elements such as character movement and dress that are determined by the theatrical and social conventions of a particular era.

personate Relating to ritual performance, the representation of a spirit being by a human actor; the transformation of the actor in bringing the presence of the spirit into the community.

perspective The painting technique used to create a sense of depth in painted scenery on the stage.

playwright The theatre artist who authors the playscripts that are frequently the starting point for theatrical creation. The playwright uses language to express dramatic action.

poetic realism Realism that is heightened through symbols, the selection of details, and eloquent language.

plot The sequence of actions that determines what happens in a play; the events that make up the play's story.

poor theatre A term used by Polish director Jerzy Grotowski to identify theatre that uses only those materials necessary to extend the expression of the actor. At the Polish Laboratory Theatre, scenery and costumes were made of the simplest, least costly materials, and no scenic elements were used merely to provide background or ornamentation.

presentational staging Staging that makes obvious use of the theatre's resources.

preview A performance that is presented to an invited audience or at a reduced ticket price to allow actors to work in front of an audience before the official opening of a play.

progression The sequence of changes that defines character development.

proscenium arch The frame, like a picture frame, defining the opening of a proscenium stage. The proscenium arch creates the sense that the audience is looking into a contained space from which one wall has been removed.

proscenium stage A rectangular theatre with the stage at one end of the rectangle.

realism A theatrical style that creates an illusion of daily life through the presentation of a detailed environment, natural actions, and language that sounds as if it were overheard in ordinary circumstances.

rehearsal The process of exploration and repetition used to prepare a play for public presentation.

rehearsal costume A temporary costume worn during rehearsal to give the actor the opportunity to construct character in response to physical costume restrictions and the psychological dimensions of the costume.

rendering A sketch or painting of scenery or costumes that is used as a visual aid by the director, the other designers, and the actors in the development of a production.

repertory The alternating presentation of more than one play at a time practiced by a theatre company such as the Oregon Shakespeare Festival.

representational staging The creation of a complete, realistic illusion on the stage that makes audience members forget that they are in the theatre.

scene 1. The smaller units that make up the acts in a play. 2. A particular moment in the performance of a play. 3. The arrangement of the scene design elements.

scene designer The theatre artist responsible for interpreting plays through shaping and defining the stage space.

scenography The work of the scene designer or combined work of the scene designer, costume designer, lighting designer, and sound designer, also known as stage design.

script The dialogue, stage directions, and character descriptions that together constitute the printed text of a play.

socialist realism A form of realistic theatre produced in the former Soviet Union, presenting an idealized view of life under Communism; heavily influenced by government manipulation.

sound reinforcement The use of microphones and amplifiers to augment the sound of actors' voices, particularly in the musical theatre.

spectacle The visual elements of a performance, including scenery, lights, costumes, and the movement of actors.

spine According to Constantin Stanislavsky, the throughline of a role or the entire play that the director and actors must identify in their preparation for performance.

stage picture The arrangement of actors on the stage to communicate character relationships.

style The combination of expressive choices made by the playwright and the director, designers, and actors that construct the world of the play.

subtext The thoughts and feelings of the character that are unspoken but expressed through gesture, facial expression, and phrasing.

superobjective A term used in method acting to identify the central motivation for a character in a play that brings together in a coherent way all of the character's smaller desires and intentions during the course of the play.

table work The reading and discussion of a play done by the cast and the director at the beginning of the rehearsal process.

technical rehearsal A rehearsal dedicated to the integration of scenery, costumes, and lighting cues into the production.

terrain The use of steps, ramps, and levels to reshape the stage floor.

theatre in the round A theatre in which the audience surrounds the stage on all sides.

theatre of the absurd Plays that focus on the lack of meaning in human existence, such as those written by Samuel Beckett, Eugène Ionesco, and Jean Genet.

theatrical conventions Elements of dramatic construction and performance accepted by theatre practitioners and audience members in a given community that facilitate the presentation of plays. Conventions of the Greek theatre include masked actors and offstage violence.

theatricalism A style of playwriting or theatrical production that makes bold use of the resources of the theatre. Theatricalism is nonrealistic and employs vivid imagery and heightened language to express the playwright's meaning. Plays produced in a theatricalist style frequently call attention to the mechanics of the theatre itself.

thespian A term used for "actor" taken from the name of Thespis, the first recognized Greek actor.

throughline The arc or progression of an actor's role that ties together all of the character's words and actions.

thrust stage A theatre space in which the audience is placed on three sides of the stage.

total theatre A theatrical style that integrates sound, words, movement, light, music, and color to create a performance that emphasizes gesture and imagery as much as or more than language.

tragedy The dramatic genre initiated by ancient Greek playwrights such as Aeschylus, Sophocles, and Euripides. Tragedy focuses on suffering and loss but celebrates the will of the individual to choose his or her own course of action.

tragicomedy A dramatic genre in which the perspective shifts between serious and comic perspectives.

trilogy Tragedies in ancient Greece were originally written as three interrelated plays called a trilogy.

typecasting A method of choosing actors for roles in a play that relies on generalizations or stereotypical notions of what characters should look like.

upstage The area of the stage farthest away from the audience.

Credits

Company; **p. 234 (top),** © Bettmann/Corbis; **p. 234 (bottom),** © Owen Carey; **p. 235,** © Oscar White/Corbis; **p. 236 (left),** AP/Wide World Photos; **pp. 236 (right) & 237,** © Bettmann/Corbis; **p. 238,** © John Springer/Corbis; **p. 239,** AP/Wide World Photos; **Chapter 9 p. 241,** Corky Lee; **p. 242,** Courtesy of Gary M. Kuwahara; **p. 244,** Corky Lee; **p. 245,** Courtesy of Stephanie Arnold; **p. 246,** Courtesy of Gary M. Kuwahara; **p. 247,** Corky Lee; **p. 249,** Courtesy of Gary M. Kuwahara; **p. 278 (top),** Photo by Doug Olsen, Courtesy of East West Players; **p. 278 (bottom),** Photo by Michael Lamont, Courtesy of East West Players; **p. 280,** Photo by James Ishida, Courtesy of East West Players; **pp. 283 & 284,** Courtesy of Gary M. Kuwahara; **pp. 285, 286, & 289,** Photo courtesy of NWAAT © Rick Wong; **Chapter 10 p. 293,** © Joan Marcus; **p. 296,** Motion Picture and Television Photo Archive; **p. 297,** Mary Gearhart/The Wooster Group; **p. 298,** © Joan Marcus; **p. 299,** © Bettmann/Corbis; **p. 302,** © Patrick Bennett; **p. 304,** 1994 Barbara Morgan/Willard & Barbara Morgan Archive © Time, Inc.; **p. 306,** © Babette Mongolte; **Chapter 11 pp. 309 & 310,** © Katy Raddatz; **p. 311,** Photo by Greg Weiner, Courtesy of Tony Kushner; **p. 313,** © Owen Carey; **p. 314,** © Katy Raddatz; **pp. 316 & 317 (bottom),** © Bettmann/Corbis; **p. 317 (top),** © Katy Raddatz; **p. 318,** Photo by Jay Thompson, Courtesy of Mark Taper Forum; **p. 319,** © Katy Raddatz; **p. 367,** © Katy Raddatz; **Part 4 Opener p. 371,** © T. Charles Erickson; **Chapter 12 p. 373,** © 1999 Liz Lauren; **p. 374,** Jennifer W. Lester; **p. 375,** Neil Hammer/Courtesy of Shakespeare and Company; **p. 376,** Photo by Jay Thompson, Courtesy of Mark Taper Forum; **p. 377,** © T. Charles Erickson; **p. 378,** Goodman Theater; **p. 379,** Photo by Rick Adams; **p. 380,** © 1999 Liz Lauren; **p. 381,** © Corky Lee; **p. 382,** Photo by Michal Daniel; **p. 384,** Photo by Rick Adams; **p. 385,** Photo by Michal Daniel; **p. 386,** Courtesy of Gary M. Kuwahara; **Chapter 13 p. 389,** © Joan Marcus; **p. 391,** © T. Charles Erickson; **p. 393,** © Ken Friedman; **p. 397,** Photo by Michal Daniel; **p. 396,** © Joan Marcus; **p. 399,** Manuel Harlan; **p. 401,** Motion Picture and Television Photo Archive; **p. 402,** Courtesy of Lucasfilm LTD; **p. 405,** Ted Allan/Motion Picture and Television Photo Archive; **Chapter 14 pp. 408, 409, 415, 428, 429, & 430,** Carol Helabian; **Chapter 15 pp. 434, 437, 440, & 441,** Photo by Michael Brosilow, Courtesy of Steppenwolf Theatre Company; **p. 444,** Photo by Michael Brosilow, Courtesy of Steppenwolf Theatre Company; **Color Sections Plate 1,** Kevin Morris; **Plate 2,** © Joan Marcus; **Plate 3,** Courtesy of the Court Theatre; **Plate 4,** Photo by Richard Feldman/Courtesy of Shakespeare and Company; **Plate 5,** Stephanie Berger © 1999; **Plates 6 & 7,** © Christopher Briscoe; **Plate 8,** Scene design Courtesy of Mike Fish; **Plate 9,** © Christopher Briscoe; **Plate 10,** Costume Design Courtesy of Candice Cain; **Plate 11,** © T. Charles Erickson; **Plate 12,** © Joan Marcus; **Plate 13,** Zane Williams Photo; **Plate 14,** Photo by Richard Feldman/Courtesy of Shakespeare and Company; **Plate 15,** Courtesy of Erik Hansen-Hansen; **Plate 16,** Courtesy of the Court Theatre; **Plate 17,** David Cooper; **Plate 18,** Photo by Richard C. Trigg, Courtesy of Actors Theatre of Louisville; **Plate 19,** Photo by Craig Schwartz, Courtesy of Mark Taper Forum; **Plate 20,** Photo by Michal Daniel; **Plate 21,** Courtesy of Eric Stone; **Plates 22 & 23,** © Joan Marcus; **Plate 24,** Photo by Marty Sohl; **Plate 25,** Photo by Michal Daniel; **Plates 26 & 27,** © Joan Marcus; **Plate 28,** © Photofest; **Plate 29,** © Joan Marcus; **Plate 30,** © Paul Kolnik; **Plates 31 & 32,** © Joan Marcus; **Plate 33,** Courtesy of Stephanie Arnold; **Plate 34,** Courtesy of Ma-Yi Theatre; **Plate 35,** © Chris Bennion; **Plates 36 & 37,** © Joan Marcus; **Plate 38,** Richard Feldman; **Plate 39,** Photo by Richard C. Trigg, Courtesy of Actors Theatre of Louisville; **Plate 40,** Photo by Rick Adams; **Plate 41,** Rico Torres/Motion Picture and Television Photo Archive; **Plate 42,** Yolanda Lopez; **Plate 43,** Carol Helabian; **Plate 44,** Photo by Scott Suchman, Courtesy of Arena Stage

Text Credits

Chapter 1 pp. 14–16 Frances McDormand from *The Actor Speaks* by Janet Sonnenberg. Copyright 1996 by Janet Sonenberg. Reprinted by permission of Crown Trade Publishers, a division of Crown Publishers, Inc. **Chapter 2 pp. 33–38** From Aeschylus, "Agamemnon", translated by Grene and Lattimore, *Complete Greek Tragedies,* 1987. Reprinted with permission from The University of Chicago Press. **Chapter 3 pp. 65, 66, 68** From *Preface to August Wilson Three Plays* by August Wilson. Copyright 1991 by University of Pittsburgh Press. Reprinted by permission of the University of Pittsburgh Press.

Index

Page numbers in **bold** indicate definitions. Page numbers in *italics* indicate photos, captions, or color plates.